THE M·G·M·STORY

THE MGM STORY

THE COMPLETE HISTORY
OF OVER FIFTY ROARING YEARS

BY
JOHN DOUGLAS EAMES

CROWN
PUBLISHERS INC.
New York

FIRST PUBLISHED IN THE USA BY
CROWN PUBLISHERS INC.
419 PARK AVENUE SOUTH, NEW YORK, 10016

REPRINTED 1976

TEXT © 1975 SUNDIAL
PUBLICATIONS LIMITED

ALL PHOTOGRAPHS
© METRO-GOLDWYN-MAYER INC.

ISBN 0 517 526131

PRINTED IN HONG KONG

AUTHOR'S NOTE

My first task in the preparation of this book – compiling a complete list of MGM pictures – presented an awkward question. What is an MGM picture? Obviously, one made by MGM. But, especially in the company's later years, there have been many MGM releases made entirely by, or in conjunction with, independent producers – and the release was not always world-wide. Where should the line be drawn? I decided to include every film distributed by MGM in both the United States and Great Britain, this being as good a rule of thumb as any. So you will find herein, along with MGM's own productions, semi-outsiders ranging from 'spaghetti westerns' to 'Gone With The Wind'.

The period covered is from 1924 (Metro-Goldwyn-Mayer officially came into being on May 17, but Mayer couldn't wait and inaugurated his studio on April 26) to 1974. During that half-century some titles underwent a sea-change when crossing the Atlantic: they have been noted in each case, the original title appearing first; both versions are listed in the index. The films are grouped according to year of completion, including post-production work. Each year has a short introduction giving a rundown on the happenings and trends in the movie world as a whole. There follows an independent description and illustration of every film completed in that year.

The help of various firms and individuals has been invaluable. I am most grateful to MGM officers in London, New York and Culver City, particularly Michael Havas, Edward Patman, Bill Edwards, Angela Dally, Martin Paley and Norman Kaphan; to Leslie Pound and Graham Smith of Cinema International Corporation; to Russell Cradick and Brian McIlmail of National Screen Service; to the personnel of the British Film Institute's library and stills archives. And, by no means least, to Metro-Goldwyn-Mayer Inc. for permission to reproduce its copyright photographs.

J. D. E.

Blueprint of a wonderland: Above, Lot 2 (photographed in part here) with its permanent outdoor sets. Outlying acreage was sold in later years. Below, the front of MGM.

Wizards of a wonderland: Top, founder Marcus Loew. Above right, studio head Louis B. Mayer. Above, production boss Irving Thalberg. Right, president Nicholas Schenck with (right and enlarged, left) international chief Arthur Loew.

FADE IN

The Hollywood that is slowly setting in the west rose in the east during the century's early 'teens, when New York-based theatre owners decided that they needed more and bigger and better movies for their rapidly multiplying audiences. These early exhibitors, such men as Marcus Loew, Adolph Zukor and William Fox, had emerged from other trades to operate nickelodeons: converted shops in which crowds, at five cents a head, sat entranced by the wonder of pictures that moved. The crowds grew, the properties mushroomed, the pictures expanded from one reel to two and even longer. Demand exceeded supply, and the early moviemakers began to ask higher terms from the exhibitors through their wholesalers, the exchanges.

The major exhibitors were controlling chains of increasingly large and comfortable theatres, and they determined to become their own suppliers. In this they were led by Zukor, who broke away from Loew's theatres in 1912 to form the Famous Players company (later Paramount). One of his best customers was Loew, until Zukor introduced the alarming practice of charging a percentage of theatre takings for his bigger pictures, instead of the customary fixed rental. At the same time he kept buying theatres and enlarging his network of exchanges to form an integrated manufacture-distribution-retail organization.

Loew resolved to do the same. Adding theatres to his imposing chain with one hand, he reached out for a studio acquisition with the other. He was offered Metro Pictures, a Hollywood outfit which had been formed in 1915 and was feeling the same need as Loew, but in reverse, by 1919: it wanted a theatre affiliation as an outlet for its product.

Its take-over by Loew's Incorporated was happily followed by the greatest success it had ever produced, *The Four Horsemen of the Apocalypse*. Not so happily, its management's shortsighted parsimony lost that film's sensational star find, Rudolph Valentino, to Paramount when he asked for a $100 salary increase and didn't get it. But Metro held on to the film's director, Rex Ingram, who gave the company almost equally big hits in *The Prisoner of Zenda* and *Scaramouche*.

Loew augmented the studio's output by signing up Jackie Coogan, the great child star of the day; making a deal with his former associate Joseph Schenck for the release of Buster Keaton features, and negotiating a non-exclusive arrangement with independent producer (and ex-Metro officer) Louis B. Mayer for four films a year.

Nevertheless, the studio set-up proved to be a constant headache for Loew. His lieutenant since the nickelodeon days was Nicholas Schenck (brother Joseph had left Loew for the production field in 1917). Schenck was now in charge of Loew's theatre interests, and reported mounting dissatisfaction with the attractions coming from Metro. Then, early in 1924, an unexpected character stepped into the scene: Lee Shubert, whose chain of houses dominated the American legitimate theatre (they still do, to some extent) but whose influence in the movie world was less apparent. He was an investor in, and a board member of, Loew's Incorporated and Goldwyn Pictures. He advised the latter's president, F. J. Godsol, to contact Loew with the idea of merging with Metro.

Goldwyn Pictures was in as shaky a state as Metro had been when Loew took it over, even though its assets and prestige were greater. It had an impressive roster of stars and directors under contract; a handsome studio built in 1915 by pioneer Thomas Ince at Culver City, near Hollywood; a string of distribution offices; and several picture palaces, including the huge Capitol on Broadway. But it was functioning far below its potential because of poor management and boardroom battles. In 1922 these had resulted in the exit of its production genius, Samuel Goldwyn, who was replaced at the top by Godsol, and who has never had any part of the company that now bears his name.

Loew saw the suggested merger as a splendid opportunity to make his studio worthy of his theatre empire. But who could mesh the combined production forces into an efficient unit? Neither the Metro nor the Goldwyn studio chiefs were up to the job. Enter another principal character: J. Robert Rubin, a shrewd lawyer who had long represented Loew's and Metro—and Mayer. Rubin gave Mayer the tip to hurry east for talks with Loew's.

Mayer, who had built up a profitable producing company during his five years in Hollywood, releasing his pictures through First National and occasionally Metro, had some talented people under contract, although not so many as Goldwyn or even Metro. He was strongest where they faltered: in management. His vigorous business sense and organizing flair were complemented in 1924 by the abilities of his principal aides—Harry Rapf, a no-nonsense supervisor of bread-and-butter movies, and Irving Thalberg. This 24-year-old, recently detached from Universal Studio by Mayer, was already being talked about as a 'boy wonder' in Hollywood, but no one could have guessed that he was the most valuable asset of all those involved in the merger under discussion.

Loew delegated the negotiations to Nicholas Schenck, and a deal was rapidly worked out. Loew's Incorporated was to absorb Goldwyn Pictures and Louis B. Mayer Productions, and the resulting Metro-Goldwyn Pictures would control production and distribution as a subsidiary of Loew's. Contracts were signed with Mayer as studio chief, Thalberg as supervisor of production and Rubin as secretary. All three were to be vice-presidents; the first two at the former Goldwyn studio, Rubin as their New York contact at Loew's headquarters.

Another unit in the giant combine was Cosmopolitan Productions, an independent company created by William Randolph Hearst to make movies starring Marion Davies. It had recently shifted its releasing outlet from Paramount to Goldwyn, and was important because of Hearst's influence on the public via his powerful group of newspapers and magazines, plus a newsreel.

Mayer and Thalberg, assisted by Rapf, had a lot of talent to call upon when they took over. They themselves brought in players Lon Chaney, Norma Shearer, Huntley Gordon, Renee Adoree and Hedda Hopper, and directors Fred Niblo, Reginald Barker, Hobart Henley and John M. Stahl. From Metro came stars Ramon Novarro, Alice Terry, Viola Dana, Jackie Coogan, Buster Keaton, Mae Busch and Monte Blue, and directors Rex Ingram and Victor Schertzinger. Goldwyn's contributions were stars Mae Murray, Conrad Nagel, Blanche Sweet, Aileen Pringle, John Gilbert, William Haines, Eleanor Boardman and (via Cosmopolitan) Marion Davies, and directors King Vidor, Marshall Neilan, Erich von Stroheim, Robert Z. Leonard, Charles Brabin and Victor Seastrom. Leo, the lion trademark, was another Goldwyn legacy, devised by Howard Dietz, who stayed on to head MGM's advertising and publicity. Writers Frances Marion and Carey Wilson and art director Cedric Gibbons were also among those in from the start in April 1924.

The studio itself was called Metro-Goldwyn-Mayer (sometimes 'Metro' for short). The movies that emerged from it at first bore the legend 'Louis B. Mayer presents . . . a Metro-Goldwyn picture'; but this was soon altered to 'Metro-Goldwyn-Mayer presents . . .' It made a hefty mouthful either way, and so it was the letters MGM that became the most famous company name in the business.

Its slogans were also famous – and vulnerable to jest. The lofty motto on Leo's scroll, 'Ars Gratia Artis' (roughly, 'art for art's sake') invited sardonic comment, and 'More Stars Than There Are in Heaven' was dropped when somebody thought it referred to the dear departed.

By the end of its second year MGM had delivered a hundred features to eagerly welcoming Loew and other theatres, which prospered mightily. The studio was already achieving prestige as well as profits, especially with *Ben-Hur*, which had been rescued from a Goldwyn impasse, and *The Big Parade*, an MGM enterprise from start to finish.

Mayer continually increased his domain's physical capacities and talent resources. After ten years the studio had 23 modern sound stages instead of the original six glass-walled structures, and had extended to 117 acres. The property also included the imposing Irving Thalberg Building of offices; standing exterior sets including a small lake and harbour, a park, a miniature jungle and streets of houses. And the world's largest film laboratory, which turned out over 150m. feet of release prints a year.

But people were the company's major asset. Of the 1934 total of about 4,000 studio employees, there were 61 stars and featured players, 17 directors and 51 writers under contract. Other companies had as many (though probably not better) directors and writers; MGM had the stars.

Its pre-eminence in this field was a result of a policy the company had followed from the outset. Although nothing was stinted in giving the pictures quality, everything else was secondary to developing and maintaining what the masses talked about, read about and wanted to see – stars.

Important in this regard was Mayer's concept of the studio as a family unit. He saw himself as a father figure, the stars as his children. He encouraged the shy ones, scolded the naughty ones, preached thrift to those who asked for more pocket-money, and warned them all of the cold, cruel world awaiting those who ran away. Remarkably few scorned this treatment (several have echoed Robert Taylor's confession that he left MGM feeling 'like a stripling leaving home') and a sense of belonging to a big family was effectively inculcated throughout the company.

Most of the studio's original stars lasted well into the talkie era: Ramon Novarro, Marion Davies and William Haines stayed for a decade, Norma Shearer for nearly two. Meanwhile, talent scouts were catching likely personalities in a web which radiated from Culver City across America and overseas. Greta Garbo was found in Berlin, Greer Garson in London, Judy Garland in Hollywood itself, where agents made MGM the No.1 goal for their clients. Besides people who had made their mark in other branches of show business, thousands of unknowns were interviewed, hundreds screen-tested, dozens contracted every year. The policy paid off even more handsomely during the second MGM decade.

The company's short subjects were also quite lucrative. They burgeoned into an average annual total of 80, including the nearby Hal Roach studio's comedies (Laurel and Hardy, Charley Chase, Our Gang, Patsy Kelly, etc.) and the output of the home studio's shorts department, headed by Fred Quimby from 1926 to 1956. It was notable for Robert Benchley's hilarious bumblings; Pete Smith's Specialties; Fitzpatrick Traveltalks with their beautiful photography and awful commentaries; the 'Crime Does Not Pay' thrillers which were a training ground for Fred Zinnemann, Joseph Losey and other directors; and the prolific cartoon section (second only to Disney's) with its indestructible, seven times Academy-Awarded cat and mouse, Tom and Jerry, created by William Hanna and Joe Barbera.

Metro-Goldwyn-Mayer was at its zenith between the late Twenties and the late Forties. Yet this period brought a most serious blow; the death in 1936 of Irving Thalberg. Although, by his own choice, his name never appeared in his film's credits, everyone in the industry knew he was the man most responsible for their excellence and for the reputation of MGM product in general. This was acknowledged by Mayer, although he never conceded an inch of his over-all authority.

The legend of Mayer as a ruthless egomaniac seems as permanently fixed in film history as that of Thalberg as a young genius, but neither could have raised MGM so high without the other. Mayer's remarkable acumen in finance, administration and showmanship was proved when he kept the studio flourishing while his partner was away ill for a year, and for years after Thalberg's death.

But the late Forties slump in the picture business hit MGM as it did every other company.

Furthermore, Leo wasn't collecting his usual lion's share of Academy Awards. Mayer had to find 'another Thalberg' to replace the cabal of executive producers which had been operating under his supervision. The choice was Dore Schary, a young man with ideas who had once been a writer at the studio, and who had risen to become production chief of RKO-Radio. Nicholas Schenck, the president of Loew's since the death in 1926 of Marcus Loew (genuinely mourned by the whole trade), approved the choice.

After a honeymoon period, Mayer and Schary came into conflict with increasing frequency and Schenck had to assert himself as peacemaker. This duplicated a situation which had cropped up from time to time between Mayer and Thalberg, even though the former held the latter in higher esteem than he did Schary. Now Mayer was also often at loggerheads with Schenck. Their hidden enmity had its roots in 1928 when Schenck and Loew's heirs had secretly sold the entire company to William Fox. (The deal was aborted by Fox's tangled finances and a US anti-trust investigation.) Mayer had then been mollified by a liberal anointment of money, but in 1951 he finally defied Schenck to choose between him and Schary. The president chose Schary: incredibly, Mayer was out. Five years later, in 1956, so was Schary.

Just as MGM had been the Hollywood studio *par excellence*, so it typified the gradual decline of the film city and its big-studio system of mass production and long-term contracts. Competition from television reduced income while ever-inflating costs increased outgoings. Studio chiefs came and went: an independent producer, Sol C. Siegel, took over in 1958, Robert Weitman followed in 1962, and Herbert Solow reigned briefly in 1969. Significantly, both the latter came from television, the movies' successor in public hypnosis. Stars, directors and producers launched out on their own; profit participation instead of (or in addition to) salary became the vogue. Although they retained a proportion of their customary production activity, the big companies increasingly turned to financing and distributing independent film-makers' products.

Meanwhile in New York the control of MGM underwent equally drastic changes. The government's anti-trust laws, which had helped to save the company in 1928, cut it in half 30 years later. Loew's became an entirely separate firm owning the theatre chain and radio station WMGM. Metro-Goldwyn-Mayer retained the studio, the distributing organization and such subsidiaries as MGM International, the overseas theatre and distribution wing developed by Arthur Loew, one of Marcus' twin sons; MGM Records; the consistently profitable Robbins–Miller–Feist music publishers; and MGM TV. This last, an example of 'if you can't beat 'em, join 'em', prospered by leasing the vast MGM backlog of movies to television (they never sold outright as some of the majors did); they also made films specifically for the medium.

Crises and convolutions in ownership and management have periodically rocked the MGM boardroom. Schenck, who had resisted changes longer than any other company's chief executive, relinquished the presidency in 1955. Arthur Loew was persuaded to take over, but had had enough within a year and resigned in favour of Joseph Vogel, a Loew's Theatres veteran of 40 years. His tenure was marked by a dramatic attempt by outside interests to gain control; among its instigators was none other than Mayer. This try for revenge was a failure, and Mayer died in 1957, an unhappy millionaire. Vice-president Robert O'Brien ascended to the presidency in 1963, followed in 1969 by James Polk Jr, another who lasted less than a year; then came James T. Aubrey Jr, ex-television executive.

Share deals and proxy battles gave behind-the-scenes control to Polk's sponsor, distillery magnate Edgar Bronfman; then to Aubrey's backer, hotel and airline financier Kirk Kerkorian, whose shareholding dominance from late 1969 continues at the present writing. Aubrey shifted MGM's headquarters from New York to the Culver City studios, where sales of company assets were announced with depressing frequency. Theatres in Australia and India, the British studio, the London-based overseas music publishers (Robbins, etc.), the MGM Record company, and parts of the Culver City acreage were liquidated. Annual reports to stockholders were saying less about films and more about the new MGM Grand Hotel in Las Vegas, into which $120m. was poured.

Finally, in October 1973, Aubrey announced the complete withdrawal of MGM from distribution. The company's product, new and old, was handed over for a ten-year period to United Artists in the USA and Canada, and to Cinema International Corporation (which already handled Paramount and Universal abroad) in the rest of the world. Simultaneously, UA bought the American arm of MGM's music publishers and CIC bought MGM International's theatres, including the Empire and Ritz in London. These transactions brought in a total of $32½m. plus a share of UA and CIC rentals from future MGM cinema and television bookings.

Aubrey resigned. Frank E. Rosenfelt, who had joined MGM's legal department in 1955, was appointed president, while Kerkorian made his control less anonymous by taking the title of chief executive. With the hotel thriving and film overheads slashed, they report booming profits.

The days when the dream factories were running full blast, peopled by almost mythical celebrities who thrived on a strange mixture of hardworking efficiency and lunatic extravagance, are long gone. But the MGM lion's roar continues, diminuendo maybe, carrying echoes of the decades when it was as loud and lusty as Hollywood itself. It even revives memories, for some, of Leo's silent miming to the accompaniment of a mighty Wurlitzer sinking below the screen. There is a flashback to every one of his films in this book – the failures (and you may recall some of those with affection) as well as the successes that lived up to the studio's motto: 'Make it good . . . make it big . . . give it class!'

IN THE BEGINNING
1924

MGM entered a growing industry. Motion pictures were the No. 1 mass entertainment and more theatres exclusively devoted to them opened every week. In the USA the total approached 20,000; in Britain it passed 4,000. Going to the movies was an all-age habit.

But the mounting rivalry of radio had to be met by making pictures bigger: the 1923 success of Cecil B. DeMille's spectacular *Ten Commandments*, and James Cruze's *Covered Wagon*, the first epic Western, inspired more big-scale productions in 1924: Rudolph Valentino in *Monsieur Beaucaire*, Mary Pickford in *Dorothy Vernon of Haddon Hall*, Douglas Fairbanks in *The Thief of Bagdad*, John Barrymore in *Beau Brummel*; D. W. Griffith's *America*, John Ford's *The Iron Horse*.

In Europe the dominant film nation was, strangely enough, Germany. A shambles five years earlier, the defeated country was creating stars and fine directors (Pola Negri, Emil Jannings; Ernst Lubitsch, Fritz Lang) faster than Hollywood could lure them away.

Besides such assets as studio equipment, stars, directors, writers and technical personnel, MGM inherited from its component companies some valuable properties for re-issue. Foremost among them were the splendid productions Rex Ingram made for Metro. The new combine successfully revived Valentino in **The Four Horsemen of the Apocalypse** *(right), which had shot him to the zenith of stardom in 1921; and* **Scaramouche** *(left), which to a less sensational degree had done the same for Ramon Novarro in 1923. This scene of Lewis Stone and Alice Terry illustrates Ingram's elegant pictorial style.*

Norma Shearer, already a popular leading lady, had only professional interest for Thalberg, her future husband, during their first busy MGM years. In **Broken Barriers** *all hell burst loose when Miss Shearer revealed to father George Fawcett, sister Ruth Stonehouse and mother Margaret McWade that she was in love with a married man. Reginald Barker, Scottish-born maker of American films since 1913, directed this emotional drama with Miss Shearer, Adolphe Menjou, James Kirkwood and Mae Busch in the major roles. Script: Sada Cowan, Howard Higgin.*

Excuse Me *was a farce about a naval officer (Conrad Nagel) and his would-be bride (Miss Shearer) who spent most of their time running up and down a train looking for a clergyman to marry them. Best-selling novelist Rupert Hughes wrote it on an off-day and it was directed by Alf Goulding, an Australian who subsequently made many movies in Britain. Also cast: Renee Adoree, John Boles, Walter Hiers, Bert Roach.*

He Who Gets Slapped *was the first film entirely ▷ prepared and produced by MGM. The six months preceding its delivery to the distributing organization in October 1924 were also occupied in completing, editing and releasing pictures originated by the Metro, Goldwyn and Mayer companies. But Mayer and Thalberg always kept in mind the importance of making this film an impressive demonstration of the new studio's powers. They assigned three stars— John Gilbert, Norma Shearer and Lon Chaney —and the celebrated Swedish director, Victor Seastrom (who also wrote the screenplay with Carey Wilson) to the story of a scientist who started a new life as a circus clown. Cast included Tully Marshall, Marc MacDermott, Ford Sterling, Paulette Duval. It was based on a Russian play staged a few years before on Broadway by the Theatre Guild: a risky choice for the studio's debut because, while it dealt with such melodramatic elements as a wicked baron pursuing the equestrienne heroine, and murder by means of a hungry lion, its effect had to be that of a moody, poetical tragedy. Happily it proved to be both an artistic and a commercial success. MGM was on its way.*

Already a major star, but with his biggest hit still in his future, Ramon Novarro had a success in **The Red Lily**, written and directed by Fred Niblo–who indeed had the same triumph yet to come in 1925: Ben Hur. Ramon and Enid Bennett played penniless lovers who eloped to Paris, she to become a prostitute known as 'the red lily', he to learn the ways of the underworld from Wallace Beery. Then usually cast as a villain, Beery in 1924 had been acting in movies for 11 years and had another quarter-century to go, the final 19 years as an MGM star. Also cast: Frank Currier, Rosemary Theby, Mitchell Lewis, Emily Fitzroy.

One of the most popular 1924 releases was Mr and Mrs Marshall Neilan's film version of Thomas Hardy's formidable novel **Tess of the d'Urbervilles** (scripted by Dorothy Farnum). Neilan was one of Hollywood's top directors, while Mrs was Blanche Sweet (her real name, believe it or not), then aged 28 and already a veteran of 15 years' filming, having started at the Biograph studio along with Mary Pickford and the Gish sisters. In this scene Tess reveals to her husband (Conrad Nagel) the shameful truth about her seduction by d'Urberville (Stuart Holmes) when she was a servant in his house. After the film was completed Mayer changed the tragic ending to a happy one, much to the annoyance of Neilan – and Hardy.

Magnificently produced and beautifully photographed in Italy, George Eliot's **Romola** was the second film in which Henry King directed Lillian Gish and Ronald Colman for Inspiration Pictures, an independent production company which chiefly consisted of King, one Charles Duell and stars Lillian Gish and Richard Barthelmess. The first was The White Sister, a successful Metro release. After Romola, Inspiration was disrupted by a sensational lawsuit brought by Lillian against Duell charging that she had been defrauded of a great deal of money due under her contract. She won. Director King and Dorothy Gish were then signed by MGM to do two pictures (neither was ever made) and in 1925 Lillian joined the MGM roster. Romola also starred Dorothy Gish and William H. Powell (that's the way he was billed then). Seen here in the wedding scene are Lillian in the title role and Powell as the villain, actually the best part in the picture.

One of the films already produced by the companies forming MGM and released just after the amalgamation was Metro's **Mademoiselle Midnight**. It was a trifle written by John Russell and Carl Harbaugh and starring Mae Murray (here with Johnny Arthur and Monte Blue) as the French heiress of a Mexican ranch. Robert Z. Leonard, the star's husband at that time, directed it. They had made a succession of popular but unmemorable pictures together under their Tiffany Productions banner, named after the famous jewellery shop rather than the gauze through which Miss Murray's close-ups were photographed.

The Valentino influence was still at full strength when Rex Ingram wrote and directed **The Arab**, with Ramon Novarro as a Bedouin tribe leader's son flaring his nostrils at the sight of Christian missionary Alice Terry. It was filmed in North Africa just before the MGM merger and Ingram edited it under the new regime. However, this fiery Irishman bridled at the very idea of supervision by studio bosses Mayer and Thalberg. He was backed by MGM's New York overlords Marcus Loew and Nicholas Schenck in his emigration to the French Riviera, where all his subsequent pictures were made.

To ensure an auspicious start with MGM, William Randolph Hearst's Cosmopolitan production company shot the works on **Janice Meredith**/The Beautiful Rebel, a great big splashy 'costume drama' directed by E. Mason Hopper and scripted by Lillie Hayward. The star was of course Marion Davies, at the centre of an American Revolution story involving the midnight ride of Paul Revere (Ken Maynard), the Boston Tea Party, a comic British sergeant (W. C. Fields) and several famous battles, not to mention Louis XVI and Marie Antoinette. It was a bit of a flop. Marion was really not at her best in the romantic dramas with which Hearst tried to make her a superstar.

Jackie Coogan, one of Hollywood's greatest child stars, was an important box-office asset for MGM during its early years. He had been famous ever since Chaplin chose him to team with him in The Kid (1919) and was still busy as a character actor in minor roles 50 years after his debut. Edward Cline directed Jackie in **Little Robinson Crusoe** as an orphan shipwrecked on an island whose natives made him a captive war god. Tom Santschi, Noble Johnson and Gloria Grey were also in Willard Mack's screenplay.

Jackie Coogan's first film made entirely under the MGM banner was **The Rag Man**. Edward Cline directed him in Willard Mack's screenplay as a kid who ran away from an orphanage fire and took refuge with a junk man (Max Davidson). Jackie was now a superstar needing an entourage of managers, press agents, secretaries, etc. He wore his Rag Man costume for this shot with his publicity chief, Lawrence Weingarten, who was soon to begin a 32-year stretch as one of MGM's most active producers – and become the husband of Sylvia Thalberg, Irving's screenplay-writing sister.

Wine of Youth was directed by King Vidor, who didn't consider it important enough to mention in his autobiography. However, it did advance the careers of three young stars-to-be: Ben Lyon, who had played the same role in the Rachel Crothers play on which the film was based, Eleanor Boardman and William Haines. Eleanor played a girl wooed by two suitors but made afraid of marriage by the quarrelling of her parents. Others in Carey Wilson's screenplay were Pauline Garon, Creighton Hale and William Collier Jr.

Virtually forgotten today, Viola Dana ranked as one of the top stars of the newly-amalgamated MGM. A lively comedienne, she enjoyed a long career which lasted until the fade-out of silent films. In **Along Came Ruth** she played a small town's live-wire who took over a furniture shop and its owner's nephew. Walter Hiers, Tully Marshall and Raymond McKee were also in the Winifred Dunn screenplay. Edward Cline directed . . . Miss Dana had to do some heavy emoting in **Revelation.** One of the dottier plots of 1924 cast her as a profligate Montmartre dancer who left her illegitimate child in a convent. An American artist was so smitten by her that he used her as the model for his painting of the Madonna, which miraculously made her reform, reclaim her child and marry the artist. George D. Baker directed from his own script based on a popular novel, 'The Rosebush of a Thousand Years'. Monte Blue and Lew Cody supported Miss Dana, seen here essaying an apache dance in the cabaret sequence.

One Night in Rome was no masterpiece, but it served to bring a great name of the American theatre to nourish MGM's budding prestige. Laurette Taylor made only three films during a triumph-studded career, all of them derived from plays by her husband, J. Hartley Manners, in which she had starred on Broadway. The first two were directed by King Vidor for Metro (Peg O' My Heart and Happiness); this third was shot in 1924 by Clarence Badger for MGM. She played a fortune-teller whose client (Warner Oland, the Swedish actor who was later to become the screen's most famous Oriental in the 'Charlie Chan' series) recognized her as the woman who had disappeared in a cloud of scandal after her husband's suicide. Tom Moore, Alan Hale and the lady billed as Miss Dupont were also in the cast.

Pauline Frederick, at the height of a long and illustrious career, made **Married Flirts** for the new company. It was one of those 'sophisticated' dramas, considered quite daring in those days of husbands being lured from wives. She played a novelist who lost her husband to a vamp, who thereupon rejected him to marry another man, who subsequently was enticed away by the novelist, who . . . Left to right: Mae Busch, Conrad Nagel, Pauline Frederick. Robert Vignola directed Julia Ivers' script from a current best-seller by Louis Joseph Vance.

Robert Z. Leonard directed **Cheaper to Marry**, from a play by Samuel Shipman, in the first of his 30 MGM years, the industry's longest association of any studio and director. That matrimony was not only a Good Thing but also a good financial deal was the moral of the film, with lawyer Conrad Nagel here making his merger bid for artist Marguerite de la Motte. Meanwhile his partner (Lewis Stone) was squandering their firm's assets on a gold-digger (Paulette Duval) and heading for suicide. Also cast: Louise Fazenda, Claude Gillingwater. Alice Duer Miller scripted.

One of the biggest moneymakers in American theatres at the time of the MGM amalgamation was Goldwyn's Three Weeks, written by Elinor Glyn and starring Aileen Pringle. Its follow-up, **His Hour**, was released in September 1924, with the box office lure of Glyn and Pringle augmented by that of John Gilbert, now just emerging as a major star, plus direction by King Vidor. Best-selling Madame Glyn (an Englishwoman, but always referred to as 'madame') and the Hollywood of the Twenties were made for each other. Both purveyed Glamour with a capital 'Gee', and never more so than in His Hour. Emily Fitzroy, Lawrence Grant and Jacqueline Gadsden supported Gilbert and Miss Pringle, who are seen here in a scene captioned: 'Gritzko manoeuvres Tamara to his lodge, she resists his advances until she collapses from exhaustion.' . . . Well, she tried.

A clutch of 1924 melos: In **The Bandolero**, Gustav von Seyffertitz (bearer of one of the screen's truly memorable names) had a difficult scene when he had to register conflicting emotions while watching Manuel Granado, as the son he thought had died years before, being married by Gordon Begg to Renee Adoree, daughter of the bandit who had kidnapped the son and reared him as a matador. Complicated, but commercial. Tom Terriss directed, mostly in Spain, from his script . . . Alice Terry was

the gentlewoman rescued from the fate worse than death by goldminer Conway Tearle in **The Great Divide**, with Wallace Beery as the nastiest man in the West. Reginald Barker directed this robust melodrama, adapted by Benjamin Glazer and Waldemar Young from a stage blood-and-thunderer that had been touring the USA for a dozen years. In 1929 he repeated the chore for First National with Dorothy Mackaill starring. It was a moneymaker every time . . . **The Dixie Handicap** was

unabashedly old-fashioned drama with everybody right in there acting for dear life. Left to right: Lloyd Hughes (hero), Otis Harlan (old retainer), Joseph Morrison (errant groom), Frank Keenan (racehorse owner), Claire Windsor (his daughter). In those days, the movies saw nothing incongruous in casting white (Harlan) and black (Morrison) actors together as Negroes. Reginald Barker directed; Waldemar Young scripted.

Sherlock, Jr, *made by Buster Keaton for Metro, was another of the early attractions to come through the new distribution set-up. It was one of the comedian's most imaginative feature-length films, with unusual photographic effects as well as the hair-raising stunts and chases that Keaton delighted in doing (without the aid of a double). He played a sleepy projectionist dreaming his way into his theatre's screen as a daredevil hero foiling the villain who kidnapped his girl. This shot shows the hero's valet, disguised as a motorcycle cop, just before he fell off the machine leaving Buster on the handlebars to hurtle through a glorious sequence of near-disasters. Jean Havez, Clyde Bruckman and Joseph Mitchell wrote the Joseph Schenck production.*

The most successful financially of all the feature-length pictures produced at Buster Keaton's studio for Metro or MGM release, **The Navigator** was, and is, considered by many Keaton buffs to be the funniest film he ever made. He played a dimwitted millionaire adrift in an ocean liner with no one else aboard but Kathryn McGuire. Approaching land, they were attacked by cannibals and escaped into the sea; the movie ended with a marvellous underwater sequence. Buster co-directed with Donald Crisp, better known as an actor, and the usual Keaton team of Jean Havez, Clyde Bruckman and Joseph Mitchell scripted.

'Sheer beauty is the only way to describe these gorgeous creatures!' said the caption for this still from **The Beauty Prize**. Lloyd Ingraham (actor of many supporting roles in later years) directed Viola Dana, Pat O'Malley, Eddie Phillips and Edward Connelly in the story of a manicurist who won a beauty contest while posing as a debutante and revealed her deception via that new craze, the radio. Written by Nina Wilcox Putnam and Winifred Dunn.

In **Lady of the Night** Norma Shearer had a shot at a dual role, playing a girl of the underworld and a daughter of luxury. The former was discharged from a reformatory on the same day as the latter graduated from finishing school. By another thumping coincidence, they both encountered a young inventor (Malcolm McGregor, here) who, bewildered by their resemblance, fell in love with both. George K. Arthur was the recipient of the bad Norma's kiss. Monta Bell directed Adela Rogers St Johns' dotty story.

Eleanor Boardman, a cool, charming actress of considerable skill, was extremely useful to MGM. Three 1924 movies were: **So this is Marriage** with Conrad Nagel. 'You're not fit to be his mother,' he snarled at her, playing domineering husband to her frivolous wife in this Hobart Henley production, which surprisingly climaxed with a biblical sequence depicting the story of David and Bathsheba. Seems that Eleanor, wearied of connubial rows, toyed with the idea of divorcing Conrad and marrying Lew Cody. The latter, noble fellow, thereupon read her the bible story, filmed in colour. Impressed, she went back to her husband, in black-and-white. Script: Carey Wilson, John Lynch, Alice D. G. Miller. Also cast: Warner Oland, John Boles, Clyde Cook, Edward Connelly, Miss Dupont, Francis McDonald, Tom O'Brien . . . Miss Boardman

took a rather unconvincing fling at male impersonation in **The Silent Accuser**. She was searching for the murderer of her stepfather. Filling her lap in this Mexican tavern scene is Edna Tichenor; dog star Peter the Great woofed through the title role as the only witness of the murder. Director was Chester Franklin, who also wrote the script with Frank O'Connor. Raymond McKee was the hero . . . Below,

Sinners in Silk: 'Here is the truth about today's flappers and lounge lizards!' claimed the advertising for this gee-whiz drama by Benjamin Glazer and Wilson. Adolphe Menjou, here playfully spiking the drinks of Hedda Hopper and Bradley Ward at a wild party, was a roué who then continued to celebrate his successful rejuvenation surgery by taking a girl home with him. His sinful intentions were thwarted when she revealed herself to be the sweetheart of his son. Miss Boardman (girl), Nagel (son), Jean Hersholt and Miss Dupont were others in the cast, directed by Henley.

Victor Schertzinger, who was to become more famous in the talkie era, directed **Bread**, a domestic drama scripted by Lenore Coffee and Albert Lewin from the best-selling novel by Charles G. Norris. He shared with Charles Chaplin the distinction of being the music composer as well as the director of his pictures. In fact, he wrote the first score for theatre musicians to play during a film: Thomas Ince's Civilization in 1916. Mae Busch and Pat O'Malley, already veterans of the silent screen, had the leads. Also cast were Robert Frazer, Wanda Hawley and Hobart Bosworth.

Robert Z. Leonard directed Mae Murray for the last time in Ibanez's story **Circe the Enchantress**; they were divorced soon afterwards. The legendary Circe could turn men into swine, and so could her 1924 counterpart as portrayed with gusto by Miss Murray. The heroine, having been corrupted by a cad when she was an innocent convent girl, proceeded to tempt and torment all the males in sight. Suddenly repenting in the middle of an orgy, she fled back to the convent, only to be paralyzed by a car crash on the way. The film ended with that 'Walk towards me . . . you can do it' treatment that has cured many a movie cripple, this time applied by hero James Kirkwood. William Haines had a featured role.

Although neither was the superstar each was soon to become, Norma Shearer and John Gilbert drew large crowds to **The Snob**, which opened in the same month (November 1924) as the more ambitious He Who Gets Slapped. This quick successor to their first romantic teaming was directed by Monta Bell from his own script, and is an example of that era's movie preoccupation with marriage and divorce. They played schoolteachers, married for love, parted by his obsessive desire for wealth and social position. Phyllis Haver, playing the blonde heiress who lured him away, shared featured billing with Conrad Nagel and Hedda Hopper (who eventually became a much-feared gossip columnist).

1924 *When MGM opened shop it found some problem items on the shelves stocked by former proprietors. A major one was Erich von Stroheim's* **Greed***, which he had finished shooting for the Goldwyn company in 1923. A year passed before its release, during which time it was cut from its original, impossible 42 reels (about four times as long as a long film should be) to 24. At this stage von Stroheim baulked, saying that this was his masterpiece and it would be ruined by further editing. He was half right: it was his masterpiece, but it wasn't ruined even after he allowed Rex Ingram to cut six reels and June Mathis, without his permission, whittled off eight more. It was an unremittingly realistic filming of a sordid novel, Frank Norris' 'McTeague', first done by World Films in 1915, and dealt with sleazy characters living in squalor, obsessed by money-love to the point of insanity. In a company and an industry dedicated to mass entertainment,* Greed *was a freak, and, as Mayer predicted, audiences found it repellent: it never recovered its cost. Nevertheless, it stands among the memorable artistic achievements in Hollywood's history. ZaSu Pitts (left with Dale Fuller) gave a dramatic performance of harrowing intensity as McTeague's wife, murdered for the money she hoarded. Von Stroheim's script also spotlighted Gibson Gowland (McTeague) and Jean Hersholt.*

The Prairie Wife, *made for MGM by a one-picture independent outfit (oddly, in view of the locale, named Eastern Productions), co-starred English actor Gibson Gowland as a result of his powerful performance as the wife-murdering dentist in* Greed. *Gowland played for almost every Hollywood company during a long career, but never had another opportunity as great as von Stroheim had given him. In the new film he was the brutal caretaker of a Western homestead, terrifying the society girl brought to it as a bride. Hugo Ballin scripted, and directed a cast that also included Dorothy Devore, Herbert Rawlinson and Boris Karloff.*

Wife of the Centaur *was King Vidor's second sex drama in succession (after* His Hour*) to star John Gilbert and Aileen Pringle. Cyril Hume's book, on which it was based, was pretty outspoken stuff for 1923 and the sensation it caused did no harm at all to the box office take of the following year's film version. Gilbert and Eleanor Boardman (together here) played a neurotic novelist and his unsophisticated wife who almost lost him to Pringle, drink and debauchery. William Haines had a supporting role in the film.*

16

SILENTLY EPIC
1925

MGM-Loew's Inc. made a profit of $4,708,631 in the studio's first full year, easily surpassing all but Paramount, which reported a million more.

Paramount had a strong star list, with Gloria Swanson, Richard Dix, Rudolph Valentino, Bebe Daniels, Thomas Meighan, Nita Naldi, Rod La Rocque, Jack Holt and the new sensation, Pola Negri.

Other studios prospered with Colleen Moore in *So Big*, Corinne Griffith in *Declassée* (with an extra named Clark Gable), Harold Lloyd in *The Freshman*, Lon Chaney in *The Phantom of the Opera*, Charlie Chaplin in *The Gold Rush* and brother Sydney in *Charley's Aunt*. Sam Goldwyn expanded his bank balance with mother-love sacrifice in *Stella Dallas* and the throbbing Vilma Banky–Ronald Colman romance of *The Dark Angel*.

They were all pretty harmless, but influential critic G. A. Atkinson told his London wireless listeners: 'Hollywood is pouring out a torrent of sophisticated barbarism . . . diabolically cynical!'

The biggest gamble of MGM's first year was inherited from the Goldwyn company. In 1923 that organization (Samuel Goldwyn had no connection with it by then) had propped up its tottering prestige by obtaining movie rights to **Ben-Hur**. *Lew Wallace's fabulous best-seller was also a huge moneymaker on the stage, and Goldwyn had had to sign away an unheard-of 50 per cent of the film's future income to get it. A massive production budget had been required: a company headed by director Charles Brabin, writer-supervisor June Mathis and star George Walsh trekked to Rome, where enormous sets were constructed. Cameras had been rolling spasmodically for three months when Goldwyn became part of MGM. News of sluggish progress so disquieted the new firm that president Marcus Loew himself sailed to the rescue with replacements: director Fred Niblo, writers Bess Meredyth and Carey Wilson, and star Ramon Novarro (here as Ben-Hur, with Francis X. Bushman as the villainous Messala). But before long there were signs that the new key people were having as disastrous a time as the old, and early in 1925 Mayer and Thalberg prevailed upon Loew to order the whole enterprise back to California where they could keep an eye on it. They did so with such efficiency – and lavish expenditure – that* Ben-Hur *emerged as the greatest world-wide success the movie industry had ever produced (except, possibly,* The Birth of a Nation*). However, its $6m. cost was never entirely recouped, thanks to that original 50 per cent royalty deal. Also cast: May McAvoy, Carmel Myers, Mitchell Lewis, Betty Bronson, Nigel de Brulier.*

The other film that really put MGM on top
▽ *was* **The Big Parade**. *Its twin New York premieres on November 19, 1925 at the Astor (where it ran 96 weeks and grossed $1.5m.) and the Capitol were the start of a furore which swept most of the world's filmgoers and critics into ecstasies of praise. In all, $15m. worth of customers loved it, and so did MGM: it had cost only $250,000 to make. Hobart Bosworth and Claire McDowell had parts in the Laurence Stallings–Harry Behn screenplay. When King Vidor had finished filming, Mayer realized the movie's immense potential and persuaded him to accept a flat payment instead of his contractual*

20 per cent of profits, which would have given him ten times as much. Mayer talked directors Victor Seastrom and Erich von Stroheim into similar revisions when it appeared beneficial to the company. A 1971 television screening of The Big Parade *(rare indeed for a silent feature) showed it to be still a moving depiction of one man's World War I, if not the towering master-work it once seemed. The love scenes of John Gilbert and Renee Adoree (right), alternately tender and vivacious, still shine; the panoramic shots of an army on the move and the closer incidents of battle remain impressive. However, the comic bits by Gilbert's buddies, Tom O'Brien and Karl Dane (second and third from left) now look pretty crude.*

MGM cameras crossed the continent from California to Maryland to film exterior shots for **The Midshipman** at the US Naval Academy ▷ at Annapolis. It was directed by Christy Cabanne who had directed Mayer's very first venture into production, The Great Secret, a 1916 serial. Ramon Novarro had to demonstrate as much athleticism as acting ability, and to somewhat greater effect: the training sequences carried more conviction than the routine plot by Carey Wilson about student (Novarro) compromised by sister (Harriet Hammond) of classmate (Wesley Barry) at instigation of nasty fiancé (Crauford Kent). The picture was a popular success and Novarro later played an undergraduate in two more.

Lights of Old Broadway/Merry Wives of Gotham *was one of the most profitable Marion Davies releases. She played orphan twins, one adopted by a rich family, the other by a poor one, with Conrad Nagel as the rich brother*

falling in love with the poor sister. Monta Bell, intently heeded by Nagel, Frank Currier and Miss Davies, wields his megaphone on the set – no director of silent films was fully equipped without this aid (thus 'megger' was slang for director) through which he broadcast his instructions before and during the action. George K. Arthur, Julia Swayne Gordon and Matthew Betz also had parts in Carey Wilson's script.

1925

Anita Stewart was the star who gave Mayer his start as a Hollywood moviemaker. Having prospered in exhibition and distribution and tried production (of a serial in New York), he decided that the latter offered the most promising future. All he needed in order to break into the Hollywood ring was a star. So in 1918 he snatched Vitagraph's biggest (causing a split with his distribution associates – Metro, ironically enough) and went to work as the producer of Anita Stewart pictures. Seven years later Anita was still box office, and Mayer signed her for MGM's **Never The Twain Shall Meet**. Peter B. Kyne's popular novel was directed by Maurice Tourneur, who gave it his usual high artistic quality. Miss Stewart played the South Seas girl taken by her father (Huntley Gordon) to San Francisco, where he died. She and his friend (Bert Lytell) went back to her native isle to marry, but he was driven by the heat and idleness of the tropics to return to his American sweetheart (Justine Johnstone).

For every epic and star vehicle MGM made it turned out several 'B' pictures to keep the Loew circuit and other cinemas supplied . . . such as **Don't** – an unfortunate title, from which filmgoers took the hint – with Sally O'Neil as a parent-defying flapper, John Patrick, Bert Roach and Ethel Wales, directed by Alf Goulding; and **The White Desert**, a melodrama about railroad tunnel builders, with Pat O'Malley and Claire Windsor, plus Robert Frazer, Frank Currier and Sojin, directed by Reginald Barker.

MGM became an assiduous gleaner of European talent, and Benjamin Christensen, gifted Danish director with 15 years in Copenhagen and Berlin studios behind him, was one of the early imports. He wrote and directed **The Devil's Circus**, with Norma Shearer and Charles Emmett Mack (here) as a trapeze artist and a pickpocket who got themselves

almost fatally involved with a lion-tamer (John Miljan) and his jealous wife (Carmel Myers). All concerned hoped for another He Who Gets Slapped – but no.

The characteristically sinister touches of author-director Tod Browning made for effective drama in **The Mystic**. Here Aileen Pringle eschews her sultry seductions for a bit of gypsy roguery. She and confederate Mitchell Lewis (here) aided the crooked guardian (Conway Tearle) of an heiress (Gladys Hulette) to get control of her fortune by means of fake seances. Scripted by Waldemar Young.

Zander the Great was the first of many MGM pictures directed by George Hill – and a loser for an untypically drab Marion Davies. She's seen here with Emily Fitzroy, British actress who appeared in dozens of Hollywood movies; and Jack Huff as Zander, a boy in search of his missing father. Marion took him out West, where a substitute father was found in a smuggler who rescued them from bandits. Holbrook Blinn, Harrison Ford, Hedda Hopper and Hobart Bosworth were also in the cast. Written by Frances Marion from Edward Fields' 1923 play.

King Vidor liked the leading lady of **Proud Flesh** better than the story he had to direct – and who could blame him? He married Eleanor Boardman, and extracted as much entertain-

ment value as possible from the yarn about a San Francisco earthquake orphan adopted by relatives in Spain and wooed by a handsome Romeo there. She turned him down and went back to a Frisco plumber. Harrison Ford (here) and Pat O'Malley played opposite Miss Boardman, with Trixie Friganza, Sojin and Margaret Seddon filling other roles. Written by Harry Behn and Agnes Christine Johnston.

The Sporting Venus was the second MGM release made by Blanche Sweet (here wearing the lowest waistline of 1925) and her director-husband, Marshall Neilan. She played a Scottish heiress who loved a medical student (Ronald Colman, with her in this scene) but was bespoken to a foreign prince (Lew Cody). Said the subtitle introducing this scene: 'Believing Donald no longer cares for her, Lady Gwendolyn plunges into the mad whirl of London night life.' Non-plungers were George Fawcett, Kate Price, Arthur Hoyt, Hank Mann. Thomas Geraghty scripted Gerald Beaumont's original.

Rex Ingram's first production made in voluntary exile was **Mare Nostrum**, scripted by Willis Goldbeck from Vicente Blasco Ibanez's 1918 war novel. It was a fine film and a potent moneyspinner. Spectacular exteriors, shot in Spain and Italy and on the Mediterranean, enhanced a vivid love story about a Spanish captain (Antonio Moreno) and a German spy (Alice Terry, here in her execution scene).

Charles Ray became a star by playing ingenuous country boys, and rarely got a chance to be anything else. In Robert Z. Leonard's **Bright Lights** he was the farm lad who fell for a Broadway dancer home for a visit (Pauline Starke, with him here), and who came a cropper trying to emulate her big-city wastrel friends (Lilyan Tashman, Ned Sparks). Original, Richard Connell; script, Jessie Burns, Lew Lipton.

Passion a la Elinor Glyn: the mysteriously titled **The Only Thing** *concerned an English duke-diplomat, mythical kingdom royalty and revolution on the shores of the Mediterranean. Conrad Nagel, who played the hero, set an all-time record by starring in 13 MGM movies in 18 months, 1924–5. Mayer rewarded him later by influencing his appointment as president of the Academy of Motion Picture Arts and Sciences. The almost equally busy Eleanor Boardman (with Nagel here) co-starred in the movie which marked the beginning of Jack Conway's long career as an MGM director. Also cast: Edward Connelly, Arthur Edmund Carewe, Vera Lewis, Dale Fuller, Ned Sparks.*

Soul Mates, *adapted by Carey Wilson from the novelist's 1911 book 'The Reason Why', was the second successive collaboration between Glyn and director Jack Conway. Aileen Pringle was the heroine, whose voluptuousness was exceeded only by the length of her train–but who was nevertheless Good, keeping a formidable banister between herself and a lustful lord (Edmund Lowe). Happily, he was allowed upstairs after paying off the mortgage held by her wicked uncle. Also cast: Phillips Smalley, Edythe Chapman, Lucien Littlefield and Ned Sparks.*

Lew Cody was to silents what William Powell became to talkies: the best of suave, man-of-the-world comedians. He had a good time in **Man and Maid** *(directed by Victor Schertzinger from an Elinor Glyn novel) playing a boulevardier who had to choose between a naughty lady and his virtuous secretary in wartime Paris. Renee Adoree (with him here) and Harriet Hammond were the alternatives in this refreshingly lighter-than-usual confection from Madame Glyn. Also cast: Paulette Duval, Alec B. Francis, Crauford Kent, Jacqueline Gadsden.*

One of the must-see performances on the New York stage in 1924 was that of Lucille La Verne as the hard-bitten mother of a Kentucky backwoods family in **Sun-Up**. *The 1925 film version recaptured the play's gritty realism under Edmund Goulding's direction, with (left to right) Pauline Starke, Miss La Verne, Edward Connelly, Conrad Nagel. Goulding scripted Lulu Vollmer's play. In this scene Nagel reveals that the army deserter they are sheltering is the son of a Prohibition officer who had shot two men of the family. 'Kill him!' says Ma.*

Antedating Walt Disney by several years, MGM banked on the universal affection elicited by elephants and made a popular movie about one. It was rather misleadingly titled **The Great Love**. *Viola Dana, Robert Agnew, ZaSu Pitts and Frank Currier were in the Marshall Neilan production (he also scripted) but the real star was Norma, seen here with veteran comic Chester Conklin as her keeper.*

Go West, *written, directed, produced by and starring Buster Keaton, was a remarkable job of one-man picture-making and one of the most lovable of silent comedies. Dragging all he owned behind him, homeless Homer took a tip from America's pioneers and decided to Go West. The only other important character in it was Brown Eyes, a cow rescued from a cattle train by Homer to become his inseparable friend.*

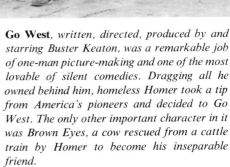

Buster Keaton directed **Seven Chances** *himself, using a Broadway farce by Roi Cooper Magrue as the scenario's basis. He had a problem in the film: on his 27th birthday he was told he would inherit $7,000,000, provided he was married by 7 pm that day. His frantic efforts to find a willing lady (Hazel Deane is the refuser in this scene) provided funny incidents, without really giving full scope to the star's talents. Joseph Schenck produced, with T. Roy Barnes, Snitz Edwards, Jean Arthur, Ruth Dwyer cast.*

A year after He Who Gets Slapped, *Victor Seastrom completed* **The Tower of Lies**, *another impressive drama in which Lon Chaney again suffered, was driven to madness, and died. And again these two fine artists struck just the right note of brooding tragedy in spite of plot elements that were sheer nickelodeon. Norma Shearer repeated her earlier success opposite Chaney; he was a Swedish farmer and she the beloved daughter who saved him from bankruptcy by eloping to the big city with their rapacious landlord. Ian Keith played the villain and William Haines, David Torrence and Claire McDowell were also involved. Mayer took producer credit for the Seastrom–Carey Wilson screenplay.*

One of the biggest hits in Lon Chaney's career was **The Unholy Three**, *a weird story written by Clarence Robbins and Waldemar Young and directed by Tod Browning. It was about circus sideshow performers: a ventriloquist (Chaney), a strong man (Victor McLaglen) and a midget (Harry Earles). Assisted by a light-fingered lady (Mae Busch) they augmented their income by picking pockets, which progressed into burglary and finally murder. Miss Busch (here with Chaney) was an Australian actress specializing in vamps and villainesses. Matt Moore and Edward Connelly were also cast.*

Lon Chaney was the Limehouse thief known as **The Blackbird**, *who used a second identity when necessary: a rescue mission keeper with contorted legs. After one robbery he killed a policeman and took cover under his usual crippled disguise, then found his joints had become permanently locked. This typical example of the writing and directing style of Tod Browning, often Chaney's collaborator, had Renee Adoree and Owen Moore (here) for romantic interest, with Doris Lloyd, Sidney Bracey and Lionel Belmore supporting.*

The Monster *is a title that might have served for four out of five Lon Chaney movies. No villainy was too vile for Lon, no disguise too grotesque. Unusually, he wore very little make-up as this particular monster (looking, in fact, remarkably like his future successor in monster-ship, Boris Karloff). He played an insane surgeon who abducted passing motorists for experiments in bringing the dead back to life. Here he is seen hypnotizing Walter James, who got all the make-up that was going in this one. Gertrude Olmstead, Hallam Cooley and Johnny Arthur were featured, and Roland West directed the Willard Mack–Albert Kenyon script, from a play by Crane Wilbur.*

In **Dance Madness** Claire Windsor played a dancer married to an alcoholic hell-raiser (the ubiquitous Conrad Nagel, cast against type). During one of their riotous parties she tested his fidelity by impersonating a notorious masked dancer (Hedda Hopper) and trying to seduce him. Those wild young pleasure-seekers of the roaring Twenties were displayed in a film which could have been inspired by the contemporary life and/or works of Scott Fitzgerald. Director Robert Z. Leonard; author, S. Jay Kaufman.

During MGM's first two years Eleanor Boardman was starred, or featured, in 11 releases. **The Way of a Girl** led her down the highway, through city streets in a mile-a-minute auto. As a speed-crazed flapper Miss Boardman survived arrests and smash-ups, only to become a hostage held by escaping convicts. Robert Vignola directed the thriller, with Matt Moore and Matthew Betz (here with Eleanor) featured. Also cast: William Russell, Charles French, Kate Price. Writers: Katherine Newlin Burt, Albert Le Vino . . . In **An Exchange of Wives** Boardman was involved in the fun and games which became commonplace in certain circles four decades later, but were a novelty in 1925. The daring (really innocent) goings-on were conducted by Hobart Henley, with the plot coming from Cosmo Hamilton's Broadway play, scripted by Frederic and Fanny Hatton. Her fellow mate-swappers, Lew Cody, Renee Adoree and Creighton Hale, were also kept very busy by MGM. The studio's stock company of contractees was much smaller than it later became.

How to keep a husband – and how to get one: the screen fairly radiated mature charm when **Daddy's Gone A'Hunting**/A Man's World brought Alice Joyce and Percy Marmont together. She had been a leading lady since the heyday of the Vitagraph company, and the English actor had recently scored a hit in If Winter Comes. The new picture – the only one either star made for MGM – was from a play by Zoe Akins, a drama of bohemian husband

versus homeloving wife. Frank Borzage directed with the accent on sentiment and with Virginia Marshall, Ford Sterling and Holmes Herbert in the cast. . . . The decor destined to be dubbed 'Early MGM' by future connoisseurs was seen in all its glory in **A Slave of Fashion**. William Haines, Lew Cody and Norma Shearer are nearly overwhelmed by the set in this scene from Hobart Henley's production, a comedy (by Samuel Shipman, Bess Meredyth, Jane Murfin) about a small-town girl who stole a train-wreck victim's lease on a New York flat in order to taste the life of luxury. When her family turned up she pretended to be the wife of the absent owner; then the owner turned up. Reader, she married him.

Victor Seastrom directed **Confessions of a Queen**, from Alphonse Daudet's 'Les Rois en Exil'. His moody Scandinavian artistry combined oddly with the French writer's ironic humour, and the film was something like an operetta without music. Left to right: Lewis Stone, Alice Terry and John Bowers, as the king-queen-prince triangle. Eugenie Besserer and Andre de Beranger were also in the Agnes Christine Johnston screenplay. After a few years with MGM, Seastrom returned to Sweden and his real name (Sjostrom); three decades later, at 77, he won world acclaim as an actor in Bergman's Wild Strawberries.

Claire Windsor was a charming beauty who held her place in the second flight of stars for many years. **The Denial** gave her a strong role. As the stern mother in this early scene she is confronted by her daughter (Lucille Rickson) asking for consent to marry a young officer (Robert Agnew). Flashback related the tragic consequences of her own mother (Emily Fitzroy) opposing her and her lover (William Haines) in the same situation. Hobart Henley directed; Agnes Christine Johnston adapted Lewis Beach's play.

Rex Beach's novel **The Auction Block** had made a hit for Goldwyn Pictures in 1917, so eight years later MGM gave it another whirl, re-scripted by Frederic and Fanny Hatton with Charles Ray and Eleanor Boardman forming a new co-starring team and Hobart Henley directing. The story–about a rich New Yorker (unusual role for Ray) and a Southern beauty contest winner who considered him an idle wastrel until he took a job in a shoe shop–was pretty thin for a novel, let alone two films. Sally O'Neil (here), as Eleanor's man-chasing friend, helped to pep it up, with David Torrence and Ned Sparks also cast.

The well-knit plot of Somerset Maugham's 1921 stage success **The Circle** provided Miss Boardman (centre) and (from left) Hale, Eulalie Jensen, Malcolm McGregor and Alec B. Francis with excellent parts. The film was directed by Frank Borzage, later to be Hollywood's foremost specialist in romantic pathos. It nicely fitted the 1925 vogue for marital infidelity in films, although it suffered by losing Maugham's urbane dialogue. Note the studio's favourite chair, last seen bearing Norma Shearer in Slave of Fashion.

In contrast to the quiet advent of Garbo, the arrival of Lillian Gish at the studio for **La Boheme** was that of a queen (their films were in production simultaneously in autumn 1925). The spotlight was on the Gish set, where King Vidor was directing the illustrious star whose signing to a long-term contract was a major MGM coup. Aided by Vidor and a passionate performance by co-star John Gilbert, Lillian gave one of her most affecting portrayals of tremulous pathos. Her technique in achieving its realism startled all concerned: for example for three days before filming Mimi's death scene she parched her lips by allowing no liquid to touch them, and trained herself to breathe without visible movement. Other characters in the Harry Behn–Ray Doyle script from Murger's 'Vie de Bohème' were played by Renee Adoree, Roy D'Arcy and Edward Everett Horton.

Twelve weeks of volcanic outbursts of temperament followed when Thalberg cast Mae Murray as **The Merry Widow** and assigned Erich von Stroheim to direct the film. Filming was frequently interrupted while star and director hurled insults at each other; at one point von Stroheim walked out of the studio and was replaced for a time by Monta Bell. There were also frequent clashes between the director and Thalberg, who had had painful past experience of the German's extravagant disregard for budget and running time (on Foolish Wives, when they were both at Universal, and Greed). One row yielded the classic Hollywood squelch: when von Stroheim explained an endless shot of a character's collection of shoes with, 'He has a foot fetish', Thalberg retorted, 'And you have a footage fetish!' But there was a happy ending: the picture proved a tremendous success. Von Stroheim had drawn the best performance of her career from Miss Murray; her bizarre personality had never been so excitingly displayed. Co-star John Gilbert also scored strongly, as did Roy D'Arcy, Tully Marshall and Edward Connelly in lesser roles. Script by the director and Benjamin Glazer.

In spite of her triumph in Greed, ZaSu Pitts received only one more big dramatic opportunity before she was restricted to the eyebrow-arching, finger-twisting comedy character who graced countless movies until she died in 1963. It was in **Pretty Ladies**, a backstage story by Adela Rogers St Johns, directed by Monta Bell. She played a pathetic Broadway star whose husband left her for one of the show's beauties. Not the blonde-wigged one in this scene: that was Lucille LeSueur, a screen newcomer playing a tiny role and hoping for bigger ones. She got 'em all right, in over 40 years of stardom as Joan Crawford. Another young hopeful playing another bit part was Myrna Loy. More prominent in the cast were Tom Moore, Norma Shearer, Lilyan Tashman, Conrad Nagel, Ann Pennington, George K. Arthur, Roy D'Arcy, Gwen Lee.

An effective script by Frederic and Fanny Hatton, well-directed by Robert Z. Leonard, gave the company a hit in **Time, the Comedian**. Mae Busch (left) played a singer with a past: she had left her husband for Lew Cody but the affair cooled when her husband committed suicide. Years later Cody and her daughter met and fell in love, whereupon mother revealed all to daughter (Gertrude Olmstead) who consoled herself with a younger suitor (Creighton Hale, right). Pipe Mae's 1925 chic.

Norma Shearer was steadily rising in popularity in 1925 and the studio made the most of it, putting her into a new film every other month. One of the less important was **His Secretary**, a comedy about an ugly duckling who overheard her boss saying he wouldn't kiss her for a thousand dollars. She went to a beautician who transformed her, and . . . you guessed it. Also cast in Hobart Henley's production were Lew Cody, Willard Louis, Karl Dane, Gwen Lee and (here, as her stunned office colleague) Ernest Gillen. Louis D. Lighton, later a top producer, and Hope Loring wrote the piffling scenario.

After two weeks of shooting **The Masked Bride** (script by Carey Wilson) director Josef von Sternberg emulated his fellow von (Stroheim) by walking out on a Mae Murray picture. It was completed by Christy Cabanne. Here apache dancer Mae defies detective Roy D'Arcy after accosting millionaire Francis X. Bushman. When not busy in bistro floor shows Mae was forced by her partner (Basil Rathbone) to rob rich men.

Real fame arrived for three young actresses via a box-office smash, **Sally, Irene and Mary**, scripted and directed by Edmund Goulding. It was about chorus girls in a Broadway show: Constance Bennett (left) was Sally, the gold-digger kept by a millionaire (Henry Kolker) who also fancied Sally O'Neil (centre) who played Mary, the girl from the slums. She rejected the primrose path to return to her poor sweetheart (William Haines); but there was no happy ending for Joan Crawford (right) as Irene, the romantic dreamer, whose wedding to a college boy (Ray Howard) was followed by death in a car crash. Soon after this film Miss Bennett left Hollywood for a few years as the wife of a real millionaire, Miss O'Neil enjoyed a fair spell of stardom, and Miss Crawford went on forever.

The 1924 success of The Rag Man called for a quick sequel. So in **Old Clothes** Jackie Coogan and Max Davidson again played partners in the junk business, with Edward Cline and Willard Mack repeating as director and writer, respectively. The new element was Joan Crawford, as a waif who took shelter with them and ended in correct storybook style with a rich young fiancé (Allan Forrest).

Late in 1925 when MGM was the talk of the industry because of blockbusters like The Merry Widow, Ben-Hur and The Big Parade, something of ultimately greater importance was going on: Greta Garbo was beginning her career at Culver City. Far from being regarded as an event worthy of mention in film history this was more a matter of trying out a new girl opposite the star, Ricardo Cortez, in **The Torrent**. Ibanez's story was of a Spanish aristocrat and a poor girl on his estate; his mother prevented their marriage, the girl became an opera star and returned to find him a middle-aged parody of her former lover (here). Director Monta Bell found that the 20-year-old newcomer was an instinctive actress, easy to guide through her role's considerable range. Cameraman William Daniels, who was to work with her during most of her career, found her unusual face a joy to photograph from any angle. And Mayer was well pleased that he had signed the leading lady of Sweden's The Story of Gosta Berling (along with its director, Mauritz Stiller, and star, Lars Hanson) during his recent European jaunt. Scenario: Dorothy Farnum. Also cast: Gertrude Olmstead, Edward Connelly, Martha Mattox.

SUCCESS OVER ALL
1926

The Jazz Age accelerated with bootleg booze as its fuel, the Charleston as its theme tune, tabloid newspapers as the chroniclers of its murder trials and sex scandals.

740 features were released by all companies, and MGM-Loew's became the industry's No. 1 with a profit of $6,388,200.

New stars were coming up: First National had Harry Langdon and Dorothy Mackaill; Fox had Janet Gaynor, Charles Farrell and Dolores Del Rio; Paramount struck oil with a comedy team, Wallace Beery and Raymond Hatton, and featured new flappers Clara Bow and Louise Brooks – the first to become a legend, the second a cult among cineastes decades after she left the screen. MGM advertised: 'Greta Garbo, discovered in stark Sweden, is setting the heart of America aflame!'. And the movie-going millions were stunned by the death of Valentino. Top hits included *Peter Pan, Beau Geste, The Circus, The Great Gatsby, Kiki* and, in a new process called Technicolor, *The Black Pirate*.

*Buster Keaton starred in and directed **Battling Butler** for MGM release, before switching to United Artists for two years. It had been a hit for Charles Ruggles as a stage musical comedy and Keaton more than made up in comedy what it lost in music. As in* The Navigator, *he played an addle-brained millionaire, this time pretending to be a champion boxer in order to win the girl (Sally O'Neil). Writers: Al Boasberg, Charles Smith, Paul Gerard Smith, Lex Neal.*

The longest actor-studio association in film history – it lasted 29 years – began with **The Barrier**, *Lionel Barrymore's first for MGM. The Rex Beach story cast Barrymore as a brutal sea captain who baulked Marceline Day's marriage to Norman Kerry by revealing Henry B. Walthall's secret of her parentage. An Alaskan storm was the climax, spectacularly staged by director George Hill. Author Beach had himself produced a version in 1917.*

Tod Browning urged the combatants on from this side of the camera in the no-holds-barred climax of **The Road to Mandalay**, *with Lon Chaney and Owen Moore throttling each other and Lois Moran stabbing Chaney. Lois, usually one of the gentler film ladies, was only 17 when this was made, and went on to more important stage and screen roles. Her name still crops up whenever another biography of Scott Fitzgerald appears. Chaney and Moore played partners in crime, with Lois as daughter of the former and sweetheart of the latter. This Browning–Herman Mankiewicz story was scripted by Elliott Clawson, with Henry B. Walthall and Sojin in minor roles.*

Tell It to the Marines, *Leo the Lion's Christmas gift to American box-offices, was second only to* Flesh and the Devil *as a 1926/7 superhit. It made an important star of William Haines and gave the versatile Lon Chaney a change of pace as a tough, heart-of-gold sergeant. The eventful plot also brought in Eleanor Boardman as a nurse, Carmel Myers as a Filipino vamp and Warner Oland as a Chinese bandit chief. George Hill directed, Richard Schayer wrote.*

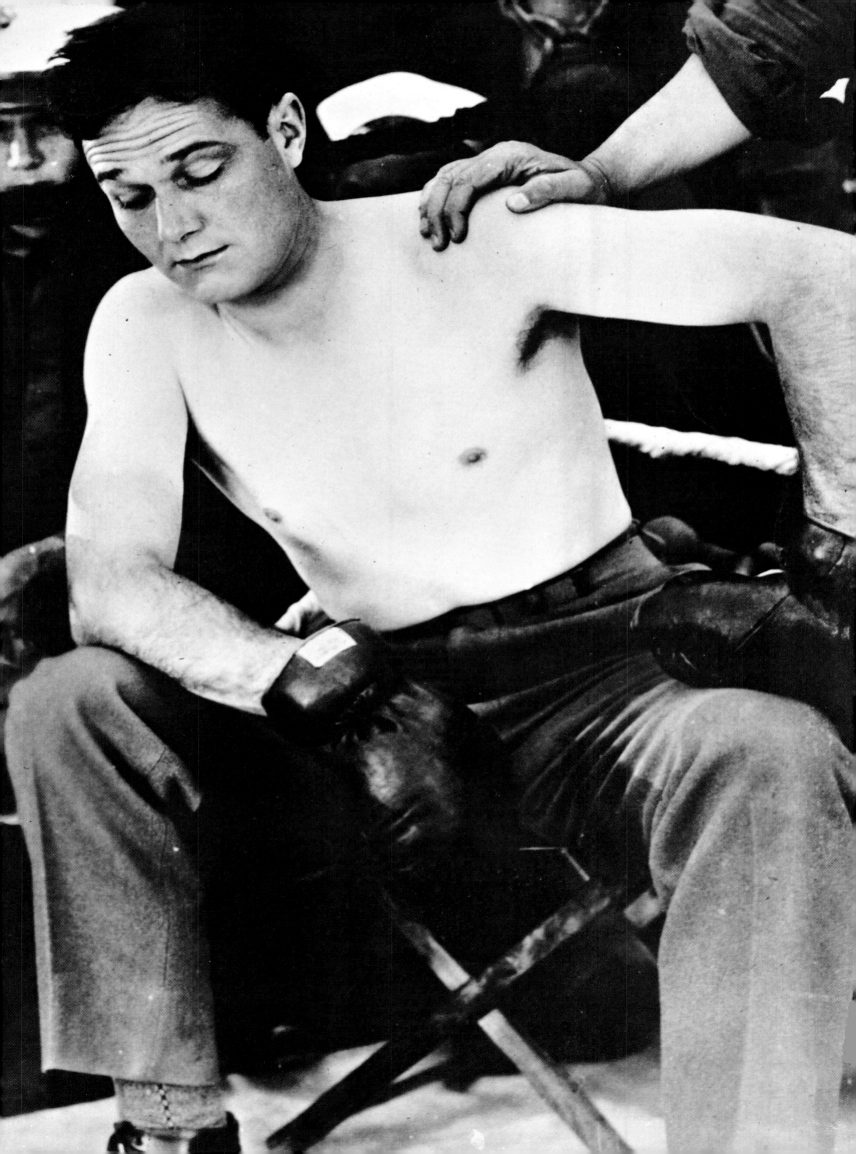

The formidable combination of director Rex Ingram, author Somerset Maugham and (left to right) international stars Russian Ivan Petrovich, American Alice Terry and German Paul Wegener gave **The Magician** *distinction.* ▷ *But the script, involving occult practices, hypnotism, a spinal operation and sinister experiments in a Monte Carlo tower, would have suited a horror specialist better than it did Ingram.*

Mayer took a look at the profits being collected by other studios with Tom Mix, Buck Jones, Hoot Gibson and the like, and decided it was about time MGM had its own Western star. He picked a genuine army officer who had lived with Indian tribes and come to Hollywood in 1922 as adviser on The Covered Wagon: Colonel Timothy John Fitzgerald McCoy. 'He's the real McCoy!' shouted the publicity department as he made his debut in **War Paint** (with Pauline Starke), which was quickly followed by **Winners of the Wilderness** (with Joan Crawford). They were shot, economically on the same location trip, by another new name on Leo's roster: W. S. Van Dyke. He had started as a 17-year-old assistant to D. W. Griffith on Intolerance in 1916, and was to become one of MGM's most prolific and successful directors.

In **Mike**, *a modest comedy-drama, Sally O'Neil* ▷ *was a girl of the railroads, living with father Charles Murray in a converted freight car and loving telegraphist William Haines. Written and directed by Marshall Neilan, with Ned Sparks, Ford Sterling, Frankie Darro and Junior Coghlan also in it . . . Haines and Claire Windsor pleased both critics and fans with* **A Little Journey**, *a charming comedy* ◁ *directed by Robert Z. Leonard. From a play by Rachel Crothers, the featherweight story was about a girl travelling to meet her fiancé, meeting a young man on the train and falling in love with him. Harry Carey had the only other significant role . . . Haines' career was boosted by* **Brown of Harvard**, *the remake of a 1917* ▽ *Essanay picture which in turn was from a 1909 play by Rida Johnson Young. Jack Conway directed Haines as a breezy lady-killer and*

Jack Pickford (here) as his bookish roommate who sacrificed himself to save the other's reputation. Mary Brian came over from Paramount to play the girl they both loved. Francis X. Bushman Jr was another collegiate type, and David Torrence a professor. Scenario by Donald Ogden Stewart and A. P. Younger.

John Gilbert and King Vidor, the star-director team of The Big Parade *and* La Bohème, *tried to make it three times lucky with* **Bardelys the Magnificent**. *However, in spite of a handsome production, the Rafael Sabatini swashbuckler didn't quite come off. Eleanor Boardman and George K. Arthur (with Gilbert here) and Roy D'Arcy and Theodore von Eltz were among those present. Script: Dorothy Farnum.*

his daughter's life and was allowed to ride in the big race. He won! Harry Carey (right) and Maurice Costello (second from left) the former matinée idol whose two beautiful daughters, Dolores and Helene, became stars, led the support. B. Reeves Eason and Archie Mayo co-directed. Gerald Beaumont and Florence Ryerson wrote the script.

Lew Cody's affaires: there were scandalous doings in **Monte Carlo**/Dreams of Monte Carlo when an American adventurer hid from pursuing detectives in the hotel room of a young schoolteacher. Christy Cabanne directed Cody and Gertrude Olmstead (here) and Roy D'Arcy, ZaSu Pitts, Harry Myers, Karl Dane and Trixie Friganza. Writers: Carey Wilson, Alice Duer Miller . . .

The Gay Deceiver led the fast set in Paris and was involved in love affairs and blackmail until he mended his ways for his daughter's sake. John M. Stahl directed the adaptation, by Benjamin Glazer, of a French play, 'Toto', with Cody in the title role, Carmel Myers (with him here) and Marceline Day, Malcolm McGregor and D'Arcy.

The studio was trying several new directors in 1926: John Francis Dillon made **Love's Blindness**. It was the one about the earl and the moneylender's daughter, as told by Elinor Glyn. (Produced under the personal supervision of Madame Glyn, warned the credits.) Antonio Moreno played the hard-up and hard-to-please milord who married luscious Pauline Starke for financial reasons only . . . but around reel seven realized it was True Love. Also cast: Lilyan Tashman, Sam de Grasse, Tom Ricketts, Kate Price, Ned Sparks and Douglas Gilmore.

MGM and Josef von Sternberg never could get along. Prior to starting and walking out on The Masked Bride in 1925 he had directed **The Exquisite Sinner**, with Conrad Nagel as a Frenchman on the run and Renee Adoree as a gypsy. The studio brass disliked the picture and gave it to Phil Rosen for extensive retakes in 1926. Others in the cast were Paulette Duval, Frank Currier, George K. Arthur and (a hint of what von Sternberg would later make of Marlene Dietrich) Myrna Loy as 'The Living Statue'. Alice Duer Miller shared writing credits with von Sternberg.

The title of **Johnny Get Your Hair Cut** was less germane to the plot than to the big publicity splurge about the maturing Jackie Coogan having his long hair shorn. An orphan, as always, he was befriended by a racehorse owner, saved

A major 1926 production, **The Fire Brigade**/ Fire!, dealt with firemen brothers and the daughter of a politician whose crooked building contracts resulted in devastating blazes. Director William Nigh got every possible frame of film filled with flaming buildings and desperate rescues. The brothers, their mother and the girl were (left to right) Charles Ray, Tom O'Brien, May McAvoy (heroine of Ben-Hur) and Eugenie Besserer. Holmes Herbert and Warner Richmond were also in the Robert Lee screenplay.

Forest fires were the highlights of two 1926 movies. In **The Flaming Forest** Technicolor was used for the climactic blaze. Here Antonio Moreno, sporting the latest in Northwest Mountie millinery, spares enough time from fighting Indians to woo Renee Adoree. They were better than their stereotyped roles deserved in the Reginald Barker production of James Oliver Curwood's action melodrama. Script: Waldemar Young. Also cast: William Austin, Tom O'Brien, Gardner James, Bert Roach . . . Some footage left over from The Flaming Forest was included in the fire that climaxed **The Understanding Heart**, trapping all four principals: Joan Crawford, Rockcliffe Fellowes, Carmel Myers and Francis X. Bushman Jr. Young Bushman, even better-looking than his father but never so famous, and Carmel are working up a blaze of their own in this scene from the Peter B. Kyne story, directed by Jack Conway.

He's chiefly remembered for his buzz-saw voice, but Ned Sparks was first prominent in silent movies. As the rum-running villain of **Money Talks** he is thwarted by gun-toting Owen Moore, who gets a 'My hero!' from Claire Windsor. Bert Roach and Kathleen Key were also in the comedy, directed by newcomer Archie Mayo who was later to be a prolific Warner Brothers film-maker. Jessie Burns and Bernard Vorhaus adapted Rupert Hughes' story.

A couple of quick Westerns were turned out by director Clifford Smith, starring Francis Mc-Donald. Edna Murphy (here) was the girl he rescued from bandits in **The Valley of Hell . . .** *In* **The Desert's Toll** *he had to prove to Kathleen Key that he didn't kill her father, as claimed by baddies Tom Santschi (torturing him here) and Anna May Wong.*

A Certain Young Man *was Ramon Novarro. He was young and a man, but none too certain in the role of an English lord over-fond of married women. This miscasting aside, Hobart Henley's comedy was amusing enough, with decorative performances by Carmel Myers and Renee Adoree (here) and Marceline Day. It was filmed in 1926 but not released until 1928. Huntley Gordon. Willard Louis and Bert Roach completed the cast.*

Sandy Wilson probably didn't know it when, decades later, he wrote his famous musical about the Twenties, but **The Boy Friend** *was a title on cinema marquees in that very era. It was a comedy about a small-town girl discontented with her family, and a boy trying to please her by throwing a high-toned party, with*

ludicrous results. Monta Bell directed the Alice Duer Miller screenplay, with Marceline Day, George K. Arthur and Gwen Lee. The boy and the girl's mother (seen here) were played by John Harron, a leading man discovered by Mary Pickford in 1921, and Elizabeth Patterson, making her screen début at the age of 50 after a long stage career. This scrawny, quavery-voiced lady gave fine film performances almost to the end of her 90 years.

Marion Davies helped the disgraced comedy star, Fatty Arbuckle, by insisting that he direct **The Red Mill,** *after a scandalous party and manslaughter trial (he was acquitted) had closed all studios' doors to him. Her generous gesture was in vain. He made the picture under the name of William Goodrich, but the 1906 Victor Herbert operetta didn't jell on the 1926 silent screen, and little more was heard of him. Owen Moore, Louise Fazenda and Karl Dane featured in the Frances Marion screenplay.*

Two Norma Shearer starrers: **The Waning Sex** *was the male, according to Frederic and Fanny Hatton's stage hit, a 1923 vote for Women's Lib brought to the cameras three years later by Robert Z. Leonard. Miss Shearer (left) was a criminal lawyer whose sex was professionally resented by Conrad Nagel, the District Attorney. She won acquittal for man-chasing widow Mary McAllister (centre) then defeated her in romancing the DA. Also in the F. Hugh Herbert screenplay: George K. Arthur, Martha Mattox . . . In* **Upstage**/The Mask of Comedy *Miss Shearer played a stagestruck girl who got bigheaded when given a break on Broadway; her career petered out until she displayed show-must-go-on courage by standing-in as target in a knife-throwing act. The film brought New York musical comedy star Oscar Shaw to Hollywood as Norma's leading man, with Gwen Lee, Dorothy Phillips and Ward Crane in support. Monta Bell directed Lorna Moon's story.*

Liking her work in Sally, Irene and Mary, *Edmund Goulding picked Joan Crawford as the female lead in his next film,* **Paris**/Shadows of Paris. *She played opposite Charles Ray in one of the many movies of that time portraying Paris as a city of sin, populated by prostitutes, their dagger-wielding apache lovers and the rich American visitors they preyed upon. Goulding's script had roles for Douglas Gilmore, Rose Dione and Michael Visaroff.*

Conrad Nagel and Claire Windsor were paired again in **Tin Hats,** *a successful starter at MGM for comedy director Edward Sedgwick. It was a funny script about three US soldiers (Nagel, George Cooper, Tom O'Brien) lost in the Rhineland on Armistice Day and accepted as conquering overlords by a village, but not by its Lady Bountiful (Miss Windsor). Albert Lewin and Lew Lipton scripted Sedgwick's original story.*

'What kind of a boy are you?' asks Antonio Moreno, assigned as bodyguard to the newly arrived Prince of Graustark and finding lingerie in his luggage. But surprise! It was really Marion Davies, as the prince's cousin, impersonating him to claim his birthright while he recovered from a skiing injury. Creighton Hale played the prince and Roy D'Arcy the villain in **Beverly of Graustark,** *a lavishly-produced comedy with a final sequence in colour. Script by Agnes Christine Johnston, it was notable as the first of a long list of MGM movies directed by Sidney Franklin, some of them among the company's finest. Not this one, though.*

*The studio picked another Ibanez novel, **The Temptress**, for Garbo's second film and assigned her Swedish mentor, Mauritz Stiller, to direct. To their dismay, Thalberg found his slow-working methods alarmingly reminiscent of von Stroheim's, and he was replaced by Fred Niblo. Garbo was again billed below the male star, in this case Antonio Moreno, but there was little doubt, either during production or in the theatres, who was the centre of excitement. Indeed, the script was built around her as the amoral woman who drove men to disgrace, murder and suicide, and herself to the gutter. Here she is fascinating H. B. Warner; other victims were Lionel Barrymore, Roy D'Arcy and Marc MacDermott. Scenario: Dorothy Farnum.*

The Garbo fuse lighted by The Torrent *and fanned by* The Temptress *really reached the dynamite with **Flesh and the Devil**. Its release* ▷ *at the end of 1926 exploded box-office records, and not only because of the sensational new star: it also had John Gilbert, sharing some of the most sizzling love scenes filmed to date. And, according to rumour spreading from gossip columns to front page headlines, these love scenes were being played offscreen as well. The movie itself was less marvellous than the stars and their publicity. Clarence Brown, who became Garbo's favourite director, made most effective use of a trashy story about a woman desiring one man, Gilbert (left), despite marriages to two others, Marc MacDermott (right) and Lars Hanson, and paying for her sins by death on an ice floe. Barbara Kent and George Fawcett also enacted Benjamin Glazer's screenplay from Hermann Sudermann's 1893 novel.*

*Setting a pattern for her screen future, Joan Crawford suffered for love in **The Taxi Dancer**.* ▷ *Although made in a hurry by a little-known director (Harry Millarde) from an obscure play, the film proved quite successful, thanks to its intriguing title and the budding popularity of its leading lady. She played a ten-cents-a-dance girl in love with a gigolo, whom she tried to save from a murder rap by offering herself to a millionaire. However, as the subtitle in this scene explained, 'He is convinced of Joslyn's purity when she refuses a cocktail before dinner'. Comparatively impure characters were played by Owen Moore, Marc MacDermott (with Joan here), Douglas Gilmore, Gertrude Astor and Rockcliffe Fellowes. Screenplay: A. P. Younger.*

The very blonde Mae Murray made an unlikely Spanish dancer in **Valencia**/The Love Song but she had a box-office hit. Credit that in some measure to the title: Valencia was America's top song of the year. Dimitri Buchowetzki, often Pola Negri's director, moved over from Paramount for this one, but couldn't make much of Alice Duer Miller's thin script. Nasty governor Roy D'Arcy and handsome sailor Lloyd Hughes were the rivals for Mae's favours.

It was daring of Thalberg to bring Beatrice Lillie to Hollywood, since the Canadian star of London and New York revues created many of her funniest effects with her voice. Movie fans of the mid-Twenties didn't quite get her subtle clowning in this silent about a repertory company's worst actress, so **Exit Smiling** failed at the box-office; she came over better in talkies later. Nevertheless Miss Lillie had some hilarious scenes, like this vamping bit with Harry Myers. Her co-star was Jack Pickford, the director was Sam Taylor, who made many of Jack's sister Mary's films. The Taylor–Tim Whelan script from Marc Connelly's play gave roles to Doris Lloyd, DeWitt Jennings, Louise Lorraine and Franklin Pangborn.

◁ Mae Murray made more headlines than films after **Altars of Desire**, with her marriages, divorces and lawsuits, and died in 1965 aged 76. It was sad when her reign as one of the original queens of the MGM lot ended. You could call her affected, artificial, absurd; but who could deny that she was the very personification of Hollywood in its dizziest days of extravagance and glamour? Altars of Desire was one of her silliest movies; a bit of fluff about an American girl sent to Paris by her father (Robert Edeson) to acquire polish. She got a fortune-hunting count (Andre de Beranger, here) as well, but hero Conway Tearle came to the rescue. Christy Cabanne directed the Alice Duer Miller–Agnes Christine Johnston screenplay.

'It's a real "A" picture,' joked MGM salesmen getting bookings for **The Scarlet Letter**. With intensely dramatic performances by Lillian Gish and Lars Hanson under Victor Seastrom's sensitive direction, the Nathaniel Hawthorne story's 'A' for Adultery could also stand for 'Art' on the screen. It was also good box-office. Miss Gish began it immediately after completion of La Bohème, having overcome opposition from Mayer, who feared it might be banned by church groups. Henry B. Walthall (her colleague in the old D. W. Griffith days), Karl Dane and Marcelle Corday led the support. Script: Frances Marion.

As **Lovey Mary**, Bessie Love looked about 17 and was actually 27, with a decade of film experience behind her (and still going strong in the Seventies on stage, screen and TV in London). She played a runaway from an orphanage in this sweet and simple story, from Alice Hegan Rice's 1903 novel, directed by King Baggott, formerly one of the earliest movie stars. She and her little companion Jackie Coombs were given a home by Mary Alden; William Haines was the boy next door; Eileen Percy and Martha Mattox supported.

The stars and director of **The Show** took time out from its heavy drama for a publicity shot purporting to show Renee Adoree teaching her colleagues French. Left to right: Adoree, director Tod Browning, John Gilbert, Lionel Barrymore. From C. T. Jackson's 1910 novel, 'The Day of Souls', the story was about a Hungarian carnival troupe. A young tearaway was reformed by a girl after her older suitor, in a ploy rarely attempted even by movie villains, tried to kill him with a poisonous lizard. Waldemar Young's screenplay also employed Edward Connelly and Gertrude Short.

1926

After pleasing the public in The Gay Deceiver Carmel Myers, wearing enough pearls to stun an ox, played opposite Lew Cody again in **The Demi-Bride**. Directed by Robert Z. Leonard, it was another comedy of the naughtiness synonymous with Paris. Norma Shearer was Carmel's stepdaughter who blackmailed Cody into marriage. Dorothy Sebastian and Lionel Belmore had bit parts in the F. Hugh Herbert–Florence Ryerson script.

Two little movies that earned their keep in 1926: **Blarney** (left), a period piece about an Irish prizefighter, Ralph Graves, involved with two New York girls, Paulette Duval (here) and Renee Adoree, directed by Marcel de Sano . . . **There You Are!**, scripted by F. Hugh Herbert from his 1925 play, with Conrad Nagel as a clerk who captured a bandit and won the boss's daughter (Edith Roberts). The latter had several changes of director; none was credited.

The Boob/The Yokel was a youthful effort by director William Wellman; by the time he made another MGM movie seven years later, he was one of the best in the business. Here's what passed for a production number in the film with the girls doing a 1926-type striptease. This innocuous piece was about a farmhand rescuing a girl from abduction by bootleggers. George K. Arthur played the boob, with Joan Crawford, Gertrude Olmstead and Charles Murray. Writers: George Scarborough, Annette Westbay, Kenneth Clarke.

Norman Kerry (left to right) with Hobart Bosworth and David Torrence. It was disappointing at the paybox and marked the beginning of a downward curve in the star's career. Script: Josephine Lovett.

GARBO ASCENDS
1927

Too many people were staying home listening to the radio: American exhibitors reported half-empty houses on the night the Jack Dempsey–Gene Tunney fight was broadcast. But the Warner Bros. were galloping to the rescue. Recently kept solvent only by their incongruous assets of Rin-Tin-Tin and John Barrymore, they had used the latter's *Don Juan* in August 1926 to test their Vitaphone process with synchronized sound (no dialogue), opening it on Broadway with supporting short subjects that talked and sang. Fox followed suit in January 1927 with Movietone – *What Price Glory?* was accompanied by talking shorts – and in June audiences could see and hear President Coolidge welcoming Lindbergh after his Atlantic flight. Strangely, none of this had so potent an impact as the silent feature *The Jazz Singer*, when Al Jolson burst into song and spoke a few words; Warners opened it on 6 October, 1927 and the audience was astounded. The movies were reborn.

The Garden of Allah *emerged from Rex Ingram's studio near Nice as his third independent production. It was the second, and probably best, version of the thrice-filmed Robert Hichens novel of sacred and profane love. Alice Terry and Ivan Petrovich (here) starred as the lovers brought together by Arab menace (Marcel Vibert) and separated by religious vows. Impressive desert exteriors were shot in North Africa. Script: Willis Goldbeck.*

*After two fine MGM pictures in a row, Lillian Gish subsided into a soggy haggis about feuding Scottish clans, **Annie Laurie**. John S. Robertson directed Creighton Hale, Miss Gish and*

*Miss Gish wasn't much luckier with Channing Pollock's anti-war play **The Enemy**, a mid-Twenties success in New York and London, which proved rather lugubrious entertainment as filmed by Fred Niblo. He's seen here (right) directing Miss Gish and Ralph Forbes as the newlyweds in an early scene. Ralph went off to war and suffered, while Lillian nearly starved and became a prostitute and suffered and their baby died and it was all a bit much for the Jazz Age moviegoers. Frank Currier and George Fawcett had secondary roles; Willis Goldbeck, Agnes Christine Johnston scripted.*

*Owen Moore, here with Sally O'Neil in **Becky**, a minor Manhattan romance, was one of three Irish brothers (Tom and Matt Moore were the others) who all went into American movies in the earliest pre-Hollywood days. All three achieved remarkably enduring prominence which lasted through the Thirties for Owen and Tom; Matt was still playing minor roles in the Fifties. Becky was the story of a salesgirl (Sally O'Neil) who got a chance in a Broadway show, attracted and was ultimately rejected by a society playboy. John P. McCarthy directed. Marian Blackton's script gave roles to Gertrude Olmstead and Harry Crocker.*

*Monta Bell wrote and directed **After Midnight**. He was better at directing. Norma Shearer and Gwen Lee played sisters in this flimsy story of New York nightlife; Norma was a cabaret hostess with a heart of gold and Gwen a gold-digger with no heart. Lawrence Gray heroed as a reformed hold-up man.*

The Joseph Conrad-Ford Madox Ford novel 'Romance' became a superior action movie in **The Road To Romance**, *a handsome production directed by John S. Robertson (it reverted to Romance in Britain). Ramon Novarro was the Spanish adventurer who rescued the girl (Marceline Day) from a Cuban prison, and Marc MacDermott and Roy D'Arcy were, as ever, the heavies. Script: Josephine Lovett.*

Given exquisite direction by Ernst Lubitsch and a lavish production, Hans Kraly's screenplay for **The Student Prince in Old Heidelberg** *proved a major hit for Ramon Novarro and Norma Shearer. The film was usually known as The Student Prince, the title of the 1924 operetta whose huge popularity was another reason for the movie's success. Lacking sound, it was really a film version of the original 1902 play, In Old Heidelberg, the bitter-sweet romance of a Ruritanian prince and an inn-keeper's niece. Miss Shearer and Novarro were supported by Jean Hersholt, Gustav von Seyffertitz and Philippe de Lacy.*

Encouraged by the success of the songless The Merry Widow and The Student Prince, MGM bought the hit musical **Rose Marie** *and filmed it* ▷ *silent. Joan Crawford was assigned the title role to further her star build-up. Lucien Hubbard, later to become a producer, wrote the screenplay and directed it. But without the music it was just another Northwest Mountie melodrama. James Murray (here with Joan) played the outlaw trapper finally felled by Mountie House Peters. Also cast: Creighton Hale and Gibson Gowland.*

The Lionel Barrymore of the Twenties was an absolute rotter, never the lovable old grouch he became in later decades. In **The Thirteenth Hour**, directed by Chester Franklin, he was a criminologist unmasked as a crook and a murderer by detective Charles Delaney and police dog Napoleon in the nick of time: here he was about to wreak further evils upon lovely Jacqueline Gadsden. The film was a baddie too. Franklin wrote it with Douglas Furber, and cast Polly Moran and Fred Kelsey in support. Barrymore had a fine old time as the heavy in the all-stops-out melodrama of **Body and Soul**, a remake of Goldwyn's 1920 The Branding Iron. First he behaved disgracefully as a doctor, then he fled to Switzerland to lust after an inn servant (Aileen Pringle), trick her skiing lover (Norman Kerry) into an accident, and finally, in an alcoholic rage of jealousy, brand the lady. Reginald Barker directed; Elliott Clawson revised Katherine Newlin Burt's original.

Ramon Novarro and Alice Terry were re-united in **Lovers?**, but the result couldn't compare with their Scaramouche, Prisoner of Zenda or The Arab. Maybe it was the absence of Rex Ingram (John Stahl directed this one), or perhaps it was the so-what story of a scandal aroused by a young man falling in love with his guardian's wife. Also cast: Edward Connelly, John Miljan and George K. Arthur. Script: Sylvia Thalberg and Douglas Furber.

Heaven on Earth was an oddity. Supposedly a brand-new production in 1927, it had the same co-stars (Renee Adoree, Conrad Nagel) and the same film editor (John English) as the 1926 Exquisite Sinner, which had been completed by the same director (Phil Rosen, who took over from Josef von Sternberg). Both were about a young Frenchman, bored with his family and their silk-mill business, running off with a band of gypsies. The different supporting cast in Heaven on Earth (Gwen Lee, Julia Swayne Gordon) indicated that Messrs Rosen and English had not quite made two movies for the price of one. Script: Harvey Gates.

'Don't step on it, it might be Lon Chaney' was a 1927 quip. Lon threw Polly Moran and millions of ticket-buyers into delicious spasms of terror in **London After Midnight**. Conrad Nagel, Marceline Day and Henry B. Walthall were also involved in the Tod Browning thriller about murder disguised as suicide and solved by hypnotism. Browning wrote the script with Waldemar Young.

Tod Browning whipped up another offbeat recipe for Lon Chaney in **The Unknown**, using a Waldemar Young script. The star played a fake armless wonder in a sideshow, mad about a girl (Joan Crawford) who couldn't bear the touch of a man's hand. So he had his arms amputated for real. Then the girl fell for an acrobat in their circus (Norman Kerry) and her peculiar aversion vanished overnight, so to speak. That's show business.

The celebrated stage thriller **Mr Wu**, filmed in Britain in 1921, was remade with Lon Chaney in Matheson Lang's old part. It was well directed by William Nigh and acted with bravura by the star and Louise Dresser (shown

here) as the English gentlewoman who stabbed him in the last reel. Her son (Ralph Forbes) wanted to marry his daughter (Renee Adoree with tilted eyelids) and Wu reacted by killing the girl and threatening the boy's family (also including Holmes Herbert and Gertrude Olmstead). Anna May Wong brought a genuine Oriental touch to the cast in Lorna Moon's version of the Maurice Vernon–Harold Owen play.

Mockery was too heavy for popular success although it was written and directed by Benjamin Christensen with dramatic power and visual beauty. Lon Chaney was impressive as a peasant who twice rescued a countess (Barbara Bedford) from Russian revolutionaries, despite having become a Bolshevik himself. Also cast: Ricardo Cortez and Emily Fitzroy.

The Big City was one of the less memorable efforts by Lon Chaney, author-director Tod Browning and scripter Waldemar Young. The star played a cabaret owner with a jewel-robbery gang as a sideline; the swag was stashed in a costume shop run by Betty Compson (here). Young love was supplied by James Murray and Marceline Day. Miss Compson, who had been in pictures since 1915, had scored opposite Chaney in The Miracle Man (1919); she continued well into the talkie era.

1927

King Vidor's **The Crowd** *was one of the most highly praised pictures in the whole history of MGM. A far cry from his* Big Parade *in scope, it was similar in that it centred on an average man pitted against situations he could not control. This postwar everyman fought on the battleground of economic serfdom. James Murray, an extra who happened to walk by when Vidor was looking for an unknown leading man, was amazingly good as the clerk with a little job in a huge office, and a little apartment in a vast city. Eleanor Boardman gave the performance of her life as his wife. Vidor wrote the story early in 1926 and worked on the film intermittently until the end of 1927. It was scripted by him with Harry Behn and John V. A. Weaver. Much of it was shot in New York, where hidden cameras recorded street scenes of a realism not seen on the screen before. The painstaking production was so unhurried that Miss Boardman (Mrs Vidor) took time out to have a baby, between scenes as it were, and Murray acted in a few lesser movies. Seven different endings were shot and it went into release with two; one left Murray as a cipher in the crowd, the other 'happy' ending gave him an unexpected windfall: exhibitors could take their choice. Although generally regarded as an artistic triumph with no paybox appeal, the film actually returned twice its cost. Minor successes were scored by Bert Roach as the boy's office pal, Del Henderson and Lucy Beaumont.*

During the leisurely production of The Crowd *its leading man, James Murray, had time for other assignments. The best of them was* **In Old Kentucky**, *a rewrite by A. P. Younger and Lew Lipton of a 1919 movie Mayer produced for First National. Murray played a drunken young war veteran who returned to find his horse-breeding family facing ruin. After their last horse won the Kentucky Derby, he reformed. Dorothy Cumming (with him here) scored a hit as his mother; others in the* John M. Stahl *picture were Helene Costello, Wesley Barry and Stepin Fetchit.*

Seven months elapsed between the completion of Flesh and the Devil *and the start of* **Love**. *Theatre owners and their patrons were loudly demanding another Garbo picture, MGM was longing for another Garbo picture, and Garbo* was refusing to make another Garbo picture. *Mayer tried persuasion, promises, threats, but for once he had met his match. 'That dumb Swede', as someone had called his young discovery, unexpectedly displayed a shrewd business sense and inflexible willpower. She had decided that $600 a week wasn't enough for a star millions were talking about and paying to see; $5,000 a week would be more appropriate. She got it, and* **Love** *went into production with John Gilbert (whom she was still on the verge of marrying, according to the headlines) co-starring and Edmund Goulding directing. As in this scene, in which the disgraced Anna Karenina steals into her former home to see the son she has abandoned, the film was less affecting than the second version of Tolstoy's tragedy which Garbo made eight years later. But it was a box-office smash. How could the masses resist billing like 'Gilbert and Garbo in Love'? Brandon Hurst as Karenin and Philippe de Lacy as the child won praise; George Fawcett and Emily Fitzroy supported in the Lorna Moon–Frances Marion screenplay.*

A surprise box office winner and a new star team arrived in **Rookies**, a riotous if unoriginal comedy with Karl Dane and George K. Arthur as tough sergeant and bumbling recruit. Paramount had similarly established the Beery–Hatton comedy team the year before with Behind the Front. *Marceline Day, Louise Lorraine and Tom O'Brien supported Dane and Arthur. Script: Byron Morgan. This was the first of the many MGM hits Sam Wood, a former Cecil B. DeMille assistant, directed.*

Two Marion Davies starrers: George Ade's **The Fair Co-Ed**/The Varsity Girl, *a Broadway hit of 20 years earlier, provided a lively role for her as a flapper who resisted going to college until she met the basketball coach (John Mack Brown in his first lead). She thereupon became the star of the girls' team and won him from the campus vamp (Jane Winton). Sam Wood directed the Byron Morgan screenplay . . .*

Miss Davies in J. M. Barrie's **Quality Street** *sounds a disastrous combination. In fact she dealt very nicely with the whimsical comedy and quiet pathos under Sidney Franklin's careful direction. Conrad Nagel played the suitor who returned from ten years at the wars and was not deceived by his aging sweetheart pretending to be her own niece. Helen Jerome Eddy, Flora Finch and Margaret Seddon were suitably quaint in support. Screenplay: Hans Kraly and Albert Lewin.*

Jackie Coogan blew a rather sour box office note with **The Bugle Call**. *Under Edward Sedgwick's direction he played a fatherless bugle boy living with his stepmother (Claire Windsor) in an 1870 frontier outpost. Herbert Rawlinson was the cavalry officer hero. The American public was given its first glimpse of its former football idol, Johnny Mack Brown, as a movie actor (far right). Script: C. Gardner Sullivan and Josephine Lovett.*

The Callahans and the Murphys *marked the MGM debut of one of the studio's best-loved stars: Marie Dressler. It didn't seem likely when the film was made in 1927; at 58 Miss Dressler had known fame in musical comedy, vaudeville and movies (Tillie's Punctured Romance, 1914). Then came hard times, and she was about to give up the show business struggle when her friend, scenarist Frances Marion, wrote this script with Marie in mind and persuaded Mayer and Thalberg to cast her in it. George Hill directed the story of two feuding slum families, the daughter of one (Sally O'Neil, with Marie here) having a baby by the son of the other (Lawrence Gray). Polly Moran and Gertrude Olmstead were also featured. The film was not well received; Irish-American societies boycotted it and it had to be withdrawn in many areas.*

Slide, Kelly, Slide *was one of William Haines' most successful vehicles. The subject was baseball, which may be America's national game, but is box office poison elsewhere – as a result it has seldom been used as a subject by Hollywood. In the case of this movie, profits in the USA alone were enough to make it a winner. Haines played the usual conceited hero who disrupted his team, then reformed. Edward Sedgwick directed A. P. Younger's screenplay. Left to right: Guinn Williams, Harry Carey, Karl Dane, Junior Coghlan, Sally O'Neil, Haines.*

In **West Point**/Eternal Youth *William Haines played a part he was doomed to reprise, with variations, in almost all his films: the arrogant know-it-all who's really a good guy au fond. In this Edward Sedgwick production, set in the US Military Academy, he was taught team spirit by girlfriend Joan Crawford and sergeant Ralph Emerson in time to score the winning touchdown against the Navy. Raymond Schrock scripted.*

Old age was creeping up on Jackie Coogan in 1927, and when **Buttons** *finished shooting he went into temporary retirement. His remarkable public appeal had lasted for seven years; at 13 he looked forward to a life of ease with the million or so dollars he had earned. But ahead lay years of litigation with his mother and stepfather who had frittered almost all of it away (resulting in a new California law requiring that the bulk of children's earnings be held in trust for them), and decades of diminishing movie roles. In his last MGM starrer, as a street urchin who became a pageboy in a transatlantic liner, he was supported by Lars Hanson, Gertrude Olmstead, Roy D'Arcy and Polly Moran (here); directed by George Hill who also wrote the story.*

The Divine Woman *was Garbo's fifth Hollywood film and the first to lift her name from second to top billing. Eager to keep its great new star happy, the studio also gave her fellow Swedes Victor Seastrom and Lars Hanson as director and leading man, and a role based on no less a fellow artist than Sarah Bernhardt. However the plot, adapted by Dorothy Farnum from Gladys Unger's play* Starlight *and substituting melodramatic fictions for many of the facts of Bernhardt's life, made it just another movie. Left to right: Lowell Sherman (as the Paris producer who made the heroine a star), Garbo, and John Mack Brown as one of her admirers. Also cast: Polly Moran, Dorothy Cumming and Paulette Duval.*

Women Love Diamonds, *the movie Garbo refused to make when she went on her salary strike, was inherited by Pauline Starke. With her were Owen Moore, Gwen Lee, Lionel Barrymore, Douglas Fairbanks Jr (with Pauline here) who had to wait a few more years to follow his father to stardom. Edmund Goulding received few plaudits for writing and directing this yarn about a girl who had an affair with a young society blade until it was disrupted by the revelation of her illegitimate birth; she made do with her former chauffeur. No fool, that Garbo.*

Aileen Pringle, a witty, cultured woman off-screen, moved away from lurid vamp roles to sophisticated comedy and a series of successes with Lew Cody, much as Myrna Loy was to do years later with William Powell. **Adam and Evil** *was a sparkling comedy by Florence Ryerson and F. Hugh Herbert based on that old favourite of scriptwriters, a confusion of twins: 'That's either your wife or your sister-in-law,'*

says Gwen Lee to Cody in this scene. Cody, married to Miss Pringle, pretended to be his twin brother while having an affair with Miss Lee. Hedda Hopper and Roy D'Arcy were their worldly friends, Robert Z. Leonard directed. . . After Adam and Evil had clicked with critics and moviegoers Pringle and Cody were quickly re-teamed in **Tea for Three.** *They were again directed by Leonard, with Owen Moore (left) as the third corner in the triangle. Hugh Herbert and Roi Cooper Megrue scripted; Dorothy Sebastian and Phillips Smalley led the supporting cast.*

Wickedness Preferred *clicked as yet another of the polished comedies teaming Miss Pringle, here displaying the 1927 mode in gown and telephone, with Lew Cody. Hobart Henley directed them in the Florence Ryerson–Colin Clements story keyed by the opening title: 'Marriage is like a cafeteria. You take the first thing that looks good and pay for it later.' Also cast: Mary McAllister, George K. Arthur, Bert Roach.*

Lars Hanson, a star in Sweden when Garbo was unknown, was rather overshadowed when they arrived simultaneously at MGM. He had the title role in **Captain Salvation,** *with Pauline Starke and George Fawcett (here). A mixture of action thriller and religious heartwringer, it didn't quite click as either. Lars played a theological student ostracized by New England villagers when he rescued a prostitute. She sailed with him in a convict ship and killed herself when the captain raped her. The hero took over the ship and converted the convicts to religion. Ernest Torrence and Marceline Day were also in the John S. Robertson production, scripted by Jack Cunningham.*

The Karl Dane–George K. Arthur team continued successfully. The old Margaret Mayo stage farce **Baby Mine** *(previously filmed by Goldwyn in 1917) was their second 1927 vehicle. Robert Z. Leonard directed their frantic antics with three babies, a midget, a case of measles for Arthur, and marriage to Charlotte Greenwood for Dane. Script: Sylvia Thalberg, F. Hugh Herbert, Lew Lipton.*

John Gilbert starred in **Twelve Miles Out**, *William Anthony McGuire's stage melodrama about bootleggers versus Prohibition agents, filmed by Jack Conway. Subject and star made it a profitable crowd-magnet. Here Gilbert interrupts an attempted seduction of Joan Crawford by rival bootlegger Ernest Torrence, who has hijacked his rum-running boat. Eileen Percy and Dorothy Sebastian had featured roles; A. P. Younger wrote the script.*

Two movies had their source in the Hearst newspapers. **Tillie the Toiler**, *a 1927 money-maker, was derived from one of their most popular comic strips, an endless saga of a dumb but happy office girl. Marion Davies, excellent in the title role, was supported by Matt Moore, Harry Crocker, George Fawcett, George K. Arthur and (with her here) Arthur Hoyt. Hobart Henley directed A. P. Younger's screenplay.* **The Lovelorn** *was inspired by the 'Advice to the Lovelorn' column, conducted by Beatrice Fairfax (Dorothy Cumming played her in the film) and read by palpitating hordes of schoolgirls and flappers. The movie was aimed at the same level and told of two sisters—played by two sisters, Sally O'Neil (here) and Molly O'Day – just crazy about the same boy, James Murray. He did this film immediately after* The Crowd *which was released later. John P. McCarthy directed; Bradley King adapted Miss Fairfax's story.*

Frisco Sally Levy *tried in vain to capitalize on the vogue for Irish–Jewish comedies started by the Broadway record-breaker* Abie's Irish Rose. *William Beaudine directed Sally O'Neil and Mickey Daniels (one of the original 'Our Gang') as children of a Jewish father (Tenen Holtz) and an Irish mother (Kate Price), with Charles Delaney as a motorcycle cop romancing Sally. Script: A. A. Cohn.*

Man, Woman and Sin *was no better than its title, according to the critics. But it did bring Jeanne Eagels to the screen after her sensational stage hit as Sadie Thompson in* Rain. *Her turbulent life (filmed in 1957 with Kim Novak) was nearing its end, hastened by drug addiction, and the personality that had thrilled Broadway seemed muted by the camera. Still, her name, the magnetism of John Gilbert – and that title – attracted the crowds to Monta Bell's drama about a reporter in love with a society editor, mistress of their newspaper's owner. Marc MacDermott in the latter role was killed by Gilbert, as in* Flesh and the Devil. *Script: Alice Duer Miller.*

On Ze Boulevard *was a crime story with oo-la-la comedy trimmings and Lew Cody playing a waiter who won a fortune. His thrifty sweetheart (Renee Adoree, here) foiled the society crooks trying to swindle him. Dorothy Sebastian and Anton Vaverka shared this scene, Roy D'Arcy was the chief crook, and Harry Millarde directed. Four literary brains created it: Florence Ryerson, F. Hugh Herbert, Richard Schayer, Scott Darling. Paris was ze locale.*

The theme of **The Latest from Paris**, *a well-received comedy by A. P. Younger, directed smartly by Sam Wood, was love in the rag trade with Norma Shearer and Ralph Forbes selling clothes for rival companies. Jewish comedians George Sidney and Tenen Holtz played their feuding bosses. Between production of* The Student Prince *and this one Norma Shearer married her real boss, becoming Mrs Irving Thalberg in September 1927.*

Meanwhile, back at the ranch (or the stockade) Tim McCoy was fighting bandits, Indians, renegades and rustlers. His 1927 movies came rolling out like tumbleweed: **California** *with Dorothy Sebastian (top left), Marc Mac-Dermott, Frank Currier, directed by W. S. Van Dyke . . .* **The Frontiersman** *with Claire Windsor (top right), Tom O'Brien, Louise Lorraine, directed by Reginald Barker . . .* **Spoilers of the West** *with William Fairbanks (bottom left), Marjorie Daw, directed by Van Dyke . . .* **The Law of the Range** *with Joan Crawford (bottom right), Rex Lease, directed by William Nigh. Along with these four Westerns, Tim McCoy squeezed in an Eastern,* **Foreign Devils**. *Van Dyke had him quelling Chinese hordes during the Boxer Rebellion and thwarting Cyril Chadwick (below) for the love of English lady Claire Windsor. Chadwick bore up under a record load of gold braid and the character name of Lord Vivien Cholmondeley. Emily Fitzroy, Frank Currier and Sojin were also involved in Marian Ainslee's version of Peter B. Kyne's story. Editor: Sam Zimbalist, a name for future MGM fame.*

William Haines pleased the fans with **Spring Fever**. *He played a shipping clerk who bluffed his way into an exclusive country club and romanced an heiress (Joan Crawford). Edward Sedgwick directed the Albert Lewin–Frank Davis adaptation of Vincent Lawrence's 1925 Broadway comedy, with George K. Arthur, Eileen Percy and George Fawcett, seen here as Haines's bemused boss.*

1928

Hollywood paused in the turmoil of converting to sound long enough to stage the first award-giving of the Academy of Motion Picture Arts and Sciences, formed in 1927. Fox and Paramount won the most, the former's Janet Gaynor as best actress for *Seventh Heaven*, *Street Angel* and *Sunrise*, Frank Borzage for directing and Benjamin Glazer for writing *Seventh Heaven*, Charles Rosher and Karl Struss for photographing *Sunrise*, also picked as best film. Paramount tied for best film with *Wings* and for writing with Ben Hecht's *Underworld* and had the best actor, Emil Jannings in *The Way of all Flesh* and *The Last Command*. MGM had to be satisfied with 'best subtitles' by Joseph Farnham for *Telling the World* and *The Fair Co-ed*. Walt Disney introduced Mickey Mouse in *Plane Crazy* a silent short; also silent were hits ranging from DeMille's *The King of Kings* with H. B. Warner as Jesus, to *Gentlemen Prefer Blondes* with Alice White. Studios were feverishly adding talking scenes to other silent movies, while Warners led again with the first all-talkie, *Lights of New York*, in July; a crude melo, it made $2m. profit.

MGM was entrusted with the distribution of **Napoleon** *although it had no hand in its production. Abel Gance's masterpiece, a landmark in French film-making, strangely failed to attract the English-speaking masses in spite of its epic story and immense spectacle. At the Tivoli in London it was thrown from three projectors onto a triple-width screen, showing either split images (as here) or one vast panorama. The idea re-emerged 24 years later as Cinerama.*

In this scene from **Telling the World** *William Haines is telling landlady Polly Moran what he thinks of her room. He was a hard-up reporter who went on to success when he caught a killer in a Frisco cafe, then broke a bigger story in China while saving an American girl (Anita Page) accused of murder. Sam Wood directed the fast-moving yarn by Dale Van Every and Raymond Schrock, with Eileen Percy, Frank Currier and Bert Roach cast . . . Haines won*

praise for his sensitive acting in **Excess Baggage**, *a drama in which he played a vaudeville acrobat whose marriage to a dancer (Josephine Dunn, a newcomer giving another*

strong performance) broke up when she became a movie star. Ricardo Cortez, Kathleen Clifford and Greta Granstedt were also under James Cruze's direction in this Frances Marion adaptation of John McGowan's 1927 Broadway hit.

Marion Davies had the biggest hit of her career in **The Patsy**/The Politic Flapper, *giving a brilliantly comic performance. It was an unexpected feather in King Vidor's cap too; he wasn't supposed to be a comedy director, but* The Patsy *proved his versatility. Marion played the downtrodden daughter of Del Henderson, both dominated by mother Marie Dressler and elder daughter Jane Winton (here). How Marion jolted them into appreciating her, via a fake love affair with Lawrence Gray (and riotously wicked impersonations of Mae Murray, Pola Negri and Lillian Gish) made rich entertainment. Agnes Christine Johnston revised Barry Connors' 1925 play.*

The Cossacks *looked like a sure thing. The John Gilbert–Renee Adoree team had never failed; Gilbert had been great in* Love, *another Tolstoy story; and all those battles on horseback would fill the screen with action. But somehow it didn't quite click. Ernest Torrence and Nils Asther supported the stars and George Hill directed the Frances Marion script, with extensive retakes by Clarence Brown.*

Buster Keaton returned to MGM as a contract star in 1928, having released a few pictures through United Artists. It was the first time he had relinquished control over his own productions, and the effect was ultimately disastrous. But **The Cameraman**, *which inaugurated his ▷ new contract, was completely successful. Edward Sedgwick directed the funny, fast-moving movie by Clyde Bruckman, Lew Lipton and Richard Schayer. It told of a tyro photographer trying to cover news events for the Hearst newsreel: the gags and stunts were, as ever, Keaton's own. Marceline Day played the girlfriend, Harry Gribbon and Harold Goodwin had bit parts.*

1928

White Shadows in the South Seas is notable as the first MGM sound film. Douglas Shearer (Norma's brother) took the completed silent picture to a New Jersey recording studio (none was available in Hollywood) and added synchronized sound effects and music in time for the New York premiere on July 31, 1928 – when the public first heard Leo roar from his trademark. Breathtaking scenic beauty won Clyde DeVinna the 1929 Academy Award for cinematography. This was the first major success for W. S. Van Dyke, who accompanied Robert Flaherty to the Marquesas Islands in the South Pacific as co-director. He soon took over entirely when Flaherty's documentary technique clashed with the studio's emphasis on a Jack Cunningham–John Colton script about a drunken doctor (Monte Blue) and a native girl (Raquel Torres).

In the summer of 1928 Mayer and Thalberg at Culver City, and Schenck in New York, acknowledged reluctantly and belatedly that the talking picture was not just a passing fad. The company's silent output was falling short of 1925/6/7 box office results, while the public rushed to see and hear other studios' talkies, especially those of Warner Bros, the previously disdained competitors whose Jazz Singer spoke the screen's first words in 1927 and who were already releasing all-dialogue movies. The first MGM star to be thrown upon the microphone's dubious mercies was William Haines in **Alias Jimmy Valentine**, scripted by Sarah Y. Mason and A. P. Younger, a remake of a 1920 Metro drama, with Karl Dane and Tully Marshall (centre and right), Lionel Barrymore and Leila Hyams. Director Jack Conway put the completed silent film back into work, re-shooting the climactic sequence with dialogue at the Paramount studio where sound equipment was already installed. Meanwhile MGM hastily built two primitive sound stages, which for several months were used in eight-hour shifts around the clock.

Beau Broadway, ostensibly one of the Lew Cody–Aileen Pringle series, featured Sue Carol more prominently than Aileen. (Miss Carol went on to play many flapper roles, then surprisingly became an actors' agent, giving special attention to the career of her husband, Alan Ladd.) Malcolm St Clair wrote and directed the piece, with Cody as a fight promoter who adopted a dying boxer's daughter, gave up his mistress, became domesticated and married the girl. Heinie Conklin was the servant in this scene with Lew and Sue.

Robert Z. Leonard liked appearing in gag publicity photos on his sets; he's seen here with Marion Davies and Nils Asther while making **The Cardboard Lover**. It was a good comedy, the first of three versions filmed by MGM from Jacques Deval's stage hit. Marion bubbled endearingly as the fan of a French tennis star who hired her to be a bogus fiancée in order to avoid his possessive mistress (Jetta Goudal). Raves for her mimicry of other stars in The Patsy cued Marion's encore in this one: she did the exotic Jetta to a turn. Carey Wilson and F. Hugh Herbert scripted.

The studio tried repeatedly to launch a dog star with the box-office bite of Rin-Tin-Tin who, single-pawed, had kept Warner Bros solvent during their lean years. Peter the Great in The Silent Accuser and Napoleon in The Thirteenth Hour had been given their chances, but retired whimpering. In 1928 the handsome animal called Flash seemed to have caught the public's fancy in Under the Black Eagle, so he was starred in **Shadows of the Night**. Human performers in the police-dog story were Lawrence Gray, Louise Lorraine, Warner Richmond and Polly Moran. It was written and directed by D. Ross Lederman.

Flash displayed his versatility by switching to a comedy role in **Honeymoon**, aided by Harry Gribbon and Polly Moran. He was a wedding gift from the groom's rival who had trained him to allow nobody, but nobody, to touch the bride. The honeymoon was saved when Flash – in a real tour de force of canine acting – fell in love with a white cat. Robert Golden directed Lew Lipton's yarn.

The Baby Cyclone, a Broadway farce by George M. Cohan, was resuscitated by F. Hugh Herbert to give Lew Cody and Aileen Pringle a change of pace but they were better in more sophisticated comedy. Robert Armstrong and Gwen Lee, with Miss Pringle here, played one of the two couples fighting over a pet peke which both women wanted. Edward Sutherland directed the silly carryings-on.

Show People was a reprise for Marion Davies and director King Vidor following the success of The Patsy. It included this famous studio lunch scene: Vidor in the foreground (light jacket) directed (left to right) William S. Hart, Marion, Douglas Fairbanks Sr, Norma Talmadge, John Gilbert, Mae Murray, Rod La Rocque, Renee Adoree, Leatrice Joy, George K. Arthur, Karl Dane, Aileen Pringle, Claire Windsor, Estelle Taylor, Hearst film columnist Louella Parsons, Dorothy Sebastian and Polly Moran. Even Charlie Chaplin and Mary Pickford made 'in person' appearances in this Hollywood comedy, which was loosely based on the career of Gloria Swanson. William Haines costarred with Marion. Wanda Tuchock, Agnes Christine Johnston and Laurence Stallings scripted.

The Actress/Trelawny of The Wells was Norma Shearer at her best, and the opening attraction at the Empire, built by MGM as London's foremost cinema in 1928. Miss Shearer charmed everyone as Sir Arthur Wing Pinero's heroine who left her fellow rep-company mummers (left to right: Lee Moran, Roy D'Arcy, Owen Moore, Gwen Lee) for a rich young aristocrat, but liked the old life better. Ralph Forbes played the boy and O. P. Heggie his crusty father. Sidney Franklin directed the Albert Lewin–Richard Schayer screenplay with a light touch.

Among the 'Bs' of 1928: Detectives, a minor Karl Dane–George K. Arthur item directed by Chester Franklin. It was set in a hotel with Polly Moran (here with George in drag) and

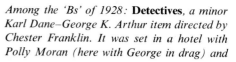

Marceline Day. . . . Under the Black Eagle, a war drama directed by W. S. Van Dyke, with Ralph Forbes rescued by his dog Flash on the battlefield (!). Marc MacDermott, Bert Roach and, again, Marceline Day (with Forbes here) were in the cast.

Masks of the Devil, a Victor Seastrom production, was notable for the technique of superimposing close-ups of John Gilbert, expressing his inner thoughts, over long-shots of the action. Also for the introduction of Eva von Berne, Irving Thalberg's much-heralded Viennese discovery, to the screen. Alas, she was seen no more. Thalberg was no match for Mayer as a star-finder. This opening scene shows amorous baron Gilbert discarding his latest plaything, Polly Ann Young (Loretta's sister) before seducing his friend's fiancée, Miss von Berne. Alma Rubens, Ralph Forbes and Theodore Roberts were others in this Frances Marion adaptation of Jacob Wassermann's 1910 novel.

Back in Tod's country–West of Zanzibar–Lon Chaney grappled with a Waldemar Young–Elliott Clawson script into which elements of practically all his previous Tod Browning thrillers had been thrown. He played a Limehouse magician paralyzed in both legs after a fight with an ivory trader (Lionel Barrymore) who had stolen his wife (Jacqueline Gadsden). They met again in Africa, where he had the trader killed by voodoo-mad natives. Meanwhile Chaney's daughter (Mary Nolan) was becoming a prostitute, so he sacrificed his life to permit her to escape with a derelict doctor whom love had regenerated. Any questions?

The Bellamy Trial, a 1927 Frances Noyes Hart best-seller adapted and filmed silent by Monta Bell in 1928, became the second picture to be partially re-shot for talking sequences. This made it a profitable release, but less so than Jimmy Valentine. The story was told in a courtroom with flashbacks illustrating the testimony. The accused and the victim were Leatrice Joy (left) and Margaret Livingston (seen here with Cosmo Kyrle Bellew). Others involved were Betty Bronson, Eddie Nugent and George Barraud.

During 1928 Karl Dane and George K. Arthur joined a circus in **Circus Rookies**, went to prison in **Brotherly Love** and took to the ocean waves in **All at Sea**. With big-top thrills augmenting their slapstick, the first was among the best of the Dane–Arthur comedies. Karl was an animal trainer, George K. a reporter, and Louise Lorraine a circus girl; a berserk gorilla provided the climax. Edward Sedgwick directed and with Lew Lipton wrote the original, scripted by Richard Schayer. The duo was also in good form in Brotherly Love. Karl played a

A Lady of Chance was Norma Shearer's last silent movie. It told a sordid story by A. P. Younger, with Miss Shearer, of all people, playing the 'badger game', luring men to her apartment to blackmail or rob them. With sound looming ahead she joined (left to right) Lowell Sherman, Gwen Lee, director Robert Z. Leonard and Johnny Mack Brown in some between-scenes vocal practice.

Diamond Handcuffs was a novelty: three separate stories linked by a diamond stolen from a South African mine which brought disaster to its successive owners. MGM used the same idea many years later with a car in The Yellow Rolls-Royce. Here: Conrad Nagel, Lena Malena (who appeared in all three episodes) and Gwen Lee in the story of a cheating wife betrayed by the diamond. John P. McCarthy directed, with Eleanor Boardman and Lawrence Gray also in the cast. Script: Carey Wilson, Willis Goldbeck, Bradley King.

MGM's showmen may have been slow to join the talkie bandwagon but, once on, they led it in new directions. They made the first real musical ever filmed, **The Broadway Melody**, late in 1928; it was also the company's first all-talkie, with dialogue by James Gleason. Its impact when it opened in February 1929 was electrify-

guard, George K. a barber, and they vied in a football match and for the warden's daughter. Her pretty face became very familiar to movie-goers over the next 25 years. She was Jean Arthur (no relation – she's American, he's Scottish), already a screen veteran at the age of 23. Charles Reisner (sometimes Riesner), former associate director with Chaplin, directed this and many subsequent MGM comedies. But when Dane and Arthur went to sea the results fell short, in laughs and paybox figures, of their army comedy Rookies. Left to right: Arthur, Dane, Josephine Dunn. Director, Alf Goulding; writers, Byron Morgan, Ann Price.

The Trail of '98 was in production through most of 1927 into 1928, and became one of the year's most important releases. Director Clarence Brown called it by far the most arduous job in his long career: he was rewarded with much acclaim for an exciting epic. The story of San Franciscans leaving their homes to get rich quick in the Alaskan goldfields was based by Benjamin Glazer and Waldemar Young on Robert W. Service's 1911 novel. Filming involved a large cast headed by Dolores Del Rio and Ralph Forbes (here) with Harry Carey, Karl Dane, Tully Marshall and about 2,000 extras. The Klondike gold rush scenes were shot near Denver at an altitude of 11,600 feet and in temperatures down to 60° below zero. The company traveled to Alaska itself for other sequences. Altogether, six men lost their lives, so dangerous were the conditions.

ing. Theatres, emblazoned with 'All Talking! All Singing! All Dancing!', were filled and encircled by excited crowds. It was not just a stunt, it was also excellent entertainment for its time and won the 'best picture' Academy Award of 1929. Edmund Goulding's simple but effective story of a sister act (Anita Page and Bessie Love, here) broken up by an amorous songwriter (Charles King) was the framework for hit numbers by Nacio Herb Brown and Arthur Freed, including the title song and 'You Were Meant for Me'. The big Technicolor production number, 'Wedding of the Painted Doll', was deemed too static by Irving Thalberg after a preview, and he ordered it to be re-shot. Sound engineer Douglas Shearer thereupon had an idea which has been used ever since. He suggested that as there was nothing wrong with the music already recorded, it should be played through loudspeakers on the set while the performers got the number right for the cameras, and the film could then be married to the pre-recording. Harry Rapf produced and Harry Beaumont was the director; his cast

included Jed Prouty, Kenneth Thompson, Mary Doran and a big chorus. The lyricist, Freed, was later to become the producer most responsible for MGM's pre-eminence in musicals.

Joan Crawford became a major star with the release of **Our Dancing Daughters**, the ideal △ screen expression of the Jazz Age, which was just then reaching its climax. Girls were cutting their hair shorter, mixing their drinks stronger, changing their bedmates faster – and millions of moviegoers rushed to see how they did it, MGM style. Miss Crawford played a wild deb who lured John Mack Brown from his hard-drinking wife, Anita Page (left). Harry Beaumont directed and Nils Asther, Dorothy Sebastian; Eddie Nugent and Dorothy Cumming were also cast. Josephine Lovett's screenplay was produced by Hunt Stromberg, but in those days he and other production supervisors (Harry Rapf, Albert Lewin, Bernard Hyman, Paul Bern) got no more screen credit from Thalberg than he gave himself: none.

Give MGM credit for developing and maintaining the superstar of stars. But there's no denying that some of Garbo's vehicles would have been novelettish nothings without her. **Wild Orchids**, scripted by Willis Goldbeck from John Colton's story 'Heat' (a title which presented billing embarrassments), was a triangle piece about a plantation owner visiting Java with his wife, who indulged in a steamy affair with a native prince. Lewis Stone and Nils Asther as husband and lover were the only others cast-listed. With Sidney Franklin directing, Garbo mesmerized her audiences once more, and again the box-office responded.

Three movies starring Ramon Novarro: **Across to Singapore** *was a new version of Ben Ames Williams' sturdy yarn, 'All the Brothers Were Valiant', first filmed by Metro in 1923. The rival sailing-ship brothers, one saintly, one devilish, were respectively and vigorously played by Ramon Novarro and Ernest Torrence. Storms at sea – emotional and climatic – were directed with gusto by William Nigh. Left to right: Joan Crawford, Frank Currier, Novarro, Edward Connelly. Script: Richard Schayer . . .* **Forbidden Hours** *scored below the*

Novarro average at the paybox, although he and Renee Adoree (here) did their best. The script by A. P. Younger had a distinct whiff of mothballs; one of those Ruritanian fancies about a king in love with a commoner who sacrificed herself to save his throne. Dorothy Cumming and Roy D'Arcy supported. Harry Beaumont directed . . . Novarro went back into ◁ *the Navy in* **The Flying Fleet**, *and if it didn't prove as big a hit as his* Midshipman, *blame it on the absence of dialogue when talkies were the new rage. It was written by Frank Wead and Schayer, excellently directed by George Hill, and produced with the co-operation of the US Naval Academy's flying school. Novarro is here getting his reward from Anita Page for surviving a perilous California–Hawaii flight with Ralph Graves, Eddie Nugent and Carroll Nye.*

Undeterred by the disappointment of The Callahans and The Murphys, *Thalberg gave Marie Dressler (centre) another and more successful chance in* **Bringing Up Father**. *She and Polly Moran (left) were teamed again, as they were to be many more times. Frances Marion's broad comedy was based, like* Tillie the Toiler, *on a famous Hearst comic strip: J. Farrell MacDonald played the henpecked Jiggs, Polly was Maggie, the social climber. Jack Conway directed them and Gertrude Olmstead, Grant Withers and Rose Dione (right).*

A Woman of Affairs *was really* The Green Hat, *Garbo version. Michael Arlen's novel, which sold in fantastic numbers, was considered so daring that the character names as well as the title had to be changed to mollify the censors. In Bess Meredyth's script the heroine still lived recklessly and died by wrecking her car, but her husband (John Mack Brown) now committed suicide because of his embezzling, not VD. John Gilbert, for the first time secondary to Garbo in both billing and footage, co-starred under Clarence Brown's direction, with Douglas Fairbanks Jr, Hobart Bosworth and (here, with the stars) Lewis Stone and Dorothy Sebastian.*

*William Haines was going from strength to strength. Having run through baseball (*Slide, Kelly, Slide*), golf (*Spring Fever*) and football (*West Point*), he continued his sporting chronicle with polo in* **The Smart Set**. *The formula was kept intact: bumptious hero lacked team spirit, was thrown out, then restored just in time to win the USA–Great Britain match. Jack Conway directed the Byron Morgan story, and Alice Day (with Haines here), Jack Holt and Hobart Bosworth were featured.*

Tim McCoy kept the action fans happy with five 1928 releases. **The Adventurer** *with Dorothy Sebastian (here) and Charles Delaney; a South American revolt story directed by Viachetslav Tourjansky (who promptly returned to Russia) . . . .* **The Bushranger** *with Marian Douglas, Russell Simpson and two*

unnamed troopers (here); an Australian bandit story directed by Chet Withey. . . . **Beyond the Sierras** *with Sylvia Beecher (right), Polly Moran (left) and Roy D'Arcy; a Californian bandit story directed by Nick Grinde. . . .* **Riders of the Dark** *with (left to right) D'Arcy, Bert Roach and Rex Lease; a Texas Ranger story also directed by Grinde. . . .* **Wyoming/** ▽ The Rock of Friendship *with Miss Sebastian and William Fairbanks; an Army versus Indians story directed by W. S. Van Dyke.*

Joan Crawford up and down: she and John Gilbert made a striking pair in **Four Walls**, *an underworld drama adapted by Alice Duer Miller from a recent Broadway winner by George Abbott and Dana Burnet. Gilbert played a gangster from New York's ghetto, jailed for manslaughter, released, then involved in the murder of his gang's leader. Carmel Myers, Vera Gordon and Robert Emmet O'Connor also responded effectively to William Nigh's strong direction.* **Dream of Love** *was supposed to be a big one for Joan but the fans wanted her as the whoopee girl of* Our Dancing Daughters *and the new movie flopped. It was based on the old French play* Adrienne Lecouvreur *whose plot, about a gypsy girl becoming a great actress and loving a prince, made a better opera than movie; script by Dorothy Farnum. Fred Niblo did it the old-fashioned way, as indicated by this scene with Warner Oland, Aileen Pringle and Nils Asther.*

1928

While the City Sleeps *was a cops-and-robbers piece by A. P. Younger with a strong cast: Lon Chaney and Anita Page (here) and Carroll Nye, Wheeler Oakman, Mae Busch and Polly Moran. Jack Conway's customary brisk direction brought conviction to the drama of a flapper who learned too much about her gangster boyfriend's boss and went to detective Chaney for help. Business was good.*

Lillian Gish and director Victor Seastrom had an artistic triumph in **The Wind**, *but it was not a box-office success, and Lillian's contract was curtailed by mutual consent. The story was basically the old favourite about the gentle girl going out to the raw West and being assaulted by a villain. The difference in this film was the extraordinary effect of mounting terror and mental aberration conveyed by actress and director. Montagu Love (here) was the man she killed before being driven mad by her conscience and the relentless winds of the plains. Lars Hanson and Dorothy Cumming were other principals in Frances Marion's screenplay.*

General Alexandroff discovers that Tania, the beautiful Russian spy, had stolen the Secret Papers in order to save her Austrian lover, so she is forced to shoot him. This sort of melodramatic nonsense did Garbo's artistic reputation no good, but **The Mysterious Lady** *was a ▽ moneymaker nevertheless. Gustav von Seyffertitz shared this scene with the star, and Conrad Nagel was her leading man for the first time. Fred Niblo directed the screenplay by Bess Meredyth.*

The Lew Cody–Aileen Pringle partnership was discontinued after **A Single Man**, *a trivial comedy in which Cody was cured of his infatuation with a young girl and proposed marriage to his secretary while the girl departed with a swain of her own age. Harry Beaumont directed (left to right) Eddie Nugent, Marceline Day, Cody and Miss Pringle in the F. Hugh Herbert–George O'Hara version of H. H. Davies' 1914 play.*

Donald Crisp, as Leif Ericsson in **The Viking**, *sights the east coast of America after a stormy voyage from Norway. Crisp had an extraordinary career. Born in London and educated at Oxford, he went to the States in 1906 in his twenties and spent a year in opera. He later began half a century in pictures, first as an actor, then as a director of stars like Douglas Fairbanks and John Barrymore, then as an actor again until the late Fifties. Meanwhile, he became important in banking circles and was a key figure in several big film financial deals. He died in 1974 at the age of 93. The Viking was an expensive flop, distinguished only (aside from Crisp's moustache) in being the first movie filmed entirely in the improved Technicolor process. Roy William Neill directed Jack Cunningham's script, and Pauline Starke, LeRoy Mason and Anders Randolf were also in the cast.*

Loretta Young started her 25-year movie career at the age of 15, in **Laugh, Clown, Laugh**. *The David Belasco stage weepie had starred Lionel Barrymore; it came to the screen as an exercise for Lon Chaney's histrionics. He played a part he had done before – a circus clown in love with a girl (Miss Young) in love with a younger man – and played it well. The lover was Nils Asther. Herbert Brenon directed and Elizabeth Meehan scripted. The film was silent but its box-office success was aided by a song of the same title which topped the 1928 hit parade.*

LAST OF THE SILENTS
1929

MGM-Loew's profits zoomed to $12,107,026, having risen gently to $6,737,205 in 1927 and $8,568,162 in 1928, and all the other companies (except Universal) were equally stimulated by the talkie boom.

Gary Cooper, Myrna Loy, Richard Arlen, Charles 'Buddy' Rogers, Lupe Velez and the entrancing Nancy Carroll were among the rising stars developed by Hollywood, but they were greatly outnumbered by famous newcomers from the stage: Ruth Chatterton, George Arliss, Helen Morgan, the Marx Brothers, Claudette Colbert, Rudy Vallee, Paul Muni, Barbara Stanwyck, Maurice Chevalier, Sophie Tucker, Walter Huston, Ann Harding, Chester Morris, Jeanette Mac-Donald, Fredric March, Ina Claire. But it was the old-timers who got the Academy Awards: Mary Pickford (*Coquette*) and Warner Baxter (*In Old Arizona*); director Frank Lloyd (*The Divine Lady*, *Weary River* and *Drag*). The talkie talk of Britain was Alfred Hitchcock's *Blackmail*.

King Vidor's prestige was so high in 1929 that he could pick his own subject, no matter how unpromising for the box office. With this carte blanche, he went totally noir for **Hallelujah!**, *written from his original by Wanda Tuchock and Richard Schayer. The drama of religion versus sin in the deep South was played entirely by unknown Negro performers, a MGM 'first' almost as revolutionary as the advent of sound. Vidor took advantage of that novelty too, adding dialogue and music to the scenes he had shot silent in Tennessee and completing interiors in one of Culver City's new sound stages. His skill and the fervent sincerity of the black cast, including Nina Mae McKinney, Daniel Haynes, and (here) Fanny Belle de Night, Victoria Spivey and Harry Gray, made* Hallelujah! *an emotional experience the critics praised unrestrainedly. Augmenting traditional songs was the first number Irving Berlin wrote for MGM, 'Waiting at the End of the Road'.*

Irving Thalberg took no chances with his wife's first talkie and gave her the title role in **The Trial of Mary Dugan**. *It was MGM's first straight all-dialogue picture and came immediately after the talk-song-and-dance* Broadway Melody. *This New York and London stage smash kept Norma Shearer listening tensely to courtroom testimony most of the time, then let her loose on a big emotional scene. Miss Shearer had never had stage experience, but she used a well-modulated voice and excellent diction to make the transition from silent stardom with immense success. Raymond Hackett (here) was her defence-lawyer brother, the role he created on Broadway. H. B. Warner, Lewis Stone, Lilyan Tashman, Olive Tell, Claude Allister and Mary Doran also scored in the Bayard Veiller thriller, directed by the author from his and Becky Gardiner's screenplay.*

There was no dialogue in **Desert Nights**; the studio was nervous about letting light-voiced he-man star John Gilbert be heard. The blonde beauty with Gilbert is Mary Nolan, who had been Imogene Wilson on Broadway until scandal-sheet publicity prompted a new start under a new name. William Nigh directed them in a diamond-mine robbery drama climaxed by a sandstorm that· trapped them and villain Ernest Torrence. Script: Lenore Coffee, Willis Goldbeck.

W. S. Van Dyke headed another South Seas expedition and came back with a major 1929 hit, **The Pagan**, with Ramon Novarro, Dorothy Janis and Donald Crisp (here) and Renee Adoree. What made it Novarro's biggest success in years was the exposure of (a) most of his torso and (b) his surprisingly melodious voice, warbling a Brown & Freed smash, 'Pagan Love Song'. The Dorothy Farnum script was an adequate frame on which to hang gorgeous scenic shots; something about a native abducting the adopted daughter of a white trader.

In and out of production for over two years, **The Mysterious Island** was finally released in 1929 with talking sequences and a Technicolor paint job. Maurice Tourneur and Benjamin Christensen made parts of it, but the directing (and scripting) credit went to Lucien Hubbard. It was an exciting, if confusing, picture of Jules Verne's underwater city fantasy, with (here) Lionel Barrymore, Jane Daly (formerly known as Jacqueline Gadsden) and Lloyd Hughes; also Montagu Love and Gibson Gowland.

Last of the Karl Dane–George K. Arthur features was **China Bound**, hilariously embroiling them in a revolution. Polly Moran and

Josephine Dunn were their respective girls. Charles Reisner directed the Sylvia Thalberg–Frank Butler story. The talkies soon finished Dane's career, and he died in 1934. Arthur continued acting for a few years, then later turned to the business side of the industry.

Spite Marriage, Buster Keaton's second film under his MGM contract and his last silent, was a backstage story with Dorothy Sebastian (here) in the most substantial role any Keaton leading lady ever had. They shared a famous scene, copied in later movies, in which she passed out after celebrating their wedding too well, and Buster tried to put her to bed with wildly funny results. Leila Hyams and Edward Earle were also in the cast; Edward Sedgwick directed, and Lawrence Weingarten produced the Ernest Pagano–Richard Schayer screenplay.

After becoming the first MGM star to face a microphone (Alias Jimmy Valentine), William Haines had another part-talkie in **The Duke Steps Out**, directed by James Cruze. It was a lively tale in which Haines dropped out of college to be a prizefighter, fell for a varsity girl (Joan Crawford) and returned to win her and the inter-collegiate boxing match. Left to right: Delmer Daves (later an important writer and director), Joan, Eddie Nugent, Haines. Script: Raymond Schrock, Dale Van Every.

The Last of Mrs Cheyney was released (July, 1929) as MGM's first film with a soundtrack; hitherto, talkies had been recorded on discs, with frequent foul-ups in the theatres when they went out of sync. Frederick Lonsdale's tightly knit play, adapted by Hans Kraly and Claudine West, found congenial actors in Norma Shearer as the jewel thief and Basil Rathbone as the cad who found her out and tried to Take Advantage. MGM's 'high class' director Sidney Franklin guided them and George Barraud, Hedda Hopper, Cyril Chadwick, Herbert Bunston and George K. Arthur through the shoals of dialogue. Although it drew less than Mary Dugan's huge receipts, it was another Shearer winner.

They Learned About Women was an odd mixture of baseball and show business themes, starring Bessie Love and vaudeville headliners Van and Schenck. Not even two top directors, Sam Wood and Jack Conway, could make much of it. Joe Schenck (no relation of the company's president), seen here with Bessie, died soon after the film was made; Gus Van continued alone for several years. Mary Doran, J. C. Nugent, Francis X. Bushman Jr, Benny Rubin and five songs were also in the Sarah Y. Mason–Arthur Baer screenplay.

The success of Excess Baggage brought an encore for William Haines and Josephine Dunn in **A Man's Man**, again directed by James Cruze. The absence of dialogue in this romance of a soda-fountain boy and a Hollywood actress was a paybox handicap. Featured in support were Mae Busch, Sam Hardy and a theme song called, no kidding, 'My Heart is Bluer Than Your Eyes, Chérie'. Forrest Halsey scripted from Patrick Kearney's 1925 play.

Speedway was William Haines' last non-talkie and, like all his films, it made a profit. It was a routine car-racing movie, with zoom-zoom motor noises and roars of the crowd synchronized to the silent footage. Here: John Miljan, Haines; also cast were Anita Page, Ernest Torrence, Polly Moran and Karl Dane. Director was Harry Beaumont. Script: Byron Morgan, Ann Price, Alfred Block.

Voice of the City was the studio's first all-talking gangster drama, made fast and cheaply. It was none too successful. Willard Mack, a Broadway veteran, wrote, directed and starred in the film, with Sylvia Field, John Miljan and Robert Ames. Mack (left) was the detective pinning a murder rap on mobster Miljan (right) to save wrongly accused Ames.

Lily Damita and Ernest Torrence turned on the heat in **The Bridge of San Luis Rey**, a worthy filming of Thornton Wilder's Pulitzer Prize novel, scripted by Alice Duer Miller, Ruth Cummings and Marian Ainslee. The multiplotted story told how the five victims of a bridge collapse in Peru happened to be there. Others in a long cast were Don Alvarado, Raquel Torres, Henry B. Walthall, Duncan Renaldo, Emily Fitzroy and Tully Marshall. Charles Brabin, veteran of the silents, had to tack on a few minutes of talk after he had completed the film.

Stage star Peggy Wood played her first film role in **Wonder of Women** with Lewis Stone, then dashed over to become the toast of London in Noël Coward's Bitter Sweet – a sharp contrast to the rather doleful movie Clarence Brown made of Bess Meredyth's script from Hermann Sudermann's novel. Stone was a composer who met Peggy on a train, settled down with her to write his masterpiece, went off with old flame Leila Hyams, then returned to Peggy, who died. The film did likewise at the box-office, partly because it was that hybrid, a part-talkie. Also cast: George Fawcett, Harry Myers, Sarah Padden, Blanche Frederici.

Replacement for the cooling Garbo–Gilbert romance in the gossip columns was the Crawford–Fairbanks thing, which resulted in marriage. Joan and Douglas Jr were also wed in **Our Modern Maidens**, the last Crawford silent. It was a follow-up but not a sequel to Our Dancing Daughters and almost as big a hit. Jack Conway directed them and Rod La Rocque, Anita Page, Eddie Nugent and Josephine Dunn in the Josephine Lovett screenplay. Many names that were to become famous on MGM credit titles worked on this film: gowns by Adrian, photography by Oliver Marsh, editing by Sam Zimbalist, music by William Axt, art direction by Cedric Gibbons.

More gore from Lon Chaney and director Tod Browning. This time they were **Where East is East**, which turned out to be Indo-China. Lon was an animal trapper whose wife (Estelle Taylor) tried to seduce their daughter's fiancé (Lloyd Hughes), so Lon killed her and himself by letting a gorilla loose. As if that weren't incredible enough, Lupe Velez was cast as the innocent daughter (here). Script: Richard Schayer, Waldemar Young.

Thunder was Lon Chaney's last silent movie, a so-so drama about a train-driver whose harsh nature alienated his sons, James Murray (here) the Crowd man, and George Duryea. Heading Chaney's support were Phyllis Haver, who had followed the Gloria Swanson path from Mack Sennett bathing beauty to star, and Murray. Both their careers were beginning to slide and Chaney himself was in poor health.

Final capitulation of the silents to the talkies was signalled by **Wise Girls**, released in September 1929. It was MGM's first movie with no silent version available for unwired theatres. Since the advent of sound, silent versions had always been made with sub-titles covering essential dialogue points; occasionally re-takes were inserted. Now, as more and more theatres were equipped for sound, silents were becoming superfluous. Wise Girls was otherwise undistinguished, a domestic comedy written by, and featuring, J. C. and Elliott Nugent, father and son, from their play 'Kempy', with (here) Norma Lee and Roland Young. Director was E. Mason Hopper.

Madame X was a highly successful directorial début for the many-sided Lionel Barrymore, who was also a talented etcher and composer. Ruth Chatterton, Paramount's first lady of the conversational film, moved her make-up box and beautiful diction over to MGM to make the movie, and brought her husband Ralph Forbes (right) to meet director Barrymore as they began shooting. Miss Chatterton was the third and best of five actresses to film this old tear-jerker about the woman who went down, down, down until defended in a murder trial by her unrecognizing son. She was preceded by Dorothy Donnelly and Pauline Frederick, followed by Gladys George and Lana Turner. Raymond Hackett, Mitchell Lewis, Sidney Toler, Carroll Nye, Richard Carle, Lewis Stone, Holmes Herbert and Eugenie Besserer supported. Script: Willard Mack.

Barrymore kept everybody acting in **The Unholy Night**, if not all to the same extent. As Sidney Jarvis pointed to an offscreen killer George Cooper looked suspicious, Natalie Moorhead mildly interested, Ernest Torrence horrified and Roland Young blank; Dorothy Sebastian simply swooned. Others lending their talents to this Ben Hecht mystery melo were Boris Karloff, John Loder, Polly Moran and John Miljan.

Adela Rogers St Johns' 1928 novel **The Single Standard** was adapted by Josephine Lovett and filmed by John S. Robertson the following year as a Garbo vehicle. As a girl out to prove that if men can get away with it, so can women, she seduced and discarded her chauffeur (Lane Chandler), cruised the South Seas with a boxer-artist (Nils Asther, here), nearly drove her husband (John Mack Brown) to suicide, and wore trousers. It was silent – but who cared, with Garbo there?

The last silent picture MGM made was **The Kiss**, completed in September 1929. As usual Garbo's expressive face needed no words, but the machine-made script by Hans Kraly was hardly worthy of her. A striking debut was made by Lew Ayres as the youth whose kiss caused her to be tried for the murder of her jealous husband. Conrad Nagel played her defending lawyer; others in the cast were Holmes Herbert and Anders Randolf. The eminent French director, Jacques Feyder, was brought over to direct.

If the Sphinx itself had spoken it could have caused little more excitement than the announcement 'Garbo Talks!' blazoned across thousands of billboards when **Anna Christie** was released. Few believed that the silent goddess could pass the microphone test, which had downed other (especially foreign-accented) Hollywood greats, with her mysterious appeal intact. And what would this glamorous temptress make of Eugene O'Neill's poor, bitter waterfront drab? Well, not only did the Garbo voice, deep and flexible, match the Garbo personality to perfection, but she gave a performance of compelling realism. Charles Bickford, George F. Marion, in his original stage part as Anna's father (he also played it in the 1923 silent version with Blanche Sweet) and Marie Dressler, stealing scenes as a drunken derelict, supported her strongly under Clarence Brown's direction in Frances Marion's screenplay. It was a tremendous hit.

1929 *Three young players from Broadway got their big break in* **So This is College**. *They were (left to right) Sally Starr, of whom little more was heard; Elliott Nugent, who became a prominent playwright and director; and Robert Montgomery, who stayed with MGM for 17 years of stardom. Cliff Edwards and Polly Moran were the comics in this rah-rah comedy with four songs and a gossamer plot about university chums sundered by a scheming co-ed. Sam Wood directed, and Al Boasberg, Delmer Daves and Joe Farnham were the writers.*

The jazz-mad revels of the Twenties were coming to an end, but Joan Crawford was still in there whooping it up in **Untamed**. *It was her first all-talkie. In this typical scene she holds back rival Gwen Lee while boyfriend Robert Montgomery gets slugged during a wild party. Joan played an heiress from the tropics, which gave her grounds for singing the theme song 'Chant of the Jungle'. Jack Conway directed, with Ernest Torrence, John Miljan and Eddie Nugent also cast. Script: Sylvia Thalberg, Frank Butler, Willard Mack.*

Marion Davies and King Vidor, the star-director duo of The Patsy *and* Show People, *made it three hits in a row with* **Not So Dumb**. *This talking remake of Constance Talmadge's 1923* Dulcy *originated in the Broadway comedy of that name by George Kaufman and Marc Connelly, the crux of which was a disastrous party thrown by a birdbrained charmer to aid her fiancé's career. Elliott Nugent, Raymond Hackett, Julia Faye and (here) Franklin Pangborn joined in the frolic, scripted by Wanda Tuchock and Edwin Justus Mayer.*

Ramon Novarro's hit song in the non-dialogue Pagan *resulted in a musical being chosen for his talkie début.* **Devil May Care** *was a light operetta set in Napoleonic France. It was no record-breaker, but it was profitable, beautifully produced, well directed by Sidney Franklin and introduced pretty Dorothy Jordan opposite the star. Herbert Stothart wrote the music, initiating a long MGM career; Marion Harris and John Miljan had featured roles; Hans Kraly and Zelda Sears adapted the plot from an 1851 French play, 'Bataille des Dames'.*

The Ship from Shanghai *was no pleasure cruiser. What with raging storms, both emotional and climatic, crazed steward Louis Wolheim running amok, and all that dialogue to remember, Holmes Herbert, Carmel Myers, Kay Johnson, Zeffie Tilbury and Conrad Nagel never had a moment's peace. Charles Brabin directed the trans-Pacific ordeal from a story by Dale Collins; script by John Howard Lawson.*

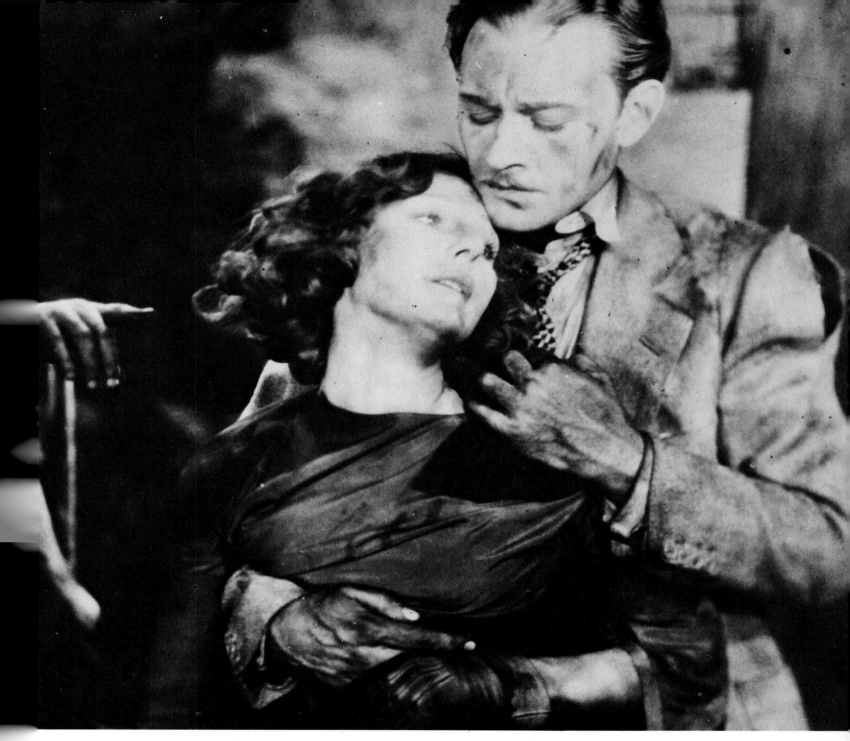

The arrival of Cecil B. DeMille at Culver City in 1929 was celebrated with the pomp befitting the king of box-office hokum. The first movie to emerge from his unit was, alas, more hokum △ than box-office. **Dynamite** concerned an heiress (Kay Johnson) forced by her grandfather's will to marry a coalminer (Charles Bickford, left) instead of her real love (Conrad Nagel). It was DeMille's first sound film; he featured a tuneful song 'How Am I to Know?', and a noisy cave-in climax. Julia Faye, Leslie Fenton and newcomer Joel McCrea were in the cast. Script by Jeanie Macpherson, John Howard Lawson, Gladys Unger.

◁ **The Idle Rich**, from Edith Ellis' Broadway success 'White Collars', was among the best early talkies. The director was William De-Mille, Cecil's brother; he didn't make 'em supercolossal–just good. The film got much unforced humour out of the inverted snobbery of a typist's family refusing to share her husband's wealth until he threatened to give it all to charity. Conrad Nagel was the million-

aire, Leila Hyams his bride; Bessie Love, James Neil and Edythe Chapman were her proletariat family. This between-scenes shot shows Nagel, Miss Hyams and director De-Mille listening to a song just recorded by Nagel for The Hollywood Revue.

Tide of Empire, a big-scale Western filmed by Allan Dwan from Waldemar Young's adaptation of Peter B. Kyne's novel, had synchronized sound–but rival Westerns were going one better by talking too. It concerned itself with ranchers, gold-seekers and outlaws in the days

when California was becoming more American than Spanish. Renee Adoree and George Duryea (here) were the leads, aided by George Fawcett, Paul Hurst, Fred Kohler and William Collier Jr.

Lord Byron of Broadway/What Price Melody? starred two New York stage singers, Charles Kaley (here, with Gwen Lee) and Ethelind Terry. Their Hollywood début seemed to send them into a camera coma, despite the efforts of two directors, William Nigh and Harry Beaumont. They went back to the stage. Cliff Edwards had another Brown–Freed song hit, 'Should I?', to follow their 'Singin' in the Rain', but otherwise–no go. Script: Crane Wilbur, Willard Mack.

The Duncan Sisters, long famous for their 'Topsy and Eva' act in vaudeville (they made a 1926 movie under that title) were starred in **It's a Great Life** *as consolation for losing the Broadway Melody leads to Bessie Love and Anita Page. It had almost the same plot, several musical numbers (here, Vivian and Rosetta doing 'Following You') and some Technicolor — but to no avail. Their personalities tended to cloy on the screen. Others appearing under Sam Wood's direction in the Al Boasberg–Willard Mack screenplay were Lawrence Gray, Jed Prouty and Benny Rubin.*

Bessie Love leads the boys and girls through the 'Everybody Tap' number in **Chasing Rainbows**. *She and Charles King hoped they had another Broadway Melody in this backstage musical, but the market was already flooded with that triumph's imitators. Still, this Bess Meredyth story was among the best of them, with Marie Dressler, Polly Moran, Jack Benny and George K. Arthur giving it strong comedy voltage, and 'Happy Days Are Here Again' supplying a smash song. Charles Reisner directed.*

Everybody but Garbo and the gateman seemed to be in **The Hollywood Revue**, *the most popular in a cycle (Fox Movietone Follies, Paramount on Parade, etc.) of musicals filmed with no story — on purpose, that is. Pictured here are Marie Dressler, Bessie Love and Polly Moran in 'Singin' in the Rain', the biggest hit of its 17 songs; and George K. Arthur, Karl Dane and Jack Benny in a comedy turn. (Dimly seen above Benny's fiddle is Ann Dvorak, then a teenage chorus girl.) Marion Davies, Buster Keaton, Norma Shearer, John Gilbert, William Haines, Laurel and Hardy, Conrad Nagel, Anita Page, Charles King, Cliff Edwards, Joan Crawford and Lionel Barrymore also contributed, augmented by two singing groups and three dancing troupes. It was a sensational success. Director Charles Reisner shot a lot of it in the 7 pm-7 am 'graveyard shift' since most of the stars were working in other movies during the day. Harry Rapf produced.*

In 1929 MGM bought the rights of Sidney Howard's play about illicit love, **They Knew What They Wanted**, and gave it to Victor Seastrom to direct as an all-talkie titled **A Lady to Love**. It was the quickest remake on record – a 1928 silent Paramount version starring Pola Negri had skirted film censorship by calling itself **The Secret Hour**. (RKO gave it a third go in 1940 with its original title.) Vilma Banky played the mail-order bride of vineyard owner Edward G. Robinson; Robert Ames was the hired hand she pressed too many grapes with. Edward G. went on to become the world's favourite gangster; Miss Banky retired. Her glamorous career, mostly co-starring with Valentino and Ronald Colman, was ended by an accent described by one critic as 'a strange mixture of Budapest and Chicago'.

The Rogue Song was the first all-Technicolor all-talkie, and Lionel Barrymore's fourth and last directing job at his home studio. (Columbia borrowed him to direct Barbara Stanwyck in **Ten Cents a Dance** before he returned to acting.) It was also the successful film début of opera star Lawrence Tibbett, who combined a splendid baritone with an ebullient personality. Vaguely based on the Franz Lehar operetta **Gypsy Love**, it was highly praised for everything except a strangely hit-less musical score. Supporting Tibbett were Judith Vosselli and Catherine Dale Owen (here), Stan Laurel and Oliver Hardy, Nance O'Neil, Ulrich Haupt, Florence Lake, Lionel Belmore, Kate Price. Script: Frances Marion and John Colton.

Bayard Veiller's spiritualist stage thriller **The Thirteenth Chair** wracked nerves nicely in Tod Browning's talkie, with Margaret Wycherly in her original role as the medium. Going into a trance every reel or so until the murderer was unmasked, she had Gretchen Holland, Bela Lugosi and Holmes Herbert (here) and Conrad Nagel, Leila Hyams, Helene Millard, Mary Forbes and Cyril Chadwick as seance table-grippers. Script: Elliott Clawson.

With Hearst keeping a beady eye on the studio to see that Marion Davies didn't get left behind in the talkie race, Thalberg hurried to give her a wartime musical, **Marianne**, directed by Robert Z. Leonard. Making her a French girl speaking broken English disguised the fact that Marion talked with a slight stammer. The movie was received with less than rapture, but it got by on the merits of six songs plus attractive performances by the star and Lawrence Gray (here) and Benny Rubin and Cliff Edwards, known on hit discs as Ukelele Ike. A separately made silent version had Oscar Shaw and Robert Ames as her leading men. Script: Dale Van Every.

The Woman Racket/Lights and Shadows offered a lacklustre story about a cop, a night-club hostess and a gang killing, with old-timers Blanche Sweet and Tom Moore and (here) John Miljan, Robert Agnew and Sally Starr as Broadway denizens. Robert Ober and Albert Kelley co-directed for the first and last time; Albert LeVino adapted the play 'Night Hostess' by Philip and Frances Dunning.

Navy Blues, a rare try by Clarence Brown at handling comedy, turned out well. The yarn about a sailor on leave and a dance-hall girl (Anita Page) proved that William Haines had lost none of his zest by going the all-talking route. Karl Dane, J. C. Nugent and Edythe Chapman helped. Nugent and his son Elliott were among the film's many writers.

The biggest star problem that faced Mayer and Thalberg when talkies arrived was John Gilbert, their top male box-office attraction until 1929. Then his first all-dialogue release, **His Glorious Night**, opened with a dull thud. Somehow his voice didn't match his face, and his impassioned love scenes with Catherine Dale Owen drew giggles instead of gasps from the fans. Lionel Barrymore's direction of this Willard Mack adaptation of Molnar's play 'Olympia' didn't help; nor did the performances of Hedda Hopper, Gustav von Seyffertitz and Nance O'Neil.

S. S. Van Dine's Philo Vance was the American Sherlock Holmes of the Twenties, a cultured eccentric whose detections kept millions of breaths bated through book after book, film upon film. Paramount made three starring William Powell, then MGM took over with Basil Rathbone in **The Bishop Murder Case**. Nick Grinde and David Burton co-directed the all-talkie about a dear old professor who called in Vance to solve a murder mystery and turned out to be the killer. L to r: Rathbone, Alec B. Francis, Leila Hyams, Clarence Geldert. Also in Lenore Coffee's screenplay: Roland Young, George F. Marion, Carroll Nye, Delmer Daves.

Norma Shearer picked him for **Their Own Desire**, a sophisticated drama about a young pair having an affair complicated by her father having an affair with his mother. So Robert Montgomery became the actor all MGM's female stars wanted – and got – as leading man. The parents in this successful talkie were Helene Millard (his), Belle Bennett and Lewis Stone (hers). Director, E. Mason Hopper; script, Frances Marion and J. G. Forbes.

Tim McCoy made four more movies in 1929, then saddled his horse and went thataway out the MGM gates—forever. All silent in a talkie world, they were: **The Desert Rider** with Raquel Torres (above), Bert Roach, Edward Connelly, directed by Nick Grinde . . . **Morgan's Last Raid** with Dorothy Sebastian, Wheeler Oakman (top right), directed by Grinde . . . **The Overland Telegraph** with Lawford Davidson (bottom right), Dorothy Janis, Frank Rice, directed by John Waters . . . **Sioux Blood** with Chief Standing Bear (middle right), Robert Frazer, Marion Douglas, directed by Waters.

THE TALKIE CRAZE
1930

The talkie craze shielded Hollywood's major companies from the world's financial crisis, and they thrived: MGM-Loew's netted a new high, $15m, which it topped only in 1946. War pictures were in the money. Howard Hughes made the most, with *Hell's Angels*, by starring a sensational blonde, Jean Harlow, opposite Ben Lyon; James Whale filmed R. C. Sherriff's great play *Journey's End;* and best of all was Lewis Milestone's version of Erich Maria Remarque's *All Quiet on the Western Front* with Louis Wolheim and Lew Ayres, which won the Academy Award.

Marlene Dietrich skyrocketed in *The Blue Angel* and *Morocco;* Edward G. Robinson in *Little Caesar* started the gangster cycle; John Wayne arrived in *The Big Trail,* Spencer Tracy in *Up the River,* Leslie Howard in *Outward Bound.* Drifting out were Norma Talmadge, Alice Joyce, Milton Sills, Corinne Griffith, Thomas Meighan, Laura La Plante, Vilma Banky, Rod La Rocque, Billie Dove and, temporarily, Lillian Gish.

An actor who had last worked on the lot as an extra in The Merry Widow *in 1925 was given a short-term contract in 1930 and cast as a gangster in Joan Crawford's* **Dance, Fools,** ▽ **Dance.** *By late 1931 he was a star, having appeared in eight more pictures with an increasingly electrifying effect on the public. The Clark Gable era at MGM had begun its 24-year span. Joan had a strong movie in this, playing a girl who became a crime reporter when her family was ruined by the stock market crash. It had much censorship trouble with a scene, which today would probably be played nude, of boys and girls stripping to their underwear for a midnight swim. Harry Beaumont's cast included Earle Foxe (left), William Bakewell, Lester Vail, Cliff Edwards and Natalie Moorhead. Script: Richard Schayer, Aurania Rouverol.*

Because it was scheduled to be John Gilbert's first talkie, Thalberg stinted nothing on **Redemption.** *He gave him a role in which John Barrymore had triumphed on the stage, Dorothy Farnum and Edwin Justus Mayer's carefully scripted version of Tolstoy's 'The Living Corpse', a strong cast including Renee Adoree, Eleanor Boardman and Conrad Nagel, epic director Fred Niblo and a lavish production.*

Result: disaster. Gilbert was quickly shunted into His Glorious Night *while the studio worked out a salvage job on* Redemption. *Several scenes – like this suicide of the hero for the sake of his wife and friend who had married since his presumed death (left to right: Gilbert, Boardman, Nagel) – were remade and the movie was eventually released as the star's second talkie. Result: flop.*

While never a superstar, William Haines was a steady moneymaker for MGM. A returned college hero and his family's astonishment at his moneymaking schemes provided spirited fun in **The Girl Said No,** *directed by Sam Wood. Marie Dressler (a one-scene riot as a drunk millionairess), Leila Hyams and Francis X. Bushman Jr were the only cast members not in this scene. Left to right: William V. Mong, Phyllis Crane, William Janney, Clara Blandick, Haines, Polly Moran, Junior Coghlan. Sarah Y. Mason and Charles MacArthur scripted.*

In **Way Out West** *Haines played a carnival gambler forced to work on a ranch to repay the cowboys he'd fleeced. Fred Niblo, the* Ben-Hur *director, made it as his last under MGM contract. Left to right: Haines, Miss Moran, Miss Hyams, Charles Middleton, Francis X. Bushman Jr, Cliff Edwards. Script: Byron Morgan, Alfred Block, Joe Farnham, Ralph Spence.*

Remote Control *gave Haines another success. It should have been a mishmash, with four directors and seven writers working on it at various times, but it turned out rather well. Malcolm St Clair and Nick Grinde wound up with direction credit. Haines played a music salesman (with Eileen Percy) turned radio announcer, foiling a crook entertainer (John Miljan) who broadcast code instructions to his gang. Charles King, Mary Doran, J. C. Nugent, Eddie Nugent (no relation) and the ubiquitous Miss Moran were also involved.*

Romance, *Garbo's second talkie, confirmed her skill with dialogue, making you believe that the Italian soprano heroine could sound like a Swedish contralto. (Strange, considering her long USA residence, that Garbo always spoke with an English–Swedish rather than an American–Swedish accent.) The old Edward Sheldon play in which Doris Keane had an international success was in sharp contrast to* Anna Christie, *and returned Garbo to an ambience of glamorous, ill-starred love. Her rather inadequate leading man was Gavin Gordon (here) as the suitor of the opera star, mistress of a rich man (Lewis Stone). Elliott Nugent, Florence Lake, Clara Blandick and Henry Armetta were also in Clarence Brown's cast. Script: Bess Meredyth, Edwin Justus Mayer.*

Fifi d'Orsay, surely the most durable mamselle in show-biz history, was still rolling her eyes and Rs in a big Broadway musical of 1972, 'Follies'. In 1930 she romped through **Those Three French Girls** *with Reginald Denny and English stage veteran George Grossmith (here) and Yola d'Avril, Sandra Ravel, Cliff Edwards and Polly Moran. Direction, Harry Beaumont; story, Arthur Freed, Dale Van Every; script, Sylvia Thalberg, Frank Butler; dialogue, P. G. Wodehouse.*

MGM's own glamour stars were working or looked the other way when **Passion Flower** *went into production, so Kay Francis was borrowed from Paramount. The movie was one for the ladies, a typical Kathleen Norris romantic novel made into a typical Kay Francis movie. In this scene she was eloping with her chauffeur (Charles Bickford) when a letter from his wife (Kay Johnson) ended their idyll, and he left Kay F. hiding a broken heart under several yards of mink. William DeMille directed, with Lewis Stone and ZaSu Pitts featured in the Martin Flavin–Laurence Johnson–Edith Fitzgerald screenplay.*

Somerset Maugham's 'The Circle', filmed silent in 1925, found its voice in **Strictly Unconventional**. *But by 1930 a teacup talkie needed strong star values to sustain it, and this one didn't have the most illustrious cast in the world. There was criticism of David Burton's stiff direction and the Sylvia Thalberg–Frank Butler treatment of the story about infidelity in two generations, with (left to right) Tyrrell Davis, Catherine Dale Owen, Paul Cavanagh and Mary Forbes; also cast were Lewis Stone, Alison Skipworth and Ernest Torrence.*

Ramon Novarro's second talkie, **In Gay Madrid**, *was a letdown after* Devil May Care. *A song-interrupted comedy, its frail Bess Meredyth–Edwin Justus Mayer–Edward Fields script about the loves of a highspirited student was directed by Robert Z. Leonard. Left to right: William V. Mong, Novarro, Beryl Mercer, Dorothy Jordan.*

An absolute winner was **The Divorcee**, *which reaped a fortune from the public, praise from the critics, and the 1929–30 best actress Oscar from the Academy for Norma Shearer. After this, her carefully planned and highly successful career ('Well, she sleeps with the boss', philosophized Joan Crawford) included many wayward wives, in sharp contrast to the offscreen Mrs Thalberg. Chester Morris (with her here), Robert Montgomery, Conrad Nagel and Florence Eldridge also sparkled in Robert Z. Leonard's production, written by Zelda Sears, Nick Grinde, John Meehan. All concerned worked wonders with not obviously ideal screen material, Ursula Parrott's novel* Ex-Wife *about a woman who shed her husband, emulated his sexual freedom, then returned to him.*

The apex of cuckoo supercolossalness was achieved by Cecil B. DeMille's **Madam Satan**, *a box-office disaster. A little pastry of a plot (by Jeanie Macpherson, Gladys Unger, Elsie Janis) about marital jealousy was covered by layer upon layer of spectacular icing until it became indigestible even to DeMillions for whom it was confected. Climax came in this scene, a costume party in a giant airship which was struck by lightning, obliging hundreds of guests to descend on New York by parachute. The stars were Kay Johnson and (here) Reginald Denny, Lillian Roth and Roland Young. Miss Roth's hectic life made a much better movie,* I'll Cry Tomorrow, *25 years later.*

Lady of Scandal/The High Road *was Frederick Lonsdale's sister-under-the-typewriter-ribbon to Pinero's 'Trelawny of the Wells'. Ruth Chatterton played the actress whose fiancé (Ralph Forbes) took her to visit his aristocratic family (Fred Kerr, Nance O'Neil). After dallying with his cousin (Basil Rathbone, here) she gave both men up and returned to the stage. Stylishly directed by Sidney Franklin, but all a bit hoity-toity for the average fan. Script: Hans Kraly, Claudine West, Edwin Justus Mayer.*

Once he could do no wrong, but in 1930 John Gilbert was slightly off-key in every try. **Way for a Sailor** *attempted to make him a tough seafarer, but sank at the box-office. Sam Wood directed (left to right) Leila Hyams, Gilbert, and Wallace Beery whose hearty humours with a pet seal occupied much footage; also writer/actor Jim Tully and Polly Moran. Laurence Stallings, W. L. River, Charles MacArthur and Al Boasberg all had a go at the script.*

◁ Chester Morris goes into solitary in **The Big House**, one of the first and best of all prison movies, and a knockout at the 1930 box office. Although it was one of the year's top money-makers, MGM did not follow it up with a burst of violence; neither Mayer nor Thalberg relished that genre. Under George Hill's direction, Morris' tough, forceful performance was matched by Wallace Beery's as a condemned convict (a role intended for Lon Chaney), and Robert Montgomery extended his acting range as a cowardly informer. Others sharing the all-round praise it received were Lewis Stone, Leila Hyams, J. C. Nugent, Karl Dane, and writer Frances Marion who won an Oscar for it. So did Douglas Shearer's sound recording.

The Big House director, writer and co-star (George Hill, Frances Marion, Wallace Beery) came up with a second 1930 super-hit in **Min and Bill**. In fact it was the biggest cash-collector of the year. But its chief asset was Marie Dressler. Her marvellous performance – of the waterfront woman who adopted a waif (Dorothy Jordan) and killed the dissolute mother (Marjorie Rambeau) who tried to reclaim her – was a real gamut-runner from slapstick to heartbreak, and won her the 1930–1 Academy Award.

With his father, J. C., Elliott Nugent (left) wrote a strong family drama and himself an effective role in **Sins of the Children**/The Richest Man in the World. He played a barber's son who stole from his employers, then became a successful inventor. As in So This is College Robert Montgomery shared honours with him under director Sam Wood. Louis Mann as the father and Leila Hyams, Mary Doran and Francis X. Bushman Jr also scored.

Joan Crawford in **Our Blushing Brides** tried a blonde wig and the patience of her suitor. The former pleased the fans less than the latter, who was Robert Montgomery. The Bess Meredyth–John Howard Lawson script, a first cousin to

Sally, Irene and Mary, detailed the amours of three shopgirls: Joan; Anita Page, who got Raymond Hackett; and Dorothy Sebastian, who got John Miljan. Director Harry Beaumont staged a big fashion parade to make doubly sure it would have the same appeal to women as the two previous 'Our' flapper epics. Also cast: Hedda Hopper, Edward Brophy, Albert Conti, Robert Emmet O'Connor, Martha Sleeper, Mary Doran, Gwen Lee, Claire Dodd.

Getting ready to write a farewell note to Robert Montgomery, the great love of her life, Garbo enacted an 'It's a far, far better thing I do now' scene with a beauty of which Gene Markey's trite script for **Inspiration** was hardly worthy. A French artists' model, and therefore immoral, she was afraid of ruining the young man's career. Many more movies like this would have ruined Garbo's. The Clarence Brown production featured Lewis Stone, Marjorie Rambeau, Karen Morley, John Miljan, Judith Vosselli, Beryl Mercer, Oscar Apfel, Edwin Maxwell, Joan Marsh, Gwen Lee, Zelda Sears.

No slouch at furthering her career, Joan Crawford talked Thalberg into giving her the important picture scheduled for his wife, who had become too pregnant to film it. It was **Paid**/Within the Law, which Sam Wood made into one of 1930's top winners and which made Joan a superstar. Discarding her flapper image, she switched on some powerful dramatic voltage in Bayard Veiller's perennial stage and screen hit, now scripted by Charles MacArthur and Lucien Hubbard. The role of a shopgirl avenging wrongful dismissal by becoming a criminal had previously served Alice Joyce in 1917 and Norma Talmadge in 1923, both under the original title Within the Law. This time, detective and hero (here with Joan) were played by John Miljan, and Kent Douglass, who later reverted to his real name, Douglass Montgomery. Also cast: Marie Prevost, Robert Armstrong, Purnell Pratt, Polly Moran and Gwen Lee.

Buster Keaton puts on a regal act with Trixie Friganza in his first talkie, **Free and Easy**. He was in great form as bumbling manager of a beauty contest winner (Anita Page), taking her and her mother (Trixie) to Hollywood, where he became an extra and she loved a star (Robert Montgomery). Edward Sedgwick had the whole MGM studio for his sets, with 'in person' appearances by William Haines, Jackie Coogan, Lionel Barrymore, Cecil B. DeMille and Fred Niblo. Script: Al Boasberg, Richard Schayer. Keaton was still big box-office at this time – but there was a long downward path ahead.

Buster Keaton claimed that he used his actual wartime experiences as material for **Doughboys**/Forward March. He must have had a riotous war; this was one of the Great Stoneface's funniest movies. Edward Sedgwick again directed him (second from left in the camp-show sequence) as the US Army's most eccentric recruit. Sally Eilers, Cliff Edwards, Edward Brophy and a few songs added to the good time had by all, including the film's exhibitors. Script: Richard Schayer.

The Girl in the Show was the first MGM movie directed by Edgar Selwyn, who has a special place in the company's history. When he, his brother Arch and Samuel Goldfish formed a company in 1916 they made its name from half of each of theirs and called it Goldwyn Pictures. (The alternative, Selfish Pictures, was instantly rejected.) The Selwyns' partner was so pleased with the corporate name that he adopted it and became Samuel Goldwyn forever after. The Girl in the Show was aimed at the double-feature market and hit its target successfully. From a John Golden–Kenyon Nicholson play about an 'Uncle Tom's Cabin' touring company, it starred Bessie Love, with Raymond Hackett and Nanci Price (here), supported by Eddie Nugent, Jed Prouty, Ford Sterling and Mary Doran.

*As on the stage, C. Aubrey Smith played the title role in **The Bachelor Father**, beginning many years as MGM's fine old English gentleman. The indefatigable Robert Z. Leonard made a zippy comedy of Edward Childs Carpenter's play, scripted by Laurence Johnson. Ralph Forbes (left) was Smith's secretary, Halliwell Hobbes and Edgar Norton his servants, and Marion Davies, Ray Milland (in one of his first movies) and Nena Quartaro (right) his illegitimate children. 'Some of the dialogue is rather risqué', warned one critic.*

*Rachel Crothers' 1929 stage comedy **Let Us be Gay** made a talkative but entertaining movie a year later, adapted by Frances Marion and with Norma Shearer and Marie Dressler (both Canadians, incidentally) sharing honours under Robert Z. Leonard's direction. To save her grand-daughter (Sally Eilers) from the clutches of Norma's ex-husband (Rod La Rocque), society matron Marie persuaded Norma to lure him back again. Raymond Hackett, Hedda Hopper and Gilbert Emery were also cast.*

*After a few so-so results with the Marie Dressler–Polly Moran comedy team, the studio suddenly hit the jackpot with **Caught Short**. The old girls had their usual story of feuding boarding-house landladies with respective children in love—but with a difference: they were playing the stock market and winning. The public was ready to start laughing at the Wall Street disaster, and big box-office ensued. Charles Reisner directed (left to right) Charles Morton, Polly, Marie, Anita Page. Greta Granstedt and T. Roy Barnes were also in the Willard Mack–Robert Hopkins screenplay.*

*Slapstick in a beauty salon made **Reducing** a popular release, but acrimony over the romances of their children was the unoriginal basic plot of another team effort by Marie Dressler, Polly Moran and director Charles Reisner. Anita Page and Sally Eilers played the comediennes' daughters, with William Collier Jr and William Bakewell as their boyfriends.*

Billy the Kid *was MGM's first big Western* ▷ *talkie, especially big in those first-run theatres where it was shown in 'Realife': 70-millimetre instead of the normal 35-millimetre film was projected. Although effective, and revived decades later, this innovation was dropped because of cost; theatres were still paying for sound installations. The studio was giving John Mack Brown a build-up (which didn't take) and he had his first starring part as Billy. Looking more like a varsity athlete than a ruthless desperado, he was cast against the wishes of director King Vidor. Wallace Beery, given a contract after his hit in* The Big House, *Kay Johnson and Wyndham Standing were featured. Script: Wanda Tuchock, Laurence Stallings, Charles MacArthur.*

*Gloom hung heavy over **This Mad World** when Basil Rathbone, a French spy visiting his mother, Louise Dresser, behind enemy lines, was recognized by Kay Johnson, wife of a German general. It meant execution for Rathbone, suicide for Kay, and no business from a misery-shunning public. William DeMille directed the Clara Beranger–Arthur Caesar screenplay.*

*Our Dancing Daughter Goes West could have been the title of the Sylvia Thalberg–Frank Butler drama, **Montana Moon**, in which Joan Crawford's wild Manhattan ways were tamed by cowboy John Mack Brown. Malcolm St Clair made it, his cast including Ricardo Cortez, Dorothy Sebastian, Cliff Edwards, Karl Dane and Benny Rubin. Critics noted a great improvement in outdoor sound recording in its ranch scenes. MGM noted unexciting receipts: the Crawford jazz-baby persona was ready for revision.*

*For the third time W. S. Van Dyke set out on a long production trek, this one for **Trader Horn**, taking into the African jungles tons of equipment and principals Edwina Booth, Duncan Renaldo and Harry Carey (here with native Mutia Omooloo). It was the first such location trip for a sound film and it lasted for seven months in 1929. Conditions were arduous, accidents abounded, Miss Booth fell ill in the tropical heat (she never fully recovered and successfully sued the company for damages), and Van Dyke kept in holiday mood with lashings of gin. Result: thousands of feet of disjointed film. Thalberg ordered them to be pulled together by retakes and added scenes at the studio and on a comparatively minor jaunt to Mexico. This took up most of 1930, but*

Top this: Mexican fisherman's daughter loves deep-sea diver; he is killed by giant sting-ray when jealous rival fouls his breathing-tube; girl offers to marry any man who captures giant sting-ray; successful candidate is escaped convict disguised as clergyman. Title: **The Sea Bat**. *Cast: Charles Bickford and Raquel Torres (here) and Nils Asther, George F. Marion, John Miljan, Gibson Gowland, Boris Karloff. Wesley Ruggles (Charles' brother) directed it, Bess Meredyth and John Howard Lawson wrote it, and people paid to see it.*

Lon Chaney was the last star of the silents (except Chaplin) to make a talkie, and his first talkie was his last. **The Unholy Three** *was completed just before his death in 1930. This photo of Chaney and director Jack Conway congratulating each other on the final scene was probably the last ever taken of the star, who died at the height of his fame. He used five different voices to supplement his make-up wizardry in this rewrite by J. C. and Elliott Nugent of his 1925 hit. Lila Lee, Elliott Nugent, John Miljan and (again as the dwarf) Harry Earles were in the new cast. MGM was to suffer two more losses of major stars in the Thirties: Marie Dressler and Jean Harlow.*

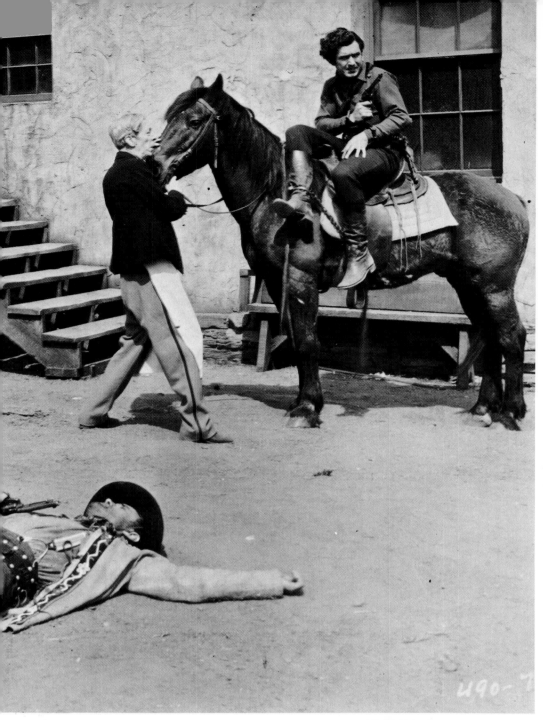

A 1927 smash on Broadway (and in London in 1928 with George Murphy playing a lead), **Good News** *made a fast-paced movie musical in 1930, directed by Nick Grinde and Edgar MacGregor. Comedian Gus Shy (here with Bessie Love) and ingénue Mary Lawlor were imported from the stage show; Stanley Smith was the singing hero, Lola Lane the college vamp, and Dorothy McNulty led the rousing 'Varsity Drag' dance number. 'The Best Things in Life Are Free' and 'Lucky in Love' were among the other DeSylva, Brown & Henderson songs that punctuated the Frances Marion–Joe Farnham script. Cliff Edwards, Thomas Jackson and Delmer Daves completed the cast.*

perseverence paid off: the film scored a tremendous success.

A certain notoriety lingered around **War Nurse**, *thanks to its source, an anonymous autobiography in which an American nurse with the French army told more or less All. But by the time it reached the screen it was cleaner than a bedbath. Robert Montgomery made a dashing aviator in this movie; the starmaking treatment was rushing him from one picture to another in 1930 and it paid off – he was the first top male star developed since talkies arrived at what was regarded as a 'woman's studio'. June Walker (here), from the New York stage, proved colourless on film. Edgar Selwyn directed them and Robert Ames, Anita Page, ZaSu Pitts, Marie Prevost, Helen Jerome Eddy, Hedda Hopper, Martha Sleeper and Eddie Nugent in the Becky Gardiner–Joe Farnham script.*

Hal Roach moved over from his MGM-affiliated shorts studio to direct a feature, **Men of the North**. *It was customary at this time for MGM to make two or three language versions simultaneously, but this routine actioner by Willard Mack and Richard Schayer about Northwest Mounties and a goldmine robbery, was for some reason chosen to be the first (and last) talkie shot in five versions: English, French, German, Spanish and Italian. Later, post-production dubbing or subtitling took care of the foreign markets. Barbara Leonard and Gilbert Roland (here), Nena Quartaro and Arnold Korff did* Men of the North *in English.*

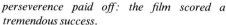

71

1930

Memories of the good old days when a tango spoke louder than words were revived by **Call of the Flesh**. And veterans Ramon Novarro, Renee Adoree and director Charles Brabin revived 'em with bravura. Ramon singing, fighting Ernest Torrence and romancing Dorothy Jordan in Technicolor added more pash to the proceedings. Script: John Colton. This was Miss Adoree's farewell appearance; after a long battle against tuberculosis she died in 1933 at the age of 35.

You've heard it but you've never seen it. **Great Day** went into production as a major musical in 1930, with Harry Pollard directing Joan Crawford, Johnny Mack Brown and Cliff Edwards. It was junked after ten days' shooting, but three of its Vincent Youmans songs have been played and sung ever since: 'Great Day', 'More Than You Know' and 'Without a Song'. It also flopped in a stage version. Another musical, The March of Time, designed as The Hollywood Revue of 1930, was given up as hopeless when near completion; two Marion Davies musicals, The 5 O'Clock Girl and Rosalie, were started and stopped. Mayer and Thalberg didn't mind letting a shaky 'B' picture go out under the MGM trademark, but not a disastrous 'A'.

Encouraged by the high paybox notes sounded by Lawrence Tibbett's Rogue Song, Mayer and Thalberg signed another Metropolitan Opera star for **A Lady's Morals**/Jenny Lind. Grace Moore was a treat to the ear as the Swedish Nightingale and much easier on the eye than most divas, but the total effect was disappointing. Left to right in this I-can't-go-on scene: Jobyna Howland, Giovanni Martino, Frank Reicher, Paul Porcasi, Miss Moore. Reginald Denny was her hero, Wallace Beery played showman P. T. Barnum (The Mighty Barnum was one of his later vehicles), and Sidney Franklin directed the Hans Kraly–Claudine West–John Meehan–Arthur Richman script.

A brisk little musical about the songwriting fraternity, **Children of Pleasure**, featured (left to right) Kenneth Thompson, leads Wynne Gibson and Lawrence Gray, Helen Johnson, Benny Rubin and May Boley. Harry Beaumont directed from a play by Crane Wilbur, adapted by Wilbur and Richard Schayer.

Leo's opera-into-movie stars, Grace Moore and Lawrence Tibbett, were teamed in a lavish version of the 1928 stage operetta **New Moon**. They did full justice to the Sigmund Romberg–Oscar Hammerstein II score, making hits all over again of 'Lover Come Back to Me', 'Softly as in a Morning Sunrise' and (despite its having the same tune as Youmans' 'No No Nanette') 'One Kiss'. Director Jack Conway relied for acting polish on Adolphe Menjou and Roland Young (seen here with Miss Moore). Miss M.'s increasing weight displeased Thalberg; her contract lapsed and she later hit her real peak at Columbia.

The life of Marion Davies was like an MGM movie, so what could be more logical than to film scenes for her 1930 musical **The Florodora Girl**/The Gay Nineties at this, her own home? One of her homes, rather: the Santa Monica 'beach house' with 118 rooms and 55 bathrooms. Marion also had a mansion in Beverly Hills, and a slightly smaller one on the MGM lot called her 'dressing-room bungalow' where she was hostess to visiting royalty, Winston Churchill, Bernard Shaw and suchlike. Furthermore, she was mistress of multi-millionaire William Randolph Hearst's gigantic California estate, San Simeon. She was also mistress of Hearst and had been since she was a Broadway chorus girl in 1918. Amazingly, she remained totally unspoiled, a generous, friendly, sunny character liked even by her more talented Hollywood rivals. The Florodora Girl was a broad satire of the Nineties, brightly written by Gene Markey and directed by Harry Beaumont, with Lawrence Gray, Ilka Chase, Walter Catlett and Claude Allister.

Robert Montgomery was destined to take over from William Haines as MGM's light comedy star, and was in fact given Haines' 1927 Spring Fever for a 1930 talkie remake, **Love in the Rough**. Several songs were added. Charles Reisner directed the Sarah Mason–Joe Farnham–Robert Hopkins screenplay, with Dorothy Jordan (here) and J. C. Nugent, Benny Rubin, and Dorothy McNulty, who became better known as Penny Singleton.

GABLE STARS
1931

The Depression deepened, and the movie-makers could not all go on prospering when millions of their customers were thrown out of work and faced actual hunger. Warner Bros, which had absorbed First National and many of the biggest music publishers during its three-year boom, reported an $8m loss. RKO-Radio, despite a blockbuster (and Academy Award winner) in *Cimarron* with Richard Dix and Irene Dunne, dipped $5½m into the red. So did Fox.

MGM and Paramount stayed solvent with $12m and $6m profits respectively, while Universal, which had lost $2½m in 1930, climbed back into the black with twin horrors: Boris Karloff in *Frankenstein* and Bela Lugosi in *Dracula*, starting a never-ending vogue.

James Cagney shocked in *Public Enemy*, and Phillips Holmes demonstrated how to drown your pregnant girlfriend so graphically in Dreiser's *An American Tragedy* that the British censor banned it.

Constance Bennett, Kay Francis, Miriam Hopkins and Sylvia Sidney became big names; Herbert Marshall, Tallulah Bankhead and Laurence Olivier took the London-to-Hollywood route.

The irresistible force meets the immovable object: Clark Gable woos Greta Garbo in **Susan Lenox, her Fall and Rise***/The Rise of* ▷ *Helga. As this shot shows, Robert Z. Leonard directed with an eye for Freudian symbolism; the stars responded with emotion-charged performances. That MGM's two most potent personalities, paired for the first and last time, failed to set the screen on fire was blamed on a meandering script toiled upon by no fewer than 14 writers; Wanda Tuchock, Zelda Sears and Edith Fitzgerald got screen credit. In support were Jean Hersholt, Alan Hale, John Miljan, Hale Hamilton, Hilda Vaughn, Ian Keith, Cecil Cunningham, Theodore Von Eltz, Helene Millard, Russell Simpson. How did Gable reach his Garbo co-star prestige? See next pages.*

MGM didn't always have the ruthless Warner Bros touch for gangster pictures, but **The Secret Six** *was a strong toughie. Wallace Beery starred as the chief mobster, and halfway down the cast list were a couple of names about to become Names: Jean Harlow and Clark Gable. Miss Harlow was rising as fast as Gable in 1931 and MGM bought her contract from Howard Hughes the following year. They are seen here with John Mack Brown (centre) who was featured beside Lewis Stone, Marjorie Rambeau, Ralph Bellamy (film début) and John Miljan. Director George Hill and writer Frances Marion (Mr and Mrs) repeated their* Big House *and* Min and Bill *hits with this.*

The Easiest Way *to luxury was horizontally, decided working girl Constance Bennett, accepting the attentions of rich Adolphe Menjou but really loving reporter Robert Montgomery. After sinning through several reels she returned to virtue in a snowstorm on Christmas Eve. The old stage shocker by Eugene Walter, filmed by Clara Kimball Young in 1917 and now scripted by Edith Ellis, was a profitable 1931 release. Others in Jack Conway's production were Anita Page, Marjorie Rambeau, J. Farrell MacDonald, Clara Blandick, Hedda Hopper and – in a bit part as a milkman – Clark Gable.*

Among the biggest in the chain of Norma Shearer successes since Mary Dugan *was* **A Free Soul**. *One reason was the sensational newcomer, Clark Gable, as her gangster lover (here). Another was the John Meehan script from a strong story by Adela Rogers St Johns, who based the character of Shearer's father on her own father, a famous criminal lawyer. Lionel Barrymore gave up directing to play this part. It included a tremendous scene when, defending Shearer on trial for Gable's murder, he addressed the jury with such passion that he fell dead at the end of the speech. Barrymore did it in one take, stole the picture, won the 1931 Academy Award for best actor, and was given a lifetime MGM contract. Leslie Howard and James Gleason were featured under Clarence Brown's direction.*

Garbo as **Mata Hari** sounded like a box-office natural, and so it proved. It was far from her best film, but allowed her to look more glamorous than ever in an eye-popping series of costumes, including a kind of spangled bikini for a Garboesque cooch-dance. It was a more interesting role than her previous spying siren in The Mysterious Lady, and Ramon Novarro made an effective romantic foil in their only movie together. George Fitzmaurice directed and Lionel Barrymore, Lewis Stone, Karen Morley, C. Henry Gordon and Alec B. Francis gave strong support. Script: Leo Birinski, Benjamin Glazer, Doris Anderson, Gilbert Emery.

A 'new' face and a lovely one. Madge Evans, starting a long MGM career, as Ramon Novarro's leading lady in **Son of India**. Madge was that rarity, a famous child actress (from the age of five she played in 32 silent movies) who returned to greater success as an adult. Jacques Feyder directed this uninspired story of a rajah's son in love with an American girl. It was pepped up with a tiger hunt, raiding bandits and a berserk elephant. Conrad Nagel, C. Aubrey Smith, Marjorie Rambeau, John Miljan, Mitchell Lewis and Nigel de Brulier had supporting roles in the Claudine West–John Meehan–Ernst Vajda script.

Bayard Veiller contrived his most ingenious (and incredible) climax in **Guilty Hands**. It came after Lionel Barrymore, who had murdered his daughter's lover, made a Free Soul-style address to a jury (imaginary this time) proving that Kay Francis (here) had done it and had put the gun in the victim's hand to make it look like suicide. Then Barrymore himself was shot dead by the corpse as its stiffening fingers pulled the trigger. Helping to make it exciting, if not plausible, were Madge Evans, C. Aubrey Smith, William Bakewell, Alan Mowbray, Polly Moran and director W. S. Van Dyke.

Everybody suffered like mad in **The Great Meadow** and no wonder. Its 1775 pioneers trekked from Virginia to Kentucky, felled forests, trapped their own food, fought Indians, and awed the small audiences their travails attracted. Charles Brabin directed Eleanor Boardman, Lucille LaVerne, William Bakewell and John Mack Brown (left to right) and Gavin Gordon, Helen Jerome Eddy and Guinn Williams. Brabin and Edith Ellis wrote it from Elizabeth Madox Roberts' novel. Miss Boardman retired during 1931, completing seven MGM years.

Politics, fifth of the Marie Dressler–Polly Moran comedies, had a stronger undercurrent of drama than their two silent and two sound predecessors. A gangster killing involving her daughter made Marie run for mayor on a clean-up-the-town campaign, with Polly as her manager. She won. So did the Dressler magic in both performance and box-office results. Polly and stuttering Roscoe Ates added hearty humour, while more dramatic angles were handled by Karen Morley, William Bakewell, John Miljan and Joan Marsh. Charles Reisner directed the screenplay by Wells Root, Malcolm Stuart Boylan and Zelda Sears.

Broadway's Helen Hayes gave a marvellous performance in a dismal mother-love tearjerker, **The Sin of Madelon Claudet**/The Lullaby. Audiences loved it, and it won Helen the best actress Academy Award in her first talkie try. The movie was based on a play by Edgar Selwyn, who directed. As scripted by the star's husband, Charles MacArthur, it was practically a rewrite of Madame X and caused one trade paper to say, 'No one will be able to watch it without a strange feeling in the throat'– referring to sobs, not nausea. Neil Hamilton (here) and Lewis Stone, Marie Prevost, Cliff Edwards, Jean Hersholt, Karen Morley and– starting a busy MGM career–Robert Young supported her.

Previewed in California as Complete Surrender with Joan Crawford and John Mack Brown, this one finally emerged as **Laughing Sinners** with Joan Crawford and Clark Gable. Chilly audience reaction prompted Thalberg to order a partial remake of the Bess Meredyth–Martin Flavin screenplay, with Gable sex-menace injected into the Salvation Army captain role. It still wasn't much of a picture, but Thalberg detected dynamite in the Crawford–Gable combination and set the story department to work on scripts for it. Neil Hamilton, Marjorie Rambeau, Guy Kibbee, Roscoe Karns and George F. Marion were others in the Harry Beaumont production.

'British' was a dirty word when applied to film production in the early Thirties. With a few exceptions, British movies were made cheaply just to fill the quota required by a law designed to temper the dominance of Hollywood on British screens. One of the exceptions was **The Outsider**, produced by Eric Hakim and directed by Harry Lachman so expertly that MGM released it in the USA as well as Britain. Frank Lawton, Joan Barry and Mary Clare (here) supported Harold Huth in his original role in Dorothy Brandon's stage hit about an unlicensed healer fighting the medical establishment over a crippled girl.

Neil Hamilton introduces his fiancée, Joan Crawford, to his parents, Emma Dunn and Hobart Bosworth, in **This Modern Age**, a minor Crawford attraction. Little did they dream that their romance would soon be wrecked by the loathsome discovery that her mother was a Kept Woman. With Pauline Frederick back on the screen as the sinning mother, Joan for once met her match in high-style histrionics. Nicholas Grinde directed the Frank Butler–Sylvia Thalberg melo.

Never the Twain Shall Meet, *remade as a talkie, introduced Broadway's favourite English actor, Leslie Howard, to MGM stardom, and Spanish dancer Conchita Montenegro in her first leading role. Much more was to be heard of Leslie, practically nothing of Conchita. The old story of conflicting civilizations didn't have much impact this time, despite direction by W. S. Van Dyke and good support by Karen Morley, C. Aubrey Smith and Clyde Cook. Ruth Cummings and Edwin Justus Mayer dusted off the 1925 scenario.*

Adolphe Menjou was **The Great Lover** *– a combination of star and title which received a who-cares response from the public. Menjou was actually in brilliant form as the temperamental, philandering opera star in this Harry Beaumont movie, with Irene Dunne (here) in one of her earliest screen roles, a budding prima donna. Also involved in Gene Markey's screenplay were Neil Hamilton, Olga Baclanova, Cliff Edwards, Ernest Torrence, Hale Hamilton, Lillian Bond, Roscoe Ates and Herman Bing.*

Whatever **The Phantom of Paris** *may have lacked, it wasn't plot. John Gilbert played a magician falsely accused of murdering the father (C. Aubrey Smith) of his girl (Leila Hyams). He escaped; she unwittingly married the real murderer (Ian Keith) who died and was impersonated by the magician after his body was taken to a plastic surgeon (Alfred Hickman, centre). Now read on. . . . Audiences were further confused by the fact that Gilbert and Keith were the most look-alike actors in Hollywood. John S. Robertson directed the Bess Meredyth–John Meehan–Edwin Justus Mayer concoction, with Lewis Stone, Jean Hersholt and Natalie Moorhead also featured.*

Remnants of Great Day, *which Harry Pollard started in 1930, turned up in his* **The Prodigal** *in 1931. One was 'Without a Song', sung by Lawrence Tibbett in the role of a Southern gent returned to his home with two disreputable pals after trying life as a hobo. Bess Meredyth and Wells Root wrote it. Esther Ralston, blonde charmer of the silents, played opposite Tibbett, with Roland Young and Cliff Edwards (here), Hedda Hopper and Purnell Pratt. It was not a success.*

Flying High/Happy Landing *was a lively musical topling Charlotte Greenwood and Pat O'Brien (here) who were establishing movie renown to match their stage fame, and Bert Lahr, the zany comedian making his screen bow in his original Broadway role: an amateur aviator who made a world-record flight because he didn't know how to land. It also had Charles Winninger, Kathryn Crawford, Guy Kibbee, Hedda Hopper. Direction was by Charles Reisner, script by Robert Hopkins, A. P. Younger and Reisner, and numbers were staged by Busby Berkeley. But they just weren't buying musicals in 1931.*

Emma *was Marie Dressler all the way, and a mighty profit-maker. She ranged from high drama to low comedy in another story by Frances Marion, writer of her Oscar-winning* Min and Bill. *Also cast was Myrna Loy in her first MGM contract assignment; years of stardom with the company lay ahead. As the housekeeper who married her employer but was unaccepted by his children, Marie (centre) was supported by Richard Cromwell, Jean Hersholt and (left to right) Barbara Kent, Purnell Pratt, Miss Loy, George Meeker, Wilfred Noy and Kathryn Crawford. Clarence Brown directed the Zelda Sears–Leonard Praskins script.*

Sheer hokum, really, but **The Champ** *was made with such superb professionalism in all departments that it achieved record business in depression-stricken 1931 – and Academy Awards for Frances Marion and Wallace Beery. It was MGM's biggest smash hit of the year. This third ideal role Miss Marion wrote for Beery was that of a brokendown boxer who made a comeback for the sake of his idolizing son, Jackie Cooper. The nine-year-old graduate from Our Gang got even greater praise than Beery from the critics, and audible sobbing from audiences. King Vidor extracted genuine pathos from both stars and good work, too, from Irene Rich, Roscoe Ates, Hale Hamilton and Edward Brophy.*

Robert Montgomery was promoted to full stardom in **Shipmates**, *a formula US Navy story which he carried breezily as the young sailor, bullied by petty officer Ernest Torrence (here), who fell for admiral's daughter Dorothy Jordan. Harry Pollard directed, and there was special praise for Clyde DeVinna's sea photography. Also cast: Gavin Gordon, Hobart Bosworth, Cliff Edwards, Joan Marsh, Eddie Nugent, Hedda Hopper. Script: Delmer Daves, Lou Edelman, Raymond Schrock, Frank Wead. . . .*

And he sparkled as **The Man in Possession**. *So did the whole profitable enterprise, with additional dialogue by P. G. Wodehouse increasing the laughs in H. M. Harwood's play about a bailiff's man posing as a butler. Sam Wood made the most of his expert cast: Montgomery, Reginald Owen and Irene Purcell (here) and Charlotte Greenwood, C. Aubrey Smith, Beryl Mercer, Alan Mowbray and Maude Eburne.*

A full-length Stan Laurel and Oliver Hardy feature was inevitable – Hal Roach's long series of shorts starring Laurel and Hardy had become so popular that they were sometimes billed bigger than the features they supported. **Pardon Us**/Jailbirds *was a prison riot in more ways than one, and a moneymaker. Director James Parrott made their idiocies all the funnier by staging them in* Big House *sets.*

The New Adventures of Get-Rich-Quick Wallingford *marked the MGM début of Jimmy 'Schnozzle' Durante, Hollywood's funniest Broadway import since the Marx Brothers. It was the first of G. R. Chester's stories to be made as a talkie—they had made movie plots since 1915—and it also held the industry's longest-title trophy for decades. Sam Wood directed this William Haines hit. Left to right: Leila Hyams, Haines, Clara Blandick and Walter Walker; also cast were Ernest Torrence, Guy Kibbee, Hale Hamilton and Henry Armetta. Script: Charles MacArthur.*

Even 'B' pictures were getting sexier in 1931. Adolphe Menjou's seductive approach to Leila Hyams was so sophisticated that he used a rectangular cocktail set in **Men Call It Love**, *a Doris Anderson script directed by Edgar Selwyn, with Mary Duncan, Norman Foster, Hedda Hopper. Lillian Bond tried a more direct technique on Reginald Denny with décolletage down to here in* **Stepping Out**, *written by Elmer Harris and Robert Hopkins, and directed by Charles Reisner, with Charlotte Greenwood, Leila Hyams, Cliff Edwards.*

William Haines was becoming more interested in interior decoration than acting, and did art direction on **Just a Gigolo**/The Dancing Partner. *The movie gave Haines a silly Hans Kraly–Claudine West–Richard Schayer script from an old Belasco play about a bachelor whose rich uncle (C. Aubrey Smith, with Haines, here) wanted him to marry, so he tried to prove all available women immoral by posing as a gigolo. Also cast in the Jack Conway production: Irene Purcell, Lillian Bond, Charlotte Granville, Albert Conti and Ray Milland.*

Preview audiences hailed John Gilbert's good performance in **Gentleman's Fate** *as a comeback, but the box-office didn't concur. Mervyn LeRoy, who was to be important at MGM years later, made his modest début there with this movie. He had just delivered a sensational gangster hit, Little Caesar, for Warners and was borrowed to direct Gilbert and Louis Wolheim as battling bootlegging brothers in Ursula Parrott's underworld yarn, scripted by Leonard Praskins. Also cast: Anita Page, Leila Hyams, John Miljan, Marie Prevost.*

John Gilbert's fabulous $250,000-a-picture contract had been negotiated by Nicholas Schenck. Some said that Mayer and Thalberg weren't trying too hard to make their New York president's talent-signing judgment look as good as theirs. Or maybe there was just a jinx on the former superstar, whose movies became progressively feebler. **West of Broadway** *with Lois Moran (here) and Madge Evans, Ralph Bellamy, El Brendel, Frank Conroy, Hedda Hopper and Gwen Lee, was directed by Harry Beaumont from a Gene Markey script about a jaded millionaire who married on the rebound, lost the girl, got her back.*

Buster Keaton rated **The Sidewalks of New York** *as one of his worst films. Never happy to be just the star, rather than the whole creative works as on his pre-MGM comedies—he was becoming increasingly frustrated and replacing inspiration with alcohol. It took four writers to concoct this story of a philanthropist trying to reform Bowery kids and two directors, Jules White and Zion Myers, whose previous achievements were short comedies enacted by trained dogs. Anita Page and Cliff Edwards headed Keaton's support.*

One of Buster Keaton's better MGM comedies, **Parlor, Bedroom and Bath**/Romeo in Pyjamas *was a 1931 remake of a 1920 Metro release starring Eugene Pallette. Edward Sedgwick directed Charlotte Greenwood, Cliff Edwards, Joan Peers, Natalie Moorhead, Edward Brophy and (here) the group around the passed-out hero: Reginald Denny, Sidney Bracey, Dorothy Christy and Sally Eilers. Script: Richard Schayer, Robert Hopkins.*

Musicals became a drug on the market in 1931. Lawrence Tibbett was axed after **Cuban Love Song** *and returned to opera and concert stardom. His last for MGM flopped, but was actually one of his most enjoyable, a free and easy romance of a US Marine and a Havana peanut-vendor (female, very—Lupe Velez in fact), directed by W. S. Van Dyke. Also cast: Karen Morley, Jimmy Durante, Ernest Torrence, Hale Hamilton and Louise Fazenda. The cast was almost outnumbered by its writers; six got screen credit.*

It's a wise star who knows her own forte. Marion Davies' was comedy, and she had a good one in **It's a Wise Child** *with (here) Lester Vail, Ben Alexander and Sidney Blackmer; also in the cast were James Gleason, Polly Moran, Marie Prevost, Emily Fitzroy, Clara Blandick and Johnny Arthur. Laurence Johnson scripted his own play, slightly de-sexed, and Robert Z. Leonard directed.*

Possessed *established Joan Crawford and Clark* ▷ *Gable as a potent co-starring team. A heady brew of politics and sex, its frank (for 1931) treatment of the latter ran it into censor trouble here and there—and high paybox returns everywhere. Wallace Ford, Skeets Gallagher, John Miljan and Frank Conroy were in the Clarence Brown production, adapted by Lenore Coffee from Edgar Selwyn's play 'The Mirage'.*

Clark Gable topped a cast for the first time in **Sporting Blood**, with Madge Evans as heroine and Lew Cody (right) back at his old studio as villain. Ernest Torrence, Marie Prevost and J. Farrell MacDonald were in it too. A good racehorse story never fails, they say, and this was a winner all the way. Charles Brabin directed with a verve that he and photographer Harold Rosson brought to maximum pitch in an audience-rousing Kentucky Derby climax. Script: Willard Mack, Wanda Tuchock. This was a Gable milestone; it proved he could carry a picture to profitability without a top female star.

Trouser-presser William Haines hoped that customer William Austin wouldn't recognize his dress suit when they were introduced by hostess Hedda Hopper. Bill borrowed it to crash the swank party that started him on the road to business success—**A Tailor-made Man**. This remake of a 1922 Charles Ray silent was written by Edgar Allan Woolf and directed by Sam Wood, with Dorothy Jordan, Joseph Cawthorn, Marjorie Rambeau, Ian Keith, Hale Hamilton, Martha Sleeper, Joan Marsh and (here) Henry Armetta.

Cecil B. DeMille filmed his favourite story, **The Squaw Man**/The White Man, for the third time. In 1913 it was the first feature-length movie made in Hollywood, and starred Dustin Farnum. Five years later DeMille directed it again with Elliott Dexter in the title role. The talking version (script by Lenore Coffee, Lucien Hubbard; dialogue by Elsie Janis, the former musical comedy star) had Warner Baxter and Lupe Velez (here) and Eleanor Boardman, Roland Young, Charles Bickford, Mitchell Lewis, Raymond Hatton, C. Aubrey Smith, Julia Faye, J. Farrell MacDonald and, in a bit part, Winifred Kingston, its leading lady in 1913. The melodrama of English gentlefolk and wild Westerners was now creaking at the joints. It was DeMille's 57th picture, and his third and last in a disappointing MGM association.

The most illustrious pair of stars in the American theatre, Alfred Lunt and Lynn Fontanne, made their one and only talkie together when Thalberg coaxed them to Hollywood to film their stage hit, **The Guardsman**. They adapted themselves smoothly to the new medium; so did the Ferenc Molnar play about a jealous actor who, heavily disguised as a guardsman, seduced his own wife. Next morning she said she'd known him all along—but had she? It was light, gay and truly sophisticated, but neither the Lunts nor the public seemed eager for an encore. Sidney Franklin directed the Ernst Vajda–Claudine West script, with Roland Young, ZaSu Pitts, Maude Eburne and Herman Bing.

Continuing his efforts to raise the movies' intelligence level, Thalberg assigned Sidney Franklin to follow The Guardsman with another witty gem from the theatre, Noël Coward's **Private Lives**. A Broadway performance of the play was filmed for the guidance of stars Norma Shearer and Robert ▽ Montgomery, director, and writers Hans Kraly, Claudine West and Richard Schayer. Miss Shearer and Montgomery coped zestfully with Coward's rapid-fire repartee and were entirely acceptable screen replacements for its renowned stage originals. Gertrude Lawrence and Coward himself. Reginald Denny and Una Merkel had the thankless roles of their dull spouses, and Jean Hersholt an interpolated bit.

Feeling the need to try a Shearer-style modern drama, Marion Davies starred in the Fannie Hurst story, **Five and Ten**/Daughter of Luxury. It was about a girl with too much money, derived from Woolworth-type chain stores. Guess who! Miss Davies got all the trimmings: director Robert Z. Leonard, lush production effects and a handpicked cast—Leslie Howard, Irene Rich, Kent Douglass, Richard Bennett (stage-star father of Constance and Joan), Ruth Selwyn, Halliwell Hobbes, Mary Duncan and Henry Armetta. But the public liked her better as a comedienne. Script: A. P. Younger, Edith Fitzgerald.

Ramon Novarro gave a polished performance as the prewar Austrian guardsman of Arthur Schnitzler's play **Daybreak**, with a delicately ▷ appealing leading lady in Helen Chandler (here) and adroit direction by Jacques Feyder. The strong cast also had Karen Morley, Kent Douglass, C. Aubrey Smith, Jean Hersholt, William Bakewell, Glenn Tryon and Clyde Cook. It was further enhanced by the newly developed supersensitive Eastman film which improved photographic values, especially in low-key lighting like this. All in vain: the crowds didn't want this movie. Script: Ruth Cummings, Zelda Sears, Cyril Hume.

A come-hither title and an excellent cast gave strong box-office impetus to **Strangers May Kiss**, with which George Fitzmaurice, French-born director of many hits for Samuel Goldwyn, made his MGM début. Practically a reprise of The Divorcee for Norma Shearer, it was based by John Meehan on another Ursula Parrott story and had the star, elegantly gowned, toying with lovers across America,

France and Spain. Left to right: Irene Rich, Robert Montgomery, Miss Shearer and Neil Hamilton; also cast were Marjorie Rambeau, Hale Hamilton, Jed Prouty, Albert Conti and Conchita Montenegro.

Clark Gable had started 1931 as a bit player and he ended it as a star in **Hell Divers**, his eighth MGM assignment that year. Scenes like this, with Marie Prevost wrapping herself around him, threw millions of female movie-goers into tizzies of rapture. George Hill's production was a thriller in other respects, with magnificent aviation sequences, Wallace Beery excellent as a US Navy veteran, and Dorothy Jordan, Conrad Nagel, Cliff Edwards, Marjorie Rambeau and John Miljan. Script: Malcolm Stuart Boylan, Harvey Gates.

1932

MGM-Loew's $8m profit seemed downright indecent in 1932 when movie profits generally were plummeting: Paramount made a $16m loss for the year, followed by bankruptcy; Fox topped that with a $17m loss, and Warner Bros. went $14m deeper into the red. Credit MGM's tremendous name power: Marie Dressler, Wallace Beery, Norma Shearer, Joan Crawford, Garbo, Clark Gable, Jean Harlow & Co. were at their zenith, and the multi-starred *Grand Hotel* was the film of the year.

With breadlines longer than the box-office queues, laughter was worth its decibels in gold; it was supplied by such clowns as Eddie Cantor, Joe E. Brown, Wheeler and Woolsey, Laurel and Hardy, Will Rogers and Jack Oakie. At Paramount, where Dietrich slunk through von Sternberg mists, Mae West arrived to prove that a sex queen could be funny on purpose. They needed laughs there; apart from their financial troubles Warner Bros had snatched three of their top stars: Ruth Chatterton, William Powell and Kay Francis. The latter two promptly scored with *One Way Passage*.

In Europe, too, light fare dominated: Gracie Fields, Jack Hulbert, Cicely Courtneidge, Jack Buchanan and Anna Neagle starred in Britain; France had Clair's *A Nous la Liberté*, and Germany enjoyed Charell's *Congress Dances* (but made more permanent impressions with Pabst's *Kameradschaft* and Sagan's *Maedchen in Uniform*). And the English censor spread mirth by insisting that *Merrily We Go to Hell* delete the title's last word; filling in the '——' drew some alarming guesses.

Lionel Barrymore was Mayer's favourite actor, and Thalberg shared his view that the great name of Barrymore lent prestige to any movie. So they grabbed brother John the minute his Warner contract ended, signed him to a $150,000-per-film pact and cast him as the gentleman thief **Arsene Lupin** *with Lionel as his detective nemesis. It was the brothers' first picture together, although each had interspersed stage roles with movies since the pre-Hollywood silent era. They struck histrionic sparks off each other and the picture was a hit. Jack Conway directed Karen Morley, John and Lionel (here) and Tully Marshall and John Miljan. Script: Carey Wilson, Leonore Coffee, Bayard Veiller.*

Jean Harlow cost MGM $60,000 when Howard Hughes sold her contract and she started earning it back in **The Beast of the City** *Walter Huston, also beginning an MGM contract, starred as the police chief. W. R. Burnett's racketeering melodrama, scripted by John Lee Mahin, began with a foreword by President Hoover and ended with police mowing down the vice gang. Left to right: Tully Marshall, J. Carrol Naish, Jean Hersholt, Harlow. Wallace Ford, Dorothy Peterson and John Miljan were also in the cast under Charles Brabin's direction.*

Clark Gable took his turn as Marion Davies' leading man in **Polly of the Circus**, *playing a clergyman who restored a fallen trapeze artiste to physical and moral health. Not even this mad caprice of casting could check Gable's career, but the resulting flop did nothing for Marion's. Alfred Santell did his sole MGM directing job on this movie, and the Carey Wilson–Laurence Johnson script updated Margaret Mayo's ancient play; in 1917 it had been filmed as the Goldwyn Company's first production, starring Mae Marsh. Also in the new version: C. Aubrey Smith, Raymond Hatton, Ruth Selwyn, Maude Eburne, Guinn Williams, Ray Milland.*

Prosperity *was the farewell appearance in tandem of Polly Moran and Marie Dressler. It had its hilarious moments, but the basic plot of a small town stricken by the Depression hit a bit too close to home for 1932 escapist entertainment. The huge Dressler following made it profitable, however, and Sam Wood's direction gave full scope to her extraordinary acting range. Anita Page, Norman Foster, Henry Armetta, John Miljan and Jacquie Lyn were also in the Eve Greene–Zelda Sears screenplay, from an original by Sylvia Thalberg and Frank Butler. Much of it was remade after a dismal preview.*

Tallulah Bankhead was lent to MGM by Paramount for **Faithless**. *Her flamboyant personality and uninhibited performances on and off the stage had kept Londoners on a vicarious spree for eight years until Paramount brought her back to the States in 1931. They starred her in five films, and she returned to the stage after this MGM job. The camera unaccountably dimmed her lustre and her crowd magnetism. Robert Montgomery partnered Tallulah in this drama of the rich impoverished by the Wall Street crash, scripted by Carey Wilson from a Mildred Cram novel. Harry Beaumont directed, with Hugh Herbert and Louise Closser Hale featured.*

Thalberg shook the industry by throwing five of the studio's biggest stars into a single picture: **Grand Hotel**. *It was a gamble which paid off ▷ richly at the box-office, and won the best film Academy Award. Vicki Baum's successful novel and play, scripted by William Drake, gave equal prominence to Garbo and John Barrymore and to Joan Crawford, Wallace Beery and Lionel Barrymore (here). That's the order in which they were billed, after much tact had been applied to stellar egos, but the chief plaudits went to Joan as Beery's hotel stenographer and Lionel as his clerk on a dying spree. Garbo was miscast as a mercurial ballerina and for once her acting seemed forced. Smoothly directed by Edmund Goulding, they were supported by Lewis Stone, Jean Hersholt, Ferdinand Gottschalk, Rafaela Ottiano, Purnell Pratt, Frank Conroy, Tully Marshall.*

1932

Marion Davies and Billie Dove felt at home in **Blondie of the Follies**. *Both Ziegfeld girls in their pre-movie days, they played friendly rivals in this backstage yarn. Robert Montgomery, Jimmy Durante, ZaSu Pitts, James Gleason, Sidney Toler, Douglass Dumbrille and Clyde Cook were also cast. With all that talent in a Frances Marion scenario with Anita Loos dialogue, directed by Edmund Goulding, it should have been as good all through as it was in one scene: a wicked take-off by Davies and Durante of Garbo and John Barrymore in Goulding's* Grand Hotel.

Frederick Lonsdale's The Last of Mrs Cheyney *gave Mrs T. one of her biggest hits, so Thalberg invited the British playwright to Culver City to write an original screenplay. The result was* **Lovers Courageous** *with Robert Montgomery and Madge Evans in the title roles—and the script was a good deal better than the title. Robert Z. Leonard expertly directed the male Cinderella story; the stars' appealing performances were aided by those of Roland Young, Fred Kerr, Reginald Owen, Halliwell Hobbes, Beryl Mercer and Alan Mowbray.*

Robert Montgomery again. In **But the Flesh is Weak**, *from Ivor Novello's stage hit 'The Truth Game', he played the fortune-hunter on the prowl in London society; Heather Thatcher was imported from the West End to play his rich quarry. The sparkling cast also had C. Aubrey Smith, Edward Everett Horton, Nora Gregor, Nils Asther, Fred Kerr and Forrester Harvey. Jack Conway, not noted for directing light comedy, showed that he could. Novello adapted his play for the screen . . . Montgomery was cast with Joan Crawford in* **Letty Lynton**. *Nothing too startling in this one to keep the matinée ladies away. Just a well-made movie with loads of glamour, two lovers for Miss Crawford, and a dash of danger when one (Asther) was accidentally poisoned and she was accused of murder before the other (Montgomery, here) proved her innocent. May*

Robson (left) celebrated her 50th year as an actress by playing Joan's mother and beginning a long MGM contract. Clarence Brown's expert direction made much of the Marie Belloc Lowndes story, scripted by John Meehan and Wanda Tuchock. Also cast: Lewis Stone, Emma Dunn, Louise Closser Hale, Walter Walker. Hunt Stromberg produced.

Jackie Cooper was the 1932 champ of child actors. In **When a Feller Needs a Friend** *he kept audiences' tear-ducts as open as his own. ('Feller' was changed to 'Fellow' in Britain just in case anybody thought it was about tree-lopping.) As a crippled boy who overcame all handicaps he was aided by Ralph Graves (here) as his father and Charles 'Chic' Sale as his ancient pal; Dorothy Peterson played Mom. Harry Pollard directed from a Sylvia Thalberg –Frank Butler script; original by William Johnston.*

Lionel Barrymore scored strongly in **Washington Masquerade**/Mad Masquerade. *He was well-rehearsed, having starred on Broadway ten years before in Henri Bernstein's 'The Claw', on which the John Meehan–Samuel Blythe screenplay was based. Karen Morley shone, too, as the sexy Washington lobbyist who married and corrupted the highminded Senator Barrymore. They and Nils Asther, C. Henry Gordon, Diane Sinclair, William Collier Sr, Rafaela Ottiano, Berton Churchill and Henry Kolker were effectively directed by Charles Brabin. But politics was never box-office.*

Divorce in the Family *was a nice little movie that didn't do much for Jackie Cooper's film career. The screenplay by Delmer Daves, who was playing college boys for MGM a few years earlier, had a happy ending for stepfather Conrad Nagel, mother Lois Wilson and son Jackie who had been won over from his father (Lewis Stone). Directed by Charles Reisner.*

Warren William, here with Verree Teasdale, was borrowed from Warners for **Skyscraper Souls** *and gave a forceful performance in the Edgar Selwyn production. A minor-league* Grand Hotel, *with interwoven stories occurring in an office building, the C. G. Sullivan–Elmer Harris screenplay from Faith Baldwin's book gave other strong roles to Maureen O'Sullivan, Gregory Ratoff, Anita Page, Norman Foster, George Barbier, Jean Hersholt, Wallace Ford and Hedda Hopper. Both Ratoff and Foster became directors.*

Keep your cool no matter how hot the situation was Myrna Loy's motto, and the secret of the appeal that was to make her a star. Meanwhile she and Neil Hamilton were among Walter Huston's supporting cast in **The Wet Parade**. *Upton Sinclair's book about the corruption created by Prohibition was produced by Hunt Stromberg, scripted by John Lee Mahin and directed by Victor Fleming, who had great MGM things ahead. Also cast: Lewis Stone, Dorothy Jordan, Jimmy Durante, Wallace Ford, John Miljan, Emma Dunn, Robert Young, Joan Marsh and Clara Blandick.*

Two successful thrillers were **Night Court**/ Justice for Sale *and* **Whistling in the Dark**. *In a scene from the former crooked judge Walter Huston (left) gets his comeuppance from New York taxi-driver Phillips Holmes, whose wife he'd framed on a prostitution charge. It was strong box-office: crime reporter Mark Hellinger and melodrama craftsman Bayard Veiller (aided by Charles Beehan and Lenore Coffee) made their specialities count in the screenplay,*

a fast-moving thriller directed by W. S. Van Dyke. Also cast: Anita Page, Lewis Stone, John Miljan, Jean Hersholt, Tully Marshall, Mary Carlisle . . . Ernest Truex, Una Merkel, Edward Arnold were hero, heroine and heavy of Whistling in the Dark, *an ingenious comedy thriller from a Broadway play by Edward Childs Carpenter and Laurence Cross about a detective story writer forced to devise a perfect crime to eliminate a gangster's enemy. It was a neat profit-winner. Elliott Nugent, erstwhile young leading man at the studio, wrote the screenplay and directed it. Cast included Nat Pendleton, destined, like Miss Merkel and Arnold, for many MGM assignments; Joseph Cawthorn, Johnny Hines and Miljan.*

Mad fools to hope they might escape unscathed! The fragile loveliness of Karen Morley had stimulated Dr Fu Manchu's appetite for evil, and Charles Starrett's virile beauty was like catnip to Fu's daughter in The Mask of Fu Manchu. *Charles Brabin directed the lavish hokum, with Boris Karloff as Sax Rohmer's insidious villain and Myrna Loy making a spectacular exit from Oriental roles as his daughter. Also cast: Lewis Stone, Jean Hersholt and David Torrence. Script was by Irene Kuhn, John Willard and Edgar Allan Woolf.*

In Kongo *Walter Huston (right) reclaimed his old stage role of the revenge-crazed, semi-paralyzed voodoo man, played in the silent* West of Zanzibar *by Lon Chaney. William Cowen directed from Leon Gordon's script, with Lupe Velez, Conrad Nagel, Virginia Bruce, C. Henry Gordon (here), Mitchell Lewis and Forrester Harvey. Ushers got little exercise.*

'Give me something that will out-horror Frankenstein' demanded Thalberg while Universal's monster was setting 1932 records. He was nonplussed when he saw what director Ted Browning had wrought in **Freaks**. Never released by the company in Britain, it was so horrible as to be downright sickening to some viewers, with cruelty, sex, dwarfs, Siamese

twins and other sideshow characters mixed in a steaming broth. But it has since become quite palatable to horror buffs, who call it Browning's best. Russia's Olga Baclanova and England's Henry Victor (here) were in it with Wallace Ford, Leila Hyams, Roscoe Ates and Edward Brophy. Script: Willis Goldbeck, Leon Gordon, Al Boasberg, Edgar Allan Woolf.

William Haines had a more serious role than usual in **Are You Listening?**, *the Dwight Taylor script from J. P. McEvoy's story about news broadcasting, with a murder hunt by radio as the climax. He also had three leading ladies: Madge Evans (here) and Anita Page and Karen Morley. Neil Hamilton, Wallace Ford, Jean Hersholt, John Miljan and Joan Marsh were also in the cast, and Harry Beaumont directed.*

She wasn't just a pretty name. Although her starring years were few and included no great movie, Helen Twelvetrees had a gift for projecting emotional force with minimum visible effort. **Unashamed** *was the first of her two MGM pictures, a Bayard Veiller variation of his* Mary Dugan *courtroom drama, directed by Harry Beaumont, about a society girl whose testimony acquitted her brother on trial for murdering her lover. Lewis Stone and Robert Warwick (here) and Robert Young, Jean Hersholt, John Miljan, Gertrude Michael, Monroe Owsley and Louise Beavers supported her.*

Drastically rewritten by Laurence Johnson and Ralph Spence to fit Buster Keaton, with Jimmy Durante as his second both in the cast and in this scene with Gilbert Roland (right), Her Cardboard Lover *was the unlikely basis for* **The Passionate Plumber**. *It turned out fairly well, with Edward Sedgwick back as Keaton's director, Polly Moran, Irene Purcell, Mona Maris, Henry Armetta and Maude Eburne in support.*

Strange Interlude (Strange Interval in Britain, whose censor removed the lewd, said wags) went a bit too far in the MGM bid for culture. On the stage Eugene O'Neill's characters spoke their thoughts, as distinct from dialogue, in long asides. It seemed that this device would become more realistic on the screen by having their thoughts on the soundtrack only. But it didn't work, whether due to faulty direction (Robert Z. Leonard), a too compressed script (C. G. Sullivan, Bess Meredyth) from the five-hour play, or inadequate acting (Clark Gable, Norma Shearer, Alexander Kirkland, Mary Alden, here; and Ralph Morgan, Robert Young, May Robson, Maureen O'Sullivan, Henry B. Walthall). Crowds were drawn by the stars and the play's fame, but were either depressed by its solemn introspections or found relief in laughing at it.

William Haines grinned his way through a snappy motorboat programmer, **Fast Life**, *waved a cheerful so-long to MGM and (except for two 1934 quickies) ended his screen career. Nearly 40 years later he was in London designing the American Ambassador's residence, having become an internationally renowned interior decorator in the intervening decades. Madge Evans played his girl in the Byron Morgan–Ralph Spence screenplay, directed by Harry Pollard, with Conrad Nagel, Arthur Byron, Cliff Edwards and Kenneth Thompson.*

Ramon Novarro, inexplicably cast as a college football hero, had one of his least successful films in **Huddle** *(tactlessly retitled The Impossible Lover in Britain). Robert Johnson, Arthur Hyman, Walton Smith and C. Gardner Sullivan combined to provide director Sam Wood with a lacklustre script, employing (left to right) Madge Evans, Kane Richmond, Martha Sleeper and Novarro; also cast were Ralph Graves, Una Merkel, John Arledge, Frank Albertson and Henry Armetta.*

The studio countered John Gilbert's complaints about his stories by letting him film one he wrote himself. **Downstairs** was unusual, a drama of life in the servants' quarters, but not dynamic enough to recharge the star's battery. He played an unscrupulous chauffeur in conflict with a virtuous butler (Paul Lukas, centre). He got the girl in reality: Virginia Bruce followed up her first MGM lead by becoming Mrs Gilbert. Hedda Hopper, Reginald Owen, Olga Baclanova and Lucien Littlefield were others in director Monta Bell's cast. Screenplay: Melville Baker, Lenore Coffee.

The old star was yielding ground to the new in **Speak Easily**, with the Ralph Spence–Laurence Johnson script, from Clarence B. Kelland's story, giving supporting comedian Jimmy Durante as many laughs as Buster Keaton. As a professor who inherited money and backed a terrible touring show, Keaton was again directed by Edward Sedgwick. Thelma Todd and Sidney Toler were featured with (left to right) Keaton, Ruth Selwyn, Hedda Hopper, Henry Armetta, Edward Brophy, Durante.

MGM had some problem productions, their release unfortunately coinciding with a general cinema slump at the end of 1932. One embarrassing flop was **The Son-Daughter**, a dramatic chop-suey by Claudine West, Leon Gordon and John Goodrich from a David Belasco–George Scarborough play about tangled loves and warring tongs in San Francisco's Chinatown. In spite of the eminence of its director (Clarence Brown) and cast, it was about as Oriental as a ham sandwich. Ramon Novarro, Lewis Stone, Helen Hayes (here) and Ralph Morgan, Warner Oland, Louise Closser Hale and H. B. Warner slanted their mascara, tucked their hands up their sleeves and let it go at that.

A box-office sensation of 1932 was **Tarzan the Ape Man**, which spawned a highly profitable series for MGM. It was the best of the dozens of movies about Edgar Rice Burroughs' hero made from 1918 to the present. Johnny Weissmuller, US swimming champion, displayed a magnificent torso and a fetching way with lines like 'Me Tarzan, you Jane'. (Ivor Novello came from London to write the dialogue for Cyril Hume's scenario.) Maureen O'Sullivan's 'Jane' had so much charm that Mayer gave her a long-term contract. W. S. Van Dyke artfully blended a studio jungle with authentic leftovers from his Trader Horn trek, and peopled it with good actors like Neil Hamilton, C. Aubrey Smith, Doris Lloyd and Forrester Harvey.

Has there ever been an army rookies comedy that flopped? Certainly not **Pack Up Your Troubles**: Laurel and Hardy's second full-length feature beat their first in laughs and profits. Ray McCarey, who directed their Hal Roach shorts, and George Marshall guided them through a fast-moving succession of gags plus a heart-tug sequence with Jacquie Lyn, a four-year-old from London whom Roach signed for 'Our Gang' shorts. Also cast: Donald Dillaway (right) and Mary Carr, Jimmy Finlayson, Muriel Evans, Grady Sutton, Charles Middleton, Billy Gilbert.

Celebrated playwrights kept coming from London as Thalberg spent MGM's money with nothing-but-the-best abandon. Following Lonsdale and Novello, John van Druten brought his 'After All' to the screen as **New Morals for Old**, collaborating with Zelda Sears and Wanda Tuchock. Robert Young, here with (left to right) Laura Hope Crews, Elizabeth Patterson and Margaret Perry, had his first top role in this moderate success about modern youth versus conservative age. Charles Brabin directed. Also cast: Lewis Stone, Myrna Loy, Donald Cook, Jean Hersholt, Ruth Selwyn, Kathryn Crawford and Louise Closser Hale.

MGM's Barrymore idolatry reached its summit with **Rasputin and the Empress**/Rasputin the ▽ Mad Monk, for which Thalberg enticed Ethel Barrymore into the movies for the first time in 14 years – and for the only time with her two brothers. Despite publicity fiction about their temperamental clashes, they worked together like good professionals, even when filming caught up with Charles MacArthur's scene rewrites. Director Richard Boleslawski let Lionel do some scenery-chewing as Rasputin, and the Bernard Hyman production had a

mixed reception. Here: Ralph Morgan (as the Czar), Tad Alexander, Ethel, John. Diana Wynyard, Edward Arnold, C. Henry Gordon and Gustav von Seyffertitz were also in the cast. There have been at least six other movies on the subject; this one had the misfortune to be the cause of a celebrated libel suit brought against MGM in London by Prince and Princess Yousoupoff. They won record damages after convincing the court that, while the Prince was Rasputin's killer, as portrayed by John Barrymore, the Princess's rape was invented.

Red-Headed Woman stirred up a storm or two. Sensational at the box-office, it gave MGM another major star in Jean Harlow, whose highly publicized platinum blonde hair was tinted for the part. It was sensational on the screen too; to such an extent that Mayer, fervent champion of morality in his public

pronouncements, was chagrined to get a rap from the industry's self-censorship body, the Hays Office, because its 'sinner must pay' code was violated. The London censor wouldn't pass it, and it has never been shown in Britain. Anita Loos' witty script from a Katharine Brush novel detailed the climb of a poor girl up a ladder of beds to wealth and happiness. Chester Morris and Leila Hyams (centre) and Lewis Stone, Una Merkel, Henry Stephenson, May Robson and—briefly—Charles Boyer were featured, with Jack Conway directing.

1932

John Ford moved over from Fox to direct **Flesh**, probably the only feature film ever made about wrestling. It is not among his most memorable movies, but he brought a performance from Wallace Beery which had critics comparing him with Emil Jannings. Karen Morley and Ricardo Cortez (here) were vivid in a cast including John Miljan, Jean Hersholt, Herman Bing and Edward Brophy; such talented writers as Edmund Goulding and Moss Hart were involved. But Beery—Flesh—wrestlers formed an unattractive image, keeping the crowds away.

For the first time since talkies came in, Norma Shearer eschewed sin and sophistication to make a movie drenched in sweetness. **Smilin' Through** had been one of Norma Talmadge's biggest hits ten years before—directed by the same Sidney Franklin—and it became a 1932 record-breaker. A battery of writers (Ernst Vajda, Claudine West, Donald Ogden Stewart, James Fagan) gave conviction to Smilin' Through's weepy romances, one told in flashback with Leslie Howard, the other (here) with Ralph Forbes and Fredric March. The latter was co-starring in his first MGM appearance. Others featured were O. P. Heggie, Beryl Mercer, Forrester Harvey. After making this movie Miss Shearer was off the screen for a year, taking Thalberg on a European trip for his health. He was exhausted after eight years of supervising MGM's output, increasing friction with Mayer about production, and recent rows with Nicholas Schenck about money.

'They were born to co-star!' screamed the ads for **Red Dust**, which brought MGM's scorching new sex symbols together – repeat together. Clark Gable and Jean Harlow generated enough heat to wither the jungle foliage the Wilson Collison story was set in. Victor Fleming vigorously directed John Lee Mahin's script, with Mary Astor also scoring as the lady ready to swap husband Gene Raymond for Gable until Harlow broke up the triangle. Tully Marshall, Donald Crisp, Forrester Harvey supported; Hunt Stromberg produced. The picture was strong enough to be a smash without the current press notoriety involving Harlow (and, by rumour, Gable) when her newly-wed husband, Paul Bern, one of Thalberg's closest associates, committed suicide.

Charles Laughton gave a stunning performance in **Payment Deferred**, repeating his London stage role of the suburban murderer. His highly individual technique, with the bizarre mannerisms not yet familiar, made a strong impact on the critics and the sparse crowds who saw the Lothar Mendes production. Scenarists Ernst Vajda and Claudine West tampered little with Jeffrey Dell's play. The star was supported by Dorothy Peterson (here) and Maureen O'Sullivan, Neil Hamilton, Ray Milland, Verree Teasdale and Halliwell Hobbes.

Confronted by two of the world's most can't-take-your-eyes-off faces, audiences risked going entrancedly cross-eyed watching Garbo and Erich von Stroheim in **As You Desire Me**. MGM, by furthering the acting career von Stroheim was to follow for the rest of his life, proved there were no hard feelings about his directorial extravagances of the Twenties. Garbo bleached her hair and he shaved his off for the scene-stealing battle that made the first part of the George Fitzmaurice production a highspot of 1932 cinema. The later scenes in Gene Markey's adaptation of the Pirandello drama were more conventionally romantic as Garbo impersonated Melvyn Douglas' longlost wife. Others supporting one of Garbo's best performances were Owen Moore, Rafaela Ottiano, Hedda Hopper and Albert Conti.

TIGHTER TIMES
1933

Cinema attendances in the US slid to 60m weekly during 1931–3 (they had doubled to 110m between 1927 and 1930) and swingeing cuts in studio overheads were applied. Even MGM was not immune – profits were at their lowest since the merger, but they were still ahead of all competitors. Warner Bros. started a new musical trend with *42nd Street* and *Gold-Diggers of 1933* ('We're in the Money' sung with fingers crossed). *King Kong* scared Fay Wray and large audiences. *Flying Down to Rio* introduced a new dance team: Fred Astaire and Ginger Rogers. James Cagney, who'd pushed half a grapefruit into Mae Clarke's face, dragged her around by the hair in *Lady Killer*. Clive Brook and Diana Wynyard were noble in *Cavalcade*. So were Margaret Sullavan and John Boles in *Only Yesterday* and Gary Cooper and Helen Hayes in *A Farewell to Arms*. Paul Muni, who deserved torture as Al Capone in *Scarface*, got it in *I am a Fugitive from a Chain Gang*. Newcomers won the Academy Awards: Katharine Hepburn for *Morning Glory*, Charles Laughton for *Henry VIII*. Joan Bennett, Douglas Fairbanks Jr, Joan Blondell, Bing Crosby, Carole Lombard, Joel McCrea, Ruby Keeler, Dick Powell, George Raft were other new stars. Marie Dressler was first at the box-office for the second year.

Heavy dramatics in **Storm at Daybreak** *started with the Sarajevo assassination, ended with a husband sacrificing his life to save his wife and her lover, and smacked of the silent movie era. Bertram Millhauser's script (from a play by Sandor Hunyady) and Richard Boleslawski's direction met with scant approval. But there were strong acting scenes for Kay Francis and Nils Asther (here, with Frank Burke, left) and Walter Huston (the husband), Phillips Holmes, Eugene Pallette, C. Henry Gordon, Louise Closser Hale and Jean Parker. Lucien Hubbard produced.*

△ *Jack Conway's direction and Harold Rosson's photography were major factors putting over* **Hell Below**, *starring Robert Montgomery and Walter Huston (here) as submarine officers. The story was formula, but the action sequences, made with US Navy co-operation (exteriors at Pearl Harbor), had crowd-drawing spectacle and dramatic guts. Madge Evans, Jimmy Durante, Robert Young, Eugene Pallette, Sterling Holloway and John Lee Mahin (who also scripted with Laird Doyle, Raymond Schrock, John Meehan) appeared.*

A lot of important talent was brought to the studio for Joan Crawford's **Today We Live**: *Gary Cooper, borrowed from Paramount where he had been a star for six years; Franchot Tone from New York's Group Theatre; Howard*

Hawks, who had just directed the stunning Scarface; William Faulkner, the great novelist writing his first screen original (script: Dwight Taylor, Edith Fitzgerald). The result was a slow triangle drama set in an unconvincing wartime England, with only the sea and air battles packing any punch. Left to right: Cooper, Robert Young, Roscoe Karns, Crawford.

Robert E. Sherwood's charming comedy **Reunion in Vienna**, *adapted by Ernst Vajda and Claudine West, was a prestige success, even though too much of a talk-piece for the millions. Director Sidney Franklin didn't have the Lunts to repeat their stage roles this time, but John Barrymore and Diana Wynyard made elegant substitutes. Barrymore was in his best bravura form as the taxi-driving, wife-stealing Hapsburg prince; so was Frank Morgan, starting a 17-year MGM stay as the bewildered husband. Henry Travers, May Robson, Una Merkel and Eduardo Ciannelli were featured.*

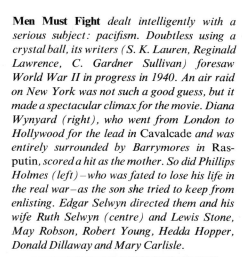

Men Must Fight dealt intelligently with a serious subject: pacifism. Doubtless using a crystal ball, its writers (S. K. Lauren, Reginald Lawrence, C. Gardner Sullivan) foresaw World War II in progress in 1940. An air raid on New York was not such a good guess, but it made a spectacular climax for the movie. Diana Wynyard (right), who went from London to Hollywood for the lead in Cavalcade and was entirely surrounded by Barrymores in Rasputin, scored a hit as the mother. So did Phillips Holmes (left) – who was fated to lose his life in the real war – as the son she tried to keep from enlisting. Edgar Selwyn directed them and his wife Ruth Selwyn (centre) and Lewis Stone, May Robson, Robert Young, Hedda Hopper, Donald Dillaway and Mary Carlisle.

showed a talent for delivering them with maximum zip. Bernard Hyman produced and Sam Wood directed smartly, with a cast including Dorothy Burgess, Guy Kibbee, Stuart Erwin and Elizabeth Patterson.

Anita Loos wrote **Hold Your Man** with Clark ▽ Gable, Jean Harlow and the box-office in mind, and it was a perfect fit. The story about a crook and his moll wasn't much, but the author of 'Gentlemen Prefer Blondes' salted its emotional conflict with what were then known as wisecracks, and Miss Harlow in particular

Since her debut in Laugh, Clown, Laugh five years before, Loretta Young had achieved stardom chiefly through her doll-like beauty. She showed she also had brains when she returned to MGM for **Midnight Mary**, a 1933 hit. In an affecting performance as an underworld girl on trial for murder, she was directed by William Wellman. Gene Markey's script, from an Anita Loos original, told the story in flashbacks from the courtroom. Here is the gang planning a heist: Ricardo Cortez, Sandy Roth, Loretta, Una Merkel, Harold Huber, Warren Hymer. Franchot Tone played the good guy, with Andy Devine and Halliwell Hobbes also cast. Lucien Hubbard produced.

Mayer's theory that family audiences always enjoy family stories got confirmation from the good reception given **This Side of Heaven.** William K. Howard directed Lionel Barrymore as a paterfamilias whose selfish brood rallied around him when he was accused of embezzlement. Left to right: Tom Brown, Mary Carlisle, Barrymore, Mae Clarke and Broadway star Fay Bainter. Also cast: Una Merkel, Onslow Stevens, Henry Wadsworth, Dickie Moore, C. Henry Gordon, Eddie Nugent. Producer: John Considine Jr. Script was by Zelda Sears, Eve Greene, Florence Ryerson and Edgar Allan Woolf, from Marjorie Paradis' original.

1933

Made on Broadway/The Girl I Made *was a smooth light comedy which triangled Robert Montgomery and Madge Evans (here) with Sally Eilers. The Gene Markey script from Courtney Terrett's original dealt with the manufacture of a star by publicity. The theme was more brilliantly used soon after in* Bombshell. *Lucien Hubbard produced and Harry Beaumont directed a cast including Eugene Pallette, Jean Parker, C. Henry Gordon, John Miljan, Raymond Hatton and Ivan Lebedeff.*

Two of 1933's crop of 'Bs':
Marion Davies had a stab at the famous Laurette Taylor role for the remake of **Peg o' My Heart** *and made a good job of it, even throwing in a bit of song-and-dance. Robert Z. Leonard directed the Frances Marion script for the masses and got 'em: it was big box office once past the metropolitan first runs. As inhabitants of the English manor coping with the roguish colleen's intrusion were Robert Greig and Onslow Stevens (here) and Juliette*

Myrna Loy started 1933 with a loan-out and played opposite John Barrymore in Topaze *so well that she was rewarded with her first MGM lead–and the year's most discreetly provocative nude scene–as Ramon Novarro's heroine in* **The Barbarian**/A Night in Cairo. *A romantic bonbon confected by Anita Loos and Elmer Harris from Edgar Selwyn's original, it proved to be Novarro's most popular movie for some time. He'd made it as* The Arab *in 1924. Sam Wood directed, with Reginald Denny, C. Aubrey Smith, Louise Closser Hale and Edward Arnold among others drifting down the Hollywood Nile.*

MGM was now making a strong comeback from its temporary slump. In **The Prizefighter and the Lady**/Everywoman's Man *John Meehan and John Lee Mahin, confusingly named aces in MGM's pack of writers, didn't veer from the classic boxing story, but their script made the pug-fights-way-to-top-then-gets-big-headed theme seem fresh. Smartly directed by W. S. Van Dyke, and produced by Hunt Stromberg, it gave showy parts to Myrna Loy, Max Baer and Walter Huston (here) and Otto Kruger. Baer, a real contender for the heavyweight crown, played the leading role with surprising ease, and the big fight climax, matching him with the gigantic Primo Carnera, refereed by Jack Dempsey, had authentic wallop.*

In 1933 Walter Wanger joined MGM's group of producers, who were emerging from their anonymity as 'supervisors' to get equal credit with directors. His **Gabriel Over the White House** *created a stir within and outside the studio. With Thalberg absent Mayer didn't realize until he saw the finished film that the Carey Wilson–Bertram Bloch script (from T. F. Tweed's British best-seller, 'Rinehard') was about a corrupt USA president. An ardent Republican, he saw it as a slur on ex-President Hoover and a boost for new President Roosevelt. He delayed its release but after a few retakes let it go–and found he had one of the most highly praised movies in years. Gregory La Cava directed Walter Huston as the party politician transformed by a car crash into a world-leading crusader against war, poverty and crime. Franchot Tone and Karen Morley (here) played his secretaries, supported by C. Henry Gordon, Jean Parker, Arthur Byron and Dickie Moore.*

Quote from a January 1933 'Film Daily' review: **'The White Sister** *is the greatest soul drama in the annals of pix. Contrast Helen Hayes' role with that of Clark Gable. Spirit warring with the flesh. Christ wins. Clark loses. And if that won't tear feminine emotions to ragged shreds, what will? A natural.' The box office confirmed that it was indeed a natural, as it had been ten years before with Lillian Gish and Ronald Colman playing nun and soldier. Hunt Stromberg produced and Victor Fleming directed the emotion-tearing, in which the stars were assisted by Lewis Stone, Edward Arnold, May Robson and Louise Closser Hale. Donald Ogden Stewart scripted F. Marion Crawford's story.*

Compton, Irene Browne and Alan Mowbray, while J. Farrell MacDonald was her ould Oirish dad. . . . Auber's operetta **The Devil's Brother**/Fra Diavolo *became a very comic opera when Hal Roach turned Laurel and Hardy loose on it. Broadway star Dennis King, with them here, had a fine voice but the music was never allowed to interrupt the flow of gags for long. Roach directed it with Charles Rogers; script by Jeanie MacPherson. Thelma Todd and Jimmy Finlayson were featured.*

Mayer tried to channel the talents of two major radio stars into films in 1933, with little success. David O. Selznick's poorest production, **Meet the Baron** surrounded Jack Pearl with other comedians–Jimmy Durante, Ted Healy, the 3 Stooges and (here with him) Edna May Oliver, ZaSu Pitts and Greta Meyer. Director Walter Lang and writers Arthur Kober, Allen Rivkin, P. J. Wolfson injected a kind of Marx Brothers anarchy into the proceedings . . . But **The Chief** was a total loss, which all Ed Wynn's famous stage and radio comedy tricks couldn't save. Charles Reisner directed (left to right) William Boyd, C. Henry Gordon, Wynn, and ex-Warner star Dorothy Mackaill, whose compatriots in England never got a chance to see the film–one of three MGM movies of the Thirties not released there. Script: Arthur Caesar, Robert Hopkins. Harry Rapf produced.

Ann Harding, Robert Montgomery, Alice Brady, Martin Burton and Myrna Loy in **When Ladies Meet**. As conversational as Reunion in Vienna, this comedy from the stage had a firmer dramatic basis which made it more widely popular with movie fans. Miss Harding as a publisher's wife and Miss Loy as his novelist mistress clashed effectively, but Miss Brady's stylized delivery of laugh lines stole the picture–the stage star's first for a dozen years. Frank Morgan also scored under Harry Beaumont's direction of the John Meehan–Leon Gordon screenplay from Rachel Crothers' play.

Lee Tracy took his quicksilver sparkle from Warners to MGM for **Clear All Wires**, the last picture completed by George Hill before his death. With Delmer Daves, Samuel and Bella Spewack adapted their Broadway hit about a foreign correspondent, enlarging its scope to take in world-wide locales. Benita Hume from London also made her début at the studio, playing opposite Tracy, with James Gleason, Una Merkel, C. Henry Gordon . . . His next,

The Nuisance/Accidents Wanted, increased his popularity. It moved almost as fast as Tracy could talk, and he had to turn on all his dynamism to ward off scene-stealing Frank Morgan. They played an ambulance-chasing insurance trickster and his doctor confederate in the Spewacks' screenplay, directed by Jack Conway. Madge Evans, Charles Butterworth, John Miljan and Herman Bing aided the fun. Lawrence Weingarten produced; MGM made a tidy profit . . . **Turn Back the Clock** allowed the

ebullient Tracy, here (second from left) with Peggy Shannon, Gordon, Otto Kruger and Mae Clarke, to round out a fuller character study than usual. The Edgar Selwyn–Ben Hecht drama, directed by Selwyn, hinged on the familiar device of a dream, in which the hard-up hero exchanged fortunes and wives with his rich friend (Kruger). Also cast: Clara Blandick and George Barbier.

Looking Forward/Service introduced two more imports by ever-Anglophile MGM: Elizabeth Allan, seen here with Lewis Stone and Phillips Holmes, and writer H. M. Harwood, with whom Bess Meredyth adapted the play by C. L. Anthony (Dodie Smith). Director Clarence Brown and the cast, which also included Lionel Barrymore, Colin Clive, Benita Hume, Douglas Walton, George K. Arthur, Halliwell Hobbes, Alec B. Francis and Doris Lloyd, gave the department-store drama an authentic English atmosphere; but trade was slow at the ticket counter.

Madge Evans and Una Merkel were the most in-demand players on MGM's roster: in 1933/4 the former was featured in 16 releases, including four loan-outs; the latter in 22, including five loan-outs. They played two of the three heroines (Florine McKinney was the third) in **Beauty for Sale**/Beauty!, another variation of the Sally, Irene and Mary story of working girls–it always had to be three, somehow–this time toiling in a beauty salon. Lucien Hubbard produced and Richard Boleslawski, rather out of his element, directed the Zelda Sears–Eve Greene script from Faith Baldwin's novel. Also cast: Alice Brady, Phillips Holmes, Otto Kruger, May Robson and Eddie Nugent.

Robert Montgomery and Madge Evans teamed for the fourth time in **Fugitive Lovers**, with Nat Pendleton, Ted Healy and the 3 Stooges, C. Henry Gordon and Ruth Selwyn. It took many writers, including Albert Hackett, Frances Goodrich and George B. Seitz, to bring forth this routine movie about an escaped convict on a New York–Los Angeles bus, but MGM's routine items had a happy knack of being better than other studios'. Richard Boleslawski directed, Lucien Hubbard produced.

King Vidor returned to MGM in 1933 to film **The Stranger's Return** *from a novel by Phil Stong, whose State Fair had just registered a major hit. The new one didn't, although Vidor captured the atmosphere of rural life with refreshing simplicity, and inspired fine work by Miriam Hopkins, Franchot Tone and Beulah Bondi (here) and Lionel Barrymore, as Miriam's grandfather dismayed by her affair with a married farmer. In support were Stuart Erwin, Irene Hervey and Grant Mitchell. Brown Holmes collaborated with Stong on the screenplay, produced by Lucien Hubbard.*

MGM continued to sail out of the 1933 doldrums with **Tugboat Annie**, *a perfect example of what Mayer (and most of the public) considered to be ideal entertainment: the hokum of husband-and-wife slapstick brawling and mother-and-son sentiment, given the warmth of life by its makers' skill. Not least that of its co-stars, Wallace Beery and Marie Dressler, aided by Robert Young (here) as their son, Maureen O'Sullivan, Willard Robertson and Frankie Darro. Its receipts were colossal. Mervyn LeRoy returned to direct them in Norman Reilly Raine's story, adapted by Zelda Sears and Eve Greene; producer, Harry Rapf.*

A quickie by MGM standards, **The Solitaire Man** *was distinguished by the first Culver City assignments of two expert performers: Herbert Marshall and Mary Boland. Although the Samuel and Bella Spewack play about double-crossing crooks was set in a cramped Paris–London airplane cabin, its tension, heightened by scenarist James K. McGuinness and director Jack Conway, gave it the illusion of action. Left to right: Lionel Atwill, May Robson, Marshall, Elizabeth Allan, Miss Boland; also present were Lucille Gleason, Ralph Forbes and Robert McWade.*

Many critics ranked **Sons of the Desert**/ Fraternally Yours *as Laurel and Hardy's best full-lengther, both for their comedy and its broad satire on American conventions. Hal Roach threw in another of his shorts stars, Charley Chase (centre), and Stan and Oliver were henpecked by Mae Busch and Dorothy Christy. William Seiter directed the Frank Craven–Byron Morgan screenplay.*

Musicals were back in fashion by late 1933, and Marion Davies had a fairly good one in **Going Hollywood**. *Its box-office appeal was guaranteed by co-star Bing Crosby, then at his crooning zenith. His acting ability not yet able to stand strain, he was cast as a crooner, with Marion (centre) as his greatest fan. Donald Ogden Stewart's screenplay, from an original by Frances Marion, was produced by Walter Wanger and directed by Raoul Walsh, with Fifi d'Orsay (right) and Stuart Erwin and Ned Sparks. Of its six songs, 'Temptation' became the big hit.*

What had been almost completed years before as a revue, The March of Time, finally saw light as **Broadway to Hollywood**/Ring Up the Curtain *with all but a smidgin of the revue jettisoned, but with a dramatic story developed from the original show-business-through-the-years idea. It turned out very well, giving strong opportunities to Frank Morgan, Jackie Cooper and Alice Brady (here) and Madge Evans, Jimmy Durante, Eddie Quillan, May Robson, Una Merkel, Russell Hardie, Nelson Eddy (début—one song). Mickey Rooney, who had been in movies since the age of four, made his MGM bow at 10. Produced by Harry Rapf, the film was a fitting farewell by its writer and director, Willard Mack, who died soon after.*

The 'B' pictures churned out at Culver City in 1933 maintained a praiseworthy standard. Shot in a couple of weeks without any of the studio's superstars, dramas like these kept release schedules filled and audiences satisfied. Madge Evans. Richard Dix (the veteran star's only MGM movie), Clarence Wilson in **Day of**

Reckoning; *written by Eve Gordon, directed by Charles Brabin, with Conway Tearle, Una Merkel, Stuart Erwin . . . Irene Hervey, Ben Lyon, Otto Kruger in* **The Women in His Life**; *written by F. Hugh Herbert, directed by George B. Seitz, with Una Merkel, Nat Pendleton, Isabel Jewell . . . Alice Brady, Maureen O'Sullivan in* **Stage Mother**; *written by Bradford Ropes, John Meehan; directed by Brabin, with Franchot Tone, Phillips Holmes, Ted Healy, C. Henry Gordon. Lucien Hubbard produced the first two, Hunt Stromberg the third.*

The Academy gave film editor Conrad Nervig an Oscar for his work on **Eskimo**/Mala the Magnificent. *Director was W. S. Van Dyke. That glutton for punishment made yet another arduous location trip for the movie, this time into the Arctic. He sailed in a whaling schooner loaded with movie technicians and equipment to the northernmost inhabited settlement in Alaska, where the ship was frozen-in for the 1932–3 winter. Their guide was Peter Freuchen, author of the book on which John Lee Mahin based his script. Clyde DeVinna got some stunning photographic effects. The native cast spoke in the Eskimo tongue, translated on film by subtitles. Mala, seen here, played the lead so winningly that producer Hunt Stromberg gave him an MGM contract. Released late in 1933 after a year in production, it got a warm reception, but some of the paybox returns had a touch of frostbite.*

Joan Crawford (right) had one of her biggest hits and the studio a record-breaker in **Dancing Lady**, a strong backstage story with musical trimmings on a lavish scale. Scripted by Allen Rivkin, Zelda Sears and P. J. Wolfson from James Warner Bellah's novel, it took her from a raided burlesque show with Winnie Lightner (left) to Broadway stardom with Fred Astaire. Their 'Rhythm of the Day' number (Fred's only appearance for his screen début) was written for the movie by Rodgers & Hart, but the one that lasted was Lane & Adamson's 'Everything I Have is Yours'. Clark Gable, overshadowed for once, co-starred, with Franchot Tone, May Robson, Ted Healy and his 3 Stooges, Grant Mitchell, Sterling Holloway, Nelson Eddy (one song) and Robert Benchley. Robert Z. Leonard directed.

Mayer called in his son-in-law, David O. Selznick, to strengthen the top production brass while Thalberg was on sick leave. Selznick started with a flourish, out-starring Grand Hotel with an astonishing cast for **Dinner at Eight**, and bringing director George Cukor over from RKO where they had turned out a succession of hits. The picture made a massive profit. The order of billing was: Marie Dressler, John Barrymore, Wallace Beery, Jean Harlow, Lionel Barrymore, Lee Tracy, Edmund Lowe, Billie Burke, Madge Evans, Jean Hersholt, Karen Morley, Phillips Holmes, May Robson, Louise Closser Hale, Grant Mitchell, Elizabeth Patterson . . . and then some. Here: Miss Burke as hostess of the dinner (which began as the film ended) and Beery and Miss Harlow as guests whose bickering was a comedy highlight. John Barrymore was outstanding as an alcoholic, suicidal actor, in the neatly jigsawed stories of the Herman Mankiewicz–Frances Marion–Donald Ogden Stewart script from the Edna Ferber–George Kaufman play.

The Secret of Madame Blanche was another dip into the Madame X–Madelon Claudet corn-bag. Irene Dunne and Douglas Walton (with Jean Parker, left) played mother and son who didn't know they were, until he committed murder, whereupon she took the blame. . . . It had the lot, including a Nineties' music hall, World War I, a big courtroom scene, and a tear-tapping performance by Irene. Charles Brabin directed the Frances Goodrich–Albert Hackett screenplay, with Phillips Holmes, Lionel Atwill, Una Merkel, C. Henry Gordon and Mitchell Lewis.

Has Phillips Holmes just murdered Mae Clarke? No–it's a frame-up! **Penthouse**/Crooks in Clover was a crime drama spiced with wit, and pointed the way for director W. S.

Van Dyke, producer Hunt Stromberg, scripters Frances Goodrich and Albert Hackett and co-star Myrna Loy to their triumphant Thin Man a year later. C. Henry Gordon (here) was the gangster heavy and Warner Baxter the lawyer hero, supported by Nat Pendleton, Charles Butterworth, Martha Sleeper, George E. Stone, Robert Emmet O'Connor and Raymond Hatton.

Laugh at yourself, Hollywood, and the world laughs with you. Jean Harlow, playing from experience, demonstrated how an actress can be glamourized and publicity-pressured into an

idol in **Bombshell**/Blonde Bombshell, an uproarious satire on the dream factories and their star-building methods. Lee Tracy (left) was her high-powered press agent and Louise Beavers her maid; others contributing were Frank Morgan, Franchot Tone, Pat O'Brien, Una Merkel, Ivan Lebedeff, Ted Healy, C. Aubrey Smith, Mary Forbes and Isabel Jewell. Director Victor Fleming and scenarists John Lee Mahin and Jules Furthman helped make the Harlow–Tracy partnership a dazzler. Hunt Stromberg produced.

Marie Dressler's last appearance was in **Christopher Bean** with Lionel Barrymore. She died, aged 65, six months after its release. Her films are not revived, so it's hard to realize

today what a powerful hold this large, unlovely woman had on the moviegoing masses. She played both drama and comedy with immense verve. If it sometimes swept her into overacting, nobody cared: the warmth of her personality was irresistible. Sidney Howard's stage hit 'The Late Christopher Bean' (from René Fauchois' 'Prenez Garde à la Peinture') revolved upon a deceased character and, strangely enough, was also the last screenplay written by Laurence Johnson (with Sylvia Thalberg) before his death. Sam Wood directed and Harry Rapf produced this comedy of an avaricious family whose housekeeper was the custodian of a posthumously famous artist's paintings. Beulah Bondi, George Coulouris, Helen Mack, Russell Hardie, H. B. Warner and Jean Hersholt supported.

Paul Osborn's play 'The Vinegar Tree' was fashioned by Bella and Samuel Spewack into an Alice Brady vehicle, **Should Ladies Behave?**, which was better than its title. The domestic comedy of three women infatuated with one man was smoothly directed by Harry Beaumont for producer Lawrence Weingarten and featured Conway Tearle and Lionel Barrymore, here with Miss Brady, aided by Katherine Alexander, Mary Carlisle, William Janney and Halliwell Hobbes. But the star's eccentric mannerisms were meeting audience resistance outside the city centres. MGM had bought Noël Coward's 'The Vortex' for her next, but censorship problems proved insoluble and she left the contract list.

Helen Hayes was splendid in **Another Language**, *adapted by Herman Mankiewicz, Gertrude Purcell and Donald Ogden Stewart from Rose Franken's play about domestic conflict, but she was challenged for critics' honours by Louise Closser Hale as her dominating mother-in-law. Sadly, Miss Hale's first leading role immediately preceded her death. This scene, in which the new bride realizes that she and her husband's family speak different languages, shows (left to right) Margaret Hamilton, Minor Watson, Miss Hale, Henry Travers, Robert Montgomery, Miss Hayes and Maidel Turner. Edward H. Griffith directed for the first time at MGM.*

What! No Beer? *was a sorry MGM swansong for Buster Keaton and allowed co-star Jimmy Durante to play first fiddle. Buster's drinking problem was now acute, and when he was able to work he had little enthusiasm for the picture. Neither had the public, although the Carey Wilson–Jack Cluett script about the partial repeal of Prohibition had its comic moments. Edward Sedgwick directed, with Roscoe Ates, Phyllis Barry, John Miljan, Henry Armetta and Edward Brophy.*

The long and painful decline of John Gilbert from topmost star to second-feature hero ended with **Fast Workers**, *which concluded his contract. Ironically, its routine script about skyscraper construction men came from Laurence Stallings, writer of his 1925 triumph, The Big Parade. Karl Brown and Ralph Wheelwright collaborated. Willard Mack and Mae Clarke (with Gilbert, here), Robert Armstrong and Sterling Holloway were featured; Tod Browning directed.*

1933 went out with one star rising and another falling in **Cat and the Fiddle.** *Jeanette MacDonald, who had scored in some Paramount frolics, was beginning her MGM career and Ramon Novarro had only two more films to go in his. The 1931 stage musical about bohemians in Brussels was adapted by the Spewacks for producer Bernard Hyman and directed by William K. Howard, with Charles Butterworth (right) and Frank Morgan, Vivienne Segal, Jean Hersholt, Henry Armetta, Joseph Cawthorn, Frank Conroy.*

The fifth and last film to star both Barrymore brothers was **Night Flight**. *With Clark Gable, Helen Hayes, Robert Montgomery, Myrna Loy and William Gargan also cast, it was intended as another all-star blockbuster but didn't measure up to* Grand Hotel *or* Dinner at Eight *at the box-office. Glamour was neglected in favour of gritty drama in the story, adapted from Antoine de Saint-Exupery's book by Oliver H. P. Garrett, about a South American airline run by John B. with ruthless disregard for his pilots' safety. Clarence Brown directed the David O. Selznick production.*

Rouben Mamoulian had Garbo's movements timed to a metronome like a ballet for the lyrical 'I am memorizing this room' scene in **Queen Christina**. *After making* As You Desire ▷ Me *Garbo had taken a year off, mostly in Sweden, leaving the world (and not least MGM) in suspense about her possible retirement. A new and lucrative contract, with script, director, photographer and cast approval rights, brought her back. The romanticized story of Sweden's 17th-century queen became the star vehicle in excelsis; it was still getting profitable bookings 40 years later. Script was by Garbo's friend Salka Viertel (with S. N. Behrman and H. M. Harwood), direction by Mamoulian, photography by her favourite William Daniels; her leading man was John Gilbert (replacing newcomer Laurence Olivier because she wanted to restore her old co-star's prestige), and production was by Walter Wanger. All was as Garbo desired it, and she responded with her finest performance to date. Lewis Stone, Ian Keith, C. Aubrey Smith, Akim Tamiroff and Reginald Owen supported reverently.*

GREAT HITS, GREAT PROFITS
1934

Weekly attendances rose 10m as the eight major companies (MGM, Paramount, Fox, Warner Bros., United Artists, Universal, RKO-Radio, Columbia) sighed with relief and upped their output to 361 features. Of these, MGM had the lion's share of hits and by far the highest net with $7½m (Warner Bros. had its fourth successive year in the red, the aggregate loss reaching $30m).
Little Columbia scooped the major Academy Awards with *It Happened One Night* and W. C. Fields made his funniest film, *It's a Gift*. Two blondes were the star sensations of the year, both via loan-outs from their studios. After dozens of supporting roles at Warners, Bette Davis came back a star from RKO's *Of Human Bondage*, while Paramount's *Little Miss Marker* gave Fox a goldmine in Shirley Temple. The latter jumped straight into the top ten money-magnets (elected annually by the exhibitors via the Motion Picture Herald), joining Will Rogers, Clark Gable, Janet Gaynor, Wallace Beery, Mae West, Joan Crawford, Bing Crosby, Marie Dressler and Norma Shearer.

One of MGM's most brilliantly successful years got off to a modestly profitable start with **The Mystery of Mr X**. *Director Edgar Selwyn, producer Lawrence Weingarten and their crew could take a bow for its authenticity. One English critic wrote: 'I have never yet seen a London policeman who looked like a London policeman in a British film. The Metro policemen, however, looked amazingly like the real thing.' Robert Montgomery played the thief and chief suspect who tracked down the actual Mr X, a maniacal killer of cops. In support were Lewis Stone, Henry Stephenson, Elizabeth Allan, Ralph Forbes, Alec B. Francis and (here) Forrester Harvey. Philip MacDonald adapted his novel with Monckton Hoffe and Howard Emmett Rogers.*

1934 brought Norma Shearer's first appearance for a year. Thalberg had recovered his health sufficiently to return to the studio, but as producer of a limited number of films rather than as overseer of its entire output. After toying with the idea of his wife doing a remake of The Green Hat, *he settled on* **Riptide** *as his unit's first. It was one of those talkative plots about adultery among the rich, and no great shakes as a movie. But the fans were glad to have Miss Shearer back, and Thalberg had better to come. Edmund Goulding wrote it and directed (left to right) Herbert Marshall,*

Miss Shearer, Robert Montgomery, Mrs Patrick Campbell (once London's most dazzling star, making her Hollywood debut at 69) and Lilyan Tashman (screen veteran at 35, who died just after this film); also Ralph Forbes, Skeets Gallagher, George K. Arthur and Halliwell Hobbes.

Jean Harlow and Patsy Kelly were a couple of gals on the make in **The Girl from Missouri**/ 100% Pure *and Franchot Tone was ready to be made by Jean. The ostensible virgin with cash-register eyes was a character very like the one she'd played in* Red-Headed Woman *but with a lot more Anita Loos humour. Many of the laughs were got by Patsy, a recruit from Hal Roach shorts, whose slam-bang delivery of dialogue enlivened scores of movies until she returned to Broadway in the seventies. Jack Conway directed the Bernard Hyman production, which featured Lionel Barrymore, Lewis Stone, Hale Hamilton, Alan Mowbray, Clara Blandick and Nat Pendleton.*

Thalberg relit the dazzling catherine wheels of musical comedy spun by director Ernst Lubitsch, Maurice Chevalier and Jeanette MacDonald in Paramount's Love Parade *and* One Hour with You *for the 1934 version of* **The Merry Widow**. *Gone were the orgiastic abandon and insinuated depravity of 1925's von Stroheim; now the widow had Jeanette's gentility, the prince had Chevalier's naughty-but-niceness, and if Lubitsch's closed bedroom doors implied a roll on the chaise-longue—well, it was all in fun. It also had Lehar's music, plus new lyrics by Lorenz Hart, plus a witty Ernst Vajda–Samson Raphaelson script, plus MGM's unparamountable opulence enhanced by Oliver Marsh's photography. (Cedric Gibbons' and Frederic Hope's art direction was Academy Awarded.) Edward Everett Horton, Una Merkel, George Barbier, Minna Gombell, Herman Bing and Donald Meek supported. Mayer and Thalberg had been trying to get its co-stars for years; they held on to MacDonald, but Chevalier's first Hollywood period was ending.*

A much less ambitious musical, **Student Tour**, *was whipped out by producer Monta Bell and director Charles Reisner in half the time and at one-tenth the cost of* The Merry Widow. *It looked it. The script by Ralph Spence and Philip Dunne about collegiates on a cruise yielded a few amusing scenes for Jimmy Durante and Charles Butterworth, but little for heroine Maxine Doyle or (left to right) Herman Brix (later Bruce Bennett), Monte Blue, Mary Loos, Phil Regan, Florine McKinney, Fay McKenzie, Bobby Gordon, Douglas Fowley and (pre-fame) Betty Grable. Nelson Eddy made another one-song appearance.*

Meanwhile still another kind of musical was hatching up the road at Hal Roach's studio. **Babes in Toyland** *was something for the kiddies, and enough of them took ma and pa along to make it a moneyspinner. That was thanks to Laurel and Hardy, at the peak of their fame; their gags were woven into Glen MacDonough's yarn about nursery rhyme characters. Gus Meins and Charles Rogers directed this version of Victor Herbert's operetta, with Stan, Harry Kleinbach, Ollie (here) and Charlotte Henry, Felix Knight and Johnny Downs.*

Early in 1934 Mayer gave Marie Dressler's morale a boost with a new contract, although he knew her illness was fatal and the studio needed a replacement for some of her scripts. He had recently let Columbia have May Robson for Frank Capra's Lady for a Day and the movie had shot her to stardom. So **You Can't Buy Everything** became a Robson vehicle. The Dudley Nichols–Lamar Trotti original was based on the true story of Hetty Green, the miserly woman who amassed millions on Wall Street. Zelda Sears' and Eve Greene's script, directed by Charles Reisner, softened the character with a strong injection of mother-love. William Bakewell (here with May), Jean Parker and Tad Alexander played the young generation and Lewis Stone, Reginald Mason, Walter Walker and Claude Gillingwater the old. Lucien Hubbard produced, with medium paybox results.

Robert Young's straightforward sincerity made him one of the best liked–and hardest worked –of actors during his dozen MGM years. In 1934 he did several loan-outs and four respectable 'Bs' on the home lot: as a Louisiana ▽ bayou boy with Jean Parker in **Lazy River**, directed by George B. Seitz, scripted and produced by Lucien Hubbard, with Ted Healy, C. Henry Gordon, Nat Pendleton, Maude Eburne . . . as an American expatriate with ▽ Una Merkel in **Paris Interlude**, directed by Edwin L. Marin, produced by Hubbard, adapted by Wells Root from an S. J. and Laura Perelman play, with Madge Evans, Otto Kruger, George Meeker, Edward Brophy . . . as a baseball professional with Madge Evans and Joseph Sauers in **Death on the Diamond**, ▽ directed by Edward Sedgwick, produced by Hubbard, story by Cortland Fitzsimmons, with Pendleton, Healy, Gordon, Paul Kelly, Mickey Rooney . . . as a football star with Stuart Erwin and Preston Foster in **The Band** ▽ **Plays On**, directed by Russell Mack, produced by Marin, with Betty Furness, Leo Carrillo, Russell Hardie, Healy, and seven writer credits.

In **Sadie McKee** Joan Crawford, not for the first time or the last, played a poor girl forced to choose between a rich man (Edward Arnold, brilliant as a happy alcoholic) and true love (Gene Raymond, who crooned the theme song 'All I Do Is Dream of You'). Clarence Brown's direction and a good cast brought dramatic vitality to this negligible bit of magazine fiction by Vina Delmar, adapted by John Meehan and produced by Lawrence Weingarten. Others involved were Franchot Tone, Joan's second husband in more or less private life, Jean Dixon (here with Joan and Gene) and Esther Ralston, Leo Carrillo, Akim Tamiroff and Zelda Sears.

Jean Parker, Charles Bickford and Mady Christians in **A Wicked Woman**. Eleventh in the cast list was Robert Taylor, an MGM discovery making his feature début there after a highly-praised short, Buried Loot, and a minor loan-out. Miss Christians, a Viennese charmer, played the title role in this story of a mother who, having killed her sadistic husband while defending her children, kept her guilty secret for ten years. Ann Austin's story, scripted by Zelda Sears and Florence Ryerson, could have been a dank weepie without her. Although an actress of note in Europe, she went on to grace other Hollywood movies without reaching deserved stardom. Also cast: Betty Furness, William Henry, Jackie Searle, Miss Sears (her last role and screenplay) and Sterling Holloway. Harry Rapf produced, Charles Brabin directed.

Every prolific director has made at least one he'd like to forget. **Laughing Boy** was W. S. Van Dyke's. A glumly dramatic tale by Oliver La Farge, noted writer about Red Indian life, was converted to a sort of screenplay by John Colton and John Lee Mahin, and produced by Hunt Stromberg, apparently while thinking of something else. Mexican stars Ramon Novarro in the mis-title role, and Lupe Velez as his

wigwam warmer, tried in vain to act like Indians. Audiences had plenty of seats to put their coats on.

Lupe Velez had a happier time in **Hollywood Party** as her temperamental self, wearing an off-the-hip number and clowning with Laurel and Hardy. Producer Harry Rapf had half the stars and directors on the lot taking a whack at this musical mishmash, but it boiled down to these three plus Jimmy Durante, Charles Butterworth, Jack Pearl, Ted Healy, June Clyde and, best of all, a Mickey Mouse cartoon sequence from Walt Disney. Richard Boleslawski got such director credit as there was. Script was by MGM's publicity chief Howard Dietz, a celebrated revue librettist in his spare time, and Arthur Kober.

Gladys George, a Broadway star, started a brief spell of Hollywood fame in **Straight is the Way**, but Karen Morley was leading lady of this minor gangster piece, a remake of the Gilbert-Crawford silent Four Walls. Producer, Lucien Hubbard; director, Paul Sloane; script, Bernard Schubert. Left to right: May Robson, Franchot Tone, Miss George. Also cast: Jack La Rue, Nat Pendleton, C. Henry Gordon and William Bakewell.

The pedigree of **Biography of a Bachelor Girl** was impeccable: producer, Thalberg; director, E. H. Griffith, who had made star Ann Harding's best movies; author, S. N. Behrman, from his Broadway hit, 'Biography', about a painter with a past who stirred up an entertaining fuss by writing her memoirs; script, Anita Loos, Horace Jackson; camera, James Wong Howe; cast, Miss Harding and Edward Arnold (here) and Robert Montgomery, Edward Everett Horton, Una Merkel. Box-office: spotty.

While MGM paid lip-service to the industry's 1934 campaign against double features, it continued delivering 'Bs' to meet stubborn public demand. Two good little programmers were: **Murder in the Private Car**/Murder on the Runaway Train, *a non-stop chase item with Russell Hardie and Charles Ruggles, and Mary Carlisle, Una Merkel and Porter Hall, produced by Lucien Hubbard, directed by Harry Beaumont, script by Ralph Spence, Edgar Allan Woolf, Al Boasberg, Harvey Thew . . .* **Have a Heart**, *a comedy about a street vendor, with Jean Parker and James Dunn, and Una Merkel, Stuart Erwin and Willard Robertson, produced by John Considine Jr, directed by David Butler, script by Florence Ryerson and Woolf.*

After Queen Christina, *the Garbo classic,* **The Painted Veil** *came as something of a letdown. The Somerset Maugham story, as adapted by John Meehan, Salka Viertel and Edith Fitzgerald, harked back to Garbo's silent movies, with Greta torn between worthy husband and passionate lover. In fact its plot hardly differed from that of* Wild Orchids, *but now Herbert Marshall, here, played the w.h. and George Brent the p.l., while China replaced Java as the exotic locale. Richard Boleslawski directed, Hunt Stromberg produced; Katherine Alexander, Warner Oland, Jean Hersholt, Beulah Bondi, Cecilia Parker and Forrester Harvey were featured.*

Besides grooming new stars, MGM knew how to revive old ones, as in the case of William Powell. After many years of stardom at Paramount, then Warners, he was fading until cast in **Manhattan Melodrama** *as the DA who had to prosecute his boyhood friend, gangster Clark Gable, and charmed the latter's mistress, Myrna Loy, away from him. It was a walloping hit. All three stars, producer David O. Selznick, director W. S. Van Dyke, author Arthur Caesar (Academy Award, best original) and scenarists Joseph Mankiewicz and Oliver H. P. Garrett were highly praised for a potent crime drama, laced with unforced fun as in this scene with Herman Bing, Loy and Powell. Leo Carrillo Isabel Jewell, Nat Pendleton and Mickey Rooney (playing Gable as a lad) were also cast.*

The tyke on the left pinched this scene in **Hide-Out** *from Robert Montgomery and Edward Arnold so easily you might have thought he was Hollywood's biggest star. It took Mickey Rooney a few more years to become that. The versatile W. S. Van Dyke made a real audience-pleaser from this Frances Goodrich–Albert Hackett script about a New York racketeer forced to take cover in the country, and taught to like it by the farmer's daughter. Maureen O'Sullivan, C. Henry Gordon, Elizabeth Patterson, Edward Brophy, Herman Bing and Henry Armetta were also in the Hunt Stromberg production.*

Marion Davies, Marjorie Gateson, and Gary Cooper carrying Jean Parker in **Operator 13**/Spy 13, *Marion's last film for MGM. It was a complicated Civil War story by Robert W. Chambers, lavishly produced by Lucien Hubbard, which hardly earned back its cost. Richard Boleslawski directed from a Harvey Thew–Zelda Sears–Eve Green script, with Mae Clarke, Douglass Dumbrille, Ted Healy, Ned Sparks, Henry B. Walthall and the four Mills Brothers (singing 'Sleepy Head'). Marion played a Northern spy assigned to liquidate Southern officer Cooper; you guessed it, they fell in love. Offscreen, Marion fell out of love with MGM when Thalberg, backed by*

Mayer, scorned her startling request to star in The Barretts of Wimpole Street *and* Marie Antoinette, *both earmarked for Norma Shearer. Later in 1934 Marion and Hearst moved her famous bungalow and his Cosmopolitan Productions over to Warners. Miss Shearer's name wasn't mentioned in Hearst newspapers for quite a while.*

'You geev Pancho beeg kees, eh?' growled Wallace Beery to Fay Wray, who rejected the invitation and got horsewhipped for her trouble in **Viva Villa!**, *a David O. Selznick near-epic, and one of the year's big winners. Howard Hawks started directing it in Mexico and Jack Conway finished it in Hollywood, getting sole credit. Between these two events there was many a foul-up. For instance, both Mexican government co-operation and Lee Tracy's contract were abruptly cancelled after the star made an intoxicated appearance on his Mexico City hotel balcony and watered a military parade passing below. Retakes with Stuart Erwin in his role ensued. Meanwhile, Beery was giving a rousing performance as the revolutionary bandit in a rip-roaring series of action scenes contrived by Ben Hecht from fact, legend and the movie stockpile. Leo Carrillo, H. B. Warner, Joseph Schildkraut, Donald Cook, George E. Stone, Katherine DeMille (Cecil's adopted daughter) and thousands of extras were in the cast.*

You can find many an oldster whose all-time favourite team is William Powell, Myrna Loy and Asta. Bill and Myrna were so easy, natural and affectionately insulting together that a large section of the public believed they were married in life, as in **The Thin Man**. Nothing △ quite like this relationship had been screened before; critics and customers were totally captivated. The never failing producer-director-writers team of Hunt Stromberg, W. S. Van Dyke and Frances Goodrich–Albert Hackett filmed Dashiell Hammett's vivid detective novel, with Maureen O'Sullivan, Nat Pendleton, Minna Gombell, Porter Hall, Henry Wadsworth, William Henry, Harold Huber, Cesar Romero, Natalie Moorhead and Edward Brophy. Edward Ellis played the thin man, a murder victim.

Men in White gave Clark Gable (here with Russell Hardie) the chance to score with quietly forceful acting instead of a personality display. And its success gave MGM a penchant for hospital doctor stories, manifest even unto the television era. Richard Boleslawski directed, with Myrna Loy as Gable's society fiancée, Elizabeth Allan as his adoring nurse, Jean Hersholt as the inevitable veteran surgeon guiding him, and Otto Kruger, C. Henry Gordon, Wallace Ford, Henry B. Walthall and Samuel S. Hinds. Monta Bell produced Waldemar Young's adaptation of Sidney Kingsley's play.

Spencer Tracy had been working none too happily at Fox since leaving Broadway in 1930, and was swapped with Robert Young for one picture in 1934. It was **The Show-Off**, George Kelly's durable comedy, filmed twice by Paramount and bought by MGM for Lee Tracy (no relation). Strangely enough, Spencer's axing from Fox the following year, which cleared the way for his MGM contract, was for the same reason that Lee had been dropped by Mayer: riotous behaviour. Meanwhile Spencer did a good job as the lovable liar in Lucien Hubbard's production, adapted by Herman Mankiewicz and directed by

Charles Reisner. Left to right: Lois Wilson, Henry Wadsworth, Tracy, Madge Evans, Alan Edwards, Clara Blandick, Grant Mitchell.

Charm was the quality J. M. Barrie's heroine lacked in his play **What Every Woman Knows**, *but Helen Hayes produced enough to clog the film sprockets. It was nevertheless an excellent reproduction of her New York stage role, and the Thalberg movie won laudatory reviews, if less than his usual paybox profits. Brian Aherne made his MGM debut as the dour hero; other impressively Scottish portrayals came from Dudley Digges (here, with Miss Hayes), Madge Evans, Lucile Watson, Donald Crisp, David Torrence and Henry Stephenson. Gregory La Cava directed the Monckton Hoffe–John Meehan screenplay.*

Only Eight Hours/Society Doctor *was chiefly* ▽ *notable for giving Robert Taylor (right) his first leading role as Chester Morris' rival for Virginia Bruce. Excepting Lionel Barrymore's, Taylor's contract at MGM lasted longer than any star's at any studio: 25 years. Morris donned Clark Gable's* Men in White *jacket for a dash round the MGM hospital corridors in this drama; Billie Burke, Raymond Walburn, William Henry, Dorothy Peterson, Johnny Hines and Donald Meek were also in Lucien Hubbard's production, directed by George B. Seitz from a Theodore Reeves story; script by Samuel Marx (later a producer) and Michael Fessier.*

John Considine Jr's production, **Sequoia**, *was a refreshing novelty. Jean Parker and Russell Hardie (here), and Samuel S. Hinds and Paul Hurst carried its slight human story, but the real stars were a deer and a mountain lion, sharing scenes with a rapport worthy of William Powell and Myrna Loy. Animal film specialist Chester Franklin directed, taking over a year to get the remarkable wildlife scenes in California's High Sierras with cameraman Chester Lyons. The Ann Cunningham–Sam Armstrong –Carey Wilson script emphasized the intelligence of animals instead of the ferocity featured in jungle epics.*

What the fans missed in Loy–Powell humour they gained in taut drama in **Evelyn Prentice**. *Myrna Loy played a wayward wife who thought she had killed her blackmailer (Harvey Stephens) and was appalled when her lawyer husband (William Powell) defended a girl (Isabel Jewell) on trial for the murder. W. E. Woodward's novel was expertly transcribed by scenarist Lenore Coffee, producer John Considine Jr and director William K. Howard. Una Merkel and Henry Wadsworth (here, with Myrna) and Rosalind Russell, Edward Brophy, Jessie Ralph and Frank Conroy were also cast.*

With the elegant Carole Lombard in her only MGM appearance, supported by Chester Morris and ZaSu Pitts, a script by Bella and Samuel Spewack and direction by Jack Conway, **The Gay Bride** *had the elements of a hit. But this comedy of a chiseling showgirl meeting her match in an amorous gangster came out looking like a Gable–Harlow reject, and the public hardly came out at all. Others in the John Considine Jr production were Nat Pendleton, Leo Carrillo and Sam Hardy.*

If there were any doubts whether Thalberg would maintain his prestige after Riptide *they were dissolved by* **The Barretts of Wimpole Street**, *a play-into-film of the highest quality and box-office power. All three stars (left to right) Fredric March, Charles Laughton and Norma Shearer, were winners of Academy Awards – for* Jekyll and Hyde, Henry VIII *and* Divorcee *respectively – and director Sidney Franklin let them go all-out for more. They didn't get them but did win much praise, especially Laughton for his repellent Papa Barrett. Like the Robert and Elizabeth Browning of March and Shearer it was ham of the most appetizing flavour. Maureen O'Sullivan, Una O'Connor, Ralph Forbes and Katherine Alexander had the next-best parts in the Ernst Vajda–Claudine West–Donald Ogden Stewart adaptation of Rudolph Besier's play.*

Louise Fazenda, usually a comic servant on screen, and the wealthy Mrs Hal Wallis off, celebrated her 20th movie year by signing an MGM contract and starring in **The Winning Ticket**, *with (left to right) Leo Carrillo, Luis Alberni and Ted Healy, whose 3 Stooges had launched out on their own. Director Charles Reisner, co-producing with Jack Cummings, squeezed as many laughs as possible out of the Ralph Spence–Richard Schayer script about an Italian barber winning the Irish Sweep. Irene Hervey, James Ellison and Akim Tamiroff were featured.*

Treasure Island was one of 1934's biggest hits, produced on the grand scale by Hunt Stromberg and directed with panache by Victor Fleming. Wallace Beery yo-ho-hoed lustily as Long John Silver (here) with Jackie Cooper as Jim Hawkins, supported by Lionel Barrymore, Otto Kruger, Lewis Stone, Nigel Bruce, Charles 'Chic' Sale, Dorothy Peterson and Douglass Dumbrille. All caught the true Stevenson spirit of adventure, as did John Lee Mahin's script and the scenic sweep of no fewer than three top cameramen: Ray June, Clyde DeVinna and Harold Rosson.

A spy drama in the sophisticated style was offered by **Stamboul Quest**, Myrna Loy's fourth success in as many months; the studio was now giving her top-star attention. She played the German heroine (a rarity in movies made between the wars) on a counter-espionage mission in Turkey, pursued by American suitor George Brent. Director Sam Wood gave a light touch to the romance and a fast pace to the dramatics in Herman Mankiewicz's screenplay. Walter Wanger produced, with Lionel Atwill, C. Henry Gordon and Mischa Auer in the cast.

Clarence Brown gave the sex magnetism of Joan Crawford and Clark Gable full rein in **Chained**, so Edgar Selwyn's uninspired story, scripted by John Lee Mahin, was a box-office wow. Otto Kruger played Joan's married paramour whom she ditched for South American rancher Gable. Also in the Hunt Stromberg production were Stuart Erwin, Una O'Connor, Marjorie Gateson and Akim Tamiroff.

Evelyn Laye had interrupted her long London career to make a movie for Sam Goldwyn in 1930. Four years later MGM signed her for her only other Hollywood picture, **The Night is Young**. Although using the celebrated talents of Vicki Baum (author), Sigmund Romberg (music), Oscar Hammerstein II (libretto) and the delightful Miss Laye opposite Ramon Novarro, the schmaltzy romance of an archduke and a ballerina fell flat. It yielded two hit songs, 'When I Grow Too Old to Dream' and the title number, but Dudley Murphy's direction was dull and producer Harry Rapf never could

recapture the musical zest of his 'Broadway Melody'. The studio now said farewell (for many years) to Novarro, the last of its original 1924 stars, except Norma Shearer, to depart. Others involved: Charles Butterworth and Una Merkel, here with Evelyn (right); Edward Everett Horton, Donald Cook, Herman Bing, Henry Stephenson, Rosalind Russell.

To give the MGM series a prestige the other 'Tarzans' never had, Mayer scheduled only one in every two years, with plenty of time and care in production. **Tarzan and his Mate** was as good entertainment as the first, and equally profitable. Cedric Gibbons, head of the art department, satisfied a yen to direct by guiding Johnny Weissmuller and Maureen O'Sullivan (seen here in the title roles) and Neil Hamilton, Paul Cavanagh, Forrester Harvey and hordes of elephants, lions and apes through eye-popping jungle adventures. The real and studio backgrounds photographed by Clyde DeVinna and Charles Clarke were so cunningly blended you couldn't tell the difference. Howard Emmett Rogers and Leon Gordon scripted for producer Bernard Hyman.

The Clark Gable–Joan Crawford crowd-attraction was reaffirmed by Bernard Hyman's production, **Forsaking all Others**, this time with Robert Montgomery making it a three-star affair. Joan, in the role Tallulah Bankhead had played on Broadway in the E. B. Roberts–F. M. Cavett comedy, was left at the altar by Bob in the first scene and left him likewise in the last, having got the Gable treatment meanwhile. W. S. Van Dyke kept the fun bubbling, helped by Joseph Mankiewicz's script and Charles Butterworth, Billie Burke, Frances Drake, Rosalind Russell and Arthur Treacher.

Thalberg persisted with his remake of Michael Arlen's The Green Hat, giving Constance Bennett the old Garbo role, rewritten by Zoe Akins. He should have left it in the files: the jaunty fatalism of the novel never came through

on film. **Outcast Lady**/A Woman of the World was the fourth of his six 1934 movies with a British background, faultlessly depicted. Miss Bennett, the only American cast, was surrounded by Hugh Williams (with her here), Herbert Marshall, Mrs Patrick Campbell, Elizabeth Allan, Robert Loraine, Ralph Forbes, Henry Stephenson, Lumsden Hare, Leo G. Carroll and Alec B. Francis. Robert Z. Leonard directed.

The 1934 production schedule finished with one of MGM's best ever: **David Copperfield** was probably the richest, most satisfying of all Dickens films, and was a great financial as well as artistic success. David O. Selznick picked George Cukor to direct, and brought in another ex-RKO colleague, Howard Estabrook, to collaborate with Hugh Walpole on the screenplay; somehow it managed to accommodate in 133 minutes' running-time all that mattered in the huge novel. W. C. Fields replaced Charles Laughton, and triumphed in a daring bit of casting as Micawber, but the most fruitful assignment for the future as well as the movie was Freddie Bartholomew (here with Fields) as young David. Selznick and Cukor found the boy while seeking locations in England; his responsive acting and precise diction made him an immediate star. The locations were never used; David Copperfield was that MGM speciality, a made-in-Hollywood British film. The long cast included Frank Lawton as David grown up, Lionel Barrymore, Madge Evans, Maureen O'Sullivan, Basil Rathbone, Edna May Oliver, Roland Young (as Uriah Heep, another successful off-casting), Lewis Stone, Elizabeth Allan, Jessie Ralph, Elsa Lanchester, Hugh Williams, Jean Cadell, Una O'Connor and dozens of others; even Walpole played a bit part.

SENSATIONAL YEARS
HARLOW AND MARX
1935

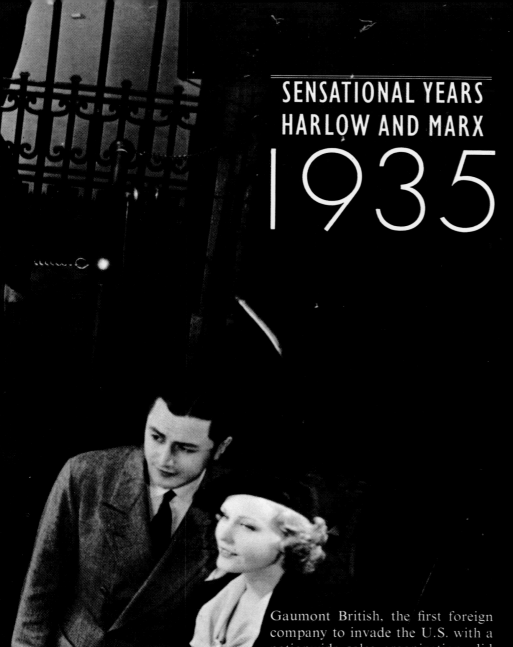

Gaumont British, the first foreign company to invade the U.S. with a nationwide sales organization, did best with Hitchcock's *39 Steps* and *The Man who Knew Too Much*: George Arliss dramas and Jessie Matthews musicals came next. Fox became 20th Century-Fox, made young Darryl Zanuck studio head and topped the ticket-selling stars list with Shirley Temple and Will Rogers, who were followed by Gable, Astaire & Rogers, Crawford, Claudette Colbert, Dick Powell, Beery, Joe E Brown and Cagney. Warners shot the works on Shakespeare with *A Midsummer Night's Dream* but made more money with new star Errol Flynn in *Captain Blood*. *Mutiny on the Bounty*, Bette Davis in *Dangerous* and Victor McLaglen in *The Informer* won Academy Awards. Paramount emerged from bankruptcy with a $3m profit (MGM netted $7½m again), reflecting the better times. Weekly world attendances rose 15% to 220m, 80m of them in the U.S.A.

Robert Taylor got top billing for the first time in **Times Square Lady**, *a melodrama about crooked gamblers, directed by George B. Seitz for the Lucien Hubbard 'B' hive. Opposite the screen's new Adonis were Helen Twelvetrees (here) and Virginia Bruce, supported by Nat Pendleton, Isabel Jewell, Jack La Rue and Pinky Tomlin, who wrote and sang its hit song, 'The Object of My Affection'. Screenplay by Albert Cohen and Robert Shannon from their original.*

George B. Seitz, one of Hollywood's most prolific directors since his Pearl White serial days, had a busy MGM year. Having launched Robert Taylor starwards in Only Eight Hours *and* Times Square Lady, *he made four good programmers in a few weeks each. Here, Seitz directing Robert Young and Madge Evans in* **Calm Yourself**, *a fast comedy starring Betty* ◁ Opposite *Furness, Nat Pendleton, Hardie Albright, Ralph Morgan; script by Arthur Kober from an Edward Hope story . . . Basil Rathbone and Aline MacMahon in* **Kind Lady**, *Bernard* △ Top Left *Schubert's adaptation of the Edward Chodorov play based on Hugh Walpole's thriller 'The Silver Casket', with Dudley Digges, Mary Carlisle, Frank Albertson, Doris Lloyd, Donald Meek . . . Maureen O'Sullivan, Joel McCrea and Adrienne Ames in* **Woman Wanted**, *a chase* △ Top Right *melodrama with Lewis Stone, Louis Calhern, Edgar Kennedy, Robert Greig and a Leonard Fields – David Silverstein script from a Wilson Collison story . . . Joseph Calleia repeating his vicious* Public Hero No. 1 *villainy in* **Exclusive** △ Above **Story**, *Michael Fessier's adaptation of Martin Mooney's newspaper-versus-gangster drama with Franchot Tone, Miss Evans, Stuart Erwin, Robert Barrat, J. Carrol Naish, Margaret Irving. Lucien Hubbard produced all but the third, a Philip Goldstone production.*

*Director Roy Del Ruth and producer John Considine Jr had one of 1935's biggest successes in **Broadway Melody of 1936** ('So new it's a year ahead!'). The original Broadway Melody song, now sung by Harry Stockwell, ushered in the movie which was otherwise no sequel to the screen's first musical. It showed what enormous technical strides had been taken in seven years of putting song, dance and stage spectacle on film. It also had fast and funny 'book' scenes by Sid Silvers, Jack McGowan and Harry Conn (from Moss Hart's original). One of those developed into the 'Sing Before Breakfast' number (here), with Eleanor Powell and Vilma and Buddy Ebsen; note the photo-montage background for the Manhattan rooftop set. Miss Powell, a whirlwind tapdancer from Broadway with toothy charm, became an instant star with this movie, which also began a long career for Ebsen; sister Vilma soon retired. Jack Benny was top-billed, sharing comedy honours with Una Merkel and scenarist Silvers; Robert Taylor and June Knight provided romance, and Frances Langford belted out the Freed–Brown songs, including 'Broadway Rhythm' and 'You Are My Lucky Star'.*

*The tried and true team – Oliver Hardy, Stan Laurel and indignant stooge Jimmy Finlayson, directed by James Horne, produced by Hal Roach – had a winner in **Bonnie Scotland**. The starring pair now appeared more remuneratively in features than in shorts and this one rolled up the biggest world-wide gross of them all. The script was by Frank Butler and Jeff Moffitt but, as usual, a prime creative contributor was Laurel; he was therefore always more highly paid than Hardy, who was solely an actor. June Lang, William Janney, Daphne Pollard and David Torrence had supporting spots.*

*Laurel and Hardy had completed a seventh full-length feature for Hal Roach (not to mention 64 shorts) by the end of 1935. It was Michael Balfe's operetta **The Bohemian Girl**, adapted by Alfred Bunn, and directed by James Horne and Charles Rogers to give maximum scope to the Stan and Ollie comedy routines. Dramatic and/or musical interludes by Mae Busch and Antonio Moreno, veterans of the silents (with them here) and Thelma Todd, Mitchell Lewis, Felix Knight and Jacqueline Wells were given*

by-the-way treatment. Jimmy Finlayson was the stars' butt again, and they were still sure-fire ticket-sellers.

*Ah, sweet mystery of showbiz! Producer Hunt Stromberg put together a soprano who acted as if every nuance had to reach the top gallery of an opera house, a baritone who didn't act at all, and an ancient (1910) operetta – and, presto, out came a smash hit establishing the screen's most successful singing team of all time. Jeanette MacDonald and Nelson Eddy in **Naughty Marietta** had cinema audiences literally applauding their Victor Herbert–Rida Johnson Young songs, 'I'm Falling in Love with Someone', 'Italian Street Song', 'Ah, Sweet Mystery of Life', etc. They were so well recorded that Douglas Shearer won an Oscar. Frank Morgan (with them here) and Elsa Lanchester, Douglass Dumbrille, Walter Kingsford, Greta Meyer, Joseph Cawthorn, Cecilia Parker and Akim Tamiroff also enacted the John Lee Mahin–Frances Goodrich and Albert Hackett screenplay, directed with W. S. Van Dyke's customary verve.*

West Point of the Air *was a successful, crowd-satisfying 1935 companion-piece to the 1928 Flying Fleet, dealing with flight training in the US Army instead of in the Navy. Wallace Beery (second from left, with Maureen O'Sullivan, Robert Young, Richard Tucker and Rosalind Russell) camera-hogged his way through the part of trainee Young's old-sweat father, supported also by Lewis Stone, James Gleason and, as Young's classmates, Russell Hardie, Robert Taylor and Henry Wadsworth. Richard Rosson directed, former director Monta Bell produced, and later producer James K. McGuinness wrote it with John Monk Saunders.*

The Flame Within was a rare solo effort in a studio given to credit-splitting: Edmund Goulding wrote the script from his own original, produced and directed it. This drama of a lady psychiatrist getting too involved with a neurotic young couple (Louis Hayward, Maureen O'Sullivan) broke no records, but it drew praise from the critics for its emotional tension, well conveyed by (left to right) Henry Stephenson, Ann Harding and Herbert Marshall.

A Night at the Opera was a smashing success, ▽ reversing the financial decline of the Marx Brothers' preceding pictures. Irving Thalberg knew what he was doing when he got the Paramount clowns to move over (dropping 'straight' brother Zeppo en route) to MGM, where they were given more opulent production and more elaborate gags, tested in a pre-filming stage tour, than ever before – although some Marx buffs deplored their yielding footage to romantic subplot and musical numbers. Sam Wood directed the George

Kaufman–Morrie Ryskind script that bristled with laugh lines for Groucho. Left to right: the monumental Margaret Dumont, singers Kitty Carlisle and Allan Jones (their hit song was 'Alone'), Chico, Groucho, Robert Emmet O'Connor, Harpo, Purnell Pratt. Walter Woolf King and Sig Ruman completed the cast.

Rosalind Russell was emerging into leading ladyship when Philo Vance gumshoed back to solve another murder in a family of neurotics, in **The Casino Murder Case**. Left to right: Paul Lukas, the new Philo; perennial butler Eric Blore; nurse Claudelle Kaye; Donald Cook (the last one you'd ever suspect); Miss Russell; serious cop Purnell Pratt; frightened maid Louise Fazenda; comic cop Ted Healy. Lukas seemed a bit heavy for Philo and the Florence Ryerson–Edgar Allan Woolf script wasn't among the best of the S. S. Van Dine series. Edwin Marin directed, Lucien Hubbard produced, with Alison Skipworth, Arthur Byron, Isabel Jewell, Leslie Fenton and Leo G. Carroll.

Public Hero Number One *harked back to the heyday of Warners' gangster cycle, and actually outclassed most of the Cagney–Robinson toughies in pace, suspense and savagery. Business was virile too. Lucien Hubbard entrusted newcomer J. Walter Ruben with direction of the Wells Root script about lawman Chester Morris (left) posing as a criminal and joining cellmate Joseph Calleia in a jail break to learn his gang's secrets. Morris had his most violently effective role since* The Big House *and Calleia, a stage actor, made a stunning movie début as a cold killer. Lionel Barrymore and Jean Arthur also starred, with Paul Kelly and Lewis Stone featured.*

Escapade, *a remake of a German hit –* Maskerade *– emerged only a year after its 1934 original. It was tailored for William Powell and Myrna Loy by producer Bernard Hyman and scenarist Herman Mankiewicz who adapted Walter Reisch's light comedy of a philandering artist in pre-war Vienna. But Myrna, having compared her MGM salary with what MGM charged other companies for her services, took a slow boat to England and awaited results. One unexpected result was a quick script rewrite for a new European discovery, Luise Rainer (here with Powell) who proceeded to waltz away with the picture. She won extraordinary raves from the critics, and Leo had a new star. Robert Z. Leonard directed, with Virginia Bruce, Mady Christians, Frank Morgan, Reginald Owen, Laura Hope Crews and Henry Travers.*

Another Myrna Loy part which made another new star while she was on strike went to Rosalind Russell in **Rendezvous**. *Signed by MGM when acting on Broadway, Rosalind had an attractively forceful style, cultivated in increasingly important roles until this one put*

her on top. William Powell played a World War I code-breaker. William K. Howard directed the ingenious screenplay devised by Bella and Samuel Spewack, P. J. Wolfson and George Oppenheimer from Major H. O. Yardley's non-fiction 'The American Black Chamber'. Binnie Barnes, Lionel Atwill, Cesar Romero, Henry Stephenson and Samuel S. Hinds were featured in the Lawrence Weingarten production.

During his brief Hollywood sojourn Hugh Walpole was kept busy by David O. Selznick. After working on (and in) David Copperfield *he collaborated with Lenore Coffee on a script from the fourth of his Herries novels. The American title* **Vanessa, Her Love Story** *(*Vanessa *in Britain) was a tip-off to the movie's emphasis on the purple romance in the book. It was a loser. William K. Howard directed (left to right) Robert Montgomery, miscast as a swaggering adventurer; Helen Hayes in the name role, which made her flee back to Broadway; and Otto Kruger as her mad husband. Also cast: May Robson, Lewis Stone, Henry Stephenson, Violet Kemble-Cooper, Donald Crisp, Jessie Ralph and George K. Arthur.*

Shakespearean actress Constance Collier, who coached MGM stars in drama and diction, brought her own formidable talents to the leading role of **Shadow of Doubt**, *an Arthur Somers Roche thriller adapted by Wells Root. George B. Seitz directed this effective 'B' for the Lucien Hubbard unit, with Ricardo Cortez and Virginia Bruce (here, with Miss Collier) and Isabel Jewell, Arthur Byron, Betty Furness, Regis Toomey and Edward Brophy.*

Always on the verge of becoming another Gable, Chester Morris found himself back in the 'Bs' after his Public Hero No. 1 *hit.* **Pursuit** *was a chase piece by Wells Root from L. G. Blochman's novel about an aviator and a female detective (Sally Eilers) hired to get a disputed child (Scotty Beckett) out of the country. Dorothy Peterson, C. Henry Gordon, Henry Travers and Minor Watson supported; Edwin L. Marin directed and Lucien Hubbard produced.*

Myrna Loy and Leo kissed and made up with a fat new contract, and within weeks of her return she had completed **Whipsaw** *with Spencer Tracy. Myrna was in a jewel-robbing gang, he was a detective, and they clashed to good box-office effect in the Howard Emmett Rogers adaptation of J. E. Grant's story, produced by Harry Rapf and directed at a fast clip by Sam Wood. Harvey Stephens, William Harrigan, Robert Warwick, Halliwell Hobbes, John Qualen and Irene Franklin supported.*

Peter Lorre's peeled-egg countenance made its Hollywood début in **Mad Love***/The Hands of* ▷ Orlac, *frightening as many moviegoers as it had in* M, *the German shocker that won him worldwide attention. The new film, based on a French story by Maurice Renard, also stemmed from Germany; it had been made silent in the Twenties with Werner Krauss in Lorre's role of a surgeon who grafted a murderer's hands on an accidentally maimed pianist. Colin Clive played the latter (Conrad Veidt in the original) with Frances Drake, Ted Healy, Sara Haden, Edward Brophy, Keye Luke and Isabel Jewell in support. The Guy Endore–John Balderston–P. J. Wolfson script dragged in some awkward comedy relief. John Considine Jr produced this last directorial effort of Karl Freund, who returned to cinematography.*

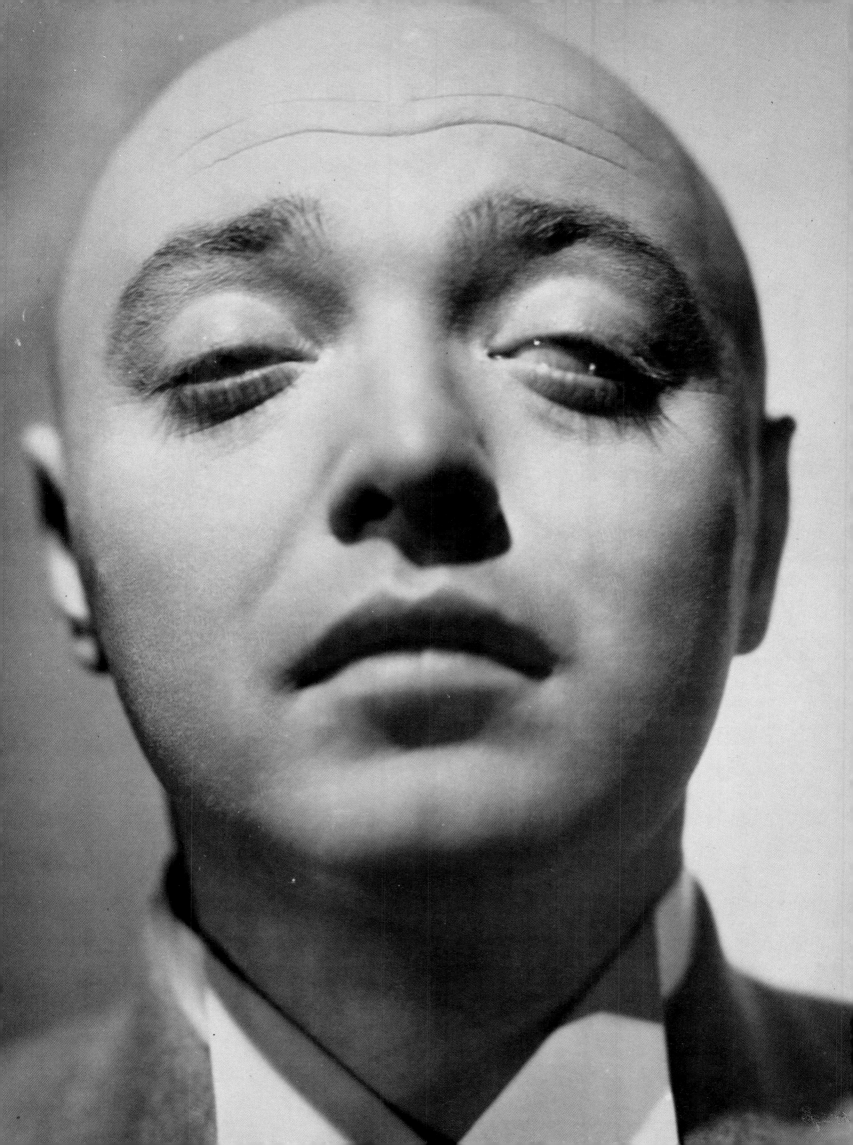

1935 *Three stars at their zenith were box-office insurance for* **China Seas**, *which hardly needed it. Thalberg's meticulous production of a good story, loaded with spectacular action sequences and zestfully directed by Tay Garnett, would have been a hit anyhow. With Wallace Beery as a modern pirate, Jean Harlow given pithy lines to snap and a loose-top-tight-bottom gown to fill, and Clark Gable in command of the ship and the screen, it became a record-breaker. Others on board were Rosalind Russell rather overdoing an English milady, Robert Benchley as a very funny drunk, Lewis Stone, Dudley Digges, C. Aubrey Smith, William Henry, Lillian Bond, Edward Brophy, Donald Meek, Emily Fitzroy and Akim Tamiroff. Screenplay by James K. McGuinness and Jules Furthman from Crosbie Garstin's novel.*

This is it: The MGM Look, personified by Joan Crawford in an Adrian gown and Oliver Marsh lighting and the adoration of two male stars, Robert Montgomery and Franchot Tone. It was the envy of competing studios, the butt of highbrow critics, and the stuff the masses' dreams were made on. **No More Ladies** exactly ▷ captured its highly polished glamour and pseudo-sophisticated romance, while the Donald Ogden Stewart–Horace Jackson script from A. E. Thomas' play supplied a dash of genuine wit. Thalberg provided the best supporting cast money could buy: Edna May Oliver, Charles Ruggles, Reginald Denny, Gail Patrick, Juliette Compton, Vivienne Osborne and Arthur Treacher. E. H. Griffith directed.

Eight years after Love, Garbo and director Clarence Brown again tackled Tolstoy's **Anna Karenina**. It gave ample evidence of how their talents had developed; Garbo, indeed, now approached perfection in screen acting. Between the two train sequences marvellously photographed by William Daniels—her first appearance through a cloud of steam, and the last sight of her rigid face in light-flashes between the moving coaches she was about to fall under—star and director made Anna as poignant a character on film as in literature. Basil Rathbone and Freddie Bartholomew won praise as her husband and son; as her lover Fredric March was a better actor than John Gilbert, if a less fiery personality. Others in the David O. Selznick production were Maureen O'Sullivan, Reginald Owen, May Robson, Reginald Denny, Phoebe Foster and Gyles Isham. Clemence Dane and Salka Viertel wrote the script.

'Look beautiful', said cameraman Milton Krasner to Robert Taylor and Jean Parker. They were abundantly equipped to do so, and not required to do much else in **Murder in the Fleet**. A so-so whodunit written and directed by Edward Sedgwick, the Lucien Hubbard production featured Ted Healy, Una Merkel, Jean Hersholt, Nat Pendleton, Donald Cook, Mischa Auer and Ward Bond.

By 1935 Jean Harlow was a shining example of MGM star-making. The gang-moll type of a few years before had been polished and refined without (Mayer forbid!) losing her frank sex attraction, and careful attention had been given to developing her acting talent, especially for comedy. **Reckless** seemingly extended her range to singing and dancing (doubles were used for both) plus some high-key dramatics. The P. J. Wolfson script was about a Broadway star almost destroyed by scandal when her husband committed suicide, a situation coolly lifted from Harlow's life. The dubious taste of this could be blamed on producer David O. Selznick, who wrote the original under the name Oliver Jeffries; otherwise he and director Victor Fleming gave evidence of their showmanship rather than artistry, later displayed in Gone With the Wind. William Powell (here) and May Robson, Ted Healy, Nat Pendleton, singers Allan Jones (début) and Nina Mae McKinney were show-business characters and Franchot Tone, Rosalind Russell, Henry Stephenson, Leon Waycoff (later Ames) and James Ellison represented Park Avenue. Two

good songs emerged: 'Everything's Been Done Before' and Jerome Kern's title number.

Spencer Tracy's illustrious 20 years under MGM contract began modestly enough with a crime reporter role in **The Murder Man**, opposite Virginia Bruce. Among their supporting cast was another new name on the company's list: James Stewart, in his first movie. Tim Whelan wrote and directed the Harry Rapf 'B', with Lionel Atwill, Harvey Stephens, Robert Barrat, William Demarest and Lucien Littlefield.

Jean Harlow and Spencer Tracy were unlikely purveyors of parental devotion in **Riffraff**, a Frances Marion screenplay about a waterfront tuna cannery, and another popular hit for Thalberg. Only this final sequence was gooey; the preceding reels were strictly hardboiled, with the co-stars either yelling insults at each other or defying the world, the fish and the devil. Joseph Calleia, Una Merkel, J. Farrell Mac-Donald and Mickey Rooney supported them; director was J. Walter Ruben.

The biting wit of Herman Mankiewicz's dialogue got the rosiest of the bouquets critics tossed at **After Office Hours**. It was bandied by Clark Gable as a newspaper editor, Constance Bennett as his you're-fired-you're-hired reporter, and Harvey Stephens (left) as the unsuspected murderer in their juiciest crime story; also cast were Billie Burke, Hale Hamilton, Katherine Alexander, Stuart Erwin and Henry Travers. They were directed by Robert Z. Leonard in the Bernard Hyman production.

One of those tiresome hate-at-first-sight romances gave Joan Crawford and Brian Aherne a hard time keeping the customers entertained in **I Live My Life**. She was a spoiled debutante, he an archaeologist who didn't dig her society crowd: Frank Morgan, Aline MacMahon, Fred Keating, Jessie Ralph, Hedda Hopper. Others in the Bernard Hyman production, directed by an off-form W. S. Van Dyke, were Eric Blore, Arthur Treacher, Etienne Girardot, Edward Brophy and Lionel Stander. Not one of Joseph Mankiewicz's best scripts, said critics.

Playing one of her bewitching bitches, Helen Vinson made her MGM bow, (producer Philip Goldstone and director Edward Ludwig were newcomers too) in **Age of Indiscretion** opposite Paul Lukas. She was his wife but sleeping around. A fight for custody of their child (David Jack Holt) was the substance of Lenore Coffee's story, scripted by Otis Garrett and Leon Gordon. Also cast: May Robson, Madge Evans, Ralph Forbes, Catherine Doucet, Beryl Mercer and Minor Watson.

*Heather Angel welcomes Cicely Courtneidge to MGM for her only Hollywood movie, **The Perfect Gentleman**/The Imperfect Lady. The title change acknowledged Cicely's fame in Britain; in America co-star Frank Morgan was the top name. Changes were also frequent during the comedy's bumpy shooting schedule in the Harry Rapf unit. Credit, if that's the right word, finally went to Tim Whelan for direction and Edward Childs Carpenter for script. Herbert Mundin, Una O'Connor, Henry Stephenson, Forrester Harvey, Mary Forbes and Doris Lloyd joined Cicely, Frank and Heather in the valiant cast.*

*Hal Roach produced one of his rare features without Laurel and Hardy in 1935 at his studio down the road from MGM. It was **Vagabond Lady**, with happy-go-lucky Robert Young snatching Evelyn Venable from stuffed-shirt Reginald Denny at the altar. Written by Frank Butler, the romantic comedy was directed by Sam Taylor, with Berton Churchill, Frank Craven, Forrester Harvey and Ferdinand Gottschalk.*

*Charles Butterworth, a good supporting comedian, lacked star quality and receipts were poor for **Baby-Face Harrington**. It kidded gangster movies by having the timid Mr. Butterworth (left) wrongly identified as America's most wanted killer, pursued by mobster Nat Pendleton as well as the cops. The Edgar Selwyn production, written by Edwin Knopf and Nunnally Johnson from a play by William LeBaron and Selwyn, was directed at a fast clip by Raoul Walsh. Also cast: Una Merkel, Harvey Stephens, Eugene Pallette, Ruth Selwyn, Eddie Nugent, Donald Meek and Claude Gillingwater.*

*Lucile Watson, Maureen O'Sullivan and Edmund Gwenn, making his Hollywood bow, in **The Bishop Misbehaves**/The Bishop's Misadventures, a Lawrence Weingarten flop. E. A. Dupont, famous for the dramatic power of his German Variety, was unaccountably the director of this mild detective comedy set in a quaintly olde worlde England, whimsically scripted from Frederick Jackson's play by Leon Gordon and George Auerbach. Reginald Owen, Dudley Digges, Lillian Bond, Melville Cooper and Robert Greig supported with British phlegm, Norman Foster with Yankee grit.*

*Harvey Stephens, Una Merkel, Franchot Tone and Leo's old friend Conrad Nagel in **One New York Night**/The Trunk Mystery. Considering the prestige of its makers – producer Bernard Hyman, director Jack Conway, cameraman Oliver Marsh, script by Frank Davis from Edward Childs Carpenter's play – this whodunit set in a big hotel was a weak sister at the paybox. Steffi Duna, Charles Starrett and Harold Huber also performed.*

Three Live Ghosts, *with Beryl Mercer and Richard Arlen in Fredrick Isham's old stage warhorse about soldiers coming home to find themselves officially listed as dead. Arlen, Claude Allister and Charles McNaughton played the title roles, with Cecilia Parker, Dudley Digges and Robert Greig also prominent. John Considine Jr produced and H. Bruce Humberstone directed the C. Gardner Sullivan screenplay.*

*Richard Thorpe had been directing quickies for ten years when Mayer had an idea he might be another W. S. Van Dyke for MGM. His first assignment, in true Van Dyke style, was a location trip to Tahiti with cameraman Clyde DeVinna to make **Last of the Pagans**, another picturesque study of native life with a superimposed melodrama (by John Farrow). It turned out rather well and established Thorpe at the studio; but a no-name cast restricted its box-office. Mala, discovery of Eskimo, stripped down in warmer climate to play Lotus Long's hero; they were the only Hollywood players cast by producer Philip Goldstone.*

*Harry Stockwell, Virginia Bruce's new leading man in **Here Comes the Band**, was a pleasant fellow with a good voice. But he made his most notable contribution to the screen at home while this movie was in production. Early in the following year his son was born: Dean Stockwell, destined to be an MGM child prodigy and a fine adult actor . . . Meanwhile, back at the studio: Ted Lewis and his band starred in this minor musical written (with Ralph Spence and Victor Mansfield) and directed by Paul Sloane, produced by Lucien Hubbard. Ted Healy, Nat Pendleton, Donald Cook, Spanky McFarland, Bert Roach and Ferdinand Gottschalk were also cast. They were all overshadowed by Billy Gilbert as a would-be singer whose slowly erupting sneezes made one of the funniest scenes of the year.*

*'If you're the heir of a rich aunt with a weak heart, take her to see this,' said one reviewer of **Mark of the Vampire**. Elizabeth Allan and Lionel Barrymore were the bemused heroine and the professor of demonology(!) in this revival of the horror cycle; old shock-and-shudder experts like director Tod Browning, writer Guy Endore and Dracula actor Bela Lugosi gave it box-office fangs. Jean Hersholt, Jessie Ralph, Henry Wadsworth, Donald Meek and Holmes Herbert were the virtuous and villainous villagers sorted out by detective Lionel Atwill. E. J. Mannix produced, a rare excursion from his studio manager duties.*

With its manhunt melodrama properly combined with its Rudolf Friml–Herbert Stothart score, the musical version of **Rose Marie** was better entertainment than the silent version had been. Jeanette MacDonald and Nelson Eddy trilled and boomed 'Indian Love Call', 'Song of the Mounties' and 'Rose Marie, I Love You' –and that last sentiment was echoed by the public to the tune of paybox millions. New star material seemed likely in James Stewart as Jeanette's brother (here), but another supporting actor, David Niven, was hardly noticed. Reginald Owen, Allan Jones, Gilda Gray, Alan Mowbray, Una O'Connor, Robert Greig and Herman Bing were also cast. Hunt Stromberg, W. S. Van Dyke and Francis Goodrich and Albert Hackett produced, directed and scripted.

Projectors burst into flame and censors dropped their scissors in shock as Jack Benny and Una Merkel threw themselves into this passionate clinch in **It's In the Air**. Benny, then America's top radio comedian, had Una as his wife and Ted Healy as his partner in a series of conman escapades concocted by scenarists Byron Morgan and Lew Lipton. Alas, the crowds stayed home listening to Benny on the radio. Charles Reisner directed the E. J. Mannix production, with Nat Pendleton, Mary Carlisle, Harvey Stephens, Johnny Arthur and Purnell Pratt.

Jackie Cooper was growing so fast they had to call in Spanky McFarland from the 'Our Gang' shorts to play him 'as a child' in **O'Shaughnessy's Boy**. Otherwise the Leonard Praskins–Otis Garrett script was pretty much the Cooper –Wallace Beery formula, but their Champ box office furore wasn't repeated. Maybe the public was growing up too. Above, Beery, having lost an arm in a tiger-taming act, returned to try it again, inspired by Jackie's 'You can do it, Dad!' and applauded by Willard Robertson and Clarence Muse. Others in the Philip Goldstone production directed by Richard Boleslawski were Leona Maricle, Sara Haden and Henry Stephenson.

MGM climaxed a remarkable year with a great film from each of its top three producers, released in quick succession towards the end of 1935. Thalberg's **Mutiny on the Bounty** was the biggest success of the three, and winner of the best picture Oscar. He bought screen rights of the book by Nordhoff and Hall from Frank Lloyd along with his services as director, and assigned Talbot Jennings, Jules Furthman and Carey Wilson to write the script. Perfectly cast were Clark Gable, splendid as Fletcher Christian–American accent regardless; and Charles Laughton as Captain Bligh, providing mimics with material for decades to come. Their conflict had even the most blasé movie-goers tense with excitement, so strong was the narrative drive and so colourful (in black-and-white) its depiction by all hands. Arthur Edeson's camerawork and editing by Margaret Booth, the studio's perennial cutting genius, were outstanding. Cast included Franchot Tone, Dudley Digges, Eddie Quillan, Herbert Mundin, Donald Crisp, Spring Byington, Henry Stephenson, Douglas Walton and Ian Wolfe . . . David O. Selznick's **A Tale of Two Cities** was even more spectacular. It was the best of several screen versions of Dickens' French Revolution story. Ronald Colman (left, with Elizabeth Allan, Edna May Oliver, Fay Chaldicott and Claude Gillingwater) miraculously removed the ham from Sydney Carton's

self-sacrifice and made a believable centrepiece for the stirring dramatics in the W. P. Lipscomb–S. N. Behrman script. Jack Conway used 17,000 extras for the Paris mob scenes, which achieved bloodcurdling fury; his long cast included Basil Rathbone, Reginald Owen, Blanche Yurka, Donald Woods, Henry B. Walthall, Fritz Leiber, Isabel Jewell, H. B. Warner, Lucille LaVerne and Tully Marshall. Oliver T. Marsh's photography, and–as in the other two films–Cedric Gibbons' art direction and Herbert Stothart's music score were notable . . . Hunt Stromberg's contribution, **Ah, Wilderness**, was much quieter, and for some critics the most memorable of the three movies. Director Clarence Brown evoked just the right mood of gentle nostalgia for Eugene O'Neill's uncharacteristic play, whose tender comedy was preserved intact in the Albert Hackett–Frances Goodrich script. Although Wallace Beery and Lionel Barrymore were top-billed, and very good, as his bibulous uncle and understanding father respectively, the film was carried by Eric Linden (here, with Spring Byington as his mother) in a painfully accurate portrait of adolescence. Linden had a busy career, but never such a good part again except his 'Golden Boy' on the London stage. Aline MacMahon, Charley Grapewin, Cecilia Parker, Mickey Rooney, Frank Albertson, Bonita Granville and Eddie Nugent also scored.

1936

There were 97,344 cinemas in the world: Russia had 34,990, the US 18,192, Germany 5,273, Britain 4,950, Italy 4,800, France 4,100, Spain 3,500, all others less than 2,000 each.

Mutiny on the Bounty continued to coin money, and with *San Francisco, Great Ziegfeld*, etc., zoomed the MGM-Loew's profit to $11m. Rivals were *Anthony Adverse, Mr Deeds Goes to Town, Story of Louis Pasteur* and *Magnificent Obsession*. Robert Taylor, Jeanette MacDonald and Gary Cooper displaced Will Rogers, Wallace Beery and James Cagney in the Top Ten star list; Claudette Colbert was still in it and was the highest-paid individual in America, receiving $302,000 for the year. Second highest, surprisingly, was Warner Baxter with $280,000.

Outside the USA the biggest attractions were Shirley Temple, Cooper, Clark Gable, Fred Astaire and Ginger Rogers, Charles Chaplin, Garbo, Marlene Dietrich, Grace Moore and Robert Taylor. New stars emerged: Tyrone Power, Humphrey Bogart, Ann Sheridan, Henry Fonda, Dorothy Lamour, Fred MacMurray, Alice Faye, Cary Grant, Madeleine Carroll. Chaplin rang down the curtain on the silents by delivering the last non-talkie, *Modern Times*.

Charley Grapewin, Spring Byington, Lionel Barrymore and Eric Linden stepped en masse *from* Ah, Wilderness *into* **The Voice of Bugle Ann**, *a drama of feuds in the Missouri backwoods climaxed by Barrymore shooting Dudley Digges for killing his foxhound. There was a happy ending for everybody (except Digges and the hound) and the movie was a small success. John Considine Jr produced and Richard Thorpe directed the Harvey Gates–Samuel Hoffenstein script from Mackinlay Kantor's novel. Maureen O'Sullivan played opposite Linden. The bitch playing the title role refused to give voice to her ululating bark, so Barrymore took her home to get her used to him. Next day, he asked his manservant, 'Has she bugled yet?' 'Yassuh!' was the reply, 'Twice on the rug and once under the piano.'*

top of her very loud voice. The Hal Roach production, directed by Harry Lachman (quite a switch from his preceding Dante's Inferno*) was freely adapted from a W. W. Jacobs story by Richard Connell, Felix Adler, Charles Rogers and Jack Jevne . . .* **Way Out West** *kept Jimmy Finlayson in his usual state of outrage. The Roach production (associate producer, Stan Laurel) worked in some hilarious song-and-dance sequences for the stars, among gags dreamed up by Rogers, Adler and James Parrott (brother of Charley Chase). Director was James Horne, Sharon Lynne and Rosina Lawrence were the girls.*

Leo returned to Viva Villa *country for* **The Robin Hood of El Dorado**, *another compound of fact and fiction about a Mexican bandit—with weaker box-office response. Warner Baxter played Joaquin Murietta, with Bruce Cabot and Margo (here) and Eric Linden, Ann Loring, J. Carrol Naish and Harvey Stephens. William Wellman's direction got plenty of action out of the script he wrote with Melvin Levy and the versatile Joseph Calleia. John Considine Jr produced.*

Laurel and Hardy continued to keep the fans happy. In **Our Relations** *they had twin brothers, sailors out on the town, and understandably confused wives. Left to right: Oliver, Stan, Daphne Pollard, Betty Healy, Lona Andre and Iris Adrian. Iris enlivened movies for the next 30 years by delivering most of her lines at the*

Florenz Ziegfeld dazzled Broadway for decades with his extravagant 'Follies' revues, but he never, even in his most spendthrift transports, approached the staggering opulence MGM lavished on his biography, **The Great Ziegfeld.** △ *Hunt Stromberg paid about $2m for three hours of film, topping the cost of* Mutiny on The Bounty *to make it the company's most expensive production since* Ben-Hur. *It re-*

turned over double its cost, and received an Academy Award (as did Luise Rainer). There were several musical numbers like this one ('You Never Looked So Beautiful Before', with Virginia Bruce glorified at top); and, memorably, the 'Pretty Girl is Like a Melody' scene with its revolving setpiece like a gigantic wedding cake bearing tons of girls, costumes, men and props, and Dennis Morgan (called Stanley

Morner and for some reason voice-dubbed by Allan Jones) singing the Irving Berlin song, written for the Ziegfeld Follies of 1919. Sets were by John Harkrider, former Ziegfeld aide, like the film's scenarist, William Anthony McGuire, and dance director, Seymour Felix. But all the dazzle would have been pointless without the strong narrative carried by William Powell as the great showman, Miss Rainer and

Myrna Loy as Anna Held and Billie Burke, his actress wives, and Frank Morgan as his right-hand man. Directed by Robert Z. Leonard, they were all excellent. Three top cameramen were credited: Oliver Marsh, Ray June and George Folsey. Also cast: Fanny Brice, Ray Bolger, Reginald Owen, Gilda Gray, Nat Pendleton, William Demarest, Ernest Cossart, Raymond Walburn and Herman Bing.

Director George B. Seitz kept 'em rolling off his assembly line: Lionel Atwill, Ann Loring and Louis Hayward in the ironically titled **Absolute Quiet**, *Harry Clork's screenplay about a planeload of shady characters forced down on a financier's ranch; with Irene Hervey, Stuart Erwin, Raymond Walburn, Wallace Ford, Matt Moore, Harvey Stephens, J. Carrol Naish; John Considine Jr produced . . . Robert Young and Betty Furness in* **The Three Wise Guys**, *a Damon Runyon yarn about Broadway sharpies, scripted by Elmer Harris; with Walburn, Bruce Cabot, Herman Bing, Stephens, Donald Meek, Thurston Hall; Harry Rapf produced . . . The fascinating English-Austrian*

Elissa Landi and Edmund Lowe in **Mad Holiday**, *a Florence Ryerson–Edgar Allan Woolf comedy whodunit in Thin Man style, from Joseph Santley's 'Murder in a Chinese Theatre'; with ZaSu Pitts, Edmund Gwenn, Ted Healy, Edgar Kennedy, Gustav von Seyffertitz, Walter Kingsford; produced by Rapf.*

'Philo Vance needs a kick in the pants' rhymed the immortal Ogden Nash about S. S. Van Dine's ineffably poised detective. Philo didn't get that, but was brought down to earth a bit by Edmund Lowe, fifth actor to play him, in **The Garden Murder Case**. *Edwin Marin directed the Bertram Millhauser screenplay about a series of murders committed under hypnosis; Lucien Hubbard produced. Left to right: Jessie Ralph, Benita Hume, Grant Mitchell, Nat Pendleton, Lowe and Virginia Bruce. Also cast: H. B. Warner, Douglas Walton, Gene Lockhart, Kent Smith, Frieda Inescort and Henry B. Walthall.*

Jackie Cooper was now a sturdy 15, and lachrymose scenes like this one in **Tough Guy** *lacked their old audience appeal. But he and Joseph Calleia (the first sympathetic role for the first Maltese movie star) were talented enough to withstand the scene-stealing of a dog unblushingly billed as Rin-Tin-Tin Jr. Several surefire elements were combined by writers Florence Ryerson and Edgar Allan Woolf and director Chester Franklin in this movie, produced by Harry Rapf: runaway rich boy, superintelligent dog and escaping gunman were pursued by cops and gangsters in a series of chase sequences. Also cast: Jean Hersholt, Harvey Stephens, Mischa Auer, Robert Warwick.*

The dear old thing charming Maureen O'Sullivan and Frank Lawton in **The Devil Doll** *is really a fiend incarnate, a creature of unspeakable evil – in short, Lionel Barrymore in drag. He had discovered how to shrink people to midget size to bend them to his wicked will. Tod Browning had lots of fun directing actors in oversize sets with huge props and furniture. Abraham Merritt's thriller, 'Burn, Witch, Burn', was adapted by Browning, Guy Endore, Garrett Fort and, an old hand at making people shrink, Erich von Stroheim. Heading the supporting cast in the E. J. Mannix production was Henry B. Walthall at the end of a career that began when the movies did.*

Roland Young, Loretta Young, Franchot Tone, Jessie Ralph and E. E. Clive in **The Unguarded Hour** *which also featured Lewis Stone, Dudley Digges, Henry Daniell (the London stage*

actor's Hollywood début), Robert Greig and Aileen Pringle. Adapted from Ladislas Fodor's play (English version, Bernard Merivale) by Howard Emmett Rogers and Leon Gordon, the plot had more twists than a pretzel. It opened with Tone as prosecutor in a murder trial and climaxed with him on trial for another murder, his wife (Loretta) holding the key to both cases. Sam Wood directed the Lawrence Weingarten production, which was quite a success.

Henry Daniell was in fine sneering form in **Under Cover of Night**, *a Lucien Hubbard quickie directed by George B. Seitz. The movie broke no records but it gave him the central role: a crazed scientist who did away with Sara Haden, Dorothy Peterson and Theodore Von Eltz and was just getting around to Florence Rice (here) when detective Edmund Lowe, cop Nat Pendleton and hero Dean Jagger broke in. Bertram Millhauser's screenplay had a university locale.*

A useful new director of bread-and-butter 'Bs' was recruited in fast-shooting Errol Taggart. His three crime thrillers of 1936, all produced by Lucien Hubbard (the first with Michael Fessier and the others with Samuel Marx) were: **Women are Trouble**, *with Florence Rice, Stuart Erwin and Paul Kelly; also Margaret*

Irving, Harold Huber and Raymond Hatton; script by Fessier from George Harmon Coxe's original . . . **The Longest Night**, *odd title for the shortest feature – a mere 50 minutes – MGM ever made; with Leslie Fenton and Julie Haydon; also Robert Young, Florence Rice,*

Ted Healy, Catherine Doucet, Janet Beecher and Sidney Toler; script by Robert Andrews from a Cortland Fitzsimmons novel . . . **Sinner Take All**, with Joseph Calleia, Margaret Lindsay, Bruce Cabot; also Stanley Ridges, Vivienne Osborne and Charley Grapewin; script by Leonard Lee and Walter Wise from Whitman Chambers' 'Murder for a Wanton'.

In case anybody thought The Thin Man *just a happy accident, the same people got together two years later and made that rarity, a sequel as good as the original.* **After the Thin Man** *was produced by Hunt Stromberg, directed by W. S. Van Dyke, written by Frances Goodrich and Albert Hackett, starred William Powell and Myrna Loy, and was a smash hit. The fun and homicide took place in San Francisco this time, involved Elissa Landi (accused), James Stewart (guilty), Joseph Calleia, Alan Marshal, Jessie Ralph, Sam Levene, Dorothy McNulty, George Zucco and Asta. Left to right: Powell, Levene, Miss Loy, Stewart.*

Buddy Ebsen, Frances Langford, Eleanor Powell, James Stewart, Sid Silvers and Una Merkel *in* **Born to Dance**, *another of the year's big grossers. Cole Porter, cleverest of songwriters, composed his first MGM score, including two everlasting hits, 'Easy to Love' and 'I've Got You Under My Skin', for this big, brassy musical directed by Roy Del Ruth and produced by Jack Cummings. Built around Miss Powell, the find of* Broadway Melody of 1936, *its script by Jack McGowan and Silvers had the nerve to make her the understudy of a temperamental revue star whom she replaced at the last moment to save the show. That she was a dancer, while the star, played by Virginia Bruce, was a singer, was a detail left unexplained for all time. The heroes were sailors on leave, another musical comedy cliché, but it was good fun, lavish and tuneful. Also cast: Raymond Walburn, Alan Dinehart and Reginald Gardiner.*

It took a battery of writers too numerous to mention to knock out the simple screenplay elevating Patsy Kelly from short to feature stardom: **Kelly the Second**. *Patsy played the trainer and Charley Chase the manager of a dimwitted prizefighter (Guinn Williams) and generated a lot of laughs in the process of making him a champ. Hal Roach produced and directed, with Pert Kelton, Harold Huber, Maxie Rosenbloom, Billy Gilbert and Edward Brophy.*

Hugh Herbert, Walter Abel *and* Charles Butterworth *as middle-aged men carefully trying to capture youth's careless rapture in* **We Went to College**/The Old School Tie. *Joseph Santley directed the amusing class-reunion comedy, written by Richard Maibaum and Maurice Rapf from a George Oppenheimer–Finley P. Dunne original. Also cast: Una Merkel, Edith Atwater, Walter Catlett. Harry Rapf produced.*

Wallace Beery movies always turned a nice profit, and playwright George Kelly whipped up a modestly entertaining script for him in **Old Hutch**. *Harry Rapf produced and J. Walter Ruben directed the comedy about a ne'er-do-well who found $100,000 in buried loot and couldn't spend it because everybody knew he hadn't earned a dollar in years. Eric Linden and Cecilia Parker reprised their* Ah, Wilderness *romance and Elizabeth Patterson (here with Beery), Donald Meek and Virginia Grey supported.*

George Fitzmaurice returned to direct Mark Reed's comedy from Broadway, **Petticoat Fever**, *Frank Davis' first MGM production. The Harold Goldman script opened out the*

action a bit, but the yarn of a sex-starved radio operator (Robert Montgomery) and the first girl he had seen for two years (Myrna Loy) was mostly talk. Reginald Owen (left) played her fiancé, crashlanded near Bob's Labrador shack, and Winifred Shotter, prominent in British movies, made a late appearance as Bob's betrothed. Although its expert players got some laughs, the Arctic chill gradually seeped through to the paybox figures.

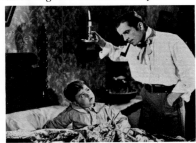

Hal Roach continued to crash the feature-length market without the aid of Laurel and Hardy, and with only mild results. **Mr Cinderella** starred Jack Haley as a barber posing as a millionaire, directed by Buster Keaton's old guide, Edward Sedgwick, in a Richard Flournoy–Arthur V. Jones–Jack Jevne screenplay. Left to right: Raymond Walburn, Betty Furness, Robert McWade, Kathleen Lockhart, Edward Brophy, Monroe Owsley, Rosina Lawrence, Haley and Tom Dugan; also cast were Iris Adrian, Arthur Treacher and Toby Wing . . . **General Spanky** incongruously teamed the elegant Phillips Holmes with Spanky McFarland, the fat tot of 'Our Gang', in a Civil War melodrama by Flournoy, Hal Yates and John Guedal. Ralph Morgan, Irving Pichel, Miss Lawrence, Hobart Bosworth and Louise Beavers also performed for directors Gordon Douglas and Fred Newmeyer.

Fury *was not one of the biggest box-office smashes, but it helped to make 1936 a vintage MGM year. Spencer Tracy gave his most telling performance to date in this superbly cinematic indictment of mob violence, directed with jolting force by Fritz Lang who also collaborated with Bartlett Cormack on the screenplay from Norman Krasna's original. Having secretly escaped a jail burned down by a lynching crowd, the innocent fugitive hid with his brothers (Frank Albertson and George Walcott, centre and right) while his persecutors were tried for causing his death. Sylvia Sidney in her only MGM film, Walter Abel, Bruce Cabot, Walter Brennan and Edward Ellis had other key roles. Joseph Mankiewicz produced.*

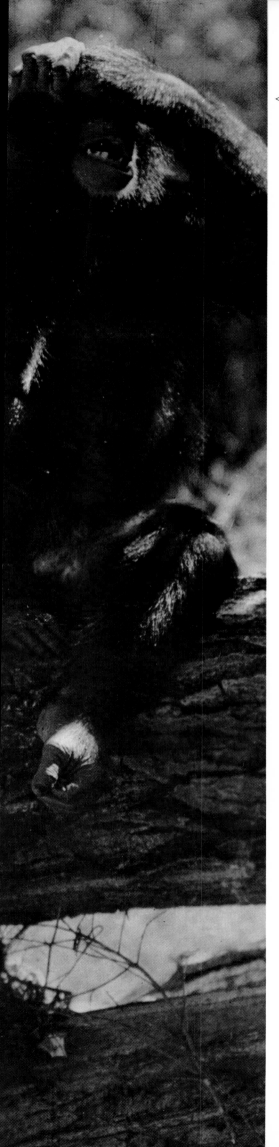

Mayer was taking no chances with the Tarzan goldmine and **Tarzan Escapes** was put back into production for virtually a complete remake after a so-so audience reaction at a preview early in 1936. Retakes were standard procedure at MGM, but this was the first wholesale job since Prosperity in 1932. It yielded rich box office ore. Johnny Weissmuller, Maureen O'Sullivan and Cheeta the chimp ran, leaped and swam through marvellously impossible jungle adventures in the Cyril Hume script, directed by Richard Thorpe. Film editor Sam Zimbalist got his first crack at producing, and John Buckler, Benita Hume, William Henry, Herbert Mundin and E. E. Clive were featured.

Romantic scenes with Chester Morris and Irene Hervey relieved the grim realism of **The Three Godfathers** in the third of four movie versions of Peter B. Kyne's story. (Offscreen, Irene became the wife of one singing star, Allan Jones, and the mother of another, Jack Jones.) Lewis Stone and Walter Brennan joined Morris to play the trio of fugitive gunmen who paused in their desert trek to rescue the newborn baby they found in a covered wagon with its dying mother. Joseph Mankiewicz produced and Richard Boleslawski directed, getting full dramatic value from the E. E. Paramore–Manuel Seff script. Also cast: Dorothy Tree, Willard Robertson, Sidney Toler.

'Hollywood is worried by star shortage. One company, MGM, has corralled most of the moneymaking names.' ('Daily Express', London, September 1936). Shedding a crocodile tear for his rivals, Leo tossed four top names into a comedy script so good it would have clicked with unknowns in the leads. With William Powell, Myrna Loy, Spencer Tracy (here) and Jean Harlow, **Libeled Lady** became a brilliant triumph. The Maurine Watkins–Howard Emmett Rogers–George Oppenheimer script, about an heiress slapping a $5m. libel suit on a newspaper, glittered with wit, and Jack Conway directed for overlapping laughs. It got them, also huge receipts. Walter Connolly, Cora Witherspoon, E. E. Clive and Charley Grapewin were prominent in the Lawrence Weingarten production.

The most sensational profit-maker of 1936 was **San Francisco**, which unexpectedly nosed past The Great Ziegfeld in the popularity stakes to become one of MGM's all-time winners. Star power was an important factor; Clark Gable, Jeanette MacDonald and Spencer Tracy were at their best in roles tailormade by Anita Loos, whose husband John Emerson co-produced with Bernard Hyman. It was also strong musically; Jeanette's songs ranged from a 'Faust' aria to a hit ballad 'Would You?' and included a title song so rousing that San Francisco has made it the city's anthem ever since. Robert Hopkins' story, set in the rowdy Barbary Coast district in 1906, had sure appeal. But the big knockout punch was the earthquake sequence, rocking and roaring for ten minutes of newsreel-like realism. Arnold Gillespie's special effects, Oliver T. Marsh's photography and Douglas Shearer's theatre-shaking sound recording created an illusion which was for many years unsurpassed among movies' technical achievements. Much of the credit for the picture's stunning impact went to director W. S. Van Dyke, whose cast included Jack Holt, Jessie Ralph, Ted Healy, Shirley Ross, Margaret Irving and Harold Huber.

Cynics who had expected Thalberg's version of **Romeo and Juliet** to be just an expensive indulgence for his wife were confounded. His infinite capacity for taking pains – not to mention retaking – resulted in a production of visual and verbal beauty, praised by the great majority of critics. The picture was so lavishly produced that it showed a bookkeeping loss of almost $1m., but MGM got its money's worth in praise and prestige. Surprisingly, the most highly lauded performance was Norma Shearer's Juliet. With no stage, let alone Shakespearean, experience, she had studied and rehearsed for months under Constance Collier and other tutors, then gave the part an air of spontaneity and a radiance all her own. She had indispensable aid from George Cukor's direction and the ardent Romeo of Leslie Howard (seen here with her between scenes). Both stars were really too old for their roles, but it didn't hurt, the rest of the cast being scaled up in age accordingly. John Barrymore could have played Mercutio with his eyes shut, and almost did; he and Basil Rathbone, C. Aubrey Smith, Ralph Forbes, Reginald Denny, Conway Tearle, Henry Kolker, Robert Warwick and Violet Kemble-Cooper were impressive; Edna May Oliver and Andy Devine struck discordant notes. Talbot Jennings' screenplay clarified without distorting.

Audiences responded faintly when three of Robert Louis Stevenson's 'Suicide Club' stories were knocked into one by E. E. Paramore and Manuel Seff for new MGM producer Louis D. Lighton's **Trouble for Two**/The Suicide Club. *It was a nice try, but the essentially modern Robert Montgomery and Rosalind Russell seemed unhappily cast as 1880 Ruritanians. J. Walter Ruben's direction was also on the fish-out-of-water side. Supporting cast: Frank Morgan (centre), Louis Hayward, Reginald Owen, E. E. Clive, Walter Kingsford, Tom Moore, Pedro de Cordoba, Robert Greig and (the stars as children) David Jack Holt, Virginia Weidler.*

The Lucien Hubbard–Edwin Marin producer-director team manufactured double-feature fodder with boundless energy in 1936. Four more were: Joseph Calleia, Robert Young, Florence Rice in **Sworn Enemy**, *with Lewis Stone, Nat Pendleton, Harvey Stephens, Leslie Fenton; crime drama by Richard Wormser, script by Wells Root . . . H. B. Warner, Katherine Alexander, Leo Carrillo, Benita Hume in* **Moonlight Murder**, *with Chester* ▽

The delectable Ann Sothern made her MGM début in **Dangerous Number**, *preceding her long contract by a couple of years. With Cora Witherspoon as her nutty ex-burlesque-queen mother, she played an actress whose caprices maddened staid husband Robert Young. Richard Thorpe directed the Lou Ostrow production from a script by Carey Wilson. Reginald Owen, Dean Jagger, Marla Shelton and Franklin Pangborn were featured.*

Wife Versus Secretary *showed what thoroughly professional writing, production and acting can do for a trite theme. The story, a typical Faith Baldwin magazine piece, was polished by Norman Krasna, Alice Duer Miller and John Lee Mahin, director Clarence Brown and producer Hunt Stromberg until it shone like the silver that poured into the box offices. A major reason for this success was the cast: a restrained and charming Jean Harlow as the secretary; Clark Gable, vital in almost every frame of the film; and May Robson as his mother, igniting the jealousy of his wife, Myrna Loy, who was at her subtle best. James Stewart, George Barbier, Hobart Cavanaugh, Gilbert Emery and Tom Dugan supported.*

fever, he had her, and W. S. Van Dyke had another in his seemingly endless series of hits. Jean Hersholt, John Eldredge, Samuel S. Hinds, Jed Prouty and Pedro de Cordoba were also in the Lawrence Weingarten production.

Three phases of Hollywood fame are represented in this shot from **Piccadilly Jim**. *Robert Montgomery and Madge Evans (right) were the stars, Aileen Pringle was an ex-star playing a small part, and the unbilled Dennis O'Keefe was emerging from the extra ranks into future stardom. The P. G. Wodehouse story, adapted by Charles Brackett and Edwin Knopf, was smartly directed by Robert Z. Leonard and performed by expert farceurs, including Frank Morgan, Eric Blore, Billie Burke, Robert Benchley, Ralph Forbes, Cora Witherspoon, Grant Mitchell, Billy Bevan and E. E. Clive. Harry Rapf produced.*

Morris, Madge Evans, Frank McHugh, Grant Mitchell, J. Carrol Naish, Duncan Renaldo; whodunit in an opera company, by Florence Ryerson, Edgar Allan Woolf . . . James Stewart, Ted Healy, Wendy Barrie in **Speed**, △ *with Una Merkel, Ralph Morgan; script by Michael Fessier from a racing car yarn by Lawrence Bachmann (future head of the MGM British studio), Milton Krims . . . . Edward Brophy, Stuart Erwin, Edmund Gwenn, Florence Rice, Robert Armstrong in* **The All-American Chump**/The Country Bumpkin, *with Harvey Stephens, E. E. Clive; con-man comedy by Lawrence Kimble.*

Robert Taylor was now so big that the London 'Observer' declared: '1936 will go on record as the year of Edward VIII, the Spanish war and Robert Taylor.' He and Barbara Stanwyck married some time after making **His Brother's Wife** *with Joseph Calleia. On-screen the Taylor–Stanwyck romance was far from smooth, as scripted by Leon Gordon and John Meehan. He was a medical researcher, she a nightclub hostess; he went out to the tropics to investigate spotted fever; she, miffed, married his brother; by the last reel she had spotted*

A wafer-thin story served to give Robert Taylor and Janet Gaynor, in her first MGM appearance, a hit in Hunt Stromberg's **Small Town Girl**. *Janet, the Fox studio's biggest attraction until Shirley Temple came along, played a rural miss picked up by playboy Taylor and married during his drunken spree. His rich fiancée demanded an annulment, whereupon he found that even while sober he preferred Janet, so have you read any good scripts lately? William Wellman directed, John Lee Mahin and Edith Fitzgerald scripted from a Ben Ames Williams novel. Also cast: Binnie Barnes, Lewis Stone, Andy Devine, Elizabeth Patterson, James Stewart, Frank Craven and Charley Grapewin.*

△ **Suzy** had practically everything; Jean Harlow and Cary Grant (here) as American showgirl and French flying ace, Franchot Tone with Irish brogue, Benita Hume as bewitching spy, the 1914 Derby, World War I, spectacular air battles and a hit theme song, 'Did I Remember?'. George Fitzmaurice got it all into 99 minutes for producer Louis D. Lighton, who had jig-sawed the scripts of Dorothy Parker, Alan Campbell, Horace Jackson and Lenore Coffee. Also cast: Lewis Stone, Inez Courtney, Reginald Mason, Theodore Von Eltz and Una O'Connor.

Producer Joseph Mankiewicz threw bushels of MGM dollars, top director Clarence Brown and one of the year's most dazzling casts into **The Gorgeous Hussy** but public response was disappointing. The teaming of Joan Crawford and Robert Taylor had been its initial attraction but the Ainsworth Morgan–Stephen M. Avery screenplay from Samuel Hopkins Adams' novel focused more interest on Lionel Barry-more and Beulah Bondi (here with Joan and Melvyn Douglas) who gave vivid performances as President Andrew Jackson and his back-woods wife. Spotlighting historical and political events had a cooling effect on the Crawford–Taylor fans. Franchot Tone, James Stewart, Alison Skipworth, Louis Calhern, Sidney Toler, Melville Cooper, Gene Lockhart and Clara Blandick had other principal roles.

Mayer took a great interest in juvenile players and made MGM the most successful studio in developing child stars. Three of them were cunningly given equal importance in the John Lee Mahin–Richard Schayer script for **The Devil is a Sissy**/The Devil Takes the Count: Mickey

Rooney as a slum kid, Freddie Bartholomew as rich Ian Hunter's son, and Jackie Cooper as a middle-class boy were thrown together in a New York school. Cooper had been a star for half a decade; Bartholomew was a big draw since David Copperfield; Rooney, then the least famous of the three, was to become the industry's number one box-office attraction for years on end. This Frank Davis production was given the golden directorial touch of W. S. Van Dyke, with Katherine Alexander, Peggy Conklin, Grant Mitchell, Etienne Girardot, Gene and Kathleen Lockhart and Andrew Tombes (as the cop) in the cast.

Joan Crawford and producer Mankiewicz snapped out of the solemnity of Gorgeous Hussy for her next, **Love on the Run**. She was back in Clark Gable's arms, when he wasn't at her heels in one long, carefree, sexy chase, and the fans were happy again. W. S. Van Dyke's direction was a breeze, and the smooth farcing of Franchot Tone (as Gable's rival reporter, also pursuing Joan), Reginald Owen, Mona Barrie, Ivan Lebedeff and William Demarest helped to make the John Lee Mahin–Manuel Seff–Gladys Hurlbut screenplay a popular hit.

Camille: tragedy on the screen, tragedy at the studio. Before its completion, its producer, Irving Thalberg, died in September 1936 at the age of 37 and at the peak of his creative power. His associate and best friend, Bernard Hyman, finished the picture, with George Cukor continuing his superlative direction. Aware of their film's excellence and in tribute to Thal-berg, an unprecedented MGM contingent attended its California premiere, including Schenck, Mayer and–rarest of public appearances–Garbo. The applause of that audience has continued ever since; it is one of the most frequently revived movies, and some consider Garbo's performance to be the finest on film. Certainly it was her best. The range of feeling expressed by the subtle play of her features and voice, from the flirtatious gaiety of the early sequences (here, with Robert Taylor respect-fully passionate as Armand, Laura Hope Crews and Rex O'Malley) to the feverish ex-haustion of her dying, was screen acting of the highest order. In the best scene of all she and Henry Daniell, as her protector, bait each other with the knowledge that her new lover is wait-ing outside her door; their barbed dialogue, his piano playing and her sardonic laughter rise to a brilliant crescendo. Daniell delighted the critics in the role Thalberg originally intended for John Barrymore, who was indisposed;

brother Lionel was present, though, to play Taylor's father in heavy-handed style. Jessie Ralph as the motherly maid and Lenore Ulric as the rival strumpet won praise, and minor roles were filled by Elizabeth Allan, Russell Hardie, E. E. Clive and Douglas Walton. The screenplay by Zoe Akins, Frances Marion and James Hilton oiled the creaks out of the old Dumas story, and William Daniels surpassed himself in photographing the star.

Thalberg had **The Good Earth** in preparation and production for three years before his death on the eve of its completion. It was twice marked by tragedy: George Hill, first chosen to direct, had shot background footage in China when he died in 1934, a suicide. Sidney Franklin eventually directed it, and very well too, with Bernard Hyman supervising after the producer's death. Although they looked un-Chinese and sounded Teutonic, Paul Muni and Luise Rainer won raves for their superlative work as the peasants of Pearl Buck's novel, which was movingly adapted by Talbot Jennings, Tess Slesinger and Claudine West. Miss Rainer got the 1937 best actress Academy Award, setting a precedent by winning for two successive years; the election of this per-formance over Garbo's Camille raised some eyebrows. The stars' artistry in the intimate scenes was matched by exterior production effects: storm, looting, famine and, above all, a terrifying locust plague (faked by Arnold Gillespie's magic department) were staged with tremendous sweep, and photographed in sepia by the masterly Karl Freund. Thalberg's associate producer was, as usual, Albert Lewin, and the cast included Walter Connolly, Tilly Losch, Keye Luke, Jessie Ralph, Charley Grapewin and Harold Huber. In a dignified dedication the picture bore the name of Thal-berg, who had never given himself screen credit. Others that he left unfinished were Maytime, A Day at the Races and Marie Antoinette; a share of the income of these and his previous productions continues to augment the fortune he left his wife and children.

COMEDY CRAZY...
1937

Hollywood output rose to 778 features, the most since 1928. Europe offered stiffer competition with hits like *Elephant Boy, Mayerling, King Solomon's Mines*. Paul Muni followed *Pasteur* with another biography, *Life of Emile Zola* which won the Academy Award, while critics applauded Ronald Colman in *Lost Horizon* and Irene Dunne and Cary Grant in *The Awful Truth*.

United Artists had a good year starring Fredric March with Janet Gaynor in *A Star is Born* and with Carole Lombard in *Nothing Sacred*; Sylvia Sidney with Joel McCrea in *Dead End* and with Henry Fonda in *You Only Live Once*; and remakes of *Prisoner of Zenda* and *Stella Dallas*. Paramount had a comedy classic: Jean Arthur and Edward Arnold in *Easy Living*. But MGM again won the box-office race by miles, netting $14½m. Universal found a mortgage lifter in Deanna Durbin, who mysteriously never made the exhibitors' top ten list. They did elect Fox's dimpled skater Sonja Henie, and Jane Withers, bad-girl foil to Shirley Temple, who topped the list again, followed by Gable, Taylor, Bing Crosby, William Powell, Astaire & Rogers, Cooper and Myrna Loy.

They don't make movies like **Rosalie** *any more, and they never will again. It would take a gold-mine and a couple of oil wells to finance just this one number: it went on for what seemed like hours, covered 60 acres of the MGM lot, and used 27 cameras to film more than 2,000 people dancing, singing or just standing there, to the tune of Cole Porter's title song. William Anthony McGuire, who learned extravagance from his ex-employer, master spendthrift Flo Ziegfeld, produced it; he also wrote the peanut of a story hidden under all the spectacle and music. The latter included one of Porter's loveliest songs, 'In The Still of The Night', sung by Nelson Eddy who co-starred with Eleanor Powell (that's her in the middle). Frank Morgan played the Ruritanian king he originated in the 1928 Ziegfeld show, whose Romberg and Gershwin numbers were dropped in favour of the new Porter score. Ray Bolger, Edna May Oliver, Ilona Massey (debut), Reginald Owen, Billy Gilbert, Janet Beecher, George Zucco and Virginia Grey also performed for director Robert Z. Leonard.*

Against Mayer's predictions of failure, Robert Montgomery, tiring of his debonair playboy image before his fans did, insisted on making **Night Must Fall**. *It was anything but a failure; the psychotic killer of Emlyn Williams' sinister play became an equally nerve-tingling movie character and opened up a whole new field for the star. Dame May Whitty, making her film*

debut at 72, was outstanding as his victim. She, Kathleen Harrison, Merle Tottenham and Matthew Boulton re-created their stage roles, while Rosalind Russell scored as the sensitive girl fascinated by the murderer. Alan Marshal, E. E. Clive and Beryl Mercer supported. Richard Thorpe's direction of the John Van Druten screenplay for producer Hunt Stromberg kept suspense taut.

Teamed for the seventh time, William Powell and Myrna Loy were again in easy command of that most difficult art, the playing of comedy. **Double Wedding**, *a giddy romp encompassing sophisticated dialogue and visual slapstick, was adapted by Jo Swerling from a Ferenc Molnar play. Richard Thorpe's direction ensured laugh-getting performances also from the secondary romantic pair, John Beal and Florence Rice, and character actors Sidney Toler, Edgar Kennedy, Jessie Ralph, Katherine Alexander and Barnett Parker. Joseph Mankiewicz produced this profit-producer.*

A 15-year-old bombshell exploded when **Broadway Melody of 1938** *(made in '37) spotlighted the MGM feature debut of Judy Garland, seen here with Buddy Ebsen in the finale. Earlier in the footage she had sung 'You Made Me Love You' to a photo of Clark Gable, snatching the movie from Robert Taylor, Eleanor Powell, George Murphy, Sophie Tucker, Binnie Barnes and Ebsen, all billed above her. Judy previously made a short with another juvenile singer, Deanna Durbin, and Mayer hit the ceiling when he discovered that Deanna's option had lapsed and that Universal had signed her for starring roles. 'We'll make Judy an even bigger star!' thundered the Czar and, sure enough, they eventually did. This Melody, like* Born to Dance, *was a lucrative hit produced by Jack Cummings, written by Sid Silvers and Jack McGowan, and directed by Roy Del Ruth; but instead of a Cole Porter score it had off-form Freed & Brown songs. Robert Benchley, Raymond Walburn, Charley Grapewin, Barnett Parker, Billy Gilbert, Broadway comedian Willie Howard and singer Igor Gorin rounded out the cast.*

The Bride Wore Red *was made by Dorothy Arzner, Hollywood's only woman director for many years. Robert Young and Franchot Tone were on Joan Crawford adoration duty for the picture and Joseph Mankiewicz again produced a Molnar work, following* Double Wedding *with this heavier piece, adapted from the playwright's 'The Girl from Trieste' by Bradbury Foote and Tess Slesinger, about a waterfront café singer posing as a society belle. It was not one of the highlights of Miss Crawford's career. Also cast: Reginald Owen, Billie Burke, George Zucco, Lynne Carver, Mary Phillips, Dickie Moore.*

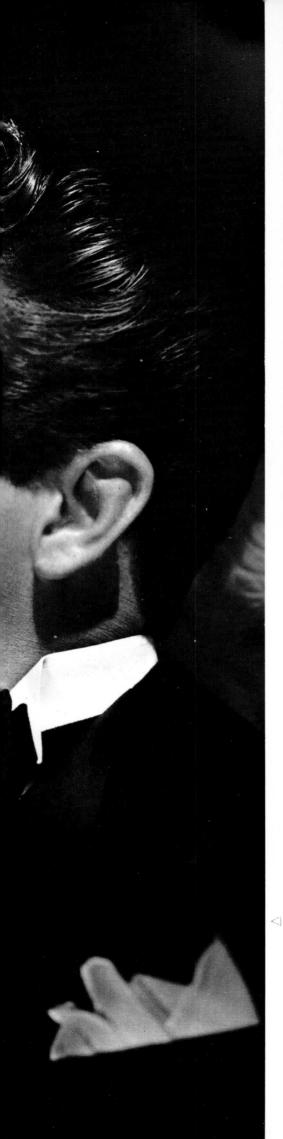

The **Thirteenth Chair** *was one of Bayard Veiller's three annuities – he also wrote* Within the Law *and* The Trial of Mary Dugan *– and had its third filming with (from left) Dame May Whitty as the medium, Janet Beecher, Ralph Forbes, Holmes Herbert (repeating his 1929 role), Heather Thatcher, Elissa Landi (hidden) and Lewis Stone; also cast were Madge Evans, Henry Daniell, Thomas Beck and Matthew Boulton. George B. Seitz directed the seance thriller for J. J. Cohn, with moderate results.*

Another remake released early in 1937 was
◁ **Personal Property**/The Man in Possession *from the H. M. Harwood comedy Robert Montgomery filmed in 1931. Hugh Mills and Ernst Vajda gave a script build-up to the heroine role so that Jean Harlow could co-star with Robert Taylor, making a torrid paybox team. It worked entertainment-wise too. W. S. Van Dyke directed the John Considine Jr production, with Reginald Owen in his original part and Henrietta Crosman, Una O'Connor, E. E. Clive, Cora Witherspoon and Marla Shelton.*

Jean Harlow had several days' work opposite Clark Gable in **Saratoga** *to finish when she* *suddenly fell ill. On June 7, 1937 she died, aged 26. By no means the brassy strumpet she often played, she was held in warm regard by her fellow workers; the mourning at MGM was sincere. Her fiancé William Powell was grief-stricken. A patch-up job was done on the movie's remaining scenes a double being filmed in long-shot where necessary. Saratoga was a pretty good picture and Jean's last performance was one of her best. Jack Conway directed the Anita Loos racetrack comedy, produced by Bernard Hyman. The loss of one MGM star coincided with the start of another's long career; Walter Pidgeon was in the cast, along with Lionel Barrymore, Frank Morgan, Una Merkel, Cliff Edwards, Frankie Darro and Hattie McDaniel.*

'Gladys George lifts herself once and for all into the thinning blue of cinema immortality', raved 'Motion Picture Daily', reviewing the 1937 version of **Madame X**. *She didn't, but she made Alexandre Bisson's old sobbie deliver its usual dramatic punch in the James K. Mc-Guinness production. John Meehan scripted and Sam Wood directed this time, with (left to right) Lynne Carver, John Beal, Emma Dunn, Miss George, Reginald Owen and Warren William; also cast were Henry Daniell, William Henry, Phillip Reed, Ruth Hussey (debut), Luis Alberni, George Zucco, Cora Witherspoon and Jonathan Hale.*

1937

Spencer Tracy's Academy Award-winning performance in **Captains Courageous** included such un-Tracylike elements as a Portuguese accent and a spot of singing. Freddie Bartholomew's acting very nearly equalled his in the role of the spoiled brat he fished out of the sea and regenerated during a whaling voyage. Victor Fleming's direction of the Kipling story was an unqualified triumph, bringing praise also to Lionel Barrymore, Melvyn Douglas, Mickey Rooney, John Carradine, Jack La Rue and Walter Kingsford. Louis D. Lighton produced the John Lee Mahin–Marc Connelly–Dale Van Every screenplay. MGM reaped massive returns.

Walter Hackett's London stage hit **Espionage** came to the screen with Madge Evans and Edmund Lowe cast as rival reporters tracking down munitions king Paul Lukas; most of the action occurred on a trans-Continental train. Manuel Seff, Leonard Lee and Ainsworth Morgan scripted and Kurt Neumann directed the Harry Rapf production as a spy-kidding comedy. Also cast: Ketti Gallian, Skeets Gallagher, Barnett Parker, Billy Gilbert, Frank Reicher and Mitchell Lewis.

In **My Dear Miss Aldrich** Walter Pidgeon carried off his first top role at MGM with practised ease. Not surprising; he had already been on stage and screen for 20 years. In the early talkie era he was, of all things, the singing hero of operetta-type musicals (and 35 years after Aldrich he was featured in MGM's Skyjacked). Flanked by Edna May Oliver as an eccentric matron, and Maureen O'Sullivan as the heiress of a New York newspaper, he put over a funny farce written by Herman Mankiewicz and directed by George B. Seitz for the J. J. Cohn unit. Also cast: Rita Johnson, Janet Beecher, Paul Harvey, Walter Kingsford, Guinn Williams, J. Farrell MacDonald and Robert Greig.

Having virtually completed **The Last of Mrs Cheyney**, Richard Boleslawski died suddenly, reducing the MGM directors list to 20 during early 1937. The players roster (including a few affiliated Hal Roach contractees) numbered 91, a fair share of whom were cast in the Frederick Lonsdale evergreen: Robert Montgomery, Joan Crawford, William Powell (here) and Frank Morgan, Jessie Ralph, Ralph Forbes, Nigel Bruce, Benita Hume, Sara Haden, Aileen Pringle and Melville Cooper. Despite this galaxy, the remake was not as popular as Norma Shearer's 1929 hit. But critics said it was an improvement; Crawford got special praise for her smooth comedy playing. The Leon Gordon–Monckton Hoffe–Samson Raphaelson script for producer Lawrence Weingarten made few alterations to the play about jewel thieves in high society.

The studio stinted nothing in giving its double-Oscar star Luise Rainer the full glamour treatment in **The Emperor's Candlesticks**. It teamed her and William Powell for the third time, with George Fitzmaurice directing and John Considine Jr producing on a generous budget. Monckton Hoffe, Herman Mankiewicz and Harold Goldman laboured to oil the creaks out of Baroness Orczy's story of spies in pre-War I European palaces. But it was unmoving movie, neglected by the fans. Also cast: Maureen O'Sullivan, Robert Young, Frank Morgan, Henry Stephenson, Douglass Dumbrille, Emma Dunn, Frank Conroy (here, with Miss Rainer), E. E. Clive, Barnett Parker.

Melvyn Douglas, Virginia Bruce and Warren William in **Arsene Lupin Returns**, a sequel to the gentleman-crook drama MGM made in 1931. It was better with the Barrymores. James K. McGuinness, Howard Emmett Rogers and George Harmon Coxe devised the new story, produced by John Considine Jr and directed by George Fitzmaurice, with John Halliday, Nat Pendleton, Monty Woolley, George Zucco, E. E. Clive, Vladimir Sokoloff and Tully Marshall, who was also in the earlier Lupin.

One of 1937's strongest pictures, dramatically if not box-officially, was **They Gave Him a Gun**. The Richard Maibaum–Cyril Hume–Maurice Rapf script from William Cowen's novel afforded the chance, fully taken, for a dual tour de force by Franchot Tone as a meek clerk transformed by his army experiences into a postwar gangster, and Spencer Tracy as a circus barker who befriended him through the years. A third telling performance came from Gladys George as an army nurse who married Tone and joined Tracy's circus when her husband was jailed. The Harry Rapf production was marred only by a contrived finish, with Tone being killed by a cop who had been his wartime gunnery instructor. W. S. Van Dyke filmed the battle scenes on the fields cultivated for The Good Earth. Also cast: Cliff Edwards, Harold Huber, Herbert Rawlinson, Mary Treen, Horace MacMahon.

Edward G. Robinson worked at MGM for the first time since 1929 in **The Last Gangster**. Meanwhile he had won immortality by snarling his way through a dozen Warner Bros. mobster epics. The movie's title admitted it was a latecomer in the genre, but gang warfare and Alcatraz sadism retained their compulsive fascination, and Robinson even managed to encompass paternal love in his public-enemy act. His leading lady was Rose Stradner, a Viennese discovery who didn't make it, and the good guy was James Stewart (that moustache had to go). J. J. Cohn produced and Edward Ludwig directed the John Lee Mahin screenplay which stemmed from a William Wellman–Robert Carson original. Douglas Scott played the child, with Lionel Stander, Alan Baxter, Grant Mitchell, Sidney Blackmer, John Carradine, Edward Brophy, Frank Conroy and Louise Beavers.

George Murphy, stage song-and-dance man, went straight when he joined MGM in 1937 — and even straighter when he left 15 years later and became US Senator from California. His first two for the company were no great shakes: **London By Night**, a kidnapping and murder thriller with Virginia Field, Forrester Harvey

and Eddie Quillan; also Rita Johnson, Leo G. Carroll, George Zucco and Montagu Love; director William Thiele; author Will Scott; producer Sam Zimbalist . . . **The Women Men Marry**, a love and murder drama with Claire Dodd (seated) and Josephine Hutchinson. Also cast were Sidney Blackmer, Cliff Edwards, John Wray, Peggy Ryan, Toby Wing, Leonard Penn and Helen Jerome Eddy. Director Errol Taggart; writers Donald Henderson Clarke, James Grant, Harry Ruskin; producer Michael Fessier.

Erich von Stroheim was the unlikely author of **Between Two Women**, a pulsating drama of love among the forceps, with Franchot Tone as the scalpel ace adored by nurse Maureen O'Sullivan (here). Sadly, Tone was in love with a ruptured appendix (Virginia Bruce) while Maureen was married to a drinking problem (Edward Norris) and many a bedpan hit the sluice before they were united. Carey Wilson scripted, George B. Seitz directed, J. J. Cohn produced, and the cast included Cliff Edwards, Janet Beecher, Leonard Penn, June Clayworth and Grace Ford.

Mannequin was the only picture Spencer Tracy and Joan Crawford made together. Although it was the Crawford formula No. 1 (tenement daughter to Broadway showgirl to millionaire's woman), she gave one of her best performances, perhaps inspired by co-star Tracy as a self-made tycoon. Directed by Frank Borzage, they brought conviction to Katherine Brush's threadbare plot. Lawrence Hazard's script, Joseph Mankiewicz's production, and supporting players Alan Curtis (a striking debut as Joan's worthless young husband), Ralph Morgan, Mary Phillips, Oscar O'Shea, Leo ('Dead End') Gorcey and Elisabeth Risdon all helped make it a hit.

Marla Shelton and Dean Jagger (mysteriously renamed Jeffrey Dean for this one movie) were tested as potential stars in the Lucien Hubbard–Michael Fessier production, **Song of the City**, a flop. The beauteous Miss Shelton soon disappeared, but Jagger developed into a major character actor. Errol Taggart directed Fessier's San Francisco drama of a seaman mixing with the rich, climaxed by a spectacular fire at sea. Margaret Lindsay, top-billed on loan from Warner Bros., Nat Pendleton, Stanley Morner, J. Carrol Naish, Charles Judels and Edward Norris completed the cast.

Man of the People was a well-made and vigorously acted programme picture, but the subject was box-office poison: politics. Thomas Mitchell (right, with Joseph Calleia), a New York stage veteran, was just starting his career as one of the screen's best actors. Others in the Lucien Hubbard production, directed by Edwin Marin, were Florence Rice, Ted Healy, Catherine Doucet and Eddie Nugent. Frank Dolan wrote the script.

After the general lack of enthusiasm for Luise Rainer in Emperor's Candlesticks, Mayer lowered her social class a few notches for **Big City** and made her the pregnant wife of a New York cab-driver. The latter was Spencer Tracy, whose talent was as untaxed as hers in the rowdy melodramatics of Norman Krasna's screenplay. The cast included two silent-era stars, Victor Varconi (right) as her brother, and Alice White in a bit part; also Janet Beecher, Charley Grapewin, Eddie Quillan, William Demarest, John Arledge, Grace Ford, Guinn Williams, Regis Toomey, Cliff Edwards, Gwen Lee and Jack Dempsey. Krasna had only himself to blame as producer, but director Frank Borzage should have known better too.

Two new producers tried their MGM wings with 'B' movies in 1937. Frederick Stephani was aided in **Beg, Borrow or Steal** by an amusing Leonard Lee–Harry Ruskin–Marion Parsonnet script about conmen on the Riviera, and an expert cast. Left to right: Herman Bing, Reginald Denny, Erik Rhodes, Frank Morgan and George Givot; also John Beal, Florence Rice, Vladimir Sokoloff, E. E. Clive and Cora Witherspoon; director was William Thiele . . .

Tom Reed had less luck with a routine melodrama about electricity power linesmen, **Bad Guy** with (left to right) Bruce Cabot, Virginia Grey, Edward Norris and Charley Grapewin; also Cliff Edwards, Jean Chatburn and Warren Hymer; directed by Edward Cahn from a script it took six writers to cook up.

Parnell was enthusiastically sponsored by Mayer, scripted by two eminent playwrights, John van Druten and S. N. Behrman, produced and directed by veteran hit-maker John M. Stahl, and starred the phenomenally popular Clark Gable and Myrna Loy. How could it miss? By being pretentious, stagey and dull, that's how. Gable as the Irish patriot orating for home rule in the House of Commons looked as though he would rather be dodging debris in the Frisco earthquake; Myrna as the wife (Alan Marshal's) he loved clandestinely seemed bored by the assignment. Also in the expensive failure were Edna May Oliver, Billie Burke, Donald Crisp, Edmund Gwenn, Montagu Love, Berton Churchill, Donald Meek, Halliwell Hobbes, J. Farrell MacDonald and George Zucco. Somewhere in this scene was Randolph Churchill, who said he earned more as a Metro Member of Parliament than as a real one.

1937

Schmaltz with a capital $ was lavishly dispensed in **Maytime**. Planned by Thalberg and eventually produced by Hunt Stromberg, it ranked as the biggest world-wide money-maker of 1937. The Sigmund Romberg–Rida Johnson Young operetta always was a winner: 20 years earlier the stage version had been so successful that two productions ran simultaneously on Broadway. The movie starred Jeanette MacDonald and Nelson Eddy in their best vocal and histrionic work to date. John Barrymore (here, with Jeanette) as the jealous Svengali to her operatic Trilby, had lost control of his waistline but not of his acting technique; his performance together with Noel Langley's screenplay provided an unusually sturdy dramatic framework for a musical. Songs ranged from 'Carry Me Back to Old Virginny' to Tchaikovsky's Fifth Symphony souped up with lyrics; Romberg's 'Will You Remember?' was the best-seller. Maestro Herbert Stothart did yeoman work and director Robert Z. Leonard added another hit to his long list. Also cast: Tom Brown, Lynne Carver, Herman Bing, Walter Kingsford, Sig Ruman, Edgar Norton, Rafaela Ottiano, Charles Judels and Paul Porcasi.

Gladys George, who scored her biggest stage hit playing a temperamental star in a comedy, had nothing but tears on the screen until **Love is a Headache** cast her as a temperamental star in a comedy. Mickey Rooney and Virginia Weidler played orphans she adopted as a publicity stunt – bad luck for Miss George and co-star Franchot Tone: the kids stole the picture. Ted Healy, Frank Jenks, Barnett Parker, Ralph Morgan, Fay Holden, Jessie Ralph and Henry Kolker rounded out the cast of Frederick Stephani's production, written by Marion Parsonnet, Harry Ruskin and William Lipman, and directed by Richard Thorpe for mild paybox results.

George Humbert, Hoagy Carmichael, Cary Grant and Constance Bennett in **Topper**, Hal ▷ Roach's first venture into sophisticated comedy, and a solid hit. Hoagy couldn't claim that his 'Old Man Moon' was sending Cary and Connie out of this world: they were already. They played ghosts awaiting acceptance into the next world who had to perform a good deed; and decided it would be to teach henpecked Mr Topper (Roland Young) how to live life to the full. Thorne Smith's fantastic novel was smartly adapted by Jack Jevne, Eddie Moran and Eric

Hatch, with Milton Bren producing for Roach. Norman Z. McLeod's bubbly direction was enhanced by Roy Seawright's photographic tricks, fading the star ghosts in and out. Also cast: Billie Burke, Eugene Pallette, Alan Mowbray, Hedda Hopper, Arthur Lake, Theodore von Eltz, J. Farrell MacDonald.

Extending his film-making empire to Britain, Mayer signed Ben Goetz as studio manager, and Michael Balcon as production chief at the Denham Studios, and assigned Robert Taylor (whose arrival caused mob scenes such as London had never seen), Maureen O'Sullivan and Lionel Barrymore to star in **A Yank at Oxford**. A shrewd choice to inaugurate MGM British, this was a story of a brash American college hero coping with the customs and traditions of the English in a way to amuse both nations; it was carefully tailored by a host of writers, seven getting screen credit: John Monk Saunders, Leon Gordon, Sidney Gilliatt, Michael Hogan, Malcolm Stuart Boylan,

Walter Ferris and George Oppenheimer. Jack Conway directed briskly and the whole enterprise bristled with success. But Balcon wouldn't be a yes-man during Mayer's tantrums and had to sit out the rest of his contract. One major row was sparked off by the casting of an unknown (to Mayer) in the second female lead; Louis B. didn't think Vivien Leigh was good enough for such an important picture. Rest of cast: Griffith Jones (here with Taylor in the Isis boat-bumping race sequence) and Edmund Gwenn, C. V. France, Edward Rigby, Morton Selten, Claude Gillingwater, Tully Marshall, Walter Kingsford, Robert Coote, Peter Croft, Noel Howlett, Edmond Breon.

Mama Steps Out *was built around Alice Brady's stock screen character of dizzy matron; producers had forgotten that her greatest New York stage triumph had been the tragic 'Strange Interlude'. Left to right: Betty Furness, Ivan Lebedeff, Guy Kibbee, Heather Thatcher, Miss Brady and Gregory Gaye in this farce about new-rich Americans on the Riviera. John Emerson produced the screenplay by his wife, Anita Loos, and George B. Seitz directed. Stanley Morner, playing opposite Miss Furness, sang his last two songs for MGM before becoming Dennis Morgan for Warner Bros.*

Don Marquis' play 'The Old Soak' provided Wallace Beery with an effective vehicle for his good-natured-slob act. **The Good Old Soak,** *adapted by A. E. Thomas, was produced by Harry Rapf, one of the company's old originals and now its most prolific producer. The script involved bootlegging, a stock market swindle and small-town family problems. Under J. Walter Ruben's direction, Beery's support included Ted Healy and Una Merkel (here), Eric Linden, Betty Furness, Janet Beecher, Robert McWade and Margaret Hamilton.*

Paradise for Three/Romance for Three *brought the fascinating Mary Astor, who had been playing leads for 15 years, to the MGM contract list. The George Oppenheimer–Harry Ruskin script, from Erich Kaestner's novel 'Three Men in the Snow', sparkled, and Edward Buzzell in his directorial bow for Leo made every laugh line count. Frank Morgan (right) scored in the central role, with Robert Young (centre) and Edna May Oliver, Florence Rice, Reginald Owen, Henry Hull, Herman Bing, Sig Ruman and Walter Kingsford helping to keep the love-in-the-Alps fun bubbling. Sam Zimbalist produced.*

Live, Love and Learn *was a fairly successful item in the 'crazy comedy' vogue of the Thirties. Robert Montgomery and Rosalind Russell co-starred as a struggling artist and his rich wife, with the priceless Maude Eburne (centre) as their Greenwich Village landlady. George Fitzmaurice directed and producer Harry Rapf gave it a strong cast, including Robert Benchley, Monty Woolley, Helen Vinson, Mickey Rooney, E. E. Clive, June Clayworth, Charles Judels, Ann Rutherford and Zeffie Tilbury. Helen Grace Carlisle's story was adapted by Charles Brackett, Cyril Hume and Richard Maibaum.*

Wallace Beery did his Viva Villa *stuff again as an outlaw in* **The Bad Man of Brimstone.** *By stretching the long arm of coincidence to snapping point, the Richard Maibaum–Cyril Hume script from a J. Walter Ruben–Maurice Rapf original managed to work in Beery's other forte, father-love, with Dennis O'Keefe as his longlost son. Harry Rapf produced with Ruben directing. Left to right: Robert Gleckler, Cliff Edwards, Joseph Calleia, Beery, Bruce Cabot, Arthur Hohl. Also cast: Virginia Bruce, Lewis Stone, Guy Kibbee, Noah Beery (acting with his brother for the first time since 1916), Scotty Beckett, Guinn Williams, John Qualen, Charley Grapewin, John Wray, Robert Barrat and Beery's co-star in the old Paramount comedies, Raymond Hatton.*

Simulating teenage enthusiasm with commendable zeal, Robert Young (30), Tom Brown (24) and James Stewart (29) played Annapolis midshipmen in **Navy Blue and Gold** *so well that audiences forgot they'd seen it all many times before. It was a winner. George Bruce incorporated the usual* esprit de corps, *dormitory horseplay and big football match in his script. Smartly paced by Sam Wood and produced by Sam Zimbalist, it also featured Lionel Barrymore, Billie Burke, Paul Kelly, Florence Rice, Frank Albertson, Samuel S. Hinds and Barnett Parker.*

Thoroughbreds Don't Cry *was the first picture to give Judy Garland top billing and the beginning of the Rooney–Garland team. Left to right: Sophie Tucker, Mickey Rooney, Ronald Sinclair (New Zealand-born, English-accented Freddie Bartholomew type) and Judy. Miss Tucker's slam-bang stage personality seemed to lose some of its gusto on the screen, and in this movie it was pretty well swamped by the three talented juveniles. The Harry Rapf production, ably directed by Alfred E. Green, was a racetrack story by J. Walter Ruben and Eleanor Griffin, scripted by Lawrence Hazard. Also cast: C. Aubrey Smith, Helen Troy, Frankie Darro, Elisha Cook Jr, Henry Kolker, Forrester Harvey, Charles D. Brown.*

Man-Proof *startled Myrna Loy fans by casting 'the perfect wife' as a predatory bachelor girl who kept stalking her prey (Walter Pidgeon) even after he'd married her rival (Rosalind Russell, right). She had to make do with Franchot Tone eventually. Unusually in this era, the comedy had no farcical elements. Rita Johnson, Nana Bryant, Ruth Hussey, Leonard Penn, John Miljan and Oscar O'Shea were also in the Louis D. Lighton production. Richard Thorpe directed the Vincent Lawrence–Waldemar Young–George Oppenheimer screenplay based on Fanny Heaslip Lea's novel 'The Four Marys'.*

Kelly the Second *having clicked, Hal Roach rolled out two more Patsy Kelly starrers in quick succession. Lyda Roberti, from Broadway musicals, teamed with her in* **Nobody's Baby**, *a maternity hospital farce by Harold Law, Hal Yates and Pat C. Flick, with Lynne Overman, Robert Armstrong and Don Alvarado, directed by Gus Meins. It had several songs, as did* **Pick a Star**, *a Hollywood comedy with most of the Roach talent, plus Mischa Auer stealing the picture as a temperamental star. Edward Sedgwick directed the Richard Flournoy–A. V. Jones–Tom Dugan story, with (left to right) Auer, Rosina Lawrence, Charles Halton, Patsy and Jack Haley. They were augmented by Lyda Roberti, Dugan, Jimmy Finlayson, and Laurel and Hardy as themselves.*

Married Before Breakfast *was something of a surprise package, a wild little comedy by Everett Freeman and George Oppenheimer which scored on novel situations and an air of spontaneity. Left to right: Irene Franklin, Hugh Marlowe, Florence Rice, Robert Young. Edwin Marin directed (his 17th picture in four years) for producer Sam Zimbalist, with June Clayworth, Barnett Parker and Warren Hymer also supporting Young and Miss Rice.*

Restive under the yoke joining her cinematically to Nelson Eddy, Jeanette Mac-Donald asked Mayer for a solo vehicle and got it: **The Firefly**. *Ironically, her new leading man, Allan Jones, had what turned out to be the big song success of the film, 'The Donkey Serenade', while Jeanette did some graceful dancing and much coy emoting as a Spanish spy during the Napoleonic war of 1808–12. The picture grossed close to* Maytime. *Rudolf Friml's 'Sympathy', 'Giannina Mia' and 'Love is Like a Firefly' came from the original 1912 stage show; the 'Donkey' song was developed from one of his piano pieces. Warren William, Douglass Dumbrille, Leonard Penn, Henry Daniell and George Zucco were involved in the hammy plot which had been assigned inexplicably to writers like Ogden Nash, Frances Goodrich and Albert Hackett; the latter pair fled MGM after this chore. Hunt Stromberg produced the overlong, overacted charade, working again with director Robert Z. Leonard.*

Racehorse owner Allan Jones and sheriff Robert Middlemass were getting on with the plot of **A Day at the Races**, *but who cared? Every audience eye was on jockey Harpo and tipster Chico Marx. Groucho, in the immortal role of Hugo Z. Hackenbush, horse doctor, was off somewhere wooing Margaret Dumont. The Marxes tested the new gags in 140 stage performances in various cities before filming; the final result was almost as funny as* A Night at the Opera *and equally profitable. Maureen O'Sullivan, Sig Ruman, Douglass Dumbrille and Esther Muir were also in the Lawrence Weingarten production, directed by Sam Wood from a Robert Pirosh–George Seaton–George Oppenheimer script.*

Mayer unknowingly laid the foundation for the most profitable series in Hollywood's history when he put most of the Ah, Wilderness cast into **A Family Affair** *in another vain effort to recapture the former's magic. Based on a*

modest Broadway success by Aurania Rouverol called 'Skidding', it was a story of Judge Hardy and his small-town family, played by (left to right) Lionel Barrymore, Julie Haydon, Cecilia Parker, Sara Haden, Eric Linden, Spring Byington and, not in this scene, Mickey Rooney. It was a Lucien Hubbard–George B. Seitz 'B' and drew a surprising number of requests from exhibitors for more like it. So its sets were kept standing and its scenarist, Kay Van Riper, was assigned to write a sequel (which eliminated the Haydon and Linden characters). The Hardy Family saga was on its way.

For the only time in Garbo's starring career, her male opposite had a more interesting role than her own in **Conquest**/Marie Walewska. ▷ *Napoleon, played by Charles Boyer, was the flame around which his Polish mistress fluttered in the Samuel Hoffenstein–Salka Viertel–S. N. Behrman script; their doomed affair was superbly acted by both stars under Clarence Brown's direction. But it lacked the bravura scenes that had made* Camille *so special; although looking utterly beautiful in Karl Freund's photography, Garbo seemed somewhat exhausted, as if still recovering from that extraordinary previous performance, and she departed for a year's rest in 1938.* Conquest, *expensively mounted by Bernard Hyman, did not earn its cost in America but was strong overseas. Supporting cast: Alan Marshal, Reginald Owen, Henry Stephenson, Dame May Whitty, Leif Erickson, C. Henry Gordon, Vladimir Sokoloff, George Zucco, Maria Ouspenskaya, Scotty Beckett. As Garbo's last dramatic vehicle, this is often included in the retrospectives that have kept her genius visible to new generations.*

The Garland career was really rolling as 1937 neared its end. Toplining **Everybody Sing**, *Judy did a blackface number that demonstrated her flair for comedy as well as her already famous talent for putting over a song. This Harry Rapf production had a funny script by Florence Ryerson and Edgar Allan Woolf about a mad theatrical family (Reginald Owen, Billie Burke, Lynne Carver) whose servants (Allan Jones, Fanny Brice) put on a Broadway show with the younger daughter (Judy). Edwin Marin directed them and Monty Woolley, Reginald Gardiner, Helen Troy, Henry Armetta and Mary Forbes.*

AND GARLAND SINGS
1938

The industry was going into another slump: most companies reported less than half the previous year's profits, with MGM-Loew's again the envy of all at $10m. Simultaneously the US Government started an anti-trust suit against the film combines to divorce theatres from studios and sales. It bedevilled the majors for years, threatening the very basis of their operation. Hollywood spent millions on publicizing the slogan 'Movies Are Your Best Entertainment', then halted it when people noticed its initials spelled 'MAYBE'.

Important releases included Walt Disney's *Snow White and the Seven Dwarfs*, new star William Holden in *Golden Boy*, Wendy Hiller in *Pygmalion*, Tyrone Power, Alice Faye and Don Ameche in *Alexander's Ragtime Band* and *In Old Chicago*.

Bette Davis won her second Oscar for *Jezebel*, Frank Capra his third for *You Can't Take It With You*. Tyrone Power, Miss Faye, Mickey Rooney and Spencer Tracy entered the Top Ten; Bing Crosby, William Powell, Gary Cooper, Fred Astaire and Ginger Rogers moved out of the list.

The second Hardy Family movie, **You're Only Young Once**, *had the cast which was to become famous: Lewis Stone and Fay Holden (an English actress oddly becoming the typical American Ma) replaced Lionel Barrymore and Spring Byington as Judge and Mrs Hardy; Mickey Rooney and Cecilia Parker carried on as their children; so did Sara Haden as Aunt Milly. Director George B. Seitz and scenarist Kay Van Riper repeated their* Family Affair *success. Lucien Hubbard had left the studio and the series, supervised by J. J. Cohn, continued without a producer credit. Also cast: Frank Craven, Ann Rutherford (a regular henceforth), Ted Pearson, Eleanor Lynn, Charles Judels.*

Mickey Rooney took over the 'Hardy' spotlight in **Judge Hardy's Children**, *and held it forever after. Here he's teaching Jacqueline Laurent a dance craze of the Thirties, the Big Apple, during the family's visit to Washington. The public was now really 'Hardy'-hooked. Director-writer team George B. Seitz and Kay Van Riper, and players Lewis Stone, Cecilia Parker, Fay Holden and Ann Rutherford continued, assisted by Robert Whitney, Ruth Hussey, Jonathan Hale, Janet Beecher, Leonard Penn, and Betty Ross Clark who temporarily replaced Sara Haden.*

The 'Hardy' series zoomed into the box-office stratosphere when its fourth instalment, **Love Finds Andy Hardy**, *outgrossed 1938 releases that cost ten times as much. The front-and-centre positioning of Mickey Rooney's role in both title and script (by William Ludwig) and the injection of Judy Garland into the cast turned the trick. The love that found Andy was a cute teenager called Lana Turner, just given a trial contract by studio executives who thought she had 'something'. Whatever it was, it lasted for 18 years at MGM. Mayer became the Hardys' foremost fan, scrutinizing every detail during production. Although there was still no screen credit for a producer, Carey Wilson, MGM stalwart since the 1924 merger, was always prominently involved. George B. Seitz again directed regulars Stone, Holden, Parker, Rutherford; and Gene Reynolds, Mary Howard, Raymond Hatton, Betty Ross Clark, Don Castle and Marie Blake.*

Rich Man, Poor Girl, *the 1938 remake of 1929's* The Idle Rich, *was chiefly notable for bringing Lew Ayres into the MGM fold for a lengthy spell; his last work there had been his 'discovery' appearance opposite Garbo in* The Kiss *nine years before. Left to right: Ruth Hussey, Robert Young, Don Castle, Ayres, Sarah Padden, Guy Kibbee and Lana Turner. A new producer-director team, Edward Chodorov and Reinhold Schunzel, filmed the Joseph Fields–Jerome Chodorov screenplay, with Rita Johnson, Gordon Jones and Virginia Grey cast.*

Hokum? Corn? Commercial soul-wallop? Whatever it was, **Boys Town** *delivered it with* ▽ *such superb professionalism that not even the toughest critics were able to resist it. The public didn't even try; they flocked in by the million, making the John Considine Jr production one of MGM's biggest winners. Spencer Tracy was a winner too, getting his second Oscar for his portrayal of Father Flanagan. The latter and his home for delinquent boys existed in real life, although the Dore Schary–John Meehan script–also Oscared–used a fictional story centred on Mickey Rooney (here with Tracy and Bobs Watson) as a roughneck refusing to reform. Norman Taurog, who had directed Jackie Cooper to boy-stardom in 1931, began an MGM long-termer with this, guiding a horde of youngsters plus adults Henry Hull, Leslie Fenton, Addison Richards, Edward Norris, Minor Watson, Jonathan Hale, Victor Kilian.*

Judy Garland and Freddie Bartholomew teamed for the only time in **Listen, Darling,** *as teenagers nudging her widowed mother, Mary Astor, into matrimony with Walter Pidgeon. The Katherine Brush story, adapted by Anne Chapin and Elaine Ryan, was trivial stuff but gave Judy a chance to sing 'Zing! Went the Strings of My Heart' which she kept in her stage repertoire to the bitter end 30 years later. Left to right: Pidgeon, Miss Astor, Judy, Freddie. Alan Hale played the suitor the youngsters didn't approve of, and Scotty Beckett, Barnett Parker, Gene Lockhart and Charley Grapewin also appeared in Jack Cummings' production, directed by Edwin Marin.*

Mayer told the Hardy unit to come up with ideas for another series, and approved one dealing with hospital doctors: young Kildare and veteran Gillespie. He thought hospital stories had universal appeal; also, he was concerned about a crippling hip injury sustained by Lionel Barrymore and realized the actor could play Gillespie in a wheelchair. So **Young Dr Kildare** went into production, and emerged only a few weeks later as a success from the word go. Kildare–Gillespie actually outlasted the Hardys; the theatrical features continued into the Forties, MGM-TV produced a weekly series for five years in the Sixties, and another new batch in the Seventies. Kildare, an apparently inexhaustible goldmine of a character, was played in the first nine movies by Lew Ayres, a quietly splendid job of acting. Max Brand's original story, scripted by Willis Goldbeck and Harry Ruskin, was directed by Harold S. Bucquet, British-born graduate

from the 'Crime Does Not Pay' shorts, and featured Nat Pendleton, Lynne Carver, Jo Ann Sayers, Samuel S. Hinds, Emma Dunn, Truman Bradley, Walter Kingsford, Monty Woolley, Marie Blake.

Even Mickey Rooney's energy was taxed by his 1938 schedule, which included overlapping assignments in eight movies, with Mick on camera most of the time. Wallace Beery shared the load in **Stablemates**: the scene-grabbing contest between these two experts in the art was a sight to behold. The surefire yarn of a broken-down vet saving a ditto racehorse owned by a stableboy was written by actor Reginald Owen and director William Thiele, adapted by Leonard Praskins and Richard Maibaum, directed by Sam Wood and produced by Harry Rapf. Margaret Hamilton, Minor Watson, Marjorie Gateson, Arthur Hohl and Oscar O'Shea completed the cast.

In **Of Human Hearts** *Clarence Brown filmed a study of rural life worthy of standing beside Vidor's* Stranger's Return *and his own* Ah, Wilderness. *Walter Huston and James Stewart were superb as religion-bound father and rebellious son, with Beulah Bondi matching them as the mother making sacrifices to help her son break away to become a surgeon. A fourth outstanding performance came from Gene Reynolds, playing Stewart as a boy. Others in the John Considine Jr production were Charles Coburn (screen debut at 61), Guy Kibbee, John Carradine (as Abraham Lincoln), Ted Healy, Gene Lockhart, Leatrice Joy Gilbert (John's daughter), Ann Rutherford and Charley Grapewin. Bradbury Foote scripted from Honore Morrow's novel. 'Benefits Forgot'. Too many fans forgot to come.*

After her previous gigantics, **Honolulu** breezed in almost like a quickie for Eleanor Powell. The dancer added a grass-skirt hip-swinger and an up-and-down-stairs routine in blackface to her repertoire, but for a musical the show was short on songs: three, none of them hits. Robert Young played a movie star and his double, which was food for comedy sequences by George Burns (centre) and Gracie Allen (right). Rita Johnson, Ruth Hussey, Clarence Kolb, Sig Rumann, Jo Ann Sayers, Ann Morriss and Eddie 'Rochester' Anderson supported. Script, Herbert Fields and Frank Partos; director, Eddie Buzzell; producer, Jack Cummings.

The Hollywood legend of extra-into-star was lived by very few hopefuls. One of them Dennis O'Keefe, had his first lead in **Hold that Kiss** a featherweight comedy with Maureen O'Sullivan (here with O'Keefe) and Mickey Rooney, George Barbier, Jessie Ralph, Edward Brophy, Fay Holden, Frank Albertson, Phillip Terry, Ruth Hussey, Barnett Parker; producer, John

Considine Jr; director, Edwin Marin; writer, Stanley Rauh . . . O'Keefe's next was **The Chaser**, a remake of Lee Tracy's The Nuisance, with Ann Morriss and Nat Pendleton; also Lewis Stone, Henry O'Neill, John Qualen, Jack Mulhall; producer, Frank Davis; director, Marin; writers, Everett Freeman, Harry Ruskin, Samuel and Bella Spewack . . . The

Book by Erich Maria Remarque and screenplay by Scott Fitzgerald (with E. E. Paramore) ◁ gave **Three Comrades** a best-seller aura heightened by the co-starring of Robert Taylor and Margaret Sullavan in her MGM début. Although he worked on several Metro scripts (A Yank at Oxford, The Women, etc.) near the end of his life, this was Fitzgerald's only screen credit among them. The downbeat story, in which three ex-soldiers (Taylor, Franchot Tone, Robert Young) were caught up in the turmoil of postwar Germany, with one being killed in a riot and the wife (Miss Sullavan) of another dying of tuberculosis, restricted mass appeal. Critics praised Frank Borzage's direction of the Joseph Mankiewicz production and the acting of the principals, who were supported by Guy Kibbee, Charley Grapewin, Henry Hull, Lionel Atwill and Monty Woolley.

Norma Shearer, who had been off the screen for two years after Thalberg's death, rose to tragic heights in the title role of **Marie Antoinette** as the French queen sank to the depths of cell, tumbril and guillotine. The movie was the 160-minute culmination of years of effort by practically everybody at MGM, from Thalberg, who had scheduled it fror Miss Shearer in 1933, to the thimble-and-thread girls in Wardrobe who put together 500 yards of white satin for Marie's Adrian-designed wedding gown, plus elaborate costumes for 151 other characters and hordes of extras. Cedric Gibbons' huge sets were dressed with equally staggering extravagance after props chief Edwin Willis had carried out a three-month ransack of antique shops in France. Meanwhile Mayer ransacked his own and other studios' contract lists for Marie's Swedish lover and came up with Tyrone Power, 20th-Fox's top male attraction. He was overshadowed histrionically by Robert Morley, imported from the London stage for the Dauphin role Thalberg had intended for Charles Laughton (who was thought to look too old). Left to right: Joseph Schildkraut, Power, Anita Louise (Marie Antoinette in Mme Du Barry, 1934), Miss Shearer and Reginald Gardiner. Others enacting the Donald Ogden Stewart–Ernst Vajda–Claudine West screenplay based on Stefan Zweig's biography were John Barrymore, still flashing traces of his old sardonic glee in his last Metro appearance, as Louis XV; Gladys George as DuBarry; Henry Daniell, Joseph Calleia, Albert Dekker, Henry Stephenson, Cora Witherspoon, Barnett Parker, Alma Kruger, Leonard Penn and George Meeker. On the eve of production Mayer and producer Hunt Stromberg had an attack of budgetitis and replaced Sidney Franklin (screen-credited for 'contributions') with the fast-shooting W. S. Van Dyke, causing dismay among cinema purists, who still shrug the film off as ostentatious hokum. But most critics and audiences thought it a splendid show whose gripping narrative was never allowed to flag.

An unusual adventure in medical detection, **Yellow Jack** had much to interest serious-minded filmgoers, as it had intrigued New York theatregoers four years earlier. Edward Chodorov adapted the Sidney Howard–Paul de Kruif play for producer Jack Cummings, and its forceful realism (that blonde in the jungle tent notwithstanding) gave George B. Seitz a bracing change from directing the Hardy family. Five US soldiers (Robert Montgomery, Alan Curtis, Buddy Ebsen, Sam Levene, William Henry) volunteered as guinea pigs to help find the cause of yellow fever in Cuba; army medicos Lewis Stone, Henry Hull, Charles Coburn and Stanley Ridges eventually spotted the mosquito as villain. Also cast: Virginia Bruce (here with Montgomery), Henry O'Neill, Janet Beecher, Andy Devine, Phillip Terry, Jonathan Hale.

Dana Burnet's 'Private Pettigrew's Girl' was filmed profitably for the third time in 1938 as **The Shopworn Angel**. Margaret Sullavan and James Stewart equalled its 1929 Paramount stars, Nancy Carroll and Gary Cooper, with their poignant performances in this Camille-like story of a kept woman having a bitter-sweet affair with a naif soldier. H. C. Potter directed; Joseph Mankiewicz produced from a screenplay by Waldo Salt, with Walter Pidgeon as the girl's rich protector, Hattie McDaniel, Alan Curtis, Nat Pendleton, Sam Levene and Charles D. Brown.

Luise Rainer, playing with a bravura that only two Oscars on an actress's mantelpiece can inspire, was **The Toy Wife**/Frou-Frou, a way- △ ward flirt in an Old Southern plantation, surrounded by ardent suitors (like Robert Young, here), julep-sipping colonels and spiritual-crooning darkies. Shades of Scarlett O'Hara? Well, having missed buying the best-seller of the decade, MGM had to do something. It gave the Zoe Akins play the sumptuous works in production (Merian C. Cooper), direction (Richard Thorpe) and cast (Melvyn Douglas, Barbara O'Neil–whose performance won her the role of Scarlett's mother in GWTW a year later–H. B. Warner, Alma Kruger, Walter Kingsford, Leonard Penn, Margaret Irving, Rafaela Ottiano, Clarence Muse, Theresa Harris). The public, however, failed to respond.

public liked him, and he went straight into **Vacation from Love**, another fast comedy, with June Knight and Brophy; also Florence Rice, Reginald Owen, Truman Bradley, Herman Bing, George Zucco; producer, Considine; director, George Fitzmaurice; writers were Patterson McNutt and Harlan Ware . . . **Burn 'Em Up O'Connor** starred O'Keefe as a speedway ace (with Harry Carey here) and Cecilia Parker, Pendleton, Alan Curtis, Charley Grapewin, Tom Neal, Terry, Bradley, Addison Richards; producer, Harry Rapf; director, Edward Sedgwick; writers, Milton Merlin and Byron Morgan, from Sir Malcolm Campbell's 'Salute to The Gods'.

Ever a publicity agent for Britain, MGM boosted Dr Barnardo's Homes, the British Mercantile Marine and the 'Queen Mary' in a made-in-Hollywood drama, **Lord Jeff**/The Boy *from Barnardo's. Mickey Rooney and Freddie Bartholomew (here with Charles Coburn) developed the fine teamwork they showed in* Devil is a Sissy *and* Captains Courageous; *but these old pros almost had their movie stolen by little Terry Kilburn, son of a London bus-driver. Peter Lawford was another new youngster in a cast including Herbert Mundin. Gale Sondergaard, George Zucco, Matthew Boulton, Walter Kingsford, Monty Woolley, Emma Dunn, Gilbert Emery. The Frank Davis production was directed by Sam Wood; script by James K. McGuinness from a Bradford Ropes–Val Burton–Endre Bohem original.*

Jeanette MacDonald and Nelson Eddy were at their peak as public idols, and sophisticates' derision had no effect on the box-office power of **The Girl of the Golden West**. *Jeanette as an 1850 saloon owner and Nelson as a bold bandit took some swallowing but, that accomplished, enjoyment of the romance, music and scenic splendour was easy. William Anthony McGuire produced on the grand scale, Robert Z. Leonard shrewdly directed the Isabel Dawn–Boyce DeGaw re-vamp of David Belasco's old stage melo. A new score was composed by Sigmund Romberg and Gus Kahn, with Gounod's 'Ave Maria' thrown in. Also cast: Walter Pidgeon, Leo Carrillo, Buddy Ebsen, Monty Woolley, Leonard Penn, H. B. Warner, Priscilla Lawson, Cliff Edwards, Noah Beery and Charley Grapewin.*

Spurred by the success of Topper *Hal Roach made another popular comedy,* **Merrily We Live**, *about a family of eccentrics, with the same production team. Except for delivery of two more Laurel and Hardy features, this concluded Roach's long association with MGM; he signed a distribution deal with United Artists in 1938. The picture was written by Jack Jevne and Eddie Moran, directed by Norman Z. McLeod with Milton Bren as associate producer, and starred Constance Bennett again. Her support included (left to right) Marjorie Rambeau, Paul Everton, Brian Aherne, Ann Dvorak, Billie Burke and Clarence Kolb; also cast were Patsy Kelly, Tom Brown, Alan Mowbray, Bonita Granville and Phillip Reed.*

Mayer was the instigator of **The Great Waltz**. *His penchant for Johann Strauss tunes found popular response when this handsome production came out–even if it was 'The Great Schmaltz' to some critics. It had a decidedly Continental flavour, with stars Luise Rainer from Vienna, Fernand Gravet from Paris and Miliza Korjus (here with Gravet) from Budapest; French director Julien Duvivier; German author Gottfried Reinhardt; Russian cameraman Joseph Ruttenberg (who won the first of his four Academy Awards); and Russian music scorer Dmitri Tiomkin. Miss Korjus was an enthusiastic soprano with great star potential but, mysteriously, her film debut was also her film farewell. Her singing of the Strauss melodies–with lyrics by Oscar Hammerstein II, 'I'm in Love with Vienna' and 'One Day When We Were Young' became best-sellers–was a highlight of the Bernard Hyman production. So were Tiomkin's gorgeous orchestrations and Ruttenberg's swirling cameras. Hugh Herbert, Lionel Atwill, Minna Gombell, Herman Bing, Sig Rumann and Henry Hull had parts in the Walter Reisch–Samuel Hoffenstein screenplay, a triangle of Strauss (Gravet), his wife (Rainer) and a temptress (Korjus).*

Port of Seven Seas, *the Hollywood version of* Fanny, *Marcel Pagnol's classic of Marseilles waterfront life, was no disgrace to the original. Wallace Beery soft-pedalled his familiar acting tricks to join Maureen O'Sullivan (with him here) and Frank Morgan in a splendid trio of performances. Henry Henigson produced, with three illustrious collaborators: director James Whale, scenarist Preston Sturges, cameraman Karl Freund. Rest of cast: John Beal, Jessie Ralph, Cora Witherspoon, Etienne Girardot.*

The morning-glory career of Luise Rainer, so quickly blooming amid critics' and Academy awards, was a rare instance of MGM failing to sustain a star's lustre. It had been wilting for some time when she made **Dramatic School**. *That did it. She left Metro, made one more movie, then retired (now a London resident of many years). Ironically, this lumbering drama about rival actresses, adapted by Ernst Vajda and Mary McCall Jr from a Hungarian play, was the first production by Mervyn LeRoy under the fabulous contract with which Mayer had lured him from Warner Bros: his annual pay of $300,000 was announced as $150,000 to keep Mayer's other producers quiet. Robert Sinclair directed Virginia Grey, Paulette Goddard, Lana Turner, Miss Rainer, Dorothy Granger and Ann Rutherford (left to right) and Alan Marshal, Genevieve Tobin, Henry Stephenson, Anthony Allan, Gale Sondergaard, Erik Rhodes, Margaret Dumont, Melville Cooper.*

Virginia Bruce never quite hit stardom, but in **The First Hundred Years** *(the hardest in any marriage, according to author-producer Norman Krasna's frothy comedy about a Manhattan couple breaking up after only five) she was particularly praised for her career-wife portrayal opposite Robert Montgomery. They were supported by Lee Bowman and Binnie Barnes (with them here) and Alan Dinehart, Harry Davenport, E. E. Clive, Nydia Westman and Jonathan Hale. Script, Melville Baker; direction, Richard Thorpe.*

Janet Gaynor, winner of the first Academy Award for an actress (1928), was coming to the end of a happy career with **Three Loves Has Nancy**. She married Adrian, whose designs for MGM stars influenced women's fashions throughout the Thirties. This movie was a crowd-pleasing comedy about a small-town girl, a novelist (Robert Montgomery) and a publisher (Franchot Tone, here) in a New York ménage à trois—quite platonic, you understand. Grady Sutton played her third love, with Claire Dodd, Guy Kibbee, Reginald Owen, Cora Witherspoon, Emma Dunn, Charley Grapewin and Lester Matthews also cast. Richard Thorpe directed the Norman Krasna production. Script: Samuel and Bella Spewack, George Oppenheimer, David Hertz.

Seeking a more rugged image for the almost too handsome Robert Taylor, the studio cast him as a prizefighter in **The Crowd Roars**. It worked, thanks to Richard Thorpe's vigorous direction of a hardboiled screenplay by Thomas Lennon, George Bruce and George Oppenheimer from Bruce's original, and to Taylor's always serious application to his profession; the box office roared. Here in the foreground: trainer Lionel Stander, boxer Taylor, father and manager Frank Morgan, promoter Charles D. Brown. Also in the Sam Zimbalist production were Edward Arnold, Maureen O'Sullivan, William Gargan, Jane Wyman, Nat Pendleton, Gene Reynolds and Isabel Jewell ... Tough guy

Taylor put up his dukes again for a run-in with Beery in **Stand Up and Fight**, a rousing melodrama of stagecoach-versus-railroad pioneering days. Producer Mervyn LeRoy got into his box-office stride with this one, directed by busy W. S. Van Dyke. Notable in support of Bob and Wally were heroine Florence Rice, black actor Clinton Rosemond, heavies Charles Bickford and Barton MacLane, Helen Broderick for laughs, and John Qualen, Charley Grapewin, Jonathan Hale, Robert Gleckler. Script by James Cain, Jane Murfin and Harvey Ferguson from a Forbes Parkhill original.

Only the horse looked bored when everybody went **Out West With the Hardys**. Title told all, but the series was now so important that three writers had to work on it: Kay Van Riper, William Ludwig, Agnes Christine Johnston. George B. Seitz directed (left to right) Sara Haden, back for good as Aunt Milly, Nana Bryant, Cecilia Parker, Fay Holden, Ralph Morgan, Virginia Weidler, Mickey Rooney and Lewis Stone. Also cast were Ann Rutherford, Don Castle, Gordon Jones, Tom Neal, Anthony Allan.

Maureen O'Sullivan, Lew Ayres and Burgess Meredith were the rather mature college kids frolicking through **Spring Madness**. A pleasant featherweight, it was unique among varsity movies in having no football or other athletic climax. The Philip Barry play 'Spring Dance' was adapted by producer Edward Chodorov with newcomer S. Sylvan Simon directing. Ruth Hussey, Ann Morriss, Frank Albertson, Joyce Compton, Jacqueline Wells, Truman Bradley, Marjorie Gateson and Sterling Holloway rounded out the cast.

MGM departed from policy to distribute the independently-produced **Flirting with Fate**. It just happened to have been made by David Loew, son of Marcus and twin brother of Arthur, MGM foreign sales chief. A so-so farce set in South America, it starred Joe E. Brown, previously Warners' top comedian, with Steffi Duna (left), Leo Carrillo (right) and Wynne Gibson, Beverly Roberts, Charles Judels, Leonid Kinskey, Irene Franklin and George Humbert. Frank McDonald directed the Joseph March–Ethel LaBlanche–Charles Melson–Harry Clork screenplay.

Franciska Gaal, whose face and style brought back memories of Mary Pickford, was imported from Budapest for three Hollywood movies; **The Girl Downstairs** was the last. Naïve to a degree as the slavey who won man-about-town Franchot Tone from her rich employer, Rita Johnson, she couldn't make a hit of the flimsy Harold Goldman–Felix Jackson–Karl Noti script, directed by Norman Taurog and produced by Harry Rapf. Tone came off best in a cast that included Walter Connolly, Reginald Owen, Reginald Gardiner, Franklin Pangborn, Robert Coote and Barnett Parker.

Laurel and Hardy again. In **Swiss Miss** they played a couple of mousetrap salesmen with no customers who took jobs in a Tyrolean hotel—which immediately became disaster-prone. Singers Della Lind from Vienna and Walter Woolf King from Broadway supported the zanies, who had comic competition from Eric Blore in the Hal Roach production directed by John Blystone. The James Parrott–Felix Adler–Charles Melson script stemmed from an original by Jean Negulesco and Charles Rogers ... **Block-Heads**, the last of the Laurel and Hardy features made by Roach for MGM, was trimmed to a fast 55 minutes. Patricia Ellis and Billy Gilbert (here with the stars) joined in their knockabout fun with élan, as did Minna Gombell and Jimmy Finlayson. Some of their gags were supplied by that great clown of the silents, Harry Langdon; other contributors were Adler, Rogers, Parrott and Arnold Belgard. Blystone directed.

Made for Christmas 1938, and given frequent annual revivals, **A Christmas Carol** radiated Dickensian warmth to the last chortle and holly berry. Reginald Owen and Terry Kilburn (foreground) were just right as Scrooge and Tiny Tim; Owen replaced Lionel Barrymore, whose lameness prevented his filming the radio characterization he broadcast every Christmas. Gene Lockhart, Barry Mackay and Lynne Carver (rear) and Leo G. Carroll, Kathleen Lockhart, Ann Rutherford, Ronald Sinclair and Lionel Braham supported. Producer, Joseph Mankiewicz; scenarist, Hugo Butler; director, Edwin Marin.

1938

Dorothy Parker was observed one day leaning out of her window in the writers' building, shouting 'Let me out – I'm as sane as you are!'. She and husband Alan Campbell were embroiled in the script of **Sweethearts**, assigned on the theory that Jeanette MacDonald and Nelson Eddy could stand some acid of wit added to their usual sugary recipe. The ancient Victor Herbert operetta seemed an unlikely subject for the experiment, but it came out as an up-dated, well-Parkerized comedy of a temperamental theatre couple, brightly acted and splendidly sung by its stars. Another daring move was shooting it all in Technicolor – a first at MGM since 1929's The Mysterious Island. Here: Florence Rice, Miss MacDonald, Eddy, Frank Morgan. Also cast: Ray Bolger, Mischa Auer, Herman Bing, George Barbier, Raymond Walburn, Gene and Kathleen Lockhart, Terry Kilburn. Another moneyspinner from the Hunt Stromberg–W. S. Van Dyke producing–directing mint.

The second MGM-British effort was even more successful than A Yank at Oxford. **The Citadel**, A. J. Cronin's best-seller about a young doctor temporarily forsaking his ideals for money made a strong vehicle for Robert Donat (left), lifted Rosalind Russell's career another notch and brought director King Vidor (right) back to the Metro fold after five years away. Victor Saville, who produced, drew upon the London theatre's acting riches for the cast: Ralph Richardson, Rex Harrison, Emlyn Williams, Mary Clare, Cecil Parker, Penelope

Dudley-Ward, Francis L. Sullivan, Nora Swinburne, Felix Aylmer, Athene Seyler, Edward Chapman. Williams also collaborated with Ian Dalrymple, Frank Wead and Elizabeth Hill (Vidor's wife) on the screenplay.

A diverting trilogy began with **Fast Company**, filmed from Marco Page's whodunit about a rare-book buff, his wife and their amateur detecting. Made to mollify exhibitors who complained of the long wait between 'Thin Man' movies, it was followed by two more with the same characters – oddly enough, played by different stars each time. The originals were Melvyn Douglas and Florence Rice, with Claire Dodd (here with Douglas) as the blonde menace, and Louis Calhern, Shepperd Strudwick, Nat Pendleton, Douglass Dumbrille, George Zucco, Horace MacMahon, Thurston Hall, Minor Watson and Mary Howard. Edward Buzzell directed and Frederick Stephani produced from Page's script. Page became a staff writer under his real name, Harry Kurnitz.

Emotions erupted in **Woman Against Woman** and **The Shining Hour**. The first had Wife No. 1 (Mary Astor) versus Wife No. 2 (Virginia Bruce) slugging it out for the love of Herbert Marshall. Edward Chodorov's screenplay, from Margaret Banning's 'Enemy Territory', was one for the ladies to catch between lunch and the hairdresser. Chodorov produced it himself, with Broadway's Robert Sinclair making his bow as a movie director, and Janet Beecher, Marjorie Rambeau, Betty Ross Clark, Zeffie Tilbury, Sarah Padden, Dorothy Christy and moppet Juanita Quigley in the cast . . . Joan Crawford, Melvyn Douglas, Margaret Sullavan, Robert Young, Fay Bainter were in **The Shining Hour**, Keith Winter's stage success fattened up with additional action by scenarists Ogden Nash and Jane Murfin. Miss Crawford played a night-club dancer taken by husband Douglas to his Wisconsin farm, where emotional involvements

with his sister-in-law, Miss Sullavan, brother Young and sister Miss Bainter gave all the acting talents concerned a good work-out. Allyn Joslyn, Frank Albertson, Hattie McDaniel and Oscar O'Shea supported them in Joseph Mankiewicz's production, directed by Frank Borzage.

Meanwhile, back on the hospital set, stetho-scopes and thermometers were handed out with the Max Factor make-up as (left to right) Florence Rice, Alan Marshal, Ann Rutherford, Mary Howard, Buddy Ebsen and Una Merkel went into a quadruple version of the studio's pet theme, **Four Girls in White**. S. Sylvan Simon directed the Nat Levine production, a Nathalie Bucknall–Endre Bohem original scripted by Dorothy Yost. Mrs Bucknall was head of the studio's research department. Cast included Kent Taylor, Jessie Ralph, Sara Haden, Phillip Terry, Tom Neal.

One of the big hits in MGM's history was ▽ scored by **Test Pilot**. With believable characters and realistic action, it had critics throwing superlatives around with abandon, and rolled up enormous grosses. Clark Gable played the title role, Myrna Loy the wife with heart in throat as he did his aerobatics, and Spencer Tracy the mechanic and best friend whom he killed in the climactic crash. Louis D. Lighton and Victor Fleming, the Captains Courageous producer and director, had a hardhitting script by Waldemar Young and Vincent Lawrence (from Frank Wead's original) to work from; Ray June contributed stunning aerial photography. Also cast: Lionel Barrymore, Samuel S. Hinds, Marjorie Main, Gloria Holden, Louis Jean Heydt, Ted Pearson, Virginia Grey, Priscilla Lawson.

Idiot's Delight, was a trenchant anti-war play by Robert E. Sherwood which the author ad-apted to star Clark Gable and Norma Shearer. Sherwood added early scenes, establishing the leads' love affair during a US vaudeville tour, to his Broadway (Lunt and Fontanne) and West End (Raymond Massey, later Lee Tracy, and Tamara Geva) smash; the European mid-section, with the girl turning up as a Russian-accented siren and disclaiming the man and their past, came straight from the play; the ending, alas, was made Hollywood-happy. Gable had a great time (he danced for the only time in his career) as the hoofer stranded in a Continental hotel as World War II began to erupt. Miss Shearer, in a role that might have suited Garbo better, attacked it with verve and almost met its extraordinary demands. Clarence Brown's direction caught every facet of the glittering Sherwood script, and Hunt Stromberg, ending MGM's 1938 production schedule on a high note, picked a strong sup-porting cast: Edward Arnold, Charles Coburn, Burgess Meredith, Laura Hope Crews, Joseph Schildkraut, Pat Paterson, Peter Willes, Skeets Gallagher, Fritz Feld, Virginia Grey, Joan Marsh. Bernadene Hayes.

Too Hot to Handle was too fast to be a flop, besides which it co-starred Clark Gable and Myrna Loy, just voted the King and Queen of Hollywood in a national poll. The 'King' label stuck to Gable for his remaining 22 years. A fine froth of action was whipped up by Jack Conway from the Laurence Stallings–John Lee Mahin script about a newsreel cameraman and an aviatrix, and the Lawrence Weingarten production proved a potent moneymaker. Also cast: Walter Pidgeon, Walter Connolly, Leo Carrillo, Johnny Hines, Virginia Weidler, Marjorie Main, Gregory Gaye, Betty Ross Clark, Henry Kolker.

GONE WITH THE WIND
1939

NBC began regular television transmissions to the American public, an event that was to prove more devastating to Hollywood in the long run than the European war which was of more immediate concern to the industry's financiers – they saw the probability of a vast market being shut down. The BBC had beaten NBC to it by three years, but only about 5,000 sets had been bought in England, so television was shrugged off by the movies as just a possible threat – to radio.

Films were strikingly higher in quality this year. The *Gone With The Wind* furore was preceded by *Stagecoach, Mr Smith Goes to Washington, Wuthering Heights, Love Affair, Of Mice and Men, Gunga Din, Jesse James, The Rains Came,* remakes of *Beau Geste* and *The Hunchback of Notre Dame,* plus a vintage crop from MGM-Loew's which harvested another $10m profit.

Bette Davis had four hits, *Dark Victory, Juarez, The Old Maid, The Private Lives of Elizabeth and Essex.* Ingrid Bergman arrived in *Intermezzo;* Marlene Dietrich came back in *Destry Rides Again.*

A lot of heavy actors did a lot of heavy acting in **Let Freedom Ring**, *an action melodrama set in Western pioneering days and climaxed by Nelson Eddy singing 'The Star Spangled Banner'. This 1939 dawn's early light wasn't very proudly hailed by MGM, but it did pretty well commercially. Ben Hecht wrote it, Jack Conway directed and Harry Rapf produced, with Edward Arnold, Victor McLaglen, Lionel Barrymore, Eddy and Virginia Bruce (left to right) and Guy Kibbee, Charles Butterworth, H. B. Warner, Raymond Walburn, Sarah Padden and Billy Bevan.*

Mickey Rooney dropped his Andy Hardy gimmicks to give a fine performance in **The Adventures of Huckleberry Finn**. *He was ably partnered by the black actor Rex Ingram (same-named as the early MGM director) who had won fame as De Lawd in The Green Pastures. Hugo Butler wrote a straightforward script from Mark Twain's masterpiece, which had been previously filmed by Paramount in 1920 and 1931. Direction by Richard Thorpe and production by Joseph Mankiewicz won general approval, as did performers Walter Connolly, William Frawley, Lynne Carver, Jo Ann Sayers, Elisabeth Risdon, Victor Kilian, Minor Watson and Clara Blandick.*

Believing that the crazy comedy vogue could stand revival, MGM signed Claudette Colbert, star of many a madcap romp since her 1934 Oscar-winning It Happened One Night, for **It's a Wonderful World**. *Producer Frank Davis cast the equally expert James Stewart with her and assigned W. S. Van Dyke as director – but no dice. The Ben Hecht script played as not so much funny as just plain silly, and ticket-buyers were scarce. Ernest Truex, Frances Drake, Sidney Blackmer, Nat Pendleton, Guy Kibbee, Richard Carle, Cecil Cunningham and Andy Clyde were also caught up in the find-the-murderer farce.*

Bridal Suite *was another comedy that caused no box-office stampede. It had (left to right) Annabella, Robert Young, Walter Connolly and Billie Burke in a Samuel Hoffenstein screenplay, from an original by Gottfried Rein-*

hardt and Virginia Faulkner, about a playboy (Young) who never turned up for his own weddings. Edgar Selwyn produced and William Thiele directed; Reginald Owen, Arthur Treacher, Gene Lockhart, Virginia Field and Felix Bressart completed the cast.

Lucky Night *was the only movie Myrna Loy and Robert Taylor made together. Individually surefire, they somehow didn't blend too well. The story of a New York couple setting out to win a fortune overnight was in the wild comedy style and required a lighter touch than Norman Taurog's heavy directorial hand provided. Joseph Allen, Henry O'Neill, Douglas Fowley, Bernard Nedell and Marjorie Main had supporting spots in the Louis D. Lighton production, written by Vincent Lawrence and Grover Jones from a yarn by Oliver Claxton.*

Joan Crawford had a winning pair of co-stars, James Stewart and Lew Ayres, in **The Ice Follies of 1939**; *but it was her biggest flop. Elaborately produced by Harry Rapf (who had guided her early career) with an eye-popping ice ballet in Technicolor to top it off, the movie fell flat on its face, tripped by Reinhold Schunzel's stodgy direction and a dreary script by Leonard Praskins, Florence Ryerson and Edgar Allan Woolf. The show-biz triangle story was better told by the silent Excess Baggage. Also cast: Lewis Stone, Lionel Stander, Mary Forbes, Truman Bradley, Marie Blake, Charles D. Brown, skating star Bess Ehrhardt.*

Lady of the Tropics *was Hedy Lamarr's MGM debut after two years under contract, a loan-out to co-star with Charles Boyer in Algiers, several false starts on I Take This Woman, and acres of 'most beautiful girl in the world' publicity. Like Greer Garson, Hedy had been discovered by Mayer during his 1937 London visit to launch A Yank at Oxford. She had been uncovered by the Czech film Ecstasy four years earlier when, as Hedy Kiesler, she shocked the then shockable world by appearing nude. Mayer renamed her after the silent screen beauty Barbara LaMarr, and personally supervised every detail of her star grooming – until Tropics flopped and his ardour cooled. Left to right: Gloria Franklin, Zeffie Tilbury, Ernest*

Cossart, Hedy, Robert Taylor. Joseph Schild-kraut, Natalie Moorhead, Charles Trowbridge, Cecil Cunningham, Frederick Worlock and Paul Porcasi were also in the Sam Zimbalist production, written to formula by Ben Hecht and directed by Jack Conway.

For once Jeanette MacDonald's voice, charm and glamour failed to get box-office response in **Broadway Serenade**/Serenade. As in Sweet-hearts, she played a stage star; Lew Ayres was her neglected husband and Ian Hunter her show's angel. Their trite triangle kept inter-rupting the musical programme, which ranged from a 'Madame Butterfly' aria to a super-colossal staged by Busby Berkeley. Robert Z. Leonard produced and directed Charles Lederer's screenplay, based on an unoriginal by Lew Lipton, John T. Foote and Hans Kraly. Others cast: Frank Morgan, Rita Johnson, Wally Vernon, William Gargan, Virginia Grey, Katherine Alexander, Al Shean, Esther Dale, Franklin Pangborn.

Eduardo Ciannelli, whose death's-head face was his fortune, played the heavy bested by hero Walter Pidgeon in **Society Lawyer**, a remake of Penthouse (the 1933 Goodrich–Hackett script was brushed up by Hugo Butler and Leon Gordon). This crime drama was otherwise notable for heroine Virginia Bruce breaking into song with 'I'm in Love with the Honorable Mr So-and-So'. Leo Carrillo, Frances Mercer, Paul Guilfoyle, Lee Bowman, Ann Morriss, Edward Brophy and Herbert Mundin were also cast. Edwin Marin directed for producer John Considine Jr.

Remember?, Greer Garson's second movie, was an inept triangle comedy with an amnesia gim-mick. It began Miss Garson's long Hollywood career by giving her the full star treatment, including a top-grade surrounding cast. Left to right: Billie Burke, Miss Garson, Robert Taylor, Reginald Owen and Lew Ayres. Also cast were Laura Hope Crews, George Barbier, Sara Haden, Halliwell Hobbes, Sig Ruman, Richard Carle, Paul Hurst. It was written by Corey Ford and Norman Z. McLeod, directed by McLeod and produced by Milton Bren, a combination taken over from Hal Roach.

Walter Brennan, Ann Sothern and William Gargan in **Joe and Ethel Turp Call on the President**. Hiding behind that formidable title was an amusing little 'B', based on one of Damon Runyon's yarns, about a couple taking their troubles right up to the White House. Its occupier turned out to be that No. 1 father-figure, Lewis Stone. Others enacting the Melville Baker script were Marsha Hunt, Tom Neal, Muriel Hutchison, Louis Jean Heydt, Mary Gordon and Jack Mulhall. Edgar Selwyn produced, Robert Sinclair directed.

Tod Browning came back to direct Henry Hull as a Houdini-like 'escapologist' and Robert Young as a sleuthing illusionist in **Miracles for Sale**, a thriller by Clayton Rawson about spiritualist mediums and stage magicians. Florence Rice, Frank Craven, Lee Bowman, William Demarest, Astrid Allwyn, Walter Kingsford, Charley Grapewin, Gloria Holden and Frederick Worlock were involved in the arcane goings-on, scripted by James Edward Grant, Marion Parsonnet and Harry Ruskin.

The era's most fascinating romance continued in **Marx Brothers at the Circus**, as Groucho subjected Margaret Dumont to new indignities and she remained in thrall to his every eyebrow-wiggle. The title tells the rest of the story, such as it is, of this moneymaker. Harpo, Chico and Groucho brought glorious anarchy to the Big Top; Kenny Baker sang Arlen–Harburg songs to Florence Rice—but singing (?) honours were snatched by Groucho's 'Lydia the Tattooed Lady'. Producer, Mervyn LeRoy; director, Edward Buzzell; script, Irving Brecher; also cast, Eve Arden, Nat Pendleton, Barnett Parker, Fritz Feld.

The Women, produced by Hunt Stromberg, was one of the year's top successes. But Clare Boothe's international stage hit had presented difficulties in filming. For one thing, the play scored some of its loudest laughs with lines no movie censor would pass: Anita Loos, scripting in collaboration with Jane Murfin, fixed that by inventing even funnier ones without weaken-ing the original's punch. Then the studio decided to cram the all-female cast with big star names, and tornadoes of temperament were forecast: director George Cukor, Holly-wood's intrepid lioness-tamer, kept them all happy, barring one clash between Norma Shearer and Joan Crawford. The film proved hugely enjoyable. Left to right: Joan Fontaine, Miss Shearer, Rosalind Russell (who stole the show as the bitchiest of the lot), Mary Boland (a riot as the ageless seeker after l'amour) and Paulette Goddard. Besides Miss Crawford, the cast also boasted Ruth Hussey, Virginia Weidler, Cora Witherspoon, Marjorie Main, Hedda Hopper, Lucile Watson, Virginia Grey, Muriel Hutchison, Florence Nash, Esther Dale, Ann Morriss, Mary Beth Hughes and, in her Broadway role, Phyllis Povah. They and a fashion parade in Technicolor were gowned by Adrian to dazzling effect.

Garbo's sense of humour, glimpsed in brief flashes during her reign as tragedy queen, was given full scope in **Ninotchka** which ranks, with Camille, Queen Christina and Anna Karenina, among the greatest Garbos, still being shown in the many special seasons of her films. Guided by the best of romantic comedy directors, Ernst Lubitsch, she gave a marvellous performance, first as a deadpan Russian commissar rapping out her lines with machine-gun speed, then transformed by Paris and Melvyn Douglas into a pleasure-loving charmer, as in this delightful drunk scene. 'Garbo Laughs!' was the ad slogan, and the world laughed with her to make it a total success. Charles Brackett, Billy Wilder and Walter Reisch adapted Melchior Lengyel's original for producer Sidney Franklin; the cast included Ina Claire, Bela Lugosi, Gregory Gaye, Edwin Maxwell, Richard Carle, and Ninotchka's hilarious trio of subordinates: Sig Ruman, Felix Bressart, Alexander Granach.

They All Come Out *started as a short in the* Crime Does Not Pay *series, grew to a four-reel 'special' and finally became a full-length feature. Producer Jack Chertok had John Higgins expanding his script and Jacques Tourneur enlarging his cast during several months. The resulting crime melodrama had documentary overtones of US prison and parole systems. Left to right: Rita Johnson, Tom Neal, Bernard Nedell, Edward Gargan; also cast were Addison Richards, John Gallaudet, Frank Thomas, Ann Shoemaker.*

The fourth screen version of Bayard Veiller's **Within the Law** *was made with Tom Neal, William Gargan, Samuel S. Hinds, Ruth Hussey. The charming Miss Hussey lacked the star quality Joan Crawford had displayed in* Paid *eight years earlier, and Charles Lederer's script was no improvement. Gustav Machaty, best known for having unveiled Hedy Lamarr in* Ecstasy, *directed for producer Lou Ostrow. Rita Johnson, Paul Kelly, Sidney Blackmer, John King and Lynne Carver were also cast.*

The triumph of **Goodbye, Mr Chips** *made the ◁ new MGM British unit's score three hits out of three tries. James Hilton's short, quiet novel about a schoolmaster turning sour until marriage sweetened his life was beautifully filled out in the screenplay by R. C. Sherriff, Claudine West and Eric Maschwitz; filmed with a sure feeling for English atmosphere by American director Sam Wood. Robert Donat's portrayal of Chips, almost unbearably poignant at times, won the Academy Award and became one of the best-loved performances ever screened. Similar audience affection was aroused by Greer Garson in the briefer role of his wife. Since being seen on the London stage and signed by Mayer in 1937 she had nearly given up hope of a film debut until this part opened up a brilliant future for her. Paul Henreid (left), and Terry Kilburn as four generations of Chips' pupils, John Mills, Lyn Harding, Austin Trevor, Edmond Breon, Jill and Judith Furse, Milton Rosmer and David Tree were in the cast assembled by producer Victor Saville. Photographed by Freddie Young, whose artistry was still serving MGM 30 years later.*

Former actor Leslie Fenton had been directing Crime Does Not Pay *shorts to learn his new job, and* **Tell No Tales**, *with Louise Platt, Melvyn Douglas and Esther Dale (here) was his first full-length work. The out-of-the-rut script (Lionel Houser; original by Pauline London and Alfred Taylor) was a series of dramatic vignettes linked by Douglas as a reporter seeking a kidnapper. In the cast, which was exceptionally large for a 'B' movie, were Gene Lockhart, Douglass Dumbrille, Sara Haden, Florence George, Halliwell Hobbes, Zeffie Tilbury, Hobart Cavanaugh and Oscar O'Shea. Edward Chodorov produced.*

Another Thin Man *was William Powell's first movie for nearly two years—a long battle with illness had kept him off the screen. His return delighted the multitudes who had been enduring imitation Thin Men. The old team—Powell, Myrna Loy, Asta, writers Frances Goodrich and Albert Hackett, director W. S. Van Dyke, producer Hunt Stromberg—was in fine form, with admirable support from C. Aubrey Smith, Ruth Hussey, Otto Kruger, Virginia Grey, Tom Neal, Marjorie Main, Nat Pendleton, Grant Mitchell and Horace MacMahon. Nick and Nora allowed themselves a little parental goo-gooing over Nick Jr (a role dribbled fetchingly by one William Anthony Poulsen) when not dealing wittily with three murders in New York's high and low society.*
Mayer wanted his new protégée, Hedy Lamarr, to get the Dietrich glamour treatment, and signed Josef von Sternberg to direct her in I Take This Woman. *It proved another false start at MGM for Joe, who was switched to Wallace Beery in* **Sergeant Madden** *(quite a*

switch!), and he actually finished this one, though not without stormy star-director incidents. Less stylish than his silent crime movies (The Drag Net, Underworld), it was still an effective melodrama, with Laraine Day making a bright debut as the wife of Beery's bad-cop son, Alan Curtis. Also in the J. Walter Ruben production were Tom Brown, Fay Holden, Marc Lawrence, Marion Martin and Horace MacMahon. Wells Root scripted the William Ullman original.

Northwest Passage *was one of the few movies shot entirely in Technicolor during the Thirties. Bought two years earlier, Kenneth Roberts' best-seller went into production in July 1939 with the script still only half-finished. When director King Vidor brought his company back from a 12-week Idaho location, he found that the book's second half was no nearer an approved screenplay, and that producer Hunt Stromberg had decided to call a halt. A little footage tying up loose ends was shot in December and 'Book 1: Rogers' Rangers' was added to the title. The story of finding the Northwest Passage through Canada was never filmed. But the preliminary campaign against marauding Indians made a robust demi-epic, well reviewed and very profitable. Robert Young, Spencer Tracy and Truman Bradley*

(here) were among the actors who endured months of swamp-wading, rapids-fording and mountain-climbing. Walter Brennan, Ruth Hussey, Nat Pendleton, Robert Barrat, Regis Toomey, Isabel Jewell, Lumsden Hare, Montagu Love, Douglas Walton, Donald MacBride and Addison Richards also had roles in the screenplay written by Talbot Jennings and Laurence Stallings.

1939 brought three more audience (and exhibitor) pleasers from the Hardy Family factory. Lewis Stone and Mickey Rooney in **The Hardys Ride High,** *in which writers Kay Van Riper, William Ludwig and Agnes Christine Johnston had them enjoying – temporarily – a million-dollar inheritance; Virginia Grey, John King, Halliwell Hobbes, Marsha Hunt, William Orr and Minor Watson were cast 'guests'. . . Helen Gilbert, Rooney, Ann Rutherford, George Breakston and Terry Kilburn in* **Andy Hardy Gets Spring Fever,** *with Andy producing his school play, 'Adrift in Tahiti' – a subject familiar to W. S. Van Dyke who replaced George B. Seitz as director just this once; Robert Kent and Addison Richards were others cast in the Van Riper script . . . Stone, Cecilia Parker and Rooney in* **Judge Hardy and Son,** *a Carey Wilson screenplay which threw the family into sombre mood when Ma Hardy suffered a near-fatal illness; cast newcomers were Henry Hull, Maria Ouspenskaya, June Preisser, Martha O'Driscoll and Joe Yule, Rooney's real-life father. Stone, Miss Parker, Fay Holden, Sara Haden and Miss Rutherford appeared in all three; Lou Ostrow produced anonymously.*

Several ingredients of old William Haines movies went into **The Kid from Texas,** *a breezy 'B' for Dennis O'Keefe. Edgar Selwyn returned to produce it, with S. Sylvan Simon directing and Florence Rice, Buddy Ebsen, Jessie Ralph, Anthony Allan, Tully Marshall, Jack Carson and Virginia Dale (the last two here with O'Keefe) in the cast. Scenarists Albert Mannheimer, Florence Ryerson and Edgar Allan Woolf let imagination run riot for the climax, a polo match between cowboys and Indians!*

150

Kildare got involved with lawbreakers in his second movie, **Calling Dr Kildare,** *and again raised the pulse-beat of the public. The latter also began to take notice of Lana Turner, now stepping out of the ingénue crowd towards the blonde-bombshell throne left vacant by Jean Harlow. Continuing from the first Kildare were Lew Ayres, Lionel Barrymore, Nat Pendleton, Lynne Carver, Samuel S. Hinds, Emma Dunn, Walter Kingsford and Marie Blake; scripters Harry Ruskin and Willis Goldbeck, director Harold Bucquet and producer (unbilled) Lou Ostrow. Newcomers were Laraine Day as nurse and Alma Kruger as matron, both to become series regulars, Phillip Terry, Donald Barry and (here with Lew and Lana) George Offerman.*

Helen Gilbert, the star patient of Lew Ayres, Lionel Barrymore and Laraine Day in **The Secret of Dr Kildare,** *is unique in Hollywood history: she became a featured actress through joining the studio orchestra and played the cello for many a soundtrack before being Discovered. She wasn't so good at playing roles – but she was beautiful. Others in this superior item in the series were Lionel Atwill, Robert Kent, Sara Haden, Grant Mitchell and Martha O'Driscoll, with regulars Nat Pendleton, Walter Kingsford, Alma Kruger and Marie Blake; Emma Dunn and Samuel S. Hinds played Kildare's parents. Harold Bucquet again directed the Willis Goldbeck–Harry Ruskin script.*

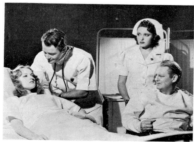

I Take This Woman *had become a laughing-stock in Hollywood long before it reached the screen. Referred to as 'I Retake This Woman' or 'Mayer's Folly', it had been in and out of production for 18 months, first under Josef von Sternberg (briefly) then Frank Borzage (only one of whose scenes was retained) and finally old troubleshooter W. S. Van Dyke. Lawrence Weingarten was nominally the producer, but Mayer himself, determined to make Hedy Lamarr the star of stars no matter what the rushes indicated, was very much in charge until even he gave up the struggle. Hedy made* Lady of the Tropics *and Spencer Tracy was lent to Fox for* Stanley and Livingstone *while various writers tinkered with the Charles MacArthur story and miles of rejected footage went into*

the bins. Ina Claire, Walter Pidgeon and Adrienne Ames disappeared from the cast; Verree Teasdale (here with Tracy and Lamarr) and Kent Taylor, Laraine Day, Jack Carson and Frances Drake were added; Paul Cavanagh, Mona Barrie, Louis Calhern, Marjorie Main and George E. Stone survived throughout. Final script credit (?) went to James K. McGuinness.

Another series, which was to last a long time and make a lot of money for MGM, began with **Maisie.** *Ann Sothern had been playing leads for five years, but this study of a flip, hard-boiled but likeable adventuress made her a real star. Robert Young (left) as the ranch-hand she lassoed, and Ian Hunter (seated) as the husband whose marital problem she solved, also scored in the J. Walter Ruben production, smartly directed by Edwin Marin. Mary McCall Jr scripted from a Wilson Collison story. Also cast: Ruth Hussey, Cliff Edwards, George Tobias, Anthony Allan, Willie Fung (centre) and Robert Middlemass (right).*

In **Congo Maisie** *Ann Sothern swung her hips and jangled her bracelets into the well-received sequel to Maisie's first adventure. She scored strongly again, and John Carroll made his MGM bow. It was a rewrite of Wilson Collison's* Red Dust *by Mary McCall Jr. That hit's Harlow–Gable–Astor triangle was completed now by Rita Johnson; Shepperd Strudwick, J. M. Kerrigan, Leonard Mudie and E. E. Clive had lesser roles. H. C. Potter directed; Ruben produced.*

Two more movies completed the whodunit career of the 'Fast' detective and his wife. **Fast and Loose** followed Fast Company, the series now given extra stellar heft in Robert Montgomery and Rosalind Russell. Edwin Marin directed with a sharp ear for the laugh lines in Harry Kurnitz's script, making it a superior programmer. Sidney Blackmer, Alan Dinehart and Donald Douglas were the only players missing from this scene—left to right: Montgomery, Ralph Morgan, Mary Forbes, Jo Ann Sayers, Reginald Owen, Anthony Allan, Tom Collins, Miss Russell, Ian Wolfe, Etienne Girardot. Frederick Stephani produced . . .

Fast and Furious, the last of the 'Fast' comedy-mysteries, starred Ann Sothern and Franchot Tone. This time Harry Kurnitz had his detective hero investigating murder in a beauty contest, helped and hindered by his none-too-trusting wife. Stephani produced and, surprisingly, Busby Berkeley directed, with Ruth Hussey, Lee Bowman, John Miljan, Allyn Joslyn, Bernard Nedell and Mary Beth Hughes cast.

Nelson Eddy and Ilona Massey in **Balalaika**. Miss Massey looked and sounded even better than in Rosalie, but the studio found her hard to cast and this was her last there for seven years. The story of Balalaika, an opulent version of Eric Maschwitz's stage hit, swooped from pre-Revolution Russia to 1938 Paris with everybody singing like mad. The Joseph Ruttenberg–Karl Freund photography and Herbert Stothart's score, incorporating music by George Posford and Bernard Gruen from the show ('Magic of Your Love', 'At the Balalaika') were stand-outs in the Lawrence Weingarten production, directed by Reinhold Schunzel from a Jacques Deval–Leon Gordon script. Also cast: Charles Ruggles, Frank Morgan, C. Aubrey Smith, Lionel Atwill, Walter Woolf King, Joyce Compton, Dalies Frantz, Phillip Terry, George Tobias, Alma Kruger.

Infrequency paid off again for the Tarzan series when **Tarzan Finds a Son** emerged almost three years after the last Johnny Weissmuller–Maureen O'Sullivan epic. Other studios produced lesser Tarzans in the interim; the big crowds were waiting for the big one and, as before, MGM gave it to 'em: more lions, elephants, monkeys, crocodiles and hokum than presented by any competitor, folks! Plus Johnny Sheffield as a jungle foundling (Tarzan and his mate somehow failed to reproduce) following his adopted Dad through every swimming and vine-swinging stunt. Cyril Hume's screenplay was directed by Richard Thorpe and produced by Sam Zimbalist, with Ian Hunter, Laraine Day, Henry Wilcoxon, Frieda Inescort and Henry Stephenson featured.

As the Rooney–Garland–Bartholomew class was graduating, younger youngsters were being developed for possible stardom; two of the best actors among them, although never the biggest names, were Virginia Weidler and Gene Reynolds. Producer Albert Levoy teamed them under William Thiele's direction in **Bad Little Angel**—a nauseating title for not a bad little movie. With them in the Dorothy Yost screenplay were Ian Hunter, Lois Wilson, Reginald Owen, Henry Hull, Guy Kibbee, Elizabeth Patterson, Mitchell Lewis, Esther Dale and subsidiary moppets Cora Sue Collins and Ann Todd.

The Wizard of Oz was the most expensive production in MGM's first 15 years. But it has had the longest continuous exposure of any picture and, never off release since it opened in 1939, has been piling up revenue non-stop. Producer Mervyn LeRoy started it with Richard Thorpe directing, stopped it after a few weeks and scrapped all footage in the grand Thalberg manner. It went back into work under Victor Fleming's direction after a brush-up of the Noel Langley–Florence Ryerson–Edgar Allan Woolf script, and the required air of dreamlike adventure came through in settings of Technicolored magnificence, peopled by fantastic characters. But the whole enterprise depended on the effectiveness of the girl who wandered through this wonderland: Fox wouldn't lend Shirley Temple, fortunately, but Judy Garland was on hand. Her awkward grace and plain-Jane beauty—not to mention her voice raised in the poignant 'Over the Rainbow', which became her lifelong theme song—made the film, and the film made her a superstar. Perfectly in key too were Jack Haley as the Tin Man, Ray Bolger as the Scarecrow and Bert Lahr as the Cowardly Lion (with her here) and Frank Morgan in the title role, Billie Burke and Margaret Hamilton as the good and wicked witches, and all the Harold Arlen–E. Y. Harburg score. 'We're Off to See the Wizard' became Australia's wartime marching song. A much inferior silent version of Frank Baum's juvenile classic had been filmed in 1925.

Their few scenes together in Calling Dr Kildare were so well received that Lew Ayres and Lana Turner were teamed in **These Glamour Girls**. It was Lana's first leading role and had critics hailing her as a new Clara Bow and/or Jean Harlow. The script by Marion Parsonnet and Jane Hall, from the latter's original, embraced six college romances and won special praise for its bright dialogue, delivered by, left to right (male), Tom Brown, Owen Davis Jr, Ayres, Richard Carlson, Peter Lind Hayes, Sumner Getchell, and (female) Ann Rutherford, Jane Bryan, Lana, Anita Louise, Marsha Hunt and Mary Beth Hughes; also cast were Ernest Truex, Tom Collins, Don Castle, Mary Forbes and Henry Kolker. S. Sylvan Simon directed the Sam Zimbalist production.

151

Zip, dash and exuberance propelled **Babes in Arms** *to great popularity, starting a cycle of 'Come on, kids, let's put on a show!' musicals. Mickey Rooney and Judy Garland dominated the proceedings with almost alarming versatility and professionalism, supported by Douglas McPhail and Betty Jaynes (top and bottom of the ladder), June Preisser, Johnny Sheffield, Leni Lynn, and adults Charles Winninger, Guy Kibbee, Grace Hayes, Henry Hull, Margaret Hamilton, Barnett Parker, Ann Shoemaker. Director Busby Berkeley omitted his old Warner Bros. chorus patterns, but not his zest in scenes like this title number, which with 'Where or When' and 'The Lady is a Tramp' survived from the Rodgers & Hart score of the 1937 Broadway show (strangely, 'Johnny One Note', 'My Funny Valentine' and 'I Wish I Were in Love Again' didn't). Producer Arthur Freed's 'I Cried for You' and 'Good Morning' were added. Script by Kay Van Riper and Jack McGowan.*

When **Gone With the Wind** *had its world premiere in Atlanta on December 14, 1939, the movie event, despite the real tragedy that started its long run three months earlier, was news everywhere. It was the culmination of the most intensively publicized production ever filmed. The furore began in June 1936 when Margaret Mitchell's 1,037-page novel was published with instantaneous success (it passed the million-copy mark in six months). David O. Selznick bought the film rights four weeks later for $50,000 – which eventually seemed so inadequate that he gave Miss Mitchell another $50,000. Although he intended it as the supreme achievement of the independent studio he had founded in 1935 after leaving MGM, Selznick was soon forced to turn to Mayer for aid. It seemed that, while casting Scarlett O'Hara, the stormy heroine, had become an international pastime, no one would accept any actor but Clark Gable in the male lead – and he was firmly tied to Metro. Also, Selznick needed an injection of cash. Presented with these needs of his son-in-law, Mayer made one of his greatest business deals: for Gable and an investment of $1,250,000 – less than a third of the total cost – MGM got the distribution rights and retained half the profits. (In 1944, after the demise of Selznick International, MGM acquired the film outright. By 1974 its estimated rentals totalled $150m.) Meanwhile, Selznick had assigned George Cukor to direct and play-wright Sidney Howard to do the screenplay, and launched a talent hunt for Scarlett that involved testing 1,400 unknowns and half the actresses in Hollywood. The first choice was Norma Shearer; a month later she announced her refusal, and the New York Times published an editorial regretting her decision! Leslie Howard and Olivia de Havilland were signed for the second leads. At last, in January 1939, Scarlett was won by Vivien Leigh, the English girl who had unknowingly tested for the part by playing the flirt (and incurring Mayer's wrath) in* A Yank at Oxford. *By this time dozens of writers ranging from Ben Hecht to Scott Fitzgerald had worked on the script (it remained chiefly Sidney Howard's, but he died in an accident before it was screened and never saw the result) and scenes of Atlanta burning in the Civil War had been shot. Main production began on January 26 and ended on July 1. After the first few weeks Selznick replaced Cukor with Victor Fleming, who had a nervous breakdown ten weeks later; Sam Wood took over while he recovered, then they co-directed. Like Cukor, both were borrowed from MGM. Also working overtime under Selznick's painstaking supervision were William Cameron Menzies, production design; Ernest Haller, camera; Lyle Wheeler, art direction; Hal Kern and James Newcom, editing; Max Steiner, music; and more than 4,000 others including actors Thomas Mitchell, Barbara O'Neil, Victor Jory, Laura Hope Crews, Hattie McDaniel, Ona Munson, Harry Davenport, Ann Rutherford, Evelyn Keyes, Carroll Nye, Paul Hurst, Isabel Jewell, Cliff Edwards, Ward Bond, Butterfly McQueen, Rand Brooks, Eddie 'Rochester' Anderson, Oscar Polk, Jane Darwell, William Bakewell, Violet Kemble-Cooper, Eric Linden, Roscoe Ates and George Meeker. Among the records it established were length (three hours, 42 minutes, plus interval), Academy Awards (ten: to Selznick, Miss Leigh, Fleming, Sidney Howard, Miss McDaniel – the first black winner of an Oscar – Menzies, Haller, Wheeler, Kern and Newcom jointly, and the picture itself); and long runs (four years at London's Ritz, for example, with queues outside even during air raids). Kept off television (except one US showing for $5m.) and given carefully spaced re-issues (with re-processed Technicolor prints enlarged from 35 to 70 millimetres in recent years), GWTW continues in its fourth decade to fill theatres and MGM's coffers. At right are Miss Leigh and Gable; above, Miss de Havilland, Bond, Gable and Howard.*

Henry Goes Arizona/Spats to Spurs, *with Frank Morgan as a tenderfoot from Broadway taking over a Western ranch, had a rough production ride involving many script changes and retakes, and it showed. Edwin Marin directed the Florence Ryerson–Milton Merlin screenplay from a story by W. C. Tuttle; Harry Rapf produced. Left to right: Gordon Jones, Douglas Fowley, Morgan, Virginia Weidler, Guy Kibbee; also cast were Slim Summerville, Owen Davis Jr, Porter Hall, Mitchell Lewis.*

Margaret Sullavan, whose special gift was to be wistful without cloying, teamed delightfully with James Stewart again in **The Shop Around the Corner**, *a box-office charmer. They played employees of a Budapest shopkeeper (Frank Morgan, excellent sans comic mannerisms) who disliked each other until a lonely-hearts bureau matched them together. Director-producer Ernst Lubitsch gave the Samson Raphaelson script (from a play by Nikolaus Lazzlo) his famous touch, gently stamping every scene with humour and sentiment. He was not alone in considering it one of his best pictures. Also cast: Joseph Schildkraut, Felix Bressart, Sara Haden; William Tracy, Inez Courtney and Edwin Maxwell.*

Ann Dvorak (centre) had become a dramatic actress of some importance since dancing in the Hollywood Revue *chorus ten years before, but the exciting, star-sized talents she evinced at times were never fully exploited. In* **Stronger Than Desire**, *a remake of* Evelyn Prentice, *she was directed by her husband, Leslie Fenton, in support of Walter Pidgeon and Virginia Bruce. This John Considine Jr production was the second Pidgeon–Bruce remake in 1939 (first,* Society Lawyer) *with Miss Bruce in a role originated by Myrna Loy. Other parts in the David Hertz–William Ludwig screenplay went to Lee Bowman, Rita Johnson, Ilka Chase, Tom Neal, Donald Douglas, Thomas Jackson and moppet Ann Todd.*

Walter Pidgeon and Rita Johnson were MGM's cliffhangers of 1939, braving a prisonful of vengeance-crazed convicts in **6,000 Enemies** *and a killer in an airliner in* **Nick Carter, Master Detective**. *The former reunited the old 'B' team, producer Lucien Hubbard and director George B. Seitz; Paul Kelly, Guinn Williams, Nat Pendleton, Tom Neal, Raymond Hatton, Grant Mitchell, Harold Huber, John Arledge, Esther Dale and Horace MacMahon were also cast. Nick Carter was the sleuth hero of countless paperbacks and the movie did well enough to start a series. Jacques Tourneur directed for Hubbard this time, with Henry Hull, Donald Meek, Stanley Ridges, Henry Victor Addison Richards and Sterling Holloway featured. Bertram Millhauser wrote both.*

In **The Earl of Chicago** *Robert Montgomery was cast against type again, at his own insistence–and equalled his* Night Must Fall *success. Starting as a comedy of contrasts, with the American hoodlum hero inheriting a British title and uneasily taking his place among the nobility, it switched to drama when he killed a confederate, was tried by his peers in the House of Lords and went to the scaffold. An unusual movie, not least in allowing the gangster earl no romantic interest. The star's clever depiction of a complex character was directed by Richard Thorpe and supported by Edward Arnold, Edmund Gwenn, Reginald Owen, E. E. Clive, Norma Varden, Halliwell Hobbes and (here with Montgomery) Ronald Sinclair. Lesser Samuels wrote the Victor Saville production from a Gene Fowler–Charles de Grandcourt story and a Brock Williams book.*

Just 19, and just made a star by the biggest of studios, Lana Turner glowed in **Dancing Co-Ed**/Every Other Inch a Lady. *The critics, who later changed their tune, went into rhapsodies over the girl; so did the public, who remained entranced for decades. Albert Mannheimer's script (story, Albert Treynor) was a smart piece of writing, set in college and movie studio and given musical ornamentation by Artie Shaw (here), subsequently the first of Lana's many husbands. Edgar Selwyn produced and S. Sylvan Simon directed. Also cast: Richard Carlson, Leon Errol, Ann Rutherford, Lee Bowman, Monty Woolley, Roscoe Karns, June Preisser, Walter Kingsford.*

Thunder Afloat, *Ralph Wheelwright's story (adapted by Wells Root and Harvey Haislip) of 1918 naval action against U-boats had unexpected topicality in the autumn of 1939 when German submarines were again prowling the Atlantic. The playing of Wallace Beery and Chester Morris brought echoes of the 1930* Big House *in which they snapped and snarled at each other to an accompaniment of crashing paybox records. This J. Walter Ruben production didn't match that scorcher, but Beery and Morris could still generate plenty of dramatic conflict. George B. Seitz directed a cast that included Carl Esmond, Virginia Grey, Douglass Dumbrille, Regis Toomey, Henry Victor, Jonathan Hale, Addison Richards, John Qualen, Phillip Terry and Mitchell Lewis.*

Lionel Barrymore and director Harold S. Bucquet took a holiday from the 'Kildare' series to make **On Borrowed Time**. *In it Sir Cedric Hardwicke coped, imperturbably as ever, with the role of Death in a tree, appearing and disappearing like the Cheshire Cat. Barrymore played an old man defying him. As scripted by Alice Duer Miller, Frank O'Neill and Claudine West and produced by Sidney Franklin, this version of Paul Osborn's play had loads of charm but a touch too much whimsy for the masses. Beulah Bondi played opposite Barrymore for the fourth time, little Bobs Watson (here) had a big part, and Grant Mitchell, Eily Malyon, Henry Travers, Nat Pendleton, Una Merkel, Phillip Terry and Ian Wolfe supported.*

Blackmail *was an unoriginal title for a wide-ranging melodrama which opened and closed with spectacular oil-well fires. In between, Edward G. Robinson, as an expert at putting them out, paid for a past crime by toiling in a chain gang. He escaped to rescue his wife (Ruth Hussey) and son (Bobs Watson) from a blackmailer, played with such slimy zest by Gene Lockhart that he became one of the few actors ever to steal scenes from Edward G. Directed by H. C. Potter, the Considine Jr production was written by David Hertz and William Ludwig from a Dorothy Yost–Endre Bohem story. John Wray (here with Robinson) and Guinn Williams, Cy Kendall, Esther Dale, Arthur Hohl, Mitchell Lewis and Victor Kilian were also cast.*

COLOUR CREEPS ON
1940

Britain, blitzed and busy, nevertheless had a cinema boom: war workers and troops on leave went to the pictures for relaxation. But with 11 countries closed to English-speaking movies, the industry's profits dropped, MGM-Loew's by $1m–but they were still top. Fox and RKO slid back into losses, the latter despite releasing two great Disney winners, *Fantasia* and *Pinocchio*.

Eighteen pictures were in Technicolor, slow growth considering it was five years since the first in the perfected process: *Becky Sharp*.

Applause for John Ford's *The Grapes of Wrath* and *The Long Voyage Home*, Preston Sturges's *The Great McGinty*, Hitchcock's *Foreign Correspondent* and *Rebecca*, the last winning the Oscar.

Mickey Rooney led the Top Ten for the second year, James Cagney and Wallace Beery returned to the list; Judy Garland and singing cowboy Gene Autry joined them; Shirley Temple was omitted after six straight years.

Escapism was still the most rewarding MGM merchandise during the Forties. Even a genre as outmoded as operetta drew huge crowds when performed by Jeanette MacDonald and Nelson Eddy, and splendiferously produced (for the second time) in **New Moon.** *The Jacques Deval–Robert Arthur re-plotting of the original story brought it no nearer life's horrid realities, and the Romberg–Hammerstein score rang out with all its old gusto. Mary Boland (left) led the supporting cast: H. B. Warner, George Zucco, Grant Mitchell, John Miljan, Stanley Fields, Dick Purcell, Cecil Cunningham, Joe Yule, Ivan Simpson. Robert Z. Leonard produced and directed.*

Strike Up The Band regrouped much of the Babes in Arms *talent–performers Mickey Rooney and Judy Garland, June Preisser and Ann Shoemaker; director Busby Berkeley and producer Arthur Freed–in a similar story and with similar crowd-drawing potency. Aside from the title and its song by Gershwin, it bore no resemblance to the Broadway show produced by Edgar Selwyn in 1928. Secondary leads William Tracy and Margaret Early are here to the left of the stars in Roger Edens'* number *'Our Love Affair'. Rounding out the cast were Paul Whiteman, with and without his orchestra, Larry Nunn, Francis Pierlot, Virginia Brissac and two veterans of the silents, Enid Bennett and Helen Jerome Eddy. Script by John Monks Jr and Fred Finklehoffe.*

First filmed in Britain seven years earlier, **Bitter Sweet** *was remade as a 1940 Jeanette MacDonald–Nelson Eddy vehicle–and satisfied only those who wanted just that. The distinctive bouquet of lavender and old spice that Noël Coward had given his original stage musical evaporated. Still, it was a pretty eyeful in Technicolor, and the ear was beguiled by 'I'll See You Again', 'Zigeuner', 'Ladies of the Town' (here with MacDonald) and 'Tokay'– but the superb 'If Love Were All' was omitted. Production by Victor Saville, direction by W. S. Van Dyke, script by Lesser Samuels. Also cast: George Sanders, Felix Bressart, Ian Hunter, Lynne Carver, Edward Ashley, Fay Holden, Sig Rumann, Janet Beecher, Curt Bois, Veda Ann Borg, Diana Lewis, Herman Bing, Greta Meyer, Charles Judels.*

Keeping Company *was announced as the first in a new series, but the studio changed its mind when the returns came in. John Shelton, Ann Rutherford, Frank Morgan and Irene Rich (left to right) headed a cast including Virginia Weidler, Virginia Grey, Dan Dailey, Gene Lockhart, Sara Haden, Henry O'Neill and Gloria DeHaven, under S. Sylvan Simon's direction. Frank Mandel's original, an innocuous piece about an engaged couple, was adapted by James Hill, Harry Ruskin and Adrian Scott; produced by Samuel Marx. With a record total of six concurrent series– 'The Hardys', 'Dr Kildare', 'Tarzan', 'Maisie', 'Thin Man', 'Nick Carter'–who needed another?*

A rewrite of Edmund Goulding's original Broadway Melody *script by Joseph Fields and Jerome Chodorov made a frame for low-budget (by Metro standards) musical numbers in* **Two Girls on Broadway**/Choose Your Partner. *George Murphy played the song-and-dance man who broke up the sister act of Lana Turner and Joan Blondell. The latter (right) already a favourite for a decade, was making the first of several MGM appearances spanning the next 30 years. Kent Taylor, Wallace Ford and Lloyd Corrigan featured in the Jack Cummings production, directed by S. Sylvan Simon.*

Little Nellie Kelly *had Judy Garland singing, dancing and showing remarkable acting maturity in her first solo starrer. She was the overriding asset in this rehash of an Irish–American stew first served up by George M. Cohan on Broadway in 1922, and unabashed corn even then. Judy played both wife and daughter of George Murphy, a smilin' New York cop, bedad. They're seen here in the lilting title number. Charles Winninger, Douglas McPhail, Arthur Shields, Rita Page, Forrester Harvey and James Burke were also in the Arthur Freed production directed by Norman Taurog. Script by Jack McGowan.*

Fred Astaire and Eleanor Powell dancing to Cole Porter's 'Begin the Beguine' in **Broadway** ▷ **Melody of 1940,** *the last and probably the best of the hit musicals bearing the famous title. Astaire had been at RKO-Radio making movie history with Ginger Rogers since his brief screen debut in* Dancing Lady *(1933) and this return to MGM began a star-studio association that lasted nearly two decades. He and Miss Powell did not blend perfectly: she was essentially a solo performer. Still, it was a great dancing show, with George Murphy also hoofing it expertly, while Frank Morgan, Ian Hunter, Florence Rice, Lynne Carver and Ann Morriss helped to put over the Leon Gordon– George Oppenheimer adaptation of a Dore Schary–Jack McGowan story. Jack Cummings produced with a lavish hand and Norman Taurog directed. Porter's score, including the haunting 'I Concentrate on You' sung by Douglas McPhail, was written specially for the film, except 'Beguine' which came from his 1935 Broadway show 'Jubilee'.*

Dr Kildare's Strange Case *drew bigger audiences than the three previous Kildares, with Lew Ayres, Lionel Barrymore, and Laraine Day coping with a mental patient by such entertaining methods as insulin shock and brain surgery—evidently what the public desired! Director was Harold S. Bucquet, script was by Willis Goldbeck and Harry Ruskin. Shepperd Strudwick, Samuel S. Hinds, Emma Dunn, Nat Pendleton, John Eldredge (the strange case), Walter Kingsford, Alma Kruger, Marie Blake, Tom Collins and Horace MacMahon assisted.*

The 'Kildare' saga continued on its disease-ridden and remunerative way with two more 1940 episodes. **Dr Kildare Goes Home** *with (left to right) Samuel Hinds, Lew Ayres and John Shelton, took him away from the big Blair hospital to establish a hometown clinic . . .* **Dr Kildare's Crisis** *injected extra name power by casting Robert Young, here with Blair regulars Nat Pendleton and Marie Blake (Jeanette MacDonald's sister). Young himself would be the doctor hero of a marathon series, TV's 'Marcus Welby MD' 30 years later. Both the new 'Kildares' were written by Willis Goldbeck and Harry Ruskin, directed by Harold S. Bucquet, and featured Ayres, Lionel Barrymore, Laraine Day, Pendleton, Miss Blake, Emma Dunn, Alma Kruger and Walter Kingsford.*

In **Andy Hardy Meets Debutante** *the Hardy series got another fillip from the reappearance of Judy Garland as Andy's hometown friend, now in New York. The deb was Diana Lewis, a newcomer who soon retired from the screen as Mrs William Powell. Except while Judy was singing 'I'm Nobody's Baby', the life and*

soul of this movie was, as usual, Mickey Rooney. George B. Seitz directed them, Lewis Stone, Cecilia Parker, Ann Rutherford, Fay Holden, Sara Haden, George Breakston, Addison Richards and George Lessey. A new scripting team, Annalee Whitmore and Thomas Seller, wrote it.

Flight Command, *another Robert Taylor box-office hit, was the first movie glorifying the US armed forces made during the war in Europe; a year later when America entered the fray, they came by the dozen. Harold Rosson's photography and Navy Air Corps co-operation on the flying scenes gave them a breathtaking excitement absent from the groundwork supplied by Harvey Haislip's and Wells Root's script. Left to right: Walter Pidgeon, Ruth Hussey, Taylor and Shepperd Strudwick. The chubby face in the background is Red Skelton, soon to be MGM's star comedian. J. Walter Ruben produced, and Frank Borzage directed a cast including Paul Kelly, Nat Pendleton, Dick Purcell, Stanley Smith, Marsha Hunt, Addison Richards, Donald Douglas.*

Completing a two-picture Edison biography in 1940, MGM acknowledged its debt to the inventor without whom . . . etc. **Young Tom Edison** was portrayed by Mickey Rooney (here with George Bancroft, Fay Bainter and Virginia Weidler) and **Edison the Man** by Spencer Tracy (below with Gene Reynolds), so there was plenty of box-office incandescence—somewhat dimmed by the solemnity of these worthy tributes. Norman Taurog directed the first, written by Bradbury Foote, Dore Schary and Hugo Butler, with Eugene Pallette, Victor Kilian, Bobby Jordan, J. M. Kerrigan, Clem Bevans, Eily Malyon and Lloyd Corrigan in the cast . . . More dramatically satisfying was the second, directed by Clarence Brown and written by the same trio plus Talbot Jennings; Charles Coburn, Rita Johnson, Lynne Overman, Henry Travers, Felix Bressart, Addison Richards, Grant Mitchell and Paul Hurst were cast. The name of John Considine Jr's associate producer on both was (fair warning) O. O. Dull.

Like the 'Hardys' and the 'Kildares', 'Maisies' cost little and earned Metro consistent profits. Unlike the others, they allowed a complete change of cast and locale every time, with the footloose showgirl, brilliantly observed by Ann Sothern, as the link. Lee Bowman shared the leads in the third, **Gold Rush Maisie**. Edwin Marin returned to direct; production by J. Walter Ruben, with Virginia Weidler, Slim Summerville, Mary Nash and Scotty Beckett in the cast. Script by Mary McCall Jr and Betty Reinhardt from a Wilson Collison original.

Two good little programmers of 1940, made while MGM continued to decry the double-feature system they fed, were **The Golden Fleecing** with (left to right) Virginia Grey, Lloyd Nolan, Lew Ayres and Marc Lawrence and **Sporting Blood** with Maureen O'Sullivan and Lewis Stone. The first, a fast farce about a timid insurance salesman embroiled with gangsters, was directed by Leslie Fenton, produced by Edgar Selwyn, and written by S. J. and Laura Perelman from a Lynn Root–John Fante–Frank Fenton original, with Leon Errol, Rita Johnson, Nat Pendleton and William Demarest. The second was a familiar racehorse story, but not the same one filmed under that title in 1931. S. Sylvan Simon got plenty of action out of the Albert Mannheimer–Dorothy Yost script from Grace Norton's original; Albert Levoy produced and Robert Young, William Gargan, Lynne Carver, Clarence Muse, Lloyd Corrigan and Russell Hicks played other leads.

Reviews and financial results were so good when Wallace Beery put on his boots, gunbelt and scowl for a trek through Death Valley in **20-Mule Team** that he spent most of his remaining movie years in the wide open spaces. Leo Carrillo played the half-breed scout who helped him get his cargo of borax across the desert, and others in the cast were Marjorie Rambeau, Anne Baxter (debut), Douglas Fowley, Noah Beery Jr (first film with his uncle), Berton Churchill, Arthur Hohl, Clem Bevans, Minor Watson. Producer, J. Walter Ruben; director, Richard Thorpe; writers, E. E. Paramore, Richard Maibaum, Cyril Hume.

1940

Pride and Prejudice *was produced by Hunt Stromberg in his best neo-Thalberg style and directed by Robert Z. Leonard with exactly the right touch to bring out the mannered charm and humour of Jane Austen's characters. They had stylish players in (left to right) Frieda Inescort, Laurence Olivier, Edward Ashley, Greer Garson; and Mary Boland, Edmund Gwenn, Edna May Oliver, Maureen O'Sullivan, Ann Rutherford, Karen Morley (back after long absence), Heather Angel, Marsha Hunt, Melville Cooper, E. E. Clive and Bruce Lester. This was Miss Garson's first Hollywood success, but Olivier, after* Wuthering Heights *and* Rebecca, *was its big crowd magnet. Miss Boland as the many-daughtered Mrs Bennet and Miss Oliver as the condescending Lady Catherine went dangerously near caricature but were enormous fun. Wit and romanticism were happily combined in the script of Aldous Huxley and Jane Murfin, based not directly on the novel but on Helen Jerome's stage version.*

The best of the 1940 crop: **The Philadelphia** ▷ **Story**, *starring Cary Grant, Katharine Hepburn and James Stewart. This brilliant comedy was a turning point in the long Hepburn career, which began with instant stardom in 1932, reached the height of an Oscar in 1933 and the depth of a 'box-office poison' rating by exhibitors in 1938. She went back to the stage and triumphed in this Philip Barry play about a household of rich offbeats invaded by a pair of magazine journalists. Its success drew bids from Hollywood, which was nonplussed to find that the shrewd Miss Hepburn's contract involved her in the film rights: if they wanted the play they had to take the 'box-office poison'. MGM took both, added two top male stars for insurance, entrusted the property to producer Joseph Mankiewicz and director George Cukor, and came up with a smash hit. Hepburn's performance, full of temperament and tenderness, should have won her another Oscar but, by some Academy caprice, Ginger Rogers was voted that year's best actress. Two Stewarts did win: James as best actor and Donald Ogden as best scenarist. The fine cast included Ruth Hussey, John Howard, Roland Young, Virginia Weidler, John Halliday, Mary Nash and Henry Daniell.*

1940

Maisie Was a Lady *was rated the best to date. Miss Sothern had the aid of two other series' stars: Lew Ayres from 'Kildare' and Maureen O'Sullivan (here with Ann and C. Aubrey Smith) from 'Tarzan'. The usual Ruben–Marin producer-director team worked from a script by Mary McCall Jr and Betty Reinhardt about a rich family's problems sorted out by our heroine, hired as a maid. Edward Ashley, Joan Perry and Paul Cavanagh were also in it.*

The Mortal Storm *was one of the year's big ones. With a perfunctory nod to the USA's official neutrality in 1940, it called Germany 'Somewhere in Europe' to set the scene for Hollywood's first major production attacking the Nazis. But no punches were pulled in the Claudine West–George Froeschel–Anderson Ellis script from Phyllis Bottome's novel about family and friends torn apart by Hitlerism. Movies like this had a telling effect on public opinion in uncommitted countries. Strength and sensitivity were evident in Frank Borzage's direction, also in the acting of Frank Morgan, Robert Young, Margaret Sullavan, Irene Rich, James Stewart, Robert Stack, Gene Reynolds and William T. Orr (left to right) and Maria Ouspenskaya, Bonita Granville, Dan Dailey (debut), Ward Bond, Esther Dale and William Edmunds. Sidney Franklin produced, without screen credit. Orr developed into a top film (Warners) and TV executive.*

Marion Martin, Albert Dekker, John Shelton, Charles Butterworth and Virginia Grey in **Blonde Inspiration**, *a dizzy farce from John Cecil Holm's play 'Four Cents a Word'. Shelton played a pulp-fiction writer who had to have a curvy dame within reaching distance or his muse (that's right) wouldn't work. Busby Berkeley directed for another new producer, B. P. Fineman; script by Marion Parsonnet; cast completed by Reginald Owen, Donald Meek, Alma Kruger, George Lessey, Rita Quigley.*

The team that never failed: William Powell and Myrna Loy in **I Love You Again**. *The tricky screenplay about a stodgy husband coming out of eight years of amnesia into his real, wild personality was good for many laughs and big business, as directed by W. S. Van Dyke and produced by Lawrence Weingarten. The George Oppenheimer–Harry Kurnitz–Charles Lederer script from a story by Maurine Watkins and Leon Gordon provided good moments for Edmund Lowe, Frank McHugh, Donald Douglas, Nella Walker, Pierre Watkin and Carl 'Alfalfa' Switzer.*

Virginia Grey, Dan Dailey and That Thing in **Hullabaloo**, *one of the first films to show a television set as home furniture. When this toy eventually started nudging movies aside as public entertainment No. 1, it was seldom allowed to show its face on the screen. Frank Morgan dominated this Louis K. Sidney production about show folk, adding song, dance and mimicry of other stars to his usual comic ditherings. Edwin L. Marin directed from a Nat Perrin script, with Billie Burke, Nydia Westman, Reginald Owen, Ann Morriss, Donald Meek, Sara Haden, Larry Nunn, Barnett Parker, Leni Lynn and deadpan singer Virginia O'Brien also cast.*

Virginia Grey, Dan Dailey (billed with 'Jr' added in his early films) and Charles Coburn in **The Captain Is a Lady**. *Coburn played the only man in an old ladies' home, surrounded and bedevilled by Beulah Bondi, Helen Broderick, Billie Burke, Helen Westley, Marjorie Main and Cecil Cunningham. Robert Sinclair directed and Frederick Stephani produced Harry Clork's amusing screenplay based on Rachel Crothers' play 'Old Lady 31'.*

Out for her third screen romp came **Dulcy**, *George S. Kaufman's and Marc Connelly's dizzy blonde, played by Constance Talmadge in 1923 and Marion Davies in 1929. Ann Sothern brought her lively comedy technique to this version, aided by Roland Young, Billie Burke, Ian Hunter, Dan Dailey, Donald Huie, Lynne Carver and Reginald Gardiner. The Albert Mannheimer–Jerome Chodorov–Joseph Fields script was produced by Edgar Selwyn with S. Sylvan Simon as director.*

Sooner or later all Metro's star comics (Buster Keaton, William Haines, Laurel and Hardy) went thataway into the wide open spaces. Sometimes the title was Way Out West, *sometimes* **Go West**, *as in the Marx Brothers' fourth opus for the company. It had its riotous moments, but the madness of Groucho, Harpo and Chico was becoming a bit mechanical. Their support included John Carroll, Diana Lewis, Walter Woolf King, Robert Barrat, June MacCloy, Tully Marshall–but not, alas, Margaret Dumont. Director, Edward Buzzell; scenarist, Irving Brecher; producer, Jack Cummings.*

The long and vituperative screen romance of Wallace Beery and Marjorie Main began in **Wyoming**/Bad Man of Wyoming. *Miss Main first caught notice as the tragic mother in Dead End but MGM developed her as a comedienne, famous for the uniquely penetrating monotone of her speech. This otherwise unremarkable Western was written by Jack Jevne and Hugo Butler, directed by Richard Thorpe and produced by Milton Bren. Also cast: Leo Carrillo, Ann Rutherford, Lee Bowman, Joseph Calleia, Bobs Watson, Paul Kelly, Henry Travers, Addison Richards.*

'Her sleepy but alert eyes are always saying things not written in the script . . . She has the soft answer that turneth away criticism' said the London 'Sunday Express' about Myrna Loy in **Third Finger, Left Hand**. Ever a critics' pet, this subtle charmer was at the peak of her public popularity when this comedy came out. She played a magazine editor who pretended to be married to Melvyn Douglas (right) for complicated reasons evolved by scenarist Lionel Houser and involving Donald Meek (left), Lee Bowman, Bonita Granville, Raymond Walburn, Felix Bressart and Ann Morriss. Director, Robert Z. Leonard; producer, John Considine Jr.

Eddie Cantor, one of the biggest names in show business after clowning and singing through dozens of Ziegfeld (stage) and Sam Goldwyn (screen) musicals, nursed the usual comedian's desire to be a straight actor. So he played a teacher in a girls' school in **Forty Little Mothers**, and was left holding the baby. This drama of deadly winsomeness unaccountably featured distinguished classical actress Dame Judith Anderson (centre), also Rita Johnson, Bonita Granville, Ralph Morgan, Nydia Westman (left), Diana Lewis and Martha O'Driscoll. The nearest thing to a musical number director Busby Berkeley – also going straight – got was something called 'Little Curly Hair in a High Chair'. Harry Rapf, whose MGM career began on MGM's first day, became semi-retired after producing this Dorothy Yost–Ernest Pagano screenplay.

From a Rachel Crothers' play, **Susan and God**/ The Gay Mrs Trexel boasted the producer-director-scenarist combination of The Women – Hunt Stromberg, George Cukor, Anita Loos – and one of its stars Joan Crawford – but their sting had lost its zing and receipts were just fair. In the role done on Broadway by Gertrude Lawrence, Miss Crawford played the first of the many self-centred queen bees she was to do so well. Fredric March and Rita Quigley were the neglected husband and daughter of this socialite caught up in a relig-

ious movement. Left to right: Ruth Hussey, Rita Hayworth (who wouldn't be in the background much longer), Miss Crawford, Nigel Bruce, Rose Hobart, Bruce Cabot; also in the cast were John Carroll, Constance Collier, Gloria DeHaven (debut), Marjorie Main, Richard Crane.

Florian, a Lipizzaner stallion, was the photogenic subject of a rather sluggish drama set in 1910–18 Austria. It was produced by Winfield Sheehan, for 20 years the Mayer of the Fox studio, owner of the only Lipizzaner horses in America, but whether MGM signed him to get Florian or Florian to get him, history recordeth not. Robert Young and Helen Gilbert are seen here getting acquainted with the hero; also cast were Charles Coburn, Lee Bowman, Reginald Owen (as Emperor Franz Josef), Lucile Watson, S. Z. Sakall, Rand Brooks and ballerina Irina Baronova. Script, from Felix Salten's novel, was by Noel Langley, Geza Herczeg, and James K. McGuinness. Edwin Marin directed.

And One Was Beautiful, another yarn about two sisters wanting the same man, featured (left to right) Robert Cummings, Jean Muir, Billie Burke and Laraine Day. Miss Muir, a delightful leading lady of the Thirties, later became a victim of the anti-Red inquisition conducted by Senator McCarthy. The entertainers so persecuted were blacklisted by the studios, including MGM – not a glorious episode in its history. Robert Sinclair directed and Frederick Stephani produced Harry Clork's adaptation of an Alice Duer Miller women's magazine story, with Ann Morriss, Esther Dale, Charles Waldron and Rand Brooks in the cast.

Frank Morgan in drag was among the anything-for-a-laugh diversions Richard Maibaum and Harry Ruskin strung together under the title of **The Ghost Comes Home** for producer Albert Levoy. Ann Rutherford and Billie Burke (seen here) and John Shelton, Reginald Owen, Donald Meek, Nat Pendleton, Frank Albertson, Harold Huber and Hobart Cavanaugh completed the cast directed by William Thiele.

In **Come Live With Me** immigrant Hedy Lamarr married US citizen James Stewart in order to stay in the country. One of those strictly business arrangements, with business getting better all the time. Clarence Brown ably produced and directed, casting Hunter, Verree Teasdale, Edward Ashley, Donald Meek, Adeline deWalt Reynolds (acting debut at 80), Barton MacLane, Horace MacMahon and, as cook and counterman with the stars here, Dewey Robinson and Frank Faylen. Story by Virginia Van Upp, script by Patterson McNutt; names to conjure with, indeed.

After 12 years' absence from MGM (since the silent Trail of '98) Dolores Del Rio turned up in **The Man from Dakota**/Arouse and Beware looking about 12 weeks older. She played a soignée Russian refugee encountered by two Union soldiers escaping from a Confederate prison during the Civil War. A likely story. But it was full of action and gave Wallace Beery (right) a good part as officer John Howard's lazy sergeant who turned hero at the end. Laurence Stallings adapted Mackinlay Kantor's novel for producer Edward Chodorov, and Leslie Fenton directed a cast that also included Donald Meek, H. B. Warner, Victor Varconi, Robert Barrat, Addison Richards and John Wray.

Waterloo Bridge was one of 1940's major successes. Like Scarlett O'Hara, its heroine was no better than she ought to have been; but unlike Scarlett she was a frail creature, who descended from ballet dancer to prostitute to suicide. Vivien Leigh proved her star quality by having as strong an effect on audiences' emotions in this second Hollywood role as in her famous first. Robert Taylor's British officer had a Nebraska accent but was otherwise convincing and praiseworthy. Their parts had been played by Mae Clarke and Douglass Montgomery in Universal's 1931 version of Robert E. Sherwood's play. Sidney Franklin produced and Mervyn LeRoy directed, reversing their usual jobs. Script was by S. N. Behrman, George Froeschel, Hans Rameau. Supporting cast: Virginia Field, Maria Ouspenskaya, Lucile Watson, C. Aubrey Smith, Steffi Duna, Leo G. Carroll.

John Shelton and Lana Turner in **We Who Are Young**. It was Lana's first try at serious acting and indicated a sensitive human being behind the glamour-girl façade. This simple story of little people in a big city, getting married, getting into debt and nearly splitting up, was modestly produced; a certain distinction in Dalton Trumbo's screenplay and Harold S.

Bucquet's direction made it worthy of more attention than it got. Gene Lockhart, Grant Mitchell, Henry Armetta, Jonathan Hale, Horace MacMahon, Ian Wolfe and Clarence Wilson were others in this Hollywood debut of Seymour Nebenzahl, producer of **M** in Germany and **Mayerling** in France.

MGM took another swipe at the Nazis with **Escape**, Mervyn LeRoy's impressively restrained filming of Ethel Vance's 1939 suspense novel, a runaway best-seller. It related how a widow was rescued from a concentration camp by her American son and a countess, mistress of a German general. These key roles were played with controlled intensity by

Nazimova, Robert Taylor and Norma Shearer (left to right) and Conrad Veidt in his Hollywood debut after 20 years of stardom in Berlin and London. Off the screen for almost that long, Nazimova returned for her second round of anti-German propaganda: she had been one of the most spectacular movie stars during World War I. Felix Bressart, Albert and Elsa Bassermann, Philip Dorn, Bonita Granville and Blanche Yurka had other parts in the Arch Oboler–Marguerite Roberts screenplay, produced by Lawrence Weingarten.

A good old MGM splurge of star-power turned a routine oil-well saga into a golden gusher at the box-office. Basically there was little difference between **Boom Town** and the roughneck melos being churned out on Poverty Row. But the same might have been said of **China Seas**

or Test Pilot. *The importance came with the big names – Clark Gable, Spencer Tracy, Claudette Colbert and Hedy Lamarr in this– and the big budget they signified, commanding top talent in every department. Sam Zimbalist gave the John Lee Mahin screenplay (from James Edward Grant's story) the 'A' production required; Jack Conway forcefully directed a narrative ranging from wildcat drilling to Wall Street finagling. Frank Morgan headed the supporting cast which included Lionel Atwill, Minna Gombell, Chill Wills, Marion Martin, Joe Yule, Sara Haden and Richard Lane.*

Aiming at the same target as Ninotchka, **Comrade X** *used farce instead of comedy for ammunition, and missed; but the Clark Gable– Hedy Lamarr names kept it in the profit column. Gable played an American reporter in Russia, Hedy a believe-it-or-not Moscow streetcar driver, and their incongruous romance ended with a Keystone Kops chase in army tanks. The film carried the prestigious name of King Vidor but little of his artistry. Gottfried Reinhardt produced the Ben Hecht– Charles Lederer screenplay based on a story by Walter Reisch, with Felix Bressart, Eve Arden, Oscar Homolka, Sig Ruman, Vladimir Sokoloff and Edgar Barrier in the cast.*

Busman's Honeymoon/Haunted Honeymoon, *a cosy murder mystery featuring Dorothy Sayers' detective Lord Peter Wimsey, played by Robert Montgomery, was the fourth MGM British production, and a lightweight compared with the unit's first three movies; it hardly caused a ripple on either side of the Atlantic. Montgomery went from Hollywood to London in 1939 to make the movie, but the outbreak of war clamped a blackout on it. So he went back to America for Earl of Chicago and returned in 1940 when London studios functioned despite air raids. Left to right, Sir Seymour Hicks, Montgomery, Constance Cummings, Leslie Banks, Robert Newton,*

Googie Withers, Frank Pettingell, Aubrey Mallalieu, Eliot Makeham and Louise Hampton also appeared under Arthur B. Woods' direction in the screenplay by Monkton Hoffe, Angus McPhail and Harold Goldman. Coincidence note: Banks and Miss Cummings had played Mr and Mrs Chips in the London stage version of the preceding MGM British film.

Strange Cargo *was Clark Gable's and Joan Crawford's eighth movie together, and in it they succumbed to that old urge again; but most of the picture dealt with the perilous escape of a boatload of cut-throats from Devil's Island. Good crowd-drawing stuff, with Frank Borzage getting colourful character studies from the stars and Peter Lorre, Paul Lukas, Albert Dekker, J. Edward Bromberg, Eduardo Ciannelli, John Arledge, Frederick Worlock, Bernard Nedell and Victor Varconi. Ian Hunter's role as a Christlike regenerating influence added a mystical overtone which didn't quite come off. Joseph Mankiewicz produced the Lawrence Hazard screenplay, from Richard Sale's novel 'Not Too Narrow, Not Too Deep'.*

Bayard Veiller's surefire courtroom thriller **The Trial of Mary Dugan** *had another outing, with Laraine Day, voted 1940's most promising new star by exhibitors, playing Norma Shearer's old part; Robert Young as her defending brother; Tom Conway as her prosecutor. Frieda Inescort, John Litel, Marsha Hunt, Marjorie Main, Henry O'Neill, Sara Haden, Addison Richards and Alma Kruger were in the cast, and Norman Z. McLeod directed for new producer Edwin Knopf. All very competent, but the shock value of MGM's first all-talkie drama had wilted.*

Seen here are Jackie Cooper, all grown up with moustache, Tommy Kelly, Leo Gorcey, Gene Reynolds, Bonita Granville and El Brendel in **Gallant Sons**, *a 'B'-minor exercise for Metro's younger generation. The William Lipman–Marion Parsonnet screenplay about a gang of kids solving a murder mystery was directed by George B. Seitz and produced by Frederick Stephani, with Ian Hunter, Gail Patrick, June Preisser, William Tracy, Edward Ashley and Minor Watson also cast.*

Walter Pidgeon played sleuth Nick Carter twice more, then the series was dropped: he had bigger things ahead. Steffi Duna was his Cuban charmer in **Phantom Raiders**, *a melo about sabotage at sea, directed by Jacques Tourneur, with Joseph Schildkraut, Florence Rice, John Carroll, Donald Meek, Nat Pendleton, Cecil Kellaway . . . In* **Sky Murder** *he held the wool for Joyce Compton while killers stalked a millionaire's private plane; George B. Seitz directed, with Karen Verne, Edward Ashley, Meek, Tom Conway, Dorothy Tree, Chill Wills, Frank Reicher and Tom Neal. William Lipman wrote both scripts for producer Frederick Stephani.*

Lewis Stone, Ian Hunter, Kathryn Grayson and Mickey Rooney in **Andy Hardy's Private Secretary**, *the last production to finish in 1940. Another 'Hardy' hit, this also had Gene Reynolds, Addison Richards and Margaret Early joining regulars Fay Holden, Ann Rutherford, Sara Haden and director George B. Seitz. As was his wont, offscreen as well as on, Mickey tried to date his new leading lady, who had just graduated from a year's course of star grooming; but Kathryn 'seemed to have something going for her higher up in the studio', said he in his 1965 autobiography. Sister Marian was written out of this script by Jane Murfin and Harry Ruskin: Cecilia Parker was blessed-eventing, as the saying went.*

GARSON AND ROONEY
1941

Every company's profits jumped even before America's war boom began in earnest. MGM-Loew's $11m topped the lot once more, followed by Paramount with $9m. Gary Cooper had two big hits, *Meet John Doe* and *Sergeant York*, the latter winning him an Oscar. The Academy ostentatiously fobbed off Orson Welles and his masterpiece, *Citizen Kane*, with a minor award because of its 'insult' to W. R. Hearst and Marion Davies. The other major winners were *How Green Was My Valley*, its director John Ford, and Joan Fontaine for *Suspicion*.

A record number of stage plays (57) were filmed, notably *The Little Foxes*, *Tobacco Road*, *Ladies in Retirement*, *The Man Who Came to Dinner*. Remakes were rampant: Tyrone Power in *Blood and Sand*, Bob Hope in *Nothing But the Truth*, Edward G. Robinson in *The Sea Wolf*, Jack Benny in *Charley's Aunt*, Margaret Sullavan in *Back Street*, Humphrey Bogart in *Maltese Falcon*. The biggest ticket-selling stars were Mickey Rooney (first for the third year running), Clark Gable, newcomers Abbott and Costello, Bob Hope, Spencer Tracy, Gene Autry, James Cagney, Bette Davis, Judy Garland and Cooper.

The military-minded 1941 public lapped up **The Bugle Sounds**, *a Wallace Beery movie about the substitution of tanks for horses in the US Cavalry. Here Marjorie Main lets stardom, or maybe an aviary, go to her head in an explosion of chic, while eye-catching young MGM finds Donna Reed and William Lundigan attend to the romance department. Cyril Hume's screenplay was produced by J. Walter Ruben and directed by S. Sylvan Simon, with Lewis Stone, George Bancroft, Chill Wills, Guinn Williams, Jerome Cowan, Jonathan Hale and Tom Dugan in the cast.*

Two-Faced Woman, *forever branded as the flop that ended Garbo's career, is surprisingly entertaining when seen again today. It was a hasty substitution for Madame Curie, shelved as too sombre for wartime. Garbo regretted that, was increasingly reluctant to work anyway (two years between her films had become the norm) and finally did what she'd been threatening for most of her 16 Hollywood years. She retired for good, still, at 36, at the height of her fame and beauty, with image and legend intact—and a lot of MGM money safely invested, thank you. In Two-Faced Woman, guided by George Cukor, supported by Constance Bennett, Melvyn Douglas and Robert Sterling (with her here), Roland Young and Ruth Gordon, Garbo gave the gimmicky story of a wife posing as her notorious twin sister a good try—even when required to perform such hotsy-totsy diversions as a wild rhumba, a bathingsuit scene and a chase finale on skis. The script, S. N. Behrman, Salka Viertel, George Oppenheimer; producer, Gottfried Reinhardt.*

Gorgeously vulgar, blindingly all-star and irresistibly supercolossal, **Ziegfeld Girl** was one of the biggest hits of 1941. Pandro S. Berman, for years the Thalberg of RKO-Radio, moved over to Culver City to produce it and show the world he could be as MGM as anybody. He threw in the lot: Edward Everett Horton, Lana Turner, Hedy Lamarr and Eve Arden (here), Judy Garland, James Stewart, Tony Martin, Jackie Cooper, Ian Hunter, Philip Dorn, Charles Winninger, Dan Dailey, Paul Kelly, Fay Holden, Felix Bressart, Rose Hobart and Mae Busch; Robert Z. Leonard to direct the narrative and Busby Berkeley the musical numbers; 100, count 'em, beautiful girls; ultra-lavish sets and gowns; song hits like 'Minnie from Trinidad' sung by Judy, 'You Stepped Out of a Dream' sung by Martin; and lots of drama. Credited to Marguerite Roberts and Sonya Levien from an original by William Anthony McGuire, it was really a granddaughter of Sally, Irene and Mary with three (inevitably) showgirls coming to customary fates: Judy to stardom, Hedy to wealthy marriage and Lana to alcoholic disaster.

Billy the Kid was a Super-Western—you could tell by the number of cattle in the stampede, all in Technicolor to boot. It also had Robert Taylor for box-office weight, and the grosses were heavy. Otherwise it didn't differ much from a hundred other oat operas of the time (there was even a current 'B'-minor series starring Buster Crabbe as Billy the Kid) or from the same story MGM filmed in 1930. Producer Irving Asher and director David Miller registered firsts; the former started his Metro contract, the latter moved up from short subjects. Gene Fowler's screenplay was enacted by Lon Chaney Jr, Brian Donlevy, Mary Howard, Olive Blakeney, Henry O'Neill and Taylor (left to right) and Ian Hunter, Guinn Williams, Gene Lockhart, Cy Kendall, Mitchell Lewis, Chill Wills, Grant Withers, Ethel Griffies and Frank Puglia.

The title **Free and Easy** had been used before, but not on this story—which had also been used before. It started as a play by Ivor Novello called The Truth Game, and was filmed in 1932 as But the Flesh is Weak; now its British uppercrust fun was reduced to short pastry in a 56-minute 'B'. Robert Cummings had Robert Montgomery's old part and was supported by Ruth Hussey and Reginald Owen (with him here), Judith Anderson, C. Aubrey Smith, Nigel Bruce, Tom Conway and Forrester Harvey. Smith and Harvey were also in the 1932 version. Script was by Marvin Borowsky, production by Milton Bren (uncredited). The movie was directed, as his first feature after nine years in the shorts department, by George Sidney, son of veteran Loew's-MGM executive Louis K. Sidney.

A quarter-century before being elected Governor of California, Ronald Reagan wooed Laraine Day in **The Bad Man**/Two-Gun Cupid while Wallace Beery beamed lethally as the bes' damn caballero in all Mehico. This third filming of Porter Browne's stage hit (First National did it in 1923 and 1930) was produced by J Walter Ruben and directed by Richard Thorpe from a script by Wells Root, and again it made money. Lionel Barrymore, Henry Travers, Chris-Pin Martin, Tom Conway, Chill Wills, Nydia Westman supported.

Two more remakes (MGM made nine this year) served as testing grounds for the studio's star-making factory. Robert Sterling, an attractive if rather bland young actor, and the versatile Marsha Hunt shared leads in **I'll Wait for You**, a re-do of 1934's Hideout, with Virginia Weidler, Paul Kelly, Fay Holden, Henry Travers, Carol Hughes, Don Costello, Veda Ann Borg, Reed Hadley; script Guy Trosper; director, Robert B. Sinclair; producer, Edwin Knopf. Sterling also featured in **The Get-Away** as one of two jail-breakers. The

other, Dan Dailey, was equally effective as hero or heavy or hoofer and proved the most successful of the newcomers. This movie was re-produced from 1933's Public Hero No. 1 by J. Walter Ruben, director of the original, who gave the job this time to Edward Buzzell, with Donna Reed (debut), Charles Winninger, Henry O'Neill and Donald Douglas in the cast. Script by Wells Root and W. R. Burnett.

Frank Morgan had a lot of fun in **The Wild Man of Borneo**, as did the rather sparse audiences who watched him play a pre-War-I super-salesman. Set mostly in a theatrical boarding house, the comedy was produced by Joseph Mankiewicz from a play by brother Herman and Marc Connelly, adapted by Waldo Salt and John McClain. Robert Sinclair directed Mary Howard, Morgan, Billie Burke, Dan Dailey, Donald Meek, Bonita Granville and Connie Gilchrist (left to right) and Marjorie Main, Andrew Tombes, Walter Catlett and Phil Silvers, later TV-famed as Sergeant Bilko.

Clark Gable and Rosalind Russell co-starred only once, as rival confidence tricksters in **They Met in Bombay**. Well-made for the paybox, as the producer-director names of Hunt Stromberg and Clarence Brown guaranteed, it showed it was 'with it' in 1941 by having the USA hero join the British army and fight in the Far East. Peter Lorre, Jessie Ralph, Reginald Owen, Eduardo Ciannelli, Matthew Boulton and Luis Alberni had roles in the Anita Loos–Leon Gordon–Edwin Justus Mayer screenplay from an original by John Kafka.

The Big Store was the Marx Brothers' fifth and last movie at MGM. (Five of their films were evidently as much as any studio could stand without falling apart—they did that many at Paramount.) Neither the best nor the worst, it gave them a whole department store to turn into a shambles. As detective Wolf J. Flywheel, Groucho was inspired by the return of old flame Margaret Dumont to give a per-

formance of scintillating verve–or something. Tony Martin had a hit number in 'Tenement Symphony'. Also cast: Virginia Grey, Douglass Dumbrille (here with the brothers), and Virginia O'Brien, Bradley Page, Marion Martin, Henry Armetta, William Tannen. Producer, Louis K. Sidney; director, Charles Reisner; writers, Sid Kuller, Hal Finberg, Ray Golden.

Greer Garson became a superstar with **Blossoms in the Dust**, which established her and Walter Pidgeon as a team of durable value to MGM; and Irving Asher's production was so lush in Technicolor that it won Academy Awards for art direction (Cedric Gibbons, Urie McCleary) and set decoration (Edwin B. Willis). 'Heart-warming' was the adjective most often used for this drama based on fact, about Edna Gladney, famous welfare worker for children. It had orphan babies gurgling all over the screen, and vast audiences gulping tears all over the world. Miss Garson and Pidgeon were supported by Felix Bressart (right), Marsha Hunt, Fay Holden, Samuel S. Hinds, William Henry, Kathleen Howard, John Eldredge, Henry O'Neill, Clinton Rosemond, Theresa Harris, George Lessey, Cecil Cunningham, Ann Morriss and Marc Lawrence. Mervyn LeRoy directed Anita Loos' screenplay, from Ralph Wheelwright's original.

Boudoir byplay alternated with bar-room brawls and gold-rush action to make **Honky Tonk** an absolute rip-snorter at the box-office. Here lady barber Veda Ann Borg gets saloon owner Clark Gable ready for a bedroom scene with Lana Turner. Pandro Berman gave potent new Gable–Turner team a worthy supporting cast: Frank Morgan, Marjorie Main, the fascinating Claire Trevor, Albert Dekker, Henry O'Neill, Chill Wills and yesteryear's Queen of Sheba, Betty Blythe. Jack Conway directed, Marguerite Roberts and John Sanford scripted, the critics said 'No' and the public said 'Wow!'.

Down in San Diego featured (left to right) Leo Gorcey, Dorothy Morris, Charles B. Smith, Henry O'Neill, Ray McDonald, Bonita Granville and Dan Dailey in a programmer about teenagers foiling spies at the US Navy base. McDonald, a young dancer from Broadway, was making his movie debut. Producer was Frederick Stephani; director, Robert B. Sinclair; writers, Harry Clark, Franz Spencer. Also cast: Frederick Worlock, Connie Gilchrist, Stanley Clements, Hobart Cavanaugh, William Tannen, Joseph Sawyer, Ludwig Stossel. It was O'Neill's hundredth film in eight years (top that).

The man-woman game was again played for smart comedy by Don Ameche, Rosalind Russell and Kay Francis in **The Feminine Touch**. The fourth corner of its romantic quadrangle was occupied by Van Heflin, signed by MGM as a result of his stage performance opposite Katharine Hepburn in The Philadelphia Story. Also present were Donald Meek, Gordon Jones, Henry Daniell, Sidney Blackmer and Grant Mitchell. The Joseph Mankiewicz production was written by George Oppenheimer, Ogden Nash and Edmund Hartmann. W. S. Van Dyke, directed.

Smilin' Through was Jeanette MacDonald's third remake in a row, and her career was beginning to get a secondhand look. Nevertheless, her faithful following ensured profitability, and the old Jane Murfin–Jane Cowl tear-jerker wore Technicolor and songs as if designed for these embellishments all along. Fans who wanted Jeanette and Nelson Eddy to love one another offscreen as well as on (they definitely didn't) had to be satisfied with her marrying Gene Raymond, who resembled Eddy and who teamed with his wife for the first time in this movie. Brian Aherne had the third lead, with Ian Hunter, Frances Robinson and Patrick O'Moore supporting. Script, Donald Ogden Stewart and John Balderston; director, Frank Borzage; producer, Victor Saville.

Meanwhile, Nelson Eddy also found himself in the remake business. Victor Saville was his producer too, but **The Chocolate Soldier** was a much gayer affair than Smilin' Through and got a warm response from press and public. It took all kinds of chances, from mating Ferenc Molnar's comedy The Guardsman with Oscar Straus' Chocolate Soldier music, to casting Eddy and a movie novice, Metropolitan Opera singer Rise Stevens in roles identified with the matchless Alfred Lunt and Lynn Fontanne. Miraculously, everything worked. Eddy suddenly acquired a talent for light comedy, Stevens displayed charming magnetism, and their voices blended well and often. Roy Del Ruth directed the screenplay by Keith Winter and Leonard Lee, with Florence Bates (right), Nigel Bruce, Nydia Westman and Charles Judels featured.

Two connubial comedies filled 'B' slots in the 1941 product schedule. Robert Young and Ruth Hussey in **Married Bachelor**, a Dore Schary screenplay from Manuel Seff's story about an unwed authority on how to be a happy spouse. Lee Bowman, Sheldon Leonard and Sam Levene also appeared in the John Considine Jr production directed by Edward Buzzell . . . Gracie Allen (for once without George Burns) and William Post Jr in **Mr and Mrs North**, a mystery-farce adapted by S. K. Lauren from Owen Davis' Broadway play. Irving Asher produced, and Robert B. Sinclair directed a cast including Paul Kelly, Rose Hobart, Tom Conway, Felix Bressart, Porter Hall, Millard Mitchell, Lucien Littlefield, Inez Cooper, Keye Luke and Jerome Cowan.

◁ **A Woman's Face** *was a major MGM hit and one of the best vehicles in Joan Crawford's long career. A strongly plotted melodrama, it had originated in a French play, 'Il Etait une Fois' by François de Croisset, and been made into a 1937 Swedish film starring Ingrid Bergman. Adapted by Donald Ogden Stewart and Elliot Paul, the movie opened with Joan's trial for the murder of Conrad Veidt (with her here) and flashbacked to show how the removal of a hideous scar had affected her life. George Cukor and Victor Saville gave it impeccable direction and production. Praise abounded for the acting of Miss Crawford, Veidt, Melvyn Douglas, Osa Massen, Reginald Owen, Albert Bassermann, Donald Meek, Marjorie Main, Henry Daniell, Connie Gilchrist, Charles Quigley, Gwili Andre, George Zucco, Henry Kolker, Robert Warwick and Gilbert Emery.*

Joan Crawford got top billing, but Greer Garson was emerging as the new First Lady of MGM, and their tacit rivalry lent edge to the remake of **When Ladies Meet**. *They had the roles played by Myrna Loy and Ann Harding in 1933, with Robert Taylor, Herbert Marshall and Spring Byington stepping into the shoes of Robert Montgomery, Frank Morgan and Alice Brady. The new Anita Loos–S. K. Lauren script from Rachel Crothers' play had the benefit of Robert Z. Leonard's polished direction and (with O. O. Dull) production. Mona Barrie and Rafael Storm filled minor parts. Business was good.*

Shadow of the Thin Man *was the fourth and not the best of the series, but it was lots better than any other detective-mystery-comedy of the time and made a handsome profit. Set in the sporting world of athletes, gamblers, touts and bookies, the Harry Kurnitz–Irving Brecher script got slapdash direction from W. S. Van Dyke. The Hunt Stromberg production marked the exit of Myrna Loy from MGM for a few years, and the debut of Barry Nelson; both, incidentally, became stage stars later. Left to right: William Powell, Henry O'Neill, Nelson, Myrna. Also cast: Donna Reed, Alan Baxter, Sam Levene, Stella Adler, Louise Beavers, and Dickie Hall as Nick Charles Jr grown to tot size.*

Don Costello, Joseph Downing, Lana Turner, Robert Taylor and Van Heflin in **Johnny Eager**. *Taylor was Johnny and Turner was eager, and their highly inflammable romance blended neatly with underworld action in the slick script of James Edward Grant and John Lee Mahin. Taylor's big-time criminal was one of his best acting jobs, but the picture was pinched by Heflin as his hanger-on, a gentle drunk; he won the year's Oscar for best supporting actor. Vivid direction by Mervyn LeRoy and strong casting—Edward Arnold, Robert Sterling, Glenda Farrell, Henry O'Neill, Patricia Dane, Barry Nelson, Diana Lewis, Charles Dingle, Paul Stewart, Connie Gilchrist—enhanced the John Considine Jr production, which amassed impressive profits.*

The Vanishing Virginian *was a charming example of that apple of Mayer's eye, the family movie. Frank Borzage's direction and Jan Fortune's script derived quiet comedy and slushless sentiment from Rebecca Yancey Williams' book about her Southern girlhood, with Kathryn Grayson trailing stardust as the author. The other young newcomers spotlighted here, Douglass Newland and Natalie Thompson, showed promise but didn't progress as Kathryn did. Spring Byington and Frank Morgan were Ma and Pa, surrounded by Elizabeth Patterson, Katherine Alexander, Scotty Beckett, Juanita Quigley, Mark Daniels and Louise Beavers. Edwin Knopf produced.*

Lady Be Good—*not one of Arthur Freed's most brilliant musicals—preserved only the title and a few Gershwin tunes from Fred and Adele Astaire's 1924 stage smash, filmed silent in 1928 by First National. A new, or rather, different story was whipped up by Jack*

McGowan, Kay Van Riper and John McClain, and the big song was an interpolation by Jerome Kern and Oscar Hammerstein II: 'The Last Time I Saw Paris' which won the Academy Award, causing controversy because it wasn't written for the film. Busby Berkeley staged a super-duper 'Fascinating Rhythm' number with Eleanor Powell and seemingly half the chorus boys in America. Norman Z. McLeod directed (left to right) Ann Sothern, Miss Powell, Red Skelton, John Carroll, Robert Young; also cast were Lionel Barrymore, Virginia O'Brien, Tom Conway, Dan Dailey, Reginald Owen, Rose Hobart and Phil Silvers.

William Powell, Gail Patrick, Myrna Loy and Jack Carson in **Love Crazy**, *Pandro S. Berman's second production for MGM and another box-office hit. Some reviewers were this side of ecstatic about making the Powell–Loy team, so superb in high comedy, go slapsticking around in this knockabout farce. The David Hertz–William Ludwig–Charles Lederer script had Powell feigning madness to prevent Loy from divorcing him, a premise that made no more sense than the incidents following. But director Jack Conway's pace was fast enough to throw audiences into a who cares, let's laugh mood. Also cast: Florence Bates, Sidney Blackmer, Sig Ruman, Vladimir Sokoloff, Sara Haden, Donald MacBride, Kathleen Lockhart, George Meeker, Elisha Cook Jr.*

Ray McDonald, Judy Garland, Richard Quine and Virginia Weidler in **Babes on Broadway**, *biggest and best of the 'youth' musicals Busby Berkeley made for MGM. Quine later became a successful director, but in this movie he and everybody else played second fiddle to Mickey Rooney, whose versatility covered practically every talent but tightrope walking. Judy partnered Mick exuberantly and had a hit song in 'How About You?' Also cast: Fay Bainter, Donald Meek, James Gleason, Emma Dunn, Luis Alberni and the celebrated critic Alexander Woollcott. Script by Fred Finklehoffe and Elaine Ryan; produced by Arthur Freed, who was building his reputation as Hollywood's ace musical-maker.*

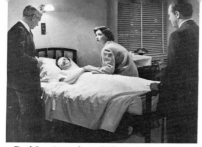

Joe Smith, American/Highway to Freedom *was the first movie from a unit headed by Dore Schary, hitherto a writer, now assigned to make 'important low-budget pictures'–a seeming contradiction in terms, but the company reaped rich profits from the results during the next two years, and Mayer upped Schary's original MGM salary from $200 to $2000. Made quickly and cheaply by director Richard Thorpe and producer Jack Chertok, it packed more drama and human interest into its 63 minutes than did many a wartime epic into twice the footage. Audiences of those days could identify completely with Robert Young's munitions factory worker and Marsha Hunt's unglamorous wife. Also in Allen Rivkin's adaptation of a Paul Gallico story were Selmer Jackson (left), Harvey Stephens (right), Darryl Hickman as the couple's son, Noel Madison, Don Costello, Russell Hicks, Mark Daniels, William Tannen.*

Also from the Schary unit: **Nazi Agent**, *with (here) Conrad Veidt, Ann Ayars and Conrad Veidt, was one of those wild ones about identical twins. Bad brother was a Nazi swine and good brother an anti-swine who–oh, you guessed. Ann Ayars was the girl for whom two Veidts didn't make a wrong; Dorothy Tree, Frank Reicher, Ivan Simpson, William Tannen, Sidney Blackmer, Martin Kosleck, Moroni Olsen, Marc Lawrence and Pierre Watkin supported. Jules Dassin graduated from the MGM Shorts Department to direct for producer Irving Asher. Script by Paul Gangelin and John Meehan Jr.*

Edward G. Robinson gambled on **Unholy Partners** *for another sensational hit like his 1931* Five Star Final *in which he was directed by Mervyn LeRoy as a Prohibition-era newspaper editor involved in crime. Same director, same role, same period, but . . . 'Best forgotten' said Edward G. in his autobiography. Somehow the gangsters' gats didn't sound so exciting while wartime guns were blazing for real. Edward Arnold (right), Laraine Day, Marsha Hunt, William T. Orr, Don Beddoe, Walter Kingsford, Charles Dingle, Joseph Downing, Don Costello and Marcel Dalio gave good support. Samuel Marx produced the Earl Baldwin–Bartlett Cormack–Lesser Samuels screenplay.*

Rejecting Scarlett in GWTW wasn't enough; two years later Norma Shearer also turned down Mrs Miniver. *Instead she chose* **We Were Dancing**, *a comedy so light and fluffy that most moviegoers didn't know it was there, judging by the receipts; and so classy that the leading actors had to wear either a white tux (Melvyn Douglas) or a monocle (Alan Mowbray). Little more than the title, from one of his 'Tonight at 8.30' playlets, gave grounds for the Noël Coward byline; Claudine West, George Froeschel and Hans Rameau were responsible for the script, Robert Z. Leonard for the direction and, with O. O. Dull, the production, Gail Patrick, Lee Bowman, Marjorie Main, Reginald Owen, Heather Thatcher, Florence Bates and Connie Gilchrist for the rest of the acting. But Norma looked a treat.*

Proud of the high-principled message disseminated by Boys Town *in 1938, and still counting the profits, Mayer asked for that camel through a needle's eye, a sequel as good as the original. With Spencer Tracy, Mickey Rooney, director Norman Taurog and producer John Considine Jr still under contract, why not? They tried, and they almost made it with* **Men of Boys Town**. *James K. McGuinness' script introduced new people–Mary Nash and Henry O'Neill, with Rooney and Tracy here; Lee J. Cobb, Darryl Hickman, Larry Nunn, George Lessey, Anne Revere, Lloyd Corrigan–and new events, but the rustle of carbon paper kept coming through. Bobs Watson, Sidney Miller and Addison Richards repeated their old roles.*

'This time Tarzan battles not only with the savage denizens of the untamed jungle but also with unscrupulous adventurers whose lust for gold threatens to destroy his earthly paradise!' said the handout for **Tarzan's Secret Treasure**. *Johnny Weissmuller and Maureen O'Sullivan went into their tenth year of Tarzan–Janeing with undiminished enthusiasm, and you could say the same about the series' fans. Richard Thorpe directed for the third time; B. P. Fineman produced the Myles Connolly–Paul Gangelin screenplay. Left to right: Philip Dorn, Barry Fitzgerald, Reginald Owen, Tom Conway, Johnny Sheffield as 'Boy', and Weissmuller holding hands with Cheeta.*

While The Philadelphia Story *was collecting awards and full houses, Katharine Hepburn moved into the second phase of her MGM campaign. She required, a somewhat dazed Mayer was informed: 1, a long-term contract with all the superstar terms, rights and privileges; 2,* **Woman of the Year**, *a script she commissioned from two little-known writers, as her next picture; 3, Spencer Tracy, whom she'd never met but admired greatly, as her co-star; and 4, George Stevens, who had made some of her RKO-Radio films, as her director. She got the lot, with producer Joseph Mankiewicz backing her up from 2 to 4. A classic comedy of two journalists whose love for each other was strained but not broken by their opposing ideas and temperaments,* Woman of the Year *won Ring Lardner Jr and Michael Kanin the Oscar for best original screenplay. With two such strongwilled stars in tandem, the movie's clash of temperaments was expected to be duplicated in reality–but it was the love story that became real, and lasted until Tracy's death a quarter-century later. Also cast: Fay Bainter and Minor Watson (with them here) and William Bendix, Reginald Owen, Dan Tobin, Roscoe Karns, William Tannen, Ludwig Stossel and Sara Haden.*

The surprise hit of **Whistling in the Dark** *started another series and made a star of Red Skelton. The play about a thriller writer caught in a real crime plot was even funnier in the new script by Albert Mannheimer, Robert Mac-Gunigle and Harry Clork than in its 1932 film version. Left to right, with assorted cops: Reed Hadley, Rags Ragland, Conrad Veidt, Skelton, Ann Rutherford, Virginia Grey and Henry O'Neill. Rest of cast: Eve Arden, Donald Douglas, Paul Stanton, Don Costello, William Tannen, Lloyd Corrigan. Director, S. Sylvan Simon; new producer George Haight.*

The People vs Dr Kildare/My Life is Yours *shifted the series locale from hospital to courtroom as the young doc was accused of malpractice. (The series name was eliminated from the title in Britain: patrons were getting confused over which 'Kildares' they'd seen and which they hadn't.) Tom Conway (brother of*

George Sanders), here cross-examining Lionel Barrymore, and Bonita Granville, Red Skelton and Diana Lewis joined the regulars: Barrymore, Lew Ayres, Laraine Day, Alma Kruger, Walter Kingsford, Marie Blake. As usual, Harold S. Bucquet directed the Willis Goldbeck–Harry Ruskin screenplay, based this time on a story by Lawrence Bachmann and Max Brand.

All that remained of the abortive start to the 'Keeping Company' series went into **This Time for Keeps**. Robert Sterling and Guy Kibbee were respectively husband and father of Ann Rutherford, who survived from the first movie along with Irene Rich as mother, Virginia Weidler as kid sister, and Samuel Marx as producer. Henry O'Neill, Connie Gilchrist and Dorothy Morris had other parts in the lacklustre Muriel Bolton–Rian James–Harry Ruskin screenplay, directed by Charles Reisner.

Three series features that couldn't miss in mid-1941, and didn't: Lionel Barrymore backed by Red Skelton, Laraine Day, Lew Ayres and Nils Asther in **Dr Kildare's Wedding Day**/Mary Names the Day *(top)* which had the usual supporting cast and director Harold S. Bucquet. New departures were the killing-off of the Day character, and the symphony orchestra supposedly conducted by Asther, the actor who played opposite MGM's female stars of an earlier era. Script by Lawrence Bachmann and Ormond Ruthven . . .

Mickey Rooney and Patricia Dane in **Life Begins for Andy Hardy** *(middle)* was the mixture as before, plus Judy Garland in her third and last appearance in a series whose stamina was the wonder of the industry. This was the biggest hit of the 11 made to date.

Miss Dane and Ray McDonald were cast newcomers in the Agnes Christine Johnston script, directed by George B. Seitz . . .

George Murphy, Ann Sothern and Robert Sterling in **Ringside Maisie**/Cash and Carry *(bottom)* from the customary writer-director-producer team of Mary McCall Jr, Edwin Marin and J. Walter Ruben. Virginia O'Brien, Jack La Rue, Natalie Thompson, Maxie Rosenbloom and Rags Ragland were also in the prizefight yarn.

Lew Ayres' performance in **Dr Kildare's Victory**/The Doctor and the Debutante *was his last as the character he made famous. For this he had a new leading lady and a new director: stage actress Ann Ayars (with him here) and W. S. Van Dyke, whose advent had no apparent effect on the established style of the series. Robert Sterling, Jean Rogers, Barry Nelson, Edward Gargan and William Bakewell were other newcomers with regulars Lionel Barrymore, Alma Kruger, Walter Kingsford, Marie Blake, Nell Craig and Frank Orth. Story by Joseph Harrington, script by Harry Ruskin and Willis Goldbeck.*

Kathleen *was Shirley Temple's one and only MGM film. The company's takeover of the star was accompanied by contract-signing photos in the papers, she dimpling happily, Mayer beaming paternally. Now he'd got the star with whom Fox had had the nerve to top his own galaxy as Box-office Draw No. 1 from 1934 to 1938! Announcements of her first Metro picture were issued and revised at frequent intervals, until late in 1941 it was finally unveiled as this shopworn domestic drama about a poor little rich girl choosing a new wife for Dad. Having been in front of the cameras for ten of her 13 years, Shirley was now more of an actress but less of a phenomenon: the public couldn't get excited, and Mayer bade her a quiet farewell. In the cast were Laraine Day, Herbert Marshall and Gail Patrick (with her here), Felix Bressart, Nella Walker and Lloyd Corrigan. Script, by Mary McCall Jr from a Kay Van Riper story; director, Harold S. Bucquet; producer, George Haight.*

The family series that went on, and on, and on: Cecilia Parker, Lewis Stone, Sara Haden, Fay Holden and Mickey Rooney in **The Courtship of Andy Hardy**. Sister Marian had made an evening dress out of a nightgown, so the others mocked her by wearing their night attire to dinner. Looked like the writers (Agnes Christine Johnston this time) were starting to scrape the bottom of the Hardy barrel. Donna Reed was the object of Andy's courtship; William Lundigan, Frieda Inescort, Harvey Stephens, Betty Wells, and Joseph Crehan were also cast with repeaters Ann Rutherford, George Breakston, George B. Seitz directing.

Rage in Heaven was Ingrid Bergman's third Hollywood film. The Christopher Isherwood–Robert Thoeren script from James Hilton's novel seemed to try for psychological depth, but the direction–started by Robert Sinclair, finished by W. S. Van Dyke–was formula suspense-movie. Robert Montgomery did his Night Must Fall maniac act in a tuxedo but neglected to adjust his American accent for the very British role of best friend to George Sanders and husband to Ingrid Bergman. Their disregard of his zombie-like demeanour while he hatched a murder plot against them made them even less credible than the nut himself. Gottfried Reinhardt (son of Max) produced, and the cast included Lucile Watson, Oscar Homolka, Philip Merivale, Matthew Boulton, Gilbert Emery and Frederick Worlock.

Barry Nelson, Laraine Day and Keye Luke in **A Yank on the Burma Road**/China Caravan, produced by Samuel Marx, directed by George B. Seitz, written by Gordon Kahn, Hugo Butler, David Lang. Also cast: Stuart Crawford, Sen Yung, Philip Ahn, Knox Manning, Matthew Boulton. If you liked the title, you loved the movie.

One of the most consistently popular stars of the world's foremost glamour studio had a face like the back of a bus and a figure like an overloaded laundry bag. He had special allure for the public when paired with a middle-aged woman with a steam-whistle voice and a total lack of attention from the studio's make-up, hair-dressing and fashion experts. Wallace Beery and Marjorie Main scored again in **Barnacle Bill**, a waterfront story by Jack Jevne and Hugo Butler which resembled Beery's early hits with Marie Dressler. Milton Bren produced and Richard Thorpe directed, with Leo Carrillo, Virginia Weidler, Donald Meek, Barton MacLane, Connie Gilchrist and Sara Haden in the cast.

King Vidor came back into his best form with **H. M. Pulham, Esq.** and gave Robert Young the most rewarding part of his career as the title character of John P. Marquand's novel. Vidor produced, directed and (with his wife, Elizabeth Hill) wrote the script. Its use of the retrospective format of Citizen Kane and the introspective monologues of Strange Interlude helped to make it an unusually absorbing film, but–perhaps because it showed conventions and traditions triumphant over romantic freedom–it was not big box-office. Opposite Young, Hedy Lamarr also gave her best performance, with expert support by Ruth Hussey, Charles Coburn, Van Heflin, Fay Holden, Bonita Granville, Leif Erickson, Phil Brown and Sara Haden. Left to right: Young, Heflin, Granville, Coburn.

Design for Scandal concluded Rosalind Russell's eight years with MGM, during which she rose from bit player to star. Silly but fun, the story had Rosalind as a professional judge and amateur sculptor, and Walter Pidgeon as a reporter assigned to get her disbarred after she'd ruled against his hot-tempered boss, Edward Arnold, in a court case. Under Norman Taurog's direction, all three milked the Lionel Houser script of every possible laugh, with aid from Guy Kibbee, Lee Bowman, Jean Rogers and Mary Beth Hughes. Producer, John Considine Jr.

Three fillers: **Washington Melodrama** was a mélange of blackmail, murder and politics, plus a spectacular water ballet that seemed to have strayed in from another movie. Kent Taylor socked Dan Dailey while Ann Rutherford screamed; Frank Morgan starred; Lee Bowman, Fay Holden, Virginia Grey, Anne Gwynne, Sara Haden, Olaf Hytten, Douglass Dumbrille and Thurston Hall supported. Script by Marion Parsonnet and Roy Chanslor from L. du Rocher Macpherson's play; director, S. Sylvan Simon; producer, Edgar Selwyn...

Larry Nunn, Virginia Weidler, Leo Gorcey and Ray McDonald in **Born to Sing**, a road company 'Babes' musical. It had a Busby Berkeley flag-waving finale, 'Ballad for Americans' sung by Douglas McPhail, and everybody tried hard–but the Rooney-Garland bezazz wasn't there. Also cast: Rags Ragland, Sheldon Leonard, Henry O'Neill, Margaret Dumont, Lester Matthews, Beverly Hudson, Joe Yule, Connie Gilchrist, moppets Dickie Hall and Darla Hood. Edward Ludwig directed the Franz Spencer–Harry Clork screenplay for producer Frederick Stephani...

Conflict over young Gene Reynolds in **The Penalty** gave Edward Arnold and Lionel Barrymore juicy roles which they chewed on with relish. Arnold wanted his son to grow up to be a big strong public enemy like his dad, while farmer Barrymore taught the boy to value Better Things. With years of collaboration on 'Crime Does Not Pay' shorts behind them, director Harold Bucquet and producer Jack Chertok knew just how to get maximum pace and punch out of the Harry Ruskin–John Higgins adaptation of Martin Berkeley's play. Also cast: Robert Sterling, Marsha Hunt, Emma Dunn, Richard Lane, Veda Ann Borg, Gloria DeHaven, Grant Mitchell, Phil Silvers.

Dr Jekyll and Mr Hyde brought Spencer ▷ Tracy the only bad reviews he ever got–even he had his limitations. The title role called for a theatrical bravura such as John Barrymore and Fredric March provided in their respective 1920 and 1931 Paramount versions. It was outside Tracy's range and he knew it: set visitor Somerset Maugham's crusher, 'Which one is he now, Jekyll or Hyde?' and the eventual reviews came as no surprise to the star. The big hit was made by Ingrid Bergman as the strumpet victimized by Hyde, a part meant for Lana Turner. Ingrid was signed to play Jekyll's sweet young thing but wanted to swap roles with Lana; the studio reluctantly agreed and was pleasantly surprised by the result. Others cast were Donald Crisp, Ian Hunter, C. Aubrey Smith, Barton MacLane, Sara Allgood, Frederick Worlock, Billy Bevan, Forrester Harvey and Lumsden Hare. It was Victor Fleming's first since GWTW which had broken his health; he got production as well as direction credit, although producer Victor Saville had been involved. John Lee Mahin adapted the R. L. Stevenson story.

THE WAR BOOM
1942

The war boom was booming and profits went into orbit: Paramount $13m, MGM–Loew's $12m, Fox $10½m, Warner Bros $8½m, Universal $3m, Columbia $1½m. The first Hollywood star to be killed on active service was Phillips Holmes of the Canadian Air Force; Carole Lombard died during a War Bond tour. Noël Coward's *In Which We Serve*, one of many impressive war pictures being turned out by British studios, won the New York Critics Award. James Cagney in *Yankee Doodle Dandy* got one of the few Academy Awards not won by *Mrs Miniver*. Humphrey Bogart and Ingrid Bergman memorably mooned at each other in *Casablanca*; Fred Astaire and Rita Hayworth glided together in *You Were Never Lovelier*; Tyrone Power and Joan Fontaine wrung tears in *This Above All*; Rosalind Russell reaped laughs in *My Sister Eileen*. *Kings Row* and Welles' *Magnificent Ambersons* gripped. Alan Ladd, Susan Hayward, Paul Henreid, Gene Tierney were new stars.

Two melodramas set in France had the most complicated plots of 1942. In **Reunion in France**/Mademoiselle France *John Wayne was a chauffeur arrested by Nazi officers Henry Daniell and Moroni Olsen. Had Joan Crawford betrayed him? Or he her? Who cared? Enough customers to make a nice profit on this web of wartime intrigue woven by Jan Lustig, Marc Connolly and Marvin Borowski from a Ladislaus Bus–Fekete story. Jules Dassin directed the Joseph Mankiewicz production, with Philip Dorn, Reginald Owen, John Carradine, Ann Ayars, Albert Bassermann, Howard da Silva, J. Edward Bromberg, Morris Ankrum,*

Odette Myrtil cast . . . William Powell was an American in pre-war Paris, with Margaret Wycherly here, in **Crossroads**, *a John Kafka–Howard Emmett Rogers story scripted by Guy Trosper, produced by Edwin Knopf, directed by Jack Conway. Hedy Lamarr played Powell's wife; Claire Trevor and Basil Rathbone the baddies who enmeshed them in a blackmail plot; also cast were Felix Bressart, Sig Ruman, H. B. Warner, Philip Merivale, Vladimir Sokoloff.*

Three fine old troupers gave the folks a good show in **Tish***: Marjorie Main in the title role,*

flanked by ZaSu Pitts and Aline MacMahon. The comedy about village spinsters adopting a baby was extracted by Annalee Whitmore and Thomas Seller from Mary Roberts Rinehart's 'Tish' stories (originally bought for Marie Dressler) and scripted by the prolific Harry Ruskin. Susan Peters proved a find in the romantic lead; others on hand were Lee Bowman, Guy Kibbee, Richard Quine, Virginia Grey, Ruby Dandridge, Al Shean and Gerald Oliver Smith. S. Sylvan Simon directed for that hapless producer who, sick of being kidded about his billing as O. O. Dull, now changed it to Orville Dull (!).

MGM reached its peak as self-appointed publicist for Britain with a Hollywood movie, **Mrs Miniver***; Churchill said its propaganda* ▷ *was worth many battleships. It was supposed to portray a typical English couple in World War II. It didn't: the Minivers were nobler and nicer than any typical couple anywhere, and well over the average income line. But what a marvellously effective movie it was, and what a sensation it caused! It swept the board in public and exhibitor polls as 1942's most popular picture, won cheers from even the crustiest critics and seven Oscars from the Academy: best film, best actress (Greer Garson), best director (William Wyler), best supporting actress (Teresa Wright), best script (Arthur Wimperis, George Froeschel, James Hilton, Claudine West), best photography (Joseph Ruttenberg) and best producer (Thalberg Memorial Award to Sidney Franklin). Shown here are Miss Garson and Walter Pidgeon as Mrs Miniver and her husband in their air-raid shelter, one of the film's more authentic sets. Also cast: Dame May Whitty, Reginald Owen, Henry Travers, Richard Ney, Tom Conway, Helmut Dantine, Christopher Severn, Brenda Forbes, Henry Wilcoxon, Clare Sanders, Rhys Williams.*

In **Random Harvest** *Ronald Colman and Greer Garson were guided by Mervyn LeRoy through the wonderful land of Amnesia, whose paths were paved with gold for moviemakers. This James Hilton romance had (a) Colman as a soldier with no identity, Garson as a music-hall girl; and (b) by a double-twist of the lost memory bit, Colman restored to health and wealth but with a blank spot for (a), and Greer as his wife, not telling him about (a) until (b) had run long enough to make a second feature unnecessary. It's easy to smile now at such contrivances, but* Miniver *producer Sidney Franklin and writers Hilton, Claudine West, George Froeschel and Arthur Wimperis had a way with them, numbing resistance at the time. The movie was a gigantic box-office hit, restoring Colman to the top echelon of stardom and clinching Miss Garson's MGM queendom. Also cast were Philip Dorn, Susan Peters, Henry Travers, Reginald Owen, Bramwell Fletcher, Rhys Williams, Una O'Connor, Margaret Wycherly, Alan Napier, Arthur Margetson, Melville Cooper, Aubrey Mather, Jill Esmond, Marta Linden, Ann Richards, Norma Varden, Ivan Simpson, Elisabeth Risdon.*

For once, MGM went to other studios to get drawing power for its first 1942 musical, **Rio Rita**. *Originally a Ziegfeld show on Broadway, it was bought from RKO Radio, who made a smash film version in 1929. For star strength, Abbott and Costello were borrowed from Universal, where they were the hottest property of the Forties. Gladys Lehman and Richard Connell wrote, and S. Sylvan Simon directed, the Pandro Berman production in routine fashion. Left to right: Kathryn Grayson and John Carroll, singing leads who occasionally managed to nudge the comedians out of camera range; Lou Costello, Joan Valerie, Bud Abbott. Also cast: Tom Conway, Patricia Dane, Barry Nelson and Eros Volusia.*

Two breadwinning 'Bs' produced by J. Walter
Ruben during his last year: **Mokey** with Bobby
Blake, Donna Reed, Dan Dailey, about a kid
getting used to his stepmother; script, Wells
Root and Jan Fortune; director, Root; also
cast, Matt Moore, Cliff Clark, Cordell Hick-
man, Etta McDaniel, Mary Field . . . **Maisie
Gets Her Man**/She Got Her Man, with Ann
Sothern, Red Skelton, took the durable heroine
back into show biz; script, Betty Reinhardt and
Mary McCall Jr; director, Roy Del Ruth; also
cast: Allen Jenkins, Leo Gorcey, Donald
Meek, Frank Jenks, Lloyd Corrigan, Walter
Catlett, Rags Ragland, Fritz Feld.

Somewhere I'll Find You clicked on the strength ▷
of its Clark Gable–Lana Turner star lure, and
contributed richly to the company's $12m.
profit ($135m. gross, highest to date) in 1942.
Gable and Robert Sterling, with Charles Dingle (left), played brothers, war correspondents,
making a play for Lana; they had an offscreen
parallel too, both joining the US Army Air
Corps after this picture. MGM's male star list
was getting thinned out by the war, a situation
soon to be eased by finds like the one playing an
unbilled bit in this: Van Johnson. The
Marguerite Roberts screenplay, adapted by
Walter Reisch from Charles Hoffman's
original, was average war and sex stuff, slickly
directed by Wesley Ruggles and produced by
Pandro Berman. Also cast: Reginald Owen,
Patricia Dane, Lee Patrick. Production was
interrupted for a few weeks when Gable
suffered severe shock after the aircrash death
of his wife, Carole Lombard.

For Me and My Gal was a nostalgic romp ▷
along the memory lane of pre-War I vaudeville
life. A smash for producer Arthur Freed and
director Busby Berkeley, it set Judy Garland
on a new pinnacle of stardom and established
Gene Kelly (bought from David O. Selznick
who signed but didn't use him after his Broadway hit in Pal Joey) as an unusual screen
personality with exciting dancing talent. Left to
right: Horace (later Stephen) McNally, Keenan Wynn, Kelly and Judy. George Murphy and
Marta Eggerth, the Polish singer also making a
Hollywood debut, were other contributors to
the musical highlights which were topped by the
title song ('The Bells are Ringing . . .'); Ben
Blue, Richard Quine and Lucille Norman supported. Script by Fred Finklehoffe, Sid Silvers
and Richard Sherman, from Howard Emmett
Rogers' original.

Fingers at the Window *starred Lew Ayres, and was his last film until 1946. He suddenly changed from an asset to an embarrassment before its release. Early in 1942, when patriotism meant belligerence and male stars from Gable on down were becoming real-life heroes, Ayres announced he was a conscientious objector. Shock waves spread from Mayer's office to fans in the smallest fleapits and back again. (Defending him, Nicholas Schenck stated solemnly that Ayres had been a vegetarian for years!) But second thoughts acknowledged that it took guts to stick to his I-won't-kill principles. In truth, there was a lot of the real Ayres in Dr Kildare and vice versa, and the parallel continued when the army sent him overseas for Medical Corps duty. Fingers, a neat thriller written by Lawrence Bachmann and Rose Caylor, was produced by Irving Asher and directed by Charles Lederer, with Laraine Day and Basil Rathbone (here) and Walter Kingsford, Miles Mander, Russell Gleason.*

*Another star in the old MGM constellation dropped out when Norma Shearer finished **Her Cardboard Lover**. This completed her six-picture contract, signed after Thalberg's death, and she called it a career. Like Garbo, she stopped with fame and beauty unfaded; again like Garbo, she had never made a movie for any studio but MGM through the years, silent and sound, of her stardom. A less happy parallel: her last was also a frothy, George Cukor-*

directed brew that went flat at the box-office. Why, with the company's vast library to choose from, she elected to film Jacques Deval's old play for a third time (Marion Davies, 1928; Buster Keaton, 1932) was known only to Norma and God. Robert Taylor co-starred in the title role, with George Sanders, Frank McHugh, Elizabeth Patterson, Chill Wills. Producer, J. Walter Ruben; script, Deval, John Collier, Anthony Veiller, William H. Wright.

*The Jeanette MacDonald–Nelson Eddy musicals, always costly, had showed signs of diminishing returns, so the company let Eddy go after starring them in **I Married an Angel**. Hunt Stromberg, producer of some of the studio's top 'A's since the silent era, also departed to go independent via United Artists. This show was notable too for having become a stage hit during the nine years it was on and off the Metro schedule. In 1933 Mayer, determined to get a reluctant Miss MacDonald to sign a long-termer, bought a Hungarian piece by Vaszary Janos for her and assigned Rodgers & Hart to write the songs. She accepted, but before work could start the then rigid Purity Code slapped a ban on the saucy story. Five years later it became a stage musical on Broadway. In 1942 the Anita Loos script about an angel luring a playboy from his terrestrial cuties broke no censorship rules. No records either. The co-stars were supported by Anne Jeffreys, Janis Carter, Marion Rosamond, Mona Maris, and Inez Cooper (here with Eddy) and Edward Everett Horton, Binnie Barnes, Reginald Owen and Douglass Dumbrille. W. S. Van Dyke directed.*

*Frankly imitative, **A Yank at Eton** had little of the warmth of A Yank at Oxford and got a comparatively mild reception. Mickey Rooney was the ebullient Yank playing havoc with the Old School conventions, represented by Freddie Bartholomew, now a lanky 18-year-old. Mickey had reached 20 and continued the longest boyhood in screen history; Freddie made a few more movies, later prospered in advertising. Tina Thayer (with them here) and Ian Hunter, Edmund Gwenn, Alan Mowbray, Marta Linden, Alan Napier, and juveniles Juanita Quigley, Peter Lawford, Raymond Severn and Terry Kilburn had roles in the George Oppenheimer–Lionel Houser–Thomas Phipps screenplay, directed by Norman Taurog and produced by John Considine Jr.*

*A prettier thing than Jean Rogers never won leading-ladyhood, which is what MGM gave her in two 'Bs'. With Mona Maris (right) in **Pacific Rendezvous**, a remake of Rendezvous, set one war later; script, Harry Kurnitz, P. J.*

*Wolfson, George Oppenheimer; director, George Sidney; producer, B. F. Zeidman; also cast, Lee Bowman, Carl Esmond, Paul Cavanagh, Blanche Yurka, William Post Jr, Arthur Shields, Frederick Worlock, Curt Bois, William Tannen, Addison Richards, Russell Hicks . . . With William Lundigan, Guy Kibbee, Dan Dailey in **Sunday Punch**, a comedy about a girl in a boarding house full of boxers; script, Fay and Michael Kanin; director, David Miller; producer, Irving Starr; also cast, J. Carrol Naish, Connie Gilchrist, Sam Levene, Leo Gorcey, Rags Ragland, Douglass Newland, Anthony Caruso.*

*A new leading man arrived for two 1942 actioners: James Craig, frequently referred to decades later in the pages of Gore Vidal's 'Myra Breckenridge'. In **The Omaha Trail** he helped haul a locomotive across the old West, with occasional pauses to woo Pamela Blake. Jesse Lasky Jr based his story on historical records, collaborating with Hugo Butler on the script; Edward Buzzell directed; Jack Chertok* ▽

*produced; Dean Jagger, Edward Ellis, Chill Wills, Donald Meek, Howard da Silva and Henry Morgan were also cast. Left: **Northwest Rangers** had Craig as a crook caught by his boyhood pal, now a Mountie. David Lang and Gordon Kahn re-scripted Arthur Caesar's Manhattan Melodrama with Craig and William Lundigan (right, with Jack Holt) in the 1934 Gable and Powell roles. Joseph Newman, a new MGM shorts graduate, directed; Samuel Marx produced; Patricia Dane, John Carradine, Keenan Wynn, Grant Withers and Darryl Hickman supported.*

Cairo *wound up Jeanette MacDonald's MGM contract: she would be back, but her heyday was over. She and Ethel Waters (here) were two of America's most famous singers but you'd never have guessed it from this movie, which mired them in a feeble espionage comedy by John McClain (from an 'idea' by Ladislaus Fodor). Ethel played a maid, obligatory for black actresses then; others involved were Robert Young, Reginald Owen, Lionel Atwill, Grant Mitchell, Eduardo Ciannelli, Mitchell Lewis, Dooley Wilson, Larry Nunn, Dennis Hoey, Mona Barrie, Rhys Williams, Cecil Cunningham. W. S. Van Dyke directed; no producer was credited.*

Franchot Tone returned to play **Pilot No. 5** in an unsuccessful but out-of-the-rut war drama by David Hertz, with Marsha Hunt and Gene Kelly sub-starred. The hero was chosen from five United Nations pilots to fly a suicide mission against Jap invaders in Java; during his absence his comrades (Kelly, Van Johnson, Alan Baxter, Dick Simmons) discussed his chequered past. George Sidney directed, B. P. Fineman produced in the Schary unit. Also cast: Steve Geray, Howard Freeman, Frank Puglia, William Tannen.

▽ **Journey for Margaret** ranked close to Miniver as a well-made heart-tugger about wartime Britain; it drew unanimous praise and massive audiences. Better yet, it created a new star in five-year-old Margaret O'Brien as the London blitz orphan adopted by an American reporter and his wife. Margaret, recruited from the crowd in Babes on Broadway, had an emotional range beyond that of most adult actresses and could turn it on like no other child before or since. It was cleverly controlled by W. S. Van Dyke in the last of his many successful efforts for MGM since 1926: he died in 1942, aged 53. The David Hertz–William Ludwig script came from war reporter W. H. White's fact-based best-seller; B. P. Fineman produced for the Schary unit. Left to right: Laraine Day, William Severn, Robert Young, Margaret; also cast were Fay Bainter, Nigel Bruce, Elisabeth Risdon, Doris Lloyd, Halliwell Hobbes, Heather Thatcher, Jill Esmond, G. P. Huntley Jr.

In **Keeper of the Flame** Spencer Tracy and ▷ Katharine Hepburn switched to drama and scored just as strongly as in their first co-starrer. George Cukor directed the tense I. A. R. Wylie story of a journalist probing a widow's secrets about her famous husband's life and death. Script by Donald Ogden Stewart; production by Victor Saville (associate Leon Gordon). Also cast: Richard Whorf, Margaret Wycherly, Forrest Tucker, Frank Craven, Audrey Christie, Horace McNally, Percy Kilbride, Darryl Hickman, Donald Meek and Howard da Silva.

Whatever became of tap-dancing? Eleanor Powell brought it to such heights of speed and grace, maybe its other exponents got discouraged. Her numbers in **Ship Ahoy** were electrifying, and while she got her breath back Red Skelton and Bert Lahr kept its large audiences amused. Harry Clork's script, climaxed by the star sending a morse code message in taps, sufficed to hold the music and gags together, and Jack Cummings' production had glitter. Edward Buzzell directed a cast also including Virginia O'Brien, William Post Jr, John Emery, Stuart Crawford, Bernard Nedell and Tommy Dorsey's band. This last had an unbilled vocalist, a skinny kid with a nice voice, named Frank Sinatra.

Worst Idea of The Year prize went to **Tarzan's New York Adventure**, which took one of the movies' great fantasy figures out of his never-never jungle into the harsh reality of Manhattan. With clothes on, the legendary superman was just another tall actor. Mayer had carefully preserved the Tarzan illusion around Johnny Weissmuller by vetoing his appearance in any other role, so this was only his sixth film in ten years under contract. In the same period Maureen O'Sullivan had made 35 pictures but she, like Johnny, now checked out. (She was off the screen for six years while she and husband John Farrow increased their family to seven children.) The Myles Connolly–William Lipman script had them flying to New York to rescue their kidnapped son (Johnny Sheffield) with Cheeta the chimp tagging along for

The critics raved over **Tortilla Flat**. John Steinbeck's novel about the indolent, pleasure-loving paisanos of California's Monterey region, was affectionately treated by Victor Fleming to preserve its offbeat charm; but—perhaps because its mood was too passive for the urgent times--business didn't measure up to what the company expected from such star power as Spencer Tracy, Hedy Lamarr and John Garfield. The most superlatives went to the tender and touching performance of Frank Morgan. Also cast: Akim Tamiroff, John Qualen, Allen Jenkins, Sheldon Leonard, Connie Gilchrist, Donald Meek, Henry O'Neill, Betty Wells. Sam Zimbalist produced, John Lee Mahin and Benjamin Glazer scripted.

With **Grand Central Murder** fast following Kid Glove Killer, Van Heflin seemed in danger of getting typed as a gumshoe, but better things were in store. Meanwhile this Peter Ruric screenplay from a whodunit by Sue MacVeigh put him in the lively setting of New York's giant station. A slick directorial job by S. Sylvan Simon; B. F. Zeidman produced. Left to right: Sam Levene, Connie Gilchrist, Betty Wells, Tom Conway, Virginia Grey, Heflin; also cast were Patricia Dane, Cecilia Parker, Samuel S. Hinds, Horace McNally (debut), Millard Mitchell, Mark Daniels.

After Kid Glove Killer Fred Zinnemann and Jack Chertok hatched another offbeat whodunit in **Eyes in the Night**, featuring Edward Arnold as a blind detective, and bringing Ann Harding back to movies. Guy Trosper and Howard Emmett Rogers scripted from Bayard Kendrick's novel 'Odor of Violets'. Reginald Denny also returned for this one, joining Donna Reed, Stanley Ridges, Horace McNally, Allen Jenkins, Katherine Emery, Rosemary DeCamp, Barry Nelson, John Emery, Steve Geray and Reginald Sheffield—plus Friday, son of silent star Flash, following in father's pawprints to play Arnold's seeing-eye dog.

comedy relief. Richard Thorpe directed, Frederick Stephani produced. Also cast: Paul Kelly and Virginia Grey (right, with the stars) and Charles Bickford, Chill Wills, Cy Kendall, Miles Mander, Russell Hicks, Charles Lane, Howard Hickman.

Kid Glove Killer scored two firsts: Van Heflin in his first top-billed role, as a scientist-detective; and Fred Zinnemann starting out as a feature director. Oscar winner for his 1938 short That Mothers Might Live, Zinnemann was another alumnus of the industry's most fruitful directors' academy, the 'Crime Does Not Pay' series. He utilized its documentary fiction style here with the same producer, Jack Chertok. John Higgins and Allen Rivkin wrote the script, enacted by (left to right) Marsha Hunt, Heflin, Eddie Quillan, Lee Bowman, James Flavin and Cliff Clark; also cast were Samuel S. Hinds, John Litel, Nella Walker.

White Cargo, the tropical sex saga that had steamed up Dad's glasses back in the Twenties, seemed a natural for Hedy Lamarr as Tondelayo, the sultry, fiery native who drove white men mad with desire. Sultry Hedy was, fiery she wasn't, and the pre-production censorship of the Forties cooled off much of the heat remaining in Leon Gordon's play. Based on Vera Simonton's novel 'Hell's Playground', it was a veteran of countless stage productions and one of the first British talkies. Gordon wrote this script, Victor Saville produced and Richard Thorpe directed. Richard Carlson and Walter Pidgeon (here with Hedy), and Bramwell Fletcher and Richard Ainley registered concupiscence as best they could under the circumstances; Frank Morgan, Reginald Owen and Clyde Cook played older, less inflammable gents.

Aside from making a small fortune on every instalment, MGM found the 'Hardy' series a fertile nursery for stars. In **Andy Hardy's Double Life** *Esther Williams, a US swimming champion, was tried for size, which looked a little large for Andy but just right for a stellar build-up. Like Judy Garland, Lana Turner, Kathryn Grayson and Donna Reed before her, she passed the 'Hardy' test to become a major studio asset. George B. Seitz directed from Agnes Christine Johnston's script, with Lewis Stone, Cecilia Parker, Fay Holden, Ann Rutherford, Sara Haden, William Lundigan, Susan Peters and Bobby Blake as support to the coruscating Mickey Rooney.*

Panama Hattie, a 1940 bell-ringer on Broadway, dropped a 1942 clanger in its movie version. Playwrights Herbert Fields and B. G. DeSylva and composer Cole Porter had tailored the show for the slam-bang, roof-raising Ethel Merman; the more insinuating charms of Ann Sothern tended to get swamped by the slapstick sailors played by Red Skelton,

Ben Blue and Rags Ragland. The real audience-rousers were the dancing Berry Brothers and the singing newcomer, Lena Horne. Marsha Hunt, Dan Dailey, Jackie Horner (here with Ann in the 'Let's Be Buddies' number), Alan Mowbray, Virginia O'Brien and Carl Esmond had 'book' parts. Producer, Arthur Freed; director, Norman Z. McLeod; script, Jack McGowan, Wilkie Mahoney.

A quick re-vamp of the 'Kildare' series to eliminate its central character was necessitated by Lew Ayres' hassle with the US draft board. **Calling Dr Gillespie** *brought in Philip Dorn as a Dutch psychiatrist working with Gillespie on a case of homicidal mania. Left to right: Phil Brown, impressive as the mental patient, Dorn, Donna Reed as the boy's fiancée, and Lionel Barrymore. Kubec Glasmon's story was scripted by Willis Goldbeck and Harry Ruskin and directed by Harold S. Bucquet, with Nat Pendleton, Ama Kruger, Mary Nash, Walter Kingsford, Nell Craig, Jonathan Hale and Charles Dingle in the cast.*

The history of **Pierre of the Plains** was more interesting than its melodramatics. Its producer, Edgar Selwyn, had written and starred in the stage version 35 years before, and a decade later joined his brother and Samuel Goldfish to form Goldwyn Pictures. In 1929 Selwyn, after returning to Broadway production for several years, became a writer-director-producer for the company that today still bears

three letters of his name. Meanwhile his old play had been filmed twice, by Artcraft in 1918 as Heart of the Wilds and by Paramount in 1922 as Over the Border. This third screen version was Selwyn's last production: he died at 67, the year after its release. George B. Seitz directed the Bertram Millhauser–Lawrence Kimble adaptation with Ruth Hussey, John Carroll and Bruce Cabot (seen here) and Phil Brown, Reginald Owen, Henry Travers, Evelyn Ankers, Frederick Worlock, Sheldon Leonard and Lois Ransom in the cast.

Robert Taylor (here with Chill Wills aboard an old destroyer on Atlantic convoy duty) played one of the many roles Robert Donat turned down after Chips *in* **Stand By for Action**/Cargo of Innocents. *For a straightforward sea drama the movie had a lot of writers: Lawrence Kirk's story about rescuing a boatload of mothers and babies was developed by Harvey Haislip and R. C. Sherriff, scripted by George Bruce, John Balderston and Herman Mankiewicz. Charles Laughton had little to do as an admiral, the bulk of footage going to Taylor. Robert Z. Leonard directed and co-produced with Orville Dull. Also cast: Brian Donlevy, Walter Brennan, Marilyn Maxwell, Henry O'Neill, Douglass Dumbrille, Richard Quine, Marta Linden, Douglas Fowley, William Tannen, Dick Simmons, Hobart Cavanaugh, Inez Cooper.*

Tennessee Johnson/The Man on America's Conscience was one of 1942's most distinguished pictures. It resulted when Mayer signed William Dieterle, the German director of Warners' prestigious biographical films, to guide Van Heflin in a role like those in which he'd directed Paul Muni and Edward G. Robinson. It told the story, dramatized by Wells Root and John Balderston, of the illiterate tailor who rose to become Lincoln's vice-president, then, after the assassination, the 17th President and the only one ever impeached (a hostile Congress failed to oust him). Heflin's strong performance was enhanced by Ruth Hussey's as his wife; others scoring in this J. Walter Ruben production were Lionel Barrymore, Regis Toomey, Marjorie Main, J. Edward Bromberg, Grant Withers, Charles Dingle, Noah Beery, Robert Warwick, Montagu Love, Lloyd Corrigan, Lynne Carver, Morris Ankrum and Carl Benton Reid. But the usual hex on political themes applied at the box office.

Producer Joe Pasternak brought his waltzy, schmaltzy, vastly popular style of musical over from Universal, where he had kept Deanna Durbin's star high. He did as much for Kathryn Grayson in **Seven Sweethearts**, a Walter Reisch–Leo Townsend romance of seven sisters. Left to right: S. Z. Sakall as their father, a Michigan Dutch restaurateur; Van Heflin as the guy who got Grayson; and (background) Dorothy Morris, Frances Raeburn, Cecilia Parker, Peggy Morris and Kathryn. Marsha Hunt and Frances Rafferty were the other two daughters. Also performing under Frank Borzage's direction: Diana Lewis, Lewis Howard, Isobel Elsom, Louise Beavers, Carl Esmond, Donald Meek.

A pretty good sequel to Whistling in The Dark, **Whistling in Dixie** became a profitable mystery farce, thanks to the popularity of Red Skelton. Ann Rutherford again supported the comedian, with George Haight and S. Sylvan Simon repeating their producer/director chores on the Nat Perrin script. Also cast: George Bancroft, Guy Kibbee, Diana Lewis, Peter Whitney, Rags Ragland, Lucien Littlefield, Mark Daniels, Pierre Watkin, Hobart Cavanaugh.

Stuck with a 'Kildare' series minus Kildare, writers Harry Ruskin, Willis Goldbeck and Lawrence Bachmann made a script out of the replacement dilemma. **Dr Gillespie's New Assistant** was to be chosen from Van Johnson (here with Lionel Barrymore, Susan Peters and Alma Kruger), Richard Quine and Keye Luke. Goldbeck took over as director, and his cast included Horace McNally, Ann Richards, Rose Hobart, Nat Pendleton, Walter Kingsford, Marie Blake, Nell Craig, George Reed and Frank Orth. A major plot element was— yes!—amnesia.

This shot caught out Richard Thorpe's grouping of his **Apache Trail** cast in the old-fashioned across-the-stage line-up that movies were supposed to have outgrown. Left to right: Grant Withers, Trevor Bardette, William Lundigan, Lloyd Nolan, Gloria Holden, Miles Mander, Ann Ayars, Frank Thomas, Connie Gilchrist, Donna Reed, Fuzzy Knight. The Maurice Geraghty script came from an Ernest Haycox story resembling his Stagecoach. Samuel Marx produced.

An over-observant servant who wrote a scandalous book about her employers caused suburban uproar in **The Affairs of Martha**/ Once Upon a Thursday, an Irving Starr production written by Isobel Lennart and Lee Gold. Jules Dassin directed a large and effective cast: Richard Carlson, Allyn Joslyn, Frances Drake, Marsha Hunt, Virginia Weidler, Melville Cooper (left to right); and Marjorie Main, Spring Byington, Barry Nelson, Inez Cooper, Sara Haden, Ernest Truex, Margaret Hamilton, Cecil Cunningham, Aubrey Mather, Grady Sutton.

Edward Arnold, Van Johnson, Jean Rogers and Richard Ney surround Fay Bainter in **The War Against Mrs Hadley**, a hit from Schary's unit. Fay, former Broadway star, had her best screen role as the selfish woman who refused to let America's war effort interfere with her comforts. This anti-Mrs Miniver was sharply written and directed, by George Oppenheimer and Harold S. Bucquet respectively, in Irving Asher's production. Sara Allgood, Spring Byington, Horace McNally, Isobel Elsom, Connie Gilchrist, Rags Ragland, Frances Rafferty, Dorothy Morris, Halliwell Hobbes, Miles Mander and Mark Daniels completed the cast.

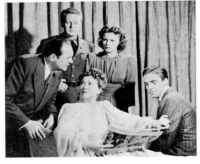

An emotional moment from **Jackass Mail**: caught in a maelstrom of conflicting desires, Wallace Beery lurches from the coy allure of Esther Howard to the voluptuous magnetism of Marjorie Main. Norman Z. McLeod wrung enough rough stuff and laughs from the Lawrence Hazard script, based on a C. G. Sullivan yarn, to make it a profitable Western for producer John Considine Jr. Additional acting by J. Carrol Naish, Darryl Hickman, William Haade, Hobart Cavanaugh, Joe Yule.

1942

In **Three Hearts for Julia** the comedy technique of Ann Sothern and Melvyn Douglas sustained a trifle almost too light even for wartime diversion. Lionel Houser's script about a music-mad wife was directed by Richard Thorpe for producer John Considine Jr. Lee Bowman, Richard Ainley, Felix Bressart, Marta Linden and Reginald Owen were featured.

Cabin in the Sky, MGM's first all-black movie since Vidor's Hallelujah! in 1929 (The Green Pastures was Hollywood's only one in the interim), ended the 1942 output on a high note. 'There's Honey in the Honeycomb' croons temptress Lena Horne in this scene, with but one possible meaning; but 'Life's Full of Consequences' croaks her seductee, Eddie 'Rochester' Anderson, as Kenneth Spencer and Rex Ingram, visitors from Heaven and Hell respectively, fight for his soul. Arthur Freed brought director Vincente Minnelli and its stage producer Albert Lewis from Broadway to film the Lynn Root play with songs by Vernon Duke and John La Touche, who added 'Happiness is a Thing Called Joe' to their original score, including 'Taking a Chance on Love' and 'Cabin in the Sky'. These three numbers were socked across by the formidable Ethel Waters, who had starred in the show, as had Ingram. Miss Horne was the sensation in a cast comprising Louis Armstrong, John 'Bubbles' Sublett, Oscar Polk, Butterfly McQueen, Ruby Dandridge, Duke Ellington and his orchestra. Script by Joseph Schrank.

STILL FIGHTING MAD
1943

Profits continued to mount, even RKO netting $7m after five years of short-earned dividends. Its hits ranged from Disney's *Bambi* to Howard Hughes' much-censored Western *The Outlaw* starring Jane Russell's mammary development. War movies flooded in, the most successful harking back to the Spanish struggle: *For Whom the Bell Tolls* with Gary Cooper and Ingrid Bergman. War-slanted musicals were Irving Berlin's *This is the Army* and the all-star *Stage*

Signe Hasso, Susan Peters and Jean Pierre Aumont in **Assignment in Brittany**, *the first of the 15 war subjects in MGM's total of 35 films completed in 1943. Helen MacInnes' best-seller about a Free French soldier in Nazi-occupied France got vigorous direction from Jack Conway, working from a script by Anthony Veiller, William Wright and Howard Emmett Rogers. Both Aumont ('Jean' was dropped from his name temporarily) and Miss Hasso, already prominent in their native France and Sweden, had their first Hollywood leads in this; also cast were Richard Whorf, Margaret Wycherly, Reginald Owen, John Emery, Miles Mander, George Coulouris, Sarah Padden, Alan Napier, Darryl Hickman, Odette Myrtil, William Edmunds, Juanita Quigley. Producer J. Walter Ruben began the picture, but died suddenly at the age of 43.*

Spencer Tracy, Barry Nelson, Esther Williams and Van Johnson in **A Guy Named Joe**, *a fanciful tale of a fighter pilot (Tracy) killed in action and sent back to the world by the Heavenly General (Lionel Barrymore) to guide a young airman (Johnson). This mélange of fantasy, combat action, comedy and love drama—Irene Dunne returned to MGM after 12 years to co-star with Tracy—could have been a disaster, but Victor Fleming's direction, Dalton Trumbo's writing (from a Chandler Sprague–David Boehm original adapted by F. H. Brennan) and the production nous of Everett Riskin (who'd scored with a similar theme in Columbia's Here Comes Mr Jordan) worked wonders with it. Business was great. Ward Bond, James Gleason, Don DeFore, Henry O'Neill, Charles Smith and Addison Richards completed the cast, the major surprise of which was Johnson. In mid-production a traffic smash-up severely injured him, leaving the alternatives of his replacement or an expensive wait for his recovery. His scenes so far shot indicated a star-making performance, and Tracy was among those who insisted he get the chance to complete it.*

Door Canteen; the latter gave the screen its only glimpse of Broadway's movie-shy superstar Katharine Cornell.
Hitchcock's *Shadow of a Doubt*, Bette Davis in *Watch on the Rhine* and with Miriam Hopkins in *Old Acquaintance*, Dana Andrews in *The Ox-Bow Incident*, Jean Arthur and Joel McCrea in *The More the Merrier* were outstanding.
Betty Grable was the pin-up goddess. She and Greer Garson had invaded the Top Ten list in 1942 and were the only women in it again this year, surrounded by Hope, Crosby, Abbott and Costello, Cooper, Bogart, Cagney, Rooney and Gable. War service then interrupted Gable's record 12 annual appearances on the list.

Two bread-and-butters that got no box-office jam: **A Stranger in Town** *and* **Harrigan's Kid**. *The first had Richard Carlson and Jean Rogers in a plot untangled by visiting judge Frank Morgan, with Porter Hall, John Hodiak (debut), Robert Barrat, Donald MacBride and Chill Wills in support; the Isobel Lennart–William Kozlenko script served to bring yet another 'Crime Does Not Pay' director, Roy Rowland, to full-length filming; Robert Sisk, also new, produced . . . The second featured Bobby Readick and William Gargan as ace jockey and sponsor in a Martin Berkeley–Alan Friedman screenplay from a racetrack yarn by Borden Chase; Charles Riesner directed and Irving Starr produced, with Frank Craven, J. Carrol Naish, Russell Hicks, Selmer Jackson.*

Five years older, Laurel and Hardy returned to MGM for **Air Raid Wardens**, *directed by another comedy veteran, Edward Sedgwick. That master of the slow burn and doubletake, Edgar Kennedy (left) almost out-mugged the star duo in a cast that included Horace McNally, Jacqueline White, Donald Meek, Howard Freeman, Nella Walker, Henry O'Neill, Robert Emmet O'Connor, William Tannen, Russell Hicks. More plot than Stan–Ollie inspiration emerged from the B. F. Zeidman production written by Martin Rackin, Jack Jevne, Charles Rogers, Harry Crane, but it paid its way.*

Best of the year's battle movies, **Bataan** *gave the home folks a harrowingly realistic impression of the American and Filipino troops' hopeless rearguard resistance after the fall of Manila. Tay Garnett directed Lloyd Nolan, Robert Taylor and Thomas Mitchell (left to right) and George Murphy, Robert Walker (whose performance as a young sailor won him an MGM long-termer), Lee Bowman, Desi Arnaz, Barry Nelson, Phillip Terry, Kenneth Spencer and Tom Dugan. Robert Andrews scripted; Irving Starr produced for Dore Schary's unit.*

Cry Havoc *was a novelty among war dramas in having an all-female cast. Stemming from a play by Allan Kenward, it was often more theatrical than realistic and some of the girls seemed to have found a beauty salon on Bataan, but it had its moments—and it ended on the right side of the ledger. Left to right: Ella Raines, Joan Blondell, Gloria Grafton, Heather Angel, Dorothy Morris, Margaret Sullavan, Frances Gifford, Diana Lewis, Ann Sothern and Marsha Hunt. Miss Sullavan (after a two-year screen absence), Miss Sothern and Miss Blondell got star billing; Fay Bainter and Connie Gilchrist were also on hand. The Paul Osborn screenplay was produced by Edwin Knopf and directed by Richard Thorpe.*

Salute to the Marines *bristled with action in red-blooded Technicolor and proved that Wallace Beery hadn't let the years dim his rowdy sergeant-major act. Fay Bainter and Marilyn Maxwell (with him here) played his wife and daughter, caught in the Philippines by Japanese bombing. John Considine Jr produced, S. Sylvan Simon directed the Wells Root–George Bruce screenplay (story, Robert Andrews). Also cast: William Lundigan, Keye Luke, Reginald Owen, Ray Collins, Noah Beery, Russell Gleason, Rose Hobart, Donald Curtis.*

MGM wanted Robert Donat in more pictures pronto after his Chips *Oscar. But his contract gave him story approval, and never was any star's approval so hard to get. After four years of rejecting parts eventually played by Spencer Tracy, Robert Montgomery, Robert Taylor, he finally accepted* **Adventures of Tartu**/Tartu, *a slick sabotage agent story by John Higgins, scripted by John Lee Mahin and Howard Emmett Rogers. The company's first British production for two years, it went to the cameras in August 1942 and didn't emerge from the cutting rooms (in Culver City) until July 1943. In the interim Irving Asher's name went off it as producer; Harold S. Bucquet's remained as director. Locales ranged from blitzed London to Nazied Prague, where Donat entertainingly impersonated a Rumanian dandy. Valerie Hobson (here) was his mysterious lady, with Glynis Johns, Walter Rilla, Martin Miller, David Ward, Phyllis Morris,*

Anthony Eustral and Percy Walsh in support. Receipts were spotty.

Hitler's Hangman *was 'suggested' by Eleanor Roosevelt and contained verses written for it by Edna St Vincent Millay. These ladies, moved by the annihilation of Lidice by the Nazis, must have been nonplussed by the movie melodramatics eventually wrought by producer Seymour Nebenzahl and director Douglas Sirk, who shot most of it independently in 1942 and added scenes when MGM picked it up in 1943. John Carradine as Heydrich, the sadist whose assassination doomed the village, left no sneer unsnarled at such phoney Czechs as Patricia Morison (with him here), and Alan Curtis, Ralph Morgan, Edgar Kennedy, Howard Freeman and Al Shean. The Peretz Hirshbein–Melvin Levy–Doris Malloy script stemmed from a factual story by Emil Ludwig and Albrecht Joseph.*

MGM turned to comedy treatment of wartime life in **Rationing** *with Wallace Beery and Marjorie Main, and* **See Here, Private Hargrove** *with Robert Walker and Donna Reed. The Beery vehicle, casting him as a shopkeeper entangled in red tape, was written by William Lipman, Grant Garrett, Harry Ruskin; directed by Willis Goldbeck, produced by Orville Dull; with Donald Meek, Dorothy Morris, Howard Freeman, Connie Gilchrist, Henry O'Neill, Douglas Fowley. It just about got by, but Hargrove was a considerable hit, thanks to Walker's bashful charm, Harry Kurnitz's tight, funny script from Marion Hargrove's army camp memoirs, and brisk direction by Wesley Ruggles. Keenan Wynn, Robert Benchley, Ray Collins, Chill Wills, Bob Crosby, Marta Linden, George Offerman, Bill Phillips, Douglas Fowley, Grant Mitchell and Donald Curtis were in the George Haight production.*

The 'Maisie' series got a topical touch when Mary McCall Jr and Robert Halff wrote her into an aircraft factory for **Swing-Shift Maisie**/ The Girl in Overalls. *Jean Rogers (left) was Ann Sothern's rival and James Craig was the test pilot they went into tailspins over. Norman Z. McLeod directed and George Haight produced, casting Connie Gilchrist, John Qualen, Kay Medford, Jacqueline White, Betty Jaynes, Marta Linden, Donald Curtis and Pierre Watkin.*

Edwin Knopf had the all-male war drama, **The Cross of Lorraine**, *shooting simultaneously with the female* Cry Havoc; *this one had more guts, but both met resistance from a battle-weary public. Left to right: Sir Cedric Hard-wicke, Joseph Calleia, Gene Kelly and Wallace Ford. Kelly, billed below Jean Pierre Aumont, showed surprising dramatic talent as one of the French prisoners (Richard Whorf, Hume Cronyn, Donald Curtis were others) tortured by German sergeant Peter Lorre. Tay Garnett directed the Michael Kanin–Ring Lardner Jr–Alexander Esway–Robert Andrews screenplay partly based on Hans Habe's autobiographical 'A Thousand Shall Fall'.*

Young Ideas *was a comedy sent in by under-graduate William Noble (a rare instance of MGM accepting unpublished material from an amateur) who was also hired to do the script with Ian McL. Hunter. Shown here are Elliott Reid and Susan Peters as college students. Herbert Marshall as their professor and Mary Astor as their mother. Miss Astor, a fine actress after 22 years in movies, was starting a five-year contract; she played a novelist, which she actually became later. Jules Dassin directed, Robert Sisk produced, with Richard Carlson and Allyn Joslyn featured.*

Du Barry was a Lady, *a Broadway smash in 1939, was a movie hit in 1943, with Lucille Ball and Red Skelton filling the Ethel Merman and Bert Lahr star spots. With songs by Cole Porter ('Do I Love You, Do I?', 'Friendship', 'Katie Went to Haiti'), it had a brassy vigour, as directed by Roy Del Ruth and produced in Technicolor by Arthur Freed, and was an improvement on the Freed–Porter–Skelton* Panama Hattie. *As in* Hattie, *some of Porter's cleverest songs were relegated to background music: 'But in the Morning, No' and 'Well, Did You Evah!'. On Broadway the latter was sung (with Betty Grable) by Charles Walters whose role was given screen zip by Gene Kelly; Walters directed the musical numbers. Also cast: Virginia O'Brien, Rags Ragland, Zero Mostel (film debut), Donald Meek, Douglass Dumbrille, George Givot, Louise Beavers, Tommy Dorsey and Band. Script by Irving Brecher.*

Planned as a cosy Joe Pasternak musical about a soldier and a colonel's daughter, **Thousands Cheer** *developed into a huge all-star extrava-ganza. Gene Kelly, Kathryn Grayson and John Boles played out the Paul Jarrico–Richard Collins story, aided by Mary Astor, pianist-conductor Jose Iturbi in his acting debut, Ben Blue, Frances Rafferty, Frank Jenks, Dick Simmons and Frank Sully. But the trimmings, in the form of an army camp con-cert, took over the screen, the publicity and the box office. There were numbers and sketches by Kelly, Miss Grayson, Iturbi, Judy Garland, Mickey Rooney, Eleanor Powell, Red Skelton, Ann Sothern, Lucille Ball, Frank Morgan, Lena Horne, Margaret O'Brien, June Allyson, Gloria DeHaven, Virginia O'Brien, Marsha Hunt, Marilyn Maxwell, Donna Reed, John Conte, Sara Haden. Plus the bands of Kay Kyser, Bob Crosby, Benny Carter. Plus a symphony orchestra. Plus a military band. Music ranged from Judy's 'The Joint is Really Jumpin' to 'United Nations on the March' commissioned by MGM from Shostakovich (any old studio could get Tchaikovsky). George Sidney directed, and the whole shebang was in Technicolor.*

Judy Garland's performance (she sang 'Every Little Movement Has a Meaning of Its Own' and proved it) made **Presenting Lily Mars** *a winner. Booth Tarkington's novel about a stagestruck girl, decorated with songs and show bands but with its warm comedy kept intact by the Richard Connell–Gladys Lehman script and Norman Taurog's direction, had key roles for Van Heflin, Richard Carlson and as producer, playwright and prima donna, Marta Eggerth. Also a great bit part for Connie Gilchrist (here with Judy) as an ex-actress theatre cleaner. Joe Pasternak produced, with Fay Bainter, Spring Byington, Ray McDonald, Leonid Kinskey and the Tommy Dorsey and Bob Crosby bands.*

After **Above Suspicion** *Joan Crawford, know-ing she was no longer news at MGM after 17 years, followed Garbo, Norma Shearer, Myrna Loy and Jeanette MacDonald through the door marked Exit. The Garson–Garland–Hepburn–Turner era had taken over. The second Helen MacInnes best-seller to hit the screen within a few months, this well-received movie starred Joan and Fred MacMurray as osten-sible honeymooners, really spies for Britain, in 1939 Germany. The Victor Saville production (associate, Leon Gordon) was directed by Richard Thorpe; script by Keith Winter, Melville Baker, Patricia Coleman. Also cast: Basil Rathbone, Reginald Owen, Richard Ainley, Cecil Cunningham, Ann Shoemaker, Felix Bressart, Sara Haden, Bruce Lester, and the brilliant Conrad Veidt, who suffered a fatal heart attack after completing his role.*

While writers whipped up a star vehicle for Margaret O'Brien, the new find did a couple of supporting assignments, one with Lionel Barry-more in **Dr Gillespie's Criminal Case**/Crazy to Kill. *This continued the story of the homicidal youth (now played by John Craven) and his frantic fiancée (Donna Reed again) begun in* Calling Dr Gillespie. *Willis Goldbeck directed the Martin Berkeley–Harry Ruskin–Lawrence Bachmann screenplay. Marilyn Maxwell, William Lundigan and Henry O'Neill appeared with hospital staffers Van Johnson, Keye Luke, Alma Kruger, Nat Pendleton, Walter Kings-ford and Marie Blake.*

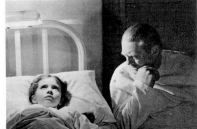

Charles Laughton, Donna Reed, Horace Mc-Nally, and Richard Carlson as the boxer in **The Man from Down Under**. All of them took the count from a heavy-handed script by Wells Root and Thomas Seller from a Bogart Rogers–Mark Kelly yarn encompassing World Wars I and II in the life of a hearty Aussie. Laughton, miscast in a Beery-type role, had Binnie Barnes as his gorblimey Marjorie Main. Clyde Cook, Arthur Sheilds, Christopher Severn, Hobart Cavanaugh and André Charlot (the revue producer, playing a priest) also performed. Likewise ill-at-ease with the material, Robert Z. Leonard directed and co-produced with Orville Dull.

Before his golden era of original musicals, Arthur Freed continued to reproduce Broadway hits. **Best Foot Forward** again starred Lucille Ball, this time playing Lucille Ball, a movie queen invited to preside over a boys' school dance. From the New York cast came young star prospects Nancy Walker (here with Harry James), Tommy Dix, June Allyson, Kenny Bowers and Jack Jordan: June was the one destined to make it big. Virginia Weidler, Gloria DeHaven and Beverly Tyler were other teenagers involved, along with adults William Gaxton, long a Broadway celebrity but a blank on film, Chill Wills, Henry O'Neill, Sara Haden, Donald MacBride, Nana Bryant and Morris Ankrum. Eddie Buzzell directed the Irving Brecher–Fred Finklehoffe adaptation of John Cecil Holm's play, while Charles Walters choreographed numbers by Hugh Martin and Ralph Blane, including the rousing 'Buckle Down, Winsocki!'

Lana Turner (here with Eugene Pallette) had a go at comedy in **Slightly Dangerous** and pleased a wide public. The Ian M. Hunter–Aileen Hamilton cliché story of a poor girl feigning amnesia and claiming to be a millionaire's longlost daughter was given cute twists by Charles Lederer and George Oppenheimer, and brisk pacing by director Wesley Ruggles. Robert Young, Dame May Whitty, Walter Brennan, Alan Mowbray, Florence Bates, Howard Freeman, Millard Mitchell, Ward Bond and Ray Collins were featured in the Pandro Berman production.

Dull thud musical of the year, **Swing Fever** had (left to right) ex-prizefighter Maxie Rosenbloom, ex-band singer Marilyn Maxwell, Nat Pendleton, Curt Bois and William Gargan struggling with an ex-original by Matt Brooks and Joseph Hoffman (script, Nat Perrin, Warren Wilson) about a shy composer whose evil-eye power caused havoc. This role was played by Kay Kyser, the band leader, whose ambitions as a star comedian this movie exposed as unwarranted. His band, Miss Maxwell and a single number by Lena Horne brought musical relief. Tim Whelan directed the Irving Starr production.

In **The Heavenly Body**, William Powell's first lead for 18 months, he was teamed with Hedy Lamarr: they'd had better luck with drama in Crossroads. He played a serious astronomer, she an astrology fan. This promising idea for matrimonial comedy, assigned to scenarists Walter Reisch, Harry Kurnitz and the renowned Michael Arlen–also eminent producer Arthur Hornblow Jr and director Alexander Hall, aiming to get their MGM contracts off to a good start–resulted in a movie that elicited more yawns than laughs. Cast included James Craig, Fay Bainter, Henry O'Neill, Spring Byington, Morris Ankrum, Connie Gilchrist, Robert Sully, Arthur Space.

Song of Russia was the last film Robert Taylor made before joining the US Navy. He was paired with Susan Peters as visiting American maestro and welcoming Soviet maiden. Pretentious and slow in its efforts to pay tribute to a war ally (later regretted by MGM when kowtowing to Senator McCarthy), it sounded Russian while Tchaikowsky (adapted by Herbert Stothart, conducted by Albert Coates) filled the soundtrack, but too often looked strictly Hollywood. Ex-actor Gregory Ratoff directed the Paul Jarrico–Richard Collins screenplay, from a story by Leo Mittler, Victor Trivas, Guy Endore; Joe Pasternak produced. Robert Benchley took time out from his hilarious 'How to . . .' shorts to provide mild comedy relief; Michael Chekhov, Vladimir Sokoloff and Leo Bulgakov stood out in the otherwise un-Russian cast: John Hodiak, Felix Bressart, Darryl Hickman, Jacqueline White.

Red Skelton, Ann Rutherford, Jean Rogers and Rags Ragland in **Whistling in Brooklyn**, *Skelton's third annual appearance as the addle-pated sleuth introduced in* Whistling in the Dark. *It hit its laugh target, but the series was not continued. S. Sylvan Simon, George Haight and Nat Perrin repeated as director/producer/writer. Also cast: Ray Collins, Henry O'Neill, William Frawley, Sam Levene, Arthur Space, Robert Emmet O'Connor, Steve Geray, Howard Freeman.*

Lost Angel *proved that Mayer hadn't lost his star-developing skill. Margaret O'Brien's* Journey for Margaret *performance brought orders from his throneroom that an ideal story must be tailored for her, if it took a year (it did). After many rejects, Isobel Lennart's script from an idea by Angna Enters clicked: a surefire yarn about a foundling, reared by scientists to be a mental prodigy, then shown the joys of normal childhood by a kindly reporter—James Craig, here with the star. Well-directed by Roy Rowland and acting with the authority of a pint-sized Garbo, Margaret carried it to great popularity. Robert Sisk produced another hit for Schary's 'B'-plus crew, casting Marsha Hunt, Philip Merivale, Henry O'Neill, Donald Meek, Keenan Wynn, Alan Napier, Sara Haden, Kathleen Lockhart, Howard Freeman, Elisabeth Risdon, Bobby Blake.*

Teenage movie fans loved **The Youngest Profession**: *it was all about them, particularly the autograph-hunting kind. It starred Virginia Weidler (right) in one of the last roles of her ten-year career as a no-nonsense child actress. Edward Buzzell directed her, Jean Porter (centre), Edward Arnold, John Carroll, Ann Ayars, Marta Linden, Agnes Moorehead, Dick Simmons, Scotty Beckett, Marcia Mae Jones, Sara Haden, Marjorie Gateson and Thurston Hall in a George Oppenheimer–Charles Lederer–Leonard Spigelgass screenplay derived from Lillian Day's popular book. Producer B. F. Zeidman got Walter Pidgeon, (left) Lana Turner, William Powell, Greer Garson and Robert Taylor to appear 'in person'.*

Judy Garland starred again with Mickey Rooney in **Girl Crazy**, *a hit. They shared honours with the George and Ira Gershwin score ('I Got Rhythm', 'Embraceable You', 'But Not for Me', 'Bidin' My Time') from Ziegfeld's 1930 Broadway show, first filmed in 1932 by RKO-Radio as a Wheeler and Woolsey vehicle. A new script by Fred Finklehoffe had the usual let's-knock-'em-in-the-aisles-kids plot, this time a musical rodeo. Here June Allyson, the blonde with a brunette voice, husks her way through one of the songs with Rooney. She and Nancy Walker worked in the picture concurrently with another Arthur Freed production,* Best Foot Forward, *but this one took longer, changing directors from Busby Berkeley to Norman Taurog midway. Rags Ragland, Guy Kibbee, Gil Stratton, Robert Strickland, Henry O'Neill, Frances Rafferty and Tommy Dorsey's band performed.*

Eleanor Powell and Red Skelton teamed for a second time in **I Dood It**/By Hook or By Crook, *which was better than its inane title (a radio catchphrase of Skelton's) but below director Vincente Minnelli's later achievements. The Fred Saidy–Sig Herzig script, based on Buster Keaton's* Spite Marriage, *about a tailor's assistant adoring a stage star, was just enough to support the abundant trimmings: Red's slapstick and pantomime; Eleanor's Hawaiian and rope-spinning dances; singer Lena Horne's and pianist Hazel Scott's production number, 'Walls of Jericho'; several*

tunes from the Jimmy Dorsey band with vocalists Helen O'Connell and Bob Eberly scoring with 'Star Eyes'. Richard Ainley, Patricia Dane, Sam Levene, John Hodiak, Thurston Hall, Butterfly McQueen, Morris Ankrum, Marjorie Gateson and Charles Judels supported them in the Jack Cummings production.

The Human Comedy *was said to be Mayer's favourite movie and was greeted with unbridled ecstasy by the Hollywood trade papers, which were not exactly impervious to his influence. Elsewhere, some critics reached for words like 'sugary' and 'over-sentimental'. William Saroyan won an Oscar for writing it in his best isn't-life-wonderful style, preserved by scripter Howard Estabrook and producer-director Clarence Brown. The latter got marvellous effects from a freckled five-year-old, Jackie Jenkins (here with Fay Bainter, Donna Reed and Dorothy Morris), who would have stolen the show had Mickey Rooney not given his finest dramatic performance. Others populating Saroyan's small town were James Craig, Marsha Hunt, Ray Collins, Van Johnson, Ann Ayars, John Craven, Mary Nash, Henry O'Neill, Katherine Alexander, Alan Baxter, Barry Nelson, Darryl Hickman, Rita Quigley, Clem Bevans and Adeline deWalt Reynolds.*

The last film (and eighth musical) that MGM finished in 1943, **Broadway Rhythm** *was light on names by the company's standards, but given lots of Technicolorful production flash by Jack Cummings. Nominally based on the 1939 Kern–Hammerstein show 'Very Warm for May', it retained little more than their lovely song, 'All the Things You Are'. Gloria DeHaven and Kenny Bowers (here) and Nancy Walker brought their youthful zest from* Best Foot Forward, *Ben Blue and Eddie 'Rochester' Anderson were comic, Hazel Scott pounded the key-*

board, Dean Murphy impersonated stars, Lena Horne scorched the screen with 'Brazilian Boogie', Tommy Dorsey and Orchestra rendered 'Milkman, Keep Those Bottles Quiet'. Top billing went to George Murphy and Ginny Simms, a radio singer beloved of Mayer; Charles Winninger played Murphy's father. Roy Del Ruth directed the Dorothy Kingsley–Harry Clork screenplay.

Lassie Come Home, *the classic boy-and-dog story, was a bonanza from Dore Schary's unit. Roddy McDowall was the star, but this scene shows two other young performers starting even more famous careers: Lassie (real name, Pal; real sex, male), the first top dog at the box office since Rin-Tin-Tin; and Elizabeth Taylor, already a beauty at 11 and, like McDowall, a London-to-Hollywood wartime evacuee. With them here are Donald Crisp, Nigel Bruce and Elsa Lanchester. Others featured in Hugo Butler's potent screenplay from the Eric Knight novel were Dame May Whitty, her husband Ben Webster, Edmund Gwenn, Alan Napier. Produced in Technicolor by Samuel Marx and directed by Fred Wilcox, risen from publicist, script clerk for King Vidor, and test director—and not hindered by being Nicholas Schenck's brother-in-law.*

Once considered too sombre for wartime success, **Madame Curie** *was dusted off for a team that in 1943 could, and did, counteract any box-office deficiency: Greer Garson and Walter Pidgeon (here with Dame May Whitty and Henry Travers as senior Curies). Scripters Paul Osborn and Paul Rameau treated Eve Curie's biography of her mother with reverence, and producer Sidney Franklin and director Mervyn LeRoy gave it their* Random Harvest *gloss. MGM gained prestige and profits, but Garson's discovery of radium stirred up no more excitement than had Tracy's invention of electric light bulbs. Albert and Elsa Bassermann, Robert Walker, C. Aubrey Smith, Victor Francen, Reginald Owen, Van Johnson and Margaret O'Brien completed the cast, the last two in mere bits.*

RE-ENTER ROMANCE
1944

Money poured in for almost anything that kept a 1944 screen alight, and MGM hit its highest net income ($14½m) since 1937 and the industry's record gross to date for any company ($166m).

Victory's approach seemed to inspire a religious cycle in movies. *Going My Way*, with Bing Crosby and Barry Fitzgerald as priests, scooped Oscars and box-office records for Paramount, while *The Song of Bernadette* made Jennifer Jones a star and worked wonders for Fox, which also turned Gregory Peck's collar around for *The Keys of the Kingdom*.

Clifford Odets (where is thy sting?) guided Cary Grant through the gloomy *None But the Lonely Heart* and Darryl Zanuck poured money into the stodgy *Wilson*, but David O. Selznick had a winner in *Since You Went Away* with Claudette Colbert, Shirley Temple, and Jennifer Jones. *Laura* and *Double Indemnity* were thrillers with a modern touch. So was Lauren Bacall, unveiled by Warners in *To Have and Have Not*.

Mrs Parkington, *Louis Bromfield's best-seller, scripted by Robert Thoeren and Polly James, whisked Greer Garson and Walter Pidgeon to the high life of millionairedom. Director Tay Garnett and producer Leon Gordon gave cohesion to the flashback-infested footage in which Greer progressed from boarding-house slavey to matriarch of a family spoiled by wealth, while Walter became a financial buccaneer and an unfaithful husband. His money-making prowess was as nothing, though, compared to the movie's: a smash. Left to right: Helen Freeman, Dan Duryea, Miss Garson, Edward Arnold, Gladys Cooper, Rod Cameron, Lee Patrick, Gerald Oliver Smith.*

*Leo rolled out the red carpet for Myrna Loy, who interrupted her wartime committee work to make **The Thin Man Goes Home** with William Powell, Lucile Watson and Harry Davenport. Maybe the surprise element of the original* Thin Man *was missed, but Nick and Nora Charles, amateur sleuths, had the same nonchalant charm as in their debut ten years before, and the box-office responded like Asta to a bone. The murder they probed was dreamed up by Robert Riskin and Harry Kurnitz; the polished script by Riskin and Dwight Taylor gave jobs to Gloria DeHaven, Anne Revere, Helen Vinson, Leon Ames, Donald Meek, Edward Brophy, Lloyd Corrigan, Donald MacBride, Minor Watson, Morris Ankrum and the quaintly-named Anita Bolster. Director, Richard Thorpe; producer, Everett Riskin.*

Nothing But Trouble *was Laurel and Hardy's last MGM release, except for a 1965 compilation of their shorts. Here Philip Merivale, Mary Boland and Henry O'Neill struggle to maintain dignity as the servant problem, i.e. Oliver and Stan, becomes acute. Not vintage L. & H., but profitable in a laugh-hungry period. Sam Taylor, director of Mary Pickford and Harold Lloyd in the old days (and famous for the credit 'by William Shakespeare; additional dialogue by Sam Taylor' on the Pickford–Fairbanks* Taming of the Shrew) *emerged from a ten-year eclipse for this B. F. Zeidman production, and was never heard of again. The Russell Rouse–Ray Golden screenplay had roles for John Warburton, Matthew Boulton and Connie Gilchrist.*

*MGM's younger generation dominated **Two Girls and a Sailor**, one of the year's most profitable musicals. June Allyson and Gloria DeHaven (here with Harry James) and Van Johnson had the title roles; Tom Drake made his screen bow. Allyson and Johnson broke through to mass popularity with their romantic scenes, written by Richard Connell and Gladys Lehman and directed by Richard Thorpe for an effect of fresh spontaneity. Jimmy Durante started a new studio contract after ten years away; Henry Stephenson, Henry O'Neill, Frank Jenks, Donald Meek and Frank Sully played straight; musical diversions featured*

Jose Iturbi and his sister Amparo at twin pianos, Lena Horne, Virginia O'Brien, Lyn and Lee Wilde, Ben Blue, Carlos Ramirez, the Xavier Cugat and James bands, and Gracie Allen performing The One-Finger Concerto (in short, 'Chopsticks') with a huge orchestra conducted by Albert Coates. Joe Pasternak produced.

*That astonishing tot, Margaret O'Brien, collected a special Academy Award in 1944 for outstanding juvenile acting. Certainly, only a child-performer allergy could prevent enjoyment of her performance in **Music for Millions**, even though watching the rest of it was like drinking a quart of raspberry syrup. With director Henry Koster joining his old Deanna Durbin producer, Joe Pasternak, this movie continued Mayer's Revenge on Universal for snatching Deanna from MGM eight years before. Marie Wilson, June Allyson and Jimmy Durante (left to right) pleased the abundant crowds for this Myles Connolly confection about a waif adopted by a symphony orchestra, to an accompaniment of classical pops. Also cast: Jose Iturbi and his piano, Larry Adler and his harmonica, Marsha Hunt, Hugh Herbert, Harry Davenport, Connie Gilchrist, Helen Gilbert with cello, Ethel Griffies.*

*Judy Garland had the best picture of her career in **Meet Me in St Louis**. Despite the fact that* ▷ *it contained fine songs, Hugh Martin and Ralph Blane's 'The Trolley Song', 'The Boy Next Door', 'Have Yourself a Merry Little Christmas', etc., it wasn't so much a musical as a charming family album brought to life by director Vincente Minnelli. Fun and unsoggy sentiment pervaded the Irving Brecher–Fred Finklehoffe script, suggested by Sally Benson's book about her girlhood. Minnelli's sense of design and period added visual distinction, and the Technicolor production, rich without being garish, began Arthur Freed's golden era. From Margaret O'Brien's Hallowe'en exploits ('I killed him!') to Marjorie Main's downright cook ('Cabbage has a cabbage smell') the supporting cast sparkled bright as Judy herself; parents Mary Astor and Leon Ames, siblings Lucille Bremer, Joan Carroll and Henry Daniels Jr, boy-next-door Tom Drake (here with Judy), grandpa Harry Davenport, and June Lockhart, Hugh Marlowe, Robert Sully, Chill Wills. It was such a hit that 20th Century-Fox made a pale copy,* Centennial Summer, *using the 1876 Philadelphia Exposition for the 1904 St Louis Fair.*

In **Gaslight**/The Murder in Thornton Square, George Cukor, producer Arthur Hornblow Jr and writers John van Druten, Walter Reisch and John Balderston demonstrated what could be done with a good old melo, given the 'A' treatment in all departments. Patrick Hamilton's play about an ostensibly loving husband driving his wife to insanity came across with renewed force five years after its British filming (with Diana Wynyard and Anton Walbrook). Now it had Ingrid Bergman conveying mental torture well enough to win a 1944 Academy Award and Charles Boyer extending his usual great-lover range to encompass sadistic villainy. Oscars went too to Cedric Gibbons, William Ferrari, Edwin B. Willis and Paul Huldchinsky for their Victorian decor. Angela Lansbury (centre), another find among London's evacuee children in Hollywood, was signed at 17 to make a striking debut: it was hard to believe she had never acted before. As a Scotland Yard man rescuing our heroine in the very nick of running-time, Joseph Cotten co-starred ('Miss Bergman and Mr Cotten through courtesy of David O. Selznick' was the billing demanded by the latter, whose studio was more like a talent agency), supported by Dame May Whitty, Barbara Everest, Edmond Breon, Halliwell Hobbes, Heather Thatcher, Lawrence Grossmith.

Another British period drama made a striking success—**The Picture of Dorian Gray**. The Pandro Berman production was scripted and directed by Albert Lewin in high style. Hurd Hatfield's Dorian had a waxwork fascination, his deadpan expression and flat mid-Atlantic voice somehow managing to suggest Oscar Wilde's English aristocrat of great beauty and limitless depravity. Suggestion was all: the undescribed vices and unshown orgies that

Lewin could only imply in the straitlaced Forties carried more punch than any director's four-lettered, full-frontal whoop-up in the Seventies. Harry Stradling's Academy Awarded photography enhanced the elegant black-and-white interiors and broke into Technicolor for the portrait (by Ivan Albright) bearing Dorian's sins. George Sanders rattled off epigrams; Angela Lansbury got her second Academy nomination (she didn't win for this or Gaslight but two nominations in her first three tries was good going). Also cast: Lowell Gilmore, Donna Reed, Peter Lawford, Miles Mander, Douglas Walton, Mary Forbes, Moyna MacGill (Angela's mother), Robert Greig, Morton Lowry, Billy Bevan, Lillian Bond.

Gentle Annie's ironic title kept away the action addicts and attracted few others to the Robert Sisk production, an offbeat Western by Lawrence Hazard based on Mackinlay Kantor's novel. James Craig played a marshal coping with two ranchers and their mother who saw no harm in an occasional bank robbery to augment their income. Donna Reed (with him here) was his beloved; Henry Morgan and Paul Langton the ranchers; Marjorie Main, mother Annie. The movie had first gone into production two years before with Robert Taylor as the marshal and W. S. Van Dyke directing. The reins dropped by the then ailing Van Dyke were picked up rather limply by Andrew Marton, with Barton MacLane, Morris Ankrum, Noah Beery and Robert Emmet O'Connor in the new cast.

Cool customer, that Marlene Dietrich. She allowed neither gold body-paint, which must have itched, nor below-title billing, which must have irked, to crack her expressionless aplomb in **Kismet**. *Ronald Colman, surveying the* ▷ *Technicolored Arabian Nights super-kitsch with detached amusement, was solo-starred in the role filmed twice (1920, 1930) by Otis Skinner, who originated it in Edward Knoblock's remarkably enduring play. In Everett Riskin's production scripted by John Meehan it resembled a musical looking for a score—which it found a decade later. Others performing under William Dieterle's heavy-handed direction were Edward Arnold, James Craig, Hugh Herbert, Joy Ann Page, Florence Bates, Harry Davenport, Robert Warwick and Hobart Cavanaugh.*

Bathing Beauty *was built around Esther Williams; of the 1944 total of 155 performers under MGM contract, she was one of ten promoted from featured players to the 'official' star list. (The others: Laraine Day, Kathryn Grayson, Van Johnson, Gene Kelly, George Murphy, Margaret O'Brien, Susan Peters, Ginny Simms, Robert Walker.) Red Skelton was co-starred for box-office insurance, and the expensive edifice was topped by a John Murray Anderson water ballet that out-Busbyed Berkeley. Other numbers promoted the current vogue for Latin American rhythms: 'Tico-Tico' played by swing organist Ethel Smith, 'Echo of a Serenade' sung by baritone Carlos Ramirez, several more by Xavier Cugat's orchestra with Lina Romay, and Harry James' band did their North American stuff. A tiny story about a girls' school emerged from the massed typewriters of Kenneth Earl, M. M. Musselman, Curtis Kenyon, Joseph Schrank, Dorothy Kingsley, Allen Boretz and Frank Waldman, giving jobs to Basil Rathbone, Bill Goodwin, Jean Porter, Nana Bryant, Donald Meek, Ann Codee, Francis Pierlot and a Marxless Margaret Dumont. George Sidney directed, Jack Cummings produced in Technicolor, and Metro made a juicy profit.*

Robert Young wound up his long stay at MGM with **The Canterville Ghost**, *a comedy of GIs billeted in a haunted castle, based more or less on Oscar Wilde's story by scenarist Edwin Blum. Charles Laughton (here with Young and Margaret O'Brien) capered frantically as the 300-year-old spook in a vain effort to stop Margaret's theft of the movie, while English atmosphere was supplied by Reginald Owen, Elisabeth Risdon, Peter Lawford, Una O'Connor and Lumsden Hare. William Gargan, Rags Ragland, Frank Faylen, Mike Mazurki and Bobby Readick played Young's buddies. Jules Dassin directed for laughs, which it didn't get enough of. Arthur Field produced.*

National Velvet *had been on Pandro Berman's must-do list since he tried to buy it for Katharine Hepburn at RKO in 1935, but Paramount grabbed the Enid Bagnold best-seller, couldn't cast it, and sold it to MGM in 1937. By 1941 Berman and* Velvet *were under the same roof; three years later a hit was born. Also a star: Elizabeth Taylor was hardly a jockey type, but she played the horse-loving title character with such 'burning eagerness tempered with sweet, fragile charm' ('N.Y. World Telegram') that not even a splendidly restrained Mickey Rooney, in his last film before army service, could steal scenes. Donald Crisp and Anne Revere, who won an Oscar (as did film editor Robert Kern), here with Liz; and Angela Lansbury, Juanita Quigley, Jackie Jenkins, Reginald Owen, Arthur Treacher, Norma Varden, Terry Kilburn and Arthur Shields also reflected the warmth of Clarence Brown's direction of the Theodore Reeves–Helen Deutsch screenplay. And it had a thundering Grand National climax – the best movie horse-race ever.*

Two more young hopefuls decorated **Three Men in White***: Marilyn Maxwell and Ava Gardner, with Lionel Barrymore wheelchairing the Blair Hospital corridors for the 13th time. Keye Luke and the ubiquitous Van Johnson continued their rivalry for Dr Gillespie's approval in a rather tired screenplay by Martin Berkeley and Harry Ruskin, directed by Willis Goldbeck. Rags Ragland was in for comedy with the series standbys Alma Kruger, Walter Kingsford, Nell Craig and George Reed.*

Nominally a 'Dr Gillespie' movie, **Between Two Women** *(not the same-named 1937 story) came out like a Van Johnson vehicle, what with the tall redhead topping popularity polls all over the map. Old Doc Barrymore had to take sub-billing along with Gloria DeHaven (here with Van), Keenan Wynn, Marilyn Maxwell, Alma Kruger, Marie Blake, Keye Luke, Nell Craig, Walter Kingsford and Leon Ames. Harry Ruskin and Willis Goldbeck repeated as writer and director, respectively, of this 14th of*

the Kildare–Gillespie scalpel-slingers. Years later in a TV series the same characters, played by Richard Chamberlain and Raymond Massey, earned MGM another mint.

Producer George Haight worked with one of the MGM old-timers on **Maisie Goes to Reno/ You Can't Do That to Me** *when Harry Beaumont, director of the original Broadway* Melody, *came out of retirement to pilot Ann Sothern through her annual 'Maisie' spree. This one was a divorce and blackmail plot devised by Harry Ruby and James O'Hanlon, given the light touch by scripter Mary McCall Jr and its always entertaining star. She had two leading men, John Hodiak and Tom Drake, supported by Paul Cavanagh and Marta Linden (with her here) Ava Gardner, Bernard Nedell, Chick Chandler, Donald Meek.*

Long absent from the studio while she became mother of the daughter who landed them both in a murder scandal 15 years later, Lana Turner returned in **Marriage Is a Private Affair** *to have a movie baby by John Hodiak. The slick triangle story (James Craig in the third corner), based by David Hertz and Lenore Coffee on Judith Kelly's novel, kept Ray June's camera focused lovingly on Lana for practically two hours' running time. Its longueurs failed to cool her popularity with the masses. Robert Z. Leonard directed; Pandro Berman produced, casting Frances Gifford, Hugh Marlowe, Natalie Schafer (first film), Keenan Wynn, Paul Cavanagh, Tom Drake, Morris Ankrum, Nana Bryant, Virginia Brissac, Addison Richards, Herbert Rudley.*

the songs were better than the production. As improbable workers in a shipyard, Powell, making his MGM bow after 11 years of musicals, and Ball sang 'In Times Like These' and Virginia memorably begged her homicidal boyfriend to 'Say that We're Sweethearts Again'. After this was released Powell stopped singing, went straight. Lahr got little chance to shine; neither did June Allyson, Rags Ragland, Steve Geray, Betty Jaynes, Howard Freeman, John Craven, Morris Ankrum. The S. M. Herzig–Fred Saidy screenplay, based on a Broadway hit, was interrupted by Vaughn Monroe and Band and Spike Jones and His City Slickers.

The 1944 crop of blondes yielded two new faces built to last. Neither Gloria Grahame, with Philip Dorn and Mary Astor in **Blonde Fever** nor Audrey Totter, with Tom Trout and Edward Arnold in **Main Street After Dark**, was a beauty exactly, but they shared a sullen sort of appeal, i.e. sex. Gloria had better luck with her debut, a smooth little marital comedy from Ferenc Molnar's 'Delilah'; script, Patricia Coleman; directed by actor Richard Whorf, produced by writer William H. Wright and acted with the featured trio by Felix Bressart, Marshall Thompson (another newcomer), Curt Bois and Elisabeth Risdon. Main Street was the product of 'Crime Does Not Pay' shorts director-producer team Edward Cahn and Jerry Bresler; the John Higgins screenplay also involved Dan Duryea, Selena Royle, Hume Cronyn and Dorothy Morris.

Mickey Rooney with Lyn and Lee Wilde in the title roles of **Andy Hardy's Blonde Trouble**, the ▽ first 'Hardy' in over a year. It allowed Andy to age enough to become a university student, but his sex life remained at the gee-whiz-she-kissed-me stage. Three writers–Harry Ruskin, William Ludwig, Agnes Christine Johnston–dug for new nuggets but the series goldmine was running out. So, alas, was the life of director George B. Seitz, maker of 13 'Hardys'. Family members Lewis Stone, Fay Holden and Sara Haden were aided by Herbert Marshall, Bonita Granville, Keye Luke, Jean Porter and Marta Linden.

Lou Costello, another star away for a year (illness), returned with straight man Bud Abbott for **Lost in a Harem**. It was directed by Charles Reisner: his last in a string of MGM comedies stretching back to the Dane and Arthur silents. Props and costumes left over from Kismet came in handy for producer George Haight, who filled out the budget with a spectacular production number to Rimsky-Korsakov's 'Scheherazade' to show this wasn't one of Universal's A & C quickies. John Conte (here with the comics), Marilyn Maxwell, Douglass Dumbrille and Jimmy Dorsey's band were featured. Screenplay: Harry Ruskin, John Grant, Harry Crane.

Virginia O'Brien, Dick Powell, Lucille Ball, Bert Lahr in **Meet the People**. It was produced by songwriter E. Y. Harburg: not surprisingly,

1944

Back to his gun-totin' bad man ways went Wallace Beery for **Barbary Coast Gent**. Getting a bit portly for this action stuff, he wasn't fast enough on the box-office draw either, this time. He's shown here hitting the dust with Binnie Barnes, Bruce Kellogg, Frances Rafferty and Ray Collins in attendance. Roy Del Ruth, directing his first Western, worked from a so-so script by William Lipman, Grant Garrett and Harry Ruskin, set in old Frisco and the Nevada goldfields. Orville Dull produced, casting John Carradine, Chill Wills, Noah Beery, Henry O'Neill, Morris Ankrum, Donald Meek, Addison Richards, Paul Hurst, Victor Kilian, Cliff Clark and Louise Beavers in support.

An American Romance got 'B' returns on an 'A' investment. King Vidor spent two years preparing the movie, shooting background footage in steel mills and car and aircraft factories in the Middle West and California; but when he was ready for narrative scenes with Spencer Tracy and Ingrid Bergman neither was available. He had to use Brian Donlevy and Ann Richards (a second-string Greer Garson from Australia), whose personalities weren't strong enough to carry the epic theme of immigrants progressing with the industrial expansion of the USA. The movie came out of prolonged editing a year later with its undercast story subordinated to the documentary spectacle: a long, long 151 minutes. Vidor directed, produced in Technicolor and wrote the original which Herbert Dalmas and William Ludwig scripted. Also cast: Walter Abel, John Qualen, Horace McNally, Mary McLeod, Robert Lowell.

Another 1944 big one that shrank in the production wash was **Dragon Seed**, Pandro Berman's production of Pearl Buck's book about Chinese peasants before and during the 1937 Japanese invasion. It drew a million customers in its first 50 days at New York's Music Hall, but elsewhere the going was tough. Critics' opinions varied widely: either it was the best Oriental drama Hollywood actors had taped their eyelids for since The Good Earth, or the worst since The Son-Daughter. Even its greatest admirers had a hard time accepting the mixed accents (everything but Chinese) of the cast. Left to right: Aline MacMahon, Walter Huston, Turhan Bey, Katharine Hepburn; also cast were Akim Tamiroff, Hurd Hatfield, J. Carrol Naish, Agnes Moorehead, Henry Travers, Frances Rafferty, Jacqueline de Wit. Jack Conway and Harold S. Bucquet co-directed the Jane Murfin–Marguerite Roberts screenplay. Lionel Barrymore delivered redundant offscreen narration.

Spencer Tracy's performance—a tour de force achieved with minimal dialogue—and Fred Zinnemann's direction were so compelling that **The Seventh Cross** succeeded despite a surfeit of escape-from-Nazis dramas. Its source novel by Anna Seghers and script by Helen Deutsch had strong suspense and colourful characters, played by Hume Cronyn and Jessica Tandy (first film), later an acclaimed stage couple, Agnes Moorehead, Herbert Rudley, Felix Bressart, Ray Collins, Alexander Granach, Katherine Locke, George Macready, Paul Guilfoyle, Steve Geray, Kurt Katch, Karen Verne, George Zucco and Eily Malyon. A romantic element was effectively supplied by Signe Hasso opposite Tracy. Pandro Berman produced.

Thirty Seconds Over Tokyo was another 1944 paybox giant, a painstaking account (almost too painstaking, said some critics: 30 Seconds took 138 minutes to unreel) of the preparation, execution and aftermath of the US bombing of Tokyo in 1942. Van Johnson and Robert Walker as two of the raid's airmen, here parting after landing in China, carried the picture effectively; Spencer Tracy had less footage as their commander, Lt Col Doolittle. Director Mervyn LeRoy, producer Sam Zimbalist and cameramen Harold Rosson and Robert Surtees saw to it that the airforce sequences kept the authenticity of pilot Ted Lawson's (Johnson's role) book, which was dramatized by Dalton Trumbo to include misty-eyed scenes with Lawson's wife, touchingly played by newcomer Phyllis Thaxter.

Also cast: Don DeFore, Tim Murdock, Horace McNally, Robert Mitchum, Donald Curtis, Louis Jean Heydt, Bill Phillips, Paul Langton, Leon Ames and Bill Williams as airmen; Ann Shoemaker, Alan Napier, Selena Royle, Jacqueline White, Dorothy Morris.

Two war pictures wound up the year's output: Tom Drake, James Gleason and Wallace Beery in **This Man's Navy** about submarine-chasing, and Laraine Day, Lee Patrick, Lana Turner and Susan Peters in **Keep Your Powder Dry** about US Women's Army Corps trainees. William Wellman brought his brisk directorial touch to the former, written by Borden Chase and produced by Samuel Marx, with Jan Clayton, Selena Royle, Noah Beery, Henry O'Neill, Steve Brodie, Paul Cavanagh, Arthur Walsh, Donald Curtis. Director Edward Buzzell had no trouble depicting the animosity between Lana and Laraine required by the Mary McCall–George Bruce script for Powder –it was for real. George Haight produced with Agnes Moorehead, Natalie Schafer, Bill Johnson, Jess Barker, June Lockhart, Marta Linden, Tim Murdock, Henry O'Neill. The gifted Susan Peters, recovered from a long illness before this film, was so crippled by an accident immediately afterwards that she never walked again.

The old Thalberg perfectionism lingered on in such typical MGM prestige pictures as **The White Cliffs of Dover**, which had sensitive performances by Irene Dunne as an American girl marrying into the British aristocracy, and Alan Marshal as her husband killed in World War I. A sentimental, patriotic, hands-across-the-sea drama based on a narrative poem by Alice Duer Miller, it drew the huge Miniver public in both countries. Credits were nothing if not high-class: director Clarence Brown, producer Sidney Franklin, writers Claudine West, Jan Lustig, George Froeschel, supporting cast Roddy McDowall, Frank Morgan, C. Aubrey Smith, Dame May Whitty, Van Johnson, Gladys Cooper, Peter Lawford (as Miss Dunne's son in World War II), John Warburton, Jill Esmond, Brenda Forbes, June Lockhart, Norma Varden and (uncredited) Elizabeth Taylor.

SONG AND DANCE
1945

British studios, amazingly active through the years of bombardment, accelerated further at war's end. Laurence Olivier's *Henry V* was applauded, but Gabriel Pascal's colossal *Caesar and Cleopatra*, with Claude Rains, Vivien Leigh and Stewart Granger, was dissected by critics. Rex Harrison in Noël Coward's *Blithe Spirit* and James Mason in *The Seventh Veil* were rolling up big business.

Hollywood's finest was *The Lost Weekend*, Charles Jackson's shattering study of alcoholism which won Oscars for Ray Milland and director Billy Wilder.

Joan Crawford celebrated 20 years on-screen with an Oscar for *Mildred Pierce*, but the durability prize went to Lillian Gish, robustly starring in *Miss Susie Slagle's* 31 years after looking too frail for this world in *Birth of a Nation*. Dorothy McGuire and James Dunn in *A Tree Grows in Brooklyn*, Bette Davis in *The Corn is Green*, Ingrid Bergman and Gregory Peck in *Spellbound* scored high. Dubious biographies, *A Song to Remember* (Chopin) and *Rhapsody in Blue* (Gershwin), had better tunes than dialogue. Van Johnson, Margaret O'Brien and sagebrusher Roy Rogers entered the Top Ten.

◁ **Ziegfeld Follies** *was the studio's third movie using the Broadway showman's name (by arrangement with widow Billie Burke), its first no-story musical since* Hollywood Revue *in 1929, and a profit-winner despite its cost. Arthur Freed had it in production during 1944 and into 1945 and frequently added and deleted items, the revue format allowing such revision even after release. Vincente Minnelli's flair for stage design was apparent in the direction, and Robert Alton choreographed. Song, dance and Technicolor spectacle dominated; comic turns faltered (a terrible Fanny Brice sketch was axed overseas) but wit sparkled in Judy Garland's send-up of a high-falutin' star, Virginia O'Brien's 'Bring on the Men', and practically every movement of Fred Astaire. He had three*

items: 'The Babbit and The Bromide' (seen above–his only appearance ever with Gene Kelly), the Gershwin ditty he and sister Adele introduced in their 1927 stage hit 'Funny Face'; a brilliant 'Limehouse Blues' with Lucille Bremer; and the luscious Freed–Warren number 'This Heart of Mine', also with Bremer. Other contributors: Lucille Ball taming panther girls (seen opposite); Lena Horne and her steamy 'Love' song; Esther Williams gliding through underwater coral; William Powell opening the show as Ziegfeld in heaven; Kathryn Grayson closing it with 'There's Beauty Everywhere', while the girls oddly drifted among clouds of soapsuds; and Red Skelton, Victor Moore, Edward Arnold, Cyd Charisse, Keenan Wynn, singers James Melton and Marion Bell.

Nothing was too good for MGM's King, back from the wars, so box-office darling Greer Garson, GWTW director Victor Fleming, ace producer Sam Zimbalist, Oscar-winning cameraman Joseph Ruttenberg and a who-cares budget were lavished on Clark Gable's first for three years, **Adventure.** *But it was a major disappointment. Frederick Hazlitt Brennan, Vincent Lawrence, Anthony Veiller and William Wright laboured over a novel by Clyde Brion Davis about a seaman and a librarian, which stubbornly refused to entertain. Left to right: Garson, Gable, Joan Blondell. Also cast: Thomas Mitchell, John Qualen, Richard Haydn, Tom Tully, Lina Romay, Philip Merivale, Harry Davenport.*

Arthur Loew spread his international distribution wing in 1945 to bring foreign productions to English-speaking territories. **The Last Chance** *was the first. One of the best movies ever made by the Swiss, it depicted in documentary style (dialogue in the characters' various languages, with subtitles where necessary) the wartime escape of refugees from Italy. Leopold Lindtberg's highly praised direction guided an inexperienced cast headed by John Hoy and Luisa Rossi (here) and E. G. Morrison and Ray Reagan. Script, Richard Schweizer; producer, Lazar Wechsler.*

Wholesome young America idealized by MGM and idolized by ticket-buyers, Van Johnson and Esther Williams made **Thrill of a Romance** *a sweet tonic for the public's war-jangled nerves. The Gladys Lehman–Richard Connell script enabled Van to sing, Esther to swim and Tommy Dorsey to trombone his band along in lushly technicolored locales. An unlikely occasion for the movie debut of famed Wagnerian tenor Lauritz Melchior, but this was a Pasternak production and Joe was a whiz at mixing musical styles. Hits in the score were 'I Should Care' and 'Please Don't Say No'. Richard Thorpe's cast included Frances Gifford, Henry Travers, Spring Byington, Carleton Young, Ethel Griffies, Donald Curtis.*

Frank Sinatra, Kathryn Grayson, Billy Gilbert and Gene Kelly (left to right) helped to make **Anchors Aweigh** *an important contributor to the $175m. Loew's Inc gross in 1945. Frankie, top-billed, had come a long way since his last MGM appearance in 1942, uncredited in* Ship Ahoy. *Principal photography was finished in 1944 but much technical work was needed on Kelly's marvellous song and dance with Jerry, the cartoon mouse. Other ace numbers were Kathryn's up-and-down-scale 'All of a Sudden My Heart Sings' and Sinatra's 'What Makes the Sunset?' and 'I Fall in Love Too Easily'. Script by Isobel Lennart, direction by George Sidney, choreography by Kelly, sumptuous production in Technicolor by Joe Pasternak. Also cast: Jose Iturbi, Dean Stockwell (first role), Pamela Britton, Rags Ragland, Henry O'Neill, Carlos Ramirez, Edgar Kennedy, Grady Sutton, Leon Ames, Sharon McManus, Henry Armetta.*

The Hoodlum Saint *was a mistake directed by Norman Taurog and produced by Cliff Reid from an original by Frank Wead and James Hill. William Powell could have phoned in his performance, Esther Williams was all at sea in her first dry role, and Angela Lansbury found herself in a flop at last. Others employed in the drama about hustlers running a charity racket in the name of St Dismas: James Gleason, Lewis Stone, Frank McHugh, Rags Ragland, Slim Summerville, Roman Bohnen, Louis Jean Heydt, Charles Trowbridge, Bill Phillips, Henry O'Neill, Matt Moore, Emma Dunn, Tom Dugan, Trevor Bardette.*

1945

They Were Expendable, was a major John Ford opus which seemed true to life (and death) in its account of torpedo boat crews fighting in the Jap-dominated Pacific. There were no phoney heroics from stars John Wayne and Robert Montgomery, here with Jack Pennick (left) and Ward Bond (right), and the obligatory romance between Wayne and nurse Donna Reed was discreetly handled. The authenticity of Montgomery's performance wasn't all due to art: he'd just finished a four-year hitch in the US Navy. Several scenes were directed by him during Ford's illness. Frank Wead's screenplay from a book by William White employed Jack Holt, Marshall Thompson, Cameron Mitchell, Paul Langton, Leon Ames, Louis Jean Heydt, Robert Barrat (as General MacArthur), Donald Curtis, Arthur Walsh.

Programme fillers, grim and giggly. Frances Rafferty, Edward Arnold, Paul Langton and Friday in **The Hidden Eye**, with Arnold reprising his blind detective role after a two-year lapse since Eyes in the Night. Script, George Harmon Coxe, Harry Ruskin; director, Richard Whorf; producer, Robert Sisk; cast, Ray Collins, Bill Phillips, Thomas Jackson, Morris Ankrum, Francis Pierlot . . . Lee and Lyn Wilde and Preston Foster in **Twice Blessed**, in which the twins switched identities and thus reunited their estranged parents, it says here. Script, Ethel Hill; director, Harry Beaumont; producer, Arthur Field; cast, Gail Patrick, Marshall Thompson, Jimmy Lydon, Richard Gaines, Jean Porter, Ethel Smith 'and her electric organ'.

Arch Oboler so startled radio fans with his play 'Alter Ego' that MGM signed him to adapt and direct it for the screen retitling it **Bewitched** and assigning Phyllis Thaxter (here with Horace McNally and Edmund Gwenn) to the central role of a schizophrenic killer. Miss Thaxter had married James Aubrey in 1944; they were divorced in 1962; he entered the MGM scene as top man in 1969. Unseen and unbilled but very much heard in this highly effective 'B' release was Audrey Totter as the voice of

Phyllis' baser self. Also cast: Henry Daniels Jr, Addison Richards, Kathleen Lockhart, Francis Pierlot, Sharon McManus, Oscar O'Shea, Minor Watson, Gladys Blake, Virginia Brissac. Producer: Jerry Bresler.

Pal, the only star who could play a bitch better than Bette Davis, emoted as both Lassie and **Son of Lassie** in Jeanne Bartlett's sequel to the famous Lassie Come Home. Other repeaters were Donald Crisp, Nigel Bruce, producer Samuel Marx, Technicolor and booming receipts. Peter Lawford (here) and June Lockhart played adult versions of the roles Roddy McDowall and Elizabeth Taylor originated (coincidentally, all four were cast the same way in White Cliffs of Dover) but now the action was shifted to Nazi-occupied Norway. Director, S. Sylvan Simon. Also cast: William Severn, Leon Ames, Nils Asther, Donald Curtis.

Another all-star dazzler, **Weekend at the Waldorf** was a pop rewrite by Samuel and Bella Spewack of Grand Hotel with (left to right) Van Johnson, Lana Turner, Ginger Rogers and Walter Pidgeon in approximately the roles first played by Lionel Barrymore, Joan Crawford, Garbo and John Barrymore. Producer Arthur Hornblow Jr spent money like there was no tomorrow, but it all came back, multiplied, at the box-office. Xavier Cugat and his bongo-bangers supplied musical moments; otherwise it was all plot and hokum, with something for everyone, including parts for Edward Arnold (the original Wallace Beery role), Keenan Wynn, Robert Benchley, Phyllis Thaxter, Leon Ames, Samuel Hinds, Lina Romay, Porter Hall, George Zucco, Miles Mander, Rosemary DeCamp, Warner Anderson, Cora Sue Collins, Michael Kirby, Nana Bryant, Moroni Olsen and Jacqueline de Wit. Robert Z. Leonard directed.

As sequels go, **What Next, Corporal Hargrove?** went pretty well. Left to right: Robert Walker as the winningly clumsy Hargrove, Keenan Wynn, Cameron Mitchell and Bill Phillips. Chill Wills, Arthur Walsh, Paul Langton, Jim Davis, Theodore Newton, Robert Kent, Jean Porter and Hugo Haas helped them reap the laughs planted in Harry Kurnitz's script. Richard Thorpe directed, George Haight produced.

Somebody turning out old scenario files blew the cobwebs off Blanche Brace's Don't Write Letters, filmed by Metro in 1922. DeVallon Scott and Alan Friedman polished it up for producer William Wright; Jules Dassin directed Marsha Hunt and John Carroll (here) and Hume Cronyn, Spring Byington, Pamela Britton, Norman Lloyd, Donald Curtis, Esther Howard and Robin Raymond . . . And so another 'B' was born–**A Letter for Evie**.

A movie theme that was old when Bertha the Sewing Machine Girl was new (servant loves employer's son) got a dash of social significance (workers strike at steel mill) in **The Valley of Decision**. They could have left out the latter and still made a fortune with the former, because it was played by box-office queen Greer Garson and Hollywood's latest male rave, Gregory Peck. Tay Garnett directed the John Meehan–Sonya Levien screenplay from Marcia Davenport's novel; Edwin H. Knopf produced. Also cast: Lionel Barrymore, Preston Foster, Donald Crisp, Marsha Hunt, Gladys Cooper, Dan Duryea, Jessica Tandy, Reginald Owen, Marshall Thompson, Barbara Everest, Geraldine Wall, John Warburton, Russell Hicks, Arthur Shields, Dean Stockwell.

Her Highness and the Bellboy was the last on MGM contract for Hedy Lamarr (here with Robert Walker). It had a big hotel locale, but as a movie it was a dump. Others trapped in this musical comedy without music or comedy were June Allyson, Carl Esmond, Agnes Moorehead, Rags Ragland, Ludwig Stossel and Warner Anderson. It was made by the producer/director/writers who had just scored a hit with Thrill of a Romance: Joe Pasternak, Richard Thorpe, Gladys Lehman–Richard Connell. Into each life some rain must fall.

Title tells all—**Bud Abbott and Lou Costello in Hollywood**—*and it's the only one ever to include any stars' full names. The rowdy comics were supported by Jean Porter (with them here) and Frances Rafferty, Warner Anderson, Mike Mazurki, Carleton Young, Donald MacBride and Marion Martin, with Lucille Ball, Preston Foster, Rags Ragland, Jackie 'Butch' Jenkins and director Robert Z. Leonard as themselves in studio scenes. S. Sylvan Simon directed; Martin Gosch produced from his original, scripted by Nat Perrin and Lou Breslow.*

The interplay of two such high-powered personalities as Wallace Beery and Margaret O'Brien had its fascination in **Bad Bascomb**, even though the main theme—bandit Beery tamed by pioneers' tot Margaret—was pure mush. Other diversions were covered wagon treks, Injun raids, wonderful Wyoming scenery enhanced by Charles Schoenbaum's camera-work. Left to right: Carrol Naish, Russell Simpson, Beery, Margaret, Marjorie Main, Warner Anderson; behind them, Renie Riano, Sara Haden, Jane Green. Also cast: Marshall Thompson, Frances Rafferty, Donald Curtis, Connie Gilchrist, Henry O'Neill. Orville Dull produced and S. Sylvan Simon directed the William Lipman–Grant Garrett screenplay from D. A. Loxley's original.

Serenely graceful, Lucille Bremer was one of the best dancing partners Fred Astaire ever had. The success of their numbers in Ziegfeld Follies *resulted in an encore,* **Yolanda and the Thief**, *again for the Vincente Minnelli–Arthur Freed team. Imaginatively staged in Technicolor by Eugene Loring, the dances delighted. But a plodding mythical-kingdom script (Irving Brecher, from a Jacques Thery–Ludwig Bemelmans story) induced yawns, and paybox cashiers finished their knitting. Also cast: Frank Morgan, Mildred Natwick, Mary Nash, Leon Ames, Ludwig Stossel, Francis Pierlot, Jane Green, Gigi Perreau.*

A much-publicized merger of MGM British and Alexander Korda's London Films had been announced with a stunning schedule (starting with War and Peace, *directed by Orson Welles, starring him and Merle Oberon). None were made, except* **Perfect Strangers**/Vacation from Marriage. *Robert Donat and Deborah Kerr starred in the movie, produced and directed by Korda. It was Donat's last for MGM, Miss Kerr's first: she followed Greer Garson's example in playing opposite him before beginning a long Hollywood career. Clemence Dane and Anthony Pelissier won Oscars for their original about a couple who joined the navy, saw the world and couldn't face returning to their humdrum marriage. Glynis Johns, Ann Todd, Roland Culver, Elliot Mason and Eliot Makeham led their supporting cast.*

Ann Sothern, having taken a year off to become a mother, returned to find nothing changed at Metro: another 'Maisie', with Harry Beaumont directing and George Haight producing again; another chaise-longue shot for the posters with co-star George Murphy. Thelma Robinson's script for **Up Goes Maisie**/Up She Goes *concentrated on dizzy comedy, climaxing in a helicopter piloted by Maisie without benefit of lesson one. Also cast: Hillary Brooke, Horace McNally, Ray Collins, Paul Harvey, Lewis Howard, Gloria Grafton, John Eldredge.*

James Craig kept busy in the 'B' hive making **Dangerous Partners** *with Edmund Gwenn and Signe Hasso and* **She Went to the Races** *with Ava Gardner. The first, a mystery thriller by Marion Parsonnet from a story by Oliver Bayer, also cast Audrey Totter, Warner Anderson, Felix Bressart, Mabel Paige, John Warburton, Henry O'Neill, Grant Withers, Horace McNally, John Eldredge; director, Edward Cahn; producer, Arthur Field. . . . Races, a comedy about professors applying science to betting, also featured Gwenn, plus Frances Gifford, Sig Ruman, Reginald Owen, J. M. Kerrigan, Charles Halton; script, Lawrence Hazard from an Alan Friedman–DeVallon Scott story; director, Willis Goldbeck; producer, Frederick Stephani.*

June Allyson and Robert Walker had better luck with **The Sailor Takes a Wife** *than with their first together,* Her Highness and the Bellboy, *despite an occasional attack of the cutes. Under Richard Whorf's direction Hugh Cronyn, Audrey Totter, Eddie 'Rochester' Anderson, Reginald Owen and Gerald Oliver Smith were audience pleasers in the Edwin Knopf production. Chester Erskine's domestic comedy was revamped from stage to screen by himself, Anne Chapin and Whitfield Cook.*

Good girl Judy Garland, bad girl Angela Lansbury and gambler John Hodiak in **The Harvey Girls**, *a big bustling Technicolor musical that everybody liked. Ray Bolger, Preston Foster, Marjorie Main, Kenny Baker, Cyd Charisse, Virginia O'Brien, Chill Wills, Selena Royle, Morris Ankrum, Bill Phillips and Horace McNally were also involved in a story of a restaurant chain conflicting with the old saloons when the railroad opened up the West. A fine Johnny Mercer–Harry Warren score included the Oscar-winning 'On the Atchison, Topeka and Santa Fe'. Arthur Freed, assisted by Roger Edens, produced; George Sidney directed. The writing credits (screenplay, Edmund Beloin, Nathaniel Curtis, Harry Crane, James O'Hanlon, Samson Raphaelson; additional dialogue, Kay Van Riper; based on a book by Samuel Hopkins Adams and an original story by Eleanore Griffin and William Rankin) indicated a rare case of too many cooks making a tasty dish.*

Portrait of Maria/Maria Candelaria *came from distinguished Mexican film-makers: stars Dolores Del Rio and Pedro Armendariz, director-writer Emilio Fernandez, cinematographer Gabriel Figueroa. The last made an especially splendid contribution to the fablelike tale of a peasant girl persecuted by fellow villagers. Despite Del Rio's command of English, she and the rest were dubbed in the version released by MGM International, to no box-office avail.*

MGM's rare ventures into the bucolic had a way of turning out just right. **Our Vines Have ▷ Tender Grapes** *delighted critics and customers, marked another triumph for Margaret O'Brien, advanced the ragamuffin career of Jackie 'Butch' Jenkins, and gave Edward G. Robinson a change of pace as a Norwegian farmer in Wisconsin. The director/producer team of Margaret's* Lost Angel, *Roy Rowland and Robert Sisk, did a fine job with Dalton Trumbo's script – not so much a story as a series of moving or amusing incidents, from a book by George Victor Martin. Also cast: James Craig, Frances Gifford, Agnes Moorehead, Morris Carnovsky, Sara Haden, Greta Granstedt, Dorothy Morris, Arthur Space, Louis Jean Heydt, Charles Middleton, Francis Pierlot.*

△ **The Clock**/Under the Clock *was the second Garland–Minnelli hit in a row for producer Arthur Freed. It's hard to believe, but Judy Garland and Robert Walker, personification of dewy young love in the movie, were already well along their paths to self-destruction when it was made in 1944–5. No such morbid idea shadowed its success or the acclaim critics gave them and director Vincente Minnelli (who became Judy's second husband). Judy's rare non-singing role in the Robert Nathan–Joseph Schrank script from Paul and Pauline Gallico's story was as a New York girl meeting and marrying a soldier on 48 hours' leave. Manhattan atmosphere was so convincing it looked like an all-location job; actually back-projection shots were dovetailed with studio street, park and station sets. James and Lucille Gleason, Keenan Wynn and Marshall Thompson played memorable bit parts. Both stars had five more MGM years ahead but their ideal partnership was never repeated.*

A perfect pair who did play encores: Spencer Tracy and Katharine Hepburn in **Without Love**, *a comedy about a misogynist marrying a manhater. It came the* Philadelphia Story *route, from Philip Barry's pen to Broadway, where it starred Hepburn, to script by Donald Ogden Stewart. It hadn't quite as much wit and charm, but enough to make it one of the season's successes. Lawrence Weingarten produced; Harold S. Bucquet directed. With Lucille Ball, Keenan Wynn, Patricia Morison, Carl Esmond, Felix Bressart, Gloria Grahame.*

A CLASSIC YEARLING
1946

World-wide cinema attendances were estimated at 235m a week: 90m in the US. 30m in Britain, 8m in France. Paramount's fantastic profit was $39m and Fox's and Warner Bros' $22m each. Thanks to a cuisine liberally sprinkled with such cornflakes as musicals, moppets and animals, the biggest MGM–Loew's profits ever were served up ($18m), although the gross income was down from 1945.

The Jolson Story made millions for Columbia and Jolson; not so for his old studio Warner Bros, which produced two other biographies: Cary Grant as Cole Porter in *Night and Day*, Ida Lupino and Olivia de Havilland as Brontë sisters in *Devotion*. Columbia made a mint with Rita Hayworth in *Gilda*. Ingrid Bergman, and Bing Crosby broke into the Top Ten list. The other eight strongest US magnets were Van Johnson, Gary Cooper, Bob Hope, Humphrey Bogart, Greer Garson, Margaret O'Brien, Betty Grable, Roy Rogers.

*There was a big public for **Courage of Lassie**, in which Lassie (née Pal), supported by Elizabeth Taylor and Frank Morgan, played a dog named Bill, making the title a misnomer. Its simple story was by Lionel Houser, its lush Technicolor photography by Leonard Smith. Tom Drake, Selena Royle, Harry Davenport, Catherine McLeod, Mitchell Lewis, Jane Green, George Cleveland, Minor Watson, Morris Ankrum and Donald Curtis were also in the Robert Sisk production, directed by Fred Wilcox.*

*James Craig, a glutton for punishment, coped with Metro's scene-stealing youngsters singly and in bunches. Survivor of two Margaret O'Briens and one Jackie 'Butch' Jenkins, he took on two more with Butch in rapid succession. **Boys' Ranch** was 'Son of Boys Town' in a Western setting, with Sharon McManus (here with Craig and Butch) and Skippy Homeier, Darryl Hickman, Dorothy Patrick,*

*Ray Collins, Geraldine Wall, Minor Watson, Arthur Space, Robert Emmet O'Connor, Moroni Olsen. Roy Rowland directed and Robert Sisk produced the William Ludwig screenplay . . . **Little Mr Jim** reunited Craig and Butch with Frances Gifford of Our Vines Have Tender Grapes; also cast were Henry O'Neill, Spring Byington, Luana Patten, Sharon McManus again, Morris Ankrum and silent star Laura La Plante. The thin story of army post families was scripted by George Bruce, directed by Fred Zinnemann, produced by Orville Dull.*

*Meanwhile, The O'Brien herself was leaving no wither unwrung in **Three Wise Fools**, aided by Thomas Mitchell and more Irish whimsy than you could shake a shillelagh at. Austin Strong's old play, first filmed by Goldwyn in 1923, was a bit icky for 1946, even as re-scripted by John McDermott and James O'Hanlon. Edward Buzzell directed and producer William Wright gave it a strong cast: Lionel Barrymore, Edward Arnold and Lewis Stone in the title roles; Jane Darwell, Harry Davenport, Cyd Charisse, Warner Anderson, Charles Dingle, Ray Collins, Henry O'Neill.*

*Dean Stockwell plus pup too much competition? Wallace Beery dozes off in **The Mighty McGurk**. William Lipman, Grant Garrett and*

Harry Clork wrote a compendium of several old Beery movies (particularly The Champ) for this one, set in the Bowery, 1900. Edward Arnold, Aline MacMahon, Cameron Mitchell, Dorothy Patrick, Aubrey Mather, Morris Ankrum and Clinton Sundberg took direction from John Waters; writer Nat Perrin turned producer for the occasion.

One of the year's best 'Bs', **Gallant Bess** brought one of MGM's oldest names, producer Harry Rapf, back to the credits; and a new process, Cinecolor, made the many exteriors look good. The movie also made a minor star of young Marshall Thompson, here with George Tobias, Clem Bevans, and the irresistible mare of the title. Jeanne Bartlett's story and script about an army horse taken home by a soldier got warm direction from Andrew Marton. Donald Curtis, Jim Davis, Chill Wills, and Wally Cassell supported the leads.

*Another boy, another pet—but **The Yearling** ▷ was at the other end of the budget scale, and among the most memorable of all MGM pictures. Claude Jarman Jr won a special Academy Award for his touching performance as the son of a poor farming couple (Gregory Peck, Jane Wyman). Oscars too to cameramen Charles Rosher, Leonard Smith and Technicolor specialist Arthur Arling; art directors Cedric Gibbons, Paul Groesse and Edwin B. Willis. Critics lauded Clarence Brown's direction of the Paul Osborn screenplay from Marjorie Kinnan Rawlings' novel, and the public responded abundantly. For producer Sidney Franklin it was a happy ending to a five-year headache that had started in 1941 when the film was shooting in Florida with a different cast headed by Spencer Tracy. Then swarms of insects hindered production, Tracy and director Victor Fleming had rows, King Vidor took over, boy and fawn grew too fast; finally Mayer ordered it shelved. In the new cast: Chill Wills, Margaret Wycherly, Clem Bevans, Forrest Tucker, Henry Travers, June Lockhart.*

Fred Zinnemann again directed Butch Jenkins in the moppet's third and best 1946 movie. Scripted by Morton Thompson from part of his book 'Joe the Wounded Tennis Player', **My Brother Talks to Horses** (great guy for titles, Morton) told an amusing tale of a kid whose gift for animal conversation proved lucrative when it came to racehorses. Peter Lawford, Charles Ruggles, Edward Arnold, Beverly Tyler, Spring Byington, O. Z. Whitehead were cast in the Samuel Marx production.

The Secret Heart *was strictly for the matinée ladies and marked, rather inauspiciously, Robert Z. Leonard's 30th anniversary as a director. It embroiled Patricia Medina, June Allyson, Marshall Thompson, Claudette Colbert, Robert Sterling (left to right) and Walter Pidgeon, Lionel Barrymore, Elizabeth Patterson, Richard Derr and Eily Malyon. The Whitfield Cook–Anne M. Chapin script from an original by Rose Franken and W. B. Meloney had a Marshall loves June/June loves Walter/Walter loves Claudette plot. Edwin H. Knopf produced.*

A. J. Cronin, modern literature's gift to the movies, had another best-seller in bookshops and cinemas with **The Green Years**. *Dean Stockwell and Charles Coburn dominated the drama of a boy growing to manhood (Tom Drake taking over the role). Dean, a grave and sensitive child, was directed by Victor Saville into a star-making performance. Others who gave their Scottish accents a workout were Hume Cronyn, Jessica Tandy, Gladys Cooper, Richard Haydn, Selena Royle, Beverly Tyler, Wallace Ford, Andy Clyde, Henry Stephenson, Norman Lloyd, Norma Varden, Henry Daniels Jr and Richard Lyon. Leon Gordon produced the Robert Ardrey–Sonya Levien screenplay.*

Robert Taylor had a strong script and a brilliant partner for his first movie after three years in the Navy. (In this he was luckier than some other stars returning from war service– Clark Gable, Mickey Rooney, Gene Kelly, Van Heflin, Red Skelton.) In **Undercurrent** *he married Katharine Hepburn and changed from hero to heavy before her very eyes. Lots of tense drama, with Robert Mitchum lurking in the woods and Vincente Minnelli in the director's chair. Pandro Berman produced the Edward Chodorov screenplay (original, Thelma Strabel), casting Edmund Gwenn, Marjorie Main, Jayne Meadows, Clinton Sundberg, Dan Tobin, Kathryn Card, Charles Trowbridge.*

Economy-minded when profits slumped late in 1946, MGM assigned Nat Perrin to write and direct a comedy about an actor–Frank Morgan –producing a movie and getting it all mixed up in the cutting room. **The Great Morgan** *thus consisted mostly of leftovers from the real MGM cutting rooms; musical out-takes featuring Eleanor Powell, Carlos Ramirez, Lucille Norman, Virginia O'Brien and the King Sisters, plus a couple of shorts by Pete Smith and John Nesbitt. Leon Ames played Morgan's studio chief. Jerry Bresler produced this mélange, released overseas only.*

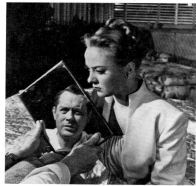

Lady in the Lake *was the first film to use the 'camera I' throughout. Robert Montgomery (here with Audrey Totter) also directed, and retained the first-person narrative of Raymond Chandler's novel by playing Philip Marlowe with every scene seen through his eyes. So audiences saw the star of this movie only when he looked in a mirror, and they resented it. Also, the subjective technique slowed down what should have been a brisk thriller. This intriguing but unpopular experiment (suggested, in fact, by the present writer) ended Montgomery's 17 MGM years. Script, Steve Fisher; producer, George Haight; cast, Lloyd Nolan, Leon Ames, Tom Tully, Jayne Meadows, Dick Simmons, Morris Ankrum, Kathleen Lockhart.*

An atmosphere of sexual tension that seldom emanated from the family-show MGM of the Forties was generated in **The Postman Always Rings Twice** *by director Tay Garnett and his excellently cast stars, Lana Turner and John Garfield. Carey Wilson produced the James Cain shocker about husband murdered by wife and lover, following the success Paramount had with Cain's similar* Double Indemnity, *and rang the box-office bell. Script by Harry Ruskin and Niven Busch. Also cast: Cecil Kellaway, Hume Cronyn, Audrey Totter, Leon Ames. Visconti had made a celebrated Italian version,* Ossessione, *in 1942.*

Sooner or later a flop had to arrive for Van Johnson; **No Leave, No Love** *was it. British musical comedy star Pat Kirkwood was imported amid fanfares to play opposite Van. Her Hollywood career ended there. Joe Pasternak produced but could shift the blame to Charles Martin, who wrote and directed the limp proceedings. Others employed: Keenan Wynn, Edward Arnold, Marie Wilson, Leon Ames, Marina Koshetz, Selena Royle, Vince Barnett, Arthur Walsh, and the Guy Lombardo and Xavier Cugat bands.*

The luscious Ilona Massey came back to sing in **Holiday in Mexico** *seven years after* Balalaika. *Xavier Cugat (with her here), Jose Iturbi and a new girl, Jane Powell, shared the musical programme with her. Jane, 16, had undergone the MGM star-grooming process so successful with teenagers Judy Garland, Kathryn Grayson and Elizabeth Taylor, and again proved its efficiency in this opulent Joe Pasternak confection. The familiar find-a-wife-for-Dad plot also involved Walter Pidgeon, Roddy McDowall (now 17), Hugo Haas, Marina Koshetz, Linda Christian, Mikhail Rasumny and Bill Phillips. Isobel Lennart's screenplay (original, William Koslenko) was directed by George Sidney. Technicolor.*

The war was over, ex-GI Mickey Rooney was two years older, and here he was, still playing Andy Hardy. Plus ça change, plus c'est la même show. **Love Laughs At Andy Hardy**, *the last in the series (for 12 years anyway), marked the ninth anniversary of Mayer's goldmine and the vein was thinning. Willis Goldbeck directed the Harry Ruskin–William Ludwig screenplay, using Holmes Herbert, Rooney, Dick Simmons, Bonita Granville (left to right) and Lewis Stone, Sara Haden, Fay Holden, Lina Romay, Dorothy Ford, Clinton Sundberg, Geraldine Wall, Addison Richards. This was the first 'Hardy' to carry a producer credit, Robert Sisk getting the dubious honour.*

A high-flier box-officially but a lame duck dramatically, **Till the Clouds Roll By** pretended to be Jerome Kern's biography, thereby cueing in a splendid album of his songs. Robert Walker played Kern (who died during its filming), sharing with Van Heflin, Lucille Bremer, Dorothy Patrick, Paul Langton, Mary Nash, Bill Phillips and (briefly) Judy Garland the narrative burden loaded by writers Guy Bolton, George Wells, Myles Connolly and Jean Holloway and directed by Richard Whorf. The musical numbers, worth the price of admission, were handled by Robert Alton; Arthur Freed produced with Technicolor prodigality. Seen here with Walker are June Allyson (who sang 'Till the Clouds Roll By' with Ray McDonald), Bremer ('I Won't Dance', 'Land Where the Good Songs Go'), Garland ('Who', 'Look for the Silver Lining', 'Sunny', all directed by husband Vincente Minnelli), Kathryn Grayson ('Make Believe', 'Long Ago and Far Away'), Heflin, Lena Horne ('Can't Help Lovin' That Man', 'Why Was I Born?'), Van Johnson ('I Won't Dance'), Tony Martin ('Make Believe', 'All the Things You Are'), Dinah Shore ('Last Time I Saw Paris'), Frank Sinatra ('Ol' Man River'). Angela Lansbury, Virginia O'Brien, Cyd Charisse and Gower Champion scored with other fine numbers.

Heavy drama set in the old West seemed an odd choice for Spencer Tracy and Katharine Hepburn, but **The Sea of Grass** turned out very well. In the Marguerite Roberts–Vincent Lawrence screenplay from Conrad Richter's novel Tracy played a ruthless cattle baron, Hepburn his sensitive wife, Melvyn Douglas the man with whom she eloped, Robert Walker their illegitimate son adopted by Tracy. The four stars drew fine reviews for their performances but disappointing business for the Pandro Berman production, directed by Elia Kazan. Also cast: Phyllis Thaxter, Harry Carey, Edgar Buchanan, Robert Armstrong, Ruth Nelson, Bill Phillips, James Bell, Robert Barrat, Charles Trowbridge, Morris Ankrum, Russell Hicks, Trevor Bardette.

Mayer was so determined to get the atom bomb for MGM that he bought off Hal Wallis, who'd started a similar subject for Paramount. President Truman supplied the title–**The Beginning or the End**. Frank Wead scripted Robert Considine's story outlining the development of nuclear fission, climaxing with the first atom bomb exploded in 1945, and asking: Is this mankind's suicide or a new era of progress?

(The jury is still out.) Well produced by Samuel Marx, it made engrossing drama but more prestige than profits. Norman Taurog directed a huge cast including (left to right) Henry O'Neill, Brian Donlevy, Hume Cronyn, Robert Walker, Warner Anderson, Tom Drake, Joseph Calleia, Hurd Hatfield, Richard Haydn, Norman Lloyd and Victor Francen; also cast were Audrey Totter, Godfrey Tearle (as Roosevelt), Barry Nelson, John Litel, Beverly Tyler, Jonathan Hale, Art Baker (as Truman), Moroni Olsen, Nella Walker, Ludwig Stossel (as Einstein), Charles Trowbridge, Paul Harvey, John Gallaudet.

The funny-ghosts gimmick popularized by the 'Topper' series was blended with domestic comedy in **The Cockeyed Miracle**/Mr Griggs Returns with Cecil Kellaway, Frank Morgan, Audrey Totter, Marshall Thompson and Gladys Cooper. Morgan, the just-deceased papa, and grandpa Keenan Wynn, 50 years dead, came back to sort out the family's chaotic affairs, which also concerned Richard Quine, Leon Ames, Jane Green, Morris Ankrum and Arthur Space. Karen de Wolf adapted George Seaton's play. S. Sylvan Simon directed the Irving Starr 'B'.

1937's Libeled Lady followed Grand Hotel/ Weekend at the Waldorf through the remake wringer to emerge as a music-added glamour piece, **Easy to Wed**. Van Johnson and Esther Williams drew their fans by the million, but the notices went to Lucille Ball in a smash comedy performance. They respectively played the original William Powell, Myrna Loy, Jean Harlow roles, while Keenan Wynn replaced Spencer Tracy. Also cast: Cecil Kellaway, June Lockhart, Carlos Ramirez (with a hit song, 'Come Closer to Me'), Ethel Smith, Ben Blue, Grant Mitchell, Paul Harvey, Jonathan Hale, James Flavin. Dorothy Kingsley did a brisk script brush-up, Edward Buzzell directed, and Jack Cummings gave it a glossy Technicolor production.

Lionel Houser's **Faithful in My Fashion** with Tom Drake, Donna Reed, Edward Everett Horton fooling in a department store. Sidney Salkow directed them and Spring Byington, Sig Ruman, Harry Davenport, Margaret Hamilton, Warner Anderson, Connie Gilchrist, Hobart Cavanaugh, Bill Phillips . . . Ralph Wheelwright's **Two Smart People** wasted a fine comedienne in a crook-chase drama, scripted by Ethel Hill and Leslie Charteris. Lucille Ball teamed with John Hodiak (pursued) and Lloyd Nolan (pursuer), then left the contract list. Directed by Jules Dassin, with Hugo Haas, Lenore Ulric, Elisha Cook Jr, Lloyd Corrigan, Vladimir Sokoloff.

'There Are Two Sides to Every Girl' trilled Kathryn Grayson (who had quite a front as well) in **Two Sisters from Boston**, a typical Joe Pasternak bon-bon stuffed with music ranging from the 'Meistersingers' Prize Song sung by Lauritz Melchior to 'G'wan Home, your Mudder's Calling' rendered by Jimmy Durante. June Allyson shared title roles with Kathryn in the Myles Connolly original set in the 1900s; Peter Lawford was their romantic target. Also directed by Henry Koster: Ben Blue, Isobel Elsom, Thurston Hall, Nella Walker.

MGM trundled out **The Show-Off** again as a vehicle for Red Skelton. There weren't many who hadn't seen it, judging by the gross. George Kelly's stage hit had been filmed by Paramount in 1926 and 1929 before Spencer Tracy did it for MGM in 1934. Marilyn Maxwell played the braggart's wife in the updated screenplay by George Wells, directed by Harry Beaumont, produced by Albert Lewis. Also cast: Marjorie Main, Virginia O'Brien, Eddie 'Rochester' Anderson, Leon Ames, Marshall Thompson, George Cleveland, Jacqueline White.

△ Top right

PROFIT UP, REPUTATION DOWN
1947

British cinemas reported income of £112m for the year. American ones took $1,565m, about $500m more than a decade earlier – but admission prices had almost doubled.

Although MGM was still regarded as the industry's No.1 company, it was in fact running behind Paramount, Warner Bros. and 20th Century-Fox in both gross income and profits. Worse, its customary domination of Academy Awards and Ten Best lists had vanished. The high-priced talents filling the vast studio were turning out too much bland escapism.

The luscious Linda Darnell was *Forever Amber*, one among many filmed books: Danny Kaye in *The Secret Life of Walter Mitty*, Tyrone Power in *Nightmare Alley*, Claudette Colbert in *The Egg and I*, Ronald Colman in *The Late George Apley* and Alfred Hitchcock's all-star *Paradine Case*.

From plays: Irene Dunne and William Powell in *Life with Father*, Eleanor Parker in *Voice of the Turtle*, William Holden in *Dear Ruth*, Rosalind Russell in *Mourning Becomes Electra*. David O. Selznick drew crowds with *Duel in the Sun*; Chaplin didn't for the first time with *Monsieur Verdoux*.

The world was seeing how good European films could be: from England, *Great Expectations*, *Black Narcissus*, *Odd Man Out*, *Brief Encounter*; from Italy, *Open City*, *Shoeshine*, *To Live in Peace*; from France, *Eternal Return*, *Children of Paradise*.

Esther Williams was back in her swimming pool in **This Time for Keeps** *and all was right with the box-office. The movie (no kin to the 1941 film with this title) reunited her* Thrill of a Romance *team: writer Gladys Lehman, director Richard Thorpe, producer Joe Pasternak. Lauritz Melchior and Technicolor also encored in the lush, lightheaded musical. Also cast: Jimmy Durante, Johnnie Johnston, Dame May Whitty, Sharon McManus, Dick Simmons, Ludwig Stossel, Xavier Cugat and his orchestra.*

Killer McCoy *shrank from heavyweight to lightweight when Mickey Rooney remade Robert Taylor's* The Crowd Roars. *It was still strong stuff, with Mickey at last allowed to act his age (25) and socking over a vivid performance, both in the boxing ring and opposite James Dunn's poignant depiction of his alcoholic father. Left to right: Sam Levene, Rooney, Dunn, David Clarke; also cast were Brian Donlevy, Ann Blyth in her first for MGM, Tom Tully, Mickey Knox, James Bell, Gloria*

Holden. Director, Roy Rowland; producer, Sam Zimbalist; script, Frederick Hazlitt Brennan, Thomas Lennon, George Bruce, George Oppenheimer.

Clark Gable's postwar false start was somewhat rectified by **The Hucksters**, *a lively adaptation of Frederick Wakeman's best-seller which lifted the lid on Madison Avenue ad agencies, commercial radio and big-business egomania. The latter was personified by Sydney Greenstreet, here getting cooled off by ad-man Gable. Deborah Kerr co-starred in her Hollywood debut, with Adolphe Menjou, Edward Arnold, Ava Gardner, Keenan Wynn, Frank Albertson, Gloria Holden, Aubrey Mather, Douglas Fowley, Connie Gilchrist, Clinton Sundberg, Richard Gaines, Kathryn Card. Jack Conway directed, Arthur Hornblow Jr produced, the Luther Davis screenplay.*

Good News *did the unusual by being better in its remake (1947, Technicolor) than in its original (1930, black-and-white). June Allyson and Peter Lawford led an enthusiastic team of collegiate types through the great old 1927 Broadway score by DeSylva, Brown and Henderson: 'The Varsity Drag', 'Lucky in Love', 'The Best Things in Life Are Free', etc. Joan McCracken, from the stage, sang and danced a sensational new number, 'Pass That Peace Pipe' by Roger Edens (who also assisted producer Arthur Freed), Hugh Martin and Ralph Blane. It also chalked up firsts for director Charles Walters, hitherto a choreographer, and scripters Betty Comden and Adolph Green. Cast included Mel Torme, Ray McDonald, Patricia Marshall, Robert Strickland, Donald MacBride, Clinton Sundberg, Tom Dugan, Morris Ankrum, Connie Gilchrist, Jane Green.*

Musicals were the MGM moneymakers and **It Happened in Brooklyn** *made more than many bigger ones. Producer Jack Cummings eschewed lavish spectacle and let the stars do their thing in uncluttered style. Like Frank Sinatra and Jimmy Durante belting out 'The Song's Gotta Have Heart', one of its Jule Styne–Sammy Cahn numbers, best of which was 'Time After Time'. Kathryn Grayson had a breezy romance with Peter Lawford and trilled some Mozart and Delibes, while soundtrack gaps were filled offscreen by a 17-year-old newcomer to the music department, pianist-composer André Previn. Richard Whorf directed Isobel Lennart's screenplay (original, Jack McGowan) and Jack Donohue staged the numbers. Also cast: Gloria Grahame, Marcy McGuire, Aubrey Mather.*

Fiesta *turned the spotlight on two young talents with decades of fame ahead: Ricardo Montalban and Cyd Charisse, whose dancing, together with the Technicolor photography of Mexican exteriors and a musical suite by Aaron Copland, were its chief assets. Esther Williams starred as a lady matador in the heavygoing script by George Bruce and Lester Cole, directed by Richard Thorpe, produced by Jack Cummings. Also cast: Mary Astor, John Carroll, Akim Tamiroff, Hugo Haas, Fortunio Bonanova, Frank Puglia, Alan Napier.*

◁ **Song of Love** *was a cut above the 'Ah, here comes Beethoven!' school of Hollywood biographies but the careful Clarence Brown production still lacked reality, settling for theatrical effect. Katharine Hepburn, Robert Walker and Henry Daniell played Clara Schumann, Brahms and Liszt. Miss Hepburn and Daniell had the requisite temperament and Paul Henreid, co-starred as Schumann, suffered nicely, but Walker was miscast. You could enjoy it with your eyes shut: glorious music, with William Steinberg conducting and Artur Rubinstein ghosting the stars' pianistics. The Ivan Tors–Irmgard von Cube–Allen Vincent–Robert Ardrey script from a play by Bernard Schubert and Mario Silva gave roles to Leo G. Carroll, Else Janssen, Gigi Perreau, Roman Bohnen, Ludwig Stossel, Tala Birell, Kurt Katch, Henry Stephenson.*

Hollywood's longest 1947 shooting schedule (five months) resulted when Gregory La Cava started **Living in a Big Way** *with Gene Kelly and Marie 'The Body' McDonald on the strength of a synopsis, written by himself, about postwar adjustment to a hasty marriage. He developed the script on the set, even letting the cast ad lib dialogue at times. The result was tedium, relieved only by two Kelly numbers which Gene choreographed with Stanley Donen, a new name on film credits. Producer, Pandro Berman; also cast, Phyllis Thaxter, Charles Winninger, Spring Byington, John Warburton, Clinton Sundberg, Jean Adair, Bill Phillips, Bernadene Hayes.*

William Powell and Myrna Loy played Nick and Nora Charles for the sixth and last time in **Song of the Thin Man,** *again making the difficult art of light comedy acting look easy. They'd co-starred in 13 films in 13 years. Leon Ames and Patricia Morison (left), Keenan Wynn, Philip Reed, Gloria Grahame, Dean Stockwell (as Nick Jr), Ralph Morgan, Don Taylor, Jayne Meadows, Warner Anderson, Connie Gilchrist, Bruce Cowling and Marie Windsor supported them in the Steve Fisher–Nat Perrin screenplay, from a whodunit by Stanley Roberts. Perrin produced, Edward Buzzell directed, exhibitors prospered.*

Two long and remarkably profitable series ended in 1947 with the final instalments of 'Maisie' and 'Dr Gillespie'. Above: **Undercover Maisie**/Undercover Girl, *Ann Sothern's tenth as the deliciously hardboiled blonde, had her wooed by Mark Daniels and Barry Nelson (left and right) while working for the police. Thelma Robinson wrote and Harry Beaumont directed the George Haight production, with Leon Ames, Clinton Sundberg, Dick Simmons, Gloria Holden, Douglas Fowley, Morris Ankrum, Nella Walker and Charles D. Brown cast . . .* **Dark Delusion**/Cynthia's Secret *featured Lucille Bremer as a neurotic patient and James Craig as yet another Dr Kildare replacement (here with nurse Geraldine Wall); Lionel Barrymore played Gillespie for the 15th time. Others directed by Willis Goldbeck in the Jack Andrews–Harry Ruskin screenplay were Edward Arnold, Jayne Meadows, Warner Anderson, Keye Luke, Alma Kruger, Henry Stephenson, Lester Matthews. As with the 'Hardy' swansong, a producer was screen-credited for the first time: Carey Wilson.*

Gladys George, Leon Ames, Dorothy Patrick and Wallace Beery in **Alias a Gentleman,** *mild stuff about an ex-con going straight. Director, Harry Beaumont; producer, Nat Perrin; script, William Lipman (who could write Beery scenes without looking by this time) from Peter Ruric's original; cast, Tom Drake, Warner Anderson, John Qualen, Sheldon Leonard, Trevor Bardette.*

Robert Taylor goes berserk under the care of asylum doctor Audrey Totter in **High Wall.** *He'd murdered his wife, or was it Herbert Marshall whodunit? Pretty tense stuff, made on a tight budget by two who learned how at Warners: director Curtis Bernhardt and producer Robert Lord. The Sydney Boehm–Lester Cole script from an Alan Clark–Bradbury Foote original gave roles to Dorothy Patrick, H. B. Warner, Warner Anderson, Elisabeth Risdon, Moroni Olsen, John Ridgely, Morris Ankrum, Vince Barnett.*

1947

Following The Show-Off *Red Skelton tried another remake of another time-tested comedy,* **Merton of the Movies**. *Paramount had filmed the George Kaufman–Marc Connelly play in 1924 with Glenn Hunter and in 1932 with Stuart Erwin (as* Make Me a Star*). In the new script by George Wells and Lou Breslow, Gloria Grahame played the Hollywood siren who attempted to besmirch Red's honour; Virginia O'Brien, Leon Ames, Hugo Haas, Alan Mowbray, Charles D. Brown and Douglas Fowley were other denizens of the old-time studios. Albert Lewis produced, and Robert Alton directed for the first time: he started his MGM career doing the rhumba with Garbo in* Two-Faced Woman, *then choreographed many big musicals.*

Tenth Avenue Angel, *starring Margaret O'Brien, was one of several projects that ran into trouble in 1946–7. It went through script and cast changes, re-takes and cutting, finally emerging 18 months after it started, and after the release of Margaret's next,* Unfinished Dance. *She played a little angel of the New York tenements, infecting everyone but the audience with her faith and joy. Harry Ruskin and Eleanore Griffin pieced together a story by Angna Enters and a sketch by Craig Rice; Roy Rowland directed, Ralph Wheelwright produced. Cast included George Murphy, Warner Anderson, Phyllis Thaxter and Margaret (above); also Angela Lansbury, Barry Nelson, Rhys Williams, Connie Gilchrist, Tom Trout.*

Richard Hart, a recruit from the New York stage, started at the top with the lead opposite Greer Garson in **Desire Me**. *He replaced Robert Montgomery, whose walk-out soon after its start in February 1946 was only one of the snags for MGM that didn't end with its September 1947 release. Script troubles bedevilled producer Arthur Hornblow Jr and director George Cukor; Garson, who needed a hit after* Adventure, *was unhappy; retakes and re-editing culminated in Cukor disowning it, so it became the company's only major*

movie carrying no director credit. Casey Robinson adapted Leonhard Frank's novel—'Karl and Anna', filmed by Paramount, also unsuccessfully, as The Homecoming *in 1925—about a soldier (Robert Mitchum), presumed dead, coming home to find his comrade-in-arms now in the arms of his wife. Scripters Zoe Akins and Marguerite Roberts tried in vain to make this hoary situation look fresh. Morris Ankrum and George Zucco had the only other significant roles.*

High Barbaree *was an example of the bland escapism overdone by Hollywood. Its authors' names, Charles Nordhoff and James Norman Hall, revived memories of their* Mutiny on the Bounty *but such adventurous scenes as this one with Van Johnson and Cameron Mitchell were outnumbered by long sugary sequences depicting the deathless love of Johnson and June Allyson, directed by the usually trenchant Jack Conway. Everett Riskin produced the Anne Chapin–Whitfield Cook–Cyril Hume screenplay casting Thomas Mitchell, Marilyn Maxwell, Claude Jarman Jr, Henry Hull, Geraldine Wall, Paul Harvey.*

Green Dolphin Street *was scripted by Samson Raphaelson from Elizabeth Goudge's book, the first winner of the annual $200,000 MGM Novel Award, a new way of buying rights before publication; later winners were never filmed. It had everything, i.e. too much for a single movie: a glorious wallow in family conflict, triangle romance, Maori uprising in old New Zealand, earthquake, tidal wave, pathos and bathos. It got the double-'A' works from producer Carey Wilson, director Victor Saville, the technicians (Oscars won by Arnold Gillespie and Warren Newcombe for visual effects, Douglas Shearer and Michael Steinore for sound effects), and a costly cast including Richard Hart, Lana Turner, Van Heflin and Gigi Perreau (here); also Donna Reed, Frank Morgan, Gladys Cooper, Reginald Owen, Edmund Gwenn, Dame May Whitty, Linda Christian, Moyna MacGill. Returns were excellent. Hart, a potential star, died at 35.*

Another MGM fling at the Arts: ballet in **The Unfinished Dance** *with Margaret O'Brien as student and Cyd Charisse as ballerina. Broadway comedian Danny Thomas and former showgirl Karin Booth had other leads in the backstage screenplay by Myles Connolly (from Paul Morand's 'Mort du Cygne'), supported by Esther Dale, Thurston Hall, Ann Codee, Ruth Brady, Gregory Gaye. The Technicolor cameras of Robert Surtees did a fine job for the old producer-director team, Joe Pasternak and Henry Koster, but box-office results were spotty.*

Mayer, aware that adolescence was the exit sign for most child stars, nurtured Elizabeth Taylor's career by buying a Broadway play about an adolescent, **Cynthia**/The Rich, Full Life, *and entrusting her to the direction of Robert Z. Leonard, glorifier of MGM females from Mae Murray on. Liz did her share by growing from lovely child to gorgeous teenager. Mary Astor and James Lydon (here as her mother and first date) supported her along with George Murphy, S. Z. Sakall, Spring Byington, Gene Lockhart, Scotty Beckett, Kathleen Howard, Morris Ankrum, Shirley Johns, Harlan Briggs and silent star Anna Q. Nilsson. Edwin Knopf produced the Harold Buchman–Charles Kaufman adaptation of Vina Delmar's play.*

Rustic charm spread through **The Romance of Rosy Ridge** *like molasses. That icky title put off some customers, but enough relished Van Johnson's performance as a wandering minstrel in post-Civil War Missouri, a rousing fight sequence, Roy Rowland's sympathetic direction, and the debut of a piquant discovery (by Norma Shearer), Janet Leigh. Lester Cole scripted Mackinlay Kantor's novel for producer Jack Cummings. Left to right: Dean Stockwell, Selena Royle, Miss Leigh, Thomas Mitchell, Johnson; also cast were Marshall Thompson, Guy Kibbee, Charles Dingle, Elisabeth Risdon, Jim Davis.*

Jeanette MacDonald, less arch than of yore, made a comeback in **Three Daring Daughters**/ The Birds and the Bees, *a Joe Pasternak confection whipped up by Albert Mannheimer, Frederick Kohner, Sonya Levien and John Meehan. With her here: Ann Todd, Jane Powell and Mary Elinor Donahue as her daughters, and Jose Iturbi, the only star ever to be equally at home as pianist, conductor and actor. Fred Wilcox directed this Technicolor excuse for a concert by singers Miss Mac-Donald and Miss Powell, and instrumentalists Iturbi, his sister Amparo and Larry Adler. Also cast: Edward Arnold, Harry Davenport, Moyna MacGill, Tom Helmore, Kathryn Card.*

Cass Timberlane *was a profitable 1947 release. The Sinclair Lewis novel, with its strong central characters of wealthy judge and poor girl who married him, was bought specifically for Spencer Tracy and Lana Turner (here with Zachary Scott). Both performed well in an interesting but unexciting picture, smoothly directed by the oddly chosen George Sidney, a musical specialist. Donald Ogden Stewart wrote the script after Tracy rejected a John O'Hara version. Arthur Hornblow Jr produced, casting Mary Astor, Tom Drake, Albert Dekker, Margaret Lindsay, Josephine Hutchinson, Rose Hobart, Mona Barrie, Selena Royle, Cameron Mitchell, John Litel, Howard Freeman.*

△ **If Winter Comes** *drenched thousands of hankies when A. S. M. Hutchinson's novel came out, and millions more when Fox filmed it in 1923. Its long-suffering hero, then Percy Marmont, was now Walter Pidgeon, flanked here by Angela Lansbury as wife and Deborah Kerr as true love. This time the exhibitors wept. Director, Victor Saville; producer, Pandro Berman; script, Marguerite Roberts, Arthur Wimperis; cast, Binnie Barnes, Janet Leigh, Dame May Whitty, Rene Ray, Reginald Owen, John Abbott, Rhys Williams, Hugh French, Dennis Hoey, Nicholas Joy, Halliwell Hobbes.*

The Arnelo Affair, *Arch Oboler's second writing/directing opus, proved less sensational than his* Bewitched *but filled its double-feature slot acceptably. Lowell Gilmore, Eve Arden and Frances Gifford (here) were caught up in a murder web woven by John Hodiak. George Murphy, Dean Stockwell, Warner Anderson, Ruby Dandridge and Joan Woodbury were others cast in the Jerry Bresler production based on a story by Jane Burr.*

B.F.'s Daughter/Polly Fulton *was Barbara Stanwyck's first at MGM for 12 years. It finished as 1947 did, and was among the year's better efforts; but the absence of action (it was basically a wealth versus socialism debate) hurt at the box office. Lots of pithy dialogue in Luther Davis' script from John P. Marquand's novel furthered the fine character acting of (left to right) Van Heflin, Miss Stanwyck, Keenan Wynn and Charles Coburn; also cast were Richard Hart, Margaret Lindsay, Marshall Thompson, Spring Byington and Barbara Laage. Robert Z. Leonard directed, Edwin Knopf produced.*

SUGAR, BUT NO SPICE

1948

Movie executives gulped tranquillizers as sales of television sets quadrupled, the US government continued to demand that major companies shed their theatre interests, and business generally drooped.

At MGM, alarm bells were ringing from President Nicholas Schenck's New York office and back. The Loew's gross was hitting a new high ($185m for the year) but studio extravagance and foul-ups brought profits down to $5m, the lowest since Depression-ridden 1932/3. Schenck told Louis B. Mayer to find another Irving Thalberg to ride hard on MGM's accident-prone producers. By mid-year he'd persuaded Dore Schary–recently the successful studio boss of RKO until running foul of Howard Hughes–to return as production head of the company he had served twice before: as writer in the late Thirties (*Boys Town*, etc.) and as producer in the early Forties (*Journey for Margaret*, etc.). His advent improved matters.

Indicative of the malaise affecting the studio early in 1948, **The Kissing Bandit** *was perpetrated by so canny a producer as Joe Pasternak. It was the big flop of Frank Sinatra's career and no help to Kathryn Grayson's, although she did get the best song, 'Love Is Where You Find It'. The deadly screenplay by Isobel Lennart and John B. Harding was sort of directed by Laslo Benedek and acted by J. Carrol Naish, Mildred Natwick, Mikhail Rasumny, Billy Gilbert, Sono Osato, Clinton Sundberg, Carleton Young. Relief came in a dance number by Ricardo Montalban, Cyd Charisse, Ann Miller, added at the last minute.*

MGM had a family interest in Enterprise Studios from the start. Co-founder of this major independent company in 1946 was David Loew, son of Marcus, brother of Arthur. Arthur took the new studio's overseas distribution for his MGM International, while United Artists handled it in the USA and Canada. In 1948 its release by MGM became world-wide, beginning with **No Minor Vices**, *starring (left to right) Dana Andrews, Lilli Palmer and Louis Jourdan. Lewis Milestone, whose* Arch of Triumph *had just laid an expensive Enterprise egg at the box office (cueing the split with UA), played safe this time with a light comedy of marital jealousy. Arnold Manoff's script had parts for Jane Wyatt, Norman Lloyd, Roy Roberts, Ann Doran, and moppets Sharon McManus, Beau Bridges.*

Receipts fell short of the Van Johnson–June Allyson average for **The Bride Goes Wild** *in which Van played a loose-living author of children's books and June a prim school-teacher. Albert Beich's breezy comedy was directed by Norman Taurog, produced by William H. Wright. Also cast were 'Butch' Jenkins, Hume Cronyn, new MGM face Arlene Dahl, old ditto Una Merkel, Richard Derr, Lloyd Corrigan, Elisabeth Risdon, Clara Blandick, Kathleen Howard.*

Force of Evil *was Abraham Polonsky's last movie for 20 years; he was blacklisted by Mayer and the other Hollywood czars during the Red scare. Excessive editing didn't help to clarify Ira Wolfert's densely written and plotted novel, 'Tucker's People'. But enough of the sombre power of both author and director came through to make it something of a collector's item, if not a popular hit. John Garfield, tough, and Beatrice Pearson, tender, were embroiled in the numbers racket along with Thomas Gomez, Roy Roberts, Marie Windsor, Barry Kelley, Paul Fix. Bob Roberts produced the picture for Enterprise.*

In **Julia Misbehaves** *the dignified Greer Garson resorted to slapstick with a troupe of acrobats to put the comedy over but, like co-star Walter Pidgeon, she was more at home in Miniver country. Their record-breaking days were over. Here Miss Garson fixes up a romance between Peter Lawford and Elizabeth Taylor. Jack Conway directed the Arthur Wimperis–William Ludwig–Harry Ruskin screenplay somewhat based on Margery Sharp's 'The Nutmeg Tree'. Producer Everett Riskin assembled expert support: Cesar Romero, Mary Boland, Nigel Bruce, Lucile Watson, Reginald Owen, Henry Stephenson, Fritz Feld, Aubrey Mather, Phyllis Morris, Ian Wolfe, Veda Ann Borg.*

Edward Sedgwick, Buster Keaton's old director, came out of retirement to put Red Skelton through his paces as a goofy spy in **A Southern Yankee**/My Hero! *Buster, whose classic Civil War comedy* The General *this wasn't as good as, supplied gags to augment Harry Tugend's script (from a Norman Panama–Melvin Frank original), produced by Paul Jones. Others cast: Arlene Dahl (here with Red) Brian Donlevy, John Ireland, Charles Dingle, Joyce Compton, Reed Hadley, George Coulouris, Lloyd Gough, Minor Watson, Art Baker, Arthur Space.*

MGM spent a lot of 1948 time on a whopping hit for 1949 exhibitors: **Little Women** *in pretty Technicolor with (left to right) Margaret O'Brien, Janet Leigh, June Allyson, Mary Astor and Elizabeth Taylor. Also cast were Peter Lawford, Rossano Brazzi (Hollywood debut), Lucile Watson, Sir C. Aubrey Smith (his last role; he died at 85 soon after this film), Elizabeth Patterson, Leon Ames, Harry Davenport, Richard Stapley, Connie Gilchrist, Ellen Corby. Producer-director Mervyn LeRoy used the Louisa May Alcott story that had given Katharine Hepburn her biggest pre-MGM success, and four members of the* Meet Me in St Louis *family, but the new movie didn't equal either of these artistically. He let saccharine clog the Andrew Solt–Sarah Mason–Victor Heerman script and Allyson's performance of the Hepburn role.*

Rouben Mamoulian, who had staged 'Oklahoma!' on Broadway, was given another slice of Americana to turn into a musical—Eugene O'Neill's 'Ah, Wilderness'. Ah, foolishness! **Summer Holiday** *coarsened the original play and its 1935 screenplay, now revised by Irving Brecher and Jean Holloway, while the added songs were hardly of Rodgers/Hammerstein quality. Arthur Freed, who hoped to match his previous period family musical,* Meet Me in St Louis, *had a hard time with this one: principal photography ended in 1946 but retakes, editing and shelving lasted until 1948. Still, there were charming moments, stylish use of Technicolor and a good cast. From top here: Walter Huston, Agnes Moorehead, Marilyn Maxwell, Mickey Rooney, Gloria DeHaven and Frank Morgan; also 'Butch' Jenkins (in Rooney's* Ah, Wilderness *part), Selena Royle, Michael Kirby, Shirley Johns, Anne Francis (debut), Virginia Brissac, Howard Freeman.*

The Sun Comes Up *was Jeanette MacDonald's last movie and in it producer Robert Sisk made her part of the most unlikely star team since Mae West and W. C. Fields got together. Miss MacDonald played a singing widow whose empty heart was filled by a backwoods boy and his dog, Claude Jarman Jr and Lassie. All three seemed nonplussed but did their best for dear old Metro, aided by director Richard Thorpe, soundtrack maestro André Previn, Technicolor and the great outdoors. Lloyd Nolan, Percy Kilbride, Margaret Hamilton, Lewis Stone and Nicholas Joy also enacted the improbable script William Ludwig and Margaret Fitts based on a novel by Marjorie Kinnan Rawlings.*

The Search *proved Fred Zinnemann's best picture since* The Seventh Cross, *and Arthur Loew's international set-up's biggest hit. Montgomery Clift played a GI in the US-occupied zone of Germany and Ivan Jandl the little war derelict he rescued. Ivan won a best juvenile Academy Award, and Richard*

Schweizer and David Wechsler got one for their screenplay. Clift, once a boy actor himself on Broadway, made a striking debut, supported by Aline MacMahon, Wendell Corey, opera star Jarmila Novotna, Mary Patton and E. G. Morrison. Lazar Wechsler produced.

John Ford's version of **Three Godfathers**, *made by his and Merian Cooper's Argosy Pictures, was at least its fourth filming, and the second released by MGM. Ford's direction of this Laurence Stallings–Frank Nugent script brought new warmth to Peter B. Kyne's story of three fugitives (John Wayne, Harry Carey Jr, Pedro Armendariz) encountering a mother and newborn baby while crossing a desert. D. W. Griffith's old star, Mae Marsh, was cast; also Ward Bond, Mildred Natwick, Jane Darwell, Ben Johnson, Charles Halton, Jack Pennick. But the real star was the Technicolor photography of Winton Hoch, who later won three Academy Awards.*

MGM jumped in with finance, a galaxy of stars and a distribution deal when Frank Capra's production company, Liberty, ran into trouble while preparing **State of the Union**/The World and His Wife. *The cast was so strong, and Capra's direction of the Anthony Veiller–Myles Connolly script from the Broadway hit by Russell Crouse and Howard Lindsay so lively, that they overcame the box-office hoodoo on political stories. The bonhomie of this scene with Adolphe Menjou, Katharine Hepburn and Spencer Tracy was sheer acting: in the movie Menjou campaigned for Tracy and Hepburn as Mr and Mrs President; in life they clashed, he supporting and they condemning Hollywood's Red witch-hunt. Also cast: Van Johnson, Angela Lansbury, Lewis Stone, Charles Dingle, Margaret Hamilton, Raymond Walburn, Maidel Turner, Art Baker, Pierre Watkin.*

Showing little of the zest of their earlier teamings, Clark Gable and Lana Turner gloomed through a surgeon/nurse love affair on the battlefront while wife Anne Baxter suffered jealous pangs back home. She just knew, somehow. **Homecoming** *had 'A'-plus names behind it—producer Sidney Franklin, director Mervyn LeRoy, author Sidney Kingsley, scripter Paul Osborn—but star power was its main asset. Others present: John Hodiak, Ray Collins (seen here with Gable and Turner) and Gladys Cooper, Cameron Mitchell, Marshall Thompson, Lurene Tuttle.*

The Secret Land *won MGM an Academy Award for best documentary of 1948. Rear-Admiral Richard Byrd returned to the South Pole 12 years after his famous 1935 expedition and made a survey of half-a-million miles of icebound territory with 4,000 men, ships and planes of the US Navy. From about 90 hours of Technicolor film shot by service cameramen, producer Orville Dull and editor Frederick Y. Smith extracted 71 enthralling minutes. Narration by Comdr Robert Montgomery, Lt Robert Taylor and Lt Van Heflin.*

Command Decision, *a drama set on an American airfield in England during the bombing of Germany, was Clark Gable's best postwar film, impressively staged by Sam Wood after eight years away from MGM. Left to right: Clinton Sundberg, Charles Bickford, Walter Pidgeon, Gable and Brian Donlevy. Also cast: Van Johnson, John Hodiak, Edward Arnold, Marshall Thompson, Richard Quine, Cameron Mitchell, Ray Collins, Warner Anderson, John McIntire, Moroni Olsen and John Ridgely. William Laidlaw and George Froeschel derived a taut script from the play by William Wister Haines. It was still running on Broadway while Sidney Franklin produced the movie.*

MGM used the title **Big City** on three different movies, all duds. This, the third one, was about a waif befriended by a Jewish cantor, a Protestant reverend and a Catholic cop. It was a great boost for atheism. Left to right: Lotte Lehmann, Karin Booth, Margaret O'Brien, George Murphy, Danny Thomas and Robert Preston. A highlight was the singing of Mme Lehmann, idol of music lovers for decades. Another debut: Betty Garrett, from Broadway musicals. Norman Taurog directed them and Edward Arnold, Jackie 'Butch' Jenkins (who then retired, aged ten), and Connie Gilchrist in the Joe Pasternak production, written by Whitfield Cook and Anne Chapin from a story by Miklos Laszlo.

The Bribe gave Ava Gardner her first star billing at MGM after a seven-year build-up. Robert Taylor loved her, hated Charles Laughton, while breaking up a war surplus racket in the tropics. This juicy chunk of melodrama was notable for its climax, a fight between Taylor and villain Vincent Price staged by Robert Z. Leonard amid a stupendous firework display. Pandro Berman produced the Marguerite Roberts screenplay (original, Frederick Nebel), casting John Hodiak, Samuel S. Hinds, John Hoyt, Tito Renaldo.

The Dore Schary touch seemed to be working already. **Act of Violence**, one of the first completed for the new studio boss, was a little 'B' that turned out to be a big 'A' in quality, audience response and press praise. Fred Zinnemann got the bulk of the last-mentioned for his direction's fast pace and harsh realism, but there was plenty too for Van Heflin's desperate fugitive and Mary Astor's prostitute with a heart of brass. The William Wright production of a non-stop suspense story by Collier Young (original) and Robert Richards (script) also had Robert Ryan, Janet Leigh, Berry Kroeger, Connie Gilchrist, Nicholas Joy.

Words and Music was so crammed with vintage Rodgers & Hart numbers that the factual distortions to which composers' movie biographies are prone bothered nobody. Least of all the writers of this Arthur Freed hit, Guy Bolton, Jean Holloway and Fred Finklehoffe. Tom Drake as Richard Rodgers and Mickey Rooney as Lorenz Hart are seen (above) with Perry Como and Cyd Charisse, visiting London to perform their 'Blue Room' (top), one of 19 numbers sung in the film. Another 17 were used instrumentally, notably 'Slaughter on Tenth Avenue' with Gene Kelly and Vera-Ellen in an electrifying eight-minute ballet. Other standouts: Rooney's and Betty Garrett's 'Manhattan', June Allyson's 'Thou Swell', Judy Garland's and Rooney's 'I Wish I Were in Love Again', Lena Horne's 'The Lady is a Tramp' and Mel Torme's 'Blue Moon' (first sung in Manhattan Melodrama, 1933, as 'The Bad in Every Man'). Norman Taurog's cast also included Ann Sothern, Janet Leigh, Marshall Thompson, Jeanette Nolan, Clinton Sundberg, Richard Quine. Robert Alton directed the numbers.

The Three Musketeers seem to have been swashing their buckles ever since movies moved, but not even Douglas Fairbanks' famous 1921 version had the lavishness of MGM's 1948 spectacle, or more acrobatic panache than Gene Kelly's d'Artagnan. Van Heflin, Gig Young and Lana Turner (with Kelly here) were accompanied in this highly commercial hokum by June Allyson, Vincent Price, Angela Lansbury, Frank Morgan, Keenan Wynn, John Sutton, Robert Coote, Reginald Owen, Ian Keith, Patricia Medina and Richard Stapley in George Sidney's dazzling cast. Robert Ardrey scripted, Pandro Berman produced in Technicolor.

Well-made and performed with conviction, not least by their star, 'Lassie' pictures were always winners. **Hills of Home**/Master of Lassie told the story of a Scottish doctor and his faithful collie. In the cast: Tom Drake and Edmund Gwenn (here with Lassie) and Donald Crisp, Janet Leigh, Rhys Williams, Reginald Owen, Edmund Breon, Alan Napier, Lumsden Hare. The Californian Sierras again played the Scottish Highlands, in Technicolor. Fred Wilcox directed and Robert Sisk produced the William Ludwig screenplay. A British film based on the same Ian MacLaren story had been directed by actor Crisp 25 years before.

Pasternak was in good form with two typical big-budget, big grossing Technicolor musicals. Dick Simmons, Cyd Charisse, Ricardo Montalban and Esther Williams in **On an Island With You**, a Dorothy Kingsley–Dorothy Cooper – Hans Wilhelm – Charles Martin screenplay about a Hollywood unit shooting in the South Seas. In Richard Thorpe's cast were Peter Lawford, Jimmy Durante, Leon Ames, Xavier Cugat and band . . . George Brent and Jane Powell as the skipper of **Luxury Liner** and his daughter whose singing came in handy to entertain the passengers. They paired off respectively with Frances Gifford and Thomas Breen; Lauritz Melchior, Marina Koshetz, the unavoidable Cugat, Richard Derr, John Ridgely, Connie Gilchrist and the Pied Pipers were on the sidelines. Script, Gladys Lehman, Richard Connell; director, Richard Whorf.

They called Carmen Miranda the Brazilian Bombshell, and her explosive personality blew the moss off many a Fox musical before her MGM first: **A Date With Judy**. She had a song hit that proved a boon to her countless mimics, 'Cuanto le Gusta', and taught Wallace Beery to dance in his only musical, a Dorothy Kingsley–Dorothy Cooper yarn. Jane Powell in the title part sang five numbers and vied with Elizabeth Taylor for Robert Stack; both girls were elevated to the hallowed MGM star list after the success of this Technicolor show, Joe Pasternak's fifth in 1948. Richard Thorpe directed, his cast including Selena Royle, Xavier Cugat and Leon Ames. Left to right: Carmen, Cugat, Jane and Liz.

Gene Kelly and Judy Garland made a marvellous pair in **The Pirate**, a vigorous and imaginative filming by Vincente Minnelli of the S. N. Behrman play that starred Alfred Lunt and Lynn Fontanne. A bit too fancy for the masses, the film did well in city centres and developed an enduring cult following. Cole Porter wrote songs that fitted its Caribbean carnival mood, but fell below his usual quota of hits. Walter Slezak, Gladys Cooper, Reginald Owen, George Zucco and the dancing Nicholas Brothers were featured in Arthur Freed's Technicolor production. Judy had been absent since her Till the Clouds Roll By numbers to give birth to Liza Minnelli in 1946.

Fred Astaire and Judy Garland as 'A Couple of Swells', a classic number from a classic musical, **Easter Parade**. Spangled with Technicolor and 17 Irving Berlin songs, showered with press praise, the Arthur Freed production stepped out into immediate box-office success and lasting fame. Astaire had announced his retirement two years before, but started another 20 years of stardom by answering MGM's SOS when Gene Kelly broke an ankle on the eve of production. Judy was at her peak and Ann Miller displayed a vivid dancing personality opposite Peter Lawford; Jules Munshin, Clinton Sundberg and Jeni LeGon shone in support. Sidney Sheldon joined Frances Goodrich and Albert Hackett to script their original story, directed by Charles Walters. Robert Alton handled the musical numbers, scoring of which won Oscars for Roger Edens and Johnny Green.

SILVER JUBILEE
1949

Hollywood's Greatest Galaxy—*indeed, the largest assembly of famous entertainers ever controlled by one organization was listed in MGM's contract roster of April 1949. On the company's 25th anniversary, these 58 of its 80 stars and featured players sat for a family portrait.* Front row: *Lionel Barrymore, June Allyson, Leon Ames, Fred Astaire, Edward Arnold, Lassie, Mary Astor, Ethel Barrymore, Spring Byington, James Craig, Arlene Dahl.* 2nd row: *Gloria DeHaven, Tom Drake, Jimmy Durante, Vera-Ellen, Errol Flynn, Clark Gable, Ava Gardner, Judy Garland, Betty Garrett, Edmund Gwenn, Kathryn Grayson, Van Heflin.* 3rd row: *Katharine Hepburn, John Hodiak, Claude Jarman Jr., Van Johnson, Jennifer Jones, Louis Jourdan, Howard Keel, Gene Kelly, Christian Kent (Alf Kjellin), Angela Lansbury, Mario Lanza, Janet Leigh.* 4th row: *Peter Lawford, Jeanette MacDonald, Ann Miller, Ricardo Montalban, Jules Munshin, George Murphy, Reginald Owen, Walter Pidgeon, Jane Powell, Ginger Rogers, Frank Sinatra, Red Skelton.* 5th row: *Alexis Smith, Ann Sothern, J. Carrol Naish, Dean Stockwell, Lewis Stone, Clinton Sundberg, Robert Taylor, Audrey Totter, Spencer Tracy, Esther Williams, Keenan Wynn. Contractees who happened to be away from the studio that day were Louis Calhern, Cyd Charisse, Gladys Cooper, Nancy Davis, Greer Garson, Jean Hagen, Lena Horne, Jose Iturbi, Deborah Kerr, Marjorie Main, Frank Morgan, Margaret O'Brien, William Powell, Paula Raymond, James Stewart, Barry Sullivan, Don Taylor, Elizabeth Taylor, Marshall Thompson, Lana Turner, Robert Walker, James Whitmore. There were 19 directors under contract at this time: Robert Alton, Compton Bennett, Clarence Brown, Edward Buzzell, George Cukor, Robert Z. Leonard, Mervyn LeRoy, Anthony Mann, Vincente Minnelli, Roy Rowland, Victor Saville, George Sidney, John Sturges, Norman Taurog, Richard Thorpe, Charles Walters, William Wellman, Sam Wood, Fred Zinnemann.*

Louis B. Mayer and Dore Schary made publicity capital of MGM's 25th-anniversary year by hosting a gigantic studio luncheon at which Leo's fabulous array of contractees ate their chicken soup in serried ranks as news cameras clicked.

Business generally was static: while MGM–Loew's managed to improve its profits a bit to $6¾m, Universal and Walt Disney went into the red for the second year running. Paramount was divested of its theatre chain by the government.

Social problems were finding more screen time and public interest, with such

The Silver Jubilee S

pictures as *Pinky, Home of The Brave, All the King's Men* and *The Snake Pit* dealing with racial prejudice, political corruption and the treatment of the insane. But comics and cowboys were the money magnets, the most popular stars being Bob Hope, Bing Crosby, Abbott and Costello, John Wayne and Gary Cooper. Former MGM hit-maker Joseph L. Mankiewicz won Oscars for writing and directing Fox's *A Letter to Three Wives*.

In Britain, Sir Laurence Olivier continued to collect awards for his *Hamlet*, but J. Arthur Rank said he'd close his studios unless entertainment tax was abolished.

At the start of 1949 post-production was completed on **Edward, My Son** which had inaugurated MGM's big new studios at Borehamwood near London in 1948. Spencer Tracy as the ruthless self-made millionaire and Deborah Kerr as his neglected, alcoholic wife starred in Donald Ogden Stewart's screenplay of the Robert Morley–Noel Langley stage hit. Mayer sent over two of his best men for it, director George Cukor and producer Edwin Knopf, but the result fell short of hopes. Critics said Tracy was not ideally cast, and the play's trick of never showing the title character who motivated the drama seemed an irritating gimmick on screen. Cast included: Ian Hunter, James Donald, Leueen MacGrath, Mervyn Johns, Felix Aylmer, Walter Fitzgerald.

Gene Kelly enjoyed tackling a straight dramatic part once in a while, and was surprisingly good at it. In **Black Hand**, set in early 1900s New York, he fought the bloodthirsty secret society that became infamous as the Mafia. Here he vows vengeance for the death of his parents, Peter Brocco and Eleanora Mendelssohn, to Marc Lawrence. Richard Thorpe got the full charge of excitement out of Luther Davis' script, replete with knifings and dynamitings, from Leo Townsend's original. William Wright produced, casting J. Carrol Naish, Teresa Celli, Frank Puglia, Barry Kelley, Bert Freed, Phyllis Morris.

Long announced by Enterprise as a vehicle for Ginger Rogers, who had script approval and didn't approve, **Caught** left its viewers as depressed as Robert Ryan and Barbara Bel Geddes in this scene. It bogged Barbara down

in the travails of that much-dramatized character, the richest girl in the world. Chief interest was stirred by the Hollywood debut of No 1 British star James Mason; also cast were Natalie Schafer, Ruth Brady, Bernadene Hayes, Curt Bois. Max Ophuls and Wolfgang Reinhardt directed and produced, with less than Teutonic efficiency, the Arthur Laurents screenplay from Libbie Block's Wild Calendar.

James Stewart returned to MGM for **The Stratton Story**. His underplaying and Sam Wood's firm direction kept the goo out of a sad story, based on fact by Douglas Morrow (who won the Oscar for best original) and Guy Trosper, about a baseball star losing his leg. Left to right: Agnes Moorehead, Stewart, June Allyson, baby William Basset and Robert Gist. Frank Morgan, Bill Williams, Bruce Cowling and Cliff Clark were in the Jack Cummings production which was well reviewed and a big moneymaker, especially in the US.

Finale for a team that made movie history: Fred Astaire and Ginger Rogers in the last number they did together, 'Manhattan Downbeat' in **The Barkleys of Broadway**. The ten years since their last movie at RKO had slowed them not at all, and this Arthur Freed production got a hearty welcome. Ginger was a late replacement for Judy Garland, whose breakdowns were becoming a serious studio problem. The conventional backstage, battling stars story by Betty Comden and Adolph Green was directed by Charles Walters (the numbers by Robert Alton), with Oscar Levant, Billie Burke, Jacques François, Gale Robbins, George Zucco, Clinton Sundberg, Inez Cooper.

Margaret O'Brien, growing fast at 12, bowed out with **The Secret Garden** and retired for several years. Later, the talent remained but movie stardom had fled. With her here are Brian Roper, Dean Stockwell and Herbert Marshall, in a cast including Gladys Cooper,

Elsa Lanchester, Reginald Owen, Aubrey Mather, Lowell Gilmore, George Zucco, Billy Bevan, Dennis Hoey, Isobel Elsom, Matthew Boulton, Norma Varden. The gentle period piece, first filmed by Paramount in 1919, ten years after Frances Hodgson Burnett wrote it, fared mildly at 1949 box-offices. Script, Robert Ardrey; director, Fred Wilcox; producer, Clarence Brown.

Yet another farewell, sadder still: Wallace Beery died soon after making **Big Jack**, his 252nd movie in 36 years. He was ailing during its production and seemed aware that he was playing the bold bandit once too often. Gene Fowler, Marvin Borowsky and Osso Van Eyss wrote it from a Robert Thoeren original and Gottfried Reinhardt produced. Richard Thorpe directed Richard Conte, Beery, Marjorie Main and Edward Arnold (left to right) and Vanessa Brown, Charles Dingle, Clinton Sundberg, Clem Bevans and Bill Phillips.

Several new films were dubbed Silver Jubilee Productions in MGM's 25th anniversary year and some of them didn't click. **The Great Sinner** had a million-dollar cast: Walter Huston, Melvyn Douglas, Gregory Peck and Ava Gardner (here) and Ethel Barrymore, Frank Morgan, Agnes Moorehead; but director Robert Siodmak and producer Gottfried Reinhardt added heavily Germanic treatment to an already doom-laden Russian story, making for a gloomy evening. Ladislas Fodor, Rene Fulop–Miller and Christopher Isherwood adapted Dostoievsky's 'The Gambler' so thoroughly that he didn't even get author credit.

Galsworthy wasn't let off lightly either. **That Forsyte Woman**/The Forsyte Saga, with Greer Garson gracious as Irene and Errol Flynn surprisingly effective as Soames, had a doggedly stagey air. American accents of the other principals–Walter Pidgeon, Robert Young, Janet Leigh, Harry Davenport (who died in 1949 after 77 years as an actor)– invalidated the Englishness demanded of the story, which scripters Jan Lustig, Ivan Tors, James B. Williams and Arthur Wimperis restricted to Book One of the Saga. But director Compton Bennett in his Hollywood debut made his dramatic points and the film was

generally popular. Leon Gordon produced it in Technicolor; with Aubrey Mather, Lumsden Hare, Gerald Oliver Smith, Halliwell Hobbes and Matt Moore. MGM had scheduled it 16 years earlier as a David Selznick production starring the three Barrymores.

Judy Garland was back in good (if overweight) form in **In the Good Old Summertime**, and Buster Keaton made his last appearance at his old studio. This was The Shop Around the Corner with Budapest taken out and several songs put in for Judy; a charming show and a moneymaker. Left to right: Spring Byington, S. Z. Sakall, Clinton Sundberg, Judy, Keaton and Van Johnson. Robert Z. Leonard directed and Albert Hackett, Frances Goodrich and Ivan Tors revamped the original script for Joe Pasternak.

The Jack Cummings musical hit **Neptune's Daughter** won an Academy Award for best song, Frank Loesser's 'Baby, It's Cold Outside', sung by Esther Williams and Ricardo Montalban, then reprised by Betty Garrett and Red Skelton. Here Miss Williams is congratulated by Keenan Wynn and Miss Garrett on winning a swim trophy in the film. Edward Buzzell directed Dorothy Kingsley's breezy screenplay, with Xavier Cugat and band, Ted de Corsia and Mike Mazurki in the cast.

Dore Schary had a penchant for hard, fast thrillers done with documentary realism and minimum expense. Two such winners in 1949: Van Johnson in **Scene of the Crime**, handcuffed

to corpse William Haade, and Ricardo Montalban in **Border Incident**, struggling with Howard da Silva. Producer credit for the first was given to Harry Rapf, but the old MGM exec had died while preparing it. Charles Schnee wrote and Roy Rowland directed, with Arlene Dahl, Gloria DeHaven, Tom Drake, Leon Ames, Donald Woods, John McIntire, Norman Lloyd, Jerome Cowan, Tom Powers, Anthony Caruso, Robert Gist, Tom Helmore . . . The second, John C. Higgins' story of Mexican farmworkers smuggled over the US border, was directed and produced by Anthony Mann and Nicholas Nayfack, with George Murphy, Teresa Celli, James Mitchell, Arnold Moss, Charles McGraw, Sig Ruman, John Ridgely.

Left to right: Angela Lansbury, Walter Pidgeon, Peter Lawford and Ethel Barrymore wondered what to do about Janet Leigh, a refugee in the British-occupied zone of Vienna, in **The Red Danube**. Bruce Marshall's novel got the full MGM works in casting and production from Carey Wilson, but the public didn't seem to care. Francis L. Sullivan, Alan Napier, Robert Coote and Melville Cooper were directed by George Sidney in the sluggish Gina Kaus–Arthur Wimperis screenplay.

The release of **Malaya**/East of the Rising Sun was delayed until after Spencer Tracy's next, while producer Edwin Knopf tried to pep it up in the cutting room. Mechanically written by Frank Fenton (original, Manchester Boddy) and directed likewise by Richard Thorpe, this melodrama was unworthy of its cast: James Stewart, Tracy, Valentina Cortese and Sydney Greenstreet (here) and Lionel Barrymore, John Hodiak, Gilbert Roland, Tom Helmore and Roland Winters.

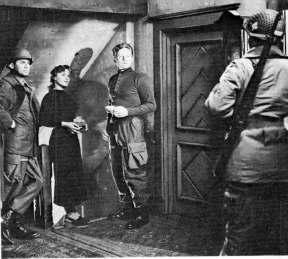

Battleground was a remarkable case of MGM history repeating itself. When Thalberg planned to make The Big Parade Mayer said no one wanted a war drama in 1925. Now Schary, the 'new Thalberg', had brought a pet project over from RKO, where Howard Hughes had vetoed it, and Mayer said no one wanted a war drama in 1949. Both movies turned out to be outstanding hits and each started a rift between Mayer, who naturally disliked being proved wrong, and his No. 2. Battleground had force in its script by Robert Pirosh (Academy Award) and realism in its direction by William Wellman. Even the glamour boys among its actors looked and sounded like GI's enduring the Battle of the Bulge. Left to right, John Hodiak, Denise Darcel, Van Johnson; also cast were Ricardo Montalban, George Murphy, Marshall Thompson, Don Taylor, Richard Jaeckel, Jerome Courtland, Leon Ames, Douglas Fowley, Bruce Cowling, James Whitmore, James Arness, Thomas Breen, Scotty Beckett. Paul Vogel's camerawork won it a second Oscar.

Don't try to get away! Richard Basehart, William Conrad, Barry Sullivan, Audrey Totter and Cyd Charisse in **Tension**, an ingenious, tightly-plotted murder story by John Klorer. Scripter Allen Rivkin and director John Berry kept the title as their watchword throughout. Producer, Robert Sisk. Also cast: Lloyd Gough, Tom d'Andrea, Tito Renaldo. Below: Geraldine Brooks, Edmund Gwenn, Lassie and Reginald Owen in **Challenge to Lassie**, for which the star (not the original) but a look-alike owned by the same trainer) had to learn sheep-herding. Adapted by William Ludwig from 'Greyfriars Bobby', the Robert Sisk production in Technicolor was directed by Richard Thorpe. Donald Crisp, Alan Webb, Henry Stephenson, Alan Napier, Sara Allgood, Arthur Sheilds, Edmond Breon and Lumsden Hare rolled Scottish Rs.

1949 *A baseball story,* **Take Me Out to the Ball Game** *(Everybody's Cheering in Britain, where the game is box-office poison) scored an entertainment home-run everywhere. Like all MGM musicals now, it was in Technicolor. With two of the world's best song-and-dance men, Frank Sinatra and Gene Kelly, how could*

it miss? Just to make sure, Arthur Freed added Esther Williams, Betty Garrett and Jules Munshin and turned them all loose on that old master of musicals, Busby Berkeley. Kelly and Stanley Donen got co-author credit for what resembled a rewrite of the 1930 flop, They Learned About Women; Harry Tugend and George Wells scripted.

But the musical that won all the critics' and customers' awards was **On the Town**, starring Betty Garrett, Frank Sinatra, Ann Miller, Jules Munshin, Vera-Ellen and Gene Kelly (left to right, above; the last two also at left). A ballet by Jerome Robbins inspired this show's triumphant career; from it Betty Comden and Adolph Green (who also played the Miller and Munshin roles) derived a 1944 Broadway hit with music by Leonard Bernstein, and, when MGM brought them to Hollywood, wrote the screenplay. Direction by Kelly and Stanley Donen had exhilarating zest; Arthur Freed's production sparkled; Roger Edens' and Lennie Hayton's scoring won an Academy Oscar. The six leads were supported by Alice Pearce, in her original stage role, and Florence Bates.

1949 **The Yellow Cab Man** starred Red Skelton as a disaster-prone inventor, here with James Gleason, Gloria DeHaven and Charles Hughes. Edward Arnold, Walter Slezak, Jay C. Flippen, Paul Harvey, Polly Moran were in it. Writers Devery Freeman and Albert Beich, director Jack Donohue and producer Richard Goldstone kept the sight gags coming almost without respite.

Once again the MGM air was heavy with imaginary anaesthetics as Pandro Berman's crew opened up the old hospital sets for **The Doctor and the Girl**, dusted off the scalpels and pulled rubber gloves on a handsome new surgeon: Glenn Ford in his first of dozens of Metro roles. Patients with him here: Janet Leigh (walking) and Gloria DeHaven (emergency). Charles Coburn, Bruce Bennett, Warner Anderson, Nancy Davis, Arthur Franz and Basil Ruysdael were also cast under Curtis Bernhardt's direction. Theodore Reeves' script streamlined 'Bodies and Souls' by Maxence van der Meersch, a massive best-seller – but not as a film.

Farley Granger and Cathy O'Donnell — golly, what those poor kids went through to get to this happy ending of **Side Street**. Audiences had their nerves frazzled too, as the lovers got caught up in robbery and murder, tensely plotted by Sydney Boehm and directed at a fast clip by Anthony Mann. He shot exteriors in Manhattan, most effectively in the climactic chase through the streets. Sam Zimbalist produced, casting James Craig against type as a vicious gangster, and Jean Hagen, Paul Jergens, Edmon Ryan, Harry Bellaver, Whit Bissell, John Gallaudet.
Bissell, John Gallaudet.

Marcia Davenport's **East Side, West Side** brought the total of novels filmed by MGM in 1949 to ten. It wasn't exactly a best-seller at the ticket-windows, but worked out at a profit thanks to its cast's drawing power: Van Heflin, Barbara Stanwyck, James Mason (left to right); plus Ava Gardner, Cyd Charisse, Gale Sondergaard, Nancy Davis, William Conrad, Raymond Greenleaf, Beverly Michaels, William Frawley. Mervyn LeRoy directed Isobel Lennart's screenplay, produced by former story department head Voldemar Vetluguin.

Top names were again sent to London for the new studio's second production, **Conspirator**, with even more disappointing results than Edward My Son, and producer Arthur Hornblow Jr faced a 'what can we do with this?' dilemma back at Culver City, where it lay on the shelf for several months. Robert Taylor reprised his Undercurrent performance of charming husband/vicious villain, while Elizabeth Taylor as his wife made a premature start as an adult actress. Sally Benson's script, from a novel by Humphrey Slater, and Victor Saville's direction were equally uninspired. Others cast: Robert Flemying, Honor Blackman, Harold Warrender, Thora Hird, Wilfrid Hyde White, Marjorie Fielding, Marie Ney, Helen Haye, Karel Stepanek.

Ann Sothern went dramatic in a minor domestic thriller, **Shadow on the Wall**. Zachary Scott co-starred, supported by little Gigi Perreau and Nancy Davis, who was to become California's first lady as Mrs Ronald Reagan; also cast were Tom Helmore, John McIntire, Marcia Van Dyke, Barbara Billingsley. Robert Sisk produced and Pat Jackson was imported from Britain to direct the William Ludwig script, from a Hannah Lees–Lawrence Bachmann story.

Any Number Can Play was a lacklustre affair, only moderately popular, although the novel by Edward Harris Heth seemed ideal Clark Gable stuff: woman trouble and business trouble for the boss of a posh gambling hell. It got the best names money could buy: writer Richard Brooks; producer Arthur Freed (what, no music?), director Mervyn LeRoy; cast Barry Sullivan, Darryl Hickman, Alexis Smith and the King himself (left to right) and Wendell Corey, Audrey Totter, Frank Morgan, Mary Astor, Lewis Stone, Marjorie Rambeau, William Conrad, Leon Ames, Edgar Buchanan, Mickey Knox, Richard Rober, Dorothy Comingore (the 'Marion Davies' in Citizen Kane).

Critics raved over **Intruder in the Dust**; Clarence Brown's production and direction of William Faulkner's novel demonstrated just how well a novel can be filmed. A master at bringing out the best in decades of MGM actors, from Garbo to Claude Jarman Jr, he got memorable performances from young Claude, Elizabeth Patterson and David Brian (here) and Juano Hernandez as the Negro they saved from lynching. Ben Maddow's script made no detours into comic or romantic relief from its grim theme of racial bigotry, personified by Porter Hall, Will Geer and Charles Kemper.

The well-cast and beautifully mounted Pandro Berman production of **Madame Bovary** took ▷ the odd course of framing the story in a depiction of Flaubert's trial for corrupting morals by writing it. Thus Emma's drama was put at one remove from the audience, who could admire without becoming engrossed. Vincente Minnelli directed the Robert Ardrey screenplay, and Jennifer Jones played the title role, Louis Jourdan (with her here), her lover. Also cast were James Mason as the author, Van Heflin as Bovary, Christopher Kent (the young Swedish actor, Alf Kjellin, renamed), Gene Lockhart, Gladys Cooper, Frank Allenby, John Abbott, Henry Morgan, George Zucco, Ellen Corby, Eduard Franz, Paul Cavanagh. Two previous versions: Hollywood, 1932 (as Unholy Love!); Paris, 1934 by Jean Renoir.

1949 *The movie of the year for many: Spencer Tracy, Judy Holliday and Katharine Hepburn in* **Adam's Rib**. *Mr and Mrs Garson Kanin (Ruth Gordon) wrote the witty story of married lawyers at professional loggerheads especially for Tracy and Hepburn, who were at their best ever. Director George Cukor and producer Lawrence Weingarten zipped them through this moneyspinner in a record 'A' schedule of 37 days. Judy's film debut as the dimwit on trial for husband-shooting was wildly funny, while three other newcomers from Broadway, David Wayne (glimpsed behind Tracy here), Tom Ewell and Jean Hagen also scored. Hope Emerson, Clarence Kolb and Polly Moran, back after 13 years, played bright bits and* ▽

Cole Porter contributed a song, 'Farewell Amanda'.

Frank Morgan's last appearance was in **Key to the City**, *an amiable, forgettable comedy teaming Clark Gable and Loretta Young (here). He died at 59 after 17 years of fine MGM work. Albert Beich's original about a convention of mayors was hoked up with gags and action by scripter Robert Crutcher and director George Sidney in Z. Wayne Griffin's production. Marilyn Maxwell, James Gleason, Raymond Burr, Lewis Stone, Raymond Walburn, Pamela Britton, Clinton Sundberg, Marion Martin, Bert Freed, Emory Parnell, Clara Blandick supported.*

A new star of the first magnitude arrived in **That Midnight Kiss***: Mario Lanza, given the ▷ lead opposite Kathryn Grayson for a debut that excited the public, had the critics talking about a new Caruso, and revived MGM's reputation for talent-spotting. In the somewhat autobiographical role of a singing truck-driver he disclosed a theatre-shaking voice and a personality to match. The Joe Pasternak musical, directed by Norman Taurog, actually gave him fourth billing below Grayson, Jose Iturbi and Ethel Barrymore, with Keenan Wynn, Jules Munshin, J. Carrol Naish, Thomas Gomez, Arthur Treacher, Marjorie Reynolds and Amparo Iturbi in support. Script: Bruce Manning, Tamara Hovey.*

Nancy Goes to Rio *was Ann Sothern's last at MGM, where she started as a chorus girl named Harriet Lake in 1929. She's shown (below) with Louis Calhern in this typically tuneful, fluffy, popular Joe Pasternak musical. Jane Powell co-starred with Ann in the Jane Hall–Frederick Kohner–Ralph Block yarn about mother and daughter chasing the same singing role and the same man (unbeknownst*

to each other, mind you), re-scripted by Sidney Sheldon from a Deanna Durbin movie Pasternak made at Universal ten years before, It's a Date. *Robert Z. Leonard directed with Carmen Miranda, Barry Sullivan, Scotty Beckett, Fortunio Bonanova, Nella Walker, Hans Conreid in the cast.*

The studio's year ended with a Yippee! as Robert Taylor rode down the wicked Apaches who dared to capture a White Woman. **Ambush** *was a superior Western, as might be expected from Sam Wood (who died at 66 soon after directing it), and it did strong business. Armand Deutsch produced Marguerite Robert's screenplay from Luke Short's story, with John Hodiak, Jean Hagen, Don Taylor, Bruce Cowling, Leon Ames, John McIntire and the beauteous Arlene Dahl (here with Taylor).*

RENAISSANCE
1950

The industry generally was in the dumps. US attendances dwindled to 60m weekly (lowest since 1933), the British average to 26m. But it was a nice little year for MGM–Loew's, the 1950 net rising a million from 1949, and a new studio vitality making itself felt with hits like *Annie Get Your Gun, Father of the Bride* and *The Asphalt Jungle*.

The weak and medium attractions were the ones chiefly affected by the fall-off in attendances; big was still big. In this category came two show business stories: Bette Davis in J. L. Mankiewicz's Academy-Awarded *All About Eve*, and William Holden in Billy Wilder's Hollywood drama *Sunset Boulevard* with its galaxy of old-timers: Gloria Swanson, Erich von Stroheim, Buster Keaton, Anna Q. Nilsson, H. B. Warner and Cecil B. DeMille. Cecil B. was up to his old epic tricks in *Samson and Delilah*. Britain's best was *The Third Man*, reuniting *Kane's* Joseph Cotten and Orson Welles.

James Stewart in *Harvey* and Gregory Peck in *12 O'Clock High* clicked. Marlon Brando made an exciting debut in *The Men. Born Yesterday* hilariously starred this year's Oscar winner, Judy Holliday, and 1949's, Broderick Crawford. Jose Ferrer also won the Academy accolade in *Cyrano de Bergerac* but it flopped, as did Harold Lloyd's last movie, *Mad Wednesday*.

With the dawn of the Fifties, Val Lewton, beloved of horror buffs for his Zombies and Cat People of the Forties, turned nice and produced **Please Believe Me**. *Maybe the ghouls resented it: it was his last picture. This romantic comedy cast (left to right) Robert Walker, Peter Lawford, Deborah Kerr and Mark Stevens; also James Whitmore, Spring Byington, J. Carrol Naish, George Cleveland. Norman Taurog directed the Nathaniel Curtis screenplay.*

Niceness also permeated **Stars In My Crown**, *a gentle drama of a country parson and his family – Joel McCrea, Ellen Drew, Dean Stockwell. Jacques Tourneur returned to direct Joe David Brown's adaptation of his own novel, scripted by Margaret Fitts, produced by William Wright. Also cast: Lewis Stone, James Mitchell, Alan Hale, Juano Hernandez, Amanda Blake, Connie Gilchrist, Arthur Hunnicutt.*

Red Skelton played three roles in **Watch the Birdie**: *a camera nut, his father and his grandfather. Three roles too many, quipped Buster Keaton buffs, faithful unto death to* The Cameraman. *Ann Miller and Arlene Dahl shared leading lady chores, supported by Leon Ames, Pamela Britton and Richard Rober. Jack Donohue directed; Harry Ruskin produced and collaborated on the script with Ivan Tors and Devery Freeman; original by Marshall Neilan Jr.*

Elizabeth Taylor, Rosemary DeCamp, Leon Ames and Van Johnson in **The Big Hangover**, *a silly failure featuring a talking dog. It did nothing for Liz, Johnson, or the auteur theory of film-making: Norman Krasna wrote, produced and directed it all by himself. Also cast: Percy Waram, Fay Holden, Edgar Buchanan, Selena Royle, Gene Lockhart, Philip Ahn, Matt Moore, Pierre Watkin, Russell Hicks...*

The Skipper Surprised His Wife *was not in the same class as* Father of the Bride, *but still a bright domestic comedy. Robert Walker starred with (left to right) Jan Sterling, Spring Byington, Joan Leslie and Edward Arnold. Dorothy Kingsley's story of an ex-captain running his home as he did his ship brought director Elliott Nugent back to MGM after 17 years. William H. Wright produced, with Leon Ames, Paul Harvey, Kathryn Card in the cast.*

The Magnificent Yankee *was Louis Calhern's great stage success: he played it for two years on Broadway and another on the road. Rewarding him for his many fine MGM supporting jobs, Schary scheduled a film version, although aware it was more of a prestige than a profit entry. Its author, Emmet Lavery, wrote the script, Armand Deutsch produced, John Sturges directed, and Ann Harding ably partnered Calhern's splendid portrayal of Oliver Wendell Holmes, the liberal US Supreme Court Justice. Eduard Franz, Philip Ober, Ian Wolfe, Richard Anderson and James Lydon were cast. Its British title,* The Man with Thirty Sons, *referred to the Harvard law graduates Holmes sponsored.*

Richard Brooks' script and direction made a real gripper of **Crisis**, *George Tabori's story of an ailing dictator and an American surgeon forced to operate on him. Brooks and Arthur Freed, producing one of his rare non-musicals, had the pleasant idea of casting erstwhile matinee idols in support of Cary Grant, Jose Ferrer and Signe Hasso: Antonio Moreno, with them here (right), was one of MGM's first stars; Ramon Novarro and Gilbert Roland were also featured with Paula Raymond, Leon Ames and Teresa Celli.*

Spencer Tracy had an even better part in **Father of the Bride** than in Adam's Rib. His superb portrait of frustrated dominance over a household in the throes of wedding fever was the centrepiece of a great comedy, scripted from Edward Streeter's book by that memorable team of the Thirties, Frances Goodrich and Albert Hackett, and affectionately directed by Vincente Minnelli. Elizabeth Taylor made such a luscious bride that she was promptly led to a real altar by her first husband. Joan Bennett, often opposite Tracy in their old Fox days, made a belated MGM debut and was just right as the wife and mother. Don Taylor, Billie Burke, Moroni Olsen, Leo G. Carroll, Melville Cooper, Taylor Holmes, Marietta Canty, Frank Orth and, as Liz's brothers, Rusty (later Russ) Tamblyn and Tom Irish completed the cast of Pandro S. Berman's enormously popular production.

1950

June Allyson and Dick Powell co-starred for the first time, after five years as Mr and Mrs, and made an amusing team in **The Reformer and the Redhead**, *a minor hit. Norman Panama and Melvin Frank wrote (from a Robert Carson original), produced and directed, casting Powell as a candidate for mayor, June as a zoo-keeper's daughter with a penchant for huge pets, including an affectionate lion. Also cast: David Wayne, Cecil Kellaway, Ray Collins, Robert Keith, Marvin Kaplan.*

After many a sad setback **Annie Get Your Gun** *came through as a tremendous hit. Arthur Freed did well to have the final print ready one year after production started in April 1949. Annie was Judy Garland at that stage, with Busby Berkeley directing. Cameras stopped when Judy suffered a complete mental and physical collapse; the studio had to wait for a Paramount picture to finish before Betty Hutton could replace her; Charles Walters took over from Berkeley; Frank Morgan died suddenly; his scenes were reshot with Louis Calhern as Buffalo Bill; Sidney took over from Walters; and so it went ... But it arrived! Though sometimes overlooked in critical surveys of the great MGM musicals, it was the biggest money-maker of them all in its time. And no mere photographed stage show! Freed's production opened out the Dorothy and Herbert Fields 'book' of the Broadway record-breaker, giving added scope to Irving Berlin's 11 songs, staged by Robert Alton and scored by Adolph Deutsch and Roger Edens (Academy Award); Sidney Sheldon scripted. Sidney directed Miss Hutton to her best performance as Annie, and Howard Keel to instant movie stardom as her rival sharpshooter. The whole cast—Benay Venuta, Keel, Miss Hutton, Calhern, Keenan Wynn (left to right) and Edward Arnold, J. C. Naish, Clinton Sundberg—performed throughout as if inspired by their finale, 'There's No Business Like Show Business'.*

The Pasternak–Taurog team which had helped the Grayson–Lanza team to score in That Midnight Kiss *gave them an even bigger hit in* **The Toast of New Orleans**, *a colourful musical. Here J. Carrol Naish admires Kathryn Grayson's 1905 Mitchell auto, but Mario Lanza has eyes only for Kathryn. A somewhat submerged third star was David Niven, with James Mitchell, Rita Moreno, Clinton Sundberg and Sig Arno also delivering the Sy Gomberg–George Wells dialogue. Lanza tested theatres' sound systems with 'Be My Love', a best-seller in the Nicholas Brodszky–Sammy Cahn score.*

Taking another whirl at musical biography of songwriters, **Three Little Words** *was less pretentious and more fun than its predecessors; a merry hit. Fred Astaire and Red Skelton played Bert Kalmar and Harry Ruby (here with Arlene Dahl as Eileen Percy, the silent movie star who married Ruby). Vera-Ellen played Mrs Kalmar; Gloria DeHaven impersonated her mother, stage star Mrs Carter DeHaven; and a cute trick named Debbie Reynolds appeared as Helen Kane, the boop-a-doop rave of the Twenties. Many a filmgoer had never heard of Kalmar & Ruby, but they'd heard their songs all right. Producer Jack Cummings, director Richard Thorpe and music supervisor André Previn crammed 14 of them into the soundtrack, while Hermes Pan staged some zingy dances for Astaire and Vera-Ellen. Script, George Wells; cast, Keenan Wynn, Gale Robbins, Phil Regan, Carleton Carpenter, Harry Shannon, Paul Harvey.*

The MGM star system was in good working order, and vehicles were still being manufactured for it. Van Johnson and Kathryn Grayson seemed a nice combination as yet untried, so Samuel Marx wrote and produced a comedy for them, **Grounds For Marriage**, ▷ *about a doctor and an opera singer, temporarily divorced. The Allen Rivkin-Laura Kerr script, directed by Robert Z. Leonard, was interrupted by gems from* Carmen *and* La Bohème. *Paula Raymond, Barry Sullivan, Lewis Stone and Reginald Owen had featured roles. Paybox response was mild.*

A period domestic comedy, with elaborate musical trimmings staged by Busby Berkeley, **Two Weeks with Love** *satisfied as both amusement and profit-maker. Here Ricardo Montalban rescues Jane Powell from a romantic-looking swoon, actually caused by putting on a surgical corset by mistake. Observers: Ann Harding, Louis Calhern, Carleton Carpenter, Debbie Reynolds, Clinton Sundberg, Tommy Rettig and Gary Gray. Jack Cummings, who gave Carpenter and Miss Reynolds a break in* Three Little Words, *allowed them more footage this time and their 1914 song, 'Aba Daba Honeymoon', became a hit all over again. Director, Roy Rowland; writers, John Larkin and Dorothy Kingsley; rest of cast, Phyllis Kirk and Charles Smith.*

How could a big shiny Pasternak musical starring Esther Williams and Van Johnson miss? **Duchess of Idaho** didn't. The conventional Dorothy Cooper–Jerry Davis script about a romantic triangle with John Lund as the third corner, was dolled up with skiing in the snow, swimming in the sun, and singing all over the place by Lena Horne, Mel Torme and Connie Haines. Robert Z. Leonard's cast included Paula Raymond, Clinton Sundberg, Amanda Blake, Dick Simmons. Jack Donohue took over to direct the numbers. Eleanor Powell, long retired as Mrs Glenn Ford, returned for a dazzling dance solo.

MGM reaped more 1950–51 income from its 1949–50 jaunting around the world, as **Kim** followed King Solomon's Mines and pre-

ceded Quo Vadis. Long on the studio's 'maybe' schedule, the Kipling classic was finally activated by the British producer-director teamwork of Leon Gordon and Victor Saville, who cast (left to right) Errol Flynn as Redbeard, Dean Stockwell as Kim and Paul Lukas as the lama, and sent a unit to India. The resulting Technicolor footage gave the adventure story, scripted by Gordon, Helen Deutsch and Richard Schayer, impressive scope and sweep. Also cast: Robert Douglas, Thomas Gomez, Cecil Kellaway, Reginald Owen, Arnold Moss, Laurette Luez.

MGM's low-budget thrillers were doing particularly well at this time. Loretta Young suffered in **Cause for Alarm** and audiences had a fine nail-biting time as her jealousy-crazed husband, Barry Sullivan, made her appear to be his murderer. As directed by Tay Garnett, the ingenious plot, confined to a few hours in a humdrum suburban locale, packed loads of suspense. It originated in a radio play by Larry Marcus, now scripted (with Mel Dinelli) and produced by Loretta's real husband, Tom Lewis. Also cast: Margalo Gillmore, Bruce Cowling, Irving Bacon, Richard Anderson and Art Baker.

Teresa, the story of an Italian GI bride, began the screen careers of four unknowns: Pier Angeli, John Ericson, Ralph Meeker and Rod Steiger. The first three were given MGM contracts. Arthur Loew, who left his international distribution desk long enough to produce it in Italy and New York, had proved himself no mean talent-picker. Left to right: Richard Bishop, Peggy Ann Garner, Tommy Lewis, Miss Angeli, Patricia Collinge and Ericson in the Coney Island sequence of the movie, which was warmly directed by Fred Zinnemann. Script by Stewart Stern from his and Alfred Hayes' original. Takings responded to a big publicity campaign for Angeli as a new star.

Devil's Doorway was sympathetic to the tribal villains of most shoot-em-ups and James Mitchell and Robert Taylor played Red Indians impressively. Anthony Mann's direction of the Nicholas Nayfack production ensured good reviews and receipts. Story and script, Guy Trosper. Also cast: Paula Raymond, Louis Calhern, Marshall Thompson, Rhys Williams, Fritz Leiber, Edgar Buchanan, Bruce Cowling.

A more conventional Western, **The Outriders** continued the revival of this genre at MGM inspired by the success of Ambush. The gunman (here) with star Joel McCrea was the Ben-Hur of yesteryear, Ramon Novarro, in a cast including Arlene Dahl, Barry Sullivan, James Whitmore, Ted de Corsia and Claude Jarman Jr. Roy Rowland directed the Irving Ravetch screenplay, produced in Technicolor by Richard Goldstone.

King Solomon's Mines was a world-wide smash. For it producer Sam Zimbalist, directors Compton Bennett and Andrew Martoni and photographer Robert Surtees took a large crew, Technicolor cameras and (left to right) Deborah Kerr, Richard Carlson and Stewart Granger on a 25,000-mile safari, and came

back with a spectacle that made the result of MGM's previous African trek, Trader Horn, look like a sideshow. The continent's natives (like the seven-foot Watusis seen here), animals, reptiles, birds, insects and scenery were superbly photographed, giving the studio priceless stock footage besides the scenes used to tell Helen Deutsch's version of the Rider Haggard novel. Some critics objected to her revisions; others were, like the public, carried away by the movie's crowded succession of exciting incidents.

That nice Marshall Thompson turned into a mad gunman in **Dial 1119**/The Violent Hour, holding a bunch of bar customers as hostages. Left to right: Virginia Field, James Bell, Keefe Brasselle, Leon Ames, Andrea King; also cast were Sam Levene, Richard Rober, William Conrad, Dick Simmons. Richard Goldstone produced John Monks Jr's taut little thriller, directed by a late graduate from short subjects, Gerald Mayer.

The big Monroe boom was still two years away when Marilyn played this unbilled bit with Dick Powell in **Right Cross**. June Allyson and Ricardo Montalban shared a triangle with Powell in Charles Schnee's entertaining prize-fight drama, produced by Armand Deutsch and directed by John Sturges. Also cast: Lionel Barrymore, Teresa Celli, Barry Kelley, John Gallaudet, Larry Keating.

Marjorie Main as a sharp-tongued widow and James Whitmore as a shyster lawyer did the title roles in **Mrs O'Malley and Mr Malone** so well that a follow-up series was planned, but it didn't happen. Left to right: Fred Clark, Ann Dvorak and Whitmore in this comedy thriller which moved as fast as the express train it was set in. Norman Taurog directed the William Wright production, with Phyllis Kirk, Dorothy Malone, Douglas Fowley, Clinton Sundberg. William Bowers scripted a story by mystery novelists Craig Rice and Stuart Palmer.

Metro signed Burt Lancaster, whose name was money in the bank after several late Forties hits, for **Vengeance Valley**, a big Western winner. He played a cattle-ranch overseer trying to straighten out his boss's wayward son, Robert Walker. (In life, Walker couldn't solve his sad drinking problem and, after two more films, died at 32.) Joanne Dru, Sally Forrest, Ray Collins, John Ireland, Hugh O'Brian, Carleton Carpenter and Ted de Corsia also figured in Luke Short's drama, scripted by Irving Ravetch, directed by Richard Thorpe and produced by Nicholas Nayfack.

Mystery Street, with Elsa Lanchester and Ricardo Montalban, began a long stay at MGM for director John Sturges. He did a fine job on this crisp 'B' about murder at Harvard, partly filmed in and around Boston. Sally Forrest, Bruce Bennett, Marshall Thompson, Jan Sterling, Edmon Ryan and Betsy Blair supported Montalban in the profitable Frank Taylor production. Script was by Sydney Boehm and Richard Brooks from a Leonard Spigelgass original.

Carey Wilson had been eager to film Owen Johnson's old 'Lawrenceville School' stories ever since he read them in the Saturday Evening Post, but was short of a script until Harry Ruskin came up with **The Happy Years**. William Wellman, also in nostalgic mood, directed before they all got on with more important things. It scored B-minus for box-office appeal. Enacting the juvenile reminiscences were Dean Stockwell and Leo G. Carroll (here) and Darryl Hickman, Scotty Beckett, Leon Ames, Margalo Gillmore.

Ask any director – or anyone else who worked with her during her 40 Hollywood years – 'Who's your favourite star?' and the answer is likely to be 'Barbara Stanwyck'. Unexpected, since her own character was often masked by the hard-hearted Hannahs she played so well, as in **To Please a Lady** with Clark Gable. This cliché-infested yarn about a tough lady journalist and a tougher racing driver was unworthy of its stars or producer-director Clarence Brown. Adolphe Menjou, Will Geer, Roland Winters, Frank Jenks and Emory Parnell had parts in the Barre Lyndon–Marge Decker screenplay.

Schary's yen for movies with a message reached the ultimate with **The Next Voice You Hear**. Its message was delivered by the voice of God when James Whitmore, Nancy Davis and Gary Gray switched on their radio. That the ludicrous was avoided and an impressive sincerity achieved proved the skill of director William Wellman, writer Charles Schnee, the cast (including Lillian Bronson, Art Smith, Tom d'Andrea, Jeff Corey) and producer Schary himself.

The disappointment jinx was still on MGM's British studio and **The Miniver Story** was an ill-advised sequel to the 1942 smash. The earlier film's win-the-war motivation made the Minivers exciting people; eight years later they were just another set of movie characters. Pretty depressing ones too, with Mrs M. (still Greer Garson, here with John Hodiak) slowly dying, and box-office results following suit. Sidney Franklin produced and H. C. Potter directed the Ronald Millar–George Froeschel screenplay. Miss Garson and Walter Pidgeon again excelled as Mr and Mrs M., with little James Fox (like brother Edward, a future leading man) catching attention as their son, Cathy O'Donnell replacing Teresa Wright as their daughter, and Henry Wilcoxon and Reginald Owen continuing their old roles. Also

in it: Leo Genn, Anthony Bushell, Peter Finch (stardom just around the corner), Alison Leggatt, Richard Gale.

A couple of photographic models, one on the way up and one on the skids, were played by Lana Turner and Ann Dvorak in **A Life of Her Own**. Unfortunately for the film, Ann committed suicide in Reel Two, leaving Lana, Ray Milland, Louis Calhern, Barry Sullivan, Tom Ewell, Jean Hagen, Phyllis Kirk, Sara Haden and director George Cukor to cope with Isobel Lennart's tedious love-versus-career script. Voldemar Vetluguin produced.

Tahiti gal Esther Williams dived for the coin tourist Howard Keel threw from his ship in **Pagan Love Song**. She swam a lot and he sang a lot, but there wasn't much coin at the box-office for this Arthur Freed musical, one of his least successful. He also wrote the lyrics for Harry Warren's songs, none of them up to the title number he and Nacio Herb Brown composed in 1929. Minna Gombell and Rita Moreno had two of the few parts in an almost imperceptible screenplay by Robert Nathan and Jerry Davis, derived from W. S. Stone's book, 'Tahiti Landfall'. Robert Alton directed, then went back to dance staging.

Three Guys Named Mike was a lightweight romance about an air hostess (Jane Wyman) and a trio of swains played by Van Johnson, Howard Keel (with Jane here) and Barry Sullivan. Charles Walters directed them and Phyllis Kirk, Jeff Donnell, Hugh Sanders, Barbara Billingsley. Sidney Sheldon scripted the Ruth Brooks Flippen original; Armand Deutsch produced. Takings hit an air pocket.

Summer Stock/If You Feel Like Singing was the MGM swansong of Judy Garland. After it had been completed, despite numerous hold-ups when Judy wore herself and everyone else to a frazzle, producer Joe Pasternak and director Charles Walters decided a flash number was needed to top it off and, fingers crossed, called Judy back. Amazingly, she zipped through this 'Get Happy' song and dance at her old brilliant best. It was a fore-taste of her next 19 legendary years, dizzily alternating disasters and triumphs. Gene Kelly co-starred in this musical, written by Sy Gomberg and George Wells and featuring Eddie Bracken, Gloria DeHaven, Phil Silvers, Marjorie Main, Ray Collins, Carleton Carpenter, Hans Conreid. It turned out pretty well, all things considered, and turned a profit.

Judy Garland was cast for the Jane Powell role in **Royal Wedding**/Wedding Bells but then missed or delayed so many rehearsals that finally Schenck, Mayer and Schary decided reluctantly to replace her once again and to risk no such disruptions in future. Judy's MGM career was over. The movie frankly cashed in on British headline-makers, not only by casting Sir Winston's daughter Sarah Churchill (here with Fred Astaire) in her only Hollywood movie, but by setting the musical in London during the Princess Elizabeth–Prince Philip wedding season. Alan Jay Lerner's book and lyrics were bright, the songs (music by Burton Lane) including a fine ballad for Miss Powell, 'Too Late Now', and a comic hit for Jane and Astaire with the all-time longest title, 'How Could You Believe Me When I Said I Love You When You Know I've Been a Liar All My Life?'. Astaire also did a memorable dance up the wall, across the ceiling and down again. Altogether a vintage Arthur Freed show, directed by Stanley Donen as his first solo effort. Also cast: Peter Lawford, Keenan Wynn, Albert Sharpe, Viola Roache, Jimmy Finlayson.

1950

The Asphalt Jungle *might be called 'Father of* ▷
the Crime', the seminal thriller from which
countless movies about big robbery plots have
sprung (including three more MGM versions
of its own W. R. Burnett original). John
Huston's script (with Ben Maddow) and
direction gave it a sinister urgency and a
gallery of vivid character portrayals by Sterling
Hayden, Anthony Caruso and Sam Jaffe (left
to right) and Louis Calhern, James Whitmore,
Jean Hagen, Marc Lawrence, John McIntire,
Teresa Celli, Dorothy Tree, Barry Kelley and
an eye-catching new blonde, Marilyn Monroe.
The Arthur Hornblow Jr production became a
great and enduring success.

Hedy Lamarr had just made a comeback in
Cecil B. DeMille's Samson and Delilah, *but*
A Lady Without Passport, *an adventure drama*
without thrills, started her downhill again.
Joseph Lewis directed and Samuel Marx pro-
duced the Howard Dimsdale screenplay, from
an original by Lawrence Taylor. John Hodiak
(Hedy is showing him her concentration camp
number here) and James Craig, George
Macready, Steve Geray, Bruce Cowling and
Trevor Bardette were in the cast.

Life became confusing for Elizabeth Taylor
when MGM rushed her back from her honey-
moon (real) to have her first baby (movie) in
Father's Little Dividend. *This quick sequel to*
Father of the Bride *completed the studio's*
1950 schedule and didn't disgrace an excellent
year, but it couldn't quite reach the original's
entertaining and moneymaking level. Every-
body took the encore: players, Liz and Don
Taylor, Spencer Tracy and Joan Bennett
(here) and Billie Burke, Moroni Olsen,
Marietta Canty, Rusty Tamblyn, Tom Irish,
Paul Harvey; producer Berman; director
Minnelli, writers Hackett and Goodrich.

ON WITH THE DANCE
1951

Although MGM-Loew's profits in 1951 ($7.6m from $178m gross) equalled those of 1950, other companies were skidding. The number of television sets in American homes doubled during the year to 15m. All companies refused to sell their huge backlogs of movies to this threatening ogre, but Columbia, Universal and Paramount announced plans to film TV material. Better news from abroad, where restrictions on Hollywood product were eased or removed by Britain, Australia, Italy, France, West Germany and Argentina.

Three films vied for any prizes *American in Paris* didn't win: Vivien Leigh (Academy Award) and Marlon Brando in *A Streetcar Named Desire*; Elizabeth Taylor and Montgomery Clift in *A Place in The Sun*, Humphrey Bogart (Academy Award) and Katharine Hepburn in *The African Queen*. Also highly regarded were Alfred Hitchcock's *Strangers on a Train*, William Wyler's *Detective Story* and Jean Renoir's *The River*. Biblical box-office: Gregory Peck and Susan Hayward as *David and Bathsheba*. Doris Day and the Dean Martin–Jerry Lewis team achieved Top Tendom, joining Wayne, Crosby, Hope, Cooper, Tracy, Betty Grable, Randolph Scott, Abbott and Costello.

Lone Star *was produced on a big scale by Z. Wayne Griffin, with proportionate box-office response. Starring Clark Gable and Ava Gardner, it was a good old slam-bang Western with Gable and Broderick Crawford slugging it out for the land and the gal. Vincent Sherman directed the stars and Lionel Barrymore and Beulah Bondi (repeating their* Gorgeous Hussy *roles), Ed Begley, James Burke, William Farnum (the Gable of 40 years earlier), Lowell Gilmore, Moroni Olsen, Russell Simpson, William Conrad. Story, Howard Estabrook; script, Borden Chase.*

Westward the Women *veered from the usual to trace the trek of a wagon train full of nubile ladies destined to help pioneering males populate the wilderness. Dore Schary personally produced the movie, an original by Frank Capra scripted by Charles Schnee and directed by William Wellman. John McIntire helped Robert Taylor quell marauding Injuns and squalling trekkers Denise Darcel, Hope Emerson, Lenore Lonergan and Julie Bishop.*

Crowds loved and critics hated **Soldiers Three** *with Cyril Cusack, Robert Newton, Stewart Granger and David Niven (from left to right). Producer Pandro Berman had won acclaim for* Gunga Din *at RKO a dozen years before, but his* Soldiers Three *was kippered Kipling. hardly worthy of the studio that had done so well by* Captains Courageous *and* Kim. *Indian location shots from the latter backgrounded the jolly horseplay directed for laughs and action, junior grade, by Tay Garnett. The Marguerite Roberts–Tom Reed–Malcolm Stuart Boylan screenplay also employed Walter Pidgeon, Greta Gynt, Frank Allenby, Robert Coote and Dan O'Herlihy.*

By Pierre of the Plains *out of* Rose Marie, *Frank Fenton's story of a trapper versus a Mountie,* **The Wild North**, *was MGM's third outdoor hit in a row. It was given a spacious production (in AnscoColor) by Stephen Ames and plenty of action by Andrew Marton. Stewart Granger and Cyd Charisse canoed and canoodled; Wendell Corey played the NWMP constable, supported by Morgan Farley, J. M. Kerrigan, Howard Petrie, and those never-out-of-work Indians.*

Home Town Story *was a cuckoo's egg in the MGM nest, laid by General Motors who had commissioned it from director-writer Arthur Pierson as a propaganda piece. It naïvely told how newsman Jeffrey Lynn learned the error of his pinko ways, realizing the goodness of Big Business when his kid sister, trapped by a cave-in, was rescued by the machinery of tycoon Donald Crisp. In this scene: Lynn, Nelson Leigh, moppet Melinda Plowman, Alan Hale Jr, Crisp and Marjorie Reynolds. Also cast: Barbara Brown, Marilyn Monroe, Glenn Tryon.*

The Red Badge of Courage *was one of the ▷ sparks that set off the final Mayer–Schary–Schenck explosion. Schary scheduled the Stephen Crane Civil War classic, Mayer vetoed it, Schary insisted, Mayer appealed to Schenck for support. He didn't get it, and this, together with other ego-bruising incidents, resulted in Mayer's exit in the summer of 1951. Meanwhile, John Huston's script and direction captured the mood of Crane's novel, although its tenuous story suffered when disastrous sneak previews cued severe cutting. Producer Gottfried Reinhardt desperately added narration (spoken by James Whitmore) to explain the action, but movie fans still couldn't get the hang of it and it failed to recover its $1.6m cost. Audie Murphy, the mild-mannered youth who won more World War II medals than any other soldier, ably led the cast: Bill Mauldin, Douglas Dick, John Dierkes, Royal Dano, Arthur Hunnicutt, Andy Devine.*

Dorothy McGuire, Elizabeth Taylor, Fred MacMurray and Howard Keel in **Callaway Went Thataway**/The Star Said No, a funny dig in Hollywood's ribs by Norman Panama and Melvin Frank. They wrote, produced and directed the popular comedy about a cowboy taking the place of a wayward movie star; Keel played both roles. Liz, Clark Gable and Esther Williams appeared as themselves.

It's a Big Country an ambitious project was in production most of 1950 and 1951. Schary marshalled an army of writers to celebrate the American way of life in nine separate episodes. By the time the film was released, seven had survived (six in Britain) but the movie itself died at the paybox. This montage shows, from California eastward: Marjorie Main and Keefe Brasselle (director, Don Weis); Bobby Hyatt, Nancy Davis, Fredric March and Angela Clarke (d., Don Hartman) S. Z. Sakall, Janet Leigh and Gene Kelly (d., Charles Vidor) Gary Cooper (d., Clarence Brown); Keenan Wynn, Ethel Barrymore and George Murphy (d., John Sturges); William Powell and James Whitmore (d., Richard Thorpe); Van Johnson, Lewis Stone (d., William Wellman). Robert Sisk produced.

The teaming of new MGM stars Pier Angeli and Stewart Granger interested the public more than the mild art-racket plot of **The Light Touch**. Not enough, however, to make it a hit. Pier confirmed the appeal of her Teresa debut but was handicapped by a toneless speaking voice. Richard Brooks, then better known as writer than director, was both for this Pandro Berman production featuring George Sanders, Kurt Kasznar, Joseph Calleia, Larry Keating, Rhys Williams, Norman Lloyd, Mike Mazurki.

After the success of Battleground Schary gave Robert Pirosh the nod to direct as well as write another war movie. Van Johnson (here with Don Haggerty) again starred in **Go For Broke!** but its appeal was a bit special, since it dealt with American soldiers of Japanese descent, played mostly by ditto actors. Good returns, nevertheless. Warner Anderson and Gianna Maria Canale added Occidental interest.

A truly affecting performance by Dorothy McGuire distinguished **Invitation**, a Jerome Weidman story scripted by Paul Osborn, based on the soap-opera situation of a rich father secretly bribing a young man to marry his daughter who had only a year to live. Love dawned after the marriage, then she found out The Truth, and – oh heavens, the agony of it all . . . Van Johnson as hired husband and Louis Calhern as fond father helped to upholster its mechanical framework; so did Gottfried Reinhardt, thankfully directing again after his Red Badge production pangs; so did producer Lawrence Weingarten and performers Ruth Roman, Ray Collins, Michael Chekhov, Barbara Ruick, Matt Moore. The piano theme by Bronislau Kaper became popular, as did the movie.

Shadow in the Sky was a quickie, but it had real force as written by the brilliant, little-known Ben Maddow, directed by Fred Wilcox, produced by William Wright and acted by (left to right) James Whitmore, Nancy Davis and Ralph Meeker. The latter vividly played a war-shocked veteran disrupting the lives of relatives giving him a home. Jean Hagen also scored as his girl, with Gladys Hurlbut, Eduard Franz, John Lupton and Jonathan Cott in minor roles. Based on a story, by Edward Newhouse.

Just This Once, with Peter Lawford, Janet Leigh and Richard Anderson, reflected the zest of young director Don Weis. Lewis Stone, Marilyn Erskine, Douglas Fowley and Benny Rubin joined them in Sidney Sheldon's screenplay, from Max Trell's story of a spendthrift millionaire tamed by a girl. Henry Berman produced.

June Allyson and Van Johnson weren't the fan raves they'd been in the Forties, but **Too Young to Kiss** turned a nice profit and pleased all but the most critical. Robert Z. Leonard and Sam Zimbalist respectively directed and produced the Frances Goodrich–Albert Hackett screenplay from Everett Freeman's comedy about a pianist pretending to be a child prodigy. Also cast: Gig Young, Paula Corday, Kathryn Givney, Larry Keating, Hans Conreid and Esther Dale.

Low-budget 'B's were back in fashion at Culver City, where ace film editor Harold Kress was promoted to director of two of them. Lassie's last MGM bark was heard in **The Painted Hills** with Gary Gray (here), Paul Kelly, Bruce Cowling, Art Smith and Ann Doran; animal movie specialist Chester Franklin produced; script by True Boardman from Alexander Hall's novel. . . Kress moved indoors for **No Questions Asked**, an insurance racket story by Berne Giler, scripted by Sidney Sheldon, produced by Nicholas Nayfack, with (left to right) Richard Anderson, Jean Hagen and Barry Sullivan; also cast were Arlene Dahl, George Murphy, Moroni Olsen, Mari Blanchard, Dick Simmons.

The none too exciting lives and loves of university teachers made for low-pressure drama in **Night Into Morning** with (left to right) Nancy Davis, Ray Milland, John Hodiak and Lewis Stone; also cast were Jean Hagen, Dawn Addams (debut), Rosemary DeCamp, Jonathan Cott, Celia Lovsky. Edwin Knopf produced and Fletcher Markle directed the Karl Tunberg–Leonard Spigelgass screenplay. . .

Metro's signing Ezio Pinza, the opera singer who scored a Broadway triumph in South Pacific, was considered quite a coup, but his charisma didn't come through on celluloid. **Mr Imperium**/You Belong to My Heart was another mistake by Knopf, who not only produced but wrote the lame tale of a movie star in love with a king in exile. Don Hartman directed and collaborated on the screenplay, colourless even in Technicolor. Left to right: Pinza, Lana Turner, Marjorie Main, Debbie Reynolds. Also cast: Barry Sullivan, Sir Cedric Hardwicke, Ann Codee.

Ezio Pinza made **Strictly Dishonourable** after Mr Imperium but it was released first to give him a better start with the film public, who didn't respond to either. As that poster disclosed, the movie was set in the Twenties, the original period of Preston Sturges' stage hit, previously filmed by Universal in 1931. Now Janet Leigh played the little Southern gal infatuated with a Broadway star, scripted into an opera singer to fit Pinza. Produced, directed and scripted by Norman Panama and Melvin Frank, with Millard Mitchell, Gale Robbins, Maria Palmer, Arthur Franz.

An off-form director, William Wellman, took Clark Gable, Technicolor cameras and a plotless Talbot Jennings script on an expensive location jaunt to Colorado, for **Across the Wide Missouri**. Like Red Badge of Courage, it suffered stringent cutting after dire preview reports. Schary, it seemed, lacked the Thalberg knack for resuscitating ailing 'A's. Adolphe Menjou (here with Gable), Ricardo Montalban, John Hodiak, Maria Elena Marques, J. Carrol Naish, Jack Holt, Alan Napier, Richard Anderson, Douglas Fowley, Russell Simpson and Frankie Darro were assorted trappers, soldiers and Indian types in the Robert Sisk production.

Texas Carnival re-teamed Esther Williams and Howard Keel to excellent box-office effect, helped by Red Skelton, Ann Miller, Keenan Wynn, Paula Raymond, Tom Tully, Glenn Strange, Donald MacBride, Hans Conreid, Thurston Hall and the Red Norvo Trio. Charles Walters kept the Jack Cummings production moving fast, giving more footage to the gags and numbers than to the George Wells–Dorothy Kingsley plot.

The busy Kingsley-Wells typewriters also disgorged **Angels in the Outfield**/Angels and The Pirates, a weird mixture of baseball and religious fantasy, unaccountably directed and produced by the distinguished Clarence Brown. No hits, no runs. Left to right: Paul Douglas, Donna Corcoran, Spring Byington, Keenan Wynn; also cast were Janet Leigh, Lewis Stone, Bruce Bennett, Ellen Corby, Marvin Kaplan, Jeff Richards, John Gallaudet.

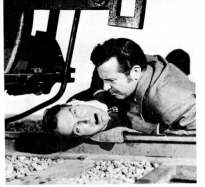

The Tall Target was Abraham Lincoln. Dick Powell played a detective searching for his would-be assassin, Leif Erickson (left) a baddie who couldn't foil our Dick. An offbeat thriller staged in and around a train, written by George Worthington Yates, Geoffrey Homes and Art Cohn and well directed by Anthony Mann. Producer, Richard Goldstone; cast, Paula Raymond, Adolphe Menjou, Marshall Thompson, Ruby Dee, Richard Rober, Will Geer, Florence Bates, Victor Kilian, Regis Toomey, Tom Powers, Jeff Richards.

Mercedes McCambridge, never one to underact, registered hate for David Brian in **Inside Straight** with Barry Sullivan bystanding. The gambling melodrama by Guy Trosper was directed by Gerald Mayer (L. B.'s nephew), produced by Richard Goldstone, with Arlene Dahl, Lon Chaney Jr, Claude Jarman Jr, Paula Raymond, John Hoyt, Monica Lewis, Roland Winters . . . In **Bannerline** Lewis Stone was the editor, Keefe Brasselle the cub reporter. Newcomer Don Weis directed and Henry Berman (Pandro's brother) produced the Charles Schnee screenplay from Samson Raphaelson's original, with Lionel Barrymore, Sally Forrest, J. Carrol Naish, Spring Byington, Larry Keating, Warner Anderson.

Rich, Young and Pretty, with (here) Marcel Dalio, Una Merkel, Fernando Lamas, Danielle Darrieux, Vic Damone, Jane Powell and Wendell Corey, was a modestly entertaining and profitable musical from the Joe Pasternak–Norman Taurog team. The story by Dorothy Cooper and Sidney Sheldon was the usual mingled romances of Jane and parent (Corey this time), which were set in Paris and interrupted by ten songs. Lamas, a star in his native Argentina, and Damone, a popular Sinatra-style singer, were starting long-term MGM contracts. Also cast: Richard Anderson, Jean Murat, Hans Conreid.

*Mysterious doings in 19th-century New York involved Barbara Stanwyck, Leslie Caron and Joseph Cotten in a flop, **The Man with a Cloak**. Much was made of the secret identity of Cotten's hero character, revealed at the end of the movie to be Edgar Allan Poe. Since this had nothing whatever to do with the story, audiences were left flummoxed. Frank Fenton's script, from a John Dickson Carr yarn, and Fletcher Markle's direction lacked tension. Stephen Ames produced, casting Louis Calhern, Joe de Santis, Jim Backus, Margaret Wycherly, Nicholas Joy, Roy Roberts, Mitchell Lewis.*

*The MGM British studio descended to an unpretentious 'B' with **Calling Bulldog Drummond**, the 22nd movie in 30 years about 'Sapper's' amateur detective, now played by Walter Pidgeon with Margaret Leighton as his unlikely Scotland Yard aide. Victor Saville's cast in the Hayes Goetz production included Robert Beatty, David Tomlinson, Peggy Evans, Charles Victor, Bernard Lee and James Hayter. Script by Howard Emmett Rogers, Gerard Fairlie and Arthur Wimperis from a Fairlie original.*

The People Against O'Hara *was a potboiler for MGM and Spencer Tracy, and Tracy's only film with Pat O'Brien, close friend for decades. Left to right: O'Brien, Tracy, John Hodiak and Yvette Duguay playing policeman, defender, DA and witness in a New York murder trial. Diana Lynn, Eduardo Ciannelli, Richard Anderson, Jay C. Flippen, Regis Toomey, James Arness (as O'Hara), William Campbell, Ann Doran, Henry O'Neill, Arthur Shields, Donald Dillaway, Emile Meyer and Jeff Richards filled John Sturges' cast in the William Wright production, written by John Monks Jr from Eleazar Lipsky's novel.*

*Greer Garson's box-office prestige wilted in **The Law and the Lady**, a third-hand vehicle that had served Norma Shearer and Joan Crawford: it was an awkward revision of Lonsdale's The Last of Mrs Cheyney, produced and directed by Edwin Knopf, whose year this definitely wasn't Left to right: Phyllis Stanley, Michael Wilding, Miss Garson and again Wilding—who, like the other top British movie male of the Forties, Stewart Granger, had just been brought to Hollywood by MGM; his double debut excited nobody. Also cast: Fernando Lamas, Marjorie Main, Hayden Rorke, Margalo Gillmore, Rhys Williams, Natalie Schafer. Rewriters: Leonard Spigelgass, Karl Tunberg.*

*Maurice Evans, Betsy Blair, Ethel Barrymore, Keenan Wynn and Angela Lansbury in **Kind Lady**, a classy remake of the nerve-twister MGM filmed in 1935. Edward Chodorov, who wrote the original play from a Hugh Walpole story, collaborated with Jerry Davis and Charles Bennett on the script which was directed with a keen sense of suspense by John Sturges. Armand Deutsch produced, casting John Williams, Doris Lloyd, Henri Letondal, Moyna MacGill (Angela's mother) and Phyllis Morris.*

*Mickey Rooney came back to MGM after a three-year absence for **The Strip**, and the company made a nice profit on a low (for a semi-musical) budget. He was supported by William Demarest, Sally Forrest and James Craig. The title referred to Hollywood Boulevard's nightlife section. Allen Rivkin's melodramatic story was produced by Joe Pasternak with cabaret spots for Vic Damone, Monica Lewis, and Louis Armstrong's band featuring Jack Teagarden, Earl 'Fatha' Hines and Barney Bigard; Mickey joined them on drums. Leslie Kardos directed, with Kay Brown, Tommy Rettig, Tom Powers, Jonathan Cott, Myrna Dell cast.*

*Colossal **Quo Vadis**—the adjective was part of the billing—generated the greatest cash flow into MGM's coffers since Gone With The Wind, its world-wide rentals exceeding $25m. Despite old Ben Hur disasters, the company chose to make it in Rome, where the new Cinecitta studio offered cheap facilities, not least in extras: 5,500 were used in this sequence, the triumphal march to Nero's palace: right, as director Mervyn LeRoy (white hat) saw it; above, as from the camera tower in right back-*

ground. LeRoy and producer Sam Zimbalist did well to bring the Technicolor super-spectacle in for $7m. in six months' shooting in 1950, followed by 1951 editing, scoring and tidying up at MGM British and Culver City. Robert Taylor, Deborah Kerr, Peter Ustinov and Leo Genn starred, with Patricia Laffan, Finlay Currie, Abraham Sofaer, Marina Berti, Buddy Baer, Felix Aylmer, Nora Swinburne, Norman Wooland, Rosalie Crutchley, 20 lions to eat Christians and two cheetahs to flank Miss Laffan's Poppaea. The script from Henryk Sienkiewicz's novel (filmed silent three times) by John Lee Mahin, S. N. Behrman and Sonya Levien was straight movie drama, representing a victory for Mayer, who ironically was fired before it reached the screen. Schary had wanted it to take a political slant, equating Nero with modern dictators; a false start had been made on it in 1949, also in Rome, John Huston directing, Arthur Hornblow producing, with Gregory Peck and Elizabeth Taylor.

The Belle of New York *had a famous title once listed for Judy Garland. She might have pepped up this perfunctory version of the old Hugh Morton play (script, Robert O'Brien, Irving Elinson), new but hitless songs by Harry Warren and Johnny Mercer. More was expected from the talents of Fred Astaire and Vera-Ellen (here dancing in the clouds), and those of producer Arthur Freed, director Charles Walters, and Marjorie Main, Keenan Wynn, Alice Pearce, Clinton Sundberg, Gale Robbins.*

An operatic musical, **The Great Caruso**, surprised many showmen by becoming an absolute smash hit, thanks chiefly to the rapidly developing Mario Lanza furore. The real Caruso's widow, Dorothy, wrote the biographical framework ornamented by the Sonya Levien–William Ludwig screenplay. It was the singingest movie ever made, featuring no fewer than 27 vocal items, most of them sung by Lanza with tremendous brio. In nine operatic scenes he was joined by Metropolitan stars Dorothy Kirsten, Blanche Thebom, Jarmila Novotna (with him here), Giuseppe Valdengo and others. The Pasternak production even yielded a pop hit, 'The Loveliest Night of the Year', sung by Ann Blyth as Caruso's wife. Richard Thorpe directed in showmanly style. In the cast: Carl Benton Reid, Eduard Franz, Ludwig Donath, Richard Hageman, Alan Napier. Douglas Shearer's sound department won an Oscar for its recording quality.

Larry Parks, a big name since portraying Al Jolson in two film biographies, starred for the last time in **Love is Better than Ever**/The Light Fantastic *opposite Elizabeth Taylor. He was then engulfed in the miasma of the McCarthy anti-Red hearings. Not much more was heard of the movie, either; a frail comedy about a dancing school, written by Ruth Brooks Flippen, directed by Stanley Donen, produced by William Wright. Also cast: Josephine Hutchinson, Tom Tully, Ann Doran, Kathleen Freeman.*

Universally acclaimed as the company's great artistic triumph of 1951, **An American in Paris** *brought the musical movie to an imaginative peak, especially in the 18-minute ballet (its 'Toulouse-Lautrec' sequence is seen here) danced by Gene Kelly and Leslie Caron. Show Boat outgrossed it as the year's most popular musical, but it brought MGM back into the Academy Award class with a bang, winning eight Oscars: best film; best story and screenplay, Alan Jay Lerner; best scoring, Johnny Green, Saul Chaplin; best art direction, Cedric Gibbons, Preston Ames, Edwin B. Willis, Keogh Gleason; best cinematography, Alfred Gilles; best costume design, Orry-Kelly, Walter Plunkett, Irene Sharaff; Thalberg Memorial Award, producer Arthur Freed; special award for choreography, Gene Kelly. The last deserved another two for his performance and his discovery of Mlle Caron in the Ballets des Champs Elysées–a new star for Metro. Vincente Minnelli's cast had only three other principals: pianist-comedian Oscar Levant, French singer Georges Guetary and the superb Nina Foch. The score was a Gershwin feast, ranging from one of George and Ira's earliest songs, 'I'll Build a Stairway to Paradise' (1922) to their last, 'Love is Here to Stay' (1937) and including 20 other numbers sung or played, plus the Concerto in F (third movement) and the title suite, which was first staged in Ziegfeld's 'Show Girl' 1929).*

A musical that always does business: **Show Boat**, *this time starring (left to right) Kathryn Grayson, Joe E. Brown and Howard Keel, with Agnes Moorehead, Marge and Gower Champion glimpsed in the background. Ava Gardner co-starred in the 'Julie' role intended for Judy Garland, and Robert Sterling, Adele Jergens, Leif Erickson, William Warfield (singing 'Ol' Man River') and Regis Toomey supported. George Sidney directed and Arthur Freed produced this handsome and hugely profitable version of Edna Ferber's goldmine, originally a best-selling novel, then a 1927*

Ziegfeld show on Broadway, then filmed twice by Universal in 1929 (mostly silent) and 1936, and revived repeatedly on New York and London stages. Jerome Kern's music, one of the best show scores ever, drew fine performances from Keel and Grayson on 'Make Believe', 'Why Do I Love You?' and 'You Are Love', while Gardner was voice-dubbed for 'Bill' and 'Cant' Help Lovin' That Man'. New songs he composed for the 1936 film were omitted, but included was 'After the Ball', which strangely is always interpolated as one of the big climactic numbers in the otherwise all-Kern score. Script: John Lee Mahin.

Excuse My Dust, *a nice little musical about a dizzy inventor of an 1895 horseless carriage, gave Red Skelton a less slapsticky role than usual, and a new girl in Sally Forrest. Script was by George Wells; director Roy Rowland; producer Jack Cummings. Macdonald Carey, Monica Lewis, Raymond Walburn (right), Jane Darwell, Lillian Bronson, Guy Anderson and Paul Harvey were cast. Arthur Schwartz and Dorothy Fields did the songs, Hermes Pan the dances, and exhibitors the no-business.*

Crime drama stalwart of the year was Walter Pidgeon, who returned to Culver City after Bulldog Drummond for two more double-feature melos. **The Sellout** *featured John Hodiak, Audrey Totter and Karl Malden (left to right) with Pidgeon as a corruption-fighting newspaper editor. Paula Raymond, Cameron Mitchell, Thomas Gomez and Everett Sloane were also in the Nicholas Nayfack–Matthew Rapf production, directed by Gerald Mayer, written by Charles Palmer from Rapf's original . . .* **The Unknown Man** *had Pidgeon as a murder trial lawyer, supported by Dawn Addams, Richard Anderson and Ann Harding (with him here) and Barry Sullivan, Keefe Brasselle, Lewis Stone, Eduard Franz, Philip Ober and Mari Blanchard. Veteran Richard Thorpe directed and newcomer Robert Thomsen produced the Ronald Millar–George Froeschel screenplay.*

247

SINGIN' IN THE RAIN
1952

This is Cinerama, with its curved picture six times the normal size, opened to great acclaim. It was the television-nagged industry's first film since sound to revive public enthusiasm via innovation, although a limited one.

Conventional screens were faring best with the super-hokum of *The Greatest Show on Earth,* so ably made by Cecil B. DeMille that it won the best film Oscar. The critics, more aware of art than box office, preferred Fred Zinnemann's *High Noon,* which did get an Academy prize for Gary Cooper. Jennifer Jones and Laurence Olivier in *Carrie,* Fredric March in *Death of a Salesman,* Burt Lancaster and Shirley Booth (Academy Award) in *Come Back, Little Sheba* were worthy but lugubrious. Cheerfulness broke in with John Wayne in Ford's *The Quiet Man,* Alec Guinness in *The Lavender Hill Mob,* Michael Redgrave in *The Importance of Being Earnest,* and Chaplin's *Limelight,* his last Hollywood movie.

A lower ratio of MGM hits dropped Loew's profits $3m below 1951, the least since 1933.

◁ *No 1952 blues while Gene Kelly and Debbie Reynolds were* **Singin' in the Rain**. *It made a star of Debbie and was the third of the really superlative musicals Kelly made for Arthur Freed; many rate it even higher than* On the Town *and* American in Paris. *It made more money, and it had more laughs, with its only slightly exaggerated picture of the studios' silents-into-talkies panic of the late Twenties, enhanced by nostalgic tunes from the Freed–Brown catalogue: the title song, 'You Were Meant for Me', 'All I Do is Dream of You', a 'Broadway Melody' ballet danced excitingly by Kelly and Cyd Charisse, plus some new ones. Like* On the Town, *it was written by Adolph Green and Betty Comden, directed by Kelly and Stanley Donen, photographed by Harold Rosson. It won applause for Donald O'Connor's clowning and dancing, and raves for Jean Hagen's wildly funny caricature of a dumb movie queen. Also cast: Millard Mitchell, Rita Moreno, Douglas Fowley, Madge Blake.*

Debbie Reynolds and Donald O'Connor (right) carried their Singin' in the Rain *ebullience into* **I Love Melvin**, *a smaller musical but large in entertainment value, and a tidy profit-maker. Don Weis directed them and Una Merkel, Allyn Joslyn, Noreen Corcoran, Richard Anderson, Jim Backus and Barbara Ruick in the George Wells production. Robert Taylor popped up in a dream sequence when Debbie sang the brilliant 'A Lady Loves' number staged, like the others, by Robert Alton. Wells scripted Laslo Vadnay's story.*

MGM filmed **The Merry Widow** *a third time, and starred Lana Turner and Fernando Lamas, directed by Curtis Bernhardt, produced by Joe Pasternak. It was once too often. No top notes at the paybox as Lehar's music played third fiddle to Technicolor glamour and the laborious sophistication of a new script by Sonya Levien and William Ludwig. Just as she had in 1934, Una Merkel led the supporting cast, now including Richard Haydn, Thomas Gomez, John Abbott, Marcel Dalio and Robert Coote.*

Skirts Ahoy!, *with Joan Evans, Vivian Blaine and Esther Williams (here) was a sex change on the customary three-sailors musical. Otherwise no surprises. But look, Gene—Esther could do her ballet under water! Isobel Lennart wrote, Sidney Lanfield directed, Joe Pasternak produced; with Barry Sullivan, Keefe Brasselle, Dean Miller, Margalo Gillmore, Jeff Donnell, Thurston Hall, and specialties by Billy Eckstine, the DeMarco Sisters, Debbie Reynolds, Bobby Van, Keenan Wynn.*

Lots of talent in **Lovely to Look At**: *Ann Miller, Zsa Zsa Gabor, Red Skelton (seated); Kurt Kasznar, Kathryn Grayson, Howard Keel, Marge and Gower Champion (standing). Two fine singers, three great dancers, a top comedian, a good character actor and an international blonde—what more could you want? Add Jerome Kern songs ('Smoke Gets in Your Eyes', 'I Won't Dance', 'Yesterdays', 'The Touch of Your Hand', 'You're Devastating', 'Lovely to Look At', etc), smooth Mervyn LeRoy direction, posh Jack Cummings production and you've got a hit. George Wells and Harry Ruby rewrote* Roberta *which was first filmed by RKO in 1934 from the Broadway show based on Alice Duer Miller's novel.*

Supporting spots in Show Boat *and* Lovely to Look At *won Marge and Gower Champion a musical of their own.* **Everything I Have is Yours**. *They practically played themselves, a brilliant, married dance team, and Dennis O'Keefe made a welcome return as their producer. Enjoyable entertainment for its none-too-crowded audiences. Robert Z. Leonard directed for writer-producer George Wells, with Monica Lewis, Dean Miller, Eduard Franz, John Gallaudet, Jonathan Cott cast.*

Jane Powell and a new talent, Bobby Van, scored in **Small Town Girl**, *a middling Pasternak musical much revised by Dorothy Cooper and Dorothy Kingsley from the 1936 Janet Gaynor movie. Farley Granger, Ann Miller, S. Z. Sakall, Robert Keith, Fay Wray, Billie Burke, Nat King Cole, Dean Miller and William Campbell took Leslie Kardos' direction, with numbers staged by Busby Berkeley.*

Plymouth Adventure *was supposed to be an epic of the 'Mayflower's' voyage to the New World, but the script sprang a leak. Helen Deutsch wrote it, from Ernest Gebler's novel. Spencer Tracy was only too convincing as the surly, contemptuous captain; audiences started wishing he'd fall overboard around Reel Three. But later it was Gene Tierney who did, leaving husband Leo Genn (right). They, Van Johnson, Dawn Addams, Lloyd Bridges, Barry Jones, John Dehner, Lowell Gilmore, Rhys Williams, Kathleen Lockhart, John Dierkes and Paul Cavanagh made quite a cast, and producer Dore Schary gave Clarence Brown quite a budget to work on. Pity.*

Surgeon and nurse were at it again in **Battle Circus.** *You had to read the credits twice to believe that this soggy romance in a Korean M.A.S.H. unit was scripted and directed by Richard Brooks and produced by the prestigious Pandro Berman. You knew it couldn't be a 'B' quickie, because up there on the screen were big stars, Humphrey Bogart and June Allyson, trying to breathe some life into it. Others cast: Keenan Wynn, Robert Keith, William Campbell, Patricia Tiernan, Jonathan Cott, Philip Ahn, Steve Forrest, Jeff Richards. Allen Rivkin and Laura Kerr wrote the 'original'.*

The last Tracy-Hepburn picture at MGM was one of their best. Written for them by Ruth Gordon and Garson Kanin, **Pat and Mike** *had Spencer as a shady sports promoter and Kate as his whiz-bang tennis and golf protégée, with Aldo Ray (right) as his bone-head boxer. Director George Cukor and producer Lawrence Weingarten gave it everything needed for a comedy winner, including a good cast: William Ching, Sammy White, Phyllis Povah, Loring Smith, George Mathews, Charles Buchinski (later Bronson), Jim Backus, Chuck Connors (debut) and sports stars Alice Marble, Donald Budge, Gussie Moran, Frank Parker, Babe Zaharias.*

Scaramouche *cut a fine dash, both in the person of Stewart Granger (in Ramon Novarro's 1923 role) and at the box-office. Janet Leigh (here sharing the happy-ending smiles) was one of his lady-loves, and Eleanor Parker the other; Mel Ferrer was his splendidly sword-swinging foe. They were supported by Henry Wilcoxon, Nina Foch, Richard Anderson, Lewis Stone (who was also in the original), Robert Coote, Elisabeth Risdon, Howard Freeman, John Dehner, John Litel. Carey Wilson supplied a Technicolorful production, briskly directed by George Sidney and much rewritten by Ronald Millar and George Froeschel from the old Rex Ingram version of Sabatini's story.*

Vittorio Gassman, a star MGM had just imported from Italy, with Nina Foch (left) and Yvonne de Carlo in **Sombrero.** *This complication of romantic dramas was directed by Norman Foster, written by him and Josefina Niggli from her novel, 'Mexican Village'. It was sleepy-time down south at the paybox, despite a strong cast that included Ricardo Montalban, Cyd Charisse, Walter Hampden, Kurt Kasznar, Rick Jason, Thomas Gomez and dancer Jose Greco. Produced in Technicolor by Jack Cummings.*

Glory Alley *was director Raoul Walsh's first at MGM for 17 years. Kurt Kasznar and Leslie Caron (foreground), Ralph Meeker, Gilbert Roland, John McIntire, Dick Simmons and Louis Armstrong in this drama set 'way down yonder in New Orleans and centred on a boxer (Meeker) and a honky-tonk dancer (Miss Caron). It didn't click. Written by Art Cohn, produced by Nicholas Nayfack.*

New Orleans also backgrounded the mingled dramas of four young people caught up by Mardi Gras fever in **Holiday for Sinners.** *Gig Young and Janice Rule (seen here), Richard Anderson and William Campbell did their best, aided by veterans Keenan Wynn, Edith Barrett, Michael Chekhov and Porter Hall and directed by Gerald Mayer, but it flopped harder than Glory Alley. 'Hush mah roar', said Leo, hurrying north. John Houseman produced the Hamilton Basso screenplay, from a story by A. I. Bezzerides.*

Director Mitchell Leisen and writer Arthur Sheekman moved over from Paramount to bring out Glenn Ford's unexpected skill as a light comedian in **Young Man With Ideas.** *Here shy businessman Ford's wife underestimates her alcoholic capacity in one of the many funny scenes in this Gottfried Reinhardt –William Wright programmer. Ruth Roman (the wife), Denise Darcel, Nina Foch, Donna Corcoran, Ray Collins, Mary Wickes, Sheldon Leonard supported.*

The acting phase of George Murphy's extraordinary career ended in 1952 after 15 MGM years. A Broadway hoofer in the Twenties, he became a politician in the sixties (after much experience of industry politics as Screen Actors Guild president, Academy vice-president and Metro's ambassador at large) and was elected as Senator from California—one up on Governor Ronald Reagan. The latter's wife, Nancy Davis, played Murphy's wife in **Talk About a Stranger** *with Billy Gray (here) as their son. This 'B'-minor drama about a family's mysterious neighbour was written by Margaret Fitts from Charlotte Armstrong's original, produced by Richard Goldstone, directed by David Bradley, and featured Kurt Kasznar and Lewis Stone.*

The success of Stratton Story *brought James Stewart another biographical drama,* **Carbine Williams,** *with Wendell Corey as the warden who couldn't stop his prisoner making the new kind of rifle he'd invented. Both actors impressed, and the Armand Deutsch production had a grim integrity, as directed by Richard Thorpe. Jean Hagen, Paul Stewart, Rhys Williams, Carl Benton Reid, James Arness, Porter Hall and Leif Erickson were also in the Art Cohn screenplay.*

The real theme of **Above and Beyond**—*the training of bomber crews for, and the execution of, the atom-bombing of Hiroshima—wasn't mentioned on the posters for box-office reasons ('The Love Story Behind the Billion Dollar Secret!' they promised). But the public soon knew, and takings were disappointing for this too-close history, powerfully depicted in the writing (with Beirne Lay), production and direction of Melvin Frank and Norman Panama. Robert Taylor and Eleanor Parker starred; James Whitmore, Larry Keating, Marilyn Erskine, Larry Gates, Stephen Dunne, Robert Burton, Jonathan Cott, Hayden Rorke, Jeff Richards, Dick Simmons, Barbara Ruick, Jim Backus supported.*

'Because You're Mine' *roared Mario Lanza's tenor above the blowing and bowing of the full MGM Studio Orchestra as flags of all nations unfurled. If you think that treatment of a tender ballad was absurd, you're reading the wrong book. Terrific audience response to such razzle-dazzle helped to shoot Nicholas Brodszky's and Sammy Cahn's song to the top of the hit parade and Joe Pasternak's movie to box-office riches. Karl Tunberg and Leonard Spigelgass provided enough script about an army-drafted opera star to fill in when Lanza or Doretta Morrow, a delightful Broadway soprano, weren't singing. Alexander Hall directed. Also cast: James Whitmore, Paula Corday, Jeff Donnell, Eduard Franz, Bobby Van, Spring Byington, Dean Miller.*

The Esther Williams of 1910-20 was Annette Kellerman, an Australian swimmer who became a movie star (she too made one called Neptune's Daughter) *and shocked even Hollywood with her contour-revealing swimsuits. Everett Freeman wrote a script about her, Arthur Hornblow Jr produced it, Mervyn LeRoy directed it:* **Million Dollar Mermaid**/ The One-Piece Bathing Suit, *starring guess who. Victor Mature (seen with Esther here), Walter Pidgeon, David Brian, Donna Corcoran, Jesse White, Maria Tallchief (as Pavlova) and Howard Freeman were in this paybox filler. The extra on the left was Creighton Hale, a leading man in Annette's era.*

The Prisoner of Zenda, *another remake of a Rex Ingram silent, was a follow-up to* Scaramouche, *and another hit. This time heroic Stewart Granger coped with dastardly James Mason. Between the 1922 original and this first Technicolor version, United Artists had nipped in with a 1937* Zenda. *Lewis Stone again bridged 30 years by appearing in first and latest editions; he was cast with Deborah Kerr, Louis Calhern, Jane Greer, Robert Douglas, Robert Coote and Francis Pierlot. Director, Richard Thorpe; producer, Pandro Berman; script, John Balderston, Noel Langley.*

The John Sturges–Armand Deutsch director-producer team passed the well-worn MGM scalpels to June Allyson and Gary Merrill (here) and Arthur Kennedy, Mildred Dunnock, Jesse White, Marilyn Erskine, Guy Anderson and James Arness for another probe into Gray's Anatomy of dramatic art, **The Girl in White**/So Bright the Flame. *But they muffed this operation by casting winsome June as a tough-minded career woman invading the man's world of slum hospital practice in 1902. Irmgard von Cube, Allen Vincent and Philip Stevenson wrote it from Emily Barringer's autobiographical 'Bowery to Bellevue'.*

Red Skelton's paybox draw had cooled off considerably, but he and Jane Greer gave touching performances as an alcoholic comedian and his divorced wife in **The Clown,** *under Robert Z. Leonard's direction. With their little son, Tim Considine, inspiring Dad to make a comeback, Martin Rackin's script carried a distinct whiff of old Wallace Beery sobbers. William H. Wright produced, casting Philip Ober, Loring Smith, Lou Lubin, Jonathan Cott, Don Beddoe, Steve Forrest.*

Lili *culminated in a ballet danced by Leslie Caron with the characters invented by the puppeteer she loved. This fantasy and the preceding fragile tale of French carnival folk might seem a perfect set-up for gooey entertainment and box-office failure. Credit these with the reverse: director Charles Walters, producer Edwin Knopf, writer Helen Deutsch (using Paul Gallico's story basis), the radiant Miss Caron with Mel Ferrer, Jean Pierre Aumont, Zsa Zsa Gabor, Kurt Kasznar, Amanda Blake. And its hugely popular theme song by Bronislau Kaper and Miss Deutsch, 'Hi Lili, Hi Lo'.*

Van Johnson was a congressman, Patricia Neal a reporter in **Washington Story**/Target for Scandal, *partly filmed in the US Capitol building and the Pentagon. Writer-director Robert Pirosh had delivered some exciting stuff to producer Schary before, but not this time. Also cast: Louis Calhern, Sidney Blackmer, Elizabeth Patterson, Philip Ober, Patricia Collinge, Reinhold Schunzel and Moroni Olsen.*

Sky Full of Moon *offered Carleton Carpenter as an ingenuous cowboy having a fling with Jan Sterling as a Las Vegas dame. Fair fun, written and directed by ex-actor Norman Foster, produced by Sidney Franklin Jr. Also cast: Keenan Wynn, Robert Burton, Elaine Stewart, Emmett Lynn, Douglass Dumbrille.*

Schary named Charles Schnee as supervisor of a new 'B' unit of seven young producers: Henry Berman, Sol Fielding, Sidney Franklin Jr, Hayes Goetz, William Grady Jr, Arthur Loew Jr and Matthew Rapf. The fact that all were relatives of MGM bigwigs caused many a merry quip over Hollywood cocktails. But their output hit a pretty high average. Berman's **You for Me** *had Peter Lawford again playing a gay (which meant happy in 1952) millionaire for director Don Weis as effectively as in* Just This Once. *Gig Young (left) and Jane Greer co-featured in the William Roberts screenplay,*

supported by Paula Corday, Barbara Ruick, Barbara Brown, Kathryn Card, Tommy Farrell . . . Howard Keel, the delightful Miss Greer again, Keenan Wynn and Dick Simmons in Rapf's **Desperate Search**, *a crashed-airline thriller scripted by Walter Doniger, directed by Joseph Lewis, with Lee Aaker, Robert Burton, Elaine Stewart, Jonathan Cott, Jeff Richards.*

Outstanding among the year's dramas, **The Bad and the Beautiful** *was a Hollywood story with an authentic look, showing the rise and fall of producer-director Kirk Douglas and the people he victimized: star Lana Turner, studio head Walter Pidgeon, writer Dick Powell and director Barry Sullivan. It picked up five Academy Awards: Gloria Grahame (best supporting actress), Charles Schnee (screenplay), Cedric Gibbons, Edward Carfagno, Edwin Willis, Keogh Gleason (art direction), Robert Surtees (photography) and Helen Rose (costume design). Director Vincente Minnelli and producer John Houseman had to be satisfied with press and public Oscars. Left to right: Turner, Kathleen Freeman, Leo G. Carroll, Pidgeon, Douglas; also cast were Gilbert Roland, Vanessa Brown, Paul Stewart, Sammy White, Elaine Stewart, Jonathan Cott, Ivan Triesault, Marietta Canty.*

Three quick thrillers: Two young English players developed by MGM in Hollywood were sent back home for **The Hour of 13**: *Peter Lawford and Dawn Addams. They played the Robert Montgomery and Elizabeth Allan roles in this modest remake of* Mystery of Mr X, *supported by Roland Culver, Derek Bond, Leslie Dwyer, Michael Hordern, Colin Gordon, Heather Thatcher, Jack McNaughton, Fabia Drake, Michael Goodliffe. Leon Gordon and Howard Emmett Rogers scripted for director Harold French and producer Hayes Goetz . . .*

Jeopardy *was wildly improbable, but Maurice Zimm's story was given so much suspense in Mel Dinelli's script, pace in John Sturges' direction and conviction in Barbara Stanwyck's and Ralph Meeker's acting that its 69 minutes stuck in the memory longer than some double-length epics. Barry Sullivan as Stanwyck's husband and Lee Aaker as their son completed the year's shortest cast in the Sol Fielding production . . .*

The built-in suspense of a ticking **Time Bomb** *served director Ted Tetzlaff and producer Richard Goldstone well in their MGM-British 'B' attraction (*Terror on a Train *in USA). Kem Bennett's script gave Glenn Ford and Maurice Denham fat acting parts bristling with urgency. Also cast: Anne Vernon, Harcourt Williams, Victor Maddern, Harold Warrender, Bill Fraser.*

Richard Greene and Peter Lawford in **Rogues March**, *an Eastern. No cowboys, but lots of Indians. Janice Rule, Leo G. Carroll, John Abbott, Patrick Aherne, Hayden Rorke, John Lupton, Michael Pate and Lester Matthews also acted for director Allan Davis. Written and produced by Leon Gordon.*

MGM at last broke through with its first British-made box-office smash since pre-war days with **Ivanhoe**. *Admittedly, it had to ▽ import four stars, producer and director from Hollywood: Robert Taylor, Elizabeth Taylor, Joan Fontaine and George Sanders; Pandro Berman and Richard Thorpe. But three of those were British-born. Not to mention Sir Walter Scott. Or adapter Aeneas MacKenzie, scripter Noel Langley, an army of technicians and a platoon of West End actors: Emlyn Williams, Finlay Currie, Felix Aylmer, Robert Douglas, Francis de Wolff, Norman Wooland, Basil Sydney, Harold Warrender, Patrick Holt, Guy Rolfe, etc. They all fell to with a will, stirring up a fine storm of Technicolored derring-do. Typical scene here: Taylor battling the wicked Sanders while Fontaine heroines helplessly.*

Van Johnson was one of Hollywood's busier actors: He was a genuine priest (right) and Paul Douglas a con-man on the run from San Quentin in **When in Rome**, a story of the 1950 pilgrimage to the Holy City. Masses on screen but not in theatres. Clarence Brown produced and directed, mainly in Italy, the Charles Schnee–Dorothy Kingsley screenplay from Robert Buckner's story, with Joseph Calleia, Tudor Owen, Carlo Rizzo, Mario Siletti, Argentina Brunetti, Emory Parnell.

The high cost of meat was, incredibly, the theme of **Confidentially Connie** with (left to right) Louis Calhern, Walter Slezak, Van Johnson and Janet Leigh, none of whom ever appeared in anything inaner. Marilyn Erskine, Gene and Kathleen Lockhart, Hayden Rorke, Barbara Ruick, Robert Burton and Arthur Space were others who could blame it on writers Max Shulman and Herman Wouk, director Edward Buzzell and producer Stephen Ames.

Carleton Carpenter got the best part in his too-brief movie career when producer Edwin Knopf and director Stanley Donen cast him as a circus employee who reported for army service with his pet lion—**Fearless Fagan**. A fresh, lively comedy, scripted by Charles Lederer from Frederick Hazlitt Brennan's adaptation of a story by Sidney Franklin Jr (associate producer) and Eldon Griffiths. Also cast: Janet Leigh, Keenan Wynn, Richard Anderson, Ellen Corby, Barbara Ruick.

My Man and I stood or fell on the charm of Ricardo Montalban, and he proved he wasn't just a pretty pair of pectorals. Claire Trevor played his employer's neglected wife who wanted to see more of this handyman; she was excellent as ever, if you could imagine anybody neglecting Claire. Montalban was more inter-

ested in a suicidal taxi-dancer—Shelley Winters in a third memorable performance, quite a score for a 'B' movie. Credit William Wellman, who directed the Stephen Ames production, written by John Fante and Jack Leonard. Wendell Corey and Jack Elam had good roles.

A strong thriller, **The Naked Spur** made a juicy profit for MGM. Here bounty hunter James Stewart keeps his cool while fugitive Ralph Meeker gives the heroine a hard time. Janet Leigh survived this and all the other trials of an action-packed Western trek, at the end of which only she and Stewart were left alive. Defunct were Meeker, Robert Ryan and Millard Mitchell. Writers, Sam Rolfe, Harold Jack Bloom; director, Anthony Mann; producer, William Wright.

Gene Kelly shelved his dancing shoes again for **The Devil Makes Three**, as a US serviceman returning to Germany and falling for Pier Angeli amid clouds of neo-Nazi intrigue. The Jerry Davis script from a Lawrence Bachmann story had suspense and a rousing chase climax; but the public never responded so well to the dramatic Kelly. Andrew Marton directed his stars, with Richard Egan, Richard Rober and a large German cast, in Munich, Salzburg and Berchtesgaden. Richard Goldstone produced.

Cowboys and/or Indians: Henry Morgan, Myron Healey, Robert Horton, Barbara Ruick, Patricia Tierman, Gene Lockhart, Glenda Farrell and Gilbert Roland in **Apache War Smoke**, a remake of Apache Trail, which had looked like a remake in the first place. Director, Harold Kress; producer, Hayes Goetz; writer, Jerry Davis, from Ernest Haycox' story . . .

253

1953

Marlon Brando was an unexpectedly accomplished Mark Antony in **Julius Caesar**. *A fine classical actor, syllable-perfect (coached by John Gielgud), had replaced mumblin' Marlon, and his fans helped to make it commercially viable. Left to right: Louis Calhern as Caesar, Brando, Greer Garson as Calpurnia and Deborah Kerr as Portia (behind them, Michael Patel, Alan Napier and John Hoyt) in John Houseman's clean-cut, forceful production of Shakespeare's drama. Director Joseph L. Mankiewicz took care to project the beauty of the language as clearly as the excitement of the plot, aided in this respect by Gielgud (Cassius) and James Mason (a magnificent Brutus). The Academy was less than generous with its Oscars, awarding only the art direction of Cedric Gibbons and Edward Carfagno. Among the vast cast were Edmond O'Brien, George Macready, Tom Powers, Ian Wolfe, Lumsden Hare, Morgan Farley, Douglas Watson, Rhys Williams, John Lupton, Douglass Dumbrille and Edmund Purdom.*

The success of Cinerama threw the industry into a frantic race to introduce technical developments for which theatres could more easily be adapted.
First off was the 3-D gimmick, which made a big winner of a claptrap melo, *Bwana Devil*, and an even bigger one of Warners' *House of Wax*. But this double-image process had lost most of its impact by the end of the year, when Fox's CinemaScope, first seen in *The Robe*, seemed set to stay. Presenting a mini-Cinerama effect, it made that Richard Burton–Jean Simmons starrer a smash, and was adopted by MGM, Columbia and Universal.

As good as Julius Caesar *in its very different way,* **The Band Wagon** *jumped close to the top* ▷ *of the Arthur Freed–Vincente Minnelli hit list, with Fred Astaire, Nanette Fabray and Jack Buchanan (here in the hilarious 'Triplets' number which Buchanan did before in another of his rare American vehicles, a 1937 Broadway show), Cyd Charisse, Oscar Levant and James Mitchell. They had a witty Betty Comden–Adolph Green script to work on, and great Schwartz–Dietz songs from the Thirties like 'Louisiana Hayride', 'I Guess I'll Have to Change My Plan', 'Dancing in the Dark', 'A Shine on Your Shoes', 'By Myself', 'Something to Remember You By', 'I Love Louisa' and 'You and the Night and the Music', topped by a new audience-rouser, 'That's Entertainment'.*

Warners, seemingly confused, announced WarnerScope, then WarnerSuperScope, then subsided into CinemaScope. Stereophonic sound also became chic. Star-power took second place to gimmick-power and bewildered exhibitors sorted out Vistarama, VistaVision, Vectograph, Variascope, Vitascope, Todd-AO, AmpoVision, Bolix 3-D, Glamorama, Moropticon, Naturama, and 3-channel, 4-channel, Warnerphonic, Kinevox Stereo, and the MGM-sponsored Perspecta sound. But those exhibitors really went into shock when Arch Oboler, maker of *Bwana Devil*, foresaw for 1965 a space-type 3-D, eliminating the theatre entirely.

Following mid-1952 MGM studio conferences masterminded by Nicholas Schenck, economy cuts in production costs, salaries and personnel were imposed. As a result, the profit slide was checked, 1953 yielding about $4½m.

1953 *Despite budget problems, MGM's big pictures seemed as star-spangled as ever.* **The Story of Three Loves** *comprised a trio of loosely linked tales lushly produced in Technicolor by Sidney Franklin, written by John Collier, Jan Lustig and George Froeschel. It had Moira Shearer and James Mason (below), directed by Gottfried Reinhardt; Leslie Caron and Farley Granger (lower right), directed by Vincente Minnelli; and Pier Angeli and Kirk Douglas (lower left) – Reinhardt again. Ethel Barrymore, Agnes Moorehead, Ricky Nelson, Zsa Zsa Gabor and Richard Anderson were in the casts, but not enough people in the audiences.*

Clark Gable's last really big winner was **Mogambo***, a remake of a film he had originally starred in: Red Dust. He was 21 years older but still throwing male magnetism around, and Ava Gardner caught it and matched it with as much femaleness as Jean Harlow once did. Adding to its paybox potency was a cool new blonde the public took to at once: Grace Kelly. John Ford directed John Lee Mahin's screenplay, now set in Africa, and Sam Zimbalist produced, casting Donald Sinden, Philip Stainton, Eric Pohlmann, Dennis O'Dea (here with the stars) and Laurence Naismith.*

Goodrich and Hackett also scripted **Give a Girl a Break** *from Vera Caspary's comedy. Left to right: Kurt Kasznar, Gower Champion, Bob Fosse, Debbie Reynolds and Lurene Tuttle. Champion was to later become a brilliant director of stage musicals; Fosse ditto, for the screen as well. The story of three girls vying for Broadway stardom – Debbie, Marge Champion and Helen Wood – was produced by Jack Cummings and trimmed with Burton Lane – Ira Gershwin songs. Stanley Donen's direction had zip.*

Passions are unleashed in **The Girl Who Had Everything***, a rewrite by Art Cohn of A Free Soul with Elizabeth Taylor, Fernando Lamas and William Powell in the roles played in 1931 by Norma Shearer, Clark Gable and Lionel Barrymore. While competently made by director Richard Thorpe and producer Armand Deutsch, it had none of the original's box-office impact. Gig Young, James Whitmore and Robert Burton completed the cast.*

MGM showed initiative in making a straight story about Negroes that was neither racial melodrama nor hot-stuff musical in **Bright Road***, although they were careful to choose beautiful people of a very light shade of black – Harry Belafonte and Dorothy Dandridge – as the stars. Philip Hepburn played the problem pupil motivating Emmet Lavery's script, from a novel by Mary Vroman, and Robert Horton was the sole white cast member. Gerald Mayer directed, Sol Fielding produced.*

The writing was on the wall for Clark Gable: his **Never Let Me Go** *was given second billing to the 3-D shorts Metroscopix in many cities. He played an American reporter who wedded Russian ballet dancer Gene Tierney, until the Iron Curtain them did part. It then developed into a routine rescue and chase drama. Clarence Brown produced and Delmer Daves directed at MGM British, casting Richard Haydn, Bernard Miles, Belita, Kenneth More, Theodore Bikel, Karel Stepanek, Anna Valentina, Frederick Valk. The Ronald Millar – George Froeschel script was based on a novel by Roger Bax.*

Frances Goodrich and Albert Hackett adapted **The Long, Long Trailer** *from a best-seller by Clinton Twiss. It brought television's 'I Love Lucy' stars to the big screen and Lucille Ball and Desi Arnaz scored a massive total of laughs and box-office returns. Marjorie Main, Keenan Wynn, Gladys Hurlbut and Moroni Olsen supported; Vincente Minnelli kept the gags flowing smoothly; Pandro Berman produced.*

Tony Martin croons to Esther Williams as they float through Florida's Cypress Gardens in **Easy to Love***. She was soon over the side, to be joined by phalanxes of Busby Berkeley's swimming and water-skiing guys and dolls in Pasternak splendour. Van Johnson augmented its strong paybox pull, John Bromfield was featured, Carroll Baker made her debut, and Charles Walters directed them in the Laslo Vadnay – William Roberts screenplay.*

Steve Forrest, Richard Widmark, Maurice Jara and William Hairston in **Take the High Ground**, another army movie from producer Schary. Directed by Richard Brooks, Millard Kaufman's screenplay centred on Widmark as a tough training sergeant; rival Karl Malden vied for Elaine Stewart, while square-bashers. Carleton Carpenter, Russ Tamblyn, Jerome Courtland and Robert Arthur sweated it out in AnscoColor. Business good.

Young Bess was scheduled for London production, but its almost all-British cast eventually performed at Culver City, and a fine job they and director George Sidney made of it. Margaret Irwin's novel of Tudor skullduggery provided rich script material for Jan Lustig and Arthur Wimperis, and Sidney Franklin's Technicolor production looked a treat. Jean Simmons and Stewart Granger, here as the young Elizabeth and Thomas Seymour, had no trouble with their love scenes, being Mr and Mrs offscreen; while Charles Laughton played a rousing reprise of his Henry VIII from memory. Also cast in this crowd-pleaser: Deborah Kerr, Guy Rolfe, Kay Walsh, Cecil Kellaway, Kathleen Byron, Rex Thompson (remarkable as the boy king Edward), Leo G. Carroll, Robert Arthur, Norma Varden, Alan Napier, Noreen Corcoran, Ivan Triesault, Elaine Stewart, Dawn Addams, Doris Lloyd, Lumsden Hare, Lester Matthews.

Bobby Van, Bob Fosse, Barbara Ruick and Debbie Reynolds injected loads of youthful vitality and talent into **The Affairs of Dobie Gillis**. Songs and dances peppered Max Shulman's college comedy, directed by Don Weis and produced by Arthur Loew Jr. Also cast: Hans Conreid, Hanley Stafford, Lurene Tuttle, Charles Lane, and Kathleen Freeman memorably leading a matronly swing group called Happy Stella Kowalski and Her Schottische Five.

The big gimmick of **Main Street to Broadway** was 'in person' appearances by Tallulah Bankhead, Ethel and Lionel Barrymore (his last film, although MGM kept him on salary until his death in 1954), Shirley Booth, Louis Calhern, Faye Emerson, Oscar Hammerstein II, Richard Rodgers, Rex Harrison, Lilli Palmer, Mary Martin, etc. Miss Bankhead, right, played herself (always a marvellous part), with Agnes Moorehead as one of the few fictional characters in Lester Cowan's production. Tom Morton, Mary Murphy, Rosemary DeCamp and Clinton Sundberg were others directed by Tay Garnett in a remarkably feeble story to be penned by Robert E. Sherwood and Samson Raphaelson.

While Mogambo was mopping up at the box-office, another old faithful emerged from the files: **All The Brothers Were Valiant**, filmed before in 1922 and 1928. Not even the modern acting styles of Stewart Granger and Robert Taylor could disguise its aged hokum; director Richard Thorpe and scripter Harry Brown didn't try to. Maybe they were right; it made money again. Ann Blyth, Betta St. John, Keenan Wynn, James Whitmore, Lewis Stone (his last film; MGM's father figure died at 74), Kurt Kasznar, Robert Burton, Jonathan Cott, John Lupton, Mitchell Lewis, Peter Whitney and James Bell were in Pandro Berman's Technicolor production.

The combined brilliance of Spencer Tracy, director George Cukor, writer Ruth Gordon and producer Lawrence Weingarten again illuminated a fine film in **The Actress**. Jean Simmons did even better in the title role than in Young Bess, but the movie was a box-office disappointment. So much for artistry. Teresa Wright played Tracy's wife and Miss Simmons their daughter in a poignant, funny story of a stagestruck girl, adapted from Miss Gordon's autobiographical play, 'Years Ago'. It featured Anthony Perkins in his debut, Ian Wolfe, Mary Wickes and Kay Williams.

The Charles Schnee unit's sports department: Horse-racing—Polly Bergen, Nina Foch and Howard Keel in Henry Berman's **Fast Company**, scripted by William Roberts, directed by John Sturges, with Marjorie Main, Robert Burton, Horace MacMahon . . . Baseball—Jeff Richards, Edward G. Robinson and Vera-Ellen in Matthew Rapf's **Big Leaguer**, scripted by Herbert Baker, directed by Robert Aldrich (his first), with William Campbell, Richard Jaeckel, Paul Langton. Both losers.

Jack Cummings snatched at Arthur Freed's laurels with a musical smash hit, **Kiss Me Kate**, which he produced in 3-D and flat versions. In the former, Ann Miller's gorgeous legs and so forth seemed to land in your lap, but this audition scene with Ron Randell (as Cole Porter), Kathryn Grayson and Howard Keel was just as effective when the three-dimension craze quickly passed. So was the whole show, directed by George Sidney and adapted by Dorothy Kingsley from the Samuel and Bella Spewack stage triumph. Porter's score, his best ever, dazzled and charmed as it set brilliant lyrics (some slightly bowdlerized for the film) to modern and (in the 'Taming of the Shrew' play within the play) Elizabethan rhythms. Among 14 songs, Ann's 'Too Darn Hot' (here) and 'Why Can't You Behave?', and the Grayson–Keel duets 'So in Love' and 'Wunderbar' became hits again; a previous Porter show-stopper, 'From This Moment On', was added for a breathtaking dance by Bob Fosse, Tommy Rall and Bobby Van. Also cast: Keenan Wynn, James Whitmore, Kurt Kasznar, Willard Parker, Claude Allister, Dave O'Brien, Ann Codee.

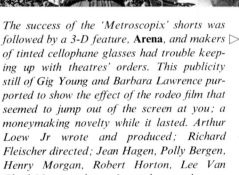

Action on the screen and at the box-office as Robert Taylor and Ava Gardner in **Ride, Vaquero** survived the machinations of big bad Anthony Quinn, Kurt Kasznar and Jack Elam. John Farrow directed Frank Fenton's screenplay in the great AnscoColored outdoors. Howard Keel co-starred; Stephen Ames produced.

MGM's first in CinemaScope was **Knights of the Round Table**, with (left to right) Robert Taylor as Lancelot, Ava Gardner as Guinevere, Anne Crawford, Stanley Baker and Mel Ferrer as King Arthur; also Felix Aylmer, Maureen Swanson, Gabriel Woolf, Anthony Forwood, Robert Urquhart and Niall McGinnis. Taylor, director Richard Thorpe, producer Pandro Berman, writer Noel Langley (with Talbot Jennings and Jan Lustig for this) and the British studio's technicians did an even better job on this spectacular adventure than they did on Ivanhoe the year before. A blockbuster.

Sliding deeper into debt the more his wife tried to keep up with the Joneses, Red Skelton was **Half a Hero**. Easygoing comedy, with Jean Hagen, little Hugh Corcoran and Charles Dingle (here) and Willard Waterman, Mary Wickes, Dorothy Patrick, Polly Bergen. Script, Max Shulman; director, Don Weis; producer, Matthew Rapf.

The success of the 'Metroscopix' shorts was followed by a 3-D feature, **Arena**, and makers of tinted cellophane glasses had trouble keeping up with theatres' orders. This publicity still of Gig Young and Barbara Lawrence purported to show the effect of the rodeo film that seemed to jump out of the screen at you; a moneymaking novelty while it lasted. Arthur Loew Jr wrote and produced; Richard Fleischer directed; Jean Hagen, Polly Bergen, Henry Morgan, Robert Horton, Lee Van Cleef, Morris Ankrum, Lee Aaker acted.

What does a cop like doing on his day off? Jeff Richards demonstrates in **Code Two** with Elaine Stewart. After many bit parts, they were given leads by producer William Grady Jr and director Fred Wilcox in Marcel Klauber's story of motorcycle police in training. Also featured: Ralph Meeker, Sally Forrest, James Craig, Keenan Wynn, Robert Horton, William Campbell, Robert Burton, Jonathan Cott.

Cry of the Hunted was one of the best pictures turned out by the Schnee 'B' unit. Here, after a gruelling chase and fight, policeman Barry Sullivan hauls escaped convict Vittorio Gassman from a Louisiana swamp. Jack Leonard's tense drama was directed by Joseph Lewis. William Grady Jr produced, casting Polly Bergen, William Conrad, Mary Zavian, Robert Burton, Harry Shannon, Jonathan Cott.

In **Torch Song** *Joan Crawford was back at MGM after ten years and still a very big name. It wasn't a very big picture though, according to the rental returns. As a Broadway star, Joan sang and danced (once in blackface, yet) and loved blind pianist Michael Wilding, who got some terrible parts at Metro. Writers John Michael Hayes and Jan Lustig bubbled sparkling dialogue into I. A. R. Wylie's soap-opera original, directed by Charles Walters, produced in Technicolor by Henry Berman and Sidney Franklin Jr. Also cast: Gig Young, Marjorie Rambeau, Henry Morgan, Dorothy Patrick, Paul Guilfoyle, Benny Rubin.*

Coveting the fortune June Allyson inherited from her murdered uncle, wicked Angela Lansbury guides her to a 19th-floor balcony while she sleepwalks. Before long, **Remains To Be Seen** *audiences were sleepsitting, despite bursts of music from June, Van Johnson and Dorothy Dandridge. Producer Arthur Hornblow, scribe Sidney Sheldon and director Don Weis made this quote comedy thriller unquote from a Howard Lindsay–Russell Crouse play. Also cast: Louis Calhern, John Beal, Barry Kelley, Sammy White, Kathryn Card, Helene Millard, Paul Harvey, Morgan Farley and Howard Freeman.*

Morocco was the location site for Mel Ferrer and Cornel Wilde in **Saadia,** *a strange mixture of desert love, bandit raids and witchcraft. Albert Lewin directed, scripted and produced in Technicolor, casting Rita Gam, Michel Simon, Cyril Cusack, Wanda Rotha, Richard Johnson. Not a box-office oasis in sight.*

Dangerous When Wet, *a bright Esther Williams musical, had her swimming the English Channel and romancing Fernando Lamas, who later became her off-screen husband. Producer George Wells added good Arthur Schwartz–Johnny Mercer songs, a Tom and Jerry underwater cartoon sequence and an enthusiastic cast: Jack Carson, Charlotte Greenwood (still high-kicking 22 years after her last MGM musical), Denise Darcel, William Demarest, Donna Corcoran. Charles Walters directed Dorothy Kingsley's screenplay.*

William Holden and Eleanor Parker succouring conked-out Richard Anderson in **Escape from Fort Bravo,** *a rousing tale of North versus South and Indians versus everybody. Frank Fenton wrote Nicholas Nayfack's Ansco-Colored production, directed by John Sturges. Also cast: John Forsythe, Polly Bergen, William Demarest, John Lupton, William Campbell and Carl Benton Reid. Profitable bookings everywhere.*

Not a whit deterred by the dull thud of The Merry Widow, Joe Pasternak starred Lana Turner in another semi-musical swooner, **Latin Lovers**, as a rich girl living it up in Rio. Ricardo Montalban co-tangoed; with Louis Calhern, John Lund, Jean Hagen, Beulah Bondi, Eduard Franz, Robert Burton and Rita Moreno. Mervyn LeRoy, who brought Lana with him to MGM 15 years before, directed as if regretting it. Script: Isobel Lennart.

Greer Garson and Walter Pidgeon reached their co-starring nadir with **Scandal at Scourie**, a tedious period piece about small-town politics, Catholic-Protestant antagonism and an adopted child. The latter gave Donna Corcoran the best part in the picture, indicating the failure of Norman Corwin, Leonard Spigelgass and Karl Tunberg to turn Mary McSherry's story into a real Garson–Pidgeon vehicle. Jean Negulesco directed and Edwin Knopf produced, vainly throwing in Technicolor. Also cast: Margalo Gillmore, Rhys Williams and Philip Ober (with the stars here) and Agnes Moorehead, Arthur Shields, John Lupton, Ian Wolfe, Philip Tonge.

Another great star of the Forties shone dimly in 1953: Mickey Rooney in **A Slight Case of Larceny** with Marilyn Erskine and Eddie Bracken. Tapping an oil company's pipeline to feed their gas station was the idea of Jerry Davis' script, directed by Don Weis and produced by Henry Berman with medium results. Elaine Stewart, Douglas Fowley, Robert Burton, Charles Halton supported.

Deborah Kerr, Movita, Betta St John, Cary Grant, Patricia Tiernan and Richard Anderson in **Dream Wife**, a bit of fluff received by press and public well this side of ecstasy. Schary produced the Sidney Sheldon–Herbert Baker–Alfred Levitt comedy, directed by Sheldon. It co-starred Walter Pidgeon, with Eduard Franz, Buddy Baer, Bruce Bennett, Dan Tobin, Gloria Holden, June Clayworth, Dean Miller, Steve Forrest.

The Great Diamond Robbery was the last for Red Skelton after 13 MGM years, Robert Leonard directed and Edwin Knopf produced the lacklustre comedy by Laslo Vadnay, with (left to right) Harry Bellaver, Skelton, George Mathews, Dorothy Stickney, Cara Williams and Kurt Kasznar; also cast were James Whitmore, Reginald Owen, Connie Gilchrist.

Two well-made 'B's in AnscoColor rounded out 1953. Earl Holliman, Dewey Martin and Keenan Wynn in a prizefight-plus-religion drama, if you can imagine it: **Tennessee Champ**, written by Art Cohn, directed by Fred Wilcox, produced by Sol Fielding; Shelley Winters and Yvette Duguay were ringside girls . . . Frances Dee, Donna Corcoran and Ward Bond gave **Gypsy Colt** his oats; Martin Berkeley scripted Eric Knight's story for the William Grady Jr–Sidney Franklin Jr production, directed by Andrew Marton, with Lee Van Cleef, Larry Keating, Bobby Hyatt.

THIS YEAR OF GRACE
1954

Warner Bros. studio and distribution were operating separately from their theatres, leaving only MGM–Loew's holding out against the US government's divorcement order. *The Caine Mutiny, The Glenn Miller Story, Rear Window, On the Waterfront, White Christmas, Three Coins in the Fountain, From Here to Eternity, Moulin Rouge, How to Marry a Millionaire, Genevieve* and *Shane* were main rivals to MGM's biggest. *Waterfront* succeeded *Eternity*, the previous winner, as the Academy's best film; Marlon Brando in the former followed William Holden in *Stalag 17* as best actor; Grace Kelly in *The Country Girl* took over from Audrey Hepburn in *Roman Holiday* as best actress. Biggest box-office star was John Wayne, in his sixth year among the Top Ten: after him came Dean Martin and Jerry Lewis, Gary Cooper, James Stewart, Marilyn Monroe, Alan Ladd, Holden, Bing Crosby, Jane Wyman and Brando.

Frances Goodrich–Dorothy Kingsley script from Stephen Vincent Benet's 'Sobbin' Women'. It was in AnscoColor and CinemaScope.

Variations on the war theme: the raw realism that keynoted **Prisoner of War** was too depressing for financial success. Steve Forrest, Dewey Martin and Ronald Reagan played Americans suffering tortures in a Korean camp, with Stephen Bekassy, Leonard Strong, Darryl Hickman, Jerry Paris and John Lupton among Andrew Marton's well-directed cast. Henry Berman produced the Allen Rivkin screenplay.

Better audience reaction greeted another Marton–Berman war movie, **Men of the** ▽ **Fighting Lady** scoring with its wild blue yonder heroics and a typically sincere performance by Van Johnson. Art Cohn's screenplay, filmed in AnscoColor, was strongly cast with Walter Pidgeon, Louis Calhern, Frank Lovejoy, Dewey Martin, Keenan Wynn, Robert Horton, Dick Simmons, Bert Freed.

Disappointingly delivering less warmth, erotic or otherwise, than its title promised, **Flame and the Flesh** dawdled through a triangle story of temptress Lana Turner and nightclub singer Carlos Thompson (here) and innocent bambina Pier Angeli. Filmed in Italy, England and Technicolor by Richard Brooks, the Auguste Bailly original was scripted by Helen Deutsch and produced by Joe Pasternak. Also cast: Bonar Colleano, Peter Illing, Charles Goldner.

John Justin and Gene Kelly in **Seagulls Over Sorrento**/Crest of the Wave, a workmanlike version of Hugh Hastings' stage success, about British and American sailors on a Scottish island. Shot in 1953 at MGM British by John and Roy Boulting, it emerged entertainingly but with little paybox impact a year later. Script: Frank Harvey and Roy Boulting. Also cast: Jeff Richards, Bernard Lee, Sidney James, Patrick Doonan, Ray Jackson, Patrick Barr.

Howard Keel could hardly believe it when Jane Powell tamed his backwoods brothers, Marc Platt, Matt Mattox, Jacques d'Amboise, Tommy Rall, Jeff Richards and Russ Tamblyn in △ **Seven Brides for Seven Brothers**. Neither could the studio when the movie became the year's most sensational hit–and it was still getting bookings around the world 20 years later. Jack Cummings produced it on the back lot, so to speak, while more expensive musicals with stage-famous titles were being made front and centre. It did for the screen what 'Oklahoma' had done for the theatre: created a new style of musical, roaring with vitality, prancing with open-air freshness. Credit Stanley Donen's direction, Michael Kidd's choreography, the Gene de Paul–Johnny Mercer songs ('When You're in Love', 'Wonderful Day', 'Bless Yore Beautiful Hide', 'Spring', 'Lonesome Polecat', etc.) and the Albert Hackett–

Betrayed ended the 24-year reign of MGM's king of stars, Clark Gable; the company found that he was no longer the surefire draw of yore, and he was eager for the lucrative freelancing which occupied his remaining six years. His last for Leo was an outdated drama of spies in German-occupied Europe, written by Ronald Millar and George Froeschel, directed by Gottfried Reinhardt at the British studio. Victor Mature (left) and Lana Turner co-starred, with Louis Calhern, Wilfrid Hyde White, O. E. Hasse, Ian Carmichael, Niall MacGinnis, Nora Swinburne, Roland Culver. Gable's subsequent percentage deals at other studios paid him better than his MGM annual salary of $500,000.

Also out, as overhead cuts reached the star list, went Greer Garson after a mere 15 years. Her great prestige had dwindled in unworthy vehicles for several years, and **Her Twelve Men** wasn't strong enough to halt the trend. She looked a treat in AnscoColor as a boys' schoolteacher in the pleasant William Roberts–Laura Z. Hobson screenplay, with Robert Ryan (right), Barry Sullivan, Richard Haydn, Barbara Lawrence, James Arness, Rex Thompson, Tim Considine, Ian Wolfe. Robert Z. Leonard directed John Houseman's production.

Carlos Thompson, Robert Taylor and Eleanor Parker in **Valley of the Kings**, or Clap Hands if You Believe in Pharaohs. Written (with Karl Tunberg) and directed by Robert Pirosh; featuring Kurt Kasznar and Victor Jory; produced in Eastman Color by one whose wish to remain anonymous we must respect.

The studio set a speed record on **Rogue Cop**, only four months elapsing between story buy and final preview. Director Roy Rowland and producer Nicholas Nayfack kept it fast on the screen too, and Robert Taylor thankfully climbed out of Valley of the Kings to higher paybox levels in the title role. Left to right: Alan Hale Jr, Taylor, Robert Simon, George Raft and Anne Francis as underworld czar Raft's floozie. Sidney Boehm's script from William McGivern's novel had parts for Steve Forrest, Vince Edwards and Robert Ellenstein.

Esther Williams was dropped from the MGM contract list after **Jupiter's Darling**; so were Marge and Gower Champion and director George Sidney (from left here with Miss Williams, George Sanders and producer George Wells). This CinemaScope musical co-starred Howard Keel and featured Richard Haydn, William Demarest, Norma Varden and Douglass Dumbrille. The product of their labours was an expensive flop, adapted by Dorothy Kingsley from Robert E. Sherwood's Broadway success of the Twenties, 'The Road to Rome'. Keel played Hannibal singing his way across the Alps; Esther swam in a mini-toga.

Off-key results, too, from **The Glass Slipper**, hopefully the successor to Lili by Leslie Caron, writer Helen Deutsch, director Charles Walters and producer Edwin Knopf. It was straight Cinderella, with Michael Wilding

swanning around in tights as Prince Charming, and Caron apparently almost as ill at ease, except while dancing with Roland Petit's Ballet de Paris. Also cast: Keenan Wynn, Elsa Lanchester, Estelle Winwood, Barry Jones, Amanda Blake, Lurene Tuttle, Liliane Montevecchi.

Victor McLaglen fixes a shotgun wedding for daughter Eleanor Parker and trapper Robert Taylor in **Many Rivers to Cross**, watched by Russ Tamblyn, Jeff Richards and Ralph Moody. About as subtle as a school performance of Taming of the Shrew, which the Guy Trosper–Harry Brown script often resembled, the backwoods comedy rattled along with uninhibited hokum and action. Nobody liked it but the public. Directed by Roy Rowland; produced by Jack Cummings in CinemaScope and Eastman Color; with James Arness, Rosemary DeCamp, Josephine Hutchinson, Sig Ruman, Alan Hale Jr, Rhys Williams.

Van Johnson joined the exodus of MGM-made stars after **The Last Time I Saw Paris**—but he would be back. Here he and Elizabeth Taylor are caught up in VE-Day celebrations in Paris during the unconvincing drama Richard Brooks and Julius and Philip Epstein based roughly on Scott Fitzgerald's story of expatriate Americans, 'Babylon Revisited'. Good acting in a handsome Technicolor production by Jack Cummings, directed by Brooks, but spotty box-office. Also cast: Walter Pidgeon, Donna Reed, Eva Gabor, Kurt Kasznar, George Dolenz, Roger Moore (debut), Celia Lovsky.

Vittorio Gassman finished his Metro contract and John Ericson started his with **Rhapsody**, a feverish romance about temperamental musicians. It had a splendid musical score (Rachmaninov, Tchaikowsky, etc.) with violinist Michael Rabin and pianist Claudio Arrau dubbing for Gassman and Ericson (with Elizabeth Taylor here). Louis Calhern, Michael Chekhov, Barbara Bates, Richard Hageman, Celia Lovsky, Richard Lupino and Stuart Whitman were in Charles Vidor's cast. Lawrence Weingarten produced the Fay and Michael Kanin screenplay from Henry Handel Richardson's 'Maurice Guest'.

Good days at Culver City when they made **Bad Day at Black Rock**. *Brooding silences, with intimations of an explosive climax at any moment, characterized Spencer Tracy's performance and the movie itself, keeping audiences in suspense and exhibitors out of the red. Lee Marvin (supine), Robert Ryan, John Ericson, Anne Francis, Dean Jagger, Walter Brennan and Ernest Borgnine performed tellingly for John Sturges in the Millard Kaufman drama, produced by Dore Schary in CinemaScope and Eastman Color.*

New stars were coming up—like a rocket, in Grace Kelly's case. She helped to sell tickets for **Green Fire**, *a so-so action drama about emerald miners, co-starring Stewart Granger (here) and Paul Douglas, with John Ericson and Murvyn Vye. Produced in Cinema-Scope and Eastman Color by Armand Deutsch; written by Ivan Goff and Ben Roberts; directed by Andrew Marton.*

You-hoo-hoos and totem tomtoms echoed through the Rockies again as **Rose Marie** *got her third MGM airing in 1954. The novelty of CinemaScope made up for the lack of Mac-Donald–Eddy box-office power in its expert singing leads, Ann Blyth and Howard Keel, but the story looked its age. Mervyn LeRoy produced and directed, Busby Berkeley stepping in for musical numbers. Also cast: Fernando Lamas, Bert Lahr, Marjorie Main, Joan Taylor, Ray Collins. New script: Ronald Millar, George Froeschel.*

Chief interest in **The Student Prince** *centred on Mario Lanza, who wasn't in it, and Edmund Purdom, the young English actor whose dashing personality made it acceptable that Lanza's voice should issue from him. The dubbing job was necessitated by Lanza's uncontrollable temperament which caused cancellation of his contract after he had recorded (magnificently) all the songs for the Joe Pasternak production. Ann Blyth (here with Edmund Gwenn and Purdom) followed* Rose Marie *with this other musical remake. MGM had not filmed the perennial stage success since 1927, so it now had sound as well as Technicolor and CinemaScope to augment the old movie's appeal. John Ericson, Louis Calhern, S. Z. Sakall, Betta St John, John Williams, Richard Anderson, Evelyn Varden, John Hoyt, Steve Rowland and John Qualen were in the William Ludwig–Sonya Levien screenplay, directed by Richard Thorpe.*

Made with great style, **Beau Brummell** *was a credit to Sam Zimbalist's production team at the British studio; the Eastman Color photography of Oswald Morris received special plaudits. Critics were split on Karl Tunberg's history-twisting script based on the old Clyde Fitch play, but most agreed about the skill and panache of Stewart Granger as Brummell and Peter Ustinov as the Prince of Wales (here with Elizabeth Taylor and Rosemary Harris). Also in Curtis Bernhardt's cast: Robert Morley as George III, James Donald, Paul Rogers, James Hayter, Noel Willman, Charles Carson, Peter Bull.*

A resounding bell-ringer arrived early in the year: **Executive Suite**, *an absorbing drama of ▷ the office manoeuvrings and private lives of a firm's board members. Big Business rarely brings big business to theatres, but Robert Wise's direction and Ernest Lehman's script from the Cameron Hawley novel made this as tense as a crime thriller, and producer John Houseman gave it a* Grand Hotel *cast of stars. Fine performances from Shelley Winters, June Allyson and (clockwise from front) Dean Jagger, Louis Calhern, Paul Douglas, Fredric March, Barbara Stanwyck, Walter Pidgeon, William Holden and Nina Foch.*

Brigadoon *was a great stage hit that went a ▷ bit awry in its CinemaScope-AnscoColor guise, as produced by Arthur Freed and directed by Vincente Minnelli. Starring Gene Kelly and Cyd Charisse (here with Barry Jones), and Van Johnson, it aroused great expectations, but Alan Jay Lerner's story of a Scottish village coming to life once every century seemed to need outdoor naturalism or stylized fantasy. It got something in between, and pretty good grosses. The great Lerner–Frederick Loewe songs, such as 'The Heather on the Hill', 'Almost Like Being in Love' and 'There But for You Go I', were its best asset. Also cast: Elaine Stewart, Albert Sharpe, Hugh Laing, Virginia Bosler, Jimmy Thompson, Eddie Quillan.*

Louis Calhern, Edmund Purdom, Steve Reeves, Richard Sabre and Jane Powell in **Athena**, *a frisky Joe Pasternak musical that just missed hit status. Richard Thorpe directed the Leonard Spiegelgass–William Ludwig comedy about a family of back-to-nature health cranks, an amusing idea not fully developed. Debbie Reynolds, Vic Damone, Evelyn Varden, Linda Christian, Ray Collins, Carl Benton Reid and Kathleen Freeman contributed.*

Sigmund Romberg, one major songwriter of Broadways' golden Twenties who hadn't been bio-filmed, had his turn in **Deep in My Heart**. Leonard Spigelgass' script was no worse than others of this ilk, and the 'Maytime', 'Student Prince', 'Desert Song' and 'New Moon' ballads held their old magic; but some of Romberg's lighter pieces could have been left in the trunk. Strong business for Roger Edens' production, directed by Stanley Donen, with a dazzling cast: Paul Stewart, Walter Pidgeon, Tamara Toumanova, Jose Ferrer (Romberg) and Merle Oberon (left to right) and opera star Helen Traubel, Paul Henreid, Howard Keel, Gene and brother Fred Kelly, Jane Powell, Vic Damone, Ann Miller, Tony Martin, Rosemary Clooney, Cyd Charisse, James Mitchell, Isobel Elsom, Jim Backus.

ROCK AROUND THE CLOCK
1955

The eight major Hollywood companies' output totalled 215 features, the lowest in the industry's history. At a weekly average of 45.8m US cinema attendances dropped to their lowest since 1923. Nevertheless, all but MGM (down a million from 1954 at $5.3m) and Fox reported higher profits: income from abroad, where the inroads of television were less severe, was healthy. The first instance of a movie giant becoming a subsidiary of a non-theatrical conglomerate came as Howard Hughes sold RKO-Radio to the General Tire and Rubber Company.

Burt Lancaster co-produced a normal-screen black-and-white little drama, *Marty*, which won Academy Awards for itself (best film), actor Ernest Borgnine, director Delbert Mann and writer Paddy Chayevsky; Lancaster also co-starred with Anna Magnani in *The Rose Tattoo* which won her the best actress award.

Other notable releases: Clouzot's unnerving *Diabolique*, de Sica's *Umberto D*, star find of the year James Dean in *Rebel Without a Cause*, Cary Grant and Grace Kelly in *To Catch a Thief*, William Holden and Jennifer Jones in *Love is a Many-Splendored Thing*, Holden and Miss Kelly in *Bridges at Toko-Ri*, James Cagney and Henry Fonda in *Mr Roberts*, Marilyn Monroe in *The Seven Year Itch* and *There's No Business Like Show Business*, Katharine Hepburn in *Summertime*.

The Blackboard Jungle *was an even faster job than* Rogue Cop, *Pandro Berman guiding it from script to release in three months. A frightening picture of violence in city schools, vividly directed by Richard Brooks, who based his script on Evan Hunter's current best-seller, it scored one of the year's paybox bulls-eyes. Unexpectedly it also ignited the world-wide wildfire of rock music, its soundtrack introducing Bill Haley's relentless 'Rock Around the Clock'. Cast: Glenn Ford, excellent as the teacher (here defying Vic Morrow's knife) and Anne Francis, Louis Calhern, Sidney Poitier, Margaret Hayes, Richard Kiley, John Hoyt, Horace MacMahon.*

ing load of kitsch, spending on sets and costumes a fortune that never came back from theatres. In this scene Lana sizes up Edmund Purdom for temple duty while swapping Maurice Zimm's awful dialogue with Louis Calhern. She could blame jewel fatigue for her performance. Others seeking excuses were James Mitchell, Taina Elg, Cecil Kellaway, Robert Coote, Henry Daniell, Francis L. Sullivan, Audrey Dalton, Neville Brand, Paul Cavanagh, John Dehner.

Moonfleet *was the only Hollywood venture of England's Joan Greenwood. She and the coolly Nordic Viveca Lindfors (left) and the volcanically Latin Liliane Montevecchi (right) kept Stewart Granger in a virile tizzy. The John Houseman production of J. Meade Falkner's adventure novel was lamely scripted by Jan Lustig and Margaret Fitts and directed by an off-form Fritz Lang. British ten-year-old Jon Whiteley had a key role, along with George Sanders, Melville Cooper, Alan Napier, Donna Corcoran, Jack Elam, Sean McClory, John Hoyt, Ian Wolfe.*

Students wondering what the prodigal son did in the bits the bible left out were advised by **The Prodigal** *that he was rubbing elbows and things with the High Priestess of the Temple of Love, née Lana Turner. Those usually adept film-makers Charles Schnee and Richard Thorpe produced and directed this excruciat-*

The dramatic intensity of **Trial** was such that even the stills were exciting, like this one of Dorothy McGuire, Katy Jurado, Rafael Campos, Glenn Ford and Arthur Kennedy. Don Mankiewicz brilliantly scripted his own novel and director Mark Robson got every atom of suspense and spectacle from the murder trial of Campos, and its communist-inspired sideshows. Stunning performances by the above and John Hodiak, Juano Hernandez (as the screen's first black judge), Robert Middleton, Elisha Cook Jr, John Hoyt, Paul Guilfoyle, Whit Bissell, Barry Kelley. Charles Schnee produced.

Hit the Deck, *the daddy of all sailors-on-leave musicals, was a Broadway smash in 1927 and filmed by RKO-Radio in 1930 and 1936 (the latter as* Follow the Fleet *with Fred Astaire, Ginger Rogers, and Irving Berlin songs). Left to right: Jane Powell, Tony Martin, Debbie Reynolds, Walter Pidgeon, Vic Damone, Gene Raymond, Ann Miller, Russ Tamblyn and Kay Armen, a rich cargo of talent. Joe Pasternak's production, directed by Roy Rowland, had a fine Vincent Youmans score, retaining 'Hallelujah', 'Sometimes I'm Happy' and 'Why Oh Why?' from the original show and 'Keeping Myself for You' from the first movie, while adding numbers from other Youmans shows. Richard Anderson, Jane Darwell and J. Carrol Naish were featured in the Sonya Levien–William Ludwig screenplay.*

Shouts of praise from the critics greeted **It's Always Fair Weather**, *starring (left to right) Gene Kelly, Cyd Charisse, Dan Dailey, Dolores Gray and Michael Kidd. But it somehow fell short of the public enthusiasm aroused by its Gene Kelly/Stanley Donen/Arthur Freed/Betty Comden–Adolph Green predecessors,* **On The Town** *and* **Singin' in the Rain**. *All the same elements were present: songs, dances, fun, wit, production style, story ideas, speed. So why didn't they add up?*

The enormously successful **Love Me or Leave Me** *brought to MGM two of the few big stars who had never worked at Culver City: Doris Day and James Cagney. Unusually for a musical about real people, the protagonists were not noble goodies: Daniel Fuchs' Oscar-winning story and his script with Isobel Lennart didn't shirk showing the ruthless ambition that took Ruth Etting from honky-tonks to Ziegfeld stardom, or the crude violence of her racketeer husband. Charles Vidor's deft direction helped Miss Day to her best performance, while Cagney fairly scorched the celluloid, again proving himself one of the most exciting actors the screen has displayed.*

Ten Ruth Etting hits of the Twenties became Doris Day hits of the Fifties in Joe Pasternak's cavalcade of Prohibition-era show business. Also cast: Cameron Mitchell, Harry Bellaver, Robert Keith, Tom Tully.

Shulman–Robert Paul Smith stage success. Celeste Holm and David Wayne increased the paybox bait, with Lola Albright, Carolyn Jones, Jarma Lewis, Tom Helmore, James Drury. Charles Walters directed Lawrence Weingarten's production.

Lucille Ball, James Mason and Desi Arnaz in **Forever Darling,** *a comedy in which Mason was an angel bringing Lucy heavenly guidance. None was forthcoming for writer Helen Deutsch, director Alexander Hall or producer Arnaz. Also cast: Louis Calhern, John Emery, Natalie Schafer, John Hoyt, Mabel Albertson.*

gave him a delicious heroine in Kay Kendall. Director Richard Thorpe and producer Pandro Berman again officiated, lavishly and colourfully transposing Sir Walter Scott's story to film via a George Froeschel–Robert Ardrey script. Also cast: Robert Morley, Wilfrid Hyde White, Duncan Lamont (right), Alec Clunes, George Cole, Marius Goring, Eric Pohlmann, Ernest Thesiger.

Guys and Dolls, $2\frac{1}{2}$ *hours of Damon Runyon's oddball characters and Frank Loesser's clever songs, directed by Joseph L. Mankiewicz, was the only Samuel Goldwyn production distributed by MGM; the deal paid off handsomely. It had been a great show and was a good film. Left to right: Marlon Brando, Jean Simmons, Frank Sinatra and Vivian Blaine. Goldwyn wanted Gene Kelly for the lead and may have had an even better movie with him in it; Brando was no song-and-dance man. On the other hand, his scenes with Miss Simmons had unusual conviction for a musical. Loesser added another winner, 'A Woman in Love', to those like 'If I Were a Bell', 'Luck Be a Lady' and 'Take Back Your Mink' of the stage smash, from which Miss Blaine, Stubby Kaye and B. S. Pully were recruited, joining Robert Keith, Sheldon Leonard, George E. Stone, Regis Toomey, Veda Ann Borg in the cast. Mankiewicz adapted the Abe Burrows–Jo Swerling play; Michael Kidd choreographed.*

Meet Me in Las Vegas/Viva Las Vegas, *a successful collaboration of producer Joe Pasternak and director Roy Rowland, teamed Cyd Charisse with Dan Dailey in a gambling story by Isobel Lennart. Here are Liliane Montevecchi, John Brascia and Miss Charisse in the exciting 'Frankie and Johnny' ballet, with off-screen singing by Sammy Davis Jr. The movie was liberally bedizened with musical numbers by the stars plus Lena Horne, Frankie Laine, Jerry Colonna and Cara Williams. Also present: Agnes Moorehead, Jim Backus, Lily Darvas, Oscar Karlweis, Paul Henreid.*

'Love is the Tender Trap' *warbled Frank Sinatra, thus simultaneously scaling the top of the music and movie hit parades in* **The Tender Trap.** *Debbie Reynolds was his bubbling, bachelor-trapping foil in this lively comedy, adapted by Julius Epstein from the Max*

The visual charms of Paris were the chief asset of **Bedevilled.** *In it Anne Baxter and Steve Forrest (brother of Dana Andrews) coped gamely with highly theatrical dramatics scripted by Jo Eisinger, directed by Mitchell Leisen – the tireless Richard Thorpe completed it when Leisen fell ill – and produced by Henry Berman. Also cast: Victor Francen, Robert Christopher and Joseph Tomelty.*

Equally theatrical but with undeniable emotional power: **Interrupted Melody,** *which was the high point of Eleanor Parker's 20-year starring career. She won much praise for a heartrending performance and William Ludwig and Sonya Levien won the script Academy Award. It was based on the true story of Australian soprano Marjorie Lawrence, stricken with polio at the height of her operatic fame. Glenn Ford as her husband matched Eleanor's acting skill, and her miming matched the dubbed voice of Eileen Farrell in eight arias; magnificent soundtrack music. Jack Cummings produced, Curtis Bernhardt directed; with Roger Moore, Cecil Kellaway, Ann Codee, Doris Lloyd, Dick Simmons.*

Quentin Durward *took Robert Taylor to MGM's British studios for the fifth time. While not a success of* Ivanhoe *proportions, it brought his London score to four hits out of five, and*

◁ **Kismet** had always looked like the libretto for a musical and it became one at last when Charles Lederer and Luther Davis adapted the old Edward Knoblock play, and Robert Wright and George Forrest composed a glorious score, the tunes borrowed from Borodin. After running for years as a stage show (originally financed by Lederer's aunt, Marion Davies) it reached CinemaScope screens in a sumptuous Arthur Freed production. Howard Keel and Dolores Gray (here), who once were rival London sensations in Oklahoma and Annie Get Your Gun respectively, appeared together for the first time and made every note of their numbers count. So did Ann Blyth and Vic Damone. But, as in Brigadoon, the usual sparkle was missing from Vincente Minnelli's direction, and business fell short of hopes. Also cast: Monty Woolley, Sebastian Cabot, Jay C. Flippen, Ted de Corsia, Jack Elam, Mike Mazurki. Its best-selling songs included 'Stranger in Paradise', 'And This is My Beloved', 'Baubles, Bangles and Beads' and the sizzling 'Not Since Nineveh'.

I'll Cry Tomorrow was the strongest of MGM's three 1955 biographical movies—all hits—about female singing stars; its depiction of acute alcoholism had more shock value than the polio of Interrupted Melody or the conflict of Love Me or Leave Me. Susan Hayward as Lillian Roth (here scraping bottom on skid row) did a highly professional job of acting, both in these sordid sequences and in the sunny days of Miss Roth's Broadway and Hollywood fame. She won the Cannes Festival award for it, but the costumes by Helen Rose got its only Academy Oscar. A batch of old songs, actually sung, surprisingly well, by Miss Hayward; the source
◁ book by Miss Roth, Mike Connolly and Gerold Frank; and Alcoholics Anonymous all got powerful plugs from its success. Director, Daniel Mann; producer, Lawrence Weingarten; cast, Eddie Albert, Richard Conte, Don Taylor, Jo Van Fleet, Ray Danton, Margo, Don Barry; script, Helen Deutsch, Jay Richard Kennedy.

Lana Turner's long MGM career ended with one of her better pictures, Edwin Knopf's handsome production of **Diane**, directed by David Miller. In Christopher Isherwood's literate script from John Erskine's romance of 16th-century France, she was Diane de Poitiers, beloved of Henry II—played by Roger Moore (here stripped for wrestling with Sean McClory). Pedro Armendariz (right), Cedric Hardwicke, Marisa Pavan (Pier Angeli's sister), Taina Elg, Torin Thatcher, Henry Daniell, John Lupton, Geoffrey Toone, Paul Cavanagh, Melville Cooper, Ian Wolfe and Gene Reynolds also performed ably, which is more than can be said for the box-office. This was the best of the few parts MGM gave Roger Moore after bringing him from England under contract; it was left to television to make him a star.

John Houseman must have been a case for the couch when his elegant all-star production of the highly regarded novel **The Cobweb** suffered a box-office trauma. William Gibson's book about psychiatrists and patients in a plush nuthouse had no mass appeal as scripted by John Paxton and directed by Vincente Minnelli. But what a cast: from front, Richard Widmark, Lauren Bacall, Charles Boyer, Lillian Gish in her first MGM movie for 22 years, John Kerr (debut), Oscar Levant, Jarma Lewis, Susan Strasberg (another debut) and Paul Stewart; also cast were Gloria Grahame, Fay Wray and Adele Jergens.

Editor at work: Ben Lewis, veteran MGM cutter, views a scene from **The Last Hunt** through his movieola. Among the most important and least publicized of film-makers, the editor usually works closely with director and/or producer to give each movie its distinctive pace, shape and character, if any. This Schary production, starring Robert Taylor as heavy and Stewart Granger as hero, dealt with the slaughter of huge herds of buffalo in the West, a subject that repelled more customers than it attracted. With Lloyd Nolan, Debra Paget, Russ Tamblyn, Constance Ford and Joe de Santis in his cast, Richard Brooks directed and wrote it from Milton Lott's original.

The King's Thief was Robert Z. Leonard's last movie in a record-breaking 31 years exclusively with MGM. It starred Edmund Purdom, Ann Blyth, George Sanders and David Niven (here), supported by Roger

Moore, Melville Cooper, Sean McClory, Isobel Elsom, Rhys Williams, Alan Mowbray, John Dehner, Paul Cavanagh; script, Christopher Knopf, from Robert Andrews' story; producer, Edwin Knopf . . . Another sword-swinger buckling its swashes rather late after Scaramouche's success: **The Scarlet Coat** with Cornel Wilde, Anne Francis and Michael Wilding (here), also Robert Douglas, John McIntire, Bobby Driscoll and Sanders, Williams, Dehner and Cavanagh again; script, Karl Tunberg; director, John Sturges; producer, Nicholas Nayfack. Both films paid their way.

1955's belle of the 'Bs' was Jarma Lewis, a fetching brunette who leading-ladied **The Marauders**, a Civil War drama with a hook-handed Keenan Wynn and Dan Duryea; also Jeff Richards, Harry Shannon, Richard Lupino; script, Earl Fenton; director, Gerald Mayer; producer, Arthur Loew Jr . . . In **It's a Dog's Life** the terrier got the best lines and Jarma got Jeff Richards; script, John Michael Hayes from Richard Harding Davis' The Bar Sinister, filmed by Pathé in 1927 as Almost Human; director, Herman Hoffman; producer, Henry Berman; cast, Edmund Gwenn, Dean Jagger, Richard Anderson, Sally Fraser, J. M. Kerrigan.

Last off the 1955 assembly line was the latest Ford model—the fourth in a year which took Glenn to the forefront of Hollywood's dramatic actors. **Ransom** showed with agonizing suspense the conflict between a kidnapped child's parents, he refusing to submit to the criminals, she (Donna Reed) eager to pay any price. Customers' nerves and theatres' seat-edges took a beating from the Cyril Hume–Richard Maibaum screenplay, tautly directed by Alex Segal. Leslie Nielsen, Juano Hernandez, Juanita Moore, Robert Keith, Mabel Albertson, Richard Gaines, Robert Burton and Alexander Scourby were in Nicholas Nayfack's production.

HIGH SOCIETY PAYS
1956

Warner Bros. and 20th-Century Fox sold their pre-1948 films to television, while MGM put a cautious toe into that whirlpool by leasing *The Wizard of Oz* for four telecasts, netting $900,000. Mary Pickford followed Chaplin in selling her share of United Artists, which they had created with Douglas Fairbanks and D. W. Griffith in 1919.

A world survey counted approximately 108,500 cinemas in operation: USA 18,500; Russia 15,500; Italy 9,500; France 5,500; West Germany 5,000; Spain 5,000; Britain 4,500; Japan 3,500; India 3,000; East Germany 3,000; Mexico 2,500; Sweden 2,500.

Practically the entire membership of the Screen Actors Guild were in Cecil B. DeMille's record-smashing remake of *The Ten Commandments* or Mike Todd's *Around The World in Eighty Days*, which won the Academy and practically every other award. (Sir Cedric Hardwicke and John Carradine managed to get into both.) King Vidor also colossaled with *War and Peace* in Italy. *Bus Stop, The King and I, Carousel, Picnic, The Man with the Golden Arm* and *Friendly Persuasion* clicked.

Frank Sinatra, Kim Novak, Marilyn Monroe, Glenn Ford and Burt Lancaster displaced Gable, Bogart, Brando, Martin and Lewis and June Allyson in the Top Ten.

The Swan, *Ferenc Molnar's romance of never-never-land royalty was released, by a triumph of timing, as Grace Kelly (with Louis Jourdan here) became Her Serene Highness Princess Grace of Monaco; an event celebrated by all news media for weeks on end (MGM even had a half-hour documentary,* **The Wedding in Monaco***). She was every inch a star as well as a princess, gentle, graceful and subtly humorous, in this remake; Lillian Gish played it in 1930 as* **One Romantic Night**. *Charles Vidor directed elegantly. Schary coaxed Alec Guinness to Hollywood as its superb co-star, with Agnes Moorehead, Brian Aherne, Jessie Royce Landis, Estelle Winwood, Leo G. Carroll and Robert Coote featured. Script: John Dighton.*

Excessive heat in the Colorado locations and in his exchanges with director Robert Wise resulted in Spencer Tracy walking out of **Tribute to a Bad Man** *and his 21-year MGM contract. So James Cagney stepped into Tracy's shoes and set a high acting example for newcomers Don Dubbins and Irene Papas in the first movie to come out of the cutting rooms in 1956. Sam Zimbalist produced Michael Blankfort's screenplay of domestic conflict on a ranch: a fairly good ticket-seller, with Stephen McNally, Onslow Stevens, Vic Morrow, Jeanette Nolan, Lee Van Cleef, Royal Dano.*

Clashing charismas and high voltage acting shook the sprockets as Anthony Quinn and Kirk Douglas took on their roles as Paul Gauguin and Vincent van Gogh in **Lust for Life**. *Douglas gave his finest performance and Quinn won the best supporting actor Oscar. Vincente Minnelli directed. The Metrocolor (new trade name) cameras of F. A. Young and Russell Harlan, filming French and Dutch exteriors and MGM-British interiors, and Norman Corwin's script (from Irving Stone's book) brought further assets to John Houseman's production. So did the work of James Donald, Pamela Brown, Everett Sloane, Niall MacGinnis, Henry Daniell, Madge Kennedy, Noel Purcell, Jill Bennett, Lionel Jeffries, Laurence Naismith, Eric Pohlmann, Jeanette Sterke and Isobel Elsom.*

A television play, one of four MGM enlarged into feature films in 1956, became **The Rack**, giving Paul Newman a star-making role as a brainwashed prisoner of the Korean war facing court martial for treason. Powerful stuff. There was much praise for Newman, Wendell Corey (right) as prosecutor, Walter Pidgeon, Anne Francis, Edmond O'Brien, Lee Marvin, Robert Burton, James Best, Cloris Leachman; also for Arnold Laven's direction of the Stewart Stern screenplay (original, Rod Serling) produced by Arthur Loew Jr. It was made before Newman's more obviously popular Somebody Up There Likes Me, but released after it in many countries.

At last MGM cameras focused on the poached-egg eyes, twenty-past-eight mouth and magnificent talent of Bette Davis. She played a proletariat Mother of the Bride in **The △ Catered Affair**/Wedding Breakfast and, despite the efforts of fellow Oscar-winners Ernest Borgnine (centre) and Barry Fitzgerald, with Debbie Reynolds (left), she commanded the audience's unblinking attention throughout. But not, alas, as much box-office attention as the adroit handling, by director Richard Brooks and scripter Gore Vidal, of Paddy Chayevsky's television play deserved. Rod Taylor, Robert Simon, silent star Madge Kennedy, Dorothy Stickney and Dan Tobin were in Sam Zimbalist's production.

Van Johnson returned to his old studio, MGM, and director, Roy Rowland, in **Slander**, for an effective performance as a victim of scandal magazine blackmail. Ann Blyth played his wife, with Steve Cochran, Marjorie Rambeau, Richard Eyer, Harold J. Stone and Lurene Tuttle in the Armand Deutsch production written by Jerome Weidman from Harry Junkin's original.

Meanwhile, back at the remake ranch, **The Barretts of Wimpole Street** was being re-enacted by Bill Travers, Jennifer Jones, Virginia McKenna and John Gielgud. Sidney

Franklin directed them, as he had Fredric March, Norma Shearer, Maureen O'Sullivan and Charles Laughton in the same parts 22 years before; but the less flamboyant dramatics of the new stars left audiences unsatisfied. Sam Zimbalist produced John Dighton's screenplay at the British studio, casting Susan Stephen, Leslie Phillips, Maxine Audley, Vernon Gray, Jean Anderson, Laurence Naismith.

Gene Kelly had worked for years on the daring experiment of an all-dance, no-dialogue film and it was a blow when **Invitation to the Dance**, his episodic ballet movie, failed to draw. Here over 22,000 amperes blaze down on him, a technical requirement for the blending of cartoon with live action in the 'Magic Lamp' sequence which was eventually released as a separate short subject. Kelly directed the Arthur Freed production, with Tamara Toumanova, Belita, Tommy Rall, Igor Youskevitch, Claire Sombert, Irving Davies, Carol Haney.

1956

Leslie Caron and John Kerr made touching war-crossed lovers in **Gaby**, if rather pale replacements for Vivien Leigh and Robert Taylor, stars of the 1940 (second) version of **Waterloo Bridge**. Robert Sherwood's play was scripted this time by Albert Hackett, Frances Goodrich and Charles Lederer for producer Edwin Knopf; Curtis Bernhardt directed at a ponderous pace. Also cast: Sir Cedric Hardwicke, Taina Elg, Margalo Gillmore, Scott Marlowe, Ian Wolfe, James Best. Business dull.

James Cagney, Barbara Stanwyck and Betty Lou Keim in **These Wilder Years**. It must have been hard to make a boring movie starring Cagney and Miss Stanwyck, but writer Frank Fenton (original, Ralph Wheelwright), director Roy Rowland and producer Jules Schermer managed it with yawns to spare. Don Dubbins played the long-lost son, Cagney's search for whom motivated the ennui; Edward Andrews, Basil Ruysdael, Dean Jones supported.

The Great American Pastime could fill baseball stadiums, but it emptied cinemas. Ann Miller, Tom Ewell and Anne Francis were wasted in Nathaniel Benchley's comedy, directed by Herman Hoffman, produced by Henry Berman, with Dean Jones, Rudy Lee, Ann Morriss.

Nine days' shooting was enough for producer Morton Fine and director David Friedkin (both television-trained fast workers) to whip up an efficient little crime thriller, **Hot Summer Night**, with (left to right) Leslie Nielsen, James Best and Colleen Miller; also Edward Andrews, Jay C. Flippen, Marjorie Hellen. Fine and Friedkin also wrote the script.

Action and suspense: Homicidal madman Louis Jourdan clutches intended victim Doris Day in **Julie**, but relief is nigh for Doris and the audience at the end of 99 minutes crammed with suspense. Writer-director Andrew Stone gave it thrilling pace; Martin Melcher (Doris' husband) produced; Barry Sullivan, Frank Lovejoy, John Gallaudet, Jack Kruschen, Carleton Young, Jack Kelly and Mae Marsh acted; and the box-office reacted profitably . . .

Deborah Kerr and John Kerr (no relation) played their stage roles, as did Leif Erickson as her husband, in **Tea and Sympathy**, filmed by Pandro Berman and Vincente Minnelli from Robert Anderson's adaptation of his long-running play. The latter dealt with a potentially homosexual adolescent whose school-master's wife showed him what he would be missing. Since any mention of h—— was taboo in a 1956 movie (and actor Kerr's obvious maturity made his schoolboy seem overdue for graduation, let alone initiation) the play's sting was softened. Still, sensitive work by both Kerrs, and its title's fame, brought good audience and box-office response. Also cast: Edward Andrews, Darryl Hickman, Dean Jones, Norma Crane, Jacqueline de Wit, Richard Tyler, Don Burnett.

The Opposite Sex added music and men to The Women, Clare Booth's scorching comedy that had made such a good all-female 1939 movie. The changes were a mistake: both press and public gave Joe Pasternak's production a cool reception. David Miller directed the strong cast: Ann Miller, Dolores Gray, Ann Sheridan, Joan Blondell (standing), and June Allyson, Joan Collins (seated); also Agnes Moorehead, Jeff Richards, Leslie Nielsen, Charlotte Greenwood, Sam Levene, Alice Pearce, Barbara Jo Allen, Alan Marshal, Carolyn Jones, Dick Shawn, Jim Backus, Harry James. Script: Fay and Michael Kanin.

Mary Astor, Cameron Prud'homme, Robert Taylor, Nicola Michaels and Burl Ives in **The Power and the Prize**, a drama of American and British commercial ethics in conflict. Alas, the big business was all on the screen. Swiss actress Elisabeth Mueller, Sir Cedric Hardwicke and Charles Coburn were also featured in Nicholas Nayfack's production, scripted by Robert Ardrey, directed by Henry Koster.

Ostensibly a biographical drama of war hero and screenwriter Frank Wead, **The Wings of Eagles** was really a good old action flick about two guys and a gal: Dan Dailey, John Wayne and Maureen O'Hara. The latter pair were the tip-off that it had the special warmth that John Ford gave such stuff. Ward Bond also represented the Ford stock company, with Edmund Lowe, Barry Kelley, Louis Jean Heydt, Jody McCrea (Joel's son), Don Burnett, Mae Marsh, May McAvoy, Dorothy Jordan, Veda Ann Borg. Charles Schnee produced Frank Fenton's screenplay.

Without so much as a by your leave to Shakespeare's agent, **Forbidden Planet** pinched the whole plot of The Tempest and turned it into a sci-fi epic starring Robby the Robot. And what's more, it credited Irving Block and Allen Adler for the basis of Cyril Hume's script. Blow, blow, thou winter wind, thou art not so unkind as Nicholas Nayfack's ingratitude. Especially as his production was a spectacular hit, winning plaudits for Walter Pidgeon, Anne Francis (here with Robby), Leslie Nielsen, Warren Stevens, Jack Kelly, Richard Anderson, Jimmy Thompson, Earl Holliman, Robert Dix, James Drury, and director Fred Wilcox.

Ava Gardner did the best work of her MGM career in **Bhowani Junction** *as the Anglo-Indian girl with three men in her life: Stewart Granger, Bill Travers and Francis Matthews (here in the Sikh religious ceremony). John Masters' best-seller about the end of British rule in India presented fiendish difficulties in complex storytelling and production. With the aid of Pandro Berman and a Sonya Levien–Ivan Moffatt script, George Cukor surmounted them to win fine reviews and generally strong business. Supporting gems by Freda Jackson, Abraham Sofaer, Peter Illing, Marne Maitland, Lionel Jeffries, Edward Chapman, and great pictures from Freddie Young's CinemaScope cameras, especially of terrifying mob riots. Filmed in England and, when India refused permission, Pakistan.*

Loading up for the showdown, Glenn Ford ignores pleas from wife Jeanne Crain in **The Fastest Gun Alive**. *Made on a minor budget by producer Clarence Greene and director Russell Rouse, this Western turned out to be the fastest draw of the season for many a happy exhibitor. Significantly, Greene, Rouse and Frank Gilroy's story all came from television. Also cast: Broderick Crawford, Russ Tamblyn, Allyn Joslyn, Leif Erickson, John Dehner, Noah Beery Jr, Rhys Williams, J. M. Kerrigan, Virginia Gregg, Bill Phillips.*

Paul Newman fought through **Somebody Up There Likes Me** *to major stardom with a hardhitting performance in and out of the ring. He played Rocky Graziano, slum hoodlum, convict and middleweight champion, in Robert Wise's box-office knockout. Charles Schnee produced Ernest Lehman's gritty screenplay, from Graziano's autobiography ghosted by Rowland Barber. Pier Angeli, movingly pathetic as Rocky's girl, headed the supporting*

cast: Harold J. Stone, Eileen Heckart, Sal Mineo, Everett Sloane, Joseph Buloff. Theodore Newton, Robert Loggia, Sammy White. The Academy awarded Joseph Ruttenberg's photography and the art direction of Cedric Gibbons (his ninth Oscar, a record) and Malcolm Brown.

Critics showered superlatives on Sidney Poitier and John Cassavetes in **Edge of the City**/A Man is Ten Feet Tall, *independently produced by David Susskind and directed by Martin Ritt. Set in grimy New York railroad yards, Robert Alan Aurthur's story of black and white friends was both harsh and uplifting. Jack Warden, Kathleen Maguire, Ruby Dee, Robert Simon and Ruth White completed the cast.*

Gene Kelly (here with Michael Redgrave and Barbara Laage) put on his director's hat again for **The Happy Road**, *a frisky lightweight about two runaway schoolchildren pursued by the mother of one and the father of the other. He also produced the Joseph Morhaim–Arthur Julian–Harry Kurnitz screenplay, in France, with Bobby Clark and Brigitte Fossey as the kids. But it played to mostly unhappy business.*

High Society *was the brightest entertainment and biggest moneymaker of 1956, a rare instance of a musicalized remake proving as good as the original. Producer Sol C. Siegel (later head of the studio) cannily allowed John Patrick to re-script Philip Barry's* Philadelphia Story *only enough to make room for nine superb Cole Porter songs. Rueing its many recent loan-outs of Grace Kelly (one,* Country Girl, *won her an Academy Award), MGM rushed her into Hepburn's old part before her departure for Monte Carlo; she sparkled in it, even singing a few bars with Bing Crosby of 'True Love', the best-selling disc of which brought royalties to her royal digs for years. Crosby also sang 'I Love You, Samantha', 'Little One', and 'Now You Has Jazz' with Louis Armstrong, who set the scene with 'High Society Calypso'. Frank Sinatra sang 'Mind if I Make Love to You?' (here) and 'You're Sensational' to Grace, 'Who Wants to Be a Millionaire?' with Celeste Holm, and 'Well, Did you Evah!' with Crosby. The last was the*

only number not written for the movie: it was performed on Broadway by Betty Grable and Charles Walters in Porter's 1939 DuBarry Was a Lady. *The same Mr Walters now brilliantly directed this film. John Lund, Louis Calhern, Margalo Gillmore, Sidney Blackmer and Lydia Reed were featured.*

MGM had bought the screen rights to one of its biggest 1956 hits, **The Teahouse of the August Moon**, *in 1952. Meanwhile John Patrick's comedy, based on a book by Vern Sneider, scored hugely in New York and London. Producer Jack Cummings and director Daniel Mann made a fine job of the movie version, giving Patrick's script open-air scope and accomplished stars. Left to right here: Marlon Brando as the Okinawan interpreter, Eddie Albert as the gone-native psychiatrist, Glenn Ford as the confused US occupation officer and Japanese star Machiko Kyo as the geisha girl. During its location work in Japan, Louis Calhern suffered a fatal heart attack, and his role was taken by Paul Ford, who had played it 1,027 times on Broadway and all but stole the picture.*

The last 1956 delivery was the first under a new MGM distribution set-up for Michael Balcon's Ealing Films, which had done much to raise post-war British movie standards. **The Man in the Sky**/Decision Against Time *was a test-pilot thriller and a true-to-life picture of a married couple, deftly combined by writers William Rose and John Eldridge, and director Charles Crichton. Fine work from leads Jack Hawkins and Elizabeth Sellars (here) and Walter Fitzgerald, John Stratton, Lionel Jeffries, Donald Pleasence, Megs Jenkins, Victor Maddern, Eddie Byrne, Raymond Francis.*

ENTER ELVIS
1957

MGM's 1957 report for the financial year ending August 31 revealed the reason for executive reshuffles in the latter half of 1956: for the first time in its history, MGM–Loew's showed a loss, going $455,000 into the red, $5.6m down from the previous year, with gross receipts $18m down at $154.3m. RKO-Radio ceased production and the studio was bought by Lucille Ball. The old Hollywood systems were in increasing disarray:- the top talents were disinclined to be long-term employees, and producers preferred cheaper, real backgrounds abroad to studio sets. Players under contract to the major companies had dwindled from 598 to 253 in ten years.

The Bridge on the River Kwai, its star Alec Guinness and director David Lean mopped up most of the year's awards. Joanne Woodward *(Three Faces of Eve)* succeeded Ingrid Bergman *(Anastasia)* as the Oscar-winning actress. Rock Hudson shot to the top of ticket-selling stars, followed by John Wayne, Frank Sinatra, William Holden, James Stewart, Pat Boone, Elvis Presley, Jerry Lewis, Yul Brynner and, in the last of his 18 wins, Gary Cooper. Hudson, Elizabeth Taylor and the late James Dean kept *Giant* in the money; smaller but more distinguished dramas were *Twelve Angry Men* and *A Hatful of Rain.*

Ten Thousand Bedrooms *was Dean Martin's first solo starrer after his years with Jerry Lewis. Despite the come-on title, it was a mild comedy with songs, set in a Rome hotel. Left to right: Paul Henreid, Eva Bartok, Martin. Also cast were Anna Maria Alberghetti, Dewey Martin, Walter Slezak, Jules Munshin, Dean Jones, Joyce Taylor, Marcel Dalio and Evelyn Varden. It was produced by Joe Pasternak, written by William Ludwig, directed by Richard Thorpe.*

Tarzan swung back to Metro via a releasing deal with Sol Lesser, who had made several in the endless saga since the great Weissmuller–O'Sullivan days. **Tarzan and the Lost Safari** *had three firsts going for it: Gordon Scott was the first jungle giant to let his muscles ripple in Technicolor; it was the series' debut in Cinema-Scope; and the first (now they told us!) to be shot in genuine African locales. Some scenes, like this with George Coulouris, Yolande Donlan, Peter Arne, Wilfrid Hyde White and Scott, were studio-made in England. Bruce Humberstone directed, John Croydon produced, Montgomery Pittman and Lillie Hayward wrote, Robert Beatty villained.*

Designing Woman *was Dore Schary's swan-song at MGM. He had not yet delivered the final print of this production when he was summoned to New York by new president Joseph Vogel at the end of 1956 and given the sack and a golden handshake of $100,000–with another $900,000 to come in deferred salary. His last film was untypical: no message, no realism, just glamorous escapist comedy with silken Vincente Minnelli direction and a box-office guarantee in Gregory Peck and Lauren Bacall, sharing this scene with Dolores Gray and Tom Helmore. George Wells wrote its Academy Award winning script and co-produced with Schary, giving parts to Chuck Connors, Sam Levene, Jack Cole, Mickey Shaughnessy. Miss Bacall's gaiety for the camera was a miracle of professionalism: at home, Humphrey Bogart was slowly dying.*

Joan Fontaine, Sandra Dee, Piper Laurie and Jean Simmons in **Until They Sail**, *a quadruplex soap opera about four sisters in a Hollywooden wartime New Zealand. Jean got Paul Newman, Joan got Charles Drake, Sandra got the glad eye from other GIs, and Piper got murdered by Wally Cassell. Robert Wise directed, Charles Schnee produced, and Robert Anderson scripted the James Michener story.*

Raintree County *introduced MGM Camera 65, a new wide-film process (three to one ratio). Producer David Lewis had to call a two-month halt in 1956 when Montgomery Clift suffered severe facial and other injuries in a car crash. Here he is with Elizabeth Taylor in a poignantly dramatic scene (her retreat into insanity), in a film that could have done with more of them. This frank attempt to make another* Gone With the Wind *failed, despite the parallels of its originating in a 1,100-page best-seller with multiple characters and Civil War sequences, and its massive production costing $6m.–then a record for any MGM movie shot in America. It made a small profit. Millard Kaufman's script didn't completely pull Ross Lockridge's sprawling story together, and there were some poor performers among Edward Dmytryk's cast, which included Eva Marie Saint, Nigel Patrick, Rod Taylor, Agnes Moorehead, Walter Abel, Tom Drake, Jarma Lewis, Lee Marvin, Rhys Williams and Myrna Hansen.*

Michael Balcon's second Ealing film for MGM starred Alec Guinness as **Barnacle Bill**/All at Sea, *a farcical dig at some British naval traditions. Too seasick to follow his ancestors into the Navy, Bill became skipper of a seaside pier complete with dance hall for teenage jivers, and started a comic feud with the local mayor (Maurice Denham). Not vintage Guinness but entertaining enough, T. E. B. Clarke's screenplay, directed by Charles Frend, had parts for Irene Browne, Victor Maddern, George Rose, Lionel Jeffries, Percy Herbert, Jackie Collins, Donald Churchill, Warren Mitchell, Miles Malleson, Eric Pohlmann, Richard Wattis, Donald Pleasence.*

Elvis Presley, after a couple of milder movies, sulked volcanically through a melodramatic role in **Jailhouse Rock**, *with frequent intervals ▷ to let the music rock and the pelvis roll. Adolescents of all ages gave it a frenzied welcome. The title song sold 2m. discs in its first fortnight of release and the movie soon brought in twice that many dollars in rentals. Richard Thorpe directed Guy Trosper's screenplay, from a story by Ned Young; Pandro Berman produced; Judy Tyler, Mickey Shaughnessy, Dean Jones and Jennifer Holden were featured.*

1957 *Eleanor Parker, thrice nominated for Academy Awards, was out to win one at last in* **Lizzie** – *or else. The role of a psycho with a three-way split gave her every chance; two-thirds of them were well taken, but director Hugo Haas (with her here; he also acted in the movie) let her overdo the third personality, a bawdy broad who suggested Nita Naldi on a hot tin roof. Richard Boone as her psychiatrist, Joan Blondell and Ric Roman were in Mel Dinelli's screenplay, from Shirley Jackson's novel 'The Bird's Nest', produced by Jerry Bresler for Kirk Douglas' Bryna Productions. Box-offices suffered an attack of depression.* ▷

The Little Hut *was a comedy that promised more than it delivered. André Roussin's play about a girl and two men on a desert island ran two years in Paris and, adapted by Nancy Mitford, almost three in London. The screenplay by F. Hugh Herbert seemed to run almost as long for spice-fanciers, lured by the tut-tuts of movie censors and posters suggesting that Ava Gardner, David Niven and Stewart Granger might strip off at any moment. It was all talk and not much action, even at the pay-box. Produced by Mark Robson and Herbert, directed by Robson, with brief appearances by Walter Chiari, Finlay Currie, Jean Cadell, Henry Oscar.*

Unlike Joe Pasternak's usual lush musicals, **This Could be the Night** *was a black-and-white comedy with incidental song numbers, a sort of minor* Guys *and* Dolls *about an innocent among Broadway nightclub wolves; in it he starred Anthony Franciosa (first film), Jean Simmons and Paul Douglas. It had sharp direction by Robert Wise; racy dialogue in Isobel Lennart's screenplay; and slick performances by the stars and Julie Wilson, Joan Blondell, J. Carrol Naish, Neile Adams, Rafael Campos, ZaSu Pitts, Tom Helmore, Murvyn Vye, Ray Anthony and his band.*

Heavily dramatic but a box-office light-weight, **I Accuse!** *dealt with the trials of Dreyfus, played by Jose Ferrer, with Viveca Lindfors as his wife. Gore Vidal's script concentrated on the accused rather than Zola as in the story's last movie version. It was well directed by Ferrer, produced by Sam Zimbalist at MGM British, and excellently acted by the above and Anton Walbrook, Leo Genn, Emlyn Williams, David Farrar, Donald Wolfit, Herbert Lom, Harry Andrews, Felix Aylmer, George Coulouris, Peter Illing, Carl Jaffe, Eric Pohlmann, John Phillips, Laurence Naismith, Michael Hordern, Ronald Howard, Charles Gray.*

Not exactly vintage MGM entertainment: Pier Angeli (left) and Michele Morgan in **The Vintage** *as sisters whose placid life in a vineyard was made turbulent by two fugitives from the law: Mel Ferrer and John Kerr. Restraint was the keynote of their acting under Jeffrey Hayden's direction, but a dash of purple passion would have done them and the movie a power of good. Written by Michael Blankfort from a novel by Ursula Keir; produced in France by Edwin Knopf, with Leif Erickson, Theodore Bikel, Jack Mullaney . . .*

Man on Fire was quickly doused by cold water from the box-office. Ranald MacDougall's literate script, directed by him, invited its audiences to shed a tear for the child of divorce, shuttling between parents. Left to right: Mary Fickett, Inger Stevens (Hollywood debut after 50 television plays), Malcolm Brodrick, Bing Crosby (good serious performance), E. G. Marshall. Sol C. Siegel produced . . .

Jack Lord, Gia Scala, Marcel Dalio, Dorothy Malone and Robert Taylor watch a mysterious follower (Martin Gabel) who is to embroil them in a smuggling racket in **Tip on a Dead Jockey**/Time for Action. Charles Lederer developed a rather disjointed script from John O'Hara's story; Knopf produced and Richard Thorpe directed for sluggish action at the paybox.

Some of **House of Numbers** was shot inside San Quentin. Parlaying two surefire movie bets, the film featured twin characters, played by Jack Palance, and a jail-break plot. One Palance's wife was played by a new Monroe-type blonde, Barbara Lang, cast with Harold J. Stone, Edward Platt, Burt Douglas. Charles Schnee produced; Russell Rouse scripted (with Don Mankiewicz, from Jack Finney's novel) and directed.

Robby the Robot was the hero, and a computer drunk with power was the heavy, in **The Invisible Boy**, a cute and fairly profitable successor to Forbidden Planet from producer Nicholas Nayfack, writer Cyril Hume and director Herman Hoffman. Actors amid the hardware were young Richard Eyer, Diane Brewster and Philip Abbott (here) and Harold J. Stone.

Blood-and-thunder on the Adriatic coast as Van Johnson and Martine Carol rescue her blind brother, Gustavo Rojo, from Red heavies in the British-made **Action of the Tiger**. Incredible but lively; James Wellard's novel was adapted by Peter Myers and scripted by Robert Carson for producer Kenneth Harper. Terence Young directed a cast including Herbert Lom, Jose Nieto, Helen Haye and, as a minor villain, Sean Connery.

Writer-director-producer Albert Lewin was off on one of his exotic sprees of drama and mysticism in **The Living Idol**, this time in Mexico. Archaeologist James Robertson Justice believed Liliane Montevecchi, loved by Steve Forrest, was haunted by Mayan sacrifices to a jaguar god centuries before. So he turned a real live jaguar loose on her (don't ask questions, just enjoy it); Steve rushed to her aid, grappled with the beast and, said synopsis, 'the whole eternal struggle between good and evil was symbolized in the battle for her soul!' . . .

Something of Value, made largely in Africa, had newsreel-like realism heightened by a fore-word from Winston Churchill, specially filmed. The bloodthirsty Mau-Mau rituals and raids on white settlers in Kenya were almost too graphically depicted in this well-received Pandro Berman production, expertly written (from Robert Ruark's best-seller) and directed by Richard Brooks. Sidney Poitier, Walter Fitz-gerald and Rock Hudson (here) were in a strong cast that included Wendy Hiller, Dana Wynter, Robert Beatty, Michael Pate, and the impressive black actors Juano Hernandez, William Marshall and Frederick O'Neal.

Westerns were in fashion (were they ever out?) after the surprise smash of Fastest Gun Alive, and MGM released two in 1957. Rory Calhoun and Anne Francis starred in **The Hired Gun**, independently produced by Calhoun and his agent, Vic Orsatti; directed by Ray Nazarro; written by Buckley Angell and David Lang; featuring Vince Edwards, John Litel, Chuck Connors, Robert Burton, Guinn Williams . . . **Gun Glory** was what Stewart Granger had when he rescued Steve Rowland and Rhonda Fleming from Arch Johnson in Nicholas Nayfack's production of William Ludwig's screenplay, from a novel by Philip Yordan; directed by Steve's father, Roy Rowland; also cast, Chill Wills and James Gregory.

The Seven Hills of Rome was a healthy money-maker on the strength of Mario Lanza's come-back. Produced by Lester Welch in Italy, the screenplay by Art Cohn and Giorgio Prosperi was about, guess what: a temperamental American singer of Italian descent who lost his job in the States and made a successful come-back in Rome. Directed by Roy Rowland and supported also by Peggie Castle, Lanza (here with Renato Rascel and Maria Allasio) put on a good show for his still extensive public. The movie was in Technirama, yet another wide-screen process, developed by Technicolor.

An absorbing, occasionally exciting re-telling of Dostoievsky's **The Brothers Karamazov** cast Yul Brynner as Dmitri and Maria Schell as Grushenka. Pandro Berman's production drew reams of publicity from an odd source: Marilyn Monroe, who, said the columnists, longed for the role given to the beauteous Maria, a sensitive actress handicapped by a perpetual smile. Happy or sad, Maria kept smilin' through while Brynner, Lee J. Cobb, Richard Basehart, William Shatner, Albert Salmi and Judith Evelyn conveyed Russian emotionalism à la Richard Brooks, who directed and got a good deal of the book into his script. It was too much for the average moviegoer, who didn't go.

Les Girls *marked Gene Kelly's last MGM appearance until* That's Entertainment, *and Cole Porter's last score written for a film. Its approving audiences included the Queen and Prince Philip at its London première. Under George Cukor's direction the story of Kelly and his three Europe-touring dancing girls (left to right: Taina Elg, Kay Kendall and Mitzi Gaynor) shimmered with elegant fun. All four principals drew praise, Miss Kendall being hailed as America's most effervescent English import since Schweppes; they were supported by Jacques Bergerac, Leslie Phillips, Henry Daniell and Patrick Macnee. Orry-Kelly won an Oscar for his costumes. But the script John Patrick wrote for producer Sol C. Siegel was a bit too sophisticated to put it in the big-money class.*

Ray Milland (here with Barbara Everest as his mother) directed **The Safecracker** *and played the criminal whom the army let out of prison to open a safe in Nazi-occupied Belgium. Milland did a good job on both counts. Scripted by Paul Monash. Produced independently by David E. Rose at MGM's British studio, with Barry Jones, Jeanette Sterke, Victor Maddern, Ernest Clark, Cyril Raymond, Melissa Stribling, Anthony Nicholls, John Welsh.*

Eleanor Parker, who had once had to stand up to comparisons with Bette Davis in one Maugham remake, Of Human Bondage, *now had the even tougher assignment of following Garbo when she starred in* **The Seventh Sin**, *a remake of his* The Painted Veil. *English director Ronald Neame took a crew to Hong Kong for exteriors, but needn't have bothered. The movie was a dead duck that not even the kiss of life from Miss Parker and Jean Pierre Aumont (here), George Sanders, Bill Travers and Françoise Rosay could revive. David Lewis produced Karl Tunberg's screenplay.*

More Garbo memories were evoked by **Silk Stockings**, *a musical* Ninotchka, *rescripted by Leonard Spigelgass. Cyd Charisse played it acceptably without coming near the original magic – except in one rapturous scene when, alone in her hotel suite, she discarded her Russian serge and donned Paris silks while dancing to Cole Porter's lovely title number. This was never sung, leaving 'All of You' as the one real hit in a below-par Porter score. Fred Astaire (here with Cyd, Joseph Buloff, Jules Munshin and Peter Lorre) was in peak form; this was his last MGM appearance until* That's Entertainment *17 years later. Janis Paige had a showy part. Directed by Rouben Mamoulian, produced by Arthur Freed, it duplicated its Broadway stage success.*

One of the year's biggest money-spinners and laugh-rousers, **Don't Go Near the Water** *told a daffy tale about US Navy press officers on a Pacific isle miles away from World War II guns. Glenn Ford winningly starred, with Anne Francis and Earl Holliman (here); also cast were Gia Scala, Keenan Wynn, Eva Gabor, Russ Tamblyn, Jeff Richards, Romney Brent. Fred Clark stole scenes wholesale as the pompous CO. The funniest gag in the Dorothy Kingsley–George Wells script (from William Brinkley's novel) had Mickey Shaughnessy, chosen for publicity as the ideal sailor, unable to speak without using that (then) unprintable word, continually bleeped out on the soundtrack. Directed by Charles Walters, produced by Lawrence Weingarten.*

TAYLOR ON A HOT TIN ROOF
1958

Company results varied widely. MGM recovered from its first losing year; 20th Century-Fox, getting royalties from oil wells on its studio property, reported a $7½m profit; Paramount zoomed to $12½m; Republic had the best of its 13 years with $1½m and Disney the best of its 18 with nearly $4m, the same as United Artists. On the other hand, Columbia dived into red ink, losing $5m; Universal lost $2m and Warner Bros. $1m.

Dramatized novels dominated the release schedules, all the way from *The Brothers Karamazov* to *Peyton Place*. Predictably, the latter was bigger box-office. Others: *The Old Man and The Sea* (Spencer Tracy), *Room at the Top* (Laurence Harvey), *Ten North Frederick* (Gary Cooper), *The Naked and The Dead* (Aldo Ray), *Lonelyhearts* (Montgomery Clift), *The Roots of Heaven* (Errol Flynn), *The Last Hurrah* (Tracy), *God's Little Acre* (Robert Ryan), *A Time to Live and a Time to Die* (John Gavin), *Marjorie Morningstar* (Natalie Wood), *The Young Lions* (Marlon Brando, Clift), *Never Love a Stranger* (Steve McQueen), *The Quiet American* (Audie Murphy), *A Farewell to Arms* (Rock Hudson, Jennifer Jones).

1958–actually one of the best years in all-round product quality during MGM's second 25–opened with a laugh or two, but not many more, from **Merry Andrew** *with Danny Kaye and Pier Angeli. The much admired comic played an English schoolmaster who became a circus clown in Paul Gallico's story, scripted by Isobel Lennart and I. A. L. Diamond. Choreographer Michael Kidd was upped to full directorship by producer Sol C. Siegel, but did a patchy job. Business varied too. Operatic basso buffo Baccaloni, Robert Coote, Noel Purcell, Rex Evans, Patricia Cutts, Tommy Rall, Walter Kingsford and six songs were in it.*

Gigi *was the biggest grosser of all Arthur Freed musicals (world rentals about $15m.), champion prizewinner of 1958, and, to many, one of the most delightful movies ever made. MGM at its best, it sparkled like the champagne here being extolled by Hermione Gingold, Louis Jourdan and Leslie Caron. The movie danced off with no fewer than ten Academy Awards: best film; best direction, Vincente Minnelli; photography, Joseph Ruttenberg; screenplay, Alan Jay Lerner; scoring, André Previn; song, 'Gigi', Lerner and Frederick Loewe; editing, Adrienne Fazan; costumes, Cecil Beaton; art direction, William Horning and Preston Ames; honorary award, Maurice Chevalier. The last-named, now a jaunty 71, had three matchless songs: 'I'm Glad I'm Not Young Any More', 'Thank Heaven for Little Girls' and, with Miss Gingold, 'I Remember It Well'. Miss Caron, either as an anxious school-girl begging her cat to 'Say a Prayer for Me Tonight' or as an assured charmer queening it at Maxim's, was exactly right; she had played Gigi in a non-musical stage version of Colette's story in London. Jourdan, with the film's biggest role, acted and sang it to perfection. Miss Gingold and Isabel Jeans were elegant old bags, wickedly funny; Eva Gabor, Jacques Bergerac and John Abbott supported handsomely.*

Two Glenn Ford movies:

The remarkable run of good Glenn Ford pictures continued with **The Sheepman**, a winning Western with an offbeat heroine in Shirley MacLaine and an on-target script by William Bowers and James Edward Grant. It had a pawky humour that made audiences and critics as happy as its exhibitors. Leslie Nielsen, Mickey Shaughnessy, Edgar Buchanan, Willis Bouchey, Slim Pickens and Pedro Gonzalez–Gonzalez (they don't make names like those any more) supported the stars, who were brightly directed by George Marshall in Edmund Grainger's production.

Red Buttons tells Glenn Ford to stick to his sergeant's stripes and stop being an **Imitation General**. Taina Elg was the girl and Dean Jones, Kent Smith, Tige Andrews and John Wilder various army types in this World War II comedy. Ford and director George Marshall blended happily again, but the William Bowers script (original, William Chamberlain) lacked the charm of The Sheepman.

Three Robert Taylor movies: **The Law and Jake Wade** took no chances at all. It had (right to left) hero Taylor, heavy Richard Widmark and heroine Patricia Owens; buried loot, an Indian raid and a final showdown in a Western ghost town. John Sturges directed. Henry Silva, Robert Middleton, DeForrest Kelley were in William Hawks' production, written by William Bowers from a novel by Marvin Albert.

Box-office response to Taylor in a tough crime drama was always good, but **Party Girl** suffered from a confusing script in which a lawyer fronting for Chicago gangsters changed sides. Joe Pasternak produced. Nicholas Ray directed the George Wells screenplay, from a story by Leo Katcher. Left to right: Lee J. Cobb,

Cyd Charisse, John Ireland and Taylor; also cast were Kent Smith, Claire Kelly, Corey Allen, David Opatoshu, Barbara Lang.

Wild brother John Cassavetes, dance-hall gal Julie London and steady brother Robert Taylor in **Saddle the Wind**. This slick Western also cast Donald Crisp, Charles McGraw, Royal Dano and Richard Erdman. Robert Pirosh directed and Armand Deutsch produced the Rod Serling screenplay, from an original by Thomas Thompson. Its box-office insurance was Taylor, most of whose remaining screen decade was spent in Westerns.

The Asphalt Jungle plot turned up in **The Badlanders** disguised as an Arizona goldmine heist. In it were Ernest Borgnine, Katy Jurado and Alan Ladd (here) and Kent Smith, Claire Kelly, Nehemiah Persoff, Barbara Baxley and Anthony Caruso (who was in Asphalt too). Directed by Delmer Daves, the new Richard Collins script was produced by Aaron Rosenberg to a hearty reception from action fans.

Kay Kendall (here with Sandra Dee, Rex Harrison, John Saxon) was superb in **The Reluctant Debutante**; her death a year later

stole a possible all-time great from the screen's future. Adapted by William Douglas Home from his stage hit, performed with urbane gaiety by these four and Angela Lansbury, Peter Myers and Diane Clare, and adroitly directed by Vincente Minnelli, this high-style comedy recalled an era when 'sophisticated' was applied to people, not machinery. Miss Kendall and Harrison (Mr and Mrs in life as in the movie) had a tax problem that required Pandro Berman to produce this very British story in Paris.

Albert Zugsmith, a specialist in sleazy melodramas, lifted the lid on dope-peddling to teenagers in **High School Confidential**, his first for MGM release. Jack Arnold directed the Robert Blees–Lewis Meltzer screenplay, with (left to right) John Drew Barrymore–son of John B. and Dolores Costello–Diane Jergens, Burt Douglas and Jan Sterling; also cast were Russ Tamblyn, Mamie Van Doren, Jerry Lee Lewis, Ray Anthony, Jackie Coogan, Charles Chaplin Jr, Robin Raymond and Lyle Talbot.

According to the Frank Davis–Franklin Coen script for **Night of the Quarter Moon**, San Francisco society was given its worst shaking since the earthquake when John Drew Barrymore's bride, Julie London, admitted to having a black grandparent. Left to right: Dean Jones, Julie, Barrymore and Agnes Moorehead. Hugo Haas' direction was as purple as the plot, enacted also by Anna Kashfi, James Edwards, Arthur Shields, Robert Warwick, Edward Andrews, Jackie Coogan, Billy Daniels, Ray Anthony and Charles Chaplin Jr, with songs from Nat King Cole and Bing's niece, Cathy Crosby. Albert Zugsmith produced.

Michael Balcon's Ealing Films came through with a moving, authentic-looking story of **Dunkirk**, one of the best movies about World War II. It drew big audiences, especially in the British Commonwealth. In this scene, a prayer for deliverance is said by Sean Barrett and Bernard Lee, as civilians whose little boat was one of the hundreds brought across from England, and John Mills, as one of the thousands of troops so rescued. Direction by Leslie Norman, production by Michael Forlong, script by David Divine and W. P. Lipscomb (based on 'The Big Pick-up' by Elleston Trevor and 'Dunkirk' by Ewan Butler and J. S. Bradford), black-and-white photography by Paul Beeson, and music by Malcolm Arnold, were all excellent. So was a huge cast including Richard Attenborough, Robert Urquhart, Ray Jackson, Meredith Edwards, Anthony Nicholls, Maxine Audley, Patricia Plunkett, Michael Gwynn, Victor Maddern, Barry Foster, Cyril Raymond, Eddie Byrne, Lionel Jeffries, Nicholas Hannen.

What was the significance of the smouldering looks exchanged by the Russian major and Lady Diana Ashmore, and how did it affect her fellow passengers on the last plane from Budapest to Vienna after the 1956 Hungarian revolt, hmmmm? Good questions, answered at great length in **The Journey** by writer George Tabori, producer-director Anatole Litvak, Yul Brynner and Deborah Kerr (here) and Jason Robards Jr, Robert Morley, E. G. Marshall, Anne Jackson, Kurt Kasznar, David Kossoff, Anouk Aimee, Ivan Petrovich, little Ronny Howard, etc. Business was slow too.

The Doctor's Dilemma had a splendid gallery of performances, directed by Anthony Asquith, and the popularity of Dirk Bogarde and Leslie Caron almost overcame the movie masses' resistance to Bernard Shaw's torrents of verbal wit. Left to right: Alastair Sim, Bogarde, John Robinson, Miss Caron, Robert Morley and Felix Aylmer. Anatole de Grunwald wrote the script and produced, casting Michael Gwynn, Maureen Delaney, Alec McCowen and Terence Alexander in minor roles.

Marshall Thompson had to use a gas mask when he got close to the **First Man Into Space**. Its audiences were not so well-equipped. The John Cooper–Lance Hargreaves script concerned a pilot who returned from a space flight as a blob-like monster. Bill Edwards played this unfortunate, with Marla Landi, Robert Ayres and Carl Jaffe also in Robert Day's cast. Produced by John Croydon and Charles Vetter Jr in England for Producers Associates, it did profitable business.

Mrs John Cassavetes, better known on stage as Gena Rowlands, made an attractive MGM debut in **The High Cost of Loving**, co-starring with its director, Jose Ferrer. They and a writer billed as Rip Van Ronkel got a lot of fun out of a tiny plot: husband thought he was losing his office job, wife thought she was starting a baby; he wasn't, she was. Milo Frank Jr produced, casting Jim Backus, Joanne Gilbert, Bobby Troup, Philip Ober, Edward Platt, Werner Klemperer.

Another pleasing MGM discovery, Dean Jones graduated from bits to the lead in **Handle with Care** as a law student building up evidence of corruption at City Hall. The script did an irritating about-face as he was proved wrong. Joan O'Brien (here holding him back from Royal Dano) and Thomas Mitchell, John

Smith, Walter Abel, Anne Seymour and Ted de Corsia were featured. David Friedkin directed, Morton Fine produced; both wrote it from Samuel and Edith Grafton's original. A double-biller.

Doris Day and Gig Young sparkled in **The Tunnel of Love**, a bright domestic comedy, produced and scripted by Joseph Fields from his Broadway hit. Richard Widmark, making a rare excursion into comedy, co-starred with Doris; in support were Gia Scala, Elisabeth Fraser and Elizabeth Wilson. Gene Kelly, completing his MGM contract, for the first time directed a movie he wasn't in.

Tarzan's Fight for Life was MGM's second and last from producer Sol Lesser, who had been tarzanning for 25 years, off and on. In it Jane, whose absence from their treetop home left Tarzan mateless for whole movies at a stretch, reappeared in the shape of Eve Brent, with Gordon Scott again doing his thing and director Bruce Humberstone telling him where and when. No CinemaScope this time, just Metrocolor. Also cast: James Edwards, Carl Benton Reid, Woody Strode, Rickie Sorensen.

Tautly exciting, **Torpedo Run** scored another hit for Glenn Ford (here with Ernest Borgnine and Dean Jones) tracking a Japanese aircraft carrier which their sub finally caught and destroyed in Tokyo Bay. The Richard Sale–William Wister Haines script had a no-nonsense directness and Joseph Pevney's direction kept up a driving pace. Diane Brewster, Paul Picerni and Robert Hardy supported in Edmund Grainger's production.

A box-office stir was caused by Tennessee Williams' **Cat on a Hot Tin Roof**. Not only was it the top moneymaker of 1958, it was the tenth biggest in all the company's years. Richard Brooks' direction and (with James Poe) script preserved the play's highly-charged atmosphere of dramatic conflict and sexual tension. The story was motivated by a husband's refusal to bed his wife, with a clear implication of his homosexual tendency, and the Lawrence Weingarten production took a step forward (or backward, as you will) in movie permissiveness from Tea and Sympathy's pussyfooting around the subject two years before. Paul Newman's brooding force as the husband came as no surprise, but Elizabeth Taylor's wife was a revelation: beautiful kitten became fiery cat in a stunning performance. Burl Ives repeated his Broadway success as Big Daddy; Jack Carson, Judith Anderson, Madeleine Sherwood and Laddy Gates supported ably.

Russ Tamblyn swung with acrobatic élan into his first star role as **Tom Thumb** (always billed as 'tom thumb'). Its production brought the full resources of MGM's British studio into play, and the heavy budget paid dividends as it became a perennial holiday booking. The Grimms' fairytale was cleverly expanded by producer-director George Pal to include songs, dances, animated puppets, and a riotous pair of villains in Peter Sellers and Terry-Thomas. Jessie Matthews was featured (23 years after being signed by MGM to star with Clifton Webb in a musical that never started) along with Bernard Miles, Alan Young, June Thorburn and Ian Wallace. Script: Ladislas Fodor.

Andy Hardy Comes Home, a faint echo of the movies that had made Mickey Rooney a star, tried to turn him into a young Judge Hardy. If the late Lewis Stone had tried to play Andy it wouldn't have been much sillier. The Hardy family, 1958: Fay Holden, Teddy Rooney (aged eight), Gina Gillespie, Patricia Breslin, Rooney, backed up by Sara Haden, Johnny Weissmuller Jr, Cecilia Parker. Very little was added to the series' $25m. in rentals by this independent production by Red Doff, directed by Howard Koch. Script: Edward Hutshing, Robert Donley.

Rod Steiger forces James Mason, Inger Stevens and their daughter Terry Ann Ross to join his plot to extort $500,000 from an airline via a planted bomb. This started a series of suspense-fraught situations in **Cry Terror**, written and directed by master withers-wringer Andrew L. Stone in his most unnerving style. Great stuff. Stone co-produced with his film editor wife, Virginia. Also cast: Neville Brand, Angie Dickinson, Jack Klugman, Kenneth Tobey, Jack Kruschen, Carleton Young and Mason's real daughter, Portland . . .

Up for a breather: Virginia Core, Ross Martin, Dan Dailey and Claire Kelly in one of the drier moments from **Underwater Warrior**, Ivan Tors' independent production about frogmen in the Pacific. Andrew Marton directed Gene Levitt's actionful script; James Gregory and Raymond Bailey completed the cast . . .

Andrew and Virginia Stone dipped their picture-making brushes into the grue again for **The Decks Ran Red**, which had captain James Mason and Dorothy Dandridge besting villain Broderick Crawford after a mutiny that killed off a shipload of actors like Stuart Whitman. David Cross, Joel Fluellen, Jack Kruschen and John Gallaudet; actionful direction by Stone. It turned a nice profit.

Some Came Running would have been a mishmash with less assured performers than Frank Sinatra, Dean Martin and Shirley MacLaine. James Jones' sprawling novel about a homecoming GI, a gambler and a goodtime girl was worked over by John Patrick and Arthur Sheekman and directed by Vincente Minnelli to yield several good scenes (mostly Miss MacLaine's), but little dramatic unity. Others in Sol C. Siegel's production were Martha Hyer, Arthur Kennedy, Nancy Gates, Leora Dana, Betty Lou Keim, Larry Gates, Steven Peck, Connie Gilchrist. The stars meant money in the paybox.

Fun on the farm with Debbie Reynolds and Tony Randall in **The Mating Game**, which transferred H. E. Bates' rambunctious 'Darling Buds of May' family to Maryland via William Roberts' adaptation. George Marshall directed, with Paul Douglas and Una Merkel as Pa and Ma Larkin, Fred Clark, Philip Ober, Charles Lane, Philip Coolidge and Trevor Bardette. Philip Barry Jr's production prospered.

An arresting new face arrived in **Nowhere to Go**: Maggie Smith, signed to a joint Ealing–MGM contract, and cast opposite George Nader as a girl giving refuge to a criminal on the run. Nader was impressive in his first movie away from Hollywood, a strong chase drama written by Seth Holt and Kenneth Tynan from Donald Mackenzie's novel and directed by Holt in London locales. Michael Balcon's production cast Bernard Lee, Geoffrey Keen, Bessie Love (her first for MGM in 28 years), Andree Melly, Howard Marion-Crawford, Harry H. Corbett, Lionel Jeffries.

BEN HUR LIVES!

1959

*Two of the greatest strokes of good fortune in MGM's history were called **Ben-Hur**. In 1925 the success or failure of the new company depended on it. In 1958 the continuance of MGM's prestige and its financial stability were risked with a $15m. investment in a remake of the same subject. A flop would have been disastrous. But its triumph was even*

MGM–Loew's, last of the hold-outs against the government's anti-trust action, finally divided itself in March into two unconnected companies: Loew's Theatres and Metro-Goldwyn-Mayer. Six months later the latter announced its profit, $7,698,951, the highest since 1951's total for the old company.

Censorship was still alive and well. The Production Code Administration (heir of the old Hays Office) refused to approve United Artists' David Niven–Mitzi Gaynor comedy *Happy Anniversary* until this speech was added: 'I never should have taken Alice to that hotel room before we were married. What

more overwhelming than the original one; it brought MGM over $80m. in world-wide rentals. Then, in 1971, it had the biggest audience for a single screening of any film when it was seen by 32,630,000 Americans on TV. Those who pigeonhole it as just an inflated supercolossal may be surprised to know that it was received by the critics, almost without exception, as a masterly piece of film-making; praise was showered on every aspect of its production, and this welcome was echoed in the Academy's prizegiving for 1959. A record 12 Oscars were voted to it as the year's best picture and for best direction (William Wyler); actor (Charlton Heston in a portrayal of great spiritual and physical strength); supporting actor (Hugh Griffith); cinematography (Robert Surtees); scoring (Miklos

Rozsa); editing (Ralph Winters, John Dunning); costumes (Elizabeth Haffenden); art direction (William Horning, Edward Carfagno); sound recording (Franklin Milton); visual effects (Arnold Gillespie, Robert MacDonald); and sound effects (Milo Lory). Those special effects were greatly responsible for the spectacular sea battle and the breathtaking chariot race sequences; they in turn were prime reasons for the phenomenal crowds it drew. It was produced in Rome by Sam Zimbalist, whose making of Quo Vadis *there was a picnic in comparison; the mounting pressure of producing this now-or-never winner hastened his death shortly before its completion. Karl Tunberg got solo credit for a script also worked on by Christopher Fry (who was on the set with Wyler throughout), Maxwell*

could I have been thinking of?' What indeed! But details in two murder trial dramas, *Compulsion* and *Anatomy of a Murder,* were unusually frank.

I Want to Live and *Separate Tables,* which had won Oscars for Susan Hayward and David Niven respectively, were hits. So were *Auntie Mame* (Rosalind Russell), *The Defiant Ones* (Tony Curtis, Sidney Poitier), *Some Like It Hot* (Marilyn Monroe, Jack Lemmon, Curtis), *The Nun's Story* (Audrey Hepburn, Peter Finch), *Pillow Talk* (Doris Day, Rock Hudson), *Rio Bravo* (John Wayne, Dean Martin).

Anderson, S. N. Behrman and Gore Vidal. Six 65-millimetre cameras were focused on its (give or take a thousand) 3,000 sets and 50,000 people, who included Stephen Boyd (at left, clashing with Heston in the chariot race) and Jack Hawkins, Haya Harareet, Martha Scott, Cathy O'Donnell, Sam Jaffe, Finlay Currie, Frank Thring, Terence Longdon, André Morell, Marina Berti, George Relph, Lawrence Payne and Duncan Lamont. Important contributions were made by second unit directors Andrew Marton, Yakima Canutt and Mario Soldati.

Shirley MacLaine and David Niven, making a comedy team as refreshing as Loy and Powell, or Hepburn and Tracy, blended their dry wit and offhand charm in **Ask Any Girl,** *a box-*

office winner for director Charles Walters and producer Joe Pasternak. George Wells' script, from a novel by Winifred Wolfe, took wicked swipes at business and merchandising morals while telling the story of how a girl who didn't smoke, drink, or anything, coped with three men about New York town. Also cast: Gig Young, Rod Taylor, Claire Kelly, Jim Backus and Elisabeth Fraser.

North by Northwest *was Alfred Hitchcock's first at MGM and, say many aficionados, his best ever. The studio replaced CinemaScope with Paramount's big-screen process, Vista-Vision, just this once; the whole production was going to be made for Paramount at one time. The movie had Cary Grant and Eva Marie Saint whirling in the vortex of Ernest Lehman's devilishly clever script to its climax among the great stone faces of Mount Rushmore. Thrilling Hitchcock touches abounded, and so did hefty grosses in all cinemas. Also cast: James Mason, Jessie Royce Landis, Leo G. Carroll, Philip Ober, Josephine Hutchinson, Martin Landau, Edward Platt, Adam Williams, Robert Ellenstein, Philip Coolidge.*

291

It Started with a Kiss which Debbie Reynolds sold to Glenn Ford for charity, then Charles Lederer's script continued at this skirt-tearing level of humour. Profitable, though. Eva Gabor, Gustavo Rojo, Fred Clark, Edgar Buchanan, Henry Morgan and Robert Warwick were in George Marshall's cast; Aaron Rosenberg produced.

Glenn Ford and Debbie Reynolds, working in perfect rapport with George Marshall, who had been directing either or both of them in five successive movies, hit the laugh jackpot with **The Gazebo**, a neat moneyspinner. Alex Coppel's black comedy featured a pet pigeon, a body that wouldn't stay buried, Carl Reiner, John McGiver, Doro Merande, Mabel Albertson and ZaSu Pitts. Screenplay, George Wells; production, Lawrence Weingarten.

'I get 'em into trouble in the first reel and keep 'em in trouble till the end' said Andrew Stone explaining his cliffhanger technique. He wrote, directed and, with editor Virginia Stone, produced **The Last Voyage**—and, boy, did he get Robert Stack and Dorothy Malone into trouble! The ship was on fire, captain George Sanders was having a crise de nerfs, Dorothy was trapped under wreckage and the water was rising steadily...Also cast: Edmond O'Brien (left), Woody Strode, Jack Kruschen and moppet Tammy Marihugh. As usual eschewing studio sets. Stone bought the famed liner 'Ile de France' which was headed for the scrapyard, filmed in and on her, and sank her as cameras turned. Short of drowning the extras, realism could go no further.

Never So Few, an uneasy mixture of comedy ▷ and action drama, sold well on the strength of its cast: Frank Sinatra and Gina Lollobrigida (here) and Steve McQueen, Peter Lawford, Brian Donlevy, Paul Henreid, Richard Johnson, Dean Jones, Charles Bronson, Philip Ahn, John Hoyt, Whit Bissell, Richard Lupino. It was whipped up by Millard Kaufman from Tom Chameles' best-seller. John Sturges directed the Edmund Grainger production.

Maurice Chevalier and Deborah Kerr in **Count Your Blessings** were sparkling players in need of something sparkling to play. The public, warned by most critics, gave a cold shoulder to this tedious filming (in Paris) of Nancy Mitford's novel 'The Blessing', whose brittle fun crumbled under the heavy hands of director Jean Negulesco, producer-scripter Karl Tunberg and actor Rossano Brazzi as Deborah's French husband. Martin Stephens as their son had a key part, with Tom Helmore, Ronald Squire, Patricia Medina, Mona Washbourne, Steve Geray and Lumsden Hare.

Emlyn Williams, Virginia McKenna, Cecil Parker, Alexander Knox, Richard Harris, Ben Wright, Peter Illing and Terence de Marney. Julian Blaustein produced at MGM British.

Also made at the London studios with profitable results, **Libel** hinged on a look-alike coincidence as phoney as The Scapegoat's. It starred Dirk Bogarde as a Sir who might really have been somebody else, Olivia de Havilland (his wife) and Robert Morley (his barrister). Paul Massie, Wilfrid Hyde White, Anthony Dawson, Richard Wattis, Martin Miller, Richard Dimbleby, Millicent Martin, Robert Shaw, Joyce Carey, Kenneth Griffith and Richard Pearson were also in Anthony Asquith's cast. A lot of talent for producer Anatole de Grunwald to lavish on a creaky melodrama, adapted by him and Karl Tunberg from Edward Wooll's 1934 play.

The first 'Tarzan' made at the MGM studios since 1942, **Tarzan the Ape Man** introduced a new, collegiate-type vine-swinger in 6' 4" Denny Miller. Both he and Joanna Barnes as Jane were less nude than their predecessors, which possibly explains why it was the company's least popular 'Tarzan'. It went back to the first (1932) MGM entry's story, re-scripted by Robert Hill, directed by Joseph Newman, produced by Al Zimbalist, with Cesare Danova and Robert Douglas featured.

Green Mansions like 'Alice in Wonderland', should not be filmed. The magic melts under the arc lights. Vincente Minnelli had briefly attempted a 1954 version with Pier Angeli and Edmund Purdom. Writer Dorothy Kingsley, director Mel Ferrer and producer Edmund Grainger now made a brave try at the W. H. Hudson classic and got generally poor reviews and receipts for their trouble. Anthony Perkins and Audrey Hepburn (then Mrs Ferrer) brought an appropriately fey quality to their jungle dalliance, and were supported by Lee J. Cobb, silent star Sessue Hayakawa, Henry Silva, Nehemiah Persoff and Michael Pate.

Dowager countess Bette Davis is confronted by bogus son Alec Guinness in the most over-dressed set of the year, and one of her too few scenes in **The Scapegoat**. Once they'd swallowed the incredible premise of Daphne du Maurier's novel (an English tourist looking and sounding so much like a French count that the latter's family couldn't tell the difference) audiences relished a tasty dish of drama confected by writers Gore Vidal and Robert Hamer, directed by Hamer for producer Michael Balcon. Also cast: Nicole Maurey, Irene Worth, Pamela Brown, Geoffrey Keen, Peter Bull and Noel Howlett.

Alfred Hitchcock had been going to direct **The Wreck of the Mary Deare** but did North by Northwest instead. He might have tightened up the suspense in Eric Ambler's script from the Hammond Innes novel; but Michael Anderson found enough dramatic conflict and action in it to make a superior thriller. Gary Cooper as captain of a deserted ship and Charlton Heston as a salvage claimer tackled their he-man roles with spirit, supported by Michael Redgrave,

1959

Output slackened in 1959, and to keep the company's overseas exchanges busy the studio packaged three features from an MGM television series, seen only in America, based on 'Northwest Passage'. Actionful programmers, they were produced by Adrian Samish and written by Gerald Drayson Adams. Shown here are Keith Larsen, Buddy Ebsen and Don △ Burnett (who were in them all) in **Fury River**, directed by Jacques Tourneur, Alan Crosland Jr, George Waggner and Otto Lang . . . the ▽ three men and Lisa Gaye in **Frontier Rangers**, directed by Tourneur, with Philip Tonge and Angie Dickinson . . . Larsen and Taina Elg in **Mission of Danger**, directed by Tourneur and Waggner, with Tonge, Alan Hale Jr and Patrick Macnee.

Mamie Van Doren almost gave her all for cinema art at frequent intervals, as Albert Zugsmith productions kept zugging. In **The Beat Generation** she generated a beat in Ray Danton. Steve Cochran, Fay Spain, Louis Armstrong, Margaret Hayes, Jackie Coogan, Jim Mitchum, Charles Chaplin Jr, Ray Anthony, Cathy Crosby, Billy Daniels, Dick Contino, Maxie Rosenbloom and one Grabowski were in the Richard Matheson–Lewis Meltzer screenplay . . . In **Girls' Town** she turned Contino on in the woods, while Mel Torme, Paul Anka, Gigi Perreau, Elinor Donahue, Sheilah Graham, Gloria Talbott and Harold Lloyd Jr joined other Zugsmith regulars Anthony, Mitchum, Chaplin, Grabowski, the Misses Hayes and Crosby to interpret Robert Smith's script. Charles Haas directed both and they made money.

The Big Operator marked a departure for ▷ Mickey Rooney, cast as a sadistic gang-leader in the movie he co-sponsored with Albert Zugsmith. A remake of Paul Gallico's Joe Smith, American, directed by Charles Haas, produced by Red Doff, scripted by Robert Smith and Allen Rivkin, it featured Steve Cochran (here getting the 'we have ways of making you talk' treatment), in Robert Young's 1941 part. Also cast: Mamie Van Doren, good as a housewife, Mel Torme, Ray Danton, Jim Backus, Ray Anthony, Jackie Coogan, Charles Chaplin Jr. Billy Daniels, Jay North, Grabowski (left), Leo Gordon (right).

Watusi was a road company King Solomon's Mines. Said caption on this scene: 'George Montgomery and Taina Elg suddenly realize that their hatred has given way to love.' Those hot African nights do it every time. The movie was scripted by James Clavell from Rider Haggard's sequel, directed by Kurt Neumann and produced by Al Zimbalist, using much stock footage from the Mines location trip. Also cast: David Farrar, Rex Ingram, Dan Seymour.

A unique spectacle was presented by a normal sized, black-and-white film, **The World, the Flesh and the Devil**, *sponsored by Harry Belafonte and Sol C. Siegel. It showed the vast canyons of Manhattan emptied by some super-weapon, and only Belafonte left alive. These sequences, brilliantly photographed by Harold Marzorati in early mornings before New York crowds and traffic got too thick to keep out of camera range, gave way to a bizarre triangle story when Inger Stevens and Mel Ferrer brought the city's population to three. Scripted and directed by Ranald MacDougall, from Ferdinand Reyher's adaptation of an M. P. Shiel tale; produced by George Englund.*

For the First Time *was Mario Lanza's ironically titled swansong. While it was drawing crowds on his name, he was dying after years of massively excessive eating and drinking; a sad waste of an extraordinary vocal gift. But he looked and sounded good in this movie featuring Zsa Zsa Gabor (here), Johanna von Koszian and Kurt Kasznar. Independently produced in Italy by Alexander Gruter, in Technirama, the Andrew Solt screenplay was directed by Rudy Mate.*

Robert Mitchum, Kieron Moore (centre) and Gia Scala in **The Angry Hills** *which also starred Elisabeth Mueller and Stanley Baker, with Theodore Bikel, Sebastian Cabot, Peter Illing, Marius Goring, Leslie Phillips and Donald Wolfit. Robert Aldrich directed the thriller for producer Raymond Stross, using A. I. Bezzerides' script from the Leon Uris novel about resistance fighters in German-occupied Greece. Fair results.*

Robert Taylor and Linda Christian in **The House of the Seven Hawks**, *a fair-to-middling adventure yarn produced in England and Holland by David E. Rose with Richard Thorpe directing. Nicole Maurey, Donald Wolfit, Eric Pohlmann and David Kossoff had parts in Jo Eisinger's script from a novel by Victor Canning.*

WELL IN THE BLACK
1960

The first full year of divorcement revealed the proportionate importance of Loew's Theatres ($2½m profit) and MGM ($9½m). No other company came near the MGM figure. But MGM production continued at a low ebb in 1960, only 12 features emerging from Culver City. Even including outside contributions, just 19 were finished for MGM release.

Britain had a rash of *Carry On* comedies, Oscar Wilde biographies (Peter Finch out-Oscaring Robert Morley), a labour union comedy, *I'm All Right, Jack*, and a ditto drama, *The Angry Silence*, both with Richard Attenborough.

Anthony Perkins starred with Gregory Peck, Ava Gardner and Fred Astaire in *On the Beach*, and with Janet Leigh in Hitchcock's most profitable shocker, *Psycho*. *South Pacific*, released in 1958, was threatening *GWTW's* long-run records.

After the *Ben-Hur* monopoly of 1959, the Academy spread its awards around a bit. Best picture, *The Apartment*; actor, Burt Lancaster in *Elmer Gantry*; actress, Elizabeth Taylor in *Butterfield 8*; director, Billy Wilder, *The Apartment*.

Winning prizes elsewhere was D. H. Lawrence's *Sons and Lovers*, directed in England by Jack Cardiff, making amends for his previous movie, *Scent of Mystery*, the first (and last?) in Smell-o-Vision.

Judy Holliday was one of the screen's true jewels, and **Bells Are Ringing**, *the last movie she made before her death in 1965, was a bright setting for her. This Betty Comden–Adolph Green musical had been a Broadway hit for Judy. Arthur Freed's production and Vincente Minnelli's direction shone, but its paybox performance disappointed: musicals were unfashionable. Dean Martin shared the excellent Comden–Green–Jule Styne score containing 'The Party's Over', 'Long Before I Knew You', 'Just in Time', 'Drop That Name' and the poignant 'I'm Going Back to The Bonjour Tristesse Brassiere Company!' Also cast: Fred Clark, Eddie Foy Jr, Jean Stapleton, Ruth Storey, Frank Gorshin, Steven Peck, Gerry Mulligan, Nancy Walters.*

To celebrate the 75th anniversary of Mark Twain's book, and perhaps earn an honest penny, Samuel Goldwyn Jr produced **The Adventures of Huckleberry Finn** *with Eddie Hodges a sprightly Huck and world light-heavyweight champ Archie Moore surprisingly*

good as Jim. It had been filmed by MGM before (and better), and twice by Paramount. This version was written by James Lee and directed by Michael Curtiz, with Tony Randall, Patty McCormack, Neville Brand, Judy Canova, Mickey Shaughnessy, Andy Devine, Buster Keaton, Finlay Currie, Josephine Hutchinson, John Carradine, Royal Dano, Sterling Holloway. Alan Jay Lerner and Burton Lane wrote four songs for it.

Edna Ferber's **Cimarron**, *once a massive hit for* ▷ *RKO-Radio, was a major box-office disappointment for MGM 30 years later. The great Oklahoma land rush of settlers staking their claims in 1889 made a thrilling sequence in CinemaScope, but the romance and marriage of adventurer Glenn Ford and city girl Maria Schell seemed to have faded since Richard Dix and Irene Dunne played them. Edmund Grainger's production went on–and on–for 140 minutes. It was directed by Anthony Mann, scripted by Arnold Schulman, with Anne Baxter, Russ Tamblyn, Mercedes McCambridge, Vic Morrow, Aline MacMahon, Arthur O'Connell, Edgar Buchanan, Robert Keith, Henry Morgan, Charles McGraw, David Opatoshu, Royal Dano, Vladimir Sokoloff.*

The funny side of family life was displayed to large audiences by **Please Don't Eat the Daisies** *with (left to right) David Niven, Spring Byington, Doris Day, Patsy Kelly, children and dog; also cast were Janis Paige, Richard Haydn, Margaret Lindsay, Jack Weston, Carmen Phillips and Mary Patton. The Joe Pasternak production was delightfully handled by director Charles Walters and scripter Isobel Lennart. Jean Kerr's book provided the screen with a rare theatre critic hero, and MGM with a hit second only to* Butterfield 8 *among new 1960 releases (1959's* Ben Hur *still dominated the scene).*

Ennui gripped audiences of **Go Naked in the World** *as Anthony Franciosa madly adored Gina Lollobrigida, took her home to meet the folks, and discovered that his father and half the town's male population had, as the saying goes, known her. This neo-Elinor Glyn drama was written and directed by Ranald Mac-Dougall from Tom Chameles' novel. Ernest Borgnine, Luana Patten, Philip Ober, Nancy Pollock, Will Kuluva, John Kellogg, John Gallaudet were in Aaron Rosenberg's production.*

While Hollywood imported the luscious Loren and Lollobrigida, it generously repaid Italy with huge masculine hunks, the most successful of whom was Steve Reeves, former Mr America, seen briefly in Athena. *He played Hercules in two Roman blockbusters, then became* **The Giant of Marathon** *to the enrichment of exhibitors, the Titanus–Galatea–Lux studios and MGM distribution. Jacques Tourneur directed the action-crammed Ennio de Concini–Augusto Frassinetti–Bruno Vailati screenplay, produced by Vailati in something called Dyaliscope. Heroine: Mylene Demongeot.*

Dan Duryea, Mickey Rooney and Terry Moore in **Platinum High School**/Rich, Young and Deadly, *an unlikely melo about an academic Alcatraz for wealthy youths. Red Doff produced for Albert Zugsmith; director, Charles Haas; script, Robert Smith, from Howard Breslin's original; cast, Conway Twitty, Warren Berlinger, Yvette Mimieux, Richard Jaeckel, Harold Lloyd Jr, Christopher Dark, Elisha Cook Jr.*

Pandro Berman, a top 'A' producer for 30 years, indulged in a cheap programmer about a gang of sadistic young terrorists, **Key Witness.** *Before release, his name came off it and so associate Kathryn Hereford took the rap. The Alfred Brenner–Sidney Michaels screenplay was directed by Phil Karlson, with Dennis Hopper and Susan Harrison (here) and Jeffrey Hunter, Pat Crowley, Joby Baker, Johnny Nash, Corey Allen, Frank Silvera.*

The novels of Jack Kerouac, chief chronicler of the beat generation, were all the rage, so MGM bought his **The Subterraneans,** *filmable or not. Not, said critics and public, as Arthur Freed's production flopped. It looked like a blue movie with all porn removed: typical was this decorous orgy involving Janice Rule, George Peppard, Leslie Caron and (right foreground) the music department's boy wonder, André Previn, understandably depressed in his camera debut. Script, Robert Thom; director, Ranald Mac-Dougall; also cast, Roddy McDowall, Anne Seymour, Jim Hutton, Scott Marlowe, Ruth Storey, Arte Johnson, Bert Freed, Gerry Mulligan, Carmen McRae.*

More restless youth, another flop: **All the Fine Young Cannibals.** *Early scenes of poor white trash in the South gave way to tiresome love tangles among the urban rich in Robert Thom's script from Rosamond Marshall's novel 'The Bixby Girls'. Michael Anderson directed Robert Wagner, George Hamilton, Natalie Wood, Susan Kohner and Jack Mullaney (left to right) and Pearl Bailey (outstanding in a brief role), Onslow Stevens, Anne Seymour, Virginia Gregg, Mabel Albertson and Louise Beavers. Pandro Berman produced.*

The Time Machine *was a fascinating thriller and a profitable grosser; George Pal did H. G. Wells proud with his production and direction, despite free changes from the original. Rod Taylor fights the monstrous Worlocks to help the gentle Elois (right Bob Barran and Yvette Mimieux); he had travelled from 1900 to 802701 AD, via stunning special effects by Gene Warren and Tim Baer which won them an Academy Award. Alan Young, Sebastian Cabot, Tom Helmore, Whit Bissell and Doris Lloyd had parts in David Duncan's screenplay.*

Dolores Hart and George Hamilton played two of the countless collegians who descended on a Florida beach resort during their Easter vacation in **Where the Boys Are**. *Joe Pasternak's exuberantly youthful comedy scored a decided hit as did this pair and Yvette Mimieux, Jim Hutton, Paula Prentiss and disc star Connie Francis, the last two making movie debuts. Henry Levin directed, George Wells scripted Glendon Swarthout's novel. Barbara Nichols, Chill Wills, Frank Gorshin were featured.*

*A grimmer, less entertaining Continental drama, **The Angel Wore Red**, offered Ava Gardner as a scarlet woman and Dirk Bogarde as a spoiled priest improbably falling in love amid an equally unconvincing Spanish Civil War. Produced for Italy's Titanus company by Goffredo Lombardo for MGM release, it was written and directed by Nunnally Johnson. Also cast: Joseph Cotten, Vittorio de Sica, Aldo Fabrizi, Arnoldo Foa, Finlay Currie, Rossana Rory, Enrico Maria Salerno, Robert Bright, Nino Castelnuovo.*

Village of the Damned, *a really sinister horror movie, emerged from MGM British to intrigue big audiences after director Wolf Rilla, producer Ronald Kinnoch and writers Stirling Silliphant, George Barclay and Rilla had worked on John Wyndham's novel 'The Midwich Cuckoos'. Here parents George Sanders and Barbara Shelley question son Martin Stephens, whose strange manner and supernatural intelligence were shared by other children born at the same time. Also cast: Michael Gwynn, Laurence Naismith, Richard Warner, Thomas Heathcote, John Phillips, Richard Vernon, Rosamund Greenwood, Bernard Archard, Peter Vaughan.*

*A good old Greco-Phoenician bash occupied the 127 minutes of an MGM pick-up, **The Colossus of Rhodes**, a profitable movie which Italian-Spanish-French producers considered so stupendous that they filmed it in Super-TotalScope. Georges Marchal and Rory Calhoun (here) were accompanied by thousands of extras, Lea Massari, Conrado Sanmartin, Angel Aranda and Jorge Rigaud under Sergio Leone's direction.*

*Elizabeth Taylor won an Oscar for her performance as the oversexed Manhattan model in **Butterfield 8**; Eddie Fisher (here) was her one platonic man friend. (Offscreen he was anything but; their marriage made front page headlines.) The film was MGM's biggest new 1960 moneymaker. Charles Schnee and John Michael Hayes freely adapted John O'Hara's novella for Pandro Berman; Daniel Mann directed a cast which included Laurence Harvey, Dina Merrill, Mildred Dunnock, Betty Field, Jeffrey Lynn, Kay Medford.*

*Two young male discoveries kept stealing the spotlight in **Home from the Hill**: George Peppard (standing) and George Hamilton (embracing Luana Patten). Both Georges were put under contract. This sombre drama about an upper-crust backwoods family was one of the studio's 1960 best. Robert Mitchum and Eleanor Parker impressed as husband and wife in conflict. Directed by Vincente Minnelli, the Edmund Grainger production was written by Harriet Frank Jr and Irving Ravetch from William Humphrey's novel. Everett Sloane, Anne Seymour and Constance Ford supported.*

*Kieron Moore, Elizabeth Sellars, Aldo Ray and Albert Sharpe in **The Day They Robbed the Bank of England**, as choice a bit of bullion burglary as could be wished. It heisted quite a paybox haul too. Peter O'Toole, Hugh Griffith, John Le Mesurier, Joseph Tomelty, Miles Malleson and Peter Myers were in Jules Buck's production, directed by John Guillermin. Script by Howard Clewes from John Brophy's novel.*

*Yves Montand and Melina Mercouri were the most striking players in a complicated game of sex and power in **Where the Hot Wind Blows**, a heavy-breathing drama set in an Italian village. Gina Lollobrigida, Marcello Mastroianni, Pierre Brasseur and Paulo Stoppa also starred effectively under Jules Dassin's direction. Roger Vailland's novel 'The Law' was the basis of Dassin's script for the French-Italian movie produced by Jacques Bar.*

PROFITS RISE
1961

Technicolor and its rivals were now decorating the vast majority of movies; soon black-and-white would have novelty value. MGM soared to its biggest profit ($12½m) in 15 years, thanks mostly to continuing *Ben-Hur* income and yet another re-issue of *Gone With the Wind*.

Hits were coming from all over the place: Italy, with the lush *La Dolce Vita* and the stark *Two Women*; Greece, *Never on Sunday*; France, *Hiroshima Mon Amour*; Brazil, *Black Orpheus*. The Academy, the critics and the public agreed on the best picture, *West Side Story*; its directors Robert Wise and Jerome Robbins, and its dancing leads, George Chakiris and Rita Moreno. Maximilian Schell in *Judgement at Nuremburg* and Sophia Loren in *Two Women* won the acting Oscars, and Paul Newman in *The Hustler* much praise.

Exhibitors elected Elizabeth Taylor as the strongest star magnet, followed by Rock Hudson, Doris Day (enjoying a second vogue, bigger than in the early Fifties), John Wayne, Cary Grant, Sandra Dee, Jerry Lewis, William Holden, Tony Curtis, Elvis Presley.

Carroll Baker and James Shigeta were touchingly effective under Etienne Perier's direction in **Bridge to the Sun** *as American wife and Japanese husband. Their trials, as she adapted herself to Oriental life and he, opposed to the war, became an outcast in his own country provided slow but holding drama, scripted by Charles Kaufman from Gwen Terasaki's autobiography. Jacques Bar made it for his French production company and MGM, neither reaping much from its release.* ▷

The Hollywood that neglected D. W. Griffith and forgot to give Garbo or Chaplin an Academy Award (until they'd left town) let the maker of Citizen Kane *waste his genius on acting in European mini-epics. Orson Welles in* **The Tartars** *joined other émigrés Victor Mature and director Richard Thorpe to tell a story described in the ads as 'Hordes storm fortress! Tartars abduct Viking beauty! Orgy celebrates conquest!' Liana Orfei, Bella Cortez, Folco Lulli and Arnoldo Foa were also in the Lux Film shot in Italy and Yugoslavia.*

The 1961 entry from George Pal, high priest of special effects movies, was **Atlantis, the Lost Continent**. *With death-ray crystals, giant-fish submarines, beast-headed humans, earthquakes, volcanoes and tidal waves, it got its share of oohs and aahs (and grosses) but lacked* The Time Machine's *grip. Daniel Mainwaring's script was based on a play by Sir Gerald Hargreaves. Cast: young newcomers Anthony Hall and Joyce Taylor (here) and John Dall, Bill Smith, Edward Platt, Berry Kroeger, Frank DeKova, Edgar Stehli.*

King of Kings *was expected to be the Big One of 1961. It went into production in April 1960 at Samuel Bronston's studios in Spain, to which MGM president Joseph Vogel paid a visit that resulted in a financial hypo from the company, as in GWTW, and plans for a major roadshow release, as for* Ben-Hur. *Neither of those precedents were followed up at the paybox, even though this epic's grosses reached eight figures after it opened to sneers from the critics and lukewarm public interest. The*

spiritual was too often secondary to the spectacular in Nicholas Ray's direction and Philip Yordan's script. Jeffrey Hunter and Siobhan McKenna (here) were a picturebook Jesus and an actressy Mary, and the other principals in an enormous cast were similarly unreal: Robert Ryan (best, as John the Baptist), Hurd Hatfield, Ron Randell, Viveca Lindfors, Rita Gam, Carmen Sevilla, Brigid Bazlen, Rip Torn, Harry Guardino, Frank Thring, Guy Rolfe, Gregoire Aslan, Royal Dano, George Coulouris.

*After 23 years in movies Bob Hope finally did one for MGM, **Bachelor in Paradise**, and Lana Turner returned to her old studio for the occasion. They were the only two singles in a California housing estate; their progress to togetherness mildly amused crowds of fairly profitable proportions. Script, Hal Kantor and Valentine Davies; original, Vera Caspary; director, Jack Arnold; producer, Ted Richmond; cast, Janis Paige, Jim Hutton, Paula Prentiss, Don Porter, Virginia Grey, Agnes Moorehead, Clinton Sundberg, John McGiver.*

Susan Hayward, director Daniel Mann and producer Lawrence Weingarten came together again for more I'll Cry Tomorrow *acclaim, but didn't get it with **Ada**, a turgid drama of power politics with weak husband and strong wife in conflict. Arthur Sheekman and William Driskill based their script on Wirt Williams' novel 'Ada Dallas'. Left to right: Dean Martin, Martin Balsam, Hayward, Ralph Meeker, Wilfrid Hyde White; also cast were Larry Gates, Robert Simon.*

*Ingrid Thulin and Paul Henreid (here) were two of the important talents trapped in the disastrous remake of **The Four Horsemen of the Apocalypse**. Glenn Ford, Charles Boyer, Paul Lukas, Yvette Mimieux, Karl Boehm and Lee J. Cobb also starred under Vincente Minnelli's direction. All were either miscast (Thulin even had to be voice-dubbed, by Angela Lansbury) or off-form or both, and Minnelli's sensitivity was out to lunch. The dialogue in the Robert Ardrey–John Gay script was so banal, and the depiction of wartime Paris in Julian Blaustein's production so faulty, that giggles punctuated its press screenings. None was heard at MGM: a $6m. flop was no laughing matter.*

The Green Helmet *had enough human interest to satisfy average audiences; but it missed the full charge of excitement its subject–racing drivers–could have sparked off. Directed by Michael Forlong and produced by Charles F. Vetter at MGM British, the Jon Cleary screenplay was based on his own novel. Left to right: Nancy Walters, Bill Travers, Ed Begley, Peter Collingwood; also cast were Sidney James, Megs Jenkins, Ursula Jeans, Sean Kelly, Tutte Lemkow, Ferdy Mayne and driving champ Jack Brabham.*

*Another respectable if unsensational programmer from the British studio, **The Secret Partner** starred Stewart Granger as a fugitive trying to prove his innocence before the law caught up with him. Director Basil Dearden and producer Michael Relph brought their experienced teamwork to bear on the David Pursall–Jack Seddon screenplay. Also cast: Haya Harareet, the* Ben Hur *heroine, Bernard Lee, Hugh Burden, Lee Montague, Melissa Stribling, Conrad Phillips, John Lee, Peter Illing and Norman Bird.*

*Long famed for her inimitable supporting performances, Margaret Rutherford became a movie star at 70 when **Murder She Said** supplied her best part since the dotty medium in* Blithe Spirit. *As Agatha Christie's Miss Marple, she detected a cunning killing and gave MGM British a tidy moneymaker, economically produced by George Brown and slickly directed by George Pollock. Also cast: Conrad Phillips and Thorley Walters (here) and Arthur Kennedy, Muriel Pavlow, James Robertson Justice, Charles Tingwell, Joan Hickson, Ronald Howard. The David Pursall–Jack Seddon script was based on Miss Christie's '4.50 from Paddington'.*

*At MGM British the sumptuous feasts of yesteryear had been replaced by double-feature fare; a smorgasbord of slapstick was served up in **Invasion Quartet**. Spike Milligan, Gregoire Aslan, John Le Mesurier and Bill Travers were the comics in the Nazi-occupied France imagined by writers Jack Trevor Story and John Briley (using a Norman Collins original), and director Jay Lewis. Ronald Kinnoch produced, casting Thorley Walters, Maurice Denham, Thelma Ruby, Millicent Martin, Cyril Luckham and (briefly) Eric Sykes.*

*Spike Milligan had British radio and TV fans slapping their knees for years, but the guffaws were too widely spaced in his first solo-starring movie, **Postman's Knock**. It was one of MGM's few London-made pictures not released in the US. Barbara Shelley played the nutty postman's loved one, supported by John Wood, Miles Malleson, Wilfred Lawson, Ronald Adam, Mario Fabrizi, Bob Todd, Warren Mitchell, Lance Percival. Written by Jack Trevor Story and John Briley, directed by Robert Lynn, produced by Ronald Kinnoch.*

*As a comedy **A Matter of WHO** was about as funny as a smallpox epidemic–and that's what it was about. Somewhere along the line the Patricia Lee–Paul Dickson story, scripted by Milton Holmes, had become a Terry-Thomas fun film when it should have been a drama about WHO (World Health Organization). Alex Nicol and Sonja Ziemann, here with the star; Richard Briers, Honor Blackman, Carol White, Guy Deghy, Geoffrey Keen, Clive Morton, Vincent Ball, Andrew Faulds and Bruce Beeby were in it. Don Chaffey directed; Walter Shenson and Holmes produced at MGM British. Spotty business.*

*Arthur Freed's **Light in the Piazza** shone fitfully. No rush to the box-office was occasioned*

by its stars (left to right) Olivia de Havilland, Rossano Brazzi, Yvette Mimieux, George Hamilton—good as they were, and magnificent as the views of Florence looked in Cinema-Scope and Metrocolor. Elizabeth Spencer's novel on which Julius Epstein based his script had a depressing element in that the Yvette Mimieux character was mentally handicapped. Guy Green directed; Barry Sullivan and Isabel Dean were featured.

Having done everything else for suspense but tie a heroine to a railroad track, Andrew Stone tried a forest blaze in **Ring of Fire**, trapping everybody including vamp Joyce Taylor, cop David Janssen and gangster Frank Gorshin. Writer-producer-director Stone and co-producer Virginia scored another hit with the nail-biting masses.

George Hamilton and Richard Boone as 1870 US Cavalry officers who fought Apache raids when not snarling at each other in **A Thunder of Drums**. The well-worn territory covered by James Warner Bellah's script was observed in a harsher light than usual by director Joseph Newman in Robert J. Enders' production. Also cast: Luana Patten, Charles Bronson, Arthur O'Connell, Richard Chamberlain (debut), Duane Eddy, James Douglas and Tammy Marihugh.

Donald O'Connor's ebullience lightened the rather heavy-handed fantasy of **The Wonders of Aladdin**, a lavish Italian production directed by Henry Levin for Lux Films. Noelle Adam (here) and Vittorio de Sica, Aldo Fabrizi and Michele Mercier had other leads in Luther Davis' screenplay. The kiddies enjoyed it.

Arthur Loew filled out his overseas release lists with three features MGM TV made for △ American home consumption. Loaded with bullets, corpses, cops and robbers, they were: . . . **The Crimebusters** with Mark Richman, Martin Gabel, Carol Rossen, Philip Ober; producer, Charles Russell; director, Boris Sagal; script, Paul Monash, Wallace Ware . . . **The Lawbreakers** with Jack Warden, Vera Miles, Robert Douglas, Arch Johnson; producer, Jaime Del Valle; director, Joseph Newman; script, Paul Monash, W. R. Burnett **The Murder Men** with Dorothy Dandridge, Mark Richman, James Coburn, Shelley Manne; producer, Paul Monash; director, John Peyser; script, Mel Goldberg.

Out of the ordinary but out of the money was **Two Loves**/Spinster, with Shirley MacLaine as an inhibited schoolteacher who backed away whenever her temperamental boyfriend (Laurence Harvey) tried to consummate their love. The audience was as frustrated as the characters by the time Julian Blaustein's production ended with Shirley still more or less pure. Director Charles Walters got some value from the unfamiliar New Zealand setting and Maori characters in Ben Maddow's adaptation of Sylvia Ashton Warner's book. The miscast stars were supported by Jack Hawkins, Nobu McCarthy, Juano Hernandez, Ronald Long and Norah Howard.

Two more beefcake epics (both remakes of Douglas Fairbanks movies) starring Steve ▽ Reeves were picked up by MGM after the success of Giant of Marathon. **The Thief of Baghdad** was directed by Arthur Lubin and produced by Bruno Vailati, with Georgia Moll, Arturo Dominici, Edy Vessel and George Chamarat. **Morgan the Pirate** was made by another Hollywood director, André de Toth, with Valerie Lagrange, Armand Mestral and Chelo Alonso. Breakneck action and spectacular production effects brought profitable bookings.

1961 was the first year in MGM's history that didn't yield one major success. **The Honeymoon Machine**, which wound it up, at least meant to be funny, and was; Lawrence Weingarten's production turned a nice profit in 1962. Based on a play by Lorenzo Semple about an officer who used his ship's computer to break the bank at a Venice casino, George Wells' screenplay got a fast pace from Richard Thorpe's direction and sprightly performances from Brigid Bazlen, Paula Prentiss, Steve McQueen and Jim Hutton (left to right) and Jack Weston, Dean Jagger, Jack Mullaney.

THE WILD WEST
1962

The twin emergence of *Cleopatra*, the most expensive movie ever made, and the 20th Century-Fox annual report of a $39,796,094 loss (the all-industry all-time record) demonstrated what one supercolossal dud can do to a company's balance-sheet. It was a pretty dismal year altogether. MGM sank $10m to a profit of $2½m.

Charlton Heston in *El Cid*, Gregory Peck in *Guns of Navarone*, Kirk Douglas in *Spartacus* and Paul Newman in *Exodus* were among the best draws after over a year in release. Best of the new ones were Britain's *A Taste of Honey* and the flamboyant display of vintage star quality by Bette Davis and Joan Crawford in *Whatever Happened to Baby Jane?*, until *Lawrence of Arabia* arrived just in time to win the Academy Award and an Oscar for director David Lean. Best performance prizes went to Peck for *To Kill a Mockingbird* and Anne Bancroft for *The Miracle Worker*. Doris Day recaptured the No. 1 spot in the *Motion Picture Herald's* Top Ten which she had held in 1960; Frank Sinatra and Burt Lancaster nudged out William Holden and Tony Curtis.

All Fall Down *came out of the cutting room to give 1962 a good start, doubly welcome after the mediocrity of 1961 product. With Warren Beatty as the dissolute wanderer and Brandon de Wilde as his idolizing young brother, plus Angela Lansbury and Karl Malden as their parents and Eva Marie Saint as their fateful visitor, John Houseman gave his production the perfect players to bring James Leo Herlihy's novel to screen life. John Frankenheimer as director and playwright William Inge as scripter were ideal casting too. Their one mistake was allowing the constant reiteration of the Beatty character's silly name, Berry-Berry, to irritate the movie's admiring (but none too numerous) spectators.*

Tarzan Goes to India *was the 36th feature filmed from Edgar Rice Burroughs' brainchild, and surefire box-office. In it a new Tarzan entrepreneur, Sy Weintraub, introduced a more mature title-roler than usual: Jock Mahoney, a top Hollywood stunt man for years. This scene shows him with elephant boy Jai and Gajendra, king (said his billing) of the elephants. John Guillermin directed the movie which was shot in India and given the full CinemaScope-Technicolor treatment. Mark Dana and Leo Gordon had parts in the Guillermin–Robert Hardy Andrews script.*

Cairo *borrowed its title from an old Jeanette MacDonald movie and its plot from* The Asphalt Jungle. *The latter, closely followed in Joanne Court's script, looked almost as good as new in its Egyptian setting, and Ronald Kinnoch's production made a useful double-biller. Directed by Wolfe Rilla, with George Sanders and Richard Johnson (here), Faten Hamama, John Meillon, Eric Pohlmann, Walter Rilla.*

Spaghetti spectaculars relished by 1962 action fans: **Damon and Pythias**/The Tyrant of Syracuse *had Guy Williams and Don Burnett as the BC pals, supported by Illaria Occhini, Liana Orfei, Arnoldo Foa and Marina Berti under Curtis Bernhardt's direction; script by Bridget Boland and Barry Oringer; produced by Sam Jaffe and Samuel Marx . . . In* **The Son of Spartacus** *vamp Gianna Maria Canale batted false eyelashes in appeal for mercy from Steve Reeves' henchmen; Jacques Sernas, Ivo Garrani and Enzo Fiermonte were featured in*

the Titanus production directed by Sergio Corbucci.

Period of Adjustment, *a bubbly comedy, came from a Tennessee Williams play. It drew smaller crowds than his breast-heavers did, but a good time was had by all while Anthony Franciosa, Jane Fonda and Jim Hutton (left to right) sorted out their matrimonial affairs with Lois Nettleton, John McGiver, Mabel Albertson and Jack Albertson. George Roy Hill directed the Isobel Lennart screenplay, Lawrence Weingarten produced.*

Cinerama joined forces with MGM to tell a story: **How the West was Won**. *After ten years ▷ of cashing in on sheer size, it needed a shot in the arm. This widest of wide-screen processes (using three linked cameras in production and three sychronized projectors in specially adapted theatres to achieve a panorama filling the whole field of vision) had exhausted its travelogue possibilities. Completed in 1962, the massive production by Bernard Smith covered the adventures of a pioneering family with enough plot twists and spectacular climaxes to equip a dozen movies. It was a prodigious money's worth–and worth approximately $50m. in world-wide rentals. Much of this came from non-Cinerama theatres, which were provided with conventional reels for one projector. Unfortunately they still showed the joins necessitated by Cinerama's triple width; incredibly, no single-camera version had been shot. Spencer Tracy's voice linked the episodes directed by Henry Hathaway, John Ford and George Marshall and enacted by Karl Malden, Carroll Baker, Debbie Reynolds and Agnes Moorehead (left to right below), also Henry Fonda, James Stewart, Gregory Peck, (with Debbie at right), John Wayne, George Peppard, Richard Widmark, Robert Preston, Carolyn Jones, Lee J. Cobb, Eli Wallach, Raymond Massey, Thelma Ritter, Walter Brennan, Brigid Bazlen, David Brian, Andy Devine, Russ Tamblyn, Henry Morgan and Mickey Shaughnessy. Writer James R. Webb, film editor Harold Kress and the MGM sound department won Academy Awards.*

1962

'How Could They Make a Movie of **Lolita**?' demanded the ads. They didn't, quite. Stanley Kubrick's handling of the Vladimir Nabokov novel, scripted by the author, threw a discreet sheet over its bedroom details (this was back in 1962) and reduced the age disparity between Humbert and Lolita by casting James Mason and Sue Lyon (here with Shelley Winters as her mother). But it remained a fascinating depiction of the games some people play, and kept its big audiences alertly amused for over 2½ hours. Peter Sellers dazzled as Quilty. Others in James B. Harris' production for Seven Arts/MGM, made in England; Marianne Stone, Diana Decker, Jerry Stovin, Gary Cockrell.

Boris Karloff played a humanitarian surgeon in **Corridors of Blood**, although its advertising strove to indicate that he was up to his monstrous old tricks. The Jean Scott Rogers script, directed by Robert Day and produced by John Croydon for Producers Associates/MGM in England, dealt with his efforts to perfect an anesthetic in the bad old days when hospitals were like torture chambers. Betta St John, Christopher Lee, Francis Matthews, Adrienne Corri, Finlay Currie, Marian Spencer, Francis de Wolff and Frank Pettingell were featured.

With **Village of Daughters**, a forced farce not released in America, Eric Sykes followed his fellow television writer-comedian Spike Milligan into MGM British stardom. He played a travelling salesman vied for by well-upholstered maidens like Scilla Gabel. Script, David Pursall and Jack Seddon; director, George

Pollock; producer, George Brown. They were all below their Murder She Said standard. Also cast: Gregoire Aslan, Yvonne Romain, John Le Mesurier, Warren Mitchell, Eric Pohlmann, Carol White, Peter Illing.

For **The Password is Courage** Andrew and Virginia Stone dropped cliffhanger fiction and moved to England to film the true story of the war hero, inappropriately named Charlie Coward, who was captured by the Germans in 1940, escaped and was recaptured seven times. Dirk Bogarde (here with Lewis Fiander and John Gardiner) was excellent as Coward; others cast were Maria Perschy, Alfred Lynch, Nigel Stock, Reginald Beckwith, Bernard Archard, Ferdy Mayne, George Pravda and Colin Blakely. Stone's script and direction gripped throughout.

The Dock Brief/Trial and Error – John Mortimer's novel comedy about a wife murderer and his useless barrister – provided Peter Sellers with a rich part as the latter. He appeared in three guises while Richard Attenborough (here with Beryl Reid and David Lodge) had six, as an imaginary trial preceded the real one. This element of fantasy frightened mass audiences away from Dimitri de Grunwald's production, directed at the British studio by James Hill. Script: Pierre Rouve.

Kill or Cure took some hearty slaps at the public funnybone by teaming Eric Sykes and Terry-Thomas in a zany script, by David Pursall and Jack Seddon, about murders in a nature cure hotel. Dennis Price, Lionel Jeffries, Moira Redmond, Katya Douglas, David Lodge, Ronnie Barker, Hazel Terry and Derrin Nesbitt joined the fun in this popular MGM-British entry from director George Pollock and producer George Brown.

Valentina Cortese and Broderick Crawford in Leonardo Bercovici's **Square of Violence**. Grim and powerful, it arrived too late in the long succession of dramas about underground resistance to Nazi brutality. Bibi Andersson was featured in the screenplay by Eric and Leonardo Bercovici...

Bigger crowds bought tickets for another stimulating drama, **Sweet Bird of Youth**, starring Paul Newman and Geraldine Page. They repeated their Broadway success in Tennessee Williams' play as the passée movie star and the stud selling himself for a chance at Hollywood. As in Cat on a Hot Tin Roof the distinctive Williams blend of raw emotionalism and poetic imagery found a vivid film translator in writer-director Richard Brooks, who had to deodorize some of the play's gamier details. Rip Torn and Madeleine Sherwood also played their stage roles, with Ed Begley (best supporting actor Academy Award), Shirley Knight, Mildred Dunnock, Philip Abbott, Corey Allen and James Douglas in the Pandro Berman production.

Boys' Night Out was more suspect morally than Lolita. It offered for laughs a story of four men, three of them married, who rented a flat and equipped it with a blonde for their use on different nights. She kept them drooling at arm's length until the wives arrived to turn the movie from unappetizing comedy into wild farce. Tony Randall was the mainstay of a cast that included Kim Novak and Janet Blair (with him here) and James Garner, Howard Duff, Patti Page, Howard Morris, Jessie Royce Landis, Oscar Homolka, Anne Jeffreys, Zsa Zsa Gabor, William Bendix, Fred Clark, Jim Backus and Larry Keating. Producer, Martin Ransohoff; director, Michael Gordon; script, Ira Wallach, Marion Hargrove, from a Marvin Worth–Arne Sultan story. Business was brisk.

Two Weeks in Another Town *scored a near-miss when Kirk Douglas, Vincente Minnelli, John Houseman and Charles Schnee tried to repeat the success of their* Bad and The Beautiful *with another drama about temperamental movie-makers. Schnee's script seemed confused and Minnelli's direction overheated; perhaps through too much cutting, the characters of Irwin Shaw's novel lost motivation. They were played at top pitch by Douglas and Cyd Charisse (here on a wild ride in Rome) and Edward G. Robinson, George Hamilton, Claire Trevor, Daliah Lavi, Rosanna Schiaffino and James Gregory.*

Scissors had apparently been used freely, too, on another movie-star story, **A Very Private Affair***, with Brigitte Bardot and Marcello Mastroianni. The bumpy continuity of Louis Malle's film gave fitful glimpses into Bardot's real life while telling the tale of a press-hounded sex symbol's loves and sorrows. MGM picked up fairly profitable bookings with a dubbed English version of the French production, written by Malle, Jean Paul Rappeneau, Jean Ferry; producer, Christine Gouze Renal.*

Escape from East Berlin/Tunnel 28 *was based on an actual escape of 28 East Berliners by digging under the Wall. Gabrielle Upton, Peter Berneis and Millard Lampell scripted the film which Don Murray sustained with one of his deeply felt performances, aided by Christine Kaufmann (here), Werner Klemperer and Karl Schell in an accomplished German cast directed by Robert Siodmak. Walter Wood's independent production, shot entirely in West Berlin, kept tension high; but grosses moderate.*

Ride the High Country/Guns in the Afternoon *has a special place in the history of Westerns. After joining forces for it. Randolph Scott and Joel McCrea, two of the genre's most durable stars, went into wealthy retirement (Scott was reputed to be Hollywood's richest actor). And it was the first cinema success for director Sam Peckinpah, long a maker of television Westerns. Unexpectedly a winner of critics' raves and international awards, it had wry humour in its N. B. Stone Jr script about two tired lawmen going into action again and finding many excitements in their last adventure. Richard Lyons produced, with Mariette Hartley, Ronald Starr, Edgar Buchanan, R. G. Armstrong, John Anderson, L. Q. Jones, Warren Oates, James Drury and John Davis Chandler in the cast.*

▽ **Jumbo**, *a big-budget circus musical that stubbornly refused to come to life either on the screen or at the paybox, failed to revive the glory that was MGM musicals; they became very few and far between. Left to right: Stephen Boyd, Doris Day, Martha Raye, Jimmy Durante. The credits bulged with important names: director Charles Walters, producers Joe Pasternak and Martin Melcher, associate Roger Edens, songs by Rodgers and Hart, script by Sidney Sheldon, original by Ben Hecht and Charles MacArthur, photography by William Daniels, and (in 36th place) second unit director Busby Berkeley. Dean Jagger and 15 circus acts supported the stars, whose best number was 'The Most Beautiful Girl in the World'. Hardly anybody used the movie's contractual title, Billy Rose's Jumbo, an acknowledgment of the stage show's producer.*

The fans liked Jim Hutton and Paula Prentiss in The Honeymoon Machine *so MGM top-starred them in* **The Horizontal Lieutenant**. *It was made by the team that paired them first in* Where the Boys Are; *producer Joe Pasternak, director Richard Thorpe and writer George Wells. This time the latter's script, based on a novel by Gordon Cotler about a 1944 clean-up operation on a Pacific island, verged on the inane and business was blah. Also cast: Charles McGraw (right), Jack Carter, Jim Backus.*

In **I Thank a Fool** *doctor Susan Hayward was convicted of mercy killing, went to jail, came out jobless, answered an ad for a nurse and discovered the advertiser was her trial prosecutor (it's a small world in movies) whose wife, Diane Cilento was having mad fits. Now read on . . . Karl Tunberg's script from Audrey Erskine Lindop's novel was directed by Robert Stevens, produced by Anatole de Grunwald and neglected by the public. Peter Finch, Kieron Moore, Cyril Cusack and Athene Seyler were in the MGM British production.*

Pat Boone was a noted advocate of purity in life and entertainment, and fan club members' eyebrows rose in unison as their idol shared scenes of illicit passion with Mai Zetterling in **The Main Attraction**. Non-members were indifferent, judging by the receipts. Daniel Petrie directed the circus melodrama, written and produced by John Patrick in England for Seven Arts/MGM. Also cast: Nancy Kwan, Kieron Moore, Yvonne Mitchell, John Le Mesurier, Warren Mitchell and Lionel Blair.

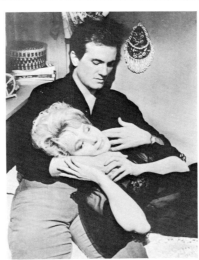

◁ The remake of **Mutiny on the Bounty** ran for 179 minutes and cost $19m. (ten times the 1935 original's budget), most of which MGM eventually got back through strong selling. Carol Reed started directing the movie in 1961, but he found the South Seas location no paradise. After many troubles—especially with Marlon Brando—he gave up and was replaced by Lewis Milestone, whose assignment recalled his exchange of cables with Harry Cohn when directing a boatload of bibulous actors in another sea epic, for Columbia in 1934. 'Hurry up, the cost is staggering', wired Cohn. 'So is the cast', replied Milestone. No such levity was suitable on the Bounty film, whose cost escalated from the staggering to the catastrophic as Brando supervised direction and script, delays multiplied and tempers frayed. It had a mixed reception and was best enjoyed by those who hadn't seen the old version. The spectacle was magnificent but the drama lost tension after the mutiny and ended dismally with the Bounty burning and Brando indulging in a long death scene. Otherwise his Fletcher Christian was more original and detailed than Clark Gable's. Trevor Howard (with him here) also impressed as Captain Bligh but—like John Gielgud in the Barretts remake—lacked the alarming flicker of madness that Charles Laughton could give his tyrants. Others in the Aaron Rosenberg production: Richard Harris, Hugh Griffith, Richard Haydn, Tim Seely, Percy Herbert, Gordon Jackson, Noel Purcell, Duncan Lamont, Chips Rafferty, Torin Thatcher, Frank Silvera, and Tarita, who became Brando's permanent offscreen partner (coincidentally, Movita, who played a major role in 1935, was once his wife; he is the father of sons by leading ladies of both Bountys). Script credit went to Charles Lederer; camera, Robert Surtees.

Polishing off his fencing foes in bunches, Stewart Granger was a 16th-century mercenary in **Swordsman of Siena**. That city's Palio horserace made the climax for Jacques Bar's Italo-French production, Étienne Perier directing the Michael and Fay Kanin–Alec Coppel script. It sold a lot of tickets. Also cast: Sylva Koscina, Christine Kaufmann, Tullio Carminati, Marina Berti, Ricardo Garrone.

Nothing if not international in 1962, MGM went south of the border down Mexico way (actually Spain) with **The Savage Guns**, a bandits versus ranchers actioner, written by Edmund Morris, directed by Michael Carreras, produced by Jimmy Sangster and Jose Maesso for Carreras' Capricorn Productions. Alex Nicol (left), Don Taylor (right) and Richard Basehart led an otherwise Spanish cast.

High-tension finish for the 1962 studio schedule: **The Hook** with (left to right) Nick Adams, Kirk Douglas, Robert Walker (son of the late star) and Enrique Magalona. To kill or not to kill their prisoner-of-war was the question turning Henry Denker's characters (from a novel by Vahe Katcha) against each other. Power in the acting and George Seaton's directing got William Perlberg's production nowhere at the box office.

INTO THE RED
1963

Chapter Two of the Wages of Extravagant Film-making came from MGM, whose release of *Mutiny on The Bounty* was followed by an appalling annual statement: $17\frac{1}{2}$m below zero. (P.S.: Marlon Brando has never been cast in another MGM picture). United Artists also dipped into the red, but only $831,000 worth, a situation corrected by its release of Steve McQueen and James Garner in *The Great Escape*, Jack Lemmon and Shirley MacLaine in *Irma La Douce*, Frank Sinatra and Laurence Harvey in *The Manchurian Candidate*, Sean Connery in the first James Bond hit, *Dr No*, and Albert Finney in *Tom Jones*. The last won the best film and best director (Tony Richardson) Oscars. Patricia Neal in *Hud* and Sidney Poitier in *Lilies of The Field* were voted the best performances.

Fellini's $8\frac{1}{2}$, Zanuck's *The Longest Day*, Rosalind Russell and Natalie Wood in *Gypsy*, and Lemmon and Lee Remick in *Days of Wine and Roses* were also impressive. Lemmon and Paul Newman joined the Top Ten list, displacing Sinatra and Burt Lancaster.

1963 opened with **The Courtship of Eddie's Father.** *Dire prospects had been indicated by the star-director-writer team who helped unsaddle* The Four Horsemen of the Apocalypse, *and one of those find-Dad-a-wife stories. So the warmth of this one surprised critics and delighted audiences. In this scene Ronny Howard, splendid as Eddie, signals to father Glenn Ford his disapproval of Dina Merrill because she has 'skinny eyes'. Shirley Jones, Stella Stevens, Roberta Sherwood and Jerry Van Dyke completed Vincente Minnelli's principals in the Joe Pasternak production, written by John Gay from a novel by Mark Toby. It later sparked off an MGM TV series.*

The V.I.P.s *was the biggest production mounted at MGM British for several years, and a potent moneymaker. Producer Anatole de Grunwald assembled top-grade talent in writing (Terence Rattigan) and directing (Anthony Asquith) as well as cast: eight stars–Elizabeth Taylor, Richard Burton and Louis Jourdan (here), Elsa Martinelli, Margaret Rutherford (who won the best supporting actress Academy Award), Maggie Smith, Rod Taylor and Orson Welles, plus Linda Christian, Robert Coote, Richard Wattis, Dennis Price, Ronald Fraser, Michael Hordern, Stringer Davis, Richard Briers, Peter Sallis, Lance Percival, Martin Miller and David Frost. The* Grand Hotel-*type collection of stories was based on London Airport and gave predominant footage to Taylor and Burton.*

In 1963 Elvis Presley started the contract that netted him and MGM millions over a ten-year stretch with movies like **It Happened at the World's Fair**. *Gone were the sneering lips and pelvic thrusts of yore as Presley went after the family trade in an innocuous tale by Si Rose and Seaman Jacobs, trimmed with several songs and a tour of the Seattle World's Fair. Produced by Ted Richmond, directed by Norman Taurog, with (left to right) Joan O'Brien, Vicky Tiu, Presley and Gary Lockwood; also Edith Atwater, H. M. Wynant, Yvonne Craig.*

With the biggest smile since Joe E. Brown's, **Flipper** *won the year's Best Dolphin Actor award from the viewers of Ivan Tors' irresistible production, a neat profit-maker. Luke Halpin was the boy sharing the creature's adventures, scripted by Arthur Weiss and directed by James Clark. Chuck Connors and Kathleen Maguire played Luke's parents.*

311

Strange that an MGM British Studio production should be made by, with and about Americans, in Riviera locales . . . Random thoughts like this served to occupy the mind while **Follow the Boys** unreeled its laborious comedy yarn about US sailors and their girls. Russ Tamblyn, Paula Prentiss, Ron Randell, Janis Paige, Roger Perry, Connie Francis, Dany Robin and Richard Long (left to right) were directed by Richard Thorpe. Lawrence Bachmann produced the David Chantler–David Osborn screenplay from his original.

Come Fly with Me also spread internationally from Leo's London lair. It was an Anatole de Grunwald production offering a sightseeing tour of Paris and Vienna plus a story of three air hostesses. Lois Nettleton, Dolores Hart and Pamela Tiffin (here) were paired with Karl Malden, Karl Boehm and Hugh O'Brian. Dawn Addams, Andrew Cruickshank, Richard Wattis, Lois Maxwell and John Crawford centre also had parts in William Roberts' screenplay, directed by Henry Levin. Bumpy box office.

Two other effective European-made, MGM-released thrillers were both about pirates. Karl Boehm played the modern kind, a jewel robber in **Rififi in Tokyo**, France's follow-up to the hugely successful Rififi, directed by Jacques Deray, produced by Jacques Bar, written by Auguste Lebreton, with Charles Vanel, Michel Vitold, Barbara Lass . . . In

Seven Seas to Calais Keith Michell was the traditional type, buccaneering under sail when not wooing Hedy Vessel. Paolo Moffa's production, written by Filippo Sanjust and directed by Rudolph Mate in Italy, featured Rod Taylor as Sir Francis Drake, Irene Worth as Elizabeth I, Anthony Dawson and Basil Dignam.

The Edgar Rice Burroughs estate continued to be one of America's most profitable institutions as its current franchise holder, Sy Weintraub, gave MGM another hit in **Tarzan's Three Challenges**. An inventive Berne Giler–Robert Day script and unfamiliar backgrounds – Day directed it all in Thailand–made it one of the series' best. Jock Mahoney (here with Earl Cameron and Ricky Der as the boy king they rescued) was the superman again and Woody Strode his equally muscular adversary.

One is innocent . . . Renato Salvatore, Jean-Claude Brialy and Anthony Perkins on trial in **Two Are Guilty**. Perkins, a rare Hollywood star to make an otherwise all-French movie, was especially good in the Alain Poiré production, picked up for international MGM distribution. André Cayatte wrote and directed the tantalizing story of a kidnap-murder committed by two unidentified young men; when police chased them out of an abandoned lighthouse three young men emerged, each claiming no knowledge of the other two. The audience was kept guessing throughout and never told which two were guilty.

Excellent acting was a strong point of **In the Cool of the Day** but the masses stayed away. An adaptation by Meade Roberts of Susan Ertz's novel, it was handsomely produced at MGM British by John Houseman. Peter Finch and Jane Fonda (here) fought against a Love that Could Not Be because they were married to others. Angela Lansbury and Arthur Hill were the others. Constance Cummings, Alexander Knox, Nigel Davenport, John Le Mesurier, Alec McCowen and Valerie Taylor were also in Robert Stevens' smoothly directed cast.

Captain Sindbad was lovely Arabian Nights nonsense, lavishly produced, and did big matinée business. Here Sindbad thrusts his sword through El Kerim only to discover that the wicked one's heart has been magicked away to an ivory tower, making him immune. Production by Frank and Herman King in Germany, with Guy Williams and Pedro Armendariz (here) and Heidi Bruhl, Abraham Sofaer, Geoffrey Toone. Written by Samuel West and Harry Relis, directed by Byron Haskin; startling special effects by Tom Howard.

The Haunting, a British thriller, eschewed the clutching hands and shrouded corpses of the haunted-house school; producer-director Robert Wise got his effects with atmospheric touches, strange sounds, and the fear reactions of Julie Harris. Also cast: Richard Johnson, Claire Bloom and Russ Tamblyn (backing her here) and Fay Compton, Rosalie Crutchley, Lois Maxwell, Valentine Dyall, Diane Clare and Ronald Adam. Nelson Giddings' script was based on a Shirley Jackson novel.

The British studio followed the success of Village of the Damned with **Children of the Damned**. It met the fate of most sequels. The fashionably international touch in John Briley's script had the unearthly moppets, representing six countries, brought by the UN to London, where they holed up in a church. Ian Hendry (here trying to force them out), Alan Badel, Barbara Ferris, Alfred Burke, Sheila Allen, Ralph Michael, Martin Miller and Bessie Love were directed by Anton Leader. Ben Arbeid produced.

Ben Arbeid also produced **Private Potter**, *a remarkable* tour de force *by Tom Courtenay as a soldier, accused of cowardice in action, who claimed he saw God. Tensely directed by Casper Wrede, who collaborated with Ronald Harwood on the script, it was liked more by critics than exhibitors. Also cast: Mogens Wieth, Ronald Fraser, James Maxwell, Ralph Michael, Frank Finlay.*

MGM's tie-up with French producer Jacques Bar brought Leo **The Day And The Hour**, *with Simone Signoret as an aloof Parisienne drawn into war activity by Stuart Whitman, a US airman escaping to Spain. René Clement directed and, with Roger Vailland, scripted André Barret's story. Genevieve Page led the supporting cast. Not many bookings for this one.*

Manuel Padilla had a brief spell of fame at the age of seven when two bright 'B's featuring him went into release at once. **Dime with a Halo** *was a comedy about five urchins with a winning sweepstake ticket they were too young to cash. Visible here: Barbara Luna, Paul Langton, Padilla and Rafael Lopez. Director, Boris Sagal; written and produced by Laslo Vadney*

and Hans Wilhelm . . . Padilla and Rory Calhoun were **The Young and the Brave** *in a Korean War drama with William Bendix, Richard Jaeckel, Richard Arlen and John Agar. Francis Lyon directed the A. C. Lyles production, written by Bierne Lay from a Ronald Davidson–Harry Slott original.*

Bob out west again: Keeping those goldurned Texas longhorns from ruining his Wyoming grasslands was Robert Taylor's aim in **Cattle King**/Guns of Wyoming *and, by jiminy, no bullets–nor even Joan Caulfield–were going to stop him. Director Tay Garnett knew how to whip into action a script like this, by Thomas Thompson, and Nat Holt's production did well in the double-feature market. Also cast: Robert Loggia, Robert Middleton, Larry Gates, Virginia Christine, William Windom.*

Nick Novarro and Pamela Austin performing in **Hootenanny Hoot**. *This frail tale by James Gordon, about television producers, served to present recording stars like Johnny Cash, Sheb Wooley and George Hamilton IV, along with Peter Breck, Ruta Lee and Joby Baker. Former dancing star Gene Nelson directed, Sam Katzman produced.*

An entertaining portfolio of stocks and blondes paid comedy dividends in **The Wheeler-Dealers**/Separate Beds *when Texas tycoon James Garner showed Wall Street business girl Lee Remick how to make a million without really trying. Director Arthur Hiller kept the George Goodman–Ira Wallach screenplay bubbling for producer Martin Ransohoff, casting Phil Harris, Chill Wills, Jim Backus, Elliott Reid and Patricia Crowley in support.*

Richard Chamberlain was one of 1963's most-seen stars as the Dr Kildare of MGM's phenomenal television series; but he had been on the cinema screen in only one minor role. Then **Twilight of Honor**/The Charge is Murder *came along, starring him as a young lawyer aided through a murder trial by Claude Rains as an old lawyer (shades of Dr Gillespie). The William Perlberg–George Seaton pro-*

duction was only moderately popular, although efficiently written by Henry Denker (from a novel by Al Dewlen) and directed by Boris Sagal. Also cast: Joey Heatherton, Nick Adams, Joan Blackman, James Gregory, Pat Buttram, Jeanette Nolan, Edgar Stehli, James Bell, Donald Barry, Bert Freed, Robin Raymond.

Lloyd Bochner, Mariette Hartley and Frankie Avalon in **Drums of Africa**. *Avalon, the pop singer, was top-billed, sound-tracked a theme song and played a sort of Andy Hardy Finds King Solomon's Mines role. The Al Zimbalist–Philip Krasne production was hardly distinguishable from* Watusi, *although a novel touch was evidenced in Quartermain, the white hunter character of the two Rider Haggard movies, now being renamed Courtemayn. Good thinking boys. Written by Robin Estridge and Arthur Hoerl, directed by James Clark, featuring Torin Thatcher and Michael Pate.*

George Pollock got a dream team for any comedy director in **Murder at the Gallop**: *Margaret Rutherford and Robert Morley, who vied for each scene to the last eyebrow-waggle and jowl-wobble. Critics called it a draw. So did exhibitors, counting the receipts. Writers David Pursall and Jack Seddon and producer George Brown repeated their treatment of an Agatha Christie mystery, this time 'After the Funeral'. Also cast: Flora Robson, Charles Tingwell, Duncan Lamont, James Villiers, Robert Urquhart, Katya Douglas, Stringer Davis.*

The Wonderful World of the Brothers Grimm was the second Cinerama movie to tell a story. George Pal produced it at Culver City on a hefty budget, using a new single-camera Cinerama technique. This eliminated the cumbersome three-projector requirement and the visible joins of the old system, but the latter's overwhelming, audience-embracing effect went too. While lacking the physical and profit-making magnitude of How the West Was Won, the movie scored well enough. Pal directed the fairytale sequences, Henry Levin the main story with (left to right) Oscar Homolka, Karl Boehm and Laurence Harvey as the Brothers, Claire Bloom and Walter Slezak. Also featured: Barbara Eden, Russ Tamblyn, Yvette Mimieux, Terry-Thomas, Beulah Bondi, Jim Backus, Buddy Hackett, Martita Hunt, Otto Kruger, Ian Wolfe, Clinton Sundberg, Tammy Marihugh, Walter Rilla and the little old lady named Cheerio Meredith. Script: David Harmon, Charles Beaumont and William Roberts.

A Global Affair gave Bob Hope ample scope for laugh-raising in an Arthur Marx–Bob Fisher–Charles Lederer script, from Eugene Vale's original, about a bachelor United Nations official taking charge of a baby abandoned in the UN Building. Lilo Pulver, Michele Mercier, Yvonne De Carlo, Elga Anderson and Miiko Taka were his glamorous baby-sitters; Robert Sterling, Nehemiah Persoff,

John McGiver, Jacques Bergerac and Mickey Shaughnessy completed Jack Arnold's cast in the profitable Hall Bartlett production for Seven Arts/MGM.

Another multi-national cast·played the incredible but entertaining drama of **The Prize**, ▷ Ernest Lehman's version of the best-seller by Irving Wallace. Paul Newman (here flanked by killers Sacha Pitoeff and Don Dubbins) starred as an American novelist in Stockholm collecting his Nobel Prize, along with an assortment of other unlikely winners: Edward G. Robinson, Micheline Presle, Gerard Oury, Sergio Fantoni, Kevin McCarthy. Robinson was kidnapped by Reds and replaced by a double in a plot switch never fully explained—but who cared, while all that action and sexy Newman–Elke Sommer by-play was going on? Not the big audiences Pandro Berman's production drew. Mark Robson directed, with Diane Baker, Leo G. Carroll, Virginia Christine, John Qualen and Anna Lee in the cast.

Hell-raising Keir Dullea needed a wife, decided Buddy Ebsen in **Mail Order Bride**/West of Montana, *a refreshing example of the new-style Western with as much ha-ha as bang-bang. Written and directed by Burt Kennedy, produced by Richard Lyons, with Lois Nettleton, Warren Oates, Barbara Luna, Paul Fix, Marie Windsor. Business was good.*

A Ticklish Affair *brought director George Sidney back to MGM. The feeble title had nothing to do with the disarming little comedy Ruth Brooks Flippen wrote from an original by Barbara Luther, chiefly concerned with the escapades of delectable Shirley Jones' three sons. Left to right: Bryan Russell, Miss Jones, Gig Young, Red Buttons, Peter Robbins and Edgar Buchanan. Another Jones charmer, Carolyn, was featured in Joe Pasternak's production.*

1963's output ended as it had begun, with a flurry of laughs. **Sunday in New York** *was a comedy gem by Norman Krasna (from his Broadway play), polished by director Peter Tewksbury and given performance sparkle by Cliff Robertson, Jane Fonda and Rod Taylor. Virginity, the story's motivation, was no longer the dirty word it had been in 1953 when it brought the wrath of censors and prosecutors down on The Moon is Blue. Everett Freeman's production for Seven Arts/MGM got praise and profits. Also cast: Robert Culp, Jim Backus, Jo Morrow.*

DULL BUT MONEYED
1964

British was beautiful in this year's movies, dominated by Rex Harrison (Academy Award) and Audrey Hepburn in *My Fair Lady* (Academy Award), and Julie Andrews (Academy Award) in *Mary Poppins*, which eventually brought Warner Bros and Disney, respectively, about $75m each. Peter O'Toole and Richard Burton in *Becket*, David Niven and Peter Sellers in *The Pink Panther*, the Beatles in *A Hard Day's Night* and Sean Connery in *From Russia With Love* were hugely popular. High praise for directors Joseph Losey (*The Servant*), Stanley Kubrick (*Dr Strangelove*), and George Cukor (*My Fair Lady*).

Efforts to bring Somerset Maugham's **Of Human Bondage** *believably back to the screen were smothered by disastrous casting of the dreamy Kim Novak and the shrewd Laurence Harvey in roles requiring the very opposite qualities. Henry Hathaway started and Ken Hughes finished directing this third movie version, with Robert Morley, Siobhan Mc-Kenna, Roger Livesey, Jack Hedley, Nanette Newman, Ronald Lacey. Screenplay by Bryan Forbes; produced by James Woolf for Seven Arts/MGM in Ireland.*

Ava Gardner and Richard Burton delivered pungent character performances in **The Night of the Iguana** *as the bawdy owner of a tumble-down Mexican hotel and the defrocked cleric turned tourist guide, whose conflicts contrasted with the gentleness of a penniless drifter, beautifully played by Deborah Kerr. They had Tennessee Williams' engrossing play, scripted (with Anthony Veiller) and directed by John Huston, to help them draw large and fascinated crowds. Sue Lyon, Grayson Hall, James Ward, Cyril Delevanti were featured in Ray Stark's MGM/Seven Arts production.*

Albert Finney and Susan Hampshire in **Night Must Fall**, *MGM's second crack at Emlyn Williams' nerve-shredder. Karel Reisz directed the new script by Clive Exton with a keen sense of suspense, and Finney was boyishly insidious as the handyman with an axe, working up to a frightening berserk climax. Critics kept harking back to Robert Montgomery's slyer performance, but ticket-buyers didn't carp. Mona Washbourne, Sheila Hancock and Michael Medwin were in the cast. Reisz and Finney produced for Lawrence Bachmann's MGM British unit.*

Critics panned *The Carpetbaggers* and Paramount cried all the way to the bank. For the third year in a row Doris Day was the star who meant most at the box-office. Lemmon, Hudson, Wayne, Grant, Presley and Newman continued in the exhibitors' Top Ten, joined by Shirley MacLaine, Ann-Margret and Richard Burton, who ungallantly bumped wife Elizabeth Taylor from the list. MGM's 1964 revenue recovered smartly from the 1963 collapse, the company announcing a $7,390,000 net from $171,360,000 income. But Cinerama suffered a $18m loss.

Still counting the receipts from The V.I.P.s, *MGM handed Anatole de Grunwald another big budget for another all-star special,* **The Yellow Rolls-Royce**. *It was nearly as good, and did nearly as well. Three separate episodes about successive owners of the Rolls were written by Terence Rattigan: millionaire Rex Harrison and his cheating wife Jeanne Moreau in the first, with Moira Lister (left), Edmund Purdom, Isa Miranda, Roland Culver, Michael Hordern and Lance Percival; Shirley Mac-Laine and Alain Delon enjoying an Italian interlude during her gangster lover's absence in the second, with George C. Scott and Art Carney; and American tourist Ingrid Bergman smuggling Omar Sharif across a Balkan border in the third, with Joyce Grenfell, Wally Cox, Guy Deghy and Carlo Groccolo (left). Anthony Asquith directed.*

▽ **Joy House**/The Love Cage *was the best of the French productions Jacques Bar supplied to MGM. René Clement directed the seamy drama, set mostly in a villa that was all Riviera sunshine outside and violence, mystery and sex within. He also wrote the script with Pascal Jardin and Charles Williams. Left to right: Jane Fonda, Lola Albright, Alain Delon.*

This was Laurence Harvey's year for flop re-△ *makes. In* **The Outrage** *(from the Japanese* Rashomon*) he was killed after seeing his wife, Claire Bloom, raped by bandit Paul Newman. Who killed him depended on which of four versions of the incident you believed; however, by the fourth replay you were wondering what to have for supper. Made rich and strange by exotic stylization in its original, this repetitive tale became a bit of an endurance test in its Western guise. Script by Michael Kanin, directed by Martin Ritt, produced by A. Ronald Lubin; with Edward G. Robinson, William Shatner, Howard da Silva, Albert Salmi.*

Robert Lewis Taylor's novel 'The Travels of Jamie McPheeters', bought years before by the studio, ended up as an MGM television series in America, and a second feature for cinemas overseas in **Guns of Diablo**. *Charles Bronson and Susan Oliver (here) and Kurt Russell, Jan Merlin and Douglas Fowley engaged in the bullet-riddled action of Berne Giler's script, directed by Boris Sagal, produced by Boris Ingster.*

Bared torso department: Richard Harrison, a hairier Steve Reeves, led six other muscle-flexers through 91 minutes of Spartan derring-do in **Gladiators 7** *produced in Rome and Madrid by Cleto Fontini and Italo Zingarelli for Joseph Fryd. Loredana Nusciak and Gerard Tichy were others directed through the profitable heroics by Pedro Lazaga.*

The Seven Faces of Dr Lao *was a typically imaginative George Pal production, but it failed to excite the public with its tricky story, scripted by Charles Beaumont from Charles Finney's novel. In this scene John Ericson is made to look like Pan to his girlfriend Barbara Eden, in one of the magic stunts Dr Lao performs when his one-man circus visits a Western town. The seven astonishing disguises Tony Randall wore as Lao won a special Oscar for MGM's veteran make-up chief, William Tuttle.*

Greta Garbo and Melvyn Douglas in Ninotchka *were among the gentler comedians whose past successes contributed to the laughs in* **MGM's Big Parade of Comedy**. *The bulk of it was slapstick scenes from such stars as Laurel and Hardy and the Marx Brothers, put together by Robert Youngson to make an 89-minute feature. The studio had previously made* Some of the Best *and* The MGM Story, *two shorter compilations which were as much trailers for future product as retrospectives.*

Julie Andrews startled her fans in **The Americanization of Emily**. *They had never expected to see their Mary Poppins popping into bed with James Garner, who also non-plussed his public by playing a shameless coward. William Bradford Huie's novel and Paddy Chayevsky's script, set in wartime London, sparkled with surprises, expertly sprung by director Arthur Hiller. Melvyn Douglas, James Coburn, Joyce Grenfell, Keenan Wynn, Liz Fraser, William Windom, Edward Binns, Gary Cockrell and Edmon Ryan were in Martin Ransohoff's production. It pulled the crowds but they weren't as big as it deserved.*

Advance to the Rear/Company of Cowards *was a rowdy Civil War comedy that pleased the masses. Melvyn Douglas and Glenn Ford (left and right) as officers in a troop of mis-fits, were easily distracted from battle plans by the town's strumpets. Stella Stevens and Joan Blondell (here leading the daughters of joy) had featured roles with Jim Backus, Alan Hale Jr, Whit Bissell and Michael Pate in the Ted Richmond production directed by George Marshall. Written by Samuel Peeples and William Bowers from originals by Jack Schaefer and William Chamberlain.*

The heroine of **The Unsinkable Molly Brown** *really existed, and her life supplied so much 'book' for the original stage show (by Richard Morris) and script for the movie (by Helen Deutsch) there was hardly room for Meredith Willson's songs, making it something of a musical manqué. Debbie Reynolds was the life and soul of the film, despite miscasting as a Colorado mining camp hellion who became a social climbing millionairess and a heroine of the 'Titanic' disaster. She and Harve Presnell, who repeated his Broadway role of Molly's husband, punched across what numbers there were. Produced on the stage by none other than Dore Schary, it was filmed by Lawrence Wein-garten on a lavish budget, amply returned from American box-offices but less so from overseas. Charles Walters directed, with Roger Edens as associate producer. Left to right: Hayden Rorke, Audrey Christie, Debbie, Hermione Baddeley and Vassili Lambrinos; also cast were Ed Begley, Jack Kruschen, Martita Hunt, Kathryn Card.*

Margaret Rutherford as Miss Marple made it three hits in a row for Lawrence Bachmann's MGM British series of Agatha Christie who-dunits. **Murder Most Foul** *again had Charles Tingwell as the Scotland Yard man astounded by her percipience (and fabulous face) as she investigated murders in a theatrical troupe. Also cast: Ron Moody, Andrew Cruickshank, Megs Jenkins, Ralph Michael, James Bolam, Francesca Annis, Stringer Davis, Pauline Jameson, Dennis Price, Terry Scott. David Pursall and Jack Seddon adapted the Christie novel 'Mrs McGinty's Dead'; George Pollock directed; Ben Arbeid produced.*

Murder Ahoy, *made by the same MGM British people who had scored with* Murder Most Foul, *was Miss Marple's last fling. Business for this series was dropping. Lionel Jeffries was the captain hopelessly outgunned by Margaret Rutherford when she snooped after a killer aboard his ship. Others concerned: Charles Tingwell, William Mervyn, Joan Benham, Stringer Davis, Nicholas Parsons, Miles Malleson, Henry Oscar, Derek Nimmo, Francis Matthews, Terence Edmond.*

Honeymoon Hotel *offered a farrago of roguish misunderstandings and wink-and-nudge dia-logue such as hadn't been displayed since Getting Gertie's Garter sent Grandpa rolling in the aisle. Inexplicably produced by Pandro Berman as a non-musical comedy, it starred two of the most talented performers of Broad-way musicals, Robert Goulet and Robert Morse, (here with Elsa Lanchester). The R. S. Allen–Harvey Bullock screenplay also em-ployed Nancy Kwan, Jill St John and Keenan Wynn, desperately directed by Henry Levin for laughs, which were in short supply.*

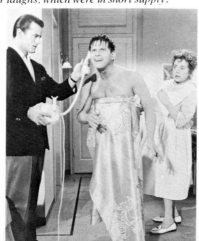

The Rounders *with Henry Fonda, Sue Ane Langdon, Hope Holiday and Glenn Ford was all fun, no guns, and pretty good profits. Chill Wills, Edgar Buchanan, Kathleen Freeman and Barton MacLane supported. The Richard Lyons production was written from Max Evans' novel and directed by Burt Kennedy.*

The stomping rhythms of Sam Katzman's 'B' musicals were blended with a dramatic story in **Your Cheatin' Heart** *and his praiseworthy production scored at the paybox in many areas. The forbidding title hid an only slightly-sugared biography of Hank Williams, who drank himself to death after writing over 500 country & western songs and singing most of*

them: his discs continued to sell in the millions even after he died. George Hamilton and Susan Oliver made a convincing Mr and Mrs Williams; Hank Jr dubbed the songs for Hamilton. Gene Nelson directed Stanford Whitmore's screenplay, with Red Buttons and Arthur O'Connell featured.

Jeffrey Hunter, 37 and still looking like the most popular undergrad on campus, took the road to Rome for a less exacting role than Jesus Christ. He co-starred with Massimo Girotti and Mylene Demongeot (with him here) and Ron Randell in **Gold for the Caesars**. *Slave revolts and Celt-Roman battles broke out all over Arnold Perl's script, from a novel by Florence Seward, directed by Andre de Toth and profitably produced by Joseph Fryd.*

1964

Hollywood's golden boy, Tab Hunter, went to Egypt to star in **The Golden Arrow** *with Rossana Podesta and (with him here) Dominique Boschero. He rode horses and magic carpets through a fast succession of Arabian Nights adventures in the Titanus production directed by Antonio Margheriti. Clever special effects in Technirama popped the eyes of its mostly juvenile audiences.*

Two minor musicals for the bubble-gum trade. Connie Francis, Jim Hutton, Susan Oliver and Joby Baker in **Looking for Love**, *produced by Joe Pasternak, directed by Don Weis, written by Ruth Brooks Flippen; with Barbara Nichols, Jay C. Flippen, Jesse White and, in cameo spots, George Hamilton, Yvette Mimieux, Paula Prentiss, Danny Thomas, Johnny Carson ...Chad Everett, Frank's girl Nancy Sinatra and Mary Ann Mobley in* **Get Yourself a College Girl**/The Swingin' Set, *produced by Sam Katzman, directed by Sidney Miller, written by Robert E. Kent; with the Dave Clark Five, the Animals, Stan Getz and Astrud Gilberto.*

One Elvis Presley wasn't enough for **Kissin'** △ **Cousins**, *a mad hill-billy romp with Pamela Austin and Yvonne Craig, here flanking a blond Elvis and a brunet Elvis. Fans didn't know which way to look. Former dancing star Gene Nelson directed and, with Gerald Drayson Adams, wrote the profitable Sam Katzman production, featuring Glenda Farrell, Arthur O'Connell, Jack Albertson and Donald Woods. Elvis shared ten songs between him.*

Viva Las Vegas/Love in Las Vegas *was Elvis Presley's most popular movie. It wasn't his usual one-man show; Ann-Margret shared his top billing, musical numbers and star voltage. Producers Jack Cummings and George Sidney gave it lots of Vegas dazzle, as in this scene of Cesare Danova and Presley bird-watching at the Tropicana. Sidney directed Sally Benson's screenplay, with William Demarest and Nicky Blair featured.*

Joanne Woodward sharing a panic with Stuart Whitman in double-biller **Signpost to Murder**, a stagey but effective thriller about an escaped prisoner from a mental hospital who forced a housewife to give him refuge. Monte Doyle's play was scripted by Sally Benson, directed by George Englund, produced by Lawrence Weingarten, with Edward Mulhare, Alan Napier cast.

Catherine Deneuve was snatched from the altar by the Gestapo and whisked to what **Vice and Virtue**'s publicity called a 'lust-crazed Nazi general's pleasure house'. Despite several orgies, more implied than shown, 'she retained her integrity'. Which was more than could be said for Roger Vadim's movie, co-produced by Gaumont and MGM in France, with Annie Girardot, Robert Hossein and O. E. Hasse taking care of the vice department. Script by Vadim and Roger Vailland.

An intriguing plot set **36 Hours** apart from other war movies (although it ended with the conventional chase) and made it a hit: a Nazi hoax convinced James Garner, US bearer of D-Day secrets, that he had been unconscious for six years and the war was long over. In it were Eva Marie Saint, Werner Peters and Garner (here) and Rod Taylor, Alan Napier, John Banner, Russell Thorson, Sig Ruman, Celia Lovsky, Martin Kosleck. George Seaton directed, and based his script on stories by Roald Dahl, Carl Hittleman and Luis Vance. Production by William Perlberg and Seaton.

Hollywood's second generation took charge of **The Young Lovers**/Chance Meeting. It was produced and directed by Samuel Goldwyn Jr and starred Henry's son Peter Fonda (here with Sharon Hugueny). They and featured players Nick Adams and Deborah Walley did well, but the Julian Halevy story and George Garrett script about university students lagged.

Flipper was the most lovable non-human star since Lassie, and **Flipper's New Adventure**/Flipper and the Pirates was one sequel that didn't disappoint. The dolphin was again Luke Halpin's pet in producer Ivan Tors' story, scripted by Art Arthur, of how they helped a stranded British yachting family: Pamela Franklin (here), Francesca Annis, Helen Cherry and Tom Helmore. Leon Benson directed it in Florida and the Bahamas. A lengthy television series ensued.

Ivan Tors veered from dolphin epics long enough to make **Rhino!** a lively movie about wild beasts. Robert Culp and Harry Guardino, having felled a lion with a harmless tranquillizing dart instead of a bullet, hunted a pair of rare white rhino in order to save them from extinction. Shirley Eaton was there to show that no such danger threatened blondes. The Arthur Weiss–Art Arthur script was produced in South Africa by Ben Chapman for Tors, who directed.

1964 ended impressively with the turbulent drama of **Young Cassidy**. Rod Taylor vigorously played Sean O'Casey's autobiographical title role in the Robert Graff–Robert Emmett Ginna production. John Ford fell ill during its shooting in Ireland and Jack Cardiff took over direction of the John Whiting screenplay. A splendid cast included Maggie Smith and Michael Redgrave as W. B. Yeats (here with Taylor) and Flora Robson, Edith Evans, Jack MacGowran, Sean Phillips, T. P. McKenna, Pauline Delany, Philip O'Flynn, and Julie Christie in a star-making performance.

DR. ZHIVAGO
1965

Nervously cheerful described the MGM outlook at the start of 1965; profits stayed even with 1964, but expenditure on *Doctor Zhivago* made the accountants shudder. Meanwhile 20th Century-Fox unveiled one of the biggest money-makers in the industry's history: *The Sound of Music*, which won the Academy Award, another Oscar for Robert Wise, and almost as many customers as *GWTW*.

The acting prizes went to Lee Marvin in *Cat Ballou* and Julie Christie in *Darling*. The latter's director, John Schlesinger, won many international citations, as did Frederico Fellini for *Juliet of the Spirits*. The annual James Bond blockbuster was *Goldfinger*; *Those Magnificent Men in Their Flying Machines* drew big crowds; Rock Hudson and Doris Day had a comedy hit in *Send Me No Flowers*; Stanley Kramer, with *It's a Mad, Mad, Mad, Mad World* in its second year of success, brought Vivien Leigh back in *Ship of Fools*, which won raves for Oskar Werner. Sean 'Bond' Connery hit the top of the star list, leading John Wayne, Doris Day, Julie Andrews, Jack Lemmon, Elvis Presley, Cary Grant, James Stewart, Elizabeth Taylor and Richard Burton.

The first feature out of the factory in 1965 was **Quick, Before it Melts**. *George Maharis, Janine Gray, Anjanette Comer and Robert Morse (left to right) topped a cast that included James Gregory, Yvonne Craig, Norman Fell and Milton Fox, the last being a penguin. It was that kind of a picture. Delbert Mann directed and co-produced with Douglas Laurence; script by Dale Wasserman from Philip Benjamin's novel.*

Still cheerful but even sillier, **Girl Happy** *had Elvis Presley chasing Shelley Fabares around Fort Lauderdale, Florida. Producer Joe Pasternak had had better luck with this locale in* Where the Boys Are. *Director Boris Sagal seemed flummoxed by the limp Harvey Bullock–R. S. Allen script, but the Presley fans came anyway. Also cast: Harold J. Stone, Gary Crosby, Joby Baker, Nita Talbot, Mary Ann Mobley, Chris Noel, Jackie Coogan.*

To Trap a Spy–*a spin-off from television's* The Man from U.N.C.L.E.–*was no great shakes on its first playdates, but the rumblings of a minor box-office earthquake could be heard in the distance. Robert Vaughn as Napoleon Solo dominated a fast-moving screenplay pieced together by Sam Rolfe, with parts for Luciana Paluzzi, Patricia Crowley, Fritz Weaver, William Marshall, Will Kuluva, David McCallum and Victoria Shaw. Don Medford directed, Norman Felton produced.*

The immortal clowning of Stan and Ollie in their early two-reelers was preserved in **Laurel and Hardy's Laughing 20's**, *compiled by Robert Youngson, whose similar MGM's Big Parade of Comedy had demonstrated how to make money without actually filming anything. The 91-minute feature was released in the same year as Laurel's death at 75; Hardy had departed eight years earlier.*

Vat 69 got a free (?) plug but the belly-dancer got nowhere in this scene of **Where The Spies Are**: *English secret agents David Niven and Nigel Davenport were too true-blue to be distracted from duty. James Leasor's 'Passport to Oblivion' was scripted (with Wolf Mankowitz), produced (with Steven Pallos) and directed by Val Guest at MGM/British, with Françoise Dorleac, John Le Mesurier, Basil Dignam, Eric Pohlmann, George Pravda, Ronald Radd and Noel Harrison. A neat thriller that got good business.*

Joy in the Morning, *Betty Smith's story of young newly-weds, lacked the poignancy of her famous* Tree Grows in Brooklyn *but it had charm, emphasized in Alex Segal's direction and the playing of Richard Chamberlain (here with Arthur Kennedy as his father) and Yvette Mimieux. Oscar Homolka, Donald Davis, Joan Tetzel, Sidney Blackmer, Virginia Gregg, Chris Noel and Harvey Stephens had parts in the Sally Benson–Alfred Hayes–Norman Lessing screenplay, produced by Henry Weinstein. Not much joy for exhibitors, though.*

Operation Crossbow, *produced in a big way by Carlo Ponti at MGM British, was almost but not quite a box-office blockbuster. The Richard Imrie–Derry Quinn–Ray Rigby script about destroying the German V-Bomb bases was impressively authentic and excitingly theatrical by turns; Erwin Hillier's photography and Tom Howard's special effects, starring supercolossal climactic explosions, were outstanding. Sophia Loren, in briefly for name value, and George Peppard, prominent throughout, are seen here. Michael Anderson directed with a sure touch, employing Trevor Howard, John Mills, Richard Johnson, Tom Courtenay, Jeremy Kemp, Anthony Quayle, Helmut Dantine, Richard Todd, Lilli Palmer, Paul Henreid, Sylvia Syms, John Fraser, Barbara Rueting, Patrick Wymark (as Churchill), Moray Watson, Richard Wattis and a thousand or so others.*

Carlo Ponti's production of Boris Pasternak's **Doctor Zhivago** gave MGM a selling problem: at first the masses couldn't pronounce the title or care less about Russian literature, and the discriminating were put off by decidedly mixed reviews. But gradually the movie was rescued by that most potent show-business asset, word-of-mouth praise, and it eventually became the company's second biggest moneymaker, ranking between GWTW and Ben-Hur with returns approaching $100m. Even David Lean's genius for covering a lot of dramatic territory in one film was taxed by the vast scale of the novel and its abundance of characters and events. But he and his screenwriter Robert Bolt kept a firm grip on both the narrative and the audience's emotions for $3\frac{1}{4}$ hours, with very few lapses through over-condensing. Bolt's script, Freddie Young's photography, John Box's and Terry Marsh's art direction, Maurice Jarre's score (the theme was a best-seller) and Phyllis Dalton's costumes won Academy Awards. A huge cast included Omar Sharif as Zhivago, Geraldine Chaplin and Julie Christie (with him above), Rod Steiger, Alec Guinness, Tom Courtenay, Siobham McKenna, Ralph Richardson, Rita Tushingham, Adrienne Corri, Geoffrey Keen, Gerard Tichy, Noel Willman, Klaus Kinski. While its makers were mostly British, it was shot in Spain and Finland.

The Loved One was anything but, so far as most critics were concerned. They dismissed it as a botch of Evelyn Waugh's hilariously scathing book on the Los Angeles way of life and death, its satire reduced to burlesque by the Terry Southern–Christopher Isherwood script and Tony Richardson's sock-it-to-'em direction. A name-spangled cast—Robert Morse (wildly miscast as the English poet 'hero'), Robert Morley, Jonathan Winters, Rod Steiger, Roddy McDowall and John Gielgud, left to right backing Anjanette Comer; and Dana Andrews, Milton Berle, James Coburn, Tab Hunter, Margaret Leighton, Liberace, Barbara Nichols, Lionel Stander—failed to draw the masses to Martin Ransohoff's Filmways/MGM production. Haskell Wexler photographed and co-produced with John Calley.

Sean Connery interrupted his lucrative James Bond career to do a real job of acting in **The Hill**, a drama of relentless, pile-driving force. Both performance and film were among the year's best. Connery, Alfred Lynch, Ossie Davis, Roy Kinnear and Jack Watson played prisoners in a desert military stockade, punished to breaking point by sadistic guards, in Ray Rigby's grim screenplay. Director Sidney Lumet really turned on the heat for audiences and actors, who included Michael Redgrave, Ian Hendry, Harry Andrews and Ian Bannen. Kenneth Hyman's Seven Arts production proved profitable for all concerned.

Shelley Winters collected an Oscar (best supporting actress) for her performance in **A Patch Of Blue** as the blowsy, overbearing mother of blind Elizabeth Hartman, who didn't know that her compassionate boyfriend, Sidney Poitier, was black. The corn was thick on the ground in Elizabeth Kata's touching story, but Guy Green never tripped up on it in his script and direction. Wallace Ford, Ivan Dixon, Elisabeth Frazer and John Qualen were also in Pandro Berman's best production for some time, a fluent profit-maker. Studio head Robert Weitman could congratulate himself on a satisfactory year.

Often glamorous lovers in Columbia movies a decade or two earlier, Glenn Ford and Rita Hayworth got together again in **The Money Trap** to play a crooked cop and a sleazy waitress. The Walter Bernstein screenplay from Lionel White's crime novel had intermittent excitement, but got only a moderate reception. Elke Sommer, Ricardo Montalban and Joseph Cotten also starred in the Max Youngstein production directed by Burt Kennedy.

Back in 1961 George Cukor had started and stopped an expensive Culver City production of △ **Lady L**, starring Gina Lollobrigida and Tony Curtis. 1965 brought the result of Peter Ustinov's try at the Romain Gary novel. It was produced by Carlo Ponti, mostly in Paris, and starred Sophia Loren and Paul Newman. Not even their box-office draw, reinforced by David Niven's, could attract full houses. Ustinov failed to establish cohesion of mood or narrative in a tale which sprawled from French brothel (here with Loren and Newman) to English stately home. Claude Dauphin, Marcel Dalio, Cecil Parker and Ustinov himself were in it.

When Steve Reeves got dressed he did to his screen career what Mary Pickford had done to

hers when she cut off her curls. Nevertheless, **Sandokan The Great** got plenty of bookings in action-at-any-price houses. Reeves fought his way through Borneo jungles and battles, accompanied by Genevieve Grad (here) and Rik Battaglia. Solly Branco's production in Techniscope was directed by Umberto Lenzi.

MGM brought Frenchmen to Hollywood to make **Once a Thief**: Jacques Bar produced and Alain Delon (here giving Ann-Margret a hard time) starred as an ex-con trying to go straight but drawn back into crime. Van Heflin returned to Leo to play Delon's policeman nemesis; Jack Palance, John Davis Chandler and Tony Musante made a chilling trio of killers. Never a dull moment in Zekial Marko's script from his own novel (he was in the cast too), directed with verve by Ralph Nelson.

While making a successful television series of Flipper, *Ivan Tors varied the formula a bit for a feature,* **Zebra in the Kitchen**, *which brought Jay North and his pet puma into an action spree during which the boy set free a whole zoo. The Art Arthur screenplay (original, Elgin Ciampi) was directed by Tors; also featured were Martin Milner, Andy Devine, Jim Davis, Joyce Meadows, Robert Lowery.*

Hysteria, *a teasing puzzle from Britain's horror wholesalers, Hammer Films, was a useful MGM release. In this scene Robert Webber, Jennifer Jayne, Lelia Goldoni, Maurice Denham and Anthony Newlands find a corpse in the shower-stall. Jimmy Sangster produced his own screenplay, leaning heavily on that old story standby, amnesia: Freddie Francis directed.*

Three from abroad: Connoisseurs of the loincloth school of acting (there were plenty of them) applauded Richard Lloyd and Kirk Morris in **Hercules, Samson and Ulysses**. *These contenders for the Steve Reeves Scholarship left little footage for Enzo Cerusico as Ulysses, and Liana Orfei as Delilah never had time to reach for the scissors. Joseph Fryd's spaghetti spectacular was written and directed by Pietro Francisci . . . In* **Greed in the Sun**

Jean Paul Belmondo interrupted his race across the Sahara with Andrea Parisy and a truckload worth $100,000 to take potshots at his pursuers. The breakneck pace, culminating in a ferocious brawl, made strange seat-fellows of action fans and French film buffs for Henri Verneuil's picture, written by Michel Audiard and produced by Alain Poire for Gaumont/ MGM. Also cast: Lino Ventura, Reginald Kernan, Gert Frobe, Bernard Blier . . . Made by

Italians, but a long way from home, was a wilder version of the 'Flipper' stories, **Tiko and the Shark**. *Produced by Goffredo Lombardo for Titanus/MGM and directed by Folco Quilici, Italo Calvino's story concerned a Polynesian boy keeping to the primitive life with his girl and his pet shark when civilization invaded their island. Beautifully filmed in the South Seas with a native cast.*

Clarence, the Cross-eyed Lion *was a feature-length try for theatre bookings in advance of another popular MGM television series, Daktari. Enjoyable, but it didn't repeat the 'U.N.C.L.E.' success. Written by star Marshall Thompson (left), Art Arthur, Alan Caillou, directed by Andrew Marton, produced by Leonard Kaufman; with Richard Haydn (right), Betsy Drake, Cheryl Miller.*

Andrew and Virginia Stone came a cropper with fantastic comedy in **The Secret of my Success**, *a three-episode story by Andrew about a dimwitted policeman (James Booth). The funniest segment concerned a dizzy husband-killer (Stella Stevens), followed by a piece featuring Honor Blackman and giant spiders, and a messy conclusion with Shirley Jones and a South American revolution. Lionel Jeffries kept turning up; ticket-buyers didn't. Left to right: Booth, Jeffries, Miss Stevens.*

Two musicals in a minor key: **Harem Scarum**/ Harem Holiday *had few rivals as the year's worst movie; in it Elvis Presley (here with Carolyn Carter) essayed a sort of singing Valentino role mixed with Fairbanks acrobatics. The comic-strip script by Gerald Drayson Adams was more or less directed by Gene Nelson, and produced by mistake and Sam Katzman. Also cast: Mary Ann Mobley, Fran Jeffries, Michael Ansara, Jay Novello, Philip Reed . . . .Katzman recovered from Harem Scarum in time to produce a cheap and cheerful remake of* Girl Crazy, *with Connie Francis and Harve Presnell assigned the hopeless task of replacing Judy Garland and Mickey Rooney.* **When the Boys Meet the Girls** *gave them fine Gershwin songs and support from Herman's Hermits, Louis Armstrong, Liberace, Sue Ane Langdon, Fred Clark, Frank Faylen, Joby Baker in a Robert E. Kent script directed by Alvin Ganzer.*

Ann-Margret, made in Sweden, in **Made in Paris**, *a wafer-thin comedy about the fashion industry. She kept the eye happily occupied while the brain dozed over Stanley Roberts' script, directed by Boris Sagal, produced by Joe Pasternak and enacted by Louis Jourdan, Richard Crenna, Chad Everett, Edie Adams, John McGiver and Marcel Dalio. Count Basie, Trini Lopez and the seductive A-M herself provided musical interludes.*

1965

The 'Man from U.N.C.L.E.' craze really lifted off with the release of **The Spy with My Face***; the television spin-off for cinemas became especially big in Britain, where MGM's distribution boss Michael Havas masterminded a sustained publicity campaign that turned these movies from bill-fillers into major money-makers. David McCallum as Illya Kuryakin, subordinated to Robert Vaughn's Napoleon Solo in the first feature, suddenly was equally idolized by the fans; Leo G. Carroll started his permanent job as the secret agents' chief; Senta Berger co-starred as their alluring enemy. It was written by Clyde Ware and Joseph Calvelli, directed by John Newland and produced by Sam Rolfe under the supervision of MGM's television executive Norman Felton.*

MGM's last releases in CinemaScope, once the wonder of the movie world (and a future headache for TV companies) were a pair of Westerns produced in Spain by Lester Welch. **Gunfighters of Casa Grande** *featured (left to right) Dick Bentley, Phil Posner, Jorge Mistral and Alex Nicol; also Steve Rowland, Mercedes Alonso, Maria Granada; director,*

Roy Rowland; writers, Patricia and Borden Chase, Clarke Reynolds . . . In **Son of a Gunfighter** *Russ Tamblyn (here flanked by Ralph Browne and Kieron Moore) was an improbable triggerman; James Philbrook, Fernando Rey and Miss Granada were also in Reynolds' screenplay. Paul Landres directed.*

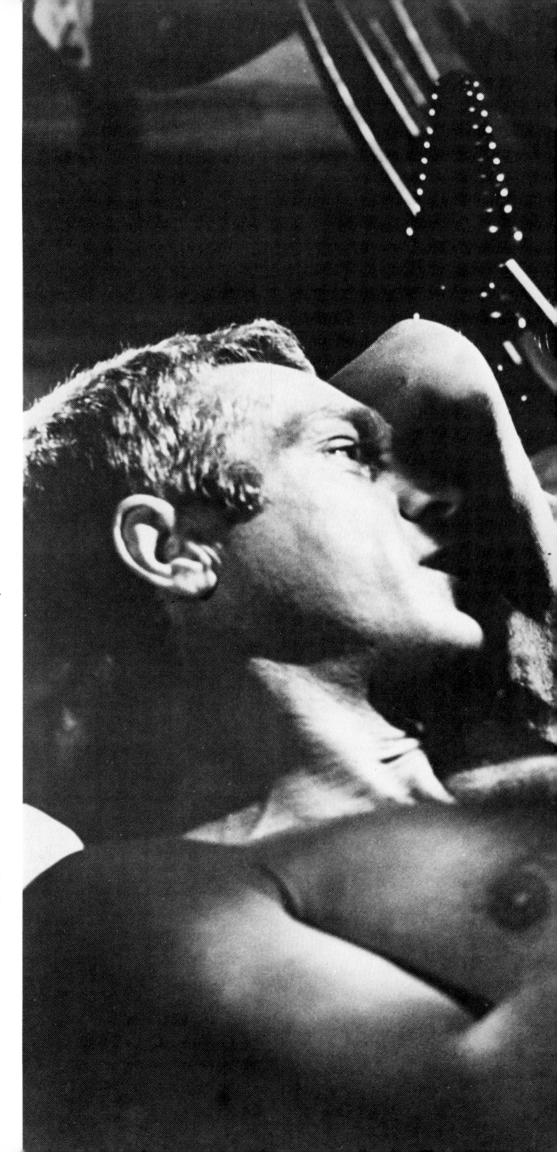

◁ Steve McQueen's fast-rising popularity was hypoed by **The Cincinnati Kid**, a hard-boiled drama about gamblers, directed with a keen eye for atmosphere and tension by Norman Jewison. He, the cast and scripters Terry Southern and Ring Lardner Jr had even card illiterates biting their nails when McQueen and Edward G. Robinson played their climactic game of stud poker. McQueen's stud play with Tuesday Weld (here) and Ann-Margaret also stirred the large audiences drawn by the Martin Ransohoff production, based on Richard Jessup's novel. Also cast: Karl Malden, Joan Blondell, Rip Torn, Jack Watson, Cab Calloway, Jeff Corey.

The Sandpiper was a dreary movie which reached 20th place on MGM's list of all-time moneymakers. Its success can only have been due to Elizabeth Taylor as beatnik mother and Richard Burton as fallen clergyman (again), playing with a commendable show of sincerity. It certainly wasn't the Dalton Trumbo–Michael Wilson script, adapted from Martin Ransohoff's story by Irene and Louis Kamp and laboriously directed by Vincente Minnelli. Ransohoff did better as producer; he gave it the magnificent background of California's Big Sur region and a luscious theme in 'The Shadow of Your Smile', which won Johnny Mandel and Paul Francis Webster the best song Academy Award. Also cast: Eva Marie Saint, Charles Bronson, Robert Webber, Morgan Mason (James' son), Tom Drake.

Seven Women was the last picture in John Ford's 48 years as a director. During filming Patricia Neal, playing the central role, collapsed and almost died in a series of strokes. Her scenes were reshot with Anne Bancroft. Left to right: Sue Lyon, Mildred Dunnock, Miss Bancroft, Margaret Leighton, Eddie Albert and Betty Field. Anna Lee, Mike Mazurki and Woody Strode were also in the grim melodrama about an American Mission menaced by Chinese bandits. Script by Janet Green and John McCormick from a Norah Lofts story. The Bernard Smith production was not a success.

329

HIGH SPYING BRINGS PROFIT

1966

Now the giant conglomerates developed an appetite for movie companies, and two old 'majors' lost their independence: Paramount became a subsidiary of Gulf and Western Industries; Warner Bros, which had become Warners-Seven Arts, was swallowed by Kinney National Service Inc. But the MGM lion bristled his whiskers with a $10m profit, defying take-overs.

A Man for All Seasons, its star Paul Scofield and director Fred Zinnemann grabbed most of the year's awards, and the beauteous Elizabeth Taylor turned herself into a blowsy bag to win the actress Oscar in *Who's Afraid of Virginia Woolf?*. Inside a human body was the unique locale for the thriller, *Fantastic Voyage*. *Alfie* and *Georgy Girl* clicked. But the biggest winner was another Bond, *Thunderball*. No surprise that Julie Andrews was voted top star magnet after *Mary Poppins* and *Sound of Music*; second was Sean Connery, then Liz Taylor, Jack Lemmon, Richard Burton, Cary Grant, John Wayne, Doris Day, Paul Newman, Elvis Presley.

The fight to the death—and big profits—between U.N.C.L.E. (United Network Command for Law and Enforcement) and the wicked THRUSH (it stood for nothing) continued ◁ with **One of Our Spies is Missing**, featuring Vera Miles, Robert Vaughan and David McCallum (left) and Maurice Evans, Leo G. Carroll, Bernard Fox, Yvonne Craig: written by Howard Rodman, Henry Slesar; director, E. Darrell Hallenbeck; producer, Boris Ingster . . . **One Spy Too Many**, the most entertaining instalment so far, followed immediately, with Rip Torn, Dorothy Provine and McCallum (above) and Vaughn, Carroll, David Opatoshu, Yvonne Craig; written by Dean Hargrove; directed by Joseph Sargent, produced by David Victor.

Imagination boggled at what villainess Janet Leigh would have done to David McCallum here if his fellow nephew of U.N.C.L.E., Robert Vaughn, hadn't arrived in time's nick. They and Jack Palance, Leo G. Carroll, Ludwig Donath, Letitia Roman and Will Kuluva had the fans jumping (and business booming) in **The Spy in the Green Hat**. But what made this one special in Norman Felton's series was a vein of uproarious satire on old gangster movies, played by Warner Bros. alumni, class of '33: Eduardo Ciannelli, Allen Jenkins, Jack La Rue, Joan Blondell, Maxie Rosenbloom, Vince Barnett and Elisha Cook Jr. Produced by David Victor and Boris Ingster, directed by Joseph Sargent, written by Peter Allan Fields.

More best-selling secret agent stuff: **The Venetian Affair**, with Elke Sommer, Robert Vaughn, Karl Boehm and Bill Weiss (left to right) and Boris Karloff, Felicia Farr, Luciana Paluzzi, Joe de Santis. E. Jack Neuman slickly scripted Helen MacInnes' novel; Jerry Thorpe directed likewise, and they co-produced to good box-office effect.

Vaughn's 'U.N.C.L.E.' sidekick, David McCallum, also had Venice on his itinerary, plus Rome, Monte Carlo and Switzerland, in **Three Bites of the Apple**. Espionage was avoided this time, but there was no less dizzy dashing about for McCallum as a tour guide with Tammy Grimes (here), and Sylva Koscina, Harvey Korman, Domenico Modugno, Aldo Fabrizi, Avril Angers, Cardew Robinson. Written by George Wells, produced and directed by Alvin Ganzer. Business was sluggish.

Rod Taylor hopped on the overcrowded secret-agent bandwagon as **The Liquidator**, and brought John Gardner's best-selling hero Boysie Oakes to the screen in robust style. Trevor Howard, Jill St John, Wilfrid Hyde White, Akim Tamiroff, Eric Sykes, David Tomlinson, Gabriella Licudi (with Taylor here), John Le Mesurier, Derek Nimmo and Jennifer Jayne were in Jack Cardiff's cast. The Peter Yeldham screenplay, climaxed with an attempt to kill Prince Philip, was produced by Jon Penington for Leslie Elliot, who gave it a touch of James Bondage by getting Shirley Bassey to sing the title song.

Peter Falk, Ian Bannen and Natalie Wood in **Penelope**, a breezy crime comedy about a neglected wife who robbed her husband's bank as a change from mere kleptomania. Arthur Loew Jr returned to produce it under Joe Pasternak's aegis, with Arthur Hiller directing George Wells' version of an E. V. Cunningham novel. Also cast: Dick Shawn, Lila Kedrova, Jonathan Winters, Lou Jacobi, Norma Crane, Jerome Cowan.

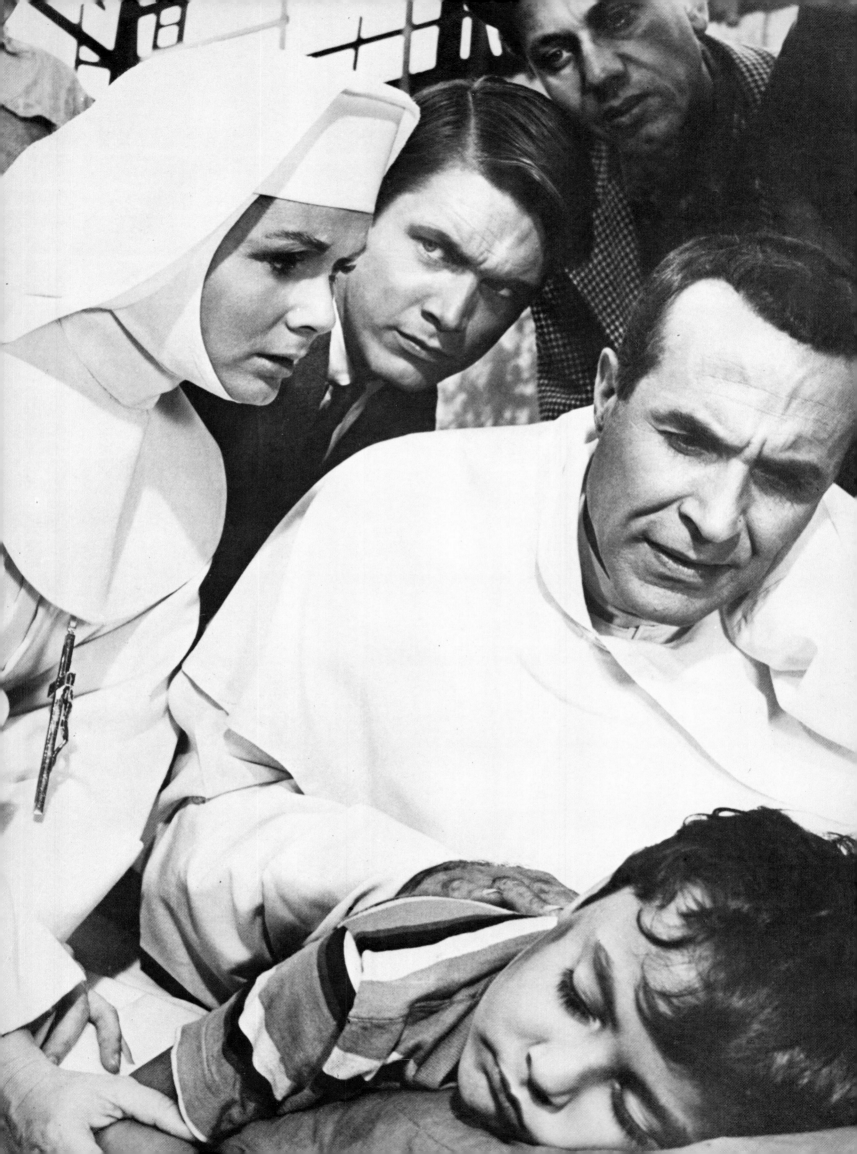

Louis B. Mayer's ghost must have been smiling down on **The Singing Nun**. It was just the family-type heart-wallop he loved; its stars – Debbie Reynolds and Ricardo Montalban (left and right) – were MGM discoveries in the good old days, and who should be playing the Mother Superior but our own Greer Garson! Commercially, Mayer would have been right, as usual: it contributed to the company's handsome 1966 profit. Based on a real character, the Belgian nun who recorded best-sellers as Soeur Sourire (it had 12 songs) the Sally Benson–John Furia Jr screenplay was directed by Henry Koster, produced by John Beck and Hayes Goetz. Also cast: Chad Everett and little Ricky Cordell (here) and Katharine Ross, Michael Pate, Agnes Moorehead, Juanita Moore, Tom Drake, Ed Sullivan, Marina Koshetz, Nancy Walters.

Hold On! was also an offspring of the disc business. It starred the British sub-Beatle group, Herman's Hermits, in particular its likeable lead singer, Peter Noone (here with Shelley Fabares). The title came from one of their hit songs, but takings indicated it could have come from another of them: 'A Must to Avoid'. Karl Green, Keith Hopwood, Derek Leckenby and Barry Whitwam of the group, Sue Ane Langdon, Herbert Anderson and Bernard Fox were in the Sam Katzman production which was written by James Gordon, directed by Arthur Lubin.

Tony Randall, Anita Ekberg and Robert Morley in **The Alphabet Murders**, a soft-boiled thriller from Lawrence Bachmann's British unit, directed by Frank Tashlin. Randall amusingly played Agatha Christie's sleuth Hercule Poirot in the David Pursall–Jack Seddon screenplay. Also cast: Maurice Denham, Guy Rolfe, Sheila Allen, Julian Glover, Clive Morton, Cyril Luckham, James Villiers, Richard Wattis, Austin Trevor.

Around the World Under the Sea was a well-made and well-received special effects thriller. In this scene Shirley Eaton, Brian Kelly, Marshall Thompson and Lloyd Bridges emerge

unscathed from a submarine volcano. David McCallum, Keenan Wynn and Gary Merrill also starred. The Art Arthur–Arthur Weiss screenplay was directed and produced for Ivan Tors by Andrew Marton.

Carlo Ponti's production **The 25th Hour** was overlong and often confusing in mood and incident, but it had the merit of being different from other war movies – maybe too much so: it drew meagre business. In it Anthony Quinn (left) playing a sort of Rumanian Don Quixote fighting the windmills of war, was taken prisoner successively by Germans, Russians and Americans. Henri Verneuil directed it in Budapest, Belgrade, Munich and Paris, casting Virna Lisi, Gregoire Aslan, Michael Redgrave, Serge Reggiani, Marcel Dalio, Alexander Knox, Marius Goring, John Le Mesurier. Script by Francoise Boyer, Wolf Mankowitz and Verneuil from C. V. Gheorghiu's novel.

Hotel Paradiso, Georges Feydeau's glorious Olympics of bed-jumping, corridor-running, door-slamming and wife-swapping, fell flat on the screen. It was produced and directed in Paris by Peter Glenville, who had successfully staged it in London (with Alec Guinness) and New York. Glenville collaborated with Jean-Claude Carriere on the script and played Feydeau in an introductory bit. Left to right: Gina Lollobrigida, Robert Morley, Peggy Mount, Leonard Rossiter and Guinness. Also cast: Akim Tamiroff, Marie Bell, Douglas Byng, Robertson Hare, Derek Fowldes, Ann Beach.

More dollars than sense: **The Glass-Bottom Boat** drew nearly $5m. from American theatres alone, thanks to dotty characters, crazy situations and Frank Tashlin's high-speed direction. And, of course, the durable popularity of Doris Day (here gagging it up with Dom de Luise). Other able farceurs who punched over Everett Freeman's script: Rod Taylor, John McGiver, Paul Lynde, Edward Andrews, Dick Martin, Eric Fleming, Elisa-

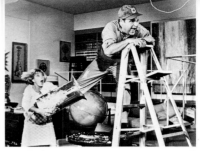

beth Fraser, Alice Pearce, George Tobias, Ellen Corby, Arthur Godfrey. Martin Melcher and Freeman produced.

The central figures of **Maya** were an elephant and her calf, in whose defence she was killed by tigers. Many customers found this hard to take: thou shalt not be cruel to elephants is a box-office commandment. Clint Walker and Jay North played an American hunter and his son in India, and John Berry directed the King Brothers production there; script by John Fante based on Gilbert Wright's adaptation of a Jalal Din–Lois Roth story.

James Garner and Jean Simmons starred in **Mr Buddwing**/Woman Without a Face, filmed from Evan Hunter's novel with considerably less success than his Blackboard Jungle. The identity problem of an amnesiac held interest, but too many romantic encounters clogged the narrative, scripted by Dale Wasserman, directed by Daniel Mann. Suzanne Pleshette, Angela Lansbury, Katharine Ross, Jack Gilford, Raymond St Jacques, Joe Mantell and ex-'Dead End Kid' Billy Halop were in the Mann–Douglas Laurence production.

The Dangerous Days of Kiowa Jones had an unusual title and a heroine who didn't look as if she'd just stepped out of a beauty shop; conviction in performance and direction set it above the average Western. Robert Horton, who'd been riding the television ranges for years, starred with Diane Baker and Sal Mineo (left and right), aided by Gary Merrill, Nehemiah Persoff and Royal Dano in the Max Youngstein–David Karr production, written by Frank Fenton and Robert Thompson, directed by Alex March.

1966

Big one of the year was **Grand Prix**, produced by Edward Lewis for Cinerama screens; it was a potent attraction in regular cinemas too. In contrast to his All Fall Down, John Frankenheimer's direction scored best in spectacular action; the intimate scenes of racing drivers and their women (written by Robert Alan Aurthur) were on the stodgy side. The race sequences, filmed on real championship circuits, had stunning impact, with remarkable camerawork by Lionel Lindon and his crew, and sound effects that won Academy Awards for Gordon Daniels and the MGM sound department. Editors Fredric Steinkamp, Henry Berman, Stewart Linder and Frank Santillo also won Oscars. Eva Marie Saint and Yves Montand (here after a crash) were cast with James Garner, Toshiro Mifune, Brian Bedford, Jessica Walter, Antonio Sabata, Francoise Hardy, Claude Dauphin, Genevieve Page, Jack Watson, Rachel Kempson, Ralph Michael and several driving champions.

Spinout/California Holiday combined all the Elvis Presley movie clichés. He played a pop singer and a racing-driver and a magnet for every girl in sight and was referred to as The Perfect American Male. What more could the Legion of El Loyalists desire? 'Critics don't buy tickets' was the motto of producer Joe Pasternak, director Norman Taurog, writers Theodore Flicker and George Kirgo. Old-timers saw that Una Merkel, Cecil Kellaway and Frederick Worlock were alive and well in a young cast: Shelley Fabares, Diane McBain, Deborah Walley, Jack Mullaney, Warren Berlinger, Dodie Marshall.

Robert Taylor, still stalwart in middle age, and young Chad Everett shared star billing and shoot-outs in **Return of the Gunfighter**, a conventional Western with such familiar badmen as Butch Cassidy (John Crawford) and the Sundance Kid (John Davis Chandler). Frank and Maurice King produced and James Neilson directed the Robert Buckner–Burt Kennedy story, featuring Ana Martin, Lyle Bettger and Michael Pate. This completed a rather undistinguished production year, its prosperity sparked by Zhivago income.

334

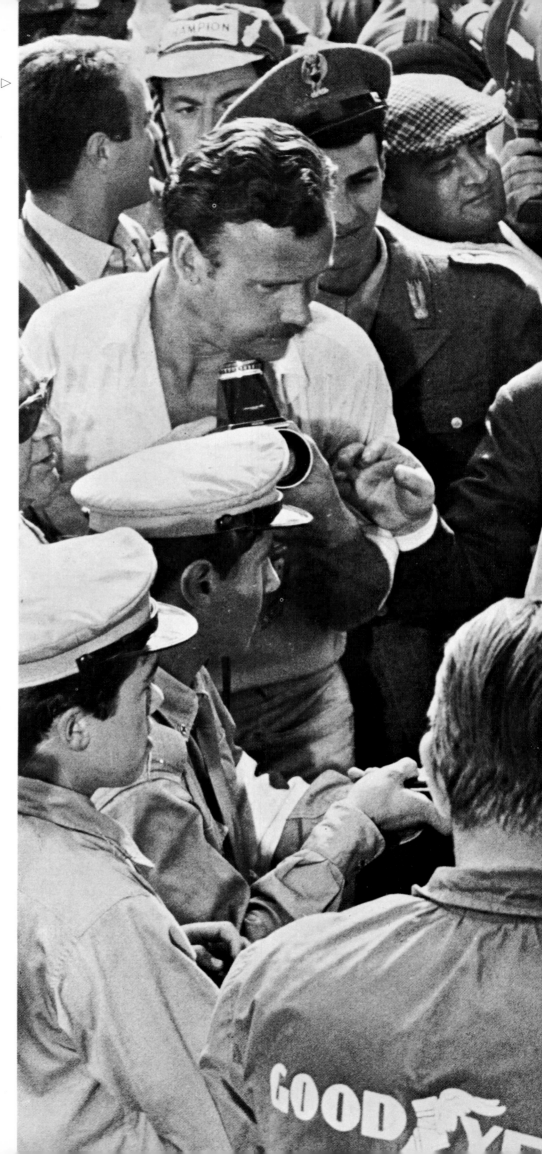

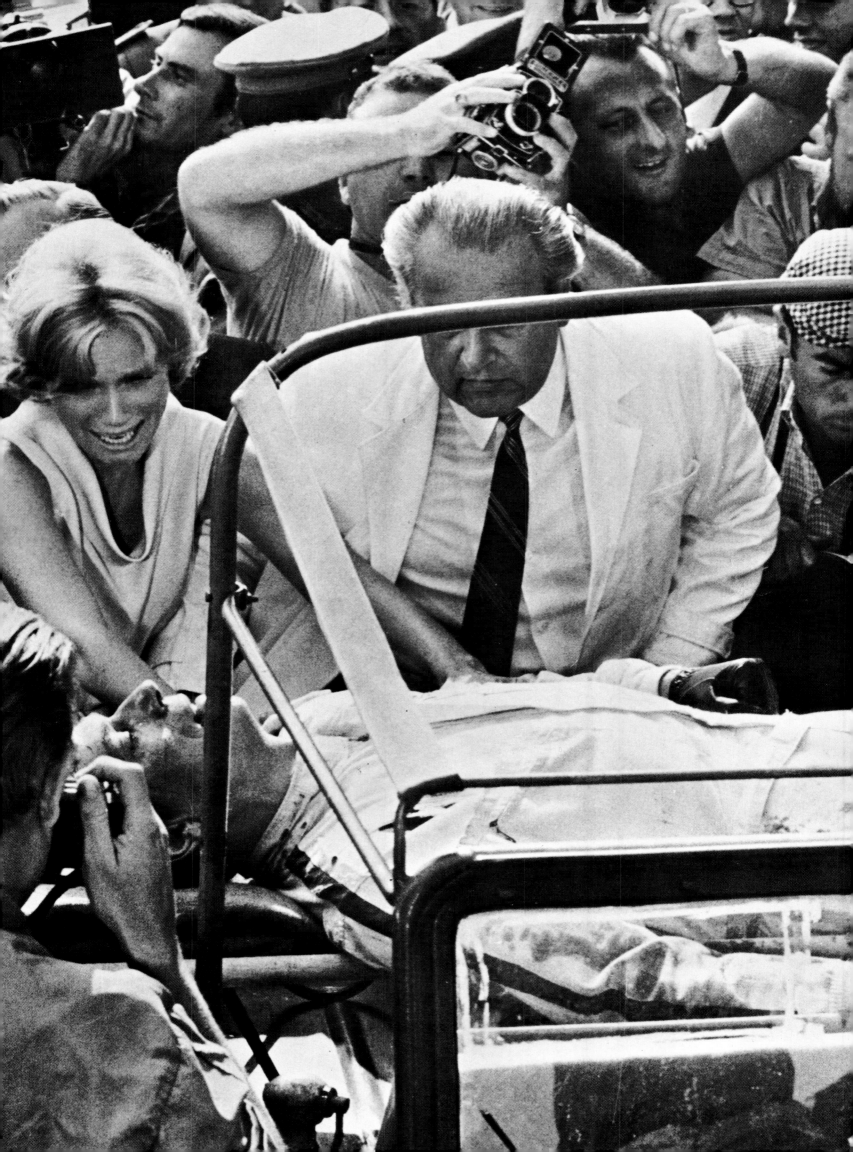

NEW DIRECTIONS

1967

Money poured into MGM's coffers: a record gross income of $227m yielding a profit of $14m. United Artists, the latest of the old-line companies to be absorbed, became a segment of Transamerica Corp.

Biggest surprise hit of the year: *Bonnie and Clyde* with Warren Beatty and Faye Dunaway made a fortune for producer Beatty and Warners. Biggest non-surprise hit: *You Only Live Twice*, yet another Bond mint for UA's new owners, who also got the Oscar winner, *In the Heat of the Night*. Rod Steiger won for his performance in this, while the best actress, said the Academy, was in Spencer Tracy's last film, *Guess Who's Coming to Dinner*: the astonishing Katharine Hepburn, whose previous Oscar was 35 years old.

The Sand Pebbles, Thoroughly Modern Millie, Barefoot in the Park and *Valley of the Dolls* were popular. France scored with *Un Homme et Une Femme* and *La Guerre est Finie*.

Double Trouble *was one of the more idiotic Elvis Presley movies. His songs came as a relief from Jo Heims' script (original, Marc Brandel) about smuggling between England and Belgium—or something. Norman Taurog directed the Judd Bernard–Irwin Winkler production, with Annette Day (here) and John Williams, Yvonne Romain, Chips Rafferty and the Wiere Brothers.*

The Comedians, *scripted by Graham Greene from his novel about a group of Europeans and Americans in voodoo-ridden Haiti, was filmed in West Africa and France: Haitian dictator Papa Doc was unwelcoming. Performances by Richard Burton and Alec Guinness (here) and Elizabeth Taylor, Peter Ustinov, Lillian Gish and Paul Ford were the movie's best assets, artistically and financially, but results were patchy. Producer and director: Peter Glenville.*

Blow-Up *had the cognoscenti discussing, dissecting and analyzing it during the late 1960's; a whole book of speculations about it was published. Non-cog crowds quickly gave up guessing what Michelangelo Antonioni was getting at and just enjoyed the 'swinging London' chic, the pervading air of mystery, the sometimes topless Vanessa Redgrave and David Hemmings (here topped), Sarah Miles 'in flagrante', and Hemmings tumbling with nude girls in his photographic studio. All of which made it a powerful ticket-seller. Antonioni brilliantly directed his baffling script, written with Tonino Guerra; Carlo Ponti produced.*

The Dirty Dozen *ousted Blow-Up as 1967's top moneymaker, and wound up as No. 6 in MGM's list of all-time winners; it had title/ cast/story chemistry that aroused instant want-to-see in the public. Director Robert Aldrich and producer Kenneth Hyman wisely went all-out for raw, rowdy action in the Nunnally Johnson–Lukas Heller screenplay about 12 soldiers, sentenced to death for murder, rape and other crimes of violence, who were instead given sabotage training and let loose on a Nazi generals' hide-out on the eve of D-Day. The dozen were John Cassavetes, Jim Brown, Telly Savalas, Donald Sutherland, Charles Bronson, Trini Lopez, Tom Busby, Al Mancini, Colin Maitland, Stuart Cooper, Ben Carruthers, and the massive Clint Walker (here attacking their trainer, Lee Marvin). Robert Ryan, Ernest Borgnine, Ralph Meeker, Richard*

Jaeckel, Robert Webber and George Kennedy were also prominent. John Poyner won an Academy Award for sound effects—mostly explosions.

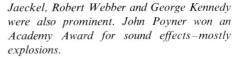

The Italian influence: **The Wild, Wild Planet** *was an Italian out-of-this-worlder with a script that Ivan Reiner may have derived from Gypsy Lazonga's Dream Book. Lisa Gastoni (here being manhandled by a gang from the outlaw planetoid Delphos in 2015 AD) was cast with Tony Russell, Massimo Serato, Franco Nero, Charles Justin and Enzo Fiermonte. Antonio Margheriti co-produced with Joseph Fryd*

and, under the name of Anthony Dawson, directed . . . Umberto Orsini, Rod Steiger and Virna Lisi in **The Girl and the General,** *an odd tale about an Italian soldier and a peasant girl who captured an Austrian general and died in a minefield. Written by Luigi Malerba, directed by Pasquale Festa Campanile, produced by Carlo Ponti, ignored by the public.*

Dangling from the lunatic fringe of cinema with James Bond and Napoleon Solo, **A Man Called Dagger** *was played by Paul Mantee (here rescuing Eileen O'Neill from a swinging scimitar). The James Peatman–Robert Weekley script titillated jaded fight connoisseurs with a climactic struggle through hundreds of hanging carcasses in a meat refrigerator. Directed by Richard Hush, produced by Lewis Horowitz; with Jan Murray, Terry Moore, Sue Ane Langdon.*

Don't Make Waves *was a comedy about glamour queens, beach boys and other freaky denizens of southern California's slide area. This rich field for satire was neglected in favour of romantic farce in the script Ira Wallach and George Kirgo based on Wallach's novel 'Muscle Beach'. Left to right: Claudia Cardinale, Tony Curtis and the ill-fated Sharon Tate. Alexander Mackendrick, who had directed Curtis in the trenchant* Sweet Smell of Success, *pulled his punches this time; box-office results went soft too. Martin Ransohoff and John Calley produced, casting Robert Webber, Joanna Barnes, Mort Sahl, Edgar Bergen, beefcake hunk David Draper.*

and Dick Kallman; also Bill Bixby, Mort Sahl, Allen Jenkins, and co-star George Hamilton.

Good actresses breathing some life into the spooky melodrama of **Eye of the Devil***: Flora Robson and Deborah Kerr. The latter replaced Kim Novak, who was injured during its production, necessitating many retakes. This tale of black magic in a mysterious French castle was total miscasting for David Niven; treating it seriously seemed less of a strain for Donald Pleasence, Edward Mulhare, Emlyn Williams, Sharon Tate, David Hemmings and John Le Mesurier. J. Lee Thompson directed the Martin Ransohoff–John Calley production, written by Robin Estridge and Dennis Murphy from Philip Lorraine's novel 'Day of the Arrow'. Exhibitors had haunted houses.*

George Hamilton and Marie Laforet were super-burglars who stole the fabulous Zaharoff jewels in **Jack of Diamonds***, a slick, entertaining programmer produced in Germany by Sandy Howard, who wrote it with Jack DeWitt. Joseph Cotten, Maurice Evans, Wolfgang Preiss and, playing themselves as robbed actresses, Carroll Baker, Zsa Zsa Gabor and Lilli Palmer were in Don Taylor's cast.*

John Gay's adaptation of Frank Robinson's book **The Power** *seemed to have strayed from the 'U.N.C.L.E.' file: its villain was that series' standby, a super-intelligence trying to gain control of the world. However, it was developed on whodunit lines and worked up quite a head of suspense. George Pal produced. Byron Haskin directed Michael Rennie, George Hamilton (here); Suzanne Pleshette, Richard Carlson, Yvonne De Carlo, Earl Holliman, Gary Merrill, Aldo Ray, Barbara Nichols, Arthur O'Connell, Nehemiah Persoff, Ken Murray.*

An illustrious MGM career recrudesced when Joan Crawford, looking as though her debut 42 years before must have been at the age of three, threw herself with typical gusto into the 'U.N.C.L.E.' maelstrom for a 'guest star' sequence in **The Karate Killers** *with Herbert Lom. Robert Vaughn, David McCallum, Curt Jurgens, Telly Savalas, Terry-Thomas, Leo G. Carroll, Kim Darby, Diane McBain, Jill Ireland and Philip Ahn were in the Boris Ingster production, written by Norman Hudis from Ingster's story, directed by Barry Shear*

Dance of the Vampires/The Fearless Vampire Killers, or Pardon Me But Your Teeth Are in My Neck *was, as the American title unsubtly indicated, a send-up of Dracula and all his ilk. It was written (with Gerard Brach) and directed by Roman Polanski, who wasn't too subtle about it either. He and his wife, Sharon Tate, Jack MacGowran (here leading a zombies' quadrille), Alfie Bass, Ferdy Mayne, Iain Quarrier and Terry Downes were featured in the Transylvanian whoop-de-do, produced by Gene Gutowski in London for Martin Ransohoff. Some audiences fell about laughing, others seemed ready to drive a stake through the movie's heart. Business varied similarly. But who could resist the credit 'Fangs by Dr Ludwig von Krankheit'?*

. . . The second 1967 'U.N.C.L.E.' spree, **The Helicopter Spies***, had Vaughn surprising Julie London with lover Roy Jenson during a hectic Dean Hargrove scenario that also involved McCallum, Carroll, Bradford Dillman, Lola Albright, Carol Lynley, John Dehner, John Carradine and Kathleen Freeman. Directed by Boris Sagal, produced by Anthony Spinner.*

Carlo Ponti starred his wife Sophia Loren in an elaborate flop, **Cinderella – Italian Style**/More Than a Miracle. *Tonino Guerra's story featured such diversions as a dishwashing contest and flying monks and got little direc-*

No organizer of a Sandra Dee Festival should omit **Doctor, You've Got to be Kidding***, in which the quondam teen-age cutie broadened her range to play a pregnant Miss with four suitors. Phillip Shuken's frantic comedy was produced by Douglas Laurence, and Peter Tewksbury directed (left to right) Sandra, the delicious Celeste Holm, Dwayne Hickman*

torial help from Francesco Rosi; it needed every ounce of box-office weight that Loren and Omar Sharif could give it. The still beautiful Dolores Del Rio played Omar's Ma, Leslie French a monk.

The Biggest Bundle of Them All, balanced uncertainly between thriller and comedy, offered Robert Wagner, Raquel Welch and Vittorio de Sica (left to right) and Edward G. Robinson, Godfrey Cambridge and Davy Kaye, as an inept gang pulling off a great train robbery. Fair response from the public. Josef Shaftel produced his own story, scripted by Sy Salkowitz and directed by Ken Annakin.

Hot Rods to Hell/52 Miles to Terror was first intended for television and then erroneously thought worthy of theatre bookings. Left to right: Jeanne Crain, Laurie Mock and Dana Andrews being menaced by malicious road-hogs in this crude melodrama. Mimsy Farmer, Paul Bertoya and Mickey Rooney Jr were in Sam Katzman's production, written by Robert E. Kent from a story by Alex Gaby, directed by John Brahm.

Exhibitors cringed when MGM salesmen offered them a **Welcome to Hard Times** and the title proved significant indeed. Business still drooped when it was changed to Killer on a Horse overseas. A pity, because it was an out-of-the-rut Western, like most directed by Burt Kennedy, who also wrote the harsh, violent script from E. L. Doctorow's novel. Janice Rule and Henry Fonda (here) and Keenan Wynn, Aldo Ray, Janis Paige, Michael Shea, Lon Chaney Jr, Alan Baxter, John Anderson, Fay Spain, Royal Dano, Edgar Buchanan, Elisha Cook Jr, Warren Oates and Paul Fix were in the Max Youngstein–David Karr production.

Roy Orbison provided the difference in another Western, **The Fastest Guitar Alive**, and his remarkably numerous fans helped the Sam Katzman production into the profit column. He played, believe it, a singing Southern spy with a bullet-shooting guitar and a bag of gold to smuggle across the Indian-seething plains. Fun for all, including (left to right) Sammy Jackson, Joan Freeman, Orbison, Maggie Pierce; also cast were Lyle Bettger, John Doucette, Ben Lessy. Director, Michael Moore; script, Robert E. Kent.

Hondo and the Apaches was Robert Taylor's MGM farewell. He died in 1969, aged 58, having made all but a few of his films for the company that discovered him in 1934. This was a good toughie, made for TV and overseas, with Ralph Taeger and Noah Beery Jr (here), also Gary Merrill, Michael Rennie, Kathie Browne, John Smith, Michael Pate, Jim Davis. Directed by Lee Katzin, scripted by producer Andrew Fenady from James Edward Grant's screenplay of a Louis l'Amour story.

Our Mother's House was a movie unlike any other. Dirk Bogarde (here with Mark Lester, Margaret Brooks, Gustav Henry and Sarah Nicholls) scored a triumph of subtle menace as the drop-out father who returned to his seedy London home to find the children living alone, pretending their mother hadn't died. These kids – Pamela Franklin, Louis Sheldon Williams, John Golgolka and Parnum Wallace were the others – carried most of the footage, including violently emotional scenes, like Old Vic veterans. Jack Clayton, who makes them seldom but well, produced and directed but the depressing tone of the drama, scripted by Jeremy Brooks and Haya Harareet from John Gloag's novel, restricted returns to MGM and Martin Ransohoff's Filmways to less than the film's due.

Startling flashbacks, flash-forwards and action-replays abounded in **Point Blank**. Brilliant British director John Boorman made this stunner in Hollywood, with Angie Dickinson, Lee Marvin and Carroll O'Connor (here) and Keenan Wynn, Lloyd Bochner, Michael Strong, John Vernon and Sharon Acker. Marvin was chilling as a brutal escaped convict, searching for his loot, in a violent screenplay based by Alexander Jacobs and David and Rafe Newhouse on Richard Stark's novel 'The Hunter', produced by Judd Bernard and Robert Chartoff. Grosses were good.

Richard Thorpe, one of MGM's most prolific moviemakers since 1935, directed and produced **The Last Challenge**/The Pistolero of Red River. Angie Dickinson again figured effectively, and the movie starred Glenn Ford as a gunfighter turned Marshal, headin' for a showdown with young killer Chad Everett. The John Sherry–Robert Emmett Ginna screenplay featured Gary Merrill, Jack Elam and Royal Dano.

A year loaded with crime and violence ended as work finished on **Sol Madrid**/The Heroin Gang, which had plenty of both. David McCallum, here being picked up as a junkie, turned out to be a drug squad agent seeking the source of the Mafia's heroin. Brian G. Hutton's direction and David Karp's script from Robert Wilder's 'Fruit of the Poppy' were tough and good. Stella Stevens, Ricardo Montalban, Rip Torn, Telly Savalas, Pat Hingle, Paul Lukas (his 40th Hollywood year) and Michael Ansara were in Hall Bartlett's production co-sponsored by Jerry Gershwin and Elliot Kastner.

OUT INTO SPACE
1968

The MGM film laboratory, acknowledged as the industry's best, helped the company to reach a $9½m profit with a 70-millimetre transformation of the 35-millimetre *GWTW*.

A disregard of the industry's Production Code and a loosening of outside censorship rules became more evident in such pictures as Frank Sinatra's *The Detective*, Deborah Kerr and David Niven in *Prudence and the Pill*, the ferocious *In Cold Blood* – and the phenomenal smash of the year: *The Graduate*, which won Mike Nichols the 1967 director Oscar, made Dustin Hoffman a star and amassed rentals near the totals of *GWTW* and *Sound of Music*. The latter's triumph inspired 20th Century-Fox to sink millions into two more musicals: *Dr Dolittle* (Rex Harrison) and *Star!* (Julie Andrews), both flops. Disney had a big one in *Jungle Book*. *Oliver* and its director Carol Reed won awards from the Academy, which surprised with acting Oscars to Cliff Robertson in *Charly* and Barbra Streisand in *Funny Girl* and Katharine Hepburn in *The Lion in Winter* – the first tie since 1932.

Guns for San Sebastian *was a big, bustling Southern filmed in Mexico by the French producer-director team, Jacques Bar and Henri Verneuil. Lots of activity (and pretty good paybox action) as villagers led by fake priest Anthony Quinn fought off Indian raids led by Charles Bronson (here with Quinn). Also in the James R. Webb screenplay, from William Faherty's story: Anjanette Comer, Sam Jaffe and Fernand Gravet, last at MGM 30 years before as star of* The Great Waltz.

△ **Dark of the Sun**/The Mercenaries *was too violent for some censor boards, but not for the public. Jim Brown and Rod Taylor led the roughneck action, which director Jack Cardiff kept moving at a terrific pace. Taylor had the year's most energetic role as he rescued a trainload of Congo villagers and a hoard of diamonds from attacking rebels. Yvette Mimieux as a refugee and Kenneth More as an alcoholic doctor co-starred in a cast that included Paul Garsten, Andre Morell, Olivier*

Despax, Guy Deghy, Calvin Lockhart and Alan Gifford. Quentin Werty and Adrian Spies scripted the George Englund production.

Arthur Kennedy and Glenn Ford in **Day of the** ▷ **Evil Gun** *were rivals who joined forces when the woman they both loved was kidnapped by Apaches. Jerry Thorpe produced and directed the stark, depressing Charles Marquis Warren– Eric Bercovici horse opera, with Dean Jagger, John Anderson, Paul Fix, Royal Dano.*

2001: A Space Odyssey, *science fiction without* ▷ *death-rays or monsters, is one of the great imaginative achievements of the movies. It was produced in Cinerama – and deep secrecy – at the MGM British studio. After an expendable prologue resembling a preview of* Planet of the Apes, *Stanley Kubrick's film took an increasingly strong grip on its audiences as it went to the moon and beyond, until its hero (Keir Dullea, here) was hurtled into the unknown regions of outer space. The final scenes were so stunningly bizarre that almost every viewer had a different explanation for them, with reactions ranging from exaltation to baffled anger. The talk it created had a cumulative effect on the box-office: initial doubts that its cost would be recouped changed to estimates of $50m. in rentals, and by 1974 it had returned $27m. in America alone. Kubrick's direction and special effects (which won an Academy Award) and, with Arthur C. Clarke, script were enhanced by a soundtrack which surprisingly featured 'The Blue Danube' and a bit of Richard Strauss' 'Thus Spake Zarathustra'; the latter became a kind of theme tune for real space flights. Also cast: Gary Lockwood as co-hero, a supercomputer named Hal as villain (with Douglas Rain's voice), William Sylvester, Daniel Richter, Leonard Rossiter, Margaret Tyzack, Robert Beatty, Sean Sullivan.*

The other extreme of science fiction was **Battle Beneath the Earth**/Battle Beneath the Sea, *a British flick about Chinese hordes tunnelling below the Pacific with laser beams to plant atom bombs under American cities. Wild, man. Montgomery Tully directed, Charles Reynolds and Charles Vetter Jr produced, L. Z. Hargreaves wrote. Also cast: Robert Ayres, Sarah Brackett and Kerwin Mathews (here) and Viviane Ventura, Peter Arne, Martin Benson, Earl Cameron, Michael McStay, Carl Jaffe.*

How to Steal the World *marked the end of 'U.N.C.L.E.', with Eleanor Parker as the last wicked victim of Robert Vaughn's and David McCallum's THRUSH-crushing exploits; Barry Sullivan, Leslie Nielsen, Tony Bill, Mark Richman, Daniel O'Herlihy, Hugh Marlowe, Ruth Warrick and Leo G. Carroll filled other leads in Anthony Spinner's production, written by Norman Hudis and directed by Sutton Roley.*

1968

Ice Station Zebra *was a 1968 thriller that tried for epic proportions with Cinerama, Ultra-Panavision, Metrocolor and a hefty budget. It just missed; but public response was good. Harry Julian Fink's script from Alistair MacLean's novel had secret agents in a nuclear submarine and at the North Pole, where a Russia versus America/Britain confrontation got wildly complicated. Exciting submarine scenes involved (left to right) Ernest Borgnine, Patrick McGoohan and Rock Hudson. Also in John Sturges' cast: Jim Brown, Tony Bill, Lloyd Nolan, Alf Kjellin, Gerald O'Laughlin. Martin Ransohoff and John Calley produced.*

Two programmes with high homicide rates: The plot of **Too Many Thieves** *was less see-through than Joanna Barnes' costume. Peter Falk (with Miss Barnes here) and Britt Ekland, Nehemiah Persoff, David Carradine, George Coulouris, Elaine Stritch and Ludwig Donath ran around in circles after stolen treasure and most of them ended up dead. Abner Biberman directed George Bellak's screenplay, a Filmways production by Richard Simons for MGM release.*

The Scorpio Letters, *with Alex Cord as an undercover agent who had his uncovered moments with Shirley Eaton. When up and about, they destroyed a blackmail gang in the Adrian Spies–Jo Eisinger script from Victor Canning's novel. Richard Thorpe produced and directed, casting Laurence Naismith, Oscar Beregi, Lester Matthews.*

Hank Williams Jr, Shelley Fabares, Donald Woods, Ed Begley and D'Urville Martin in **A Time to Sing**, *written country-style by Robert E. Kent and Orville Hampton, directed by Arthur Dreifuss, produced by Sam Katzman. A time to stay home and watch an old MGM movie on television.*

Elvis Presley supplied box-office insurance and an unusually animated performance in **Stay Away, Joe** *with Burgess Meredith and Katy Jurado as his Indian parents. Peter Tewksbury gave the zany script (Michael Hoey, from Dan Cushman's book) an infectious air of high spirits. Joan Blondell, Thomas Gomez, Henry Jones, Quentin Dean, I. Q. Jones and Anne Seymour were in Douglas Laurence's production.*

The power blackout that had paralyzed New York a few years before inspired **Where Were You When the Lights Went Out?** *Doris Day and Terry-Thomas had some madly funny moments in this strong ticket-seller, as did Robert Morse, Patrick O'Neal, Lola Albright, Jim Backus, Steve Allen and Ben Blue, under Hy Haverback's expert comedy guidance. The Everett Freeman–Karl Tunberg script was produced by Freeman and Martin Melcher.*

The makers of **The Extraordinary Seaman** *went in for extraordinary credits: 'Directed by John Frankenheimer; produced by Edward Lewis; a co-production of John Frankenheimer Productions and Edward Lewis Productions Inc; an Edward Lewis Production; a John Frankenheimer Film.' So critics knew where to lay the blame for a silly wartime comedy. Not on stars David Niven and Faye Dunaway (here) or on Alan Alda, Mickey Rooney, Jack Carter, Juano Hernandez, Barry Kelley. Writers: Philip Rock and Hal Dresner.*

The Presley formula was varied slightly in **Speedway** *to allow him a song-and-dance co-star for the first time since Viva Las Vegas: Nancy Sinatra played a mini-skirted income tax collector chasing Elvis, once again a racing-driver. Their musical numbers made up for the lack of novelty in Phillip Shuken's trivial script, Norman Taurog's direction and Douglas Laurence's profitable production. Bill Bixby, Gale Gordon and Carl Ballantine were in support.*

Patricia Neal miraculously recovered from the severe strokes she had suffered while making Seven Women *and returned to the screen in* **The Subject Was Roses**, *with her dramatic powers not only intact but intensified. Martin Sheen (here) as her son and Jack Albertson in an Oscar-winning performance as her husband retained their stage roles in Frank Gilroy's screenplay of his Broadway success. Producer Edgar Lansbury and director Ulu Grosbard, who also repeated their work on the play, gave the drama of family tensions added realism by using actual locations in and around New York. No box-office strength, though.*

Also a paybox dud, but with less artistic claim to be anything else, **The Legend of Lylah Clare** *served an indigestible stew about a Hollywood director-genius who, obsessed by the death of his wife, a star, found her double and tried to make her a star too. In this scene, after mutual torso appraisal, Kim Novak and Gabriele Tinti begin an affair under the jealous eye of Peter Finch. Ernest Borgnine, Milton Selzer, Rossella Falk, Valentina Cortese, Coral Browne and Jean Carroll were other unbelievable movie-town characters in the Hugo Butler–Jean Rouverol script. Production and direction by Robert Aldrich.*

Live a Little, Love a Little, *Elvis Presley's 28th movie, offered the unique sight of the singing idols of different generations of teenagers acting together: Rudy Vallee, whose screaming, swooning fans were as numerous and idiotic in 1930 as Presley's in 1960–70, supported the latter in this amusing lightweight. So did Michele Carey, Eddie Hodges, Don Porter, Sterling Holloway and Dick Sargent. Presley was directed by Norman Taurog for the ninth time and produced by Douglas Laurence for the third. Their big mistake was changing one of the great titles of all time: Michael Hoey's script was based on Dan Greenburg's 'Kiss My Firm But Pliant Lips'.*

Irwin Winkler and Robert Chartoff followed Point Blank *with another Richard Stark crime thriller,* **The Split**, *in which Jim Brown and Julie Harris played gangleaders in a football stadium robbery. Clever twists in the script (Robert Sabaroff) and sharp direction (Gordon Flemyng) made it a moneyspinner. Diahann Carroll, Ernest Borgnine, Gene Hackman, James Whitmore, Donald Sutherland, Jack Klugman and Warren Oates helped, as did the Quincy Jones music.*

John Frankenheimer and Edward Lewis made amends for Extraordinary Seaman *with* **The Fixer**. *Those crazy credits were still there, but this time they really were credits, especially Frankenheimer's for his powerful direction of an almost unbearably grim story. He helped Alan Bates (left) to a memorable performance as a persecuted Jew in Czarist Russia; also Ian Holm (brimmed hat), Dirk Bogarde (right), Elizabeth Hartman, Hugh Griffith, David Warner, Carol White, Thomas Heathcote and Georgia Brown in shorter but no less vivid parts. The script that Dalton Trumbo, who had learned about persecution in the McCarthy hearings, wrote from Bernard Malamud's novel retained its force – and an emphasis on misery that deterred entertainment-seekers.*

Hot Millions, *an endearingly daffy comedy, featured Peter Ustinov as an ingenious embezzler outwitting Karl Malden's computer, and Maggie Smith as a secretary good at taking down. Produced in Britain by American Mildred Freed Alberg and directed by Canadian Eric Till, the Ustinov–Ira Wallach screenplay delighted audiences which should have been bigger. Bob Newhart, Robert Morley and Cesar Romero were featured.*

Peter Noone and his group, Herman's Hermits (Karl Green, Keith Hopwood, Derek Leckenby, Barry Whitwam) bounced back for a chaotic comedy mixing pop songs and greyhound racing, **Mrs Brown, You've Got a Lovely Daughter**. *Less than lovely business for Allen Klein's British production, written by Thaddeus Vane, directed by Saul Swimmer. Lance Percival, Marjorie Rhodes and Noone (here) and Stanley Holloway, Mona Washbourne, Sheila White and Sarah Caldwell were cast.*

There's nothing new about rebellious youth versus foolish parents, but Sam Katzman produced an effectively emotional little drama on the theme in **The Young Runaways**, *with Lynn Bari and Patty McCormick (here as mother and daughter), Richard Dreyfuss, Kevin Coughlin, Lloyd Bochner, Norman Fell, Quentin Dean and James Edwards. Arthur Dreifuss ably directed the Orville Hampton screenplay.*

Kenner *was an inept chase drama filmed in Bombay and shelved for over a year. Bookings were few. Steve Sekely directed the Harold Clemens–John Loring script, from a story by*

Mary Murray, who produced. In the cast: Jim Brown (here) and Madlyn Rhue, Ricky Cordell, Robert Coote, Charles Horvath.

The Shoes of the Fisherman *was a long, lavish filming of Morris West's best-seller, produced in Italy by George Englund on a big budget and given major attention as a top 'A' release by MGM. The public failed to respond in requisite numbers. Vatican scenes like this, with Anthony Quinn as a Russian Pope (Leo McKern, left, as a cardinal), his election, and his troubled friendship with a Jesuit (Oskar Werner) were splendidly acted, written and staged. Less absorbing, and sometimes downright phoney, were his secret pact with Russian and Chinese leaders, and a subplot about an American reporter, expressionlessly played by David Janssen. Michael Anderson directed West's screenplay. Also cast: Barbara Jefford, Vittorio de Sica, Laurence Olivier, John Gielgud, Clive Revill, Rosemary Dexter, Paul Rogers, Niall MacGinnis, Frank Finlay, George Pravda and Arnoldo Foa.*

The Culver City old guard supplied the surprise hit among so many 'outside' independent productions of 1968. George Wells wrote, William Daniels photographed and Lawrence Weingarten produced **The Impossible Years**, *a generation-gap comedy which easily bridged the gap between cost and receipts, with a few million to spare. David Niven, in his best form, and a vivacious young beauty, Cristina Ferrare, took good care of the father and daughter leads, with Chad Everett, Lola Albright, Ozzie Nelson and Jeff Cooper in support. Michael Gordon directed the adaptation of a play by Bob Fisher and Arthur Marx (Groucho's son).*

Vittorio Gassman, Sophia Loren and Mario Adorf in **Ghosts–Italian Style** *(the sameness of Miss Loren's titles was started by her 1964 hit* Marriage–Italian Style*). The fast and funny screenplay by Tonino Guerra was from Eduardo de Filippo's play, produced by Carlo Ponti and directed by Renato Castellani. Bookings in English-speaking countries were sparse.*

WHERE EAGLES DARE

1969

The year of the long knives at MGM's New York headquarters (James Polk Jr, who followed Robert O'Brien as president, lasted for less than a year before he was replaced by James T. Aubrey Jr) was also the year of the company's short production list.

Total receipts of American cinemas, thanks partly to rising admission prices, were the highest since 1957, $1,097m—but the public spent eight times as much on television, radio and records. In Britain, the prices had risen 50 per cent in five years and admissions had dropped from 343m to 215m.

The story of a male prostitute, *Midnight Cowboy*, Maggie Smith in *The Prime of Miss Jean Brodie*, John Wayne in *True Grit*, Jane Fonda and Gig Young in *They Shoot Horses, Don't They?*; *Oh What a Lovely War* and *Z* won many international awards. Katharine Hepburn, 37 years a star, at last made the exhibitors' Top Ten list, joining such upstarts as Paul Newman, John Wayne, Steve Mc-Queen, Dustin Hoffman, Clint Eastwood, Sidney Poitier, Lee Marvin, Jack Lemmon and Barbra Streisand.

Burt Lancaster's demise in **The Gypsy Moths** *came a bit too early in the movie for its box-office good. He played one of three dare-devil parachutists—Scott Wilson (with him here) and Gene Hackman played the other two—who fell apart when Lancaster, bemused after a nude tumble on a sofa with Scott's aunt (Deborah Kerr), omitted to pull the ripcord on his next jump. Script by William Hanley from a novel by James Drought. Sheree North, William Windom and Bonnie Bedelia were featured in the John Frankenheimer–Edward Lewis production, directed by Frankenheimer, produced by Hal Landers and Bobby Roberts.*

The year's biggest moneymaker, **Where Eagles Dare** *starred Richard Burton (right) and Clint Eastwood (at bar) as Allied fighters who parachuted to a Gestapo stronghold and posed as German officers in order to free an important prisoner. Alistair MacLean's plot got so complicated towards the end that audiences gave it up and just enjoyed the action, which was nonstop. Elliott Kastner produced and Brian G. Hutton directed at MGM British. Also cast: Mary Ure, Patrick Wymark, Michael Hordern, Donald Houston, Ingrid Pitt (foreground), Peter Barkworth, William Squire, Robert Beatty, Brock Williams, Neil McCarthy, Vincent Ball, Anton Diffring, Ferdy Mayne, Derren Nesbitt.*

The Five-Man Army *was a lively example of the genre known in the trade as spaghetti Western. Peter Graves and Nino Castelnuovo (here) and James Daly, Bud Spencer and Tetsuro Tamba slaughtered approximately 500 foes on their way to a $500,000 gold hoard. Exhibitors did pretty well out of the caper too. Directed by Don Taylor in Italy, set in Mexico by writers Dario Argento and Marc Richards, produced by Italo Zingarelli.*

Fredric March, at 72 still one of the best actors in the business, played mayor to George Kennedy's old sheriff and Jim Brown's new sheriff in **Tick . . . Tick . . . Tick**. *They were sitting on a racial time-bomb when Brown was elected as their Southern town's first black law-enforcer. The movie had tension and well-developed climaxes as written by James Lee Barrett and directed by Ralph Nelson. They also produced, giving Lynn Carlin, Don Stroud, Janet MacLachlan and Richard Elkins key roles.*

MGM signed television's Dan Rowan and Dick Martin, whose 'Laugh-In' had drawn the highest series ratings in the history of the box, and came out with one of the silliest pictures in the history of the movies, **The Maltese Bippy**. *Mildred Natwick (with them here) and Carol Lynley, Robert Reed, Julie Newmar and Fritz Weaver worked hard for laughs in the Everett Freeman–Robert Enders production written by Freeman and Ray Singer, directed by Norman Panama. It was photographed by William Daniels, who used to be Garbo's cameraman.*

Marlowe *was the fifth movie about Raymond Chandler's detective. For it James Garner stepped into Philip Marlowe's gumshoes formerly worn by Humphrey Bogart, George Montgomery, Dick Powell and Robert Montgomery. Gayle Hunnicutt played the most attractive of the offbeat characters he met in the maze of murder, blackmail, dope and sex that Stirling Silliphant scripted from Chandler's 'The Little Sister'. Also in the cast were Carroll O'Connor, Rita Moreno, Sharon Farrell, Jackie Coogan (at the studio where he starred 45 years before) and Bruce Lee (in his first exhibition of the Kung Fu mayhem which became a film craze four years later). Paul Bogart directed the fairly successful Gabriel Katzka–Sidney Beckerman production.*

This shot of Raquel Welch was the advertising come-on for **Flare-Up**, *an MGM post-production pick-up written by Mark Rodgers, directed by James Neilson, produced by Leon Fromkess. The star was hardly ever off-camera, as she danced at the Pussy-a-Go-Go, was chased by a mad killer (Luke Askew), betrayed by a homosexual drug addict (Ron Rifkin), bedded by a car-hop (James Stacy), and finally grabbed a handy can of gasoline to turn the heavy into a human torch. Popcorn on sale in the lobby.*

Michelangelo Antonioni's first American work was **Zabriskie Point**. Very warm there. And in this scene it's getting warmer as Mark Frechette and Daria Halprin obey their impulses, which director Antonioni extended to a whole desert vista of pairs coupling and trios tripling. This was too much for some censors, who obliged MGM by cutting, X-rating, and getting headline publicity for the $6m. movie. It needed the help; popular appeal was strangely lacking despite its fashionable youth versus establishment theme and sensational treatment. Rod Taylor co-starred with Mark and Daria, both of whom made their debuts in the Carlo Ponti production, written by Antonioni with Sam Shepard, Fred Gardner, Tonino Guerra and Clare Peploe.

The Green Slime, a Japanese-made shrieker, resembled a 90-minute case of DTs, what with giant blobs of jelly multiplying all over the place and relentlessly enveloping the entire cast. Just to make it more difficult for heroes Robert Horton and Richard Jaeckel, it all happened in a space station beyond help from Earth. MGM picked the movie up from producers Ivan Reiner and Walter Manley and gave it the works in ballyhoo, with spotty results. Director, Kinji Fukasaku; writers, Charles Sinclair, William Finger, Tom Rowe; heroine, Luciana Paluzzi.

Business was somnolent when beautiful people Marcello Mastroianni and Faye Dunaway drifted through luxury villas and Alpine scenery to find **A Place for Lovers**. Vittorio de Sica directed their dreamy perambulations, concluded by the disclosure that Faye had one of those fatal movie diseases that don't show. Caroline Mortimer and Karin Engh played the only other principals invented by the combined brainpower of Julian Halevy, Peter Baldwin, Ennio de Concini, Tonino Guerra and Cesare Zavattini. Carlo Ponti produced in Italy.

*Carlo Ponti also produced **The Best House in London**, this time in Britain. It was a much livelier affair; Denis Norden put enough plots for three movies into a bawdy period piece which involved David Hemmings, versatile fellow, in the dual roles of wicked womanizer and male virgin, Joanna Pettet (with him here) as an early Women's Libber), Dany Robin as a high-class brothelkeeper, Warren Mitchell as a dotty airship inventor, George Sanders as an old rake, Martita Hunt as a schoolma'am, John Bird as the Home Secretary, and Maurice Denham as editor of The Times. Director Philip Saville kept the fun going at a spanking pace; box-office pace varied.*

*Although **Alfred the Great** was consigned to the drop-dead file by some audiences and critics, others applauded its spectacular action sequences and an unusual character study of the 9th-century king, part religious scholar, part violent warrior, in the Ken Taylor–James R. Webb script directed by Clive Donner. Whether David Hemmings proved the right choice for the complex role was a moot point. With him in this scene are Prunella Ransome as his queen and Michael York as his Viking enemy. Also cast in the Bernard Smith–James Webb film, produced by Smith: Colin Blakely, Julian Glover, Ian McKellen, Vivian Merchant, Alan Dobie, Peter Vaughan, Barry Jackson.*

*MGM hopefully entered **The Appointment** at the Cannes Festival, where it was all but jeered off the screen by the assembled cognoscenti; then never so much released as let out the back-door to television. Anouk Aimee and Omar Sharif (here) were directed by Sidney Lumet in this James Salter screenplay, produced in*

Italy by Martin Poll. The glum drama of a man suspecting his wife of sparetime prostitution dragged on for many a long reel, but it hardly deserved its fate. Lotte Lenya's sinister madam won the few kind words it got.

*A stirring Western: in **Heaven with a Gun** ▽ Glenn Ford proved that you can't fool around with a preacher, pardner, when he's an ex-gunfighter. The fast-drawing reverend settled a feud between sheepmen and cattle ranchers in the King Brothers production, featuring Carolyn Jones, David Carradine (victim here), J. D. Cannon, Barbara Hershey and Noah Beery Jr. Richard Carr's screenplay got sharp direction from Lee Katzin, and good business.*

*MGM hadn't taken on Jules Verne in the 40 years since The Mysterious Island. Now his durable hero turned up again in **Captain** ▷ **Nemo and the Underwater City**, causing far fewer production headaches, and got good response from juveniles of all ages. Robert Ryan and Nanette Newman led a cast that included Chuck Connors, Luciana Paluzzi, Bill Fraser, Kenneth Connor and John Turner, directed by James Hill. R. Wright Campbell, Pip and Jane Barker wrote the script, Bertram Ostrer produced for Steven Pallos at MGM British.*

The major MGM headache of 1969's output was another expensive British production that fell below box-office hopes: **Goodbye Mr Chips**, *given roadshow treatment as the year's Big One. Entertainment-wise, it was just that: director Herbert Ross and producer Arthur Jacobs did a fine job of turning MGM's classic 1939 weepie into a musical, and Peter O'Toole made a superb Chips, with pop singer Petula Clark surprisingly effective in the expanded role of his wife. But they couldn't supplant oldsters' memories of Robert Donat and Greer Garson, and youngsters didn't dig Leslie Bricusse's songs. Terence Rattigan updated the story from World War I to World War II in his script. Also cast: Sir Michael Redgrave,*

George Baker, Michael Bryant, Jack Hedley, Sean Philips, Michael Culver, Barbara Couper.

The Trouble With Girls *allowed Elvis Presley too little singing and more than enough acting. Script troubles stymied this Lester Welch production of a property that had been on MGM's shelf for years: 'Chautauqua', the Day Keene–Dwight Babcock novel about a travelling tent show in the Twenties. Marlyn Mason, Vincent Price, Edward Andrews, John Carradine and Joyce Van Patten were others directed by Peter Tewksbury in the Arnold and Lois Peyser screenplay.*

The Phantom Tollbooth *was MGM's first feature-length cartoon. It starred, not the studio's long-famed Tom and Jerry, but a bored little boy (live action) who became an adventurous little boy (animated drawing) when he drove his toy car into a cartoon wonderland. Bookings were sparse for this imaginative effort, but deserved profits may eventually accrue from children's shows, television screenings, etc. It was based on Norton Juster's book and produced by Chuck Jones, Abe Levitow and Les Goldman. Jones and Goldman had won the Academy Award with their short MGM cartoon,* The Dot and The Line.

VIOLENCE IN VOGUE
1970

MGM closed its studio in Britain and amalgamated with EMI there, in production as well as distribution, thus increasing British releases in Britain and America. World-wide, the company sustained an operating loss of $8,228,000, recouped only by the sales of assets totalling $9,801,000.

The phenomenon of the year came at the end: *Love Story* with no major stars, no famous book or play source and no praise from the critics, began pouring cash into Paramount's bank account.

Before that, the year's big attractions were Burt Lancaster in *Airport*, Disney's *The Aristocats*, Warners' pop festival documentary *Woodstock*, *M.A.S.H.*, and *Patton*.

1969 releases still thriving were *Butch Cassidy and the Sundance Kid*, *Midnight Cowboy* and Disney's *Love Bug*. *Easy Rider*, *Alice's Restaurant* and *Five Easy Pieces* were new-wave hits.

Patton, its star George C. Scott and director Franklin Schaffner, and Glenda Jackson in *Women in Love* were Oscar-winners.

The real Presley finally found his way onto the screen in **Elvis–That's The Way It Is**. *Unencumbered by a fatuous script or his own acting limitations, he simply came on and belted out song after song, and the full force of his stage personality came through the camera for the first time. His off-stage sense of humour also shone in the documentary feature showing his rehearsals and performance at the International Hotel, Las Vegas, with interpolated comments by his fans, most of them weird. Brilliantly directed by Denis Sanders and photographed by Lucien Ballard, it made 108 minutes of solid entertainment–and a barrel of money.*

Strange triangle in **Country Dance**/Brotherly Love*: Peter O'Toole, who was in love with his sister, Susannah York, who knew it, and Michael Craig, who wanted to keep her as his wife. It was played with authority, especially by O'Toole, whose role ranged from gentle pathos to insane violence. James Kennaway's script and J. Lee Thompson's direction dealt with promiscuity and incest delicately, perhaps too much so for the movie's box-office good. Harry Andrews, Judy Cornwell, Cyril Cusack and Brian Blessed were in Robert Emmett Ginna's fine production.*

In **The Strawberry Statement**, *as in reality, vague youthful urges to be 'into something meaningful' escalated to bloody clashes with the law. The movie's climactic confrontation was excitingly staged by Stuart Hagmann; the preceding hour and a half held only spasmodic interest, and public reaction was disappointing. Irwin Winkler and Robert Chartoff produced, featuring Bruce Davison, Kim Darby (left) and Danny Goldman, Kristina Holland, Bud Cort, James Coco, and Israel Horovitz, who also scripted from a book by James Kunen. Several songs sound-tracked, including the inevitable Lennon–McCartney 'Give Peace a Chance'.*

Meanwhile, university drop-outs were being examined (and better acted) in an even more tenuous story, **The Magic Garden of Stanley Sweetheart**. *It was explicit about sex, but still didn't draw the crowds, who may have been deterred by the terrible title. Don Johnson played Stanley (here getting turned on by Michael Greer while Victoria Racimo, Dianne Hull and Linda Gillin wait for the weed to come round). Robert Westbrook's novel (script by himself) was filmed in New York by Leonard Horn for producer Martin Poll.*

Zigzag/False Witness *had a dazzlingly original plot which made a tense and exciting movie for those who could follow its convolutions without getting dizzy. Not very many tried: it had little cast magnetism, though it featured several good actors, headed by George Kennedy (foreground) as an innocent man pretending to be guilty of kidnapping to collect the ransom, and Eli Wallach as his trial lawyer. Others in the picture were Anne Jackson, Steve Ihnat, William Marshall, Anita O'Day. Script by John Kelley, from Robert Enders' original. Richard Colla directed, Enders and Everett Freeman produced.*

Censorship, which permitted children to watch all kinds of suffering and killing, slapped an 'X' on **The Body** *for this scene of one of life's great joys. Copulation was shown as a natural part of human experience along with birth, youth, maturity and dying (but not, strangely, death) in this remarkable documentary feature. Producer Tony Garnett and Director Roy Battersby included astonishing Technicolor film of internal functions, as well as of matter-of-fact nudity. Commentaries spoken by Vanessa Redgrave and Frank Finlay. The Kestrel-Anglo-EMI production was excellently received.*

Brewster McCloud *was a comedy about a youth building mechanical wings to fly with and committing several murders. There was a good deal about birds and bird-droppings by the way. 'I couldn't explain it,' said director Robert Altman, and neither could anybody else. Altman had made M.A.S.H. which may have persuaded MGM and producer Lou Adler that he could make a success of anything. Bud Cort and Sally Kellerman (here) were supported by Michael Murphy, William Windom, Shelley Duvall, Rene Auberjonois, Stacy Keach and Margaret Hamilton (the Wicked Witch of Oz) in Doran Cannon's screenplay.*

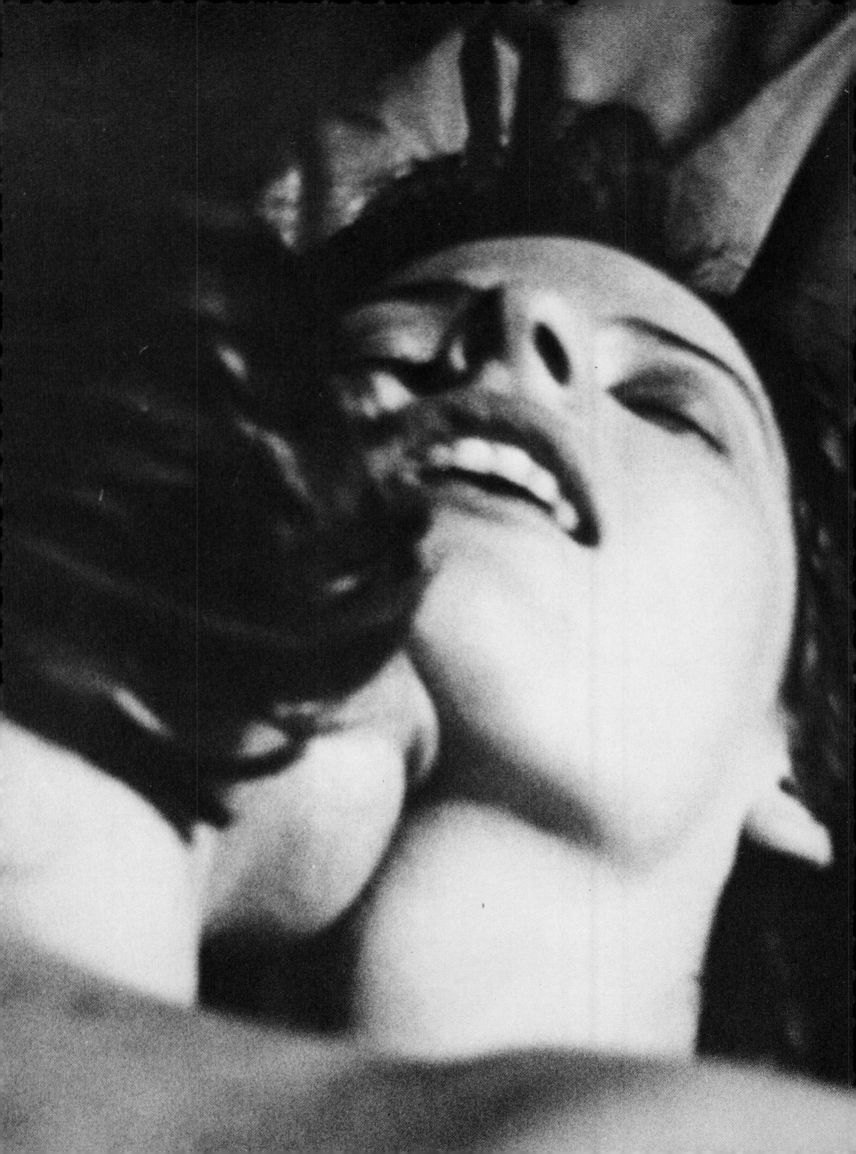

Once again MGM got a hit-maker one movie removed from his hit: **Alex in Wonderland** was directed by Paul Mazursky, who'd had a winner in Bob & Carol & Ted & Alice. The new one was a disjointed study of a Hollywood director at loose ends, its brilliant moments insufficient to attract ticket-buying crowds. Donald Sutherland (here with Jeanne Moreau in one of two sequences shot on Hollywood Boulevard) made a long, difficult role look easy; Mazursky himself scintillated in a satirical sketch of a producer; Ellen Burstyn was fine as the director's wife. Larry Tucker produced and collaborated on the script with Mazursky.

Dirty Dingus Magee was one of Burt Kennedy's jolly Westerns and rowdier than most. Frank Sinatra (here with Michele Carey) had a high old time as a carefree outlaw in the Tom and Frank Waldman–Joseph Heller comedy from David Markson's novel, and its exhibitors enjoyed good response. Also cast: George Kennedy, Anne Jackson, Lois Nettleton, Jack Elam, John Dehner, Harry Carey Jr, Paul Fix.

Charming love scenes (including one in the obligatory Seventies' nude) between Sarah Miles and Christopher Jones relieved the otherwise sombre drama of **Ryan's Daughter**, David ▷ Lean's first film since Doctor Zhivago. With his usual background of war (the 1916 Irish revolt this time) it was essentially a simple triangle story of these two and Robert Mitchum as the village schoolmaster. Hence the public's expectation of another Lean super-epic—furthered by MGM's having to treat it as such in order to get back its incredible $12m. cost—was disappointed. Nevertheless, it was a splendidly acted, beautifully made picture, that won Oscars for John Mills' supporting performance as a hideous half-wit and Freddie Young's gorgeous photography. Trevor Howard, Leo McKern and Barry Foster had other leads in Robert Bolt's screenplay, produced by Anthony Havelock-Allan. MGM distribution could take bows during 1970–73 for reaping approximately double the cost of its prolonged 1969–70 production.

Kelly's Heroes was a hit in the USA and an ▷ outright smash in the UK and some other countries. The movie followed the wild adventures of Donald Sutherland, Clint Eastwood and Telly Savalas (left to right) along with Don Rickles, Carroll O'Connor, Hal Buckley, Stuart Margolin, Dick Davalos and other GIs robbing a bank behind the German lines. This was war? Troy Kennedy Martin wrote the Gabriel Katzka–Sidney Beckerman production, directed by Brian Hutton for slam-bang action.

Author Hugh Leonard's funny idea of a penis transplant was tediously developed in **Percy**, delivering little of what its subject matter promised to spice-seekers. 'Percy', the hero's coy name for his new organ, was never seen—mercifully or disappointingly, according to taste—but its box-office potency was decidedly

The year's most mixed-up family figured in **My Lover, My Son**, *with Romy Schneider as mother giving son Dennis Waterman an incestuous come-on because she got him confused in her mind with her dead lover; sonny almost co-operated but instead went for a nude scene with Patricia Brake in a Thames houseboat; meanwhile father Donald Houston was bedding secretary Alexandra Bastedo, but came home in time for the big climax in which he got killed by Romy, who let Dennis think he'd done it, and do you remember the Hardy Family? Directed by John Newland, produced by Wilbur Stark, scripted by William Marchant and Jenni Hall from a story by Stark and a novel by Edward Grierson.*

evident. Hywel Bennett was the recipient of the transplant, George Best (right) a footballer in a game Bennett imagined while searching for the identity of his member's original owner. Ralph Thomas' cast in the Betty Box EMI production also featured Elke Sommer, Britt Ekland, Denholm Elliott, Cyd Hayman, Janet Key, Patrick Mower, Pauline Delany, Adrienne Posta, Julia Foster.

British releases on both sides of the Atlantic increased; an average example in quality and drawing power was **The Walking Stick** *– good, but not very good. David Hemmings and Samantha Eggar deftly played characters who were more interesting in themselves than in what they did: an introverted girl and a seductive thief. The robbery climax of George Bluestone's script, from Winston Graham's novel, missed much of its potential suspense. Emlyn Williams, Phyllis Calvert, Ferdy Mayne, Francesca Annis, Bridget Turner and Dudley Sutton were in the Elliot Kastner–Alan Ladd Jr production, directed by Eric Till.*

After Easy Rider *came out, American highways were crammed with leather-jacketed, black-glassed motorcycled wanderers aged 17, going on 30, who were either living life like it really is, man, or making more movies like* Easy Rider. *One of the latter.* **Then Came Bronson**, *was a television pilot released overseas with minimal box-office repercussions. Michael Parks played the drop-out and Bonnie Bedelia the pick-up, supported by Akim Tamiroff, Gary Merrill, Sheree North, Martin Sheen and Bert Freed. Written by Denne Bart Petticlerc, directed by William Graham, produced by Robert Justman.*

Dark Shadows/House of Dark Shadows *was brought up to date only by extra violence; otherwise all the old vampire clichés were on view in this hearse-opera based on a popular television series. Here Kathryn Leigh Scott, Joan Bennett and Louis Edmonds discover one of the movie's many corpses. Dan Curtis produced and directed the Sam Hall–Gordon Russell screenplay. Also cast: Grayson Hall, Jonathan Frid and Roger Davis.*

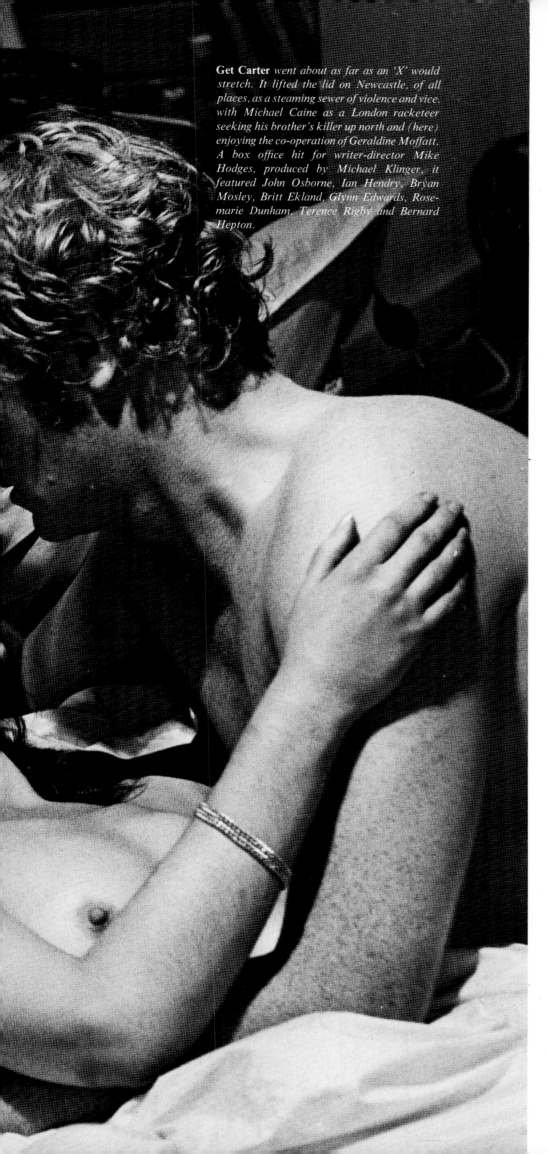

Get Carter *went about as far as an 'X' would stretch. It lifted the lid on Newcastle, of all places, as a steaming sewer of violence and vice. with Michael Caine as a London racketeer seeking his brother's killer up north and (here) enjoying the co-operation of Geraldine Moffatt. A box office hit for writer-director Mike Hodges, produced by Michael Klinger, it featured John Osborne, Ian Hendry, Bryan Mosley, Britt Ekland, Glynn Edwards, Rosemarie Dunham, Terence Rigby and Bernard Hepton.*

The vogue for violence: 'First time I've had to fry a lady', said hot-seat operator Stacy Keach to murderess Mariana Hill in **The Traveling Executioner**, *which went into loving detail over the use of a 1918 electric chair that didn't always work. After a good deal of whoring and unofficial killing, he ended up in the chair himself, with his teen-age assistant Bud Cort throwing the switch. This fragrant nosegay was gathered by producer-director Jack Smight from author Garry Bateson and tossed to a wincing public, who ducked . . .*

Ex-star Cornel Wilde produced and directed **No Blade of Grass**, *a British contribution to MGM's share of the violence that filled the screens, but not always the cinemas, in 1970. The Sean Forestal–Jefferson Pascal screenplay was from John Christopher's novel. Wilde intended the tale of a future famine to be anti-pollution propaganda wrapped in exciting fiction, but it came out as conventional action melodrama. In this scene, Nigel Davenport, John Hamill and Anthony May arrive too late to save Jean Wallace and Lynne Frederick from some raping marauders.*

In **The Moonshine War** *the bullets flew as thick as when Warner Bros. had a franchise on the Prohibition era, but the public didn't seem to care any more. The movie starred Patrick McGoohan as a revenue agent and Richard Widmark as a bootlegger fighting over a booze-making still in Kentucky. Alan Alda, Lee Hazlewood, Will Geer, Melodie Johnson and Harry Carey Jr were in the Martin Ransohoff production, written by Elmore Leonard, directed by Richard Quine.*

DRUGS AND DREAMS
1971

MGM announced a healthy turnaround from 1970's operating loss; the 1971 operating profit was $7,835,000, which with further asset disposals of $8,523,000 brought the net income to $16,358,000 – the highest for 25 years.

Other companies prospered with the drug thriller *The French Connection*, the James Bond *Diamonds Are Forever*, the near-pornographic *Carnal Knowledge* and the nostalgic *Summer of '42*.

British payboxes were filled by spin-offs from television: *Dad's Army, On the Buses, Up Pompeii*, although cinemas had dwindled there to 1,529 (a third of their peak number) and attendances to 193m. *The French Connection*, its star Gene Hackman and director William Friedkin, and Jane Fonda in *Klute* took the Academy Awards. Walter Matthau, George C. Scott, Ali MacGraw and Sean Connery replaced Jack Lemmon, Barbra Streisand, Sidney Poitier and Katharine Hepburn in the Top Ten.

Production delays while producers Lester Perskey and Lewis Allen backed and filled about how close to the wind director Harvey Hart should sail with **Fortune and Men's Eyes** *resulted in this study of male homosexuality arriving well after the more entertaining* Boys in the Band *had pre-empted the subject's novelty value. The heartless story of a normal youth (Wendell Burton) debauched by a prison population incredibly devoted to sexual activities was filmed in a Quebec jail with, also incredibly, Canadian government assistance. Here aggressive hunter Zooey Hall and flam-*

boyant queen Michael Greer appraise the new fish in their tank. Greer, who played the same role on the stage, and Danny Freedman, as a pathetic cellmate, were outstanding. Script was by John Herbert from his Broadway play.

The Boy Friend, *Sandy Wilson's little satire of Twenties musical comedies, with pretty tunes and ingenuous story, was staged in London originally in 1953 and became an international smash. MGM bought screen rights in 1956, but producers were afraid of its sheer simplicity; such a famous property had to be a BIG movie – but how? Lap-dissolve to 1971, London again; enter writer-director-producer Ken Russell, afraid of nothing. He gave the original show a backstage story outside the story, superimposed on the Twenties stage spoof a satire of Thirties movie musicals in the Busby Berkeley style, and added some Freed–Brown hits from the MGM music library. It was all brilliantly done and overdone. Here ex-model phenomenon Twiggy (disarmingly amateur) and ex-ballet star Christopher Gable are singing 'I Could Be Happy with You'. In an exuberant supporting cast Tommy Tune did a sensational Charleston and Glenda Jackson an unbilled bit; also Max Adrian, Brian Pringle, Murray Melvin, Moyra Fraser, Georgina Hale, Barbara Windsor. Box-office was patchy.*

1971

An early 1971 arrival, **The Night Digger**, followed the sad course of too many MGM properties in the Seventies: lacking obvious box-office appeal, it was shelved for a while, then not so much released as allowed to escape. The Alan Courtney–Norman Powell British production was written by Roald Dahl (from a novel by Joy Cowley) for his wife, Patricia Neal, and had much of the repellent fascination of its obvious forebear, Night Must Fall. Here, Nicholas Clay, outside looking in, waits for blind Pamela Brown and adopted daughter Patricia to employ him as a handyman: they are unaware of his penchant for nocturnal rape and murder. A tragic Clay–Neal love affair was excellently acted by both. Alastair Reid directed. Also cast: Jean Anderson, Graham Crowden, Yootha Joyce and Peter Sallis.

Mad Dogs and Englishmen was a documentary that repeated the stimulating effect of Elvis–That's the Way It Is, although it lacked the Presley box-office charisma. Director Pierre Adidge lived with rock singer Joe Cocker and his entourage during a two-month US tour, and filmed 62 hours of performances and offstage activities which were edited to 117 minutes. Pianist-bandleader Leon Russell was featured in the Adidge–Harry Marks–Robert Abel production; executive producer Jerry Moss.

Believe in Me, a downbeat drama of drug addiction which made no concession to the box office, and vice versa, was made by the Strawberry Statement team: writer, Israel Horovitz; director, Stuart Hagmann; producers, Irwin Winkler and Robert Chartoff. Michael Sarrazin and Jacqueline Bisset totally convinced as a young couple descending from romantic bliss to hopeless degradation via experiments with amphetamines. At times it was painful to watch, as when Sarrazin injected

'speed' into his tongue. Jon Cypher and Allen Garfield led the supporting cast; Geraldine Fitzgerald and George Rose were left on the cutting-room floor.

Nothing could be further removed from an 'X' movie than **Tales of Beatrix Potter**/Peter Rabbit and Tales of Beatrix Potter, a musical interpretation of some of the author's stories, danced by members of the Royal Ballet. Its appeal was primarily to tiny tots, then to adults attuned to its special artistry, but surprisingly they were augmented by enough everyday filmgoers to make it a money-spinning success, especially in its native Britain. Ann Howard as Jemima Puddle-Duck and Robert Mead as Mr Fox are the dancers in this scene, choreographed like the rest by Frederick Ashton to music by John Lanchbery. Production by John Brabourne and Richard Goodwin; adapted by Goodwin and its designer, Christine Edzard; directed by Reginald Mills.

John Huston was replaced by Richard Fleischer as director of **The Last Run**. George C. Scott starred in the Carter DeHaven production, with Tony Musante and Trish Van Devere, who later became Mrs Scott. He played a retired driver for a Chicago mob, persuaded to do one more job, driving an escaped convict and his girl across Spain, then dying from a pursuer's bullet. Colleen Dewhurst, the previous Mrs Scott, was also featured in this pretty good chase thriller by Alan Sharp.

The Jerusalem File was an action drama which depicted the confusion following the Six Day War all too convincingly. Troy Kennedy Martin's script, and John Flynn's direction, caught the tension of the time but tangled their Israeli and Arab students and terrorists in a knot of plot obscurities. Left to right: Nicol Williamson, Bruce Davison, Donald Pleasence. Daria Halprin, the Zabriskie Point girl, and Ian Hendry were also in the Ram Ben Efraim production, shot in Jerusalem and Tel Aviv.

The odorous mishmash of sex and murder produced and written by Gene Roddenberry from Francis Pollini's novel, **Pretty Maids All in a Row** was directed by Roger Vadim–imported from Paris for the occasion–as a jaunty black comedy. Rock Hudson played a high school instructor who seduced girl pupils in his office and killed them if they took it seriously; John David Carson was a young boy whose virginity Hudson persuaded teacher Angie Dickinson to remove. Telly Savalas, Roddy McDowall, Keenan Wynn, William Campbell and Joy Bang (sic) were also in the cast.

Familiar stuff was given an up-to-date sheen in **Villain** by four-letter dialogue and the limit in brutality. Here gangsters Richard Burton and Ian McShane, unaware that the police are trailing them, abduct Joss Ackland from hospital because he knows where their loot is hidden. Burton, good in the psychopathic title role, was supported also by Nigel Davenport, Donald Sinden, Fiona Lewis, T. P. McKenna, Cathleen Nesbitt, Colin Welland. An Elliott Kastner–Alan Ladd Jr–Jay Kantor production directed by Michael Tuchner; script, Dick Clement and Ian La Frenais from Al Lettieri's adaptation of James Barlow's The Burden of Proof.

Old friends on view via US television and reaching theatre screens overseas: Lew Ayres, 30 years after 'Kildare', and Tony Franciosa in **Earth II**, a space thriller directed by Tom Gries, written and produced by William Read Woodfield and Allan Balter, with Gary Lockwood (space-typed by 2001), Scott Hylands, Mariette Hartley, Hari Rhodes, Gary Merrill, Inga Swenson . . . From MGM's television Medical Center came Edward G. Robinson and Maurice Evans in **Operation Heartbeat**, a suture-snipper directed by Boris Sagal, written by A. C. Ward and produced by Frank Glicks-

man, with Richard Bradford, Kim Stanley, Kevin McCarthy, William Windom, James Daly, Shelley Fabares, James Shigeta, J. D. Cannon, William Marshall.

Also TV-generated, **Night of Dark Shadows**, a second spin-off from the 'Dark Shadows' shudder series, was shot entirely at millionaire Jay Gould's old mansion in Tarrytown, New York, by Dan Curtis, with (left to right) Grayson Hall, John Karlen and James Storm; David Selby, Lara Parker, Kate Jackson and Christopher Pennock. It was written by Grayson's husband, Sam Hall.

A fast and entertaining Western directed in Spain by Sam Wanamaker for producer Euan Lloyd, **Catlow** starred Yul Brynner and Richard Crenna as gunslingers on opposite sides of the law who joined forces when danger threatened—which it continually did. Written by Scot Finch and J. J. Griffith from Louis l'Amour's novel, it gave roles to Leonard Nimoy, Daliah Lavi, Jo Ann Pflug, Jeff Corey, David Ladd, Bessie Love. Good business.

An attraction that didn't attract: Robert Mitchum's first film after Ryan's Daughter, **Going Home**. Its study of a father-son relationship after 13 years' separation (father had been jailed for killing son's mother) failed to connect with audiences. Brenda Vaccaro as Dad's new woman and Jan-Michael Vincent

as the boy had the only other significant roles in Lawrence Marcus' script, produced and directed by Herbert B. Leonard.

Producers Irwin Winkler and Robert Chartoff plummeted from the tragic Believe in Me to the frantic **The Gang that Couldn't Shoot Straight**. Jimmy Breslin's book about the inept capers of Italian lowlife in New York was scripted by Waldo Palt and directed by James Goldstone. The cast, which sometimes outnumbered its audience, included (left to right) Leigh Taylor-Young, Carmine Caridi, James Sloyan, Jerry Orbach, Jo Van Fleet, Herve Villechaize, Sam Coppola; also Lionel Stander, Robert de Niro.

Leslie Caron had often been better cast than in **Chandler**, a commonplace shoot-and-chase drama produced by her husband, Michael S. Laughlin. Warren Oates played her private-eye lover in John Sacret Young's script from a Paul Magwood story, directed by Magwood, with Alex Dreier, Mitchell Ryan, Charles McGraw, Gloria Grahame, Royal Dano.

Most unexpected flop of 1971: **Wild Rovers**. Like the recent winner Butch Cassidy and The Sundance Kid, it was a big-scale Western about two bad, lovable cowboys getting in and out of trouble; it was produced (with Ken Wales), written and directed by habitual hit-maker Blake Edwards; and starred Ryan O'Neal, top man in the record-breaking Love Story (here defending co-star William Holden in a brawl, observed by bartender Bruno VeSota). But . . . No waiting, seats in all parts. Karl Malden, Rachel Roberts, Joe Don Baker, Lynn Carlin, Moses Gunn and Leora Dana were featured.

Most unexpected smash of 1971: **Shaft**, a crime drama with an almost all black (formerly Negro) cast headed by Richard Round-tree—here conking a honky (formerly White) intruder. Described as a 'cool, hip, black private eye', Shaft was in the middle of a blood-and-thunder melo bloodier and more thunderous than anything Chandler or Hammett private eyes ever saw, and the fans loved it. Director, Gordon Parks; producer, Joel Freeman; script, Ernest Tidyman and John D. F. Black, based on the former's book; cast, Moses Gunn (outstanding as a Harlem boss), Charles Cioffi, Christopher St. John, Gwenn Mitchell, Lawrence Pressman. Isaac Hayes' Oscar-winning theme tune topped the charts.

Corky offered Robert Blake and Charlotte Rampling in an unpleasant story about a stock-car racing roughneck. Few bookings and fewer plaudits for Bruce Geller's production, written by Eugene Price, directed by Leonard Horn, with Patrick O'Neal, Chris Connelly, Pamela Payton-Wright, Ben Johnson, Laurence Luckinbill.

There was nastiness, but some excitement and payboxactivity, in **Sitting Target**. Ian McShane and Oliver Reed (the latter here getting his unfaithful wife into his sights) were escaped convicts who left a trail of corpses behind them as they rushed to their own violent deaths. Jill St. John, Edward Woodward, Frank Finlay, Freddie Jones, Robert Beatty, Jill Townsend and Tony Beckley were also directed by Douglas Hickox in Alexander Jacobs' version of Laurence Henderson's novel. It was produced in England by Barry Kulick.

BARE AND BLACK
1972

Movies with black casts and movies with nude casts became surefire at American box-offices. The former, although savagely violent, were exported profitably. But other countries banned the second kind, which displayed every imaginable sexual activity in detail. Orthodox producers often found their releases being outgrossed by 'sexploitation' shockers like *Deep Throat* and *The Devil in Miss Jones*.

However, they and all the rest of the year's output were dwarfed by *The Godfather*. Paramount's Mafia bloodbath rapidly became the biggest moneymaker in the industry's history, just ahead of *Sound of Music*, which ranked just ahead of *GWTW*. The latter, 33 years old, was estimated to have retained the record for number of admissions. Other notable attractions were *Fiddler on the Roof*, *Deliverance*, *A Clockwork Orange*, *What's Up Doc?* *Godfather* also won the Oscar; Marlon Brando irked the Academy (like George C. Scott two years before) by refusing his award. Liza Minnelli and director Bob Fosse got Oscars for the superb *Cabaret*.

The Shaft grosses proved that black is beautiful, and MGM turned out four 1972 features in that suddenly profitable category. The first was **Cool Breeze**, yet another remake of *Asphalt Jungle*, with Judy Pace and Jim Watkins in the roles originated by Jean Hagen and Sterling Hayden; also cast were Thalmus Rasulala, Raymond St Jacques, Lincoln Kilpatrick, Sam Laws, Margaret Avery, Paula Kelly, Pamela Grier. Director Barry Pollack made only minor changes in his script of W. R. Burnett's crime classic for producer Gene Corman. Now how about a musical version?

Back to trendy brutality and mindless action with Shaft, Richard Roundtree again playing the Harlem hard guy in **Shaft's Big Score**. It didn't equal the original's box-office but turned a nice profit. For a climax, baddies chased our hero through the Brooklyn Navy Yard in a helicopter, machine-gun blazing. They missed: another sequel was on the schedule. Again written by Ernest Tidyman (who produced with Roger Lewis) and directed by Gordon Parks. Moses Gunn, Joseph Mascolo, Kathy Imrie, Wally Taylor, Julius Harris were in it.

Pamela Grier, who was becoming the Ava Gardner of black movies, starred in **Hit Man**, a quick black remake of Get Carter. Writer-director George Armitage shifted the Ted Lewis original to LA's underworld, which made Newcastle's look like Disneyland. Bernie Casey played the Michael Caine part, supported by Lisa Moore, Bhetty Waldron, Sam Laws and Don Diamond. Gene Corman produced.

Customers turned on by the Italian billings and 'Adults' rating of **Weekend Murders** may have expected bursting bodices and passions. What they got was an Agatha Christie-type family-gathering thriller(?) in an English mansion. Playboy Giacomo Rossi Stuart and black girl-friend Beryl Cunningham added a muted dolce vita note. Michele Lupo directed and Antonio Mazza produced the Fabio Pittorru–Massimo Felisatti screenplay, with Lance Percival and opera star Anna Moffo also cast.

Calvin Lockhart was the best black actor involved in the new trend; he looked capable of following Sidney Poitier up the ladder to real stardom, given the right opportunities. But in **Melinda** he was the usual storm centre of criminal violence. Story by Raymond Cistheri, script by Lonne Elder III, directed by Hugh Robertson, produced by Pervis Atkins. Also cast: Rosalind Cash, Vonetta McGee, Paul Stevens, Rockne Tarkington.

For vulgarity and violence, it would be hard to beat **Kansas City Bomber**, which for some reason was co-sponsored by the gorgeous Raquel Welch. This 'MGM presentation of a Levey–Gardner–Laven–Raquel Welch–Artists Entertainment Complex Production' made her appear about as attractive as a garbage truck. Its Thomas Rickman–Calvin Clements script loosely connected a series of professional roller-skating races in which men and women tripped and bashed each other around while fans screamed encouragement. In towns where such bouts are staged it did good business. Left to right: Raquel, Richard Lane, Patti 'Moo-Moo' Cavin, an actual pro skater. Also in the cast were Kevin McCarthy, Helen Kallianiotes, Norman Alden, Mary Kay Pass, Jeanne Cooper. Produced by Marty Elfand, directed for maximum ugh by Jerrold Freedman.

Big things were expected of **Travels With my Aunt**, long scheduled for Katharine Hepburn, then switched to Maggie Smith (here discussing her next scene with George Cukor, one of Hollywood's foremost directors for over 40 years, most of them with MGM). But this was not to be the company's badly needed smash hit. Maggie was allowed, or directed, to overact as Graham Greene's outrageous heroine, so that both she and the film alternated between the entertaining and the tiresome. Alec McCowen, as the prim nephew she transformed, shone in a cast that included Robert Stephens, Lou Gossett, Cindy Williams, Jose Luis Lopez Vasquez and Valerie White. The Jay Allen–Hugh Wheeler screenplay was produced by Robert Fryer and James Cresson. Anthony Powell's costumes won an Oscar.

The platonic friendship of young woman and old man was one of the nice things about **One is a Lonely Number**, a touching study of a deserted wife, written by David Seltzer from a New Yorker story by Rebecca Morris and directed by Mel Stuart. Here divorcée Trish Van Devere and widower Melvyn Douglas are overcome by their private griefs while watching a performance of King Lear. A sharp, brassy performance by ex-ingénue Janet Leigh stood out in a cast that included Monte Markham, Jane Elliot, Jonathan Lippe and Paul Jenkins. Stan Margulies produced for executive David Wolper. Lonely numbers in the cinemas.

The reappearance of Rita Hayworth lent a glimmer of interest to **The Wrath of God** as Robert Mitchum, armed with crucifix and machine-gun, swashbuckled through preposterous Central American exploits. Ralph Nelson directed his script, from James Graham's story, produced by Peter Katz and William Gilmore Jr to no acclaim. Also cast: Frank Langella, Victor Buono, Ken Hutchison, John Colicos.

Another old (well, older) face: Victor Mature, who had retired from the screen in 1960, returned in **Every Little Crook and Nanny**. Neither he nor the refreshing Lynn Redgrave could rescue a hopelessly confused script Mixmastered from Evan Hunter's novel by Cy Howard, Jonathan Axelrod and Robert Klane. Howard also directed Leonard Ackerman's production, featuring Paul Sand, Maggie Blye, Dom DeLuise and John Astin. No business.

Peter Lawford (right, with Katharine Ross and James Garner) was one of the players in **They Only Kill Their Masters** who brought echoes of MGM's palmy days. June Allyson, so often

his co-star, was in it, as were Tom Ewell, Edmond O'Brien and Andy Hardy's steady date, Ann Rutherford. Hal Holbrook, Harry Guardino, Christopher Connelly and Arthur O'Connell had other leads in Lane Slate's screenplay, directed by James Goldstone, produced by William Belasco. This awkwardly titled whodunit held audience interest but had little paybox appeal.

Ken Russell returned from his Boy Friend holiday to his true work: the dramatization of the artistic temperament. **Savage Messiah** depicted the mercurial relationship between French sculptor Henri Gaudier-Brzeska and the Polish woman 20 years his senior who gave him her name. It was vintage Russell: vital, unconventional, and romantic despite his assuming deafness in cast and audience – dialogue was shouted rather than spoken. Its box-office results were reported in whispers. In the cast: Scott Antony and Dorothy Tutin (here) splendid in the leads; Helen Mirren, spectacularly nude; Lindsay Kemp, John Justin and Michael Gough. Written by Christopher Logue from the sculptor's biography by H. S. Ede.

The producer-director team of **Elvis on Tour**, Pierre Adidge and Robert Abel, announced it as 'A close-up of the birth and life of an American phenomenon', and recalled that when the Beatles met Presley one of them told him, 'Before you, there was nothing'. So it was a relief to see in this documentary feature that Elvis had not yet disappeared in a nimbus of sainthood, but was still in there rockin' and rollin' and sockin' it to the million-dollar crowds in a series of one-night stands. An entertaining and profitable release.

Nearest thing to a major hit in 1972 was ▷ **Skyjacked**; strictly conventional fiction about an airliner, eastbound from Los Angeles, with a passenger (James Brolin, second from left) who threatened to blow it up unless its crew (left to right: James Swofford, Charlton Heston,

Yvette Mimieux, Mike Henry) took him to Moscow. The mini-dramas of other passengers (Walter Pidgeon, still handsomely authoritative at 75; Jeanne Crain, Claude Akins, Leslie Uggams, Roosevelt Grier, Mariette Hartley, etc.) filled in between crises in David Harper's main story, scripted by Stanley Greenberg. Produced by Walter Seltzer and directed by John Guillermin for crowd-rousing excitement, it had a good deal of MGM's old confident professionalism. Its paybox power was partly due also to Heston, one of the few veteran stars maintaining their magnetism into the 1970s.

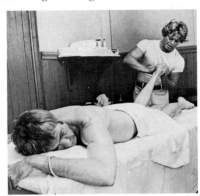

Sinister masseurs cropped up in two thrillers, much the better of which was **The Carey Treatment**. James Coburn, a doctor investigating a fatal abortion case, discovered that rubber Michael Blodgett was really a drug-pushing killer in the William Belasco production. Jeffery Hudson's brilliant mystery novel was scripted by James Bonner and directed by Blake Edwards, with Jennifer O'Neill, Pat Hingle, Dan O'Herlihy, Elizabeth Allen, Alex Dreier, James Hong, Regis Toomey – and Skye Aubrey, the daughter of MGM chief James T. Aubrey Jr (and Phyllis Thaxter); her vivid talent obviated nepotism . . . In **The Black Belly**

of the Tarantula Barbara Bouchet got the table treatment from Ezio Marano before being murdered. The violent Italian whodunit was directed by Paolo Cavara; Marcello Danon produced his own story, scripted by Lucille Laks.

Nicholas Roeg exited after five days of directing **Nightmare Honeymoon** and was replaced by Elliot Silverstein. Here Rebecca Dianna Smith and Dack Rambo, heiress and Vietnam veteran, are distracted from their just-married activities by seeing a murder being done. The bride was raped by the killers in the course of S. Lee Pogostin's distressing screenplay, from a novel by Lawrence Block. John Beck, Pat Hingle, Jeanette Nolan and Roy Jenson were others in Hugh Benson's production.

No wonder that scientists Stuart Whitman and Janet Leigh and daughter Melanie Fullerton look upset in **Night of the Lepus**; a rabbit they injected with something or other has escaped,

and now all Arizona is menaced by rabbits the size of horses, and carnivorous to boot. The terror Alfred Hitchcock could evoke with normal-sized birds William Caxton couldn't with giant bunnies. A. C. Lyles' production of the Don Holliday–Gene Kearney screenplay from Russell Braddon's novel cast Rory Calhoun, De Forrest Kelley, Paul Fix.

Private Parts was the unequivocal title of a Gene Corman production that began with teen-age heroine Ayn Ruymen spying on a normal sex act, and continued with nothing else normal in a seedy Los Angeles hotel, where kinky photographer John Ventantonio subjected her to the needle and other peculiar experiences. In the USA MGM used an alias, Premier Productions, to present it; in Britain the censor chopped five minutes out before giving it an 'X'. Lucille Benson and Laurie Main were in the fetid Philip Kearney-Les Rendelstein screenplay, directed by Paul Bartel.

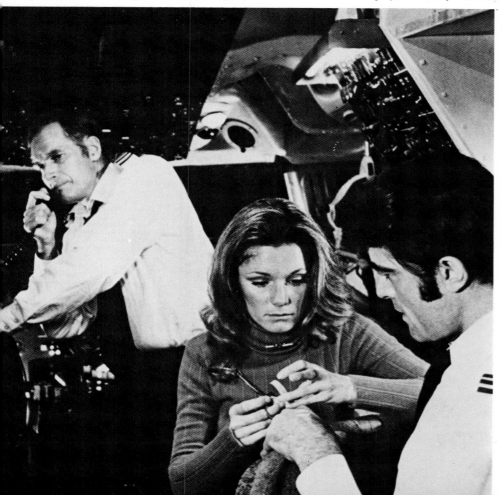

Andrew Stone, who used to keep crowds tenterhooked on suspense thrillers, went soft with a rich Viennese pastry, **The Great Waltz**. People who had been avoiding permissive movies sank with relief into its romance, lilting melodies and après garde technique. It dealt with Johann Strauss II and his music, like Duvivier's 1938 film of the same name, but seemed comparatively old-fashioned, even with Metrocolor and Panavision. Left to right: Horst Buchholz as Strauss, singer Mary Costa as his wife and Rossano Brazzi as her former lover. Also cast: Nigel Patrick, Yvonne Mitchell, James Faulkner as other Strausses.

Lolly Madonna XXX/The Lolly-Madonna War could arouse little public interest in a squalid rural feud imagined by Sue Grafton, who wrote the script with producer Rodney Carr-Smith from her novel. Here Robert Ryan tells Rod Steiger and Katherine Squire that two of their sons have raped his daughter, Joan Goodfellow. Others in Richard Sarafian's cast: Scott Wilson, Jeff Bridges, Ed Lauter.

MGM hoped, again in vain, that Visconti's **Ludwig** would halt its procession of flops and near-misses. At great length and with prodigal opulence the movie outlined the drama of the 19th-century Bavarian king from his succession, through his sponsoring Wagner's operas, his thwarting the marriage hopes of Austria's empress (Romy Schneider) and his two obsessions—wooing handsome young men and building fantastic castles—to the madness that increased until his mysterious death. Left to right: Helmut Berger as Ludwig, Sylvana Mangano as Wagner's Cosima and Trevor Howard as the composer. Visconti wrote the script with Enrico Medioli and used Ludwig's real castles, plus Cinecitta studio sets, for Ugo Santalucia's visually magnificent production. Gert Frobe, Helmut Grien, John Moulder-Brown, Umberto Orsini were in a huge cast.

RUNNING DOWN
1973

MGM issued its last financial statement as a major distributor, showing a net income of $9,267,000 (1972's was $10,737,000). But those figures included sales of studio properties, overseas theatres and music companies, without which the 1973 net would have been $809,000, and 1972's $7,849,000. That fast slide in operating profits was one reason why MGM liquidated its world-wide distributing organization, overseas theatres and US music publishers in October.

20th Century-Fox's *The Poseidon Adventure* was the year's box-office champ. *Last Tango in Paris* made a mint by bridging art and sexploitation. The jazzy *Jesus Christ Superstar*, Sam Peckinpah's violent *The Getaway*, Ryan O'Neal and daughter in *Paper Moon*, Barbra Streisand and Robert Redford in *The Way We Were* and Roger Moore as the new James Bond in *Live and Let Die* were big.

John Wayne was the most popular star of the decade, followed in order by Doris Day, Cary Grant, Rock Hudson, Elizabeth Taylor, Jack Lemmon, Julie Andrews, Paul Newman, Sean Connery, Elvis Presley, Sidney Poitier and Lee Marvin.

Slither *was the first of the few movies completed at MGM in 1973. Trailer-camp denizens in this scene are James Caan, Louise Lasser and Sally Kellerman. Surprise twists in W. D. Richter's script and a sense of fun in Howard Zieff's direction made this thriller stand out, but not as a ticket-seller. Peter Boyle and Allen Garfield were in it; Jack Sher produced.*

No fun in **Wicked, Wicked** *and not much box-office either. David Bailey played the house dick and Randolph Roberts the psycho handyman in a hotel with special room service for blondes: they got murdered. Writer-director-producer Richard L. Bare spared the audience no grisly details. Also cast: Tiffany Bolling, Scott Brady, Edd Byrnes, Diane McBain, Madeleine Sherwood, Arthur O'Connell. The William T. Orr production had novelties in the use of split-screen action and* Phantom of the Opera *organ music written for the 1925 silent thriller.*

Westworld *was the top moneymaker for MGM* ▽ *in the 1973 output—although well down in the all-companies hit list. It was something really new in Westerns. Here, tourist Richard Benjamin (watched by another, James Brolin) shoots and kills Yul Brynner, or so he thinks. But Yul is just a robot worked by computers, like all the natives of this fake Western holiday resort. Writer-director Michael Crichton couldn't maintain the audience's suspension of disbelief when the robots ran wildly out of control. Good try, though. Produced by Paul Lazarus III. Also cast: Norman Bartold, Alan Oppenheimer, Victoria Shaw and Dick Van Patten.*

Disappointing results from the in-fashion Sam Peckinpah's **Pat Garrett and Billy the Kid**, *in which the director's flair for blending violence and a poetic vision of the West was only fitfully apparent. Pat and Billy got more paybox action when they were Wallace Beery and Johnny Mack Brown in 1930, or Brian Donlevy and Robert Taylor in 1941. Rudolph Wurlitzer's*

script about the former outlaw pals, now hunter and hunted, was hard to follow: James T. Aubrey was said to have ordered extensive cuts, resulting in fragmented roles for all but James Coburn as Pat and Kris Kristofferson as Billy (seen here at the end) and Bob Dylan, whose narrative songs were largely unintelligible. Also cast: Richard Jaeckel, Katy Jurado, Jason Robards Jr, Chill Wills, Jack Elam, Slim Pickens, John Beck, R. G. Armstrong, Paul Fix. Producer, Gordon Carroll.

Soylent Green *was Edward G. Robinson's last* ▽ *movie; he died in 1973, 50 years after his film debut and 80 after his birth. This original thriller pictured the horrendous future of a New York in which pollution and over-population had made everything scarce except people. Harry Harrison's story, scripted by Stanley Greenberg, hinged on the discovery by hero Charlton Heston (here cornering Chuck Connors) that the staple food for the masses, processed by a monopoly, was made from human corpses. Strong action and mob scenes; lively box-office response. Also cast: Leigh Taylor-Young, Joseph Cotten, Brock Peters, Paula Kelly, Mike Henry, Roy Jenson, Whit Bissell, Celia Lovsky. Director, Richard Fleischer; production, Walter Seltzer, Russell Thacher.*

The Man Who Loved Cat Dancing *had lots going for it: it was a love story combined with Western action, from a current best-seller (by Marilyn Durham), and starred Burt Reynolds and Sarah Miles, who received acres of news space when location filming was*

Trader Horn *was a remake of the 1930 epic in name and locale only. Every possible (and impossible) African jungle cliché was crammed into the tale as Rod Taylor quelled villainous natives, various beasts and detachments of the British and German armies in the unintentionally funny William Norton–Edward Harper screenplay. It was directed by Reza Badiyi after a fashion, produced by Lewis Rachmil. Also cast: Anne Heywood, Jean Sorel, Don Knight.*

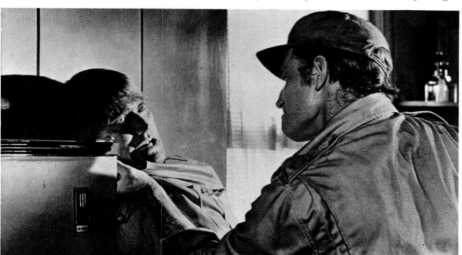

Black power was declining at the box-office, even for the third Shaft punch-up, Shaft in Africa, *and the series continued on television. Richard Roundtree (here with most of the well-developed Neda Arneric) was cast with Frank Finlay, Vonetta McGee and Marne Maitland; directed by John Guillermin; produced by Roger Lewis; written by Stirling Silliphant . . . Also aboard ship in momentary non-violence were Jim Brown and Judy Pace in* The Slams *(meaning prison; also the reviews it got) a jail-break caper directed by Jonathan Kaplan; produced by Gene Corman; written by Richard Adams. Also cast: Roland Harris, Paul E. Harris and Frank de Kova.*

interrupted by the strange death of her male secretary. But the MGM paybox jinx was still on. Richard Sarafin directed and Martin Poll produced with Eleanor Perry, who wrote the script. Left to right: Miss Miles, Bo Hopkins, Reynolds; also cast were George Hamilton, Jack Warden, Lee J. Cobb, Robert Donner, Larry Littlebird, Jay Silverheels.

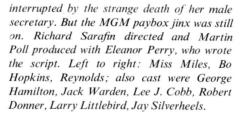

The exploits of the gun-totin' pair featured in Deaf Smith and Johnny Ears *were less out of the ordinary than their movie's title. The one novelty in its Texas turmoil, Italian style, was a deaf-mute hero (Anthony Quinn) whose affliction didn't prevent him and his younger pal (Franco Nero) from wiping out an entire garrison of baddies. Oscar Saul and Harry Essex, heading a posse of Italian writers, provided a script in which action fortunately precluded much dubbed dialogue. Director, Paolo Cavara; producers, Joseph Janni and Luciano Perugia; heroine, Pamela Tiffin.*

Robert Ryan co-starred in The Outfit, *his 80th and next-to-last movie: he died in 1973, aged 64. Here Robert Duvall forces information from Felice Orlandi, watched by Karen Black in this tough thriller about one man's war on a crime organization to avenge his brother's murder. Also in Carter DeHaven's production, written (from Richard Stark's novel) and directed by John Flynn: Joe Don Baker, Sheree North, Timothy Carey, Richard Jaeckel, Jane Greer, Marie Windsor, Elisha Cook Jr, Roy Roberts, Emile Meyer, Roy Jenson, singer Anita O'Day, boxer Archie Moore, tennist Tony Trabert.*

GOLDEN ENTERTAINMENT
1974

On January 4 the MGM Grand Hotel, Las Vegas, completed its first month of operation and reported capacity bookings. The world's largest resort hotel, with 2,084 rooms, it cost $120m. (estimated cost when construction started in April 1972 was $90m.) and had advance reservations into 1982.

Universal won its first best picture Academy Award since 1930's *All Quiet On The Western Front* with *The Sting*, which took seven Oscars altogether, including one to director George Roy Hill. Jack Lemmon in *Save the Tiger* was elected best actor and Glenda Jackson in *A Touch of Class* best actress. MGM won nothing, had few films on current release via its new distributors, and fewer imminent. But the 50th anniversary of the studio's opening on April 26th, 1924, was celebrated in the light of new President Frank E. Rosenfelt's statement: 'One of our principal objectives will be to provide a climate at MGM which will attract creative film-makers... Contrary to recent public speculation, the roar of Leo the Lion will not be reduced to a weak meow.'

The Super Cops *looked like the wildest fiction; actually it told the true story of two New York crime-crushers who racked up a record total of arrests and convictions in the tough, drug-ridden ghetto of Bedford-Stuyvesant. Nicknamed 'Batman and Robin' by the press, they are Dave Greenberg and Bob Hatz, seen here in the background in minor roles, with David Selby as Hantz and Ron Leibman as Greenberg in the foreground. The script by Lorenzo Semple Jr (from L. H. Whittemore's book) and direction by Gordon Parks gave the William Belasco production cartoon-like speed and violence. Sheila Frazier, Pat Hingle, Dan Frazer and Joseph Sirola were featured.*

During 1974 Michelangelo Antonioni made his third film for MGM, produced by Carlo Ponti for 1975 release. **The Passenger** *had his usual fascinating ambiguities draped around a sturdy framework constructed by 25-year-old English writer Mark Peploe. Jack Nicholson, at the top of his profession after a succession of hits from* Easy Rider *to* Chinatown, *starred as a disenchanted television journalist taking*

on the identity of a look-alike dead man –and his surprising past. Here he encounters Maria Schneider (the Last Tango in Paris *girl), playing a nameless hippie who stayed to share his new life. Ian Hendry and Jennie Runacre had other leads in the drama, filmed in Spain, Algeria, Germany and England.*

Kazablan *was made in Tel Aviv with Israeli star Yehoram Gaon (centre) leading an all-singing, all-dancing. all-chutzpah street gang. High spirits, low grosses. Menahem Golan produced, directed and (with Haim Hefer) scripted the jolly Jewish musical.*

A contract for Dean Martin to headline at the MGM Grand Hotel included a movie commitment, so he made **Mr Ricco**. *They loved him in Las Vegas, but not in this minor murder melo, directed by Paul Bogart, scripted by Robert Hoban, produced by former MGM vice-president Douglas Netter. Thalmus Rasulala shared this brawl with him and featured billing with Cindy Williams, Geraldine Brooks, Eugene Roche, Philip Thomas, Denise Nicholas.*

That's Entertainment *was a rousing tribute to the first 50 MGM years and a heartening pace-setter for the second. It was completed in time for a May 1974 première and the most enthusiastic reception for any of the company's movies in years. Musical highlights from MGM's vast archives were dovetailed into a 132-minute feature written, directed and produced by Jack Haley Jr under the aegis of the studio's production chief, Daniel Melnick. Linked by newly filmed introductions and voice-over comments by Fred Astaire (right, in his astonishing walls-and-ceiling dance in* Royal Wedding*), Bing Crosby, Gene Kelly, Peter Lawford, Liza Minnelli, Donald O'Connor, Debbie Reynolds, Mickey Rooney, Frank Sinatra, James Stewart and Elizabeth Taylor, the excerpts made a dazzling show. Above, Jean Harlow in* Reckless. *Below, Deanna Durbin and Judy Garland in their film debut, the short* Every Sunday. *'While many may ponder the future of Metro-Goldwyn-Mayer', said* Variety *in its rave review, 'nobody can deny that it has one hell of a past!'*

RECORDS GO BOOM
1975

Inflation? Unemployment? International crises? 'Forget 'em and go to the movies' was one public reaction, especially in the USA and Canada, where cinema income reached $2 billion, the all-time high. More encouraging yet, the number of tickets sold was the highest for 12 years. Universal's *Jaws* chewed a big chunk of that total, becoming the greatest money-maker ever released (of course, thanks partly to ever-rising seat prices), with *The Towering Inferno, Earthquake, Young Frankenstein, The Godfather Part 2, Shampoo*, the British *Murder on the Orient Express* and *Tommy* among the runners-up in 1975 prosperity.

MGM joined the record-breaking spree: net profits ($31,862,000) were the best in the company's history. Over a third of the operating income came from feature films, despite the scarcity of new product—striking proof that the scrapping of distribution had worked. The remainder came from the MGM Grand, Las Vegas, now believed to be the most profitable hotel in the world.

Completed as the year ended, **That's Entertainment, Too!** *was planned by studio generalissimo Daniel Melnick as a sequel in spirit to the previous year's winner, and more than that in substance. Along with musicals from MGM's bulging storehouse of golden oldies, some of its most renowned 'straight' successes were also represented (that still of Garbo and Taylor in* Camille *at the top of this set is indicative), and a good deal of new material was filmed under the direction of Gene Kelly, here reunited with Fred Astaire. In short—nostalgia, plus. Saul Chaplin, long a contributor to Leo's musicals (he won Oscars for* An American in Paris *and* 7 Brides for 7 Brothers*) co-produced with Melnick.*

Inexplicably, movies about movies seldom attract many moviegoers. **Hearts of the West**, *with Jeff Bridges (Academy-nominated for his work in* The Last Picture Show*) as a B-picture cowboy softening crusty production manager Blythe Danner, was praised for its evocation of 1930s Hollywood but met box-office apathy. Andy Griffith, Donald Pleasence and Alan Arkin were others in Rob Thompson's warm comedy, directed by Howard Zieff and produced by Tony Bill, the young actor who made it big as a producer with* The Sting.

Sean Connery in **The Wind and the Lion** *had one of his best parts since turning in his 007 badge. As the last of the Barbary Pirates, he played a 1904 forerunner of today's terrorists kidnapping an American woman (Candice Bergen) in Morocco and making huge ransom demands on President Theodore Roosevelt (Brian Keith). John Milius directed his screenplay in Spain, with emphasis on spectacular action; Herb Jaffe produced; John Huston co-starred. MGM and Columbia collaborated in its making (a new Hollywood idea that once*

would have given L.B. Mayer and Harry Cohn coronaries) and shared its income. This split-the-risk procedure on an expensive project was also followed on the 20th Century-Fox/Warner Bros. Towering Inferno.

△ *A geriatric joy,* **The Sunshine Boys** *scored a resounding hit for the company and for Walter Matthau (right) and George Burns (returning to the screen at, incredibly, 79). Their character studies of ex-vaudeville partners who loved to hate each other were comedy acting of the richest quality, relished by critics and crowds alike. Director Herbert Ross smartly paced the laugh-peppered dialogue of Neil Simon, who scripted from his Broadway success, and producer Ray Stark gave it showbiz authenticity via New York location filming.*

The names on this page have not been included in the index.

METRO'S GREAT MUSICALS

Many of the movies illustrated here were represented in *That's Entertainment*. After its trailblazing 1929 *Broadway Melody*, the company bumped along with its competitors as the public fell in and out of love with this genre during the Thirties. But in the Forties and Fifties other studios were consistently surpassed by the musical flair, inventiveness and expertise of MGM. Under producers such as Jack Cummings, Joe Pasternak and (most importantly) Arthur Freed, it assembled a galaxy of talents – performers, directors, song-writers, choreographers, arrangers, orchestraters, instrumentalists – that has never been equalled in the history of popular music.

The golden era was ushered in by **The Wizard of Oz** *(right). It made Judy Garland a major star.*

Judy presented a future star, daughter Liza Minnelli, in the final scene of **In the Good Old Summertime** *with Van Johnson.*

Mickey Rooney conga-ed with Judy in one of their biggest hits, **Strike Up The Band.**

Many rate **Meet Me In St Louis** *as the best Garland of all. Left to right: Leon Ames, Judy, Harry Davenport, Lucille Bremer, Joan Carroll, Henry Daniels Jr., Mary Astor.*

△ *A 12-minute highlight of* **The Band Wagon** *was a private-eye ballet, 'The Girl Hunt', danced by Fred Astaire and Cyd Charisse.*

Fred and Ginger Rogers reprised their old Gershwin hit, 'They Can't Take That Away from Me', in **The Barkleys of Broadway**.

Another **Barkleys of Broadway** *number: Fred in the camera-tricky 'Shoes with Wings On'.*

Astaire and Eleanor Powell in their breathtaking **Broadway Melody of 1940** *tap routine.*

The loveliest dancer he paired with, Cyd Charisse, was with Astaire in Cole Porter's **Silk Stockings**, *the musical* Ninotchka.

Not one to bruise female egos when asked to name his best partner, Fred picks Gene Kelly. They were together only in **Ziegfeld Follies**.

Vera-Ellen teamed with Astaire in the Kalmar & Ruby biopic, **Three Little Words**. ▷

Six of the fastest legs in show business putting over 'Be a Clown' in **The Pirate**: Gene Kelly and the Nicholas Brothers, above. Right: Gene's genius was again enhanced by a Cole Porter score in **Les Girls**, with Mitzi Gaynor, Kay Kendall and Taina Elg.

But the most popular success in the hit-studded Kelly career was **Singin' in the Rain**, co-starring Debbie Reynolds and Donald O'Connor (below). Its dramatic ballet blending 'Broadway Melody' and 'Broadway Rhythm' paired Cyd Charisse with Gene (above); while he had another Nacio Herb Brown-Arthur Freed oldie all to himself: the

title number, sung and danced with a wonderful Astaire-like ease (below). O'Connor was a

show-stopper with 'Make 'em Laugh' (re-markably close in tune and lyric to 'Be a Clown').

Harve Presnell and Debbie Reynolds romped through **The Unsinkable Molly Brown**.

Love Me or Leave Me gave Doris Day *(centre) more solos than any other film: 13.*

⊲ *Best of the many hits MGM derived from stage musicals:* **Kiss Me Kate**, *with Howard Keel and Kathryn Grayson.*

The whoopee girl of 1929, Joan Crawford, sings 'Got a Feelin' for You' in **The Hollywood Revue** *(above).*

Jane Powell, who got the full MGM star-making treatment, singing 'It's a Most Un-usual Day' in **A Date with Judy**.

Not really singers or dancers, June Allyson and Peter Lawford still made **Good News** *swing.*

Viva Las Vegas, *says Elvis Presley, surrounded by showgirls and Cesare Danova.*

Ann Miller steers those gorgeous legs around a surrealist band in **Small Town Girl**.

Esther Williams and Howard Keel in **Pagan Love Song**.

⊲ **Deep in My Heart** *had ballerina Tamara Toumanova as one of its stars.*

Not the least entertaining of the many film usages of Irving Berlin's 'Puttin' On the Ritz' was in **Idiot's Delight**, *by Gable of-all-people.*

A dazzling dance team on screen – Marge and Gower Champion in **Lovely to Look At** *(above) and* **Everything I Have is Yours** *(below).*

377

The **Band Wagon** featured Fred Astaire and Cyd Charisse exquisitely 'Dancing in the Dark'.

Mario Lanza with Kathryn Grayson in **The Toast of New Orleans** (above) and Doretta Morrow in **Because You're Mine** (right).

Collector's item: Sinatra and Crosby singing 'Well, Did You Evah!' in **High Society**.

Two unforgettably lavish eye-bogglers, made 15 years apart: 'A Pretty Girl is Like a Melody' in **The Great Ziegfeld** *(above); Leslie Caron and Gene Kelly in the* **American in Paris** *ballet (right).*

▽ *The song and dance talents of Frank Sinatra and Gene Kelly blended so happily in* **Anchors Aweigh** *that they were teamed twice more.*

Cyd Charisse and Dee Turnell dance to 'On Your Toes' in **Words and Music**.

Total enchantment: **Gigi**, with Louis Jourdan, Leslie Caron and Maurice Chevalier singing 'Thank Heaven for little Girls'. Below, Howard

Kelly and Sinatra in **Take Me Out to the Ball**

The phenomenal barn-raising number in **Seven Brides for Seven Brothers**, above. Below, Nelson Eddy and Jeanette MacDonald in the

Keel and Dolores Gray in the melodious **Kismet**. Below, Mickey Rooney, aged 10, takes a bow in **Broadway to Hollywood**.

Game. Two remakes: Above, Petula Clark sings 'London is London' in **Goodbye, Mr Chips**. Below, **Show Boat** sails that ol' man river.

second (1935) **Rose Marie**. In **Luxury Liner**, below, Jane Powell sings 'Spring Came Back to Vienna' to Shirley Johns.

Inventing excuses for Esther Williams to get into water, and things for her to do when she got there, taxed MGM brains for a dozen years. Spectacular numbers resulted, as in **Neptune's Daughter** *(here),* **Million Dollar**

Mermaid *(below) and* **Dangerous When Wet** *(right). This last borrowed an idea from* **Anchors Aweigh** *(lower right) in which Gene Kelly danced with Jerry the mouse; for Esther, the cartoon studio also supplied Tom*

the cat and other co-swimmers.

Van Johnson and Esther made a surefire box-office team for the 4th time in **Easy to Love**.

Busby Berkeley staged the 'Totem Tomtom' number for the third version of **Rose Marie**.

The stars of **Three Little Words** *had some of their spotlight stolen by young newcomers Debbie Reynolds and Carleton Carpenter.*

'Anything You Can Do I Can Do Better', sing Betty Hutton and Howard Keel in **Annie Get Your Gun**, *a stage-to-screen smash.*

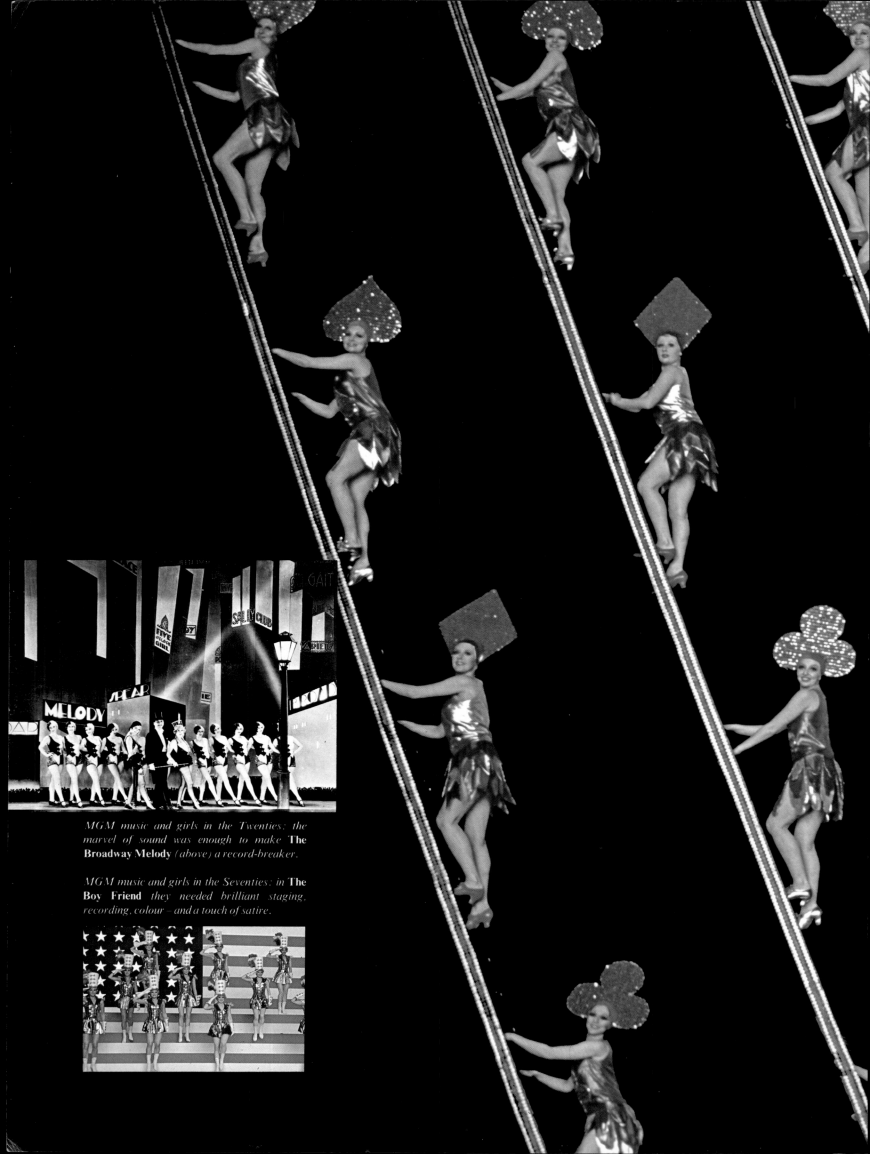

MGM music and girls in the Twenties: the marvel of sound was enough to make **The Broadway Melody** (above) a record-breaker.

MGM music and girls in the Seventies: in **The Boy Friend** they needed brilliant staging, recording, colour – and a touch of satire.

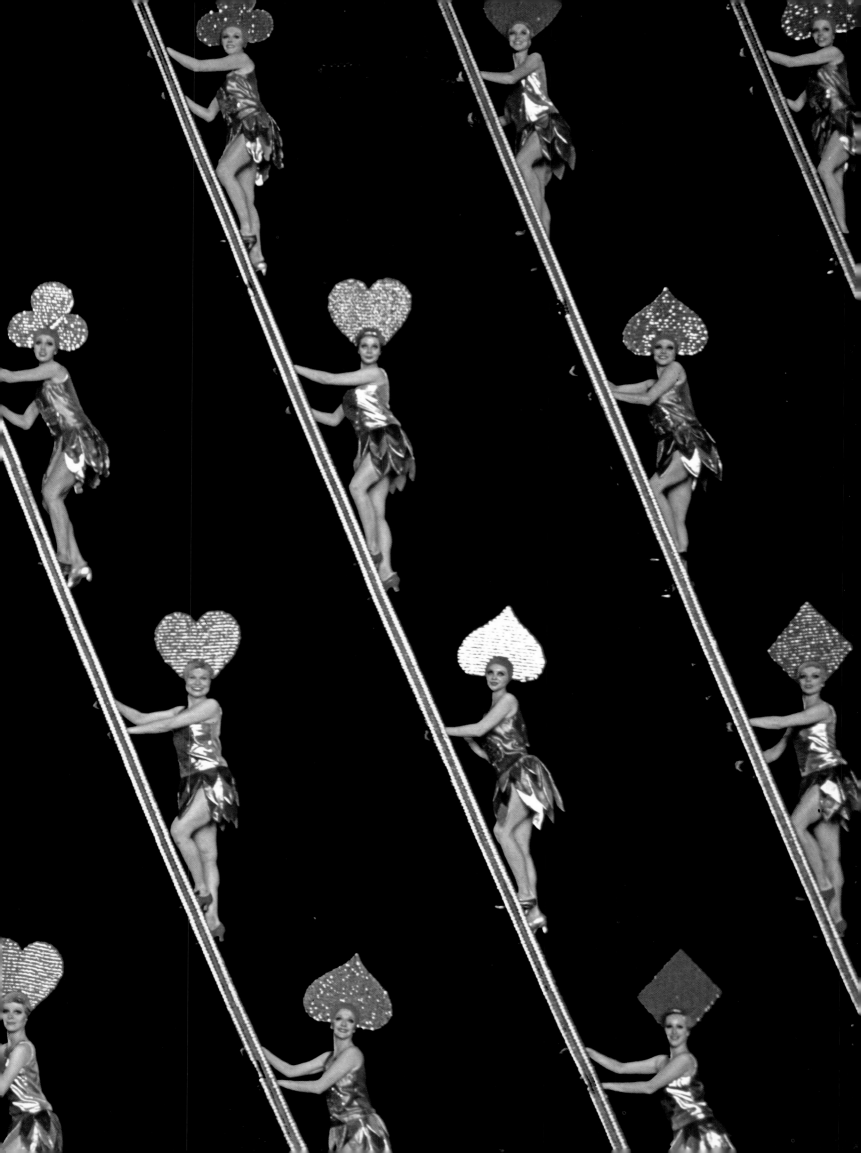

Simultaneously celebrating the première of **That's Entertainment** and the 50th anniversary of MGM were some of the players starred or featured by the company during its first half-century. From left, back row: Howard Keel, June Allyson, Adele Astaire, Fred Astaire, George Burns, Marge Champion, Cyd Charisse, Jackie Cooper, Dan Dailey, Vic Damone, Tom Drake, Buddy Ebsen, Nanette Fabray, Glenn Ford, Eva and Zsa Zsa Gabor, Jack Haley, Ava Gardner, Charlton Heston, George Hamilton. Middle Row: Gene Kelly, Phyllis Kirk, Janet Leigh, Myrna Loy, Marjorie Main, Tony Martin, Dennis Morgan, the Nicholas Brothers, Merle Oberon, Margaret O'Brien, Virginia O'Brien, Donald O'Connor, Donna Reed, Debbie Reynolds, Ginger Rogers, Ann Rutherford, Alexis Smith. Front row: Craig Stevens, Gloria Swanson, James Stewart, Johnny Weissmuller, Russ Tamblyn, Audrey Totter, Elizabeth Taylor, Keenan Wynn, Shirley MacLaine, Roddy McDowall with a descendant of Lassie, and Jimmy Durante. Which three of these people never appeared in an MGM picture? You, dear reader, having absorbed and retained every word of this book, need not be told. Others will be able to work out the answer with the aid of The Index.

INDEX

A Nous la Liberté 82
Aaker, Lee 252, 258
'*Aba Daba Honeymoon*' 234
Abbott, Bud 166, 177, 185, 197, 223, 240
Abbott, George 51
Abbott, John 215, 228, 249, 252, 284
Abbott, Philip 281, 306
Abel, Robert 360, 364
Abel, Walter 123, 198, 278, 287
Abie's Irish Rose 43
Above and Beyond 251
Above Suspicion 187
Absolute Quiet 122
Academy Awards 8, 9, 49, 54, 66, 67, 69, 74, 75, 76, 77, 82, 90, 95, 100, 103, 105, 109, 121, 127, 128, 132, 138, 142, 143, 146, 149, 152, 156, 166, 169, 171, 176, 192, 194, 204, 206, 210, 218, 225, 232, 234, 240, 247, 249, 252, 254, 262, 268, 271, 273, 274, 277, 278, 280, 284, 290, 296, 298, 300, 304, 306, 311, 316, 322, 325, 329, 334, 336, 337, 340, 342, 351, 352, 358, 362, 368
Academy of Motion Picture Arts and Sciences 21, 44, 362
Accidents Wanted 94
Acker, Sharon 339
Ackerman, Leonard 364
Ackland, Joss 360
Across the Wide Missouri 243
Across to Singapore 51
Act of Violence 219
Action of the Tiger 281
Actress, The 47
Actress, The 257
Ada 302
Ada Dallas 302
Adair, Jean 213
Adam and Evil 42
Adam, Noelle 303
Adam, Ronald 302, 312
Adams, Edie 327
Adams, Gerald Drayson 294, 320, 327
Adams, Neile 280
Adams, Nick 309, 313, 321
Adam's Rib 230
Adams, Richard 367
Adams, Samuel Hopkins 127, 204
Adamson, Harold 98
Addams, Dawn 243, 247, 250, 252, 257, 312
Ade, George 41
Adidge, Pierre 360, 364
Adler, Allen 276
Adler, Felix 120, 143
Adler, Larry 192, 215
Adler, Lou 352
Adler, Stella 171
Adoree, Renee 8, 10, 13, 18, 21, 23, 24, 31, 32, 35, 39, 43, 44, 47, 51, 56, 61, 66, 72
Adorf, Mario 345
Adrian 57, 115, 141, 143, 147
Adrian, Iris 120, 123
Adrian, Max 358
Adrienne Lecouvreur 51
Advance to the Rear 319
Adventure 201, 214
Adventurer, The 51
Adventures of Huckleberry Finn, The 146, 296
Adventures of Tartu 186
Affairs of Dobie Gillis, The 257
Affairs of Martha, The 183
African Queen, The 240
After All 86
After Midnight 36
After Office Hours 116
'*After the Ball*' 297
After the Funeral 313
After the Thin Man 123
Agar, John 313
Age of Indiscretion 116
Agnew, Robert 21, 24, 64
'*Ah, Sweet Mystery of Life*' 110
Ah, Wilderness 119, 120, 123, 136, 139, 218
Aherne, Brian 105, 116, 142, 169, 274
Aherne, Patrick 252
Ahn, Philip 174, 232, 250, 292, 338
Aimee, Anouk 287, 350
Ainley, Richard 182, 183, 187, 191
Ainslea, Marion 43, 57
Air Raid Wardens 186
Airport 352
Akins, Claude 364
Akins, Zoe 24, 107, 127, 141, 214
Alberg, Mildred Freed 345
Alberghetti, Ann Maria 278
Alberni, Luis 131, 168, 171
Albert, Eddie 273, 277, 329
Albert, Marvin 286
Albertson, Frank 85, 109, 119, 123, 135, 140, 144, 163, 210
Albertson, Jack 320, 344
Albertson, Mabel 271, 273, 292, 298, 304
Albright, Hardie 109
Albright, Ivan 194
Albright, Lola 271, 317, 338, 344, 345
Alcott, Louisa May 216
Alda, Alan 344, 357
Alden, Mary 35, 85
Alden, Norman 362
Aldrich, Robert 257, 295, 337, 344
Alex in Wonderland 354
Alexander, Ben 78
Alexander, Katherine 97, 103, 105, 116, 126, 127, 128, 147, 171, 191
Alexander, Tad 87, 102
Alexander, Terence 287
Alexander's Ragtime Band 138
Alfie 330
Alfred the Great 350
Algiers 146
Alias a Gentleman 213
Alias Jimmy Valentine 46, 47, 56
Alice in Wonderland 293
Alice's Restaurant 352
All about Eve 232
All American Chump, The 126
All at Sea 48
All at Sea 278
All Fall Down 304, 334
'*All I Do is Dream of You*' 102, 249
'*All of a Sudden My Heart Sings*' 201
'*All of You*' 283
All Quiet on the Western Front 66, 368
All the Brothers were Valiant 51, 257
All the Fine Young Cannibals 298
All the King's Men 223
'*All the Things You Are*' 191, 209
Allan, Anthony 142, 143, 150, 151,
Allan, Elizabeth 94, 95, 100, 104, 107, 117, 119, 127, 252
Allasio, Marisa 281
Allen, Barbara Jo 276
Allen, Corey 286, 298, 306
Allen, Elizabeth 364
Allen, Gracie 140, 169, 192
Allen, Jay 362
Allen, Joseph 146
Allen, Lewis 358
Allen, R.S. 319, 322
Allen, Sheila 312, 333
Allen, Steve 344
Allenby, Frank 228, 240
Allgood, Sara 174, 183, 225
Allister, Claude 54, 72, 117, 257
Allwyn, Astrid 147
Allyson, June 187, 188, 191, 192, 197, 203, 208, 209, 210, 214, 216, 219, 222, 224, 234, 236, 242, 250, 251, 259, 266, 274, 276, 364, 377, 384
Almost Human 273
'*Almost Like Being in Love*' 266
'*Alone*' 111
Along Came Ruth 13
Alonso, Chelo 303
Alonso, Mercedes 328
Alphabet Murders, The 333
Altars of Desire 35
Alter Ego 202
Altman, Robert 352
Alton, Robert 201, 209, 214, 219, 220, 222, 224, 234, 237, 249
Alvarado, Don 57, 136
Ambler, Eric 293
Ambush 231, 236
Ameche, Don 138, 169
America 10
American Black Chamber, The 112
American in Paris, An 240, 247, 249, 378
American Romance, An 198
American Tragedy, An 74
Americanization of Emily, The 319
Ames, Adrienne 109, 150
Ames, Leon 116, 192, 198, 201, 202, 203, 208, 209, 213, 214, 216, 219, 220, 222, 225, 228, 231, 232, 236, 244, 370
Ames, Preston 247, 284
Ames, Robert 56, 64, 71
Ames, Stephen 240, 253, 258
AmpoVision 255
Anastasia 278
Anatomy of a Murder 291
Anchors Aweigh 201, 378, 380
And One Was Beautiful 163
Anderson, Doris 76, 78
Anderson, Eddie 'Rochester' 140, 152, 183, 191, 203, 209
Anderson, Elga 314
Anderson, Guy 247, 251
Anderson, Herbert 333
Anderson, Jean 275, 360
Anderson, John 307, 339, 340
Anderson, John Murray 195
Anderson, Judith 163, 168, 289
Anderson, Maxwell 291
Anderson, Michael 293, 298, 322, 345
Anderson, Richard 232, 235, 242, 243, 244, 247, 249, 250, 253, 256, 259, 261, 266, 270, 273, 276, 278
Anderson, Robert 276
Anderson, Warner 202, 203, 206, 209, 213, 214, 215, 218, 228, 242, 243
Andersson, Bibi 306
Andre, Gwili 171,
Andre, Lona 120
Andrews, Dana 185, 216, 271, 325, 339
Andrews, Edward 276, 286, 333, 351
Andrews, Harry 280, 326, 352
Andrews, Jack 213
Andrews, Julie 316, 319, 322, 330, 340, 366
Andrews, Robert Hardy 123, 186, 187, 273, 304
Andrews, Tige 286
Andy Hardy Comes Home 289
Andy Hardy Gets Spring Fever 150
Andy Hardy Meets Debutante 158
Andy Hardy's Blonde Trouble 197
Andy Hardy's Double Life 182
Andy Hardy's Private Secretary 165
Angel, Heather 117, 160, 186
Angel Wore Red, The 299
Angeli, Pier 235, 242, 253, 256, 263, 273, 277, 280, 284, 293
Angell, Buckley 281
Angels and the Pirates 243
Angels in the Outfield 243
Angers, Avril 331
Angry Hills, The 295
Angry Silence, The 296
Animals, The 320
Anka, Paul 294
Ankers, Evelyn 182
Ankrum, Morris 176, 182, 188, 191, 192, 194, 196, 197, 198, 202, 204, 206, 208, 209, 210, 213, 214, 258
Anna Christie 58, 67
Anna Karenina 115, 148
Annabella 146
Annakin, Ken 339
Annie Get Your Gun 232, 234, 273, 380
Annie Laurie 36
Annis, Francesca 319, 321, 355
Ann-Margret 317, 320, 326, 327, 329
Another Language 98
Another Thin Man 149
Ansara, Michael 327, 339
AnscoColor 240, 257, 258, 259, 261, 263, 264, 266
Anthony Adverse 120
Anthony, C.L.: see Smith, Dodie
Anthony, Ray 280, 286, 294
Antonioni, Michelangelo 336, 348, 368
Antony, Scott 364
Any Number Can Play 228
'*Anything You Can Do*' 380
Apache Trail 183, 253
Apache War Smoke 253
Apartment, The 296
Apfel, Oscar 69
Appointment, The 350
Arab, The 12, 39, 92
Aranda, Angel 299
Arbeid, Ben 312, 313, 319
Arbuckle, Fatty 32
Arch of Triumph 216
Archard, Bernard 299, 306
Arden, Eve 147, 165, 168, 172, 215
Ardrey, Robert 208, 213, 219, 224, 228, 271, 276, 302
Are You Listening? 85
Arena 258
Argento, Dario 345
Argosy Pictures 218
Aristocats, The 352
Arledge, John 85, 133, 154, 165
Arlen, Harold 151
Arlen, Michael 51, 107, 188
Arlen, Richard 54, 117, 313
Arling, Arthur 206
Arliss, George 54, 109
Armen, Kay 270
Armendariz, Pedro 204, 218, 273, 312
Armetta, Henry 67, 78, 80, 82, 85, 86, 98, 103, 136, 169, 201
Armitage, George 362
Armstrong, Charlotte 250
Armstrong, Louis 183, 244, 250, 277, 294, 327
Armstrong, R.G. 307, 366
Armstrong, Robert 46, 69, 98, 126, 136, 209
Armstrong, Sam 105
Arnaz, Desi 186, 256, 271
Arne, Peter 278, 342
Arnelo Affair, The 215
Arneric, Neda 367
Arness, James 225, 244, 251, 264
Arno, Sig 234
Arnold, Edward 85, 87, 92, 102, 103, 128, 143, 145, 154, 171, 172, 174, 181, 183, 191, 192, 194, 197, 201, 202, 206, 208, 210, 213, 215, 218, 219, 222, 224, 228, 232, 234, 314
Arnold, Jack 286, 302
Arnold, Malcolm 287
Around the World in 80 Days 274
Around the World Under the Sea 333
Arouse and Beware 163
Arrau, Claudio 264
Arsene Lupin 82
Arsene Lupin Returns 132
Artcraft Pictures 182
Arthur, Art 321, 327, 333
Arthur, George K. 15, 19, 27, 30, 31, 32, 35, 39, 41, 42, 43, 47, 48, 56, 63, 94, 100, 112
Arthur, Jean 21, 48, 112, 128, 185
Arthur, Johnny 12, 22, 78, 119
Arthur, Robert 156, 257
Arzner, Dorothy 128
As You Desire Me 89, 98
Asher, Irving 168, 169, 172, 179, 183, 186
Ashley, Edward 156, 160, 162, 163, 165
Ashton, Frederick 360
Ask Any Girl 291
Askew, Luke 347
Aslan, Gregoire 300, 302, 306, 333
Asphalt Jungle, The 232, 238, 286, 304, 362
Asquith, Anthony 287, 293, 311, 317
Assignment in Brittany 184
'Asta' 104, 123, 149, 192
Astaire, Adele 171, 201, 384
Astaire, Fred 90, 97, 109, 120, 128, 138, 156, 171, 176, 201, 203, 220, 222, 224, 234, 237, 245, 247, 254, 270, 283, 296, 368, 372, 378, 384
Asther, Nils 44, 46, 49, 51, 52, 57, 71, 84, 90, 173, 202
Astin, John 364
Astor, Gertrude 33
Astor, Mary 89, 135, 139, 144, 150, 187, 192, 197, 211, 214, 215, 216, 219, 222, 228, 276, 370
'*At the Balalaika*' 151
Ates, Roscoe 76, 77, 85, 98, 152
Athena 266, 298
Atkins, Pervis 362
Atkinson, G.A. 18
Atlantis, the Lost Continent 300
Attenborough, Richard 287, 296, 306
Atwater, Edith 123, 311
Atwill, Lionel 95, 97, 107, 112, 116, 117, 122, 141, 142, 150, 151, 165, 179,
Auberjonois, Rene 352
Aubrey, James T., Jr. 9, 202, 346, 364, 366
Aubrey, Skye 364
Auction Block, The 24
Audiard, Michel 327
Audley, Maxine 275, 287
Auer, Mischa 107, 115, 122, 136, 144
Auerbach, George 117
Aumont, Jean Pierre 184, 187, 251, 283
Auntie Mame 291
Aurthur, Robert Alan 277, 334
Austen, Jane 160
Austin, Anne 102
Austin, Pamela 313, 320
Austin, William 31, 80
Autry, Gene 156, 166
Avalon, Frankie 313
'*Ave Maria*' 142
Avery, Margaret 362
Avery, Stephen M. 127
Awful Truth, The 128,
Axelrod, Jonathan 364
Axt, William 57
Ayars, Ann 172, 173, 176, 183, 191
Aylmer, Felix 144, 224, 245, 252, 258, 280, 287
Ayres, Lew 58, 66, 138, 139, 143, 146, 147, 150, 151, 158, 159, 162, 173, 179, 182, 360
Ayres, Robert 287, 342

'*Babbitt and the Bromide, The*' 201
Babcock, Dwight 351
Babes in Arms 152, 156
Babes in Toyland 100
Babes on Broadway 171, 180
Baby Cyclone, The 46
Baby-face Harrington 117
'*Baby, It's Cold Outside*' 225
Baby Mine 42
Babylon Revisited 264
Bacall, Lauren 192, 273, 278
Baccaloni 284
Bachelor Father, The 70
Bachelor in Paradise 302
Bachmann, Lawrence P. 126, 173, 179, 183, 187, 228, 253, 312, 316, 319, 333
Back Street 166,
Backus, Jim 244, 249, 250, 251, 267, 271, 276, 287, 291, 294, 306, 307, 313, 314, 315, 319, 344
Baclanova, Olga 77, 85, 86
Bacon, Irving 235
Bad and the Beautiful, The 252, 307
Bad Bascomb 203
Bad Day at Black Rock 266
Bad Guy 133
'*Bad in Every Man, The*' 219
Bad Little Angel 151
Bad Man, The 168,
Bad Man of Brimstone 135
Bad Man of Wyoming 162
Baddeley, Hermione 319
Badel, Alan 312
Badger, Clarence 13
Badiyi, Reza 367
Badlanders, The 286
Baer, Arthur 56
Baer, Buddy 245, 261
Baer, Max 92
Baer, Tim 298
Baggott, King 35
Bagnold, Enid 196
Bailey, David 366
Bailey, Pearl 298
Bailey, Raymond 289
Bailly, Auguste 263
Bainter, Fay 91, 144, 159, 171, 172, 180, 183, 186, 187, 188, 191
Baker, Art 209, 216, 218, 235
Baker, Carroll 256, 300, 304, 338
Baker, Diane 314, 333
Baker, George 351
Baker, George D. 13
Baker, Herbert 257, 261
Baker, Joby 298, 313, 320, 322, 327
Baker, Joe Don 361, 367
Baker, Kenny 147, 204
Baker, Melville 86, 142, 147, 187
Baker, Stanley 258, 295
Bakewell, William 66, 70, 76, 81, 102, 152, 173
Balalaika 151, 208
Balcon, Michael 134, 277, 278, 287, 289, 293
Balderston, John 112, 169, 182, 194, 251
Baldwin, Earl 172
Baldwin, Faith 84, 94, 126
Baldwin, Peter 348
Balfe, Michael 110
Ball, Lucille 187, 188, 197, 201, 203, 204, 209, 256, 271, 278
Ball, Vincent 302, 346
'*Ballad for Americans*' 174
Ballantine, Carl 344
Ballard, Lucien 352
Ballets des Champs Elysees 247
Ballin, Hugo 16
Balsam, Martin 302
Balter, Allan 360
Bambi 184,
Bancroft, Anne 304, 329
Bancroft, George 159, 166, 183
Band Plays On, The 102
Band Wagon, The 254, 372, 378
Bandolero, The 13
Bang, Joy 360
Bankhead, Tallulah 74, 82, 107, 257
Banks, Leslie 165,
Banky, Vilma 18, 64, 66
Bannen, Ian 326, 331
Banner, John 321
Bannerline 243
Banning, Margaret C. 144
Bar, Jacques 299, 300, 309, 312, 313, 317, 326, 340
Bar Sinister, The 273
Barbarian, The 92
Barbary Coast Gent 198
Barber, Rowland 277
Barbera, Joe 8
Barbier, George 84, 94, 100, 140, 144, 147
Barclay, George 126, 299
Bardelys the Magnificent 30
Bardette, Trevor 183, 201, 209, 213, 238, 289
Bardot, Brigitte 307
Bare, Richard L. 366
Barefoot in the Park 336
Bari, Lynn 345
Barker, Jess 198
Barker, Pip and Jane 350
Barker, Reginald 8, 10, 13, 20, 31, 39, 43
Barker, Ronnie 306
Barkleys of Broadway, The 224, 372
Barkworth, Peter 346
Barlow, James 360
Barnacle Bill 174
Barnacle Bill 278
Barnes, Binnie 112, 126, 128, 142, 179, 188, 198, 215
Barnes, Joanna 293, 338, 344
Barnes, T. Roy 21, 70
Barnett, Vince 208, 213, 331
Baronova, Irina 163
Barr, Patrick 263
Barran, Bob 298
Barrat, Robert 109, 116, 135, 149, 162, 163, 186, 202, 209
Barraud, George 47, 56
Barret, Andre 313
Barrett, Edith 250
Barrett, James Lee 347
Barrett, Sean 287
Barretts of Wimpole Street, The 103, 105, 275, 309
Barrie, J.M. 41, 105
Barrie, Mona 127, 150, 171, 179, 215
Barrie, Wendy 126
Barrier, Edgar 165
Barrier, The 28
Barringer, Emily 251
Barry, Donald 150, 273, 313
Barry, Joan 76
Barry, Philip 143, 160, 204, 277
Barry, Philip Jr. 289
Barry, Phyllis 98
Barry, Wesley 19, 40
Barrymore, Ethel 86, 87, 222, 224, 225, 231, 242, 244, 256, 257
Barrymore, John 10, 36, 52, 66, 82, 84, 87, 90, 92, 97, 98, 125, 127, 141, 174, 202, 286
Barrymore, John Drew 134, 286
Barrymore, Lionel 28, 33, 35, 39, 42, 46, 47, 52, 56, 57, 63, 64, 69, 75, 76, 82, 84, 86, 91, 94, 95, 97, 98, 100, 105, 107, 112, 117, 119, 120, 122, 127, 131, 132, 134, 135, 136, 138, 139, 143, 145, 146, 150, 154, 158, 168, 171, 173, 174, 182, 183, 184, 187, 196, 198, 202, 206, 208, 213, 222, 225, 236, 240, 243, 256, 257
Bartel, Paul 365
Barthelmess, Richard 12
Bartholomew, Freddie 107, 115, 127, 132, 135, 139, 142, 151, 179
Bartlett, Hall 314, 339
Bartlett, Jeanne 202, 206
Bartok, Eva 278
Bartold, Norman 366
Basehart, Richard 225, 281, 309
Basie, Count 327
Bass, Alfie 338
Bassermann, Albert 164, 171, 176, 191
Bassermann, Elsa 164, 191
Basset, William 224
Bassey, Shirley 331
Basso, Hamilton 250
Bastedo, Alexandra 355
Bataan 186,
Bataille des Dames 60
Bates, Alan 345
Bates, Barbara 264
Bates, Florence 169, 171, 172, 188, 194, 227, 243
Bates, H.E. 289
Bateson, Garry 357
Bathing Beauty 195
Battaglia, Rik 326
Battersby, Roy 352
Battle Beneath the Earth, The 342
Battle Beneath the Sea, The 342
Battle Circus 250
Battleground 225, 242
Battling Butler 28
Baum, L. Frank 151,
Baum, Vicki 82, 107
Bax, Roger 256
Baxley, Barbara 286
Baxter, Alan 132, 171, 180, 191, 339
Baxter, Anne 159, 218, 271, 296
Baxter, Warner 54, 80, 97, 120
Bayer, Oliver 203
Bazlen, Brigid 300, 303, 304
'*Be a Clown*' 374
'*Be My Love*' 234
Beach, Ann 333
Beach, Lewis 24
Beach, Rex 24, 28
Beahan, Charles 84
Beal, John 128, 131, 133, 142, 259
Beast of the City, The 82
Beat Generation, The 294
Beatles, The 316, 333, 364
Beaton, Cecil 284
Beatty, Robert 244, 278, 281, 342, 346, 361
Beatty, Warren 304, 336
Beau Broadway 46
Beau Brummel 10, 266
Beau Geste 28, 146
Beaudine, William 43
Beaumont, Charles 314, 317
Beaumont, Gerald 20, 31
Beaumont, Harry 49, 51, 52, 56, 61, 66, 67, 69, 72, 76, 77, 78, 82, 85, 92, 94, 97, 103, 196, 202, 203, 209, 213
Beaumont, Lucy 40
Beautiful Rebel, The 12
Beauty! 94
Beauty for Sale 94

Beauty Prize, The 15
Beavers, Louise 85, 97, 123, 132, 171, 183, 187, 198, 298
Because You're Mine 251, 378
'*Because You're Mine*' 251
Beck, John 333, 365, 366
Beck, Thomas 131
Beckerman, Sidney 347, 354
Becket 316
Beckett, Scotty 112, 135, 136, 139, 159, 171, 191, 214, 225, 231, 236
Beckley, Tony 361
Beckwith, Reginald 306
Becky 36
Becky Sharp 156
Beddoe, Don 172, 251
Bedelia, Bonnie 346, 355
Bedevilled 271
Bedford, Barbara 39
Bedford, Brian 334
Beeby, Bruce 302
Beecher, Janet 123, 128, 131, 132, 133, 135, 138, 141, 144, 156
Beecher, Sylvia 51
Beery, Noah 135, 142, 182, 186, 194, 198
Beery, Noah Jr. 159, 277, 317, 339, 350
Beery, Wallace 12, 13, 28, 41, 67, 69, 70, 72, 75, 77, 81, 82, 87, 95, 97, 100, 103, 107, 109, 110, 114, 119, 120, 123, 135, 139, 142, 143, 149, 154, 156, 159, 162, 163, 166, 168, 174, 183, 186, 198, 202, 203, 206, 213, 220, 224, 251, 366
Beeson, Paul 287
Beg, Borrow or Steal 133
Begg, Gordon 13
'*Begin the Beguine*' 156
Beginning or the End, The 209
Begley, Ed 240, 302, 306, 319, 344
Behind the Front 41
Behn, Harry 18, 20, 24, 40
Behrman, S.N. 98, 102, 119, 133, 136, 164, 167, 220, 245, 291
Beich, Albert 216, 228, 230
Bekassy, Stephen 263
Bel Geddes, Barbara 224
Belafonte, Harry 256, 295
Belasco, David 52, 78, 86, 142
Belasco, William 364, 368
Belgard, Arnold 143
Believe in Me 360, 361
Belita 256, 275
Bell, James 209, 210, 236, 257, 313
Bell, Marie 333
Bell, Marion 201
Bell, Monta 15, 19, 27, 32, 36, 43, 47, 86, 100, 104, 110
Bellah, James Warner 98, 303
Bellak, George 344
Bellamy, Ralph 75, 78
Bellamy Trial, The 47
Bellaver, Harry 228, 261, 270
Belle of New York, The 247
Bellew, Cosmo Kyrle 47
Bells Are Ringing 296
Belmondo, Jean Paul 327
Belmore, Lionel 23, 35, 64
Beloin, Edmund 204
Bemelmans, Ludwig 203
Benchley, Nathaniel 276
Benchley, Robert 8, 98, 114, 126, 128, 135, 186, 188, 202
Bendix, William 172, 306, 313
Benedek, Laslo 216
Benefits Forgot 139
Benet, Stephen Vincent 263
Benham, Joan 319
Ben-Hur 8, 18, 27, 31, 66, 120, 244, 290, 296, 298, 300, 302, 325
Benjamin, Philip 322
Benjamin, Richard 366
Bennett, Belle 64
Bennett, Bruce 100, 228, 236, 243, 261
Bennett, Charles 244
Bennett, Compton 222, 224, 236
Bennett, Constance 27, 74, 75, 80, 107, 116, 134, 142, 167
Bennett, Enid 12, 156
Bennett, Hywel 355
Bennett, Jill 274
Bennett, Joan 80, 90, 233, 238, 355
Bennett, Kem 252
Bennett, Richard 80
Benny, Jack 63, 110, 119, 166
Benson, Hugh 365
Benson, Leon 321
Benson, Lucille 365
Benson, Martin 342
Benson, Sally 192, 228, 320, 321, 322, 333
Bentley, Dick 328
Beranger, Clara 70
Bercovici, Eric 306, 341
Bercovici, Leonardo 306
Beregi, Oscar 344
Bergen, Edgar 338
Bergen, Polly 257, 258, 259
Berger, Helmut 365
Berger, Senta 328
Bergerac, Jacques 283, 284, 314
Bergman, Ingmar 24
Bergman, Ingrid 146, 171, 174, 176, 184, 194, 198, 201, 206, 278, 317
Berkeley, Busby 77, 147, 151, 152, 156, 162, 163, 168, 171, 174, 178, 191, 195, 226, 234, 249, 256, 266, 307, 358, 380
Berkeley, Martin 174, 186, 187, 196, 261
Berle, Milton 325
Berlin, Irving 54, 121, 184, 220, 234, 270, 377
Berlinger, Warren 298, 334
Berman, Henry 242, 243, 252, 257, 259, 261, 263, 271, 273, 276, 334
Berman, Pandro S. 168, 169, 171, 177, 178, 188, 194, 196, 198, 208, 209, 213, 215, 219, 228, 233, 238, 240, 242, 243, 250, 251, 252, 256, 257, 258, 268, 271, 276, 277, 278, 281, 286, 298, 299, 306, 314, 319, 326
Bern, Paul 49, 89
Bernard, Judd 336, 339
Berneis, Peter 307
Bernhardt, Curtis 213, 228, 249, 266, 271, 276, 304
Bernstein, Henri 84
Bernstein, Leonard 227
Bernstein, Walter 326
Berry Brothers 182
Berry, John 225, 333
Bertha the Sewing Machine Girl 202
Berti, Marina 245, 291, 304, 309
Bertoya, Paul 339
Besier, Rudolph 105
Besserer, Eugenie 24, 31, 57
Best Foot Forward 188, 191
Best, George 355
Best House in London, The 350
Best, James 275, 276
'*Best Things in Life Are Free, The*' 71, 210
Betrayed 264
Bettger, Lyle 334, 339
Between Two Women 133
Between Two Women 196
Betz, Matthew 19, 24
Bevan, Billy 126, 146, 174, 194, 224
Bevans, Clem 159, 191, 206, 224
Beverly of Graustark 32
Bewitched 202, 215
Bey, Turhan 198,
Beyond the Sierras 51
Bezzerides, A.I. 250, 295
B.F.'s Daughter 215
Bhowani Junction 277
Biberman, Abner 344
Bickford, Charles 58, 61, 67, 71, 80, 102, 143, 181, 218
'*Bidin' My Time*' 191
Big City 133
Big City 219
Big City, The 39
Big Hangover, The 232
Big House, The 69, 70, 75, 77, 112, 154
Big Jack 224
Big League r 257
Big Operator, The 294
Big Parade, The 8, 18, 27, 30, 40, 98, 225
Big Pick-up, The 287
Big Store, The 168
Big Trail, The 66
Bigard, Barney 244
Biggest Bundle of Them All, The 339
Bikel, Theodore 256, 280, 295
'*Bill*' 247
Bill, Tony 342, 344
Billingsley, Barbara 228, 237
Billy Rose's Jumbo 307
Billy the Kid 70, 168
Bing, Herman 77, 80, 87, 94, 100, 103, 107, 119, 121, 122, 133, 134, 135, 141, 142, 144, 156
Binns, Edward 319
Biograph Studio 12
Biography 102
Biography of a Bachelor Girl 102
Bird, John 350
Bird, Norman 302
Birds and the Bees, The 215
Bird's Nest, The 280
Birell, Tala 213
Birinski, Leo 76
Birth of a Nation, The 18, 201
Bishop, Julie 240
Bishop Misbehaves, The 117
Bishop Murder Case, The 64
Bishop, Richard 235
Bishop's Misadventures, The 117
Bissell, Whit 228, 269, 292, 298, 319, 367
Bisset, Jacqueline 360
Bisson, Alexandre 131
Bitter Sweet 57, 156
Bixby, Bill 338, 344
Bixby Girls, The 298
Black Belly of the Tarantula, The 364
Black Hand 224
Black, John D.F. 361
Black, Karen 367
Black Narcissus 210
Black Orpheus 300
Black Pirate, The 28
Blackbird, The 23
Blackboard Jungle, The 268, 333
Blackmail 54
Blackmail 154
Blackman, Honor 228, 302, 327
Blackman, Joan 313
Blackmer, Sidney 78, 132, 133, 146, 149, 151, 169, 171, 172, 251, 277, 322
Blackton, Marian 36
Blaine, Vivian 249, 271
Blair, Betsy 236, 244
Blair, Janet 306
Blair, Lionel 309
Blair, Nicky 320
Blake, Amanda 232, 235, 251, 264
Blake, Bobby 178, 182, 190
Blake, Gladys 202
Blake, Madge 249
Blake, Marie 138, 139, 146, 150, 158, 173, 183, 187, 196
Blake, Pamela 179
Blake, Robert 361
Blakely, Colin 306, 350
Blakeney, Olive 168,
Blanchard, Marie 242, 247
Blandick, Clara 66, 67, 75, 78, 84, 94, 100, 105, 127, 146, 216, 230
Blane, Ralph 188, 192, 210
Blankfort, Michael 274, 280
Blarney 35
Blaustein, Julian 293, 302, 303
Blees, Robert 286
'*Bless Yore Beautiful Hide*' 263
Blessed, Brian 352
Blessing, The 292
Blier, Bernard 327
Blinn, Holbrook 20
Blithe Spirit 201, 302
Bloch, Bertram 92
Blochman, L.G. 112
Block, Alfred 56, 66
Block-Heads 143
Block, Irving 276
Block, Lawrence 365
Block, Libbie 224
Block, Ralph 231
Blodgett, Michael 364
Blonde Bombshell 97
Blonde Fever 197
Blonde Inspiration 162
Blondell, Joan 156, 186, 201, 276, 280, 319, 329, 331, 344
Blondie of the Follies 84
Blood and Sand 166
Bloom, Claire 312, 314, 317
Bloom, Harold Jack 253
Blore, Eric 111, 116, 126, 143
Blossoms in the Dust 169
Blow-Up 336, 337
Blue Angel, The 66
Blue, Ben 178, 182, 187, 191, 192, 209, 344
'*Blue Banube, The*' 342
Blue, Monte 8, 12, 13, 46, 100
'*Blue Moon*' 219
'*Blue Room, The*' 219
Bluestone, George 355
Blum, Edwin 195
Blye, Maggie 364
Blystone, John 143
Blyth, Ann 210, 247, 257, 266, 273, 275
Blythe, Betty 169
Blythe, Samuel 84
Boardman, Eleanor 8, 12, 15, 16, 20, 21, 24, 28, 30, 40, 48, 66, 76, 80
Boardman, True 242
Boasberg, Al 28, 60, 63, 67, 69, 85, 103
Bob and Carol and Ted and Alice 354
Bochner, Lloyd 313, 339, 345
Boddy, Manchester 225
Bodies and Souls 228
Body, The 352
Body and Soul 39
Boehm, David 184
Boehm, Karl 213, 302, 312, 314, 331
Boehm, Sydney 228, 236, 264
Bogarde, Dirk 287, 293, 299, 306, 339, 345
Bogart, Humphrey 120, 166, 176, 185, 206, 240, 250, 274, 278, 347
Bogart, Paul 347, 368
Bohem, Endre 142, 145, 154
Bohemian Girl, The 110
Bohnen, Roman 201, 213
Bois, Curt 156, 179, 188, 197, 224
Bolam, James 319
Boland, Bridget 304
Boland, Mary 95, 147, 156, 160, 192, 216
Boles, John 10, 15, 90, 187
Boleslawski, Richard 86, 90, 94, 102, 103, 104, 119, 125, 132
Boley, May 72
Bolger, Ray 121, 128, 144, 151, 204
Bolix 3D 255
Bolling, Tiffany 366
Bolster, Anita 192
Bolt, Robert 325, 354
Bolton, Guy 209, 219
Bolton, Muriel 173
Bombshell 92, 97
Bonanova, Fortunio 211, 231
Bond, Derek 252
Bond, Lillian 77, 78, 114, 117, 194
Bond, Ward 115, 152, 162, 184, 188, 202, 218, 261, 276
Bondi, Beulah 95, 97, 103, 127, 139, 154, 162, 240, 261, 314
Bonner, James 364
Bonnie and Clyde 336
Bonnie Scotland 110
Boob, The 35
Boom Town 164
Boone, Pat 278, 309
Boone, Richard 280, 303
Boorman, John 339
Booth, Edwina 70
Booth, James 327
Booth, Karin 214, 219
Booth, Margaret 119
Booth, Shirley 249, 257
Boothe, Clare 147, 276
Border Incident 225
Boretz, Allen 195
Borg, Veda Ann 156, 168, 169, 174, 216, 271, 276
Borgnine, Ernest 266, 268, 275, 286, 287, 293, 337, 344, 345
Born to Dance 123, 126
Born to Sing 174
Born Yesterday 232
Borodin, Alexander 273
Borowski, Marvin 168, 176, 224
Borzage, Frank 24, 44, 133, 141, 144, 150, 158, 162, 165, 169, 171, 183,
Boschero, Dominique 320
Bosler, Virginia 266
Bosworth, Hobart 15, 18, 20, 36, 51, 76, 77, 123,
Bottome, Phyllis 162,
Bouchet, Barbara 365
Bouchey, Willis 286
Boulting, John and Roy 263
Boulton, Matthew 128, 131, 142, 168, 174, 192, 224
Bow, Clara 28, 151
Bowers, John 24
Bowers, Kenny 188, 191
Bowers, William 236, 286, 319
Bowery to Bellevue 251
Bowman, Lee 142, 147, 151, 154, 159, 162, 163, 169, 172, 174, 176, 179, 181, 183, 186
Box, Betty 355
Box, John 325
Boy Friend, The 32
Boy Friend, The 358, 364
Boy from Barnardo's, The 142
'*Boy Next Door, The*' 192
Boyd, Stephen 291, 307
Boyd, William 94
Boyer, Charles 87, 136, 146, 194, 273, 302
Boyer, Francoise 333
Boylan, Malcolm Stuart 76, 81, 134, 240
Boyle, Peter 366
Boys in the Band, The 358
Boy's Night Out 306
Boys' Ranch 206
Boys Town 138, 172, 216
Brabham, Jack 302
Brabin, Charles 8, 18, 57, 60, 72, 76, 80, 82, 84, 85, 86, 95, 97, 102
Brabourne, John 360
Brace, Blanche 202
Bracey, Sidney 23, 78
Brach, Gerard 338
Bracken, Eddie 237, 261
Brackett, Charles 126, 135, 148
Brackett, Sarah 342
Braddon, Russell 365
Bradford, J.S. 287
Bradford, Richard 361
Bradley, David 250
Bradley, Truman 139, 141, 143, 146, 149
Brady, Alice 94, 95, 97, 135, 171
Brady, Ruth 214, 224
Brady, Scott 366
Braham, Lionel 143
Brahm, John 339
Brake, Patricia 355
Branco, Solly 326
Brand, Max 139, 173,
Brand, Neville 268, 289, 296
Brandel, Marc 336
Branding Iron, The 39
Brando, Marlon 232, 240, 254, 262, 271, 274, 277, 284, 309, 310, 362
Brandon, Dorothy 76
Brascia, John 271
Brasselle, Keefe 236, 242, 243, 247, 249
Brasseur, Pierre 299
'*Brazilian Boogie*' 191
Brazzi, Rossano 216, 292, 303, 365
Bread 15
Breakston, George 150, 158, 173,
Brecher, Irving 147, 162, 171, 187, 188, 192, 203, 218
Breck, Peter 313
Breen, Thomas 219, 225
Bremer, Lucille 192, 201, 203, 209, 213, 370
Bren, Milton 134, 142, 147, 162, 168, 174
Brendel, El 78, 165
Brennan, Frederick Hazlitt 184, 201, 210, 253
Brennan, Walter 123, 125, 147, 149, 182, 188, 266, 304
Brenner, Alfred 298
Brenon, Herbert 52, 134
Brent, Eve 287
Brent, George 103, 107, 219
Brent, Romney 283
Breon, Edmond 149, 194, 219, 225
Bresler, Jerry 197, 202, 208, 215, 280
Breslin, Howard 298
Breslin, Jimmy 361
Breslin, Patricia 289
Breslow, Lou 203, 214
Bressart, Felix 146, 148, 154, 156, 159, 163, 164, 165, 168, 169, 173, 176, 183, 187, 188, 197, 198, 203, 204
Brewster, Diane 281, 287
Brewster McCloud 352
Brialy, Jean-Claude 312
Brian, David 228, 243, 251, 304
Brian, Mary 30
Bribe, The 219
Brice, Fanny 121, 136, 201
Bricusse, Leslie 351
Bridal Suite 146
Bride Goes Wild, The 216
Bride Wore Red, The 128
Bridge of San Luis Rey, The 57
Bridge on the River Kwai, The 278
Bridge to the Sun 300
Bridges at Toko-Ri, The 268
Bridges, Beau 216
Bridges, Jeff 365
Bridges, Lloyd 250, 333
Brief Encounter 210
Briers, Richard 302, 311
Brigadoon 266, 273
Briggs, Harlan 214
Bright Lights 20
Bright Road 256
Bright, Robert 299
Briley, John 302, 312
'*Bring on the Men*' 201
Bringing Up Father 51
Brinkley, William 283
Brissac, Virginia 156, 196, 202, 218
British Broadcasting Corp. 146
Britton, Pamela 201, 202, 230, 232
Brix, Herman: see Bennett, Bruce
Broadway Melody, The 48, 54, 63, 107, 110, 156, 196, 249, 370, 382
'*Broadway Melody, The*' 48, 374
Broadway Melody of 1936 110, 123
Broadway Melody of 1938 128
Broadway Melody of 1940 156, 372
Broadway Rhythm 191
'*Broadway Rhythm*' 110, 374
Broadway Serenade 147
Broadway to Hollywood 95, 379
Brocco, Peter 224
Broderick, Helen 143, 162
Brodie, Steve 198
Brodrick, Malcolm 281
Brodszky, Nicholas 234, 251
Broken Barriers 10
Brolin, James 364, 366
Bromberg, J. Edward 165, 176, 182
Bromfield, John 256
Bromfield, Louis 192
Bronfman, Edgar 9
Bronson, Betty 18, 47
Bronson, Charles 250, 292, 303, 317, 329, 337, 340
Bronson, Lillian 237, 247
Bronston, Samuel 300
Brook, Clive 90
Brook, Hillary 203,
Brooks, Geraldine 225, 368
Brooks, Jeremy 339
Brooks, Louise 28
Brooks, Margaret 339
Brooks, Matt 188
Brooks, Rand 152, 163
Brooks, Richard 228, 232, 236, 242, 250, 257, 263, 264, 268, 273, 275, 281, 289, 306
Brophy, Edward 69, 77, 78, 85, 86, 87, 98, 102, 103, 104, 105, 112, 114, 116, 123, 126, 132, 140, 141, 147, 192
Brophy, John 299
Brotherly Love 48
Brotherly Love 352
Brothers Karamazov, The 281, 284
Brown, Barbara 240, 252
Brown, Charles D. 135, 141, 143, 146, 213, 214
Brown, Clarence 33, 44, 48, 51, 57, 58, 64, 67, 69, 75, 77, 78, 84, 86, 94, 98, 102, 107, 115, 119, 126, 127, 136, 139, 145, 159, 163, 168, 191, 196, 198, 206, 213, 222, 224, 228, 237, 242, 243, 250, 253, 256
Brown, George 302, 306, 313
Brown, Georgia 345
Brown, Harry 257, 264
Brown, Jim 337, 340, 344, 345, 347, 367
Brown, Joe David 232
Brown, Joe E. 82, 109, 143, 247, 311
Brown, Johnny Mack 41, 42, 48, 49, 51, 57, 70, 72, 75, 76, 365
Brown, Karl 98
Brown, Kay 244
Brown, Malcolm 277
Brown, Nacio Herb 49, 56, 61, 237, 358, 374
Brown of Harvard 30
Brown, Pamela 274, 293, 360
Brown, Phil 174, 182
Brown, Tom 91, 134, 135, 142, 149, 151
Brown, Vanessa 224, 252
Browne, Coral 344
Browne, Irene 92, 278
Browne, Kathie 339
Browne, Porter 168
Browne, Ralph 328
Browning, Tod 20, 23, 28, 35, 39, 47, 57, 64, 85, 98, 117, 122, 147
Bruce, George 135, 143, 182, 186, 198, 206, 210, 211
Bruce, Nigel 107, 132, 163, 168, 169, 180, 191, 202, 216
Bruce, Virginia 85, 86, 105, 109, 112, 116, 117, 121, 122, 123, 132, 133, 135, 141, 144, 146, 147, 154
Bruckman, Clyde 14, 15, 44
Bruhl, Heidi 312
Brunetti, Argentina 253
Brush, Katharine 87, 133, 139
Bryan, Jane 151
Bryant, Michael 351
Bryant, Nana 136, 143, 188, 195, 196, 202
Bryna Productions 280
Brynner, Yul 278, 281, 287, 361, 366
Buchanan, Edgar 209, 228, 232, 236, 286, 292, 296, 307, 315, 319, 339
Buchanan, Jack 82, 254
Buchholz, Horst 365
Buchman, Harold 214
Buchowetski, Dimitri 35
Buck, Jules 299
Buck, Pearl S. 127, 198
'*Buckle Down, Winsocki*' 188
Buckler, John 125
Buckley, Hal 354
Bucknall, Nathalie 145
Buckner, Robert 253, 334
Bucquet, Harold S. 139, 150, 154, 158, 164, 173, 174, 182, 183, 186, 198, 204
Bud Abbott and Lou Costello in Hollywood 203
Budge, Donald 250
Bugle Call, The 41
Bugle Sounds, The 166
Bulgakov, Leo 188
Bull, Peter 266, 293
Bullock, Harvey 319, 322
Buloff, Joseph 277, 283
Bunn, Alfred 110
Bunston, Herbert 56
Buono, Victor 364
Burden, Hugh 302
Burden of Proof, The 360
Burgess, Dorothy 91
Buried Loot 102
Burke, Alfred 312
Burke, Billie 97, 105, 107, 116, 121, 126, 128, 133, 134, 135, 136, 142, 146, 147, 151, 162, 163, 168, 201, 224, 233, 238, 249
Burke, Frank 90
Burke, James 156, 240
Burn 'Em Up O'Connor 141
Burn, Witch, Burn 122
Burnet, Dana 51, 141
Burnett, Don 276, 294, 304
Burnett, Frances Hodgson 224
Burnett, W.R. 82, 168, 238, 303, 362
Burns, George 140, 169, 384
Burns, Jessie 20, 31
Burr, Jane 215
Burr, Raymond 230
Burroughs, Edgar Rice 86, 304, 312
Burrows, Abe 271
Burstyn, Ellen 354
Burt, Katherine Newlin 24, 39
Burton, David 64, 67
Burton, Martin 94
Burton, Richard 254, 311, 316, 317, 322, 329, 330, 336, 346, 360
Burton, Robert 251, 252, 253, 256, 257, 258, 261, 273, 275, 281
Burton, Val 142,
Burton, Wendell 358
Bus Stop 274

Busby, Tom 337
Busch, Mae 8, 10, 13, 15, 23, 27, 52, 56, 95, 110, 168
Busch, Niven 208
Bus-Fekete, Ladislaus 176
Bushell, Anthony 237
Bushman, Francis X. 18, 27, 30
Bushman, Francis X. Jr 31, 56, 66, 69
Bushranger, The 51
Busman's Honeymoon 165
'But In the Morning, No' 187
'But Not for Me' 191
But the Flesh is Weak 84, 168
Butch Cassidy and the Sundance Kid 352, 361
Butler, David 103
Butler, Ewan 287
Butler, Frank 56, 60, 67, 70, 76, 82, 84, 110, 117
Butler, Hugo 143, 146, 147, 159, 162, 174, 179, 191, 344
Butterfield 8 296, 298, 299
Butterworth, Charles 94, 97, 98, 100, 102, 107, 117, 123, 146, 162
Buttons 42
Buttons, Red 286, 315, 319
Buttram, Pat 313
Buzzell, Edward 135, 140, 144, 147, 162, 168, 169, 179, 180, 188, 191, 198, 206, 209, 213, 222, 225, 253
Bwana Devil 254, 255
By Hook or By Crook 191
'By Myself' 254
Byington, Spring 119, 120, 136, 138, 171, 183, 187, 188, 201, 202, 206, 209, 213, 214, 215, 222, 225, 232, 243, 251, 298
Byng, Douglas 333
Byrd, Richard 218
Byrne, Eddie 277, 287
Byrnes, Edd 366
Byron, Arthur 85, 92, 111, 112
Byron, Kathleen 257

Caan, James 366
Cabanne, Christy 19, 27, 31, 35
Cabaret 362
Cabin in the Sky 183
Cabot, Bruce 120, 122, 123, 133, 135, 163, 182
Cabot, Sebastian 273, 295, 298
Cadell, Jean 107, 280
Caesar and Cleopatra 201
Caesar, Arthur 70, 94, 103, 179
Cagney, James 74, 90, 109, 112, 120, 156, 166, 176, 185, 268, 270, 274, 276
Cahn, Edward 133, 197, 203
Cahn, Sammy 210, 234, 251
Caillou, Alan 327
Cain, James M. 143, 208
Caine, Michael 356, 362
Caine Mutiny, The 262
Cairo 179
Cairo 304
Caldwell, Sarah 345
Calhern, Louis 109, 127, 144, 150, 222, 231, 232, 234, 236, 237, 238, 242, 244, 251, 253, 254, 257, 259, 261, 263, 264, 266, 268, 271, 277
Calhoun, Rory 281, 299, 313, 365
California 43
California Holiday 334
Call of the Flesh 72
Callahans and the Murphys, The 41, 51
Callaway Went Thataway 242
Calleia, Joseph 109, 112, 116, 120, 122, 123, 126, 133, 135, 141, 162, 187, 209, 242, 253
Calley, John 325, 338, 344
Calling Bulldog Drummond 244
Calling Dr Gillespie 182, 187
Calling Dr Kildare 150, 151
Calloway, Cab 329
Calm Yourself 109
Calvelli, Joseph 328
Calvert, Phyllis 355
Calvino, Italo 327
Cambridge, Godfrey 339
Cameraman, The 44, 232
Cameron, Earl 312, 342
Cameron, Rod 192,
Camille 127, 136, 141, 148
Campanila, Pasquale Festa 337
Campbell, Alan 127, 144
Campbell, Malcolm 141
Campbell, Mrs Patrick 100, 107
Campbell, R. Wright 350
Campbell, William 244, 249, 250, 257, 258, 259, 360
Campos, Rafael 269, 280
Canale, Gianna Maria 242, 304
Canning, Victor 344
Cannon, Doran 352
Cannon, J.D. 350, 361
Canova, Judy 296
'Can't Help Lovin' That Man' 209, 247
Canterville Ghost, The 195
Cantor, Eddie 82, 163
Canty, Marietta 233, 238, 252
Canutt, Yakima 291
Capra, Frank 102, 138, 218, 240
Capricorn Productions 309
Captain Blood 109
Captain is a Lady, The 162
Captain Nemo and the Underwater City 350
Captain Salvation 42
Captain Sindbad 312
Captains Courageous 132, 142, 145, 240
Carbine Williams 251
Card, Kathryn 208, 210, 215, 232, 252, 259, 319
Cardboard Lover, The 46
Cardiff, Jack 296, 321, 331, 341
Cardinale, Claudia 338
Carewe, Arthur Edmund 21
Carey, Harry 30, 31, 41, 48, 70, 141, 209
Carey, Harry Jr. 218, 354, 357
Carey, Joyce 293
Carey, Macdonald 247
Carey, Michele 345, 354
Carey, Timothy 367
Carey Treatment, The 364
Carfagno, Edward 252, 254, 290
Cargo of Innocents 182
Caridi, Carmen 361
Carle, Richard 57, 146, 148
Carlin, Lynn 347, 361
Carlisle, Helen Grace 135
Carlisle, Kitty 111
Carlisle, Mary 85, 91, 97, 103, 109, 119
Carlson, Richard 151, 154, 182, 183, 186, 187, 188, 236, 338
Carmichael, Hoagy 134
Carmichael, Ian 264
Carminati, Tullio 309
Carnal Knowledge 358
Carnera, Primo 92
Carney, Art 317
Carnovsky, Morris 204
Carol, Martine 281
Carol, Sue 46
Caron, Leslie 244, 247, 250, 251, 256, 264, 276, 284, 287, 298, 361, 378, 379
Carousel 274
Carpenter, Carleton 234, 236, 237, 252, 253, 257, 380
Carpenter, Edward Childs 70, 85, 117
Carpetbaggers, The 317
Carr, John Dickson 244
Carr, Mary 86
Carr, Richard 350
Carradine, David 344, 350
Carradine, John 132, 139, 176, 179, 186, 198, 274, 296, 338, 351
Carreras, Michael 309
Carrie 249
Carriere, Jean-Claude 333
Carrillo, Leo 102, 103, 105, 126, 142, 143, 145, 147, 159, 162, 164, 174
Carroll, Diahann 345
Carroll, Gordon 366
Carroll, Jean 344
Carroll, Joan 192, 370
Carroll, John 150, 162, 163, 165, 171, 177, 182, 191, 202, 211
Carroll, Leo G. 107, 111, 133, 143, 213, 233, 236, 252, 257, 274, 291, 314, 328, 331, 338, 342
Carroll, Madeleine 120,
Carroll, Nancy 54, 141
Carr-Smith, Rodney 365
Carruthers, Ben 337
'Carry Me Back to Old Virginny' 134,
Carry On comedies 296
Carson, Charles 266
Carson, Jack 150, 171, 259, 289
Carson, John David 360
Carson, Johnny 320
Carson, Robert 132, 234, 281
Carter, Benny 187
Carter, Carolyn 327
Carter, Jack 307, 344
Carter, Janis 179
Caruso, Anthony 179, 225, 238, 286
Caruso, Dorothy 247
Carver, Lynne 128, 131, 134, 136, 139, 143, 146, 149, 150, 156, 159, 162, 172
Casablanca 176
Casey, Bernie 362
Cash and Carry 173
Cash, Johnny 313
Cash, Rosalind 362
Casino Murder Case, The 111
Caspary, Vera 256, 302
Cass Timberlane 215
Cassavetes, John 277, 286, 287, 337
Cassell, Wally 206, 278
Castellani, Renato 345
Castelnuovo, Nino 346
Castle, Don 138, 143, 151
Castle, Peggie 281
Cat and the Fiddle 98
Cat Ballou 322
Cat on a Hot Tin Roof 298, 306
Catered Affair, The 275
Catlett, Walter 72, 123, 168, 178,
Catlow 361
Cattle King 313
Caught 224
Caught Short 70
Caulfield, Joan 313
Cause for Alarm 235
Cavalcade 90, 91
Cavanagh, Paul 67, 107, 150, 162, 179, 196, 198, 228, 250, 268, 273
Cavanaugh, Hobart 126, 149, 163, 169, 182, 183, 188, 194, 209
Cavara, Paolo 365, 367
Cavett, F.M. 107
Cavin, Patty 362
Cawthorn, Joseph 80, 85, 98, 110
Caxton, William 365
Cayatte, Andre 312
Caylor, Rose 179
Celli, Teresa 224, 225, 232, 236, 238
Centennial Summer 192
Certain Young Man, A 32
Cerusico, Enzo 327
Chadwick, Cyril 43, 56, 64
Chaffey, Don 302
Chained 107
Chakiris, George 300
Chaldicott, Fay 119
Challenge to Lassie 225
Chamarat, George 303
Chamberlain, Richard 196, 303, 313, 322
Chamberlain, William 286, 319
Chambers, Robert W. 103
Chambers, Whitman 123
Chameles, Tom 292, 298
Champ, The 77, 119, 206
Champion, Gower 209, 247, 249, 256, 264, 377
Champion, Marge 247, 249, 256, 264, 377, 384
Chance Meeting 321
Chandler 361
Chandler, Chick 196
Chandler, Helen 81
Chandler, John Davis 307, 326, 334
Chandler, Lane 57
Chandler, Raymond 208, 347, 361
Chaney, Lon 8, 10, 18, 22, 23, 28, 39, 47, 52, 57, 69, 71, 85
Chaney, Lon Jr. 168, 243, 339
Chanslor, Roy 174
'Chant of the Jungle' 60
Chantler, David 312
Chapin, Anne M. 139, 203, 208, 214, 219
Chaplin, Charles 12, 15, 18, 47, 48, 71, 120, 210, 249, 274, 300
Chaplin, Charles Jr. 120, 286, 294
Chaplin, Geraldine 325
Chaplin, Saul 247
Chaplin, Sydney 18
Chapman, Ben 321
Chapman, Edward 144, 277
Chapman, Edythe 21, 61, 64
Charell, Eric 82
Charge is Murder, The 313
Charisse, Cyd 201, 204, 206, 209, 211, 214, 216, 219, 222, 225, 228, 240, 249, 250, 254, 266, 267, 270, 271, 283, 286, 307, 372, 374, 378, 384
Charley's Aunt 18, 166
Charlot, Andre 188
Charly 340
Charteris, Leslie, 209
Chartoff, Robert 339, 345, 352, 360, 361
Chase, Borden 186, 198, 240, 328
Chase, Charley 8, 95, 120, 123
Chase, Ilka 72, 154
Chase, Patricia 328
Chaser, The 140,
Chasing Rainbows 63
Chatburn, Jean 133,
Chatterton, Ruth 54, 57, 67, 82
Chautauqua 351
Chayevsky, Paddy 268, 275, 319
Cheaper to Marry 13
'Cheeta' 125, 172, 180
Chekhov, Michael 188, 242, 250, 264
Cherry, Helen 321
Chertok, Jack 149, 172, 174, 179, 181
Chester, G.R. 78
Chevalier, Maurice 54, 100, 284, 292, 379
Chiari, Walter 280
Chief, The 94
Children of Paradise 210
Children of Pleasure 72
Children of the Damned 312
China Bound 56
China Caravan 174
China Seas 114, 164
Chinatown 368
Ching, William 250
Chocolate Soldier, The 169
Chodorov, Edward 109, 138, 141, 143, 144, 149, 163, 208, 244
Chodorov, Jerome 138, 156, 162
Choose Your Partner 156
Chopin, Frederic 201
'Chopsticks' 192
Christensen, Benjamin 20, 39, 56
Christian, Linda 208, 214, 266, 295, 311
Christians, Mady 102, 112
Christie, Agatha 302, 313, 319, 333
Christie, Audrey 180, 319
Christie, Julie 321, 322, 325
Christine, Virginia 313, 314
Christmas Carol, A 143
Christopher Bean 97
Christopher, John 357
Christopher, Robert 271
Christy, Dorothy 78, 95, 144
Churchill, Berton 84, 117, 133, 159
Churchill, Donald 278
Churchill, Randolph 133
Churchill, Sarah 237
Churchill, Winston 72, 176, 237, 281, 322
Ciampi, Elgin 327
Ciannelli, Eduardo 90, 147, 165, 168, 179, 244, 331
Cilento, Diane 307
Cimarron 74, 296
Cincinnati Kid, The 329
Cinderella, Italian Style 338
Cinecitta Studio 365
Cinecolor 206
Cinema International Corp. 9
CinemaScope 254, 255, 258, 263, 264, 266, 273, 277, 278, 287, 291, 296, 303, 304, 328
Cinerama 44, 254, 304, 314, 317, 334, 342, 344
Cioffi, Charles 361
Circe the Enchantress 15
Circle, The 28
Circus, The 28
Circus Rookies 48
Cistheri, Raymond 362
Citadel, The 144
Citizen Kane 166, 174, 228, 232, 300
Civilization 15
Clair, Rene 82
Claire, Ina 54, 148, 150
Clare, Diane 286, 312
Clare, Mary 76, 144
Clarence, the Cross-Eyed Lion 327
Clark, Alan 213
Clark, Betty Ross 138, 144, 145
Clark, Bobby 277
Clark, Cliff 178, 181, 198, 224
Clark, Ernest 283
Clark, Fred 236, 283, 289, 292, 296, 306, 327
Clark, James 311, 313
Clark, Petula 351, 379
Clarke, Angela 242
Clarke, Arthur C. 342
Clarke, Charles 107
Clarke, David 210
Clarke, Donald Henderson 133
Clarke, Kenneth 35
Clarke, Mae 90, 91, 94, 97, 98, 103, 164
Clarke, T.E.B. 278
Clavell, James 294
Claw, The 84
Clawson, Elliott 28, 39, 47, 64
Claxton, Oliver 146
Clay, Nicholas 360
Clayton, Jack 339
Clayton, Jan 198
Clayworth, June 133, 135, 136, 261
Clear All Wires 94
Cleary, Jon 302
Clemens, Harold 345
Clement, Dick 360
Clement, Rene 313, 317
Clements, Calvin 362
Clements, Colin 42
Clements, Stanley 169
Cleopatra 304
Cleveland, George 206, 209, 232
Clewes, Howard 299
Clifford, Kathleen 44
Clift, Montgomery 218, 240, 278, 284
Cline, Edward 12, 13, 27
Clive, Colin 94, 112
Clive, E.E. 122, 125, 126, 127, 128, 131, 132, 133, 135, 142, 150, 154, 160
Clock, The 204
Clockwork Orange, A 362
Clooney, Rosemary 267
Clork, Harry 122, 143, 162, 163, 169, 172, 174, 180, 191, 206
Clouzot, Henri-Georges 268
Clown, The 251
Cluett, Jack 98
Clunes, Alec 271
Clyde, Andy 146, 208
Clyde, June 102
Coates, Albert 188, 192
Cobb, Lee J. 172, 281, 286, 293, 302, 304, 367
Coburn, Charles 139, 141, 142, 145, 159, 162, 163, 174, 208, 215, 228, 276
Coburn, James 303, 319, 325, 364, 366
Cobweb, The 273
Cochran, Steve 275, 294
Cocker, Joe 360
Cockeyed Miracle, The 209
Cockrell, Gary 306, 319
Coco, James 352
Code Two 258
Codee, Ann 195, 214, 243, 257, 271
Cody, Lew 13, 15, 20, 21, 24, 27, 31, 35, 42, 43, 46, 52, 80
Coen, Franklin 286
Coffee, Lenore 15, 56, 64, 78, 80, 82, 84, 86, 105, 112, 116, 127, 196
Coghlan, Junior 30, 41, 66
Cohan, George M. 46, 156
Cohen, Albert 109
Cohn, A.A. 43
Cohn, Art 243, 250, 251, 256, 261, 263, 281
Cohn, Harry 309
Cohn, J.J. 131, 132, 133, 138
Colbert, Claudette 54, 109, 120, 146, 165, 192, 208, 210
Cole, George 271
Cole, Jack 278
Cole, Lester 211, 213, 214
Cole, Nat 'King' 249, 286
Coleman, Patricia 187, 194
Colette 284
Colicos, John 364
Colla, Richard 352
Colleano, Bonar 263
Collier, Constance 112, 125, 163
Collier, John 179, 256
Collier, William 61, 84
Collier, William Jr. 12, 70
Collinge, Patricia 235, 251
Collingwood, Peter 302
Collins, Cora Sue 151, 202
Collins, Dale 60
Collins, Jackie 278
Collins, Joan 276
Collins, Norman 302
Collins, Ray 186, 188, 189, 191, 198, 202, 203, 206, 218, 234, 236, 237, 242, 250, 266
Collins, Richard 187, 188, 286
Collins, Tom 151, 158
Collison, Wilson 89, 109, 150, 159
Colman, Ronald 12, 18, 20, 64, 92, 119, 128, 177, 194, 210
Colonna, Jerry 271
Colossus of Rhodes, The 299
Colton, John 46, 49, 64, 72, 102
Columbia Pictures 64, 72, 100, 102, 176, 184, 206, 240, 254, 284, 309, 326
Comden, Betty 210, 224, 227, 249, 254, 270, 296
Come Back, Little Sheba 249
'Come Closer to Me' 209
Come Fly with Me 312
Come Live with Me 163
Comedians, The 336
Comer, Anjanette 322, 325, 340
Comingore, Dorothy 228
Command Decision 218
Como, Perry 219
Company of Cowards 319
Complete Surrender 76
Compson, Betty 39
Compton, Fay 312
Compton, Joyce 143, 151, 165, 216
Compton, Juliette 92, 115
Compulsion 291
Comrade X 165
'Concerto in F' 247
Confessions of a Queen 24
Confidentially Connie 253
Congo Maisie 150
Congress Dances 82
Conklin, Chester 21
Conklin, Heinie 46
Conklin, Peggy 127
Conn, Harry 110
Connell, Richard 20, 120, 177, 187, 192, 201, 203, 219
Connelly, Christopher 361, 364
Connelly, Edward 15, 21, 23, 27, 35, 39, 51, 65
Connelly, Marc 35, 60, 132, 162, 168, 176, 214
Connery, Sean 281, 310, 316, 322, 326, 330, 358, 366
Connolly, Mike 273
Connolly, Myles 172, 180, 192, 209, 214, 218
Connolly, Walter 125, 127, 143, 145, 146
Connor, Kenneth 350
Connors, Barry 44
Connors, Chuck 250, 278, 281, 311, 350, 367
Conquest 136
Conrad, Joseph 36
Conrad, William 225, 228, 236, 240, 258
Conreid, Hans 231, 237, 242, 243, 257
Conroy, Frank 78, 82, 98, 105, 132,
Considine, John W. Jr. 91, 103, 105, 110, 112, 117, 120, 122, 131, 132, 138, 139, 140, 141, 147, 154, 159, 163, 169, 171, 172, 174, 179, 183, 186,
Considine, Robert 209
Considine, Tim 251, 264
Conspirator 228
Conte, John 187, 197
Conte, Richard 224, 273
Conti, Albert 69, 78, 81, 89
Contino, Dick 294
Conway, Jack 21, 30, 31, 43, 46, 51, 52, 56, 57, 60, 71, 72, 75, 78, 82, 84, 87, 90, 94, 95, 100, 103, 105, 117, 119, 125, 131, 134, 145, 146, 147, 165, 169, 171, 176, 184, 198, 210, 214, 216
Conway, Tom 165, 168, 169, 171, 172, 176, 177, 181
Coogan, Jackie 7, 8, 12, 27, 31, 41, 42, 69, 286, 294, 322, 347
Cook, Clyde 15, 77, 81, 84, 182, 188
Cook, Donald 86, 103, 107, 111, 115, 117
Cook, Elisha Jr. 135, 171, 209, 269, 298, 331, 339, 367
Cook, Whitfield 203, 208, 214, 219
Cool Breeze 362
Cooley, Hallam 22
Coolidge, Calvin 36
Coolidge, Philip 289, 291
Coombs, Jackie 35
Cooper, Dorothy 219, 220, 235, 243, 249
Cooper, Gary 54, 90, 103, 120, 128, 138, 141, 166, 184, 185, 206, 223, 240, 242, 249, 262, 278, 284, 293
Cooper, George 32, 57
Cooper, Gladys 192, 198, 202, 208, 209, 214, 218, 220, 222, 224, 228
Cooper, Inez 169, 179, 182, 183, 224
Cooper, Jackie 77, 84, 95, 107, 119, 122, 127, 138, 165, 168, 384
Cooper, Jeanne 362
Cooper, Jeff 345
Cooper, John 287
Cooper, Melville 117, 127, 132, 142, 160, 177, 183, 233, 225, 268, 273
Cooper, Merian C. 141, 218
Cooper, Stuart 337
Coote, Robert 134, 143, 219, 225, 240, 249, 250, 251, 268, 274, 284, 311, 345
Copland, Aaron 211
Coppel, Alex 292, 309
Coppola, Sam 361
Coquette 54
Corbett, Harry H. 289
Corbucci, Sergio 304
Corby, Ellen 216, 228, 243, 253, 333
Corcoran, Donna 243, 250, 251, 259, 261, 268
Corcoran, Hugh 258
Corcoran, Noreen 249, 257
Cord, Alex 344
Corday, Marcelle 35
Corday, Paula 242, 251, 252
Cordell, Ricky 333, 345
Core, Virginia 289
Corey, Jeff 237, 329, 361
Corey, Wendell 218, 228, 240, 243, 251, 253, 275
Corky 361
Cormack, Bartlett 123, 172
Corman, Gene 362, 365, 367
Corn is Green, The 201
Cornell, Katharine 185
Cornwell, Judy 352
Corri, Adrienne 306, 325
Corridors of Blood 306
Corrigan, Lloyd 156, 159, 172, 173, 178, 182, 192, 209, 216
Cort, Bud 352, 357
Cortese, Valentina 225, 306, 344
Cortez, Bella 300
Cortez, Ricardo 27, 39, 44, 70, 87, 91, 112
Corwin, Norman 261, 274
Cosmopolitan Productions 7, 8, 12, 103
Cossacks, The 44
Cossart, Ernest 121, 147
Costa, Mary 365
Costello, Dolores 31, 286
Costello, Don 168, 171, 172
Costello, Helene 31, 40
Costello, Lou 166, 177, 185, 197, 223, 240
Costello, Maurice 31
Cotler, Gordon 307
Cott, Jonathan 242, 243, 244, 249, 250, 251, 252, 257, 258
Cotten, Joseph 194, 232, 244, 299, 326, 338, 367
Coughlin, Kevin 345
Coulouris, George 97, 184, 216, 278, 280, 300, 344
Count Your Blessings 292
Country Bumpkin, The 126
Country Dance 352
Country Girl, The 262, 277
Couper, Barbara 351

'Couple of Swells, A' 220
Courage of Lassie 206
Court, Joanne 304
Courtenay, Tom 313, 322, 325
Courtland, Jerome 225, 257
Courtneidge, Cicely 82, 117
Courtney, Alan 360
Courtney, Inez 127, 154
Courtship of Andy Hardy, The 173,
Courtship of Eddie's Father, The 310
Covered Wagon, The 10, 30
Cowan, Jerome 166, 169, 225, 331
Cowan, Lester 257
Cowan, Sada 10
Coward, Noel 57, 80, 97, 156, 172, 176, 201
Cowen, William 85, 132
Cowl, Jane 169
Cowley, Joy 360
Cowling, Bruce 213, 224, 225, 231, 235, 236, 238, 242
Cox, Wally 317
Coxe, George Harmon 122, 132, 202
Crabbe, Buster 168
Craig, James 179, 187, 188, 190, 191, 194, 196, 203, 204, 206, 213, 222, 228, 238, 244, 258
Craig, Michael 352
Craig, Nell 173, 182, 183, 196
Craig, Yvonne 311, 320, 322, 331
Crain, Jeanne 277, 339, 364
Cram, Mildred 82
Crane, Harry 186, 197, 204
Crane, Norma 276, 331
Crane, Phyllis 66
Crane, Richard 163
Crane, Stephen 240
Crane, Ward 32
Craven, Frank 95, 117, 126, 138, 147, 180, 186
Craven, John 187, 191
Crawford, Anne 258
Crawford, Broderick 232, 240, 277, 289, 306
Crawford, F. Marion 92
Crawford, Joan 27, 30, 31, 32, 33, 35, 36, 39, 42, 43, 49, 51, 56, 57, 60, 63, 66, 67, 69, 70, 72, 76, 78, 82, 84, 90, 97, 100, 102, 107, 109, 115, 116, 127, 128, 132, 133, 144, 146, 147, 149, 163, 165, 171, 176, 187, 201, 202, 244, 259, 304, 338, 377
Crawford, John 312, 334
Crawford, Kathryn 77, 86
Crawford, Stuart 174, 180
Crazy to Kill 187
Crehan, Joseph 173
Crenna, Richard 327, 361
Cresson, James 362
Crest of the Wave 263
Crews, Laura Hope 86, 112, 127, 145, 147, 152
Crichton, Charles 277
Crichton, Michael 366
Crime Does Not Pay 8, 139, 149, 174, 181, 186, 197
Crimebusters, The 303
Crisis 232, 240
Crisp, Donald 15, 52, 56, 89, 105, 112, 119, 133, 174, 191, 196, 202, 219, 225, 286
Crocker, Harry 36, 43
Croft, Peter 134
Cromwell, Richard 77
Cronin, A.J. 144, 208
Cronyn, Hume 187, 197, 198, 202, 203, 208, 209, 216
Crooks in Clover 97
Crosby, Bing 90, 95, 100, 128, 138, 185, 192, 206, 223, 240, 262, 277, 281, 367, 378
Crosby, Bob 186, 187
Crosby, Cathy 286, 294
Crosby, Gary 322
Crosland, Alan Jr. 294
Crosman, Henrietta 131
Cross, David 289
Cross, Laurence 85
Cross of Lorraine, The 187
Crossroads 176, 188
Crothers, Rachel 12, 30, 70, 94, 162, 163, 171
Crouse, Russell 218, 259
Crowd, The 40, 43, 57
Crowd Roars, The 143, 210
Crowden, Graham 360
Crowley, Patricia 298, 313, 322
Croydon, John 278, 287, 306
Cruickshank, Andrew 312, 319
Crutcher, Robert 230
Crutchley, Rosalie 245, 312
Cruze, James 44, 56
Cry Havoc 186, 187
Cry of the Hunted 258
Cry Terror 289
'Cuanto le Gusta' 220
Cuban Love Song 78
Cugat, Xavier 192, 195, 202, 208, 210, 219, 220, 225
Cukor, George 97, 107, 125, 127, 147, 152, 160, 163, 167, 171, 179, 180, 194, 214, 222, 224, 230, 237, 250, 257, 277, 283, 316, 326, 362
Culp, Robert 315, 321
Culver, Michael 351
Culver, Roland 203, 252, 264, 317
Cumming, Dorothy 40, 42, 43, 49, 51, 52
Cummings, Constance 165, 312
Cummings, Jack 105, 123, 128, 139, 140, 141, 156, 162, 180, 191, 195, . 209, 210, 211, 214, 224, 225, 234, 243, 247, 249, 250, 256, 257, 263, 264, 271, 277, 320, 370
Cummings, Robert 163, 168,
Cummings, Ruth 54, 77, 81
Cunningham, Ann 105
Cunningham, Beryl 362
Cunningham, Cecil 74, 146, 147, 156, 162, 169, 179, 183, 187
Cunningham, E.V. 331
Cunningham, Jack 42, 46, 52
Curie, Eve 191
Currie, Finlay 245, 252, 280, 291, 296, 299, 306
Currier, Frank 12, 19, 20, 21, 31, 36, 43, 44, 51
Curtis, Alan 133, 141, 149, 186
Curtis, Dan 355, 361
Curtis, Donald 186, 187, 198, 201, 202, 203, 206
Curtis, Nathaniel 204, 232
Curtis, Tony 291, 300, 304, 326, 338
Curtiz, Michael 296
Curwood, James Oliver 31
Cusack, Cyril 240, 259, 307, 352
Cushman, Dan 344
Cutts, Patricia 284
Cynthia 214
Cynthia's Secret 213
Cypher, Jon 360
Cyrano de Bergerac 232

Daddy's Gone a-Hunting 24
Dad's Army 358
Dahl, Arlene 216, 222, 225, 231, 232, 234, 236, 242, 243
Dahl, Roald 321, 360
Dailey, Dan 156, 162, 168, 169, 171, 174, 178, 179, 182, 270, 271, 276, 289, 384
Daktari 327
Dale, Esther 147, 149, 151, 154, 162, 163, 214, 242
Dale, Virginia 150
Dalio, Marcel 172, 243, 249, 278, 281, 326, 327, 333
Dall, John 300
Dalmas, Herbert 198
Dalrymple, Ian 143
Dalton, Audrey 268
Dalton, Phyllis 325
Daly, James 346, 361
Daly, Jane: see Gadsden, Jacqueline
d'Amboise, Jacques 263
Damita, Lily 57
Damon and Pythias 304
Damone, Vic 243, 244, 266, 267, 270, 273, 384
Dana, Leora 289, 361
Dana, Mark 304
Dana, Viola 8, 13, 15, 21
Dance, Fools, Dance 66
Dance Madness 24
Dance of the Vampires 338
Dancing Co-Ed 154
'Dancing in the Dark' 254, 378
Dancing Lady 97, 156
Dancing Partner, The 78
d'Andrea, Tom 225, 237
Dandridge, Dorothy 256, 259, 289, 303
Dandridge, Ruby 176, 183, 215
Dane, Clemence 115, 203
Dane, Karl 18, 27, 31, 32, 35, 41, 42, 46, 47, 48, 56, 63, 64, 69, 70
Dane, Patricia 171, 173, 177, 178, 179, 181, 191
Dangerous 109
Dangerous Days of Kiowa Jones, The 333
Dangerous Number 126
Dangerous Partners 203
Dangerous When Wet 259, 380
Daniell, Henry 122, 127, 131, 136, 141, 160, 169, 171, 174, 213, 268, 273, 274, 283
Daniels, Bebe 18
Daniels, Billy 286, 294
Daniels, Gordon 334
Daniels, Henry Jr. 192, 202, 208, 370
Daniels, Mark 171, 172, 181, 183, 213
Daniels, Mickey 43
Daniels, William 27, 98, 115, 127, 307, 345, 347
Dano, Royal 240, 274, 286, 287, 296, 300, 333, 339, 341, 361
Danon, Marcello 365
Danova, Cesare 293, 320, 377
Dante's Inferno 120
Dantine, Helmut 176, 322
Danton, Ray 273, 294
Darby, Kim 338, 352
Darcel, Denise 225, 240, 250, 259
D'Arcy, Roy 24, 27, 30, 31, 32, 33, 35, 36, 42, 43, 47, 51
Dark Angel, The 18
Dark, Christopher 298
Dark Delusion 213
Dark of the Sun 341
Dark Shadows 355, 361
Dark Victory 146
Darling 322
Darling Buds of May, The 289
Darling, Scott 43
Darnell, Linda 210
Darrieux, Danielle 243
Darro, Frankie 30, 95, 131, 135, 243
Darvas, Lily 271
Darwell, Jane 152, 206, 218, 247, 270
da Silva, Howard 176, 179, 180, 225, 317
Dassin, Jules 172, 176, 183, 187, 195, 202, 209, 299
Date with Judy, A 220, 377
Daudet, Alphonse 24
Daughter of Luxury 80
Dauphin, Claude 326, 334
Davalos, Dick 354
Dave Clark Five, The 320
Davenport, Harry 142, 152, 192, 194, 201, 206, 209, 215, 216, 224, 370
Davenport, Marcia 202, 228
Davenport, Nigel 312, 322, 357, 360
Daves, Delmer 56, 60, 64, 71, 77, 84, 94, 256, 286
David and Bathsheba 240
David Copperfield 107, 112, 127
Davidson, Lawford 65
Davidson, Max 12, 27
Davidson, Ronald 313
Davies, H.H. 52
Davies, Irving 275
Davies, Marion 7, 8, 12, 19, 20, 32, 41, 43, 44, 46, 47, 60, 63, 64, 70, 72, 78, 80, 82, 84, 92, 95, 103, 162, 166, 179, 273
Davies, Valentine 302
Davis, Allan 252
Davis, Bette 100, 109, 138, 146, 166, 185, 201, 202, 232, 275, 283, 293, 304
Davis, Clyde Brion 201
Davis, Donald 322
Davis, Frank 43, 117, 123, 127, 140, 142, 146, 286
Davis, Jerry 235, 237, 244, 253, 261
Davis, Jim 202, 206, 214, 327, 339
Davis, Luther 210, 215, 224, 273, 303
Davis, Nancy 222, 228, 237, 242, 243, 250
Davis, Ossie 326
Davis, Owen 169
Davis, Owen Jr. 151, 154
Davis, Richard Harding 273
Davis, Roger 355
Davis, Sammy Jr. 271
Davis, Stringer 311, 313, 319
Davis, Tyrrell 67
Davison, Bruce 352, 360
d'Avril, Yola 67
Daw, Marjorie 43
Dawn, Isabel 142
Dawson, Anthony 293, 312, 337
Day, Alice 51
Day and the Hour, The 313
Day, Annette 336
Day at the Races, A 127, 136
Day, Doris 240, 270, 276, 287, 291, 298, 300, 304, 307, 317, 322, 330, 333, 344, 366, 377
Day, Laraine 149, 150, 151, 158, 163, 165, 168, 172, 173, 174, 179, 180, 195, 198
Day, Lillian 191
Day, Marceline 28, 31, 32, 36, 39, 41, 42, 44, 47, 52
Day of Reckoning 95
Day of Souls, The 35
Day of the Arrow 338
Day of the Evil Gun 341
Day, Robert 287, 306, 312
Day They Robbed the Bank of England, The 299
Daybreak 81
Days of Wine and Roses 310
Dead End 128, 162
Deaf Smith and Johnny Ears 367
Dean, Isabel 303
Dean, James 268, 278
Dean, Jeffrey 133
Dean, Quentin 344, 345
Deane, Hazel 21
Dear Ruth 210
Dearden, Basil 302
Death of a Salesman 249
Death on the Diamond 102
de Beranger, Andre 24, 35
de Brulier, Nigel 18, 76
DeCamp, Rosemary 181, 202, 232, 243, 257, 264
De Carlo, Yvonne 250, 314, 338
Decision Against Time 277
Decker, Diana 306
Decker, Marge 237
Decks Ran Red, The 289
Declassee 18
de Concini, Ennio 298, 348
de Cordoba, Pedro 126
de Corsia, Ted 225, 236, 273, 287
de Croisset, François 171
Dee, Frances 261
Dee, Ruby 243, 277
Dee, Sandra 278, 286, 300, 338
Deep in My Heart 267, 377
Deep Throat 362
de Filippo, Eduardo 345
Defiant Ones, The 291
DeFore, Don 184, 198
DeGaw, Boyce 142
Deghy, Guy 302, 317, 341
de Grandcourt, Charles 154
de Grasse, Sam 31
de Grunwald, Anatole 287, 293, 307, 311, 312, 317
de Grunwald, Dimitri 306
DeHaven, Carter 234, 360, 367
DeHaven, Gloria 156, 163, 174, 187, 188, 191, 192, 218, 222, 225, 228, 234, 237
de Havilland, Oliva 152, 206, 293, 303
Dehner, John 250, 268, 273, 277, 338, 354
Dekker, Albert 141, 162, 165, 169, 215
DeKova, Frank 300, 367
de Kruif, Paul 141
de Lacy, Philippe 36, 40
de la Motte, Marguerite 13
Delaney, Charles 39, 43, 51
Delaney, Maureen 287
Delany, Pauline 321, 355
Delevanti, Cyril 316
Delibes, Clement 210
Delilah 197,
Deliverance 362
Dell, Jeffrey 89
Dell, Myrna 244
Delmar, Vina 102, 214
Delon, Alain 317, 326
Del Rio, Dolores 28, 48, 163, 204, 339
Del Ruth, Roy 110, 123, 128, 169, 178, 187, 191, 198
de Luise, Dom 333, 364
Del Valle, Jaime 303
DeMarco Sisters 249
Demarest, William 116, 121, 127, 133, 147, 159, 244, 259, 264, 320
de Marney, Terence 293
Demi-Bride, The 35
DeMille, Cecil B. 10, 41, 44, 61, 67, 69, 80, 232, 238, 249, 274
DeMille, Katherine 103
DeMille, William C. 61, 70
Demongeot, Mylene 298, 319
Dempsey, Jack 36, 92, 133
Deneuve, Catherine 321
Denham, Maurice 252, 278, 302, 327, 333, 350
Denham Studios 134
Denial, The 24
de Night, Fanny Belle 54
de Niro, Robert 361
Denker, Henry 309, 313
Denny, Reginald 67, 72, 78, 80, 92, 115, 117, 125, 133, 181
de Paul, Gene 263
Der, Ricky 312
Deray, Jacques 312
Derr, Richard 208, 216, 219
de Saint-Exupery, Antoine 98
de Sano, Marcel 35
de Santis, Joe 244, 273, 331
Desert Nights 56
Desert Rider, The 65
Desert Song, The 267
Desert's Toll, The 32
de Sica, Vittorio 268, 299, 303, 339, 345, 348
Design for Scandal 174
Designing Woman 278
Desire Me 214
Despax, Olivier 341
Desperate Search 252
Destry Rides Again 146
De Sylva, B.G. 182
De Sylva, Brown and Henderson 71, 210
Detective, The 340
Detective Story 240
Detectives 47
de Toth, Andre 303, 319
Deutsch, Adolph 234
Deutsch, Armand 231, 232, 236, 237, 244, 251, 256, 266, 275, 286
Deutsch, Helen 196, 198, 235, 236, 250, 251, 263, 264, 271, 273, 319
Deval, Jacques 46, 151, 156, 179
Devil Doll, The 122
Devil in Miss Jones, The 362
Devil is a Sissy, The 127, 142
Devil Makes Three, The 253
Devil May Care 60, 67
Devil Takes the Count, The 127
Devil's Brother, The 92
Devil's Circus, The 20
Devil's Doorway 236
Devine, Andy 91, 125, 126, 141, 240, 296, 304, 327
DeVinna, Clyde 46, 77, 95, 107, 117
Devore, Dorothy 16
Devotion 206
Dewhurst, Colleen 360
de Wilde, Brandon 304,
de Wit, Jacqueline 198, 202, 276
DeWitt, Jack 338
Dewlen, Al 313
de Wolf, Karen 209
de Wolff, Francis 252, 306
Dexter, Elliott 80
Dexter, Rosemary 345
Diabolique 268
Dial 1119 236
Diamond, Don 362
Diamond Handcuffs 48
Diamond, I.A.L. 284
Diamonds Are Forever 358
Diane 273
Dick, Douglas 240
Dickens, Charles 107, 119, 143
Dickinson, Angie 289, 294, 339, 360
Dickson, Paul 302
'Did I Remember?' 127
Dierkes, John 240, 250
Dieterle, William 182, 194
Dietrich, Marlene 31, 66, 82, 120, 146, 149, 194
Dietz, Howard 8, 102, 254
Diffring, Anton 346
Digges, Dudley 105, 109, 114, 117, 119, 120, 122
Dighton, John 274, 275
Dignam, Basil 312, 322
Dillaway, Donald 86, 91, 244
Dillman, Bradford 338
Dillon, John Francis 31
Dimbleby, Richard 293
Dime with a Halo 313
Dimsdale, Howard 238
Din, Jalal 333
Dinehart, Alan 123, 142, 151
Dinelli, Mel 235, 252, 280
Dingle, Charles 171, 172, 178, 182, 206, 214, 216, 218, 224, 258
Dinner at Eight 97, 98
Dione, Rose 32, 51
Dirty Dingus Magee 354
Dirty Dozen, The 337
Disney, Walt 8, 21, 44, 102, 138, 156, 184, 222, 284, 316, 340, 352
Divine, David 287
Divine Lady, The 54
Divine Woman, The 42
Divorce in the Family 84
Divorcee, The 67, 81, 105
Dix, Richard 18, 74, 95, 296
Dix, Robert 276
Dix, Tommy 188
Dixie Handicap, The 13
Dixon, Ivan 326
Dixon, Jean 102
Dmytryk, Edward 278
'Do I Love You, Do I?' 187
Dobie, Alan 350
Dock Brief, The 306
Doctor and the Debutante, The 173
Doctor and the Girl, The 228
Doctor Dolittle 340
Dr Gillespie's Criminal Case 187
Dr Gillespie's New Assistant 183
Dr Jekyll and Mr Hyde 105, 174
Dr Kildare Goes Home 158
Dr Kildare's Crisis 158
Dr Kildare's Strange Case 158
Dr Kildare's Victory 173
Dr Kildare's Wedding Day 173
Dr No 310
Dr Strangelove 316
Doctor, You've Got to be Kidding 338
Doctor Zhivago 322, 325, 334, 354
Doctorow, E.L. 339
Doctor's Dilemma, The 287
Dodd, Claire 69, 133, 143, 144
Doff, Red 289, 294, 298
Dolan, Frank 133
Dolenz, George 264
Dominici, Arturo 303
Don Juan 36
Donahue, (Mary) Elinor 215, 294
Donald, James 224, 266, 274
Donat, Robert 144, 149, 182, 186, 203, 351
Donath, Ludwig 247, 331, 344
Donen, Stanley 213, 226, 227, 237, 247, 249, 253, 256, 262, 267, 270
Doniger, Walter 252
'Donkey Serenade, The' 136
Donlan, Yolande 278
Donlevy, Brian 168, 182, 198, 209, 210, 216, 218, 292, 365
Donley, Robert 289
Donnell, Jeff 237, 249, 251
Donnelly, Dorothy 57
Donner, Clive 350
Donner, Robert 367
Donohue, Jack 210, 228, 232, 235
Don't 20
Don't Go Near the Water 283
Don't Make Waves 338
Don't Write Letters 202
Doonan, Patrick 263
Doran, Ann 216, 242, 244, 247
Doran, Mary 49, 54, 56, 66, 69
Dorleac, Francoise 322
Dorn, Philip 164, 168, 172, 176, 177, 182, 197
Dorothy Vernon of Haddon Hall 10
d'Orsay, Fifi 67, 95
Dorsey, Jimmy 191, 197
Dorsey, Tommy 180, 187, 191, 201
Dostoievsky, Feodor 244, 281
Dot and the Line, The 351
Double Indemnity 192, 208
Double Trouble 336
Double Wedding 128
Doucet, Catherine 116, 123, 133
Doucette, John 339
Doughboys 69
Douglas, Burt 281, 286
Douglas, Donald 151, 154, 158, 162, 168, 172
Douglas, Gordon 123
Douglas, James 303, 306
Douglas, Katya 306, 313
Douglas, Kirk 252, 256, 274, 280, 304, 307, 309
Douglas, Marion 51, 65
Douglas, Melvyn 89, 127, 132, 141, 144, 148, 149, 163, 167, 171, 172, 183, 209, 224, 317, 319, 364
Douglas, Paul 243, 253, 266, 280, 289
Douglas, Robert 235, 251, 252, 273, 293, 303
Douglass, Kent: see Montgomery, Douglass
Dove, Billie 66, 84
Down in San Diego 169
Downes, Terry 338
Downing, Joseph 171, 172
Downs, Johnny 100
Downstairs 86
Doyle, Laird 90
Doyle, Maxine 100
Doyle, Monte 320
Doyle, Ray 24
Dracula 74
Drag 54
Drag Net, The 149
Dragon Seed 198
Drake, Betsy 327
Drake, Charles 278
Drake, Fabia 252
Drake, Frances 107, 112, 146, 150, 183
Drake, Tom 192, 196, 198, 206, 208, 209, 213, 215, 219, 222, 225, 278, 329, 333, 384
Drake, William 82
Dramatic School 142
Draper, David 338
Dream of Love 51
Dream Wife 261
Dreams of Monte Carlo 31
Dreier, Alex 361, 364
Dreifuss, Arthur 344, 345
Dreiser, Theodore 74
Dresner, Hal 344
Dresser, Louise 39, 70
Dressler, Marie 41, 44, 51, 58, 63, 66, 69, 70, 71, 76, 77, 82, 90, 95, 97, 100, 102, 174, 176
Drew, Ellen 232
Dreyfuss, Richard 345
Driscoll, Bobby 273
Driskill, William 302
'Drop That Name' 296
Drought, James 346
Dru, Joanne 236
Drums of Africa 313
Drury, James 271, 276, 307
DuBarry was a Lady 187, 277
Dubbins, Don 274, 276, 314
Duchess of Idaho 235
Dudley-Ward, Penelope 144
Duel in the Sun 210
Duell, Charles 12
Duff, Howard 306
Dugan, Tom 123, 126, 136, 166, 186, 201, 210
Duguay, Yvette 244, 261
Duke Steps Out, The 56
Duke, Vernon 183
Dulcy 60, 162
Dull, Orville O. 159, 171, 172, 176, 182, 186, 188, 198, 203, 206, 218
Dullea, Keir 315, 342
Dumas, Alexandre 127
de Maurier, Daphne 293
Dumbrille, Douglass 84, 103, 107, 110, 132, 136, 144, 149, 154, 169, 174, 179, 182, 187, 197, 252, 254, 264
Dumont, Margaret 111, 136, 142, 147, 162, 168, 174, 195
Duna, Steffi 117, 143, 164, 165
Dunaway, Faye 336, 344, 348
Duncan, David 298
Duncan, Mary 78, 80
Duncan Sisters 63

Dunham, Rosemarie 356
Dunkirk 287
Dunn, Emma 76, 84, 131, 132, 139, 142, 143, 150, 158, 171, 174, 201
Dunn, James 103, 201, 210
Dunn, Josephine 44, 48, 56, 57
Dunn, Winifred 13, 15
Dunne, Finley P. 123
Dunne, Irene 74, 77, 97, 128, 184, 198, 210, 296
Dunne, Philip 100
Dunne, Stephen 251
Dunning, John 290
Dunning, Philip and Frances 64
Dunnock, Mildred 251, 299, 306, 329
Dupont, E.A. 117
Dupont, Miss 13, 15
Durante, Jimmy 78, 84, 85, 86, 90, 94, 95, 98, 100, 102, 192, 209, 210, 219, 222, 307, 384
Durbin, Deanna 128, 183, 192, 231, 368
Durham, Marilyn 367
Duryea, Dan 192, 197, 202, 273, 298
Duryea, George 57, 61
Duval, Paulette 10, 13, 21, 31, 35, 42
Duvall, Robert 367
Duvall, Shelley 352
Duvivier, Julien 142, 365
Dvorak, Ann 63, 142, 154, 236, 237
Dwan, Allan 61
Dwyer, Leslie 252
Dwyer, Ruth 21
Dyaliscope 298
Dyall, Valentine 312
Dylan, Bob 366
Dynamite 61

E.M.I. Ltd 352, 355
Eagels, Jeanne 43
Ealing Films 277, 278, 287, 289
Earl, Kenneth 195
Earl of Chicago, The 154, 165,
Earle, Edward 56
Earles, Harry 23, 71
Early, Margaret 156, 165,
Earth II 360
Easiest Way, The 75
Eason, B. Reeves 31
East of the Rising Sun 225
East Side, West Side 228
Easter Parade 220
Eastern Productions 16
Eastman Color 264, 266
Eastman Film 81
Eastwood, Clint 346, 354
Easy Living 128
Easy Rider 352, 355, 368
Easy to Love 256, 380
'*Easy to Love*' 123
Easy to Wed 209
Eaton, Shirley 321, 333, 344
Eberly, Bob 191
Ebsen, Buddy 110, 123, 128, 141, 142, 145, 150, 294, 315, 384
Ebsen, Vilma 110
Eburne, Maude 77, 80, 82, 85, 102, 135
'*Echo of a Serenade*' 195
Eckstine, Billy 249
Ecstasy 146, 149
Eddy, Duane 303
Eddy, Helen Jerome 41, 71, 76, 133, 156
Eddy, Nelson 95, 97, 100, 110, 119, 128, 134, 136, 142, 144, 146, 151, 156, 169, 179, 266, 379
Ede, H.S. 364
Edelman, Lou 77
Eden, Barbara 314, 317
Edens, Roger 156, 201, 204, 220, 227, 234, 267, 307, 319
Edeson, Arthur 119
Edeson, Robert 35
Edge of the City 227
Edinburgh, Duke of 283
Edison the Man 159
Edmond, Terence 319
Edmonds, Louis 355
Edmunds, William 162, 184
Edward My Son 224, 228
Edward VIII 126
Edwards, Alan 105
Edwards, Bill 287
Edwards, Blake 361, 364
Edwards, Cliff 60, 61, 63, 64, 66, 67, 69, 70, 71, 72, 76, 77, 78, 81, 85, 131, 132, 133, 135, 142, 150, 152
Edwards, Glynn 356
Edwards, James 286, 287, 345
Edwards, Meredith 287
Edwards, Snitz 21
Edwards, Vince 264, 281
Edzard, Christine 360
Efraim, Ram Ben 360
Egan, Richard 253
Egg and I, The 210
Eggar, Samantha 355
Eggerth, Marta 178, 187
Ehrhardt, Bess 146
8½ 310
Eilers, Sally 69, 70, 78, 92, 112
Eisinger, Jo 271, 295, 344
Ekberg, Anita 333
Ekland, Britt 344, 355, 356
El Cid 304
Elam, Jack 253, 258, 268, 273, 339, 354, 366
Elder, Lonne III 362
Eldredge, John 126, 158, 169, 203
Eldridge, Florence 67
Eldridge, John 277
Elephant Boy 128
Elfand, Marty 362
Elg, Taina 268, 273, 276, 283, 286, 294, 374
Elinson, Irving 247
Eliot, George 12
Elizabeth II 283
Elkins, Richard 347
Ellenstein, Robert 264, 291
Ellington, Duke 183
Elliot, Jane 364
Elliot, Leslie 331
Elliott, Denholm 355
Ellis, Anderson 162
Ellis, Edith 61, 75, 76
Ellis, Edward 104, 123, 179
Ellis, Patricia 143
Ellison, James 105, 116
Elmer Gantry 296
Elsom, Isobel 183, 209, 224, 267, 273, 274
Elvis on Tour 364
Elvis – That's the Way It is 352, 360
'*Embraceable You*' 191
Emerson, Faye 257
Emerson, Hope 230, 240
Emerson, John 125, 135
Emerson, Ralph 42
Emery, Gilbert 70, 76, 126, 142, 171, 174
Emery, John 180, 181, 184, 271
Emery, Katherine 181
Emma 77
Emperor's Candlesticks, The 132, 133
Enders, Robert J. 303, 347, 352
Endore, Guy 112, 117, 122, 188
Enemy, The 36
Enemy Territory 144
Engh, Karin 348
English, John 39
Englund, George 295, 321, 341, 345
Enterprise Studio 216, 224
Enters, Angna 190, 214
Epstein, Julius 264, 271, 303
Epstein, Philip 264
Erdman, Richard 286
Erickson, Leif 136, 174, 243, 247, 251, 277, 280
Ericson, John 235, 264, 266, 317
Errol, Leon 154, 159
Erskine, Chester 203
Erskine, John 273
Erskine, Marilyn 242, 251, 253, 261
Ertz, Susan 312
Erwin, Stuart 91, 95, 102, 103, 107, 109, 116, 122, 126, 214
Escapade 112
Escape 164
Escape from East Berlin 307
Escape from Fort Bravo 259
Eskimo 95, 117
Esmond, Carl 179, 182, 183, 203, 204
Esmond, Jill 177, 180, 198
Espionage 132
Essanay Pictures 30
Essex, Harry 367
Estabrook, Howard 107, 191, 240
Estridge, Robin 313, 338
Esway, Alexander 187
Eternal Return 210
Eternal Youth 42
Etting, Ruth 270
Eustral, Anthony 186
Evans, Edith 321
Evans, Joan 249
Evans, Madge 76, 78, 80, 84, 85, 90, 92, 94, 95, 97, 102, 105, 107, 109, 116, 126, 131, 132
Evans, Maurice 244, 331, 338, 360
Evans, Max 319
Evans, Muriel 86
Evans, Peggy 244
Evans, Rex 284
Evelyn, Judith 281
Evelyn Prentice 105, 154
Everest, Barbara 194, 202, 283
Everett, Chad 320, 327, 333, 334, 339, 345
Everton, Paul 142
Every Little Crook and Nanny 364
'*Every Little Movement*' 187
Every Other Inch a Lady 154
Every Sunday 136
Everybody Sing 136
'*Everybody Tap*' 63
Everybody's Cheering 226
'*Everything I Have is Yours*' 97
Everything I Have is Yours 249, 377
'*Everything's Been Done Before*' 116
Everywoman's Man 92
Ewell, Tom 230, 237, 276, 364
Excess Baggage 44, 56, 146
Exchange of Wives, An 24
Exclusive Story 109
Excuse Me 10
Excuse My Dust 247
Executive Suite 266
Exit Smiling 35
Exodus 304
Exquisite Sinner, The 31, 39
Exton, Clive 316
Extraordinary Seaman, The 344, 345
Ex-Wife 67
Eye of the Devil 338
Eyer, Richard 275, 281
Eyes in the Night 181, 202

Fabares, Shelley 322, 333, 334, 344
Fabray, Nanette 254, 384
Fabrizi, Aldo 299, 303, 331
Fabrizi, Mario 302
Factor, Max 145
Fagan, James 87
Faherty, William 340
Fair Co-Ed, The 41, 44
Fairbanks, Douglas 10, 47, 52, 192, 219, 274, 303
Fairbanks, Douglas Jr. 42, 51, 57, 90
Fairbanks, William 43, 51
Fairfax, Beatrice 43
Fairlie, Gerard 244
Faithful in My Fashion 209
Faithless 82
Falk, Peter 331, 344
Falk, Rossella 344
Falkner, J. Meade 268
False Witness 352
Family Affair, A 136, 138
Famous Players Co. 7
Fanny 142
Fantasia 156
Fantastic Voyage 330
Fante, John 159, 253, 333
Fantoni, Sergio 314
'*Farewell, Amanda*' 230
Farewell to Arms, A 90, 284
Farley, Morgan 240, 254, 259
Farmer, Mimsy 339
Farnham, Joseph 44, 60, 66, 71, 72
Farnum, Dorothy 12, 27, 30, 33, 42, 51, 56, 66
Farnum, Dustin 80
Farnum, William 240
Farr, Felicia 331
Farrar, David 280, 294
Farrell, Charles 28
Farrell, Eileen 271
Farrell, Glenda 171, 253, 320
Farrell, Sharon 347
Farrell, Tommy 252
Farrow, John 117, 180, 258
'*Fascinating Rhythm*' 171
Fast and Furious 151
Fast and Loose 151
Fast Company 144, 151
Fast Company 257
Fast Life 85
Fast Workers 98
Fastest Guitar Alive, The 339
Fastest Gun Alive, The 277, 281
Father of the Bride 232, 233, 238
Father's Little Dividend 238
Fauchois, Rene 97
Faulds, Andrew 302
Faulkner, James 365
Faulkner, Virginia 146
Faulkner, William 90, 228
Faust 125
Fawcett, George 10, 20, 33, 36, 40, 42, 43, 57, 61
Faye, Alice 120, 138
Faye, Julia 60, 61, 80
Faylen, Frank 163, 195, 327
Fazan, Adrienne 284
Fazenda, Louise 13, 32, 78, 105, 111
Fearless Fagan 253
Fearless Vampire Killers, The 338
Feist Music 9
Feld, Fritz 145, 147, 178, 216
Felisatti, Massimo 362
Felix, Seymour 121
Fell, Norman 322, 345
Fellini, Frederico 310, 322
Fellowes, Rockcliffe 31, 33
Felton, Norman 322, 328, 331
Feminine Touch, The 169
Fenady, Andrew 339
Fenton, Earl 273
Fenton, Frank 159, 225, 240, 244, 258, 259, 276, 333
Fenton, Leslie 60, 111, 122, 126, 138, 149, 154, 159, 163
Ferber, Edna 97, 247, 296
Ferguson, Harvey 143
Fernandez, Emilio 204
Ferrare, Christina 345
Ferrari, William 194
Ferrer, Jose 232, 267, 280, 287
Ferrer, Mel 250, 251, 258, 259, 280, 293, 295
Ferris, Barbara 312
Ferris, Walter 134
Ferry, Jean 307
Fessier, Michael 105, 109, 122, 126, 133
Fetchit, Stepin 40
Feydeau, Georges 333
Feyder, Jacques 58, 76, 81
Fiander, Lewis 306
Fickett, Mary 281
Fiddler on the Roof 362
Field, Arthur 195, 202, 203
Field, Betty 299, 329
Field, Mary 178
Field, Sylvia 56
Field, Virginia 132, 146, 164, 236
Fielding, Marjorie 228
Fielding, Sol 252, 256, 261
Fields, Dorothy 234, 247
Fields, Edward 20, 67
Fields, Gracie 82
Fields, Herbert 140, 182, 234
Fields, Joseph 138, 156, 162, 287
Fields, Leonard 109
Fields, Peter Allan 331
Fields, Stanley 156
Fields, W.C. 12, 100, 107, 218
Fiermonte, Enzo 304, 337
Fiesta 211
52 Miles to Terror 339
Figueroa, Gabriel 204
Filmways Productions 325, 339, 344
Finberg, Hal 169
Finch, Flora 41
Finch, Peter 237, 291, 296, 307, 312, 344
Finch, Scot 361
Fine, Morton 276, 287
Fineman, B.P. 162, 172, 180
Finger, William 348
Fingers at the Window 179
Fink, Harry Julian 344
Finklehoffe, Fred 156, 171, 178, 191, 192, 219
Finlay, Frank 313, 345, 352, 361, 367
Finlayson, Jimmy 86, 92, 110, 120, 136, 143, 237
Finney, Albert 310, 316
Finney, Charles 317
Finney, Jack 281
Fire! 31
Fire Brigade, The 31
Firefly, The 136
First Hundred Years, The 142
First Man into Space 287
First National 7, 28, 40, 168, 171
Fisher, Bob 314, 345
Fisher, Eddie 299
Fisher, Steve 208, 213
Fitch, Clyde 266
Fitts, Margaret 218, 232, 250, 268
Fitzgerald, Barry 172, 192, 275
Fitzgerald, Edith 67, 74, 80, 90, 103, 126
Fitzgerald, F. Scott 24, 28, 141, 152, 264
Fitzgerald, Geraldine 360
Fitzgerald, Walter 224, 277, 281
Fitzmaurice, George 76, 81, 89, 123, 127, 132, 135, 141
Fitzpatrick Traveltalks 8
Fitzroy, Emily 12, 13, 20, 24, 39, 40, 43, 57, 114
Fitzsimmons, Cortland 102, 123
Five and Ten 80
Five Easy Pieces 352
Five-Man Army, The 346
Five O'Clock Girl, The 72
Five Star Final 172
Fix, Paul 315, 339, 341, 354, 365, 366
Fixer, The 345
Flaherty, Robert 46
Flame and the Flesh 263
Flame Within, The 111
Flaming Frontiers, The 31
Flare-Up 347
'Flash' 46, 47, 181
Flaubert, Gustave 228
Flavin, James 181, 209
Flavin, Martin 67, 76
Fleischer, Richard 258, 360, 367
Fleming, Eric 333
Fleming, Rhonda 281
Fleming, Victor 84, 89, 92, 97, 107, 116, 132, 145, 151, 152, 174, 181, 184, 201, 206
Flemyng, Gordon 345
Flemyng, Robert 228
Flesh 87
Flesh and the Devil 28, 33, 40, 43
Fletcher, Bramwell 177, 182
Flick, Pat C. 136
Flicker, Theodore 334
Flight Command 158
Flippen, Jay C. 228, 244, 273, 276, 320
Flippen, Ruth Brooks 237, 245, 315, 320
Flipper 311, 321, 327
Flipper and the Pirates 321
Flipper's New Adventure 321
Flirting with Fate 143
Florodora Girl, The 72
Florian 163
Flournoy, Richard 123, 136
Fluellen, Joel 289
Flying Down to Rio 90
Flying Fleet, The 51, 110
Flying High 77
Flynn, Errol 109, 222, 224, 235, 284
Flynn, John 360, 367
Foa, Arnoldo 299, 300, 304, 345
Foch, Nina 247, 250, 257, 266
Fodor, Ladislas 122, 179, 224, 289
Follies 67
Follow the Boys 312
Follow the Fleet 270
'*Following You*' 63
Folsey, George 121
Fonda, Henry 120, 128, 268, 304, 317, 339
Fonda, Jane 304, 312, 315, 317, 346, 358
Fonda, Peter 321
Fontaine, Joan 147, 166, 176, 252, 278
Fontanne, Lynn 80, 145, 169, 220
Fontini, Cleto 317
Foolish Wives 27
Foote, Bradbury 128, 139, 159, 213
Foote, John T. 147
For Me and My Gal 178
For The First Time 295
For Whom the Bell Tolls 184
Forbes, Brenda 176, 198
Forbes, Bryan 316
Forbes, J.G. 64
Forbes, Mary 64, 67, 97, 117, 136, 146, 151, 194
Forbes, Ralph 36, 39, 43, 47, 48, 67, 70, 87, 95, 100, 105, 107, 116, 125, 126, 131, 132
Forbidden Hours 51
Forbidden Planet 276, 281
Force of Evil 216
Ford, Constance 273, 299
Ford, Corey 147
Ford, Dorothy 208
Ford, Ford Maddox 36
Ford, Glenn 228, 235, 250, 252, 268, 269, 271, 273, 274, 277, 283, 286, 287, 292, 296, 302, 310, 319, 326, 339, 341, 350, 384
Ford, Grace 133
Ford, Harrison 20
Ford, John 10, 87, 156, 166, 202, 218, 249, 256, 276, 304, 321, 329
Ford, Paul 277, 336
Ford, Wallace 78, 82, 84, 85, 104, 122, 156, 187, 208, 326
Foreign Correspondent 156
Foreign Devils 43
Forestal, Sean 357
Forever Amber 210
Forever Darling 271
Forlong, Michael 287, 302
Forrest, Allan 27
Forrest, George 273
Forrest, Sally 236, 243, 244, 247, 258
Forrest, Steve 250, 251, 256, 261, 263, 264, 271, 281
Forsaking All Others 107
Forsyte Sage, The 224
Forsythe, John 259
Fort, Garrett 122
Fortune and Men's Eyes 358
Fortune, Jan 171, 178
Forty Little Mothers 163
42nd Street 90
Forward March 69
Forwood, Anthony 258
Fosse, Bob 256, 257, 362
Fossey, Brigitte 277
Foster, Barry 287, 354
Foster, Julia 355
Foster, Norman 78, 82, 84, 117, 250, 252
Foster, Phoebe 115
Foster, Preston 102, 202, 203, 204
Four Cents a Word 162
4.50 from Paddington 302
Four Girls in White 145
Four Horsemen of the Apocalypse, The 7, 10, 302, 310
Four Marys, The 136
Four Walls 51, 102
Fowldes, Derek 333
Fowler, Gene 154, 168, 224
Fowley, Douglas 100, 146, 154, 159, 182, 186, 210, 213, 214, 225, 236, 242, 243, 249, 261
Fox, Bernard 331, 333
Fox, Edward 237
Fox Films 28, 36, 44, 74, 82, 87, 100, 104, 109, 126, 128, 141, 150, 151, 156, 163, 173, 176, 192, 206, 210, 215, 220, 223, 254, 268, 274, 284, 304, 322, 340
Fox, James 237
Fox Movietone Follies 63
Fox, William 7, 9
Foxe, Earle 66
Foy, Eddie Jr. 296
Fra Diavolo 92
France, C.V. 134
Francen, Victor 191, 209, 271
Franciosa, Anthony 280, 298, 304, 360
Francis, Alec B. 21, 24, 64, 76, 94, 100, 107
Francis, Anne 218, 264, 266, 268, 273, 275, 276, 281, 283
Francis, Connie 298, 312, 320, 327
Francis, Freddie 327
Francis, Kay 67, 74, 76, 82, 90, 169
Francis, Raymond 277
Francisci, Pietro 327
Francois, Jacques 224
Frank, Gerold 273
Frank, Harriet Jr. 299
Frank, Leonhard 214
Frank, Melvin 216, 234, 242, 243, 251
Frank, Milo Jr. 287
Franken, Rose 98, 208
Frankenheimer, John 304, 334, 344, 345, 346
Frankenstein 74, 85
'*Frankie and Johnny*' 271
Franklin, Chester 15, 39, 47, 105, 122, 242
Franklin, Gloria 146
Franklin, Irene 112, 136, 143
Franklin, Pamela 321, 339
Franklin, Sidney 32, 41, 47, 49, 56, 60, 67, 72, 80, 87, 90, 105, 127, 141, 148, 154, 162, 164, 176, 177, 191, 198, 206, 218, 237, 256, 257, 275
Franklin, Sidney Jr. 252, 253, 259, 261
Frantz, Dalies 151
Franz, Arthur 228, 243
Franz, Eduard 228, 232, 242, 247, 249, 251, 261
Fraser, Bill 252, 350
Fraser, Elisabeth 287, 291, 326, 333
Fraser, John 322
Fraser, Liz 319
Fraser, Moyra 358
Fraser, Ronald 311, 313
Fraser, Sally 273
Frassinetti, Augusto 298
Fraternally Yours 95
Frawley, William 146, 189, 228
Frazer, Dan 368
Frazer, Robert 15, 20, 65
Frazier, Sheila 368
Freaks 85
Frechette, Mark 348
Frederici, Blanche 57
Frederick, Lynne 357
Frederick, Pauline 13, 57, 76
Free and Easy 69
Free and Easy 168
Free Soul, A 75, 76
Freed, Arthur 49, 56, 61, 67, 152, 156, 171, 178, 182, 183, 187, 188, 191, 192, 201, 203, 204, 209, 210, 216, 219, 220, 224, 226, 227, 228, 232, 234, 237, 247, 249, 254, 257, 266, 270, 273, 275, 283, 284, 296, 298, 302, 358, 370, 374
Freed, Bert 224, 230, 263, 298, 313, 355
Freedman, Danny 358
Freedman, Jerrold 362
Freeman, Devery 228, 232
Freeman, Everett 136, 140, 242, 251, 315, 333, 344, 347, 352
Freeman, Helen 192
Freeman, Howard 180, 186, 188, 189, 190, 215, 218, 250, 251, 259
Freeman, Joan 339
Freeman, Joel 361
Freeman, Kathleen 247, 252, 257, 266, 319, 338
French, Charles 24
French Connection, The 358
French, Harold 252
French, Hugh 215
French, Leslie 339
Frend, Charles 278
Freshman, The 18
Freuchen, Peter 95
Freund, Karl 112, 127, 136, 142, 151
Frid, Jonathan 355
'Friday' 181, 202
Friedkin, David 276, 287
Friedkin, William 358
Friedman, Alan 186, 202, 203
Friendly Persuasion 274
'*Friendship*' 187
Friganza, Trixie 20, 31, 69
Friml, Rudolf 119, 136
Frisco Sally Levy 43
Frobe, Gert 327, 365
Froeschel, George 162, 164, 172, 176, 177, 198, 218, 237, 247, 250, 256, 264, 266, 271
From Here to Eternity 262
From Russia with Love 316
'*From This Moment On*' 257
Fromkess, Leon 347
Frontier Rangers 294
Frontiersman, The 43
Frost, David 311
Frou-Frou 141

Fruit of the Poppy 339
Fry, Christopher 290
Fryd, Joseph 317, 319, 327, 337
Fryer, Robert 362
Fuchs, Daniel 270
Fugitive Lovers 94
Fukasaku, Kinji 348
Fuller, Dale 16, 21
Fullerton, Melanie 365
Fulop-Miller, Rene 224
Fung, Willie 150
Funny Face 201
Funny Girl 340
Furber, Douglas 39
Furia, John Jr. 333
Furness, Betty 102, 109, 112, 122, 123, 135
Furse, Jill 149
Furse, Judith 149
Furthman, Jules 97, 114, 119
Fury 123
Fury River 294

Gaal, Franciska 143
Gabel, Martin 281, 303
Gabel, Scilla 306
Gable, Christopher 358
Gable, Clark 18, 66, 74, 75, 76, 78, 80, 81, 82, 85, 91, 92, 97, 98, 100, 103, 104, 105, 107, 109, 112, 114, 116, 119, 120, 125, 126, 127, 128, 131, 133, 145, 150, 152, 165, 166, 168, 169, 178, 179, 185, 201, 208, 210, 218, 222, 228, 230, 237, 240, 242, 243, 256, 264, 274, 309, 377
Gabor, Eva 264, 283, 284, 292, 384
Gabor, Zsa Zsa 249, 251, 256, 295, 306, 338, 384
Gabriel Over the White House 92
Gaby 276
Gaby, Alex 339
Gadsden, Jacqueline 13, 21, 39, 47, 56
Gaines, Richard 202, 210, 273
Gale, Richard 237
Gallagher, Skeets 78, 100, 132, 145
Gallant Bess 206
Gallant Sons 165
Gallaudet, John 149, 209, 228, 236, 243, 249, 276, 289, 298
Gallian, Ketti 132
Gallico, Paul 172, 204, 251, 284, 294
Gallico, Pauline 204
Galsworthy, John 224
Gam, Rita 259, 300
Gambler, The 224
Gance, Abel 44
Gang That Couldn't Shoot Straight, The 361
Gangelin, Paul 172,
Ganzer, Alvin 327, 331
Gaon, Yehoram 368
Garbo, Greta 8, 24, 27, 28, 33, 40, 42, 49, 51, 52, 57, 58, 63, 67, 69, 74, 76, 82, 84, 89, 98, 103, 107, 120, 127, 136, 138, 145, 148, 167, 179, 187, 190, 202, 214, 228, 283, 300, 317, 347
Garden Murder Case, The 122
Garden of Allah, The 36
Gardiner, Becky 54, 71
Gardiner, John 306
Gardiner, Reginald 123, 136, 141, 143, 162
Gardner, Ava 196, 203, 210, 219, 222, 224, 228, 240, 247, 256, 258, 277, 289, 296, 299, 316, 362, 384
Gardner, Fred 348
Gardner, John 331
Garfield, Allen 360, 366
Garfield, John 181, 208, 216
Gargan, Edward 149, 173
Gargan, William 98, 143, 147, 149, 159, 186, 188, 195
Garland, Judy 8, 128, 135, 136, 138, 139, 151, 152, 156, 158, 166, 168, 171, 173, 174, 178, 182, 187, 191, 192, 201, 204, 208, 209, 219, 220, 222, 224, 225, 234, 237, 247, 327, 368, 370
Garner, James 306, 310, 313, 319, 321, 333, 334, 347, 364
Garner, Peggy Ann 235
Garnett, Tay 114, 186, 187, 192, 202, 208, 235, 240, 257, 313
Garnett, Tony 352
Garon, Pauline 12
Garrani, Ivo 304
Garrett, Betty 219, 222, 225, 226, 227
Garrett, George 321
Garrett, Grant 186, 198, 203, 206
Garrett, Oliver H.P. 98, 103
Garrett, Otis 116, 119
Garrone, Ricardo 309
Garson, Greer 8, 146, 147, 149, 160, 169, 171, 177, 185, 187, 191, 192, 198, 201, 202, 203, 206, 214, 216, 222, 224, 237, 244, 254, 261, 264, 333, 351
Garsten, Paul 341
Garstin, Crosbie 114
Gary, Romain 326
Gaslight 194
Gassman, Vittorio 250, 258, 264, 345
Gastoni, Lisa 337
Gates, Harvey 39, 81, 120
Gates, Larry 251, 289, 302, 313
Gates, Nancy 289
Gateson, Marjorie 103, 107, 139, 143, 191
Gaumont British 109, 327
Gaumont (France) 321
Gavin, John 284
Gaxton, William 188
Gay Bride, The 105
Gay Deceiver, The 31, 35
Gay, John 302, 310, 338
Gay Mrs Trexel, The 163
Gay Nineties, The 72
Gaye, Gregory 135, 145, 148, 214
Gaye, Lisa 294
Gaynor, Janet 28, 44, 100, 126, 128, 143, 249
Gaynor, Mitzi 283, 290, 374
Gazebo, The 292
Gebler, Ernest 250
Geer, Will 228, 237, 243, 357
Geller, Bruce 361
General, The 216
General Motors 240
General Spanky 123
Genevieve 262
Genn, Leo 237, 245, 250, 280
Gentle Annie 194
Gentleman's Fate 78
Gentlemen Prefer Blondes 44, 91
George, Florence 149
George, Gladys 57, 102, 131, 132, 134, 141, 213
Georgy Girl 330
Geraghty, Maurice 183
Geraghty, Thomas 20
Geray, Steve 180, 181, 189, 197, 198, 238, 292
Gershwin, George 128, 156, 171, 191, 201, 247, 372
Gershwin, Ira 191, 256
Gershwin, Jerry 339
Get Carter 356, 362
'*Get Happy*' 237
Get Yourself a College Girl 320
Getaway, The 168
Getaway, The 366
Getchell, Sumner 151
Getting Gertie's Garter 319
Getz, Stan 320
Geva, Tamara 145
Gheorghiu, C.V. 333
Ghost Comes Home, The 163
Ghosts, Italian Style 345
'*Giannina Mia*' 136
Giant 278
Giant of Marathon, The 298, 303
Gibbons, Cedric 8, 57, 100, 107, 119, 141, 169, 194, 206, 297, 252, 254, 277
Gibson, Hoot 30
Gibson, William 273
Gibson, Wynne 72, 143
Giddings, Nelson 312
Gielgud, John 254, 275, 309, 325, 345
Gifford, Allan 341
Gifford, Frances 186, 196, 201, 203, 204, 206, 215, 219
Gigi 284, 379
Gilbert, Billy 86, 117, 123, 128, 132, 143, 201, 216
Gilbert, Helen 150, 163, 192
Gilbert, Joanne 287
Gilbert, John 8, 10, 13, 15, 16, 18, 24, 27, 30, 33, 35, 40, 43, 44, 47, 51, 56, 57, 63, 64, 66, 67, 77, 78, 86, 98, 102, 115
Gilbert, Leatrice Joy 139
Gilberto, Astrud 320
Gilchrist, Connie 168, 169, 171, 172, 173, 174, 179, 181, 183, 186, 187, 188, 192, 203, 209, 210, 213, 214, 216, 219, 232, 261, 289
Gilda 206
Giler, Berne 242, 312, 317
Gilford, Jack 333
Gillen, Ernest 27
Gilles, Alfred 247
Gillespie, A. Arnold 125, 127, 214, 290
Gillespie, Gina 289
Gilliatt, Sidney 134
Gillin, Linda 352
Gillingwater, Claude 13, 102, 117, 119, 134
Gillmore, Margalo 235, 236, 244, 149, 261, 276, 277
Gilmore, Douglas 31, 32, 33
Gilmore, Lowell 194, 215, 224, 240, 250
Gilmore, William, Jr. 364
Gilroy, Frank 277, 344
Gingold, Hermione 284
Ginna, Robert Emmett 321, 339, 352
Girardot, Annie 321
Girardot, Etienne 116, 127, 142, 151
Girl and the General, The 337
Girl Crazy 191, 327
Girl Downstairs, The 143
Girl from Missouri, The 100
Girl from Trieste, The 128
Girl Happy 322
'*Girl Hunt, The*' 372
Girl I Made, The 92
Girl in Overalls, The 187
Girl in the Show, The 69
Girl in White, The 251
Girl of the Golden West, The 142
Girl Said No, The 66
Girl Who Had Everything, The 256
Girls Town 294
Girotti, Massimo 319
Gish, Dorothy 12
Gish, Lillian 12, 24, 35, 36, 44, 52, 66, 92, 201, 273, 274, 336
Gist, Robert 224, 225
Give a Girl a Break 256
'*Give Peace a Chance*' 352
Givney, Kathryn 242
Givot, George 133, 187
Gladiators 7 317
Glamorama 255
Glasmon, Kubec 182
Glass Bottom Boat, The 333
Glass Slipper, The 264
Glazer, Benjamin 13, 15, 27, 31, 33, 44, 48, 76, 181
Gleason, James 48, 75, 78, 84, 94, 110, 171, 184, 198, 204, 228, 230
Gleason, Keogh 247, 252
Gleason, Lucille 95, 204
Gleason, Russell 179, 186
Gleckler, Robert 135, 143
Glenn Miller Story, The 262
Glenville, Peter 333, 336
Glicksman, Frank 360
Gloag, John 339
Global Affair, A 314
Glory Alley 250
Glover, Julian 333, 350
Glyn, Elinor 21, 31, 298
Go for Broke! 242
Go Naked in the World 298
Go West 21
Go West 162
Goddard, Paulette 142, 147
Godfather, The 362
Godfrey, Arthur 333
God's Little Acre 284
Godsol, F.J. 7
Goetz, Ben 134
Goetz, Hayes 244, 252, 253, 333
Goff, Ivan 266
Going Hollywood 95
Going Home 361
Going My Way 192
Golan, Menahem 368
Gold Diggers of 1933 90
Gold for the Caesars 319
Gold, Lee 183
Gold Rush, The 18
Gold Rush Maisie 159
Goldbeck, Willis 20, 36, 48, 49, 56, 85, 139, 150, 158, 173, 182, 183, 186, 187, 196, 203, 208, 213
Goldberg, Mel 303
Golden Arrow, The 320
Golden Boy 119, 138
Golden Fleecing, The 159
Golden, John 69
Golden, Ray 169, 192
Golden, Robert 46
Goldfinger 322
Goldman, Danny 352
Goldman, Harold 123, 132, 143, 165
Goldman, Les 351
Goldner, Charles 263
Goldoni, Lelia 327
Goldstone, James 361, 364
Goldstone, Philip 109, 116, 117, 119
Goldstone, Richard 228, 236, 243, 250, 252, 253
Goldwyn Pictures 7, 8, 18, 24, 69, 82, 182, 206
Goldwyn, Samuel 7, 18, 39, 42, 69, 81, 107, 163, 271
Goldwyn, Samuel Jr. 296, 321
Golgolka, John 339
Gombell, Minna 100, 104, 142, 143, 165, 237
Gomberg, Sy 234, 237
Gomez, Thomas 216, 231, 235, 247, 249, 250, 344
Gone With The Wind 116, 141, 146, 152, 172, 174, 201, 244, 278, 296, 300, 322, 325, 340, 362
Gonzales-Gonzalez, Pedro 286
Good Earth, The 127, 132, 198
'*Good Morning*' 152
Good News 71, 210, 377
Good Old Soak, The 135
Goodbye, Mr Chips 149, 182, 186, 351, 379
Goodfellow, Joan 365
Goodliffe, Michael 252
Goodman, George 313
Goodrich, Frances 94, 97, 103, 104, 110, 119, 123, 136, 147, 149, 220, 225, 233, 238, 242, 256, 263, 276
Goodrich, John 86
Goodrich, William 32
Goodwin, Bill 195
Goodwin, Harold 44
Goodwin, Richard 360
Gorcey, Leo 133, 165, 169, 174, 178, 179
Gordon, Bobby 100
Gordon, C. Henry 76, 84, 85, 87, 90, 91, 92, 94, 95, 97, 102, 103, 104, 107, 112, 136
Gordon, Colin 252
Gordon, Eve 95
Gordon, Gale 344
Gordon, Gavin 67, 76, 77
Gordon, Huntley 8, 20, 32
Gordon, James 313, 333
Gordon, Julia Swayne 19, 39
Gordon, Leo 294, 304
Gordon, Leon 85, 86, 94, 107, 116, 117, 122, 126, 132, 134, 147, 151, 156, 162, 168, 180, 182, 187, 192, 208, 225, 235, 252
Gordon, Mary 147
Gordon, Michael 306, 345
Gordon, Ruth 167, 230, 250, 257
Gordon, Vera 51
Gorgeous Hussy, The 127, 240
Gorin, Igor 128
Goring, Marius 271, 295, 333
Gorshin, Frank 296, 298, 303
Gosch, Martin 203
Gossett, Lou 362
'*Got a Feelin' for You*' 377
Gottschalk, Ferdinand 82, 117
Goudal, Jetta 46
Goudge, Elizabeth 214
Gough, Lloyd 216, 225
Gough, Michael 364
Gould, Jay 361
Goulding, Alf 10, 20, 48
Goulding, Edmund 21, 27, 32, 40, 42, 49, 82, 84, 87, 100, 111, 156
Goulet, Robert 319
Gounod, Charles 142
Gowland, Gibson 16, 36, 56, 71
Grable, Betty 100, 185, 187, 206, 240, 277
Grabowski 294
Grad, Genevieve 326
Graduate, The 340
Grady, William Jr. 252, 258, 261
Graff, Robert 321
Grafton, Gloria 186, 203
Grafton, Samuel and Edith 287
Grafton, Sue 365
Graham, James 364
Graham, Sheilah 294
Graham, William 355
Graham, Winston 355
Grahame, Gloria 197, 204, 210, 214, 252, 273, 361
Grainger, Edmund 286, 287, 292, 293, 296, 299
Granach, Alexander 148, 198
Granada, Maria 328
Granado, Manuel 13
Grand Central Murder 181
Grand Hotel 82, 84, 97, 98, 202, 209, 266, 311
Grand Prix 334
Granger, Dorothy 142
Granger, Farley 228, 249, 256
Granger, Stewart 201, 236, 240, 242, 244, 250, 251, 257, 266, 268, 273, 277, 280, 281, 302, 309
Granstedt, Greta 44, 70, 204
Grant, Cary 120, 127, 128, 134, 160, 192, 207, 232, 261, 268, 291, 300, 317, 322, 330, 366
Grant, James Edward 112, 133, 147, 165, 171, 286, 339
Grant, John 197
Grant, Lawrence 13
Granville, Bonita 119, 142, 162, 163, 164, 165, 168, 169, 173, 174, 197, 208
Granville, Charlotte 78
Grapes of Wrath, The 156
Grapewin, Charley 119, 120, 123, 125, 126, 127, 128, 133, 135, 139, 141, 142, 143, 147
Graves, Peter 346
Graves, Ralph 35, 51, 84, 85
Gravet, Fernand 142, 340
Gray, Billy 250
Gray, Charles 280
Gray, Dolores 270, 273, 276, 278, 379
Gray, Gary 234, 237, 242
Gray, Gilda 119, 121
Gray, Harry 54
Gray, Janine 322
Gray, Lawrence 36, 41, 44, 46, 48, 63, 64, 72
Gray, Vernon 275
Grayson, Kathryn 165, 171, 177, 182, 183, 187, 195, 201, 208, 209, 210, 216, 222, 231, 234, 247, 249, 257, 377, 378
Graziano, Rocky 277
Great American Pastime, The 276
Great Caruso, The 247
Great Day 72, 77
Great Diamond Robbery, The 261
Great Divide, The 13
Great Escape, The 310
Great Expectations 210
Great Gatsby, The 28
Great Love, The 21
Great Lover, The 77
Great McGinty, The 156
Great Meadow, The 76
Great Morgan, The 208
Great Secret, The 19
Great Sinner, The 224
Great Waltz, The 142, 340, 365
Great Ziegfeld, The 120, 125, 378
Greatest Show on Earth, The 249
Greco, Jose 250
Greed 16, 27
Greed in the Sun 327
Green, Adolph 210, 224, 227, 249, 254, 270, 296
Green, Alfred E. 135
Green Dolphin Street 214
Green Fire 266
Green, Guy 303, 326
Green Hat, The 51, 100, 107
Green Helmet, The 302
Green, Jane 203, 206, 209, 210
Green, Janet 329
Green, Johnny 220, 247
Green, Karl 333, 345
Green Mansions 293
Green Pastures, The 146, 183
Green Slime 348
Green Years, The 208
Greenberg, Dave 368
Greenberg, Stanley 364, 367
Greenburg, Dan 345
Greene, Clarence 277
Greene, Eve 82, 91, 94, 95, 102, 103
Greene, Graham 336, 362
Greene, Richard 252
Greenleaf, Raymond 228
Greenstreet, Sydney 210, 225
Greenwood, Charlotte 42, 77, 78, 259, 276
Greenwood, Joan 268
Greenwood, Rosamund 299
Greer, Jane 251, 252, 367
Greer, Michael 352, 358
Gregg, Virginia 277, 298, 322
Gregor, Nora 84
Gregory, James 281, 289, 307, 313, 322
Greig, Robert 92, 109, 117, 119, 122, 126, 132, 194
Grenfell, Joyce 317, 319
Grey, Gloria 12
Grey, Virginia 123, 128, 133, 142, 145, 147, 149, 150, 154, 156, 159, 162, 169, 172, 174, 176, 181, 302
Greyfriar's Bobby 225
Gribbon, Harry 44, 46
Grien, Helmut 365
Grier, Pamela 362
Grier, Roosevelt 364
Grierson, Edward 355
Gries, Tom 360
Griffies, Ethel 168, 192, 201
Griffin, Eleanore 135, 204, 214
Griffin, Z. Wayne 230, 240
Griffith, Corinne 18, 66
Griffith, D.W. 30, 35, 218, 274, 300
Griffith, Edward H. 98, 102, 115
Griffith, Hugh 290, 299, 309, 345
Griffith, J.J. 361
Griffith, Kenneth 293
Griffiths, Eldon 253
Grimes, Tammy 331
Grinde, Nick 51, 64, 65, 66, 67, 71, 76
Groccolo, Carlo 317
Groesse, Paul 206
Grosbard, Ulu 344
Grossmith, George 67
Grossmith, Lawrence 194
Grounds for Marriage 234
Gruen, Bernard 151
Gruter, Alexander 295
Guardino, Harry 300, 321, 364
Guardsman, The 80, 169
Guedal, John 123
Guerra, Tonino 336, 338, 345, 348
Guess Who's Coming to Dinner 336
Guest, Val 322
Guetary, Georges 247
Guilfoyle, Paul 147, 198, 259, 269
Guillermin, John 299, 304, 364, 367
Guinness, Alec 249, 274, 278, 293, 325, 333, 336
Guilty Hands 76
Gulf and Western Industries 330
Gun Glory 281
Gunfighters of Casa Grande 328
Gunga Din 146, 240
Gunn, Moses 361, 362
Guns for San Sebastian 340
Guns in the Afternoon 307
Guns of Diablo 317
Guns of Navarone 304
Guns of Wyoming 313
Gutowski, Gene 338
Guy Named Joe, A 184
Guys and Dolls 271, 280
'*G'wan Home, Your Mudder's Calling*' 209
Gwenn, Edmund 117, 122, 126, 133, 134, 154, 160, 179, 191, 202, 203, 208, 214, 219, 222, 225, 266, 273
Gwynn, Michael 287, 299
Gwynne, Anne 174
Gynt, Greta 240
Gypsy 310
Gypsy Colt 261
Gypsy Love 64
Gypsy Moths, The 346

H.M. Pulham, Esq 174
Haade, William 183, 225
Haas, Charles 294, 298
Haas, Hugo 202, 208, 209, 211, 214, 280, 286
Habe, Hans 187
Hackett, Albert 94, 97, 103, 104, 110, 119, 123, 136, 147, 149, 225, 233, 238, 242, 256, 263, 276
Hackett, Buddy 314
Hackett, Raymond 54, 57, 60, 69, 70, 220
Hackett, Walter 132
Hackman, Gene 345, 346, 358
Haden, Sara 112, 119, 122, 132, 136, 138, 143, 145, 147, 149, 150, 154, 156, 158, 162, 165, 171, 172, 173, 174, 182, 183, 187, 188, 190, 191, 197, 203, 204, 208, 237, 289
Hadley, Reed 168, 172, 216
Haffenden, Elizabeth 290
Hageman, Richard 245, 264
Hagen, Jean 222, 228, 230, 231, 237, 238, 242, 243, 249, 251, 258, 261, 362
Haggard, H. Rider 236, 294, 313
Haggerty, Don 242
Hagmann, Stuart 352, 360
Haight, George 172, 173, 183, 187, 189, 196, 197, 198, 202, 203, 208, 213
Haines, Connie 235
Haines, William 8, 12, 15, 16, 23, 24, 27, 28, 30, 35, 41, 42, 43, 46, 47, 51, 56, 63, 64, 66, 69, 72, 78, 80, 85, 150, 162
Haines, William Wister 218, 287
Hairston, William 257
Haislip, Harvey 154, 158, 182
Hakim, Eric 76
Hale, Alan 13, 74, 139, 232
Hale, Alan Jr. 240, 264, 294, 319
Hale, Creighton 12, 24, 27, 32, 36, 251
Hale, Georgina 358
Hale, Jonathan 131, 138, 141, 142, 143, 154, 164, 166, 182, 209
Hale, Louise Closser 82, 84, 86, 90, 92, 97, 98
Halevy, Julian 321, 348
Haley, Bill 268
Haley, Jack 123, 136, 151, 384
Haley, Jack Jr. 368
Half a Hero 258
Halff, Robert 187
Hall, Alexander 188, 242, 251, 271
Hall, Anthony 300
Hall, Dickie 171, 174
Hall, Grayson 316, 355, 361
Hall, James Norman 214
Hall, Jane 151, 231
Hall, Jenni 355
Hall, Porter 103, 104, 154, 169, 186, 202, 228, 250, 251
Hall, Sam 355, 361
Hall, Thurston 122, 144, 174, 191, 209, 214, 249
Hall, Zooey 358
Hallelujah! 54, 183
'*Hallelujah!*' 270
Hallenbeck, E. Darrell 331
Haller, Ernest 152
Halliday, John 132, 160
Halop, Billy 333
Halpin, Luke 311, 321
Halprin, Daria 348, 360
Halsey, Forrest 96
Halton, Charles 136, 203, 218, 261
Hamama, Faten 304
Hamer, Robert 293
Hamill, John 357
Hamilton, Aileen 188
Hamilton, Cosmo 24
Hamilton, George 298, 303, 307, 319, 320, 338, 367, 384
Hamilton, George IV 313
Hamilton, Hale 74, 77, 78, 80, 81, 100, 116
Hamilton, Margaret 98, 135, 139, 151, 152, 183, 209, 218, 352
Hamilton, Neil 76, 77, 81, 84, 85, 86, 89, 107
Hamilton, Patrick 194

Hamlet 223
Hammer Films 327
Hammerstein, Oscar II 72, 107, 142, 156, 171, 191, 218, 257
Hammett, Dashiell 104, 361
Hammond, Harriet 19, 21
Hampden, Walter 250
Hampshire, Susan 316
Hampton, Louise 165
Hampton, Orville 344, 345
Hancock, Sheila 316
Handle With Care 287
Hands of Orlac, The 112
Haney, Carol 275
Hanley, William 346
Hanna, William 8
Hannen, Nicholas 287
Hansen, Myrna 278
Hanson, Lars 27, 33, 35, 42, 52
Hantz, Bob 368
Happiness 13
'*Happiness is a Thing Called Joe*' 183
Happy Anniversary 290
'*Happy Days are Here Again*' 63
Happy Landings 77
Happy Road, The 277
Happy Years, The 236
Harareet, Haya 291, 302, 339
Harbaugh, Carl 12
Harburg, E.Y. 147, 151, 197
Hard Day's Night, A 316
Hardie, Russell 95, 97, 102, 103, 104, 105, 110, 127
Harding, Ann 54, 94, 102, 111, 171, 181, 232, 234, 247
Harding, John B. 216
Harding, Lyn 149
Hardwicke, Cedric 154, 187, 273, 274, 276
Hardy, Francoise 334
Hardy, Oliver 8, 63, 64, 77, 82, 86, 92, 95, 100, 102, 110, 117, 120, 123, 136, 142, 143, 162, 186, 192, 317, 322
Hardy, Robert 287
Hardy, Sam 56, 105
Hardy, Thomas 12
Hardys Ride High, The 150
Hare, Lumsden 107, 149, 174, 195, 219, 225, 254, 257, 292
Hare, Robertson 333
Harem Holiday 327
Harem Scarum 327
Hargreaves, Gerald 300
Hargreaves, Lance 287
Hargreaves, L.Z. 342
Hargrove, Dean 331, 338
Hargrove, Marion 186, 306
Harkrider, John 121
Harlan, Otis 13
Harlan, Russell 274
Harlow, Jean 66, 71, 75, 82, 87, 89, 91, 97, 100, 105, 114, 116, 125, 126, 127, 131, 150, 151, 209, 256, 368
Harmon, David 314
Harper, David 364
Harper, Edward 367
Harper, Kenneth 281
Harrigan, William 112
Harrigan's Kid 186
Harrington, Joseph 173
Harris, Elmer 78, 84, 92, 122
Harris, James B. 306
Harris, Julie 312, 345
Harris, Julius 362
Harris, Marion 60
Harris, Paul E. 367
Harris, Phil 313
Harris, Richard 293, 309
Harris, Roland 367
Harris, Rosemary 266
Harris, Theresa 141, 169
Harrison, Harry 367
Harrison, Kathleen 128
Harrison, Noel 322
Harrison, Rex 144, 201, 257, 286, 316, 317, 340
Harrison, Richard 317
Harrison, Susan 298
Harron, John 32
Hart, Dolores 298, 312
Hart, Frances Noyes 47
Hart, Harvey 358
Hart, Lorenz 97, 100, 152, 179, 219, 307
Hart, Moss 87, 110
Hart, Richard 214, 215
Hart, William S. 47
Hartley, Mariette 307, 313, 360, 364
Hartman, Don 242, 243
Hartman, Elizabeth 326, 345
Hartmann, Edmund 169
Harvey 232
Harvey, Forrester 84, 85, 86, 87, 89, 100, 103, 107, 117, 132, 135, 156, 168, 174
Harvey, Frank 263
Harvey Girls, The 204
Harvey, Laurence 284, 299, 303, 310, 314, 316, 317
Harvey, Paul 132, 203, 209, 214, 228, 232, 234, 238, 247, 259
Harwood, H.M. 77, 94, 98, 131
Harwood, Ronald 313
Haskin, Byron 312, 338
Hasse, O.E. 263, 321
Hasso, Signe 184, 198, 203, 232
Hastings, Hugh 263
Hatch, Eric 134
Hathaway, Henry 304, 316
Hatfield, Hurd 194, 198, 209, 300
Hatful of Rain, A 278
Hatton, Frederic and Fanny 24, 27, 32
Hatton, Raymond 28, 41, 80, 82, 92, 97, 122, 135, 138, 154
Haunted Honeymoon 165
Haunting, The 312
Haupt, Ulrich 64
Havas, Michael 328
Have a Heart 103
'*Have Yourself a Merry Little Christmas*' 192
Havelock-Allan, Anthony 354
Haver, Phyllis 15, 57
Haverback, Hy 344
Havez, Jean 14, 15
Hawkins, Jack 277, 291, 303
Hawks, Howard 90, 103
Hawks, William 286
Hawley, Cameron 266
Hawley, Wanda 15
Hawthorne, Nathaniel 35
Hayakawa, Sessue 293
Haycox, Ernest 183, 253
Hayden, Jeffrey 280
Hayden, Sterling 238, 364
Haydn, Richard 201, 208, 209, 249, 256, 264, 298, 309, 327
Haydon, Julie 122, 136
Haye, Helen 228, 281
Hayes, Alfred 235, 322
Hayes, Bernadene 145, 213, 224
Hayes, Grace 152
Hayes, Helen 76, 86, 90, 92, 98, 105, 112
Hayes, Isaac 361
Hayes, John Michael 259, 273, 299
Hayes, Margaret 268, 294
Hayes, Peter Lind 151
Hayman, Cyd 355
Haynes, Daniel 54
Hays, Will (Hays Office) 87, 290
Hayter, James 244, 266
Hayton, Lennie 227
Hayward, Lillie 12, 278
Hayward, Louis 111, 122, 125
Hayward, Susan 176, 240, 273, 291, 302, 307
Hayworth, Rita 163, 176, 206, 326, 364
Hazard, Lawrence 133, 135, 165, 183, 194, 203
Hazlewood, Lee 357
He Who Gets Slapped 10, 15, 20, 23
Healey, Myron 253
Healy, Betty 120
Healy, Ted 94, 95, 97, 102, 103, 105, 111, 112, 115, 116, 117, 119, 122, 123, 125, 126, 133, 134, 135, 139
Hearst, William Randolph 7, 12, 64, 72, 103, 166
Heart of the Wilds 182
Heat 49
Heathcote, Thomas 299, 345
'*Heather on the Hill, The*' 266
Heatherton, Joey 313
Heaven on Earth 39
Heaven with a Gun 350
Heavenly Body, The 183
Hecht, Ben 44, 57, 94, 103, 146, 147, 152, 165, 307
Heckart, Eileen 277
Hedley, Jack 316, 351
Heerman, Victor 216
Hefer, Haim 368
Heflin, Van 169, 171, 174, 181, 182, 183, 187, 208, 209, 214, 215, 218, 219, 222, 228, 326
Heggie, O.P. 47, 87
Heims, Jo 336
Helicopter Spies, The 338
Hell Below 90
Hell Divers 81
Hellen, Marjorie 276
Heller, Joseph 354
Heller, Lukas 337
Hellinger, Mark 84
Hell's Angels 66
Hell's Playground 182
Helmore, Tom 215, 225, 228, 271, 278, 280, 292, 298, 321
Hemmings, David 336, 338, 350, 355
Henderson, Del 40, 44
Henderson, Laurence 361
Hendry, Ian 312, 326, 356, 360, 368
Henie, Sonja 128
Henigson, Henry 142
Henley, Hobart 8, 15, 24, 27, 32, 42, 43
Henreid, Paul 149, 176, 213, 267, 271, 278, 292, 302, 322
Henry, Charlotte 100
Henry Goes Arizona 154
Henry, Gustav 339
Henry, Mike 364, 367
Henry V 201
Henry, William 102, 104, 105, 114, 125, 131, 141, 169
Hepburn, Audrey 262, 291, 293, 316
Hepburn, Katharine 90, 160, 169, 172, 180, 187, 196, 198, 204, 208, 209, 213, 216, 218, 222, 230, 240, 250, 268, 277, 291, 336, 340, 346, 358, 362
Hepburn, Philip 256
Hepton, Bernard 356
Her Cardboard Lover 85, 179
Her Highness and the Bellboy 203
Her Twelve Men 264
Herbert, F. Hugh 32, 35, 42, 43, 46, 52, 95, 280
Herbert, Holmes 24, 31, 39, 57, 58, 60, 64, 117, 131, 208
Herbert, Hugh 42, 82, 123, 142, 192, 194
Herbert, John 358
Herbert, Percy 278, 309
Herbert, Victor 32, 100, 110, 144
Hercules, Samson and Ulysses 327
Herczeg, Geza 163
Here Comes Mr Jordan 184
Here Comes the Band 117
Hereford, Kathryn 298
Herlihy, James Leo 304
Herman's Hermits 327, 333, 345
Hernandez, Juano 228, 232, 269, 273, 281, 303, 344
Heroin Gang, The 339
Hershey, Barbara 350
Hersholt, Jean 15, 16, 36, 74, 76, 77, 80, 81, 82, 84, 85, 86, 87, 97, 98, 103, 104, 115, 117, 122, 126
Hertz, David 143, 154, 171, 180, 196
Hervey, Irene 95, 105, 122, 125
Herzig, Sig M. 191, 197
Heston, Charlton 290, 291, 293, 304, 364, 367, 384
Heth, Edward Harris 228
Heydt, Louis Jean 145, 147, 198, 201, 202, 204, 276
Heywood, Anne 367
'*Hi Lili Hi Lo*' 251
Hichens, Robert 36
Hickman, Alfred 77
Hickman, Cordell 178
Hickman, Darryl 172, 179, 180, 183, 184, 188, 191, 206, 228, 236, 263, 276
Hickman, Dwayne 338
Hickman, Howard 181
Hickox, Douglas 361
Hicks, Russell 159, 172, 179, 181, 186, 202, 209, 232
Hicks, Seymour 165
Hickson, Joan 302
Hide-Out 103, 168
Hidden Eye, The 202
Hiers, Walter 10, 13
Higgin, Howard 10
Higgins, John C 149, 174, 181, 186, 197, 225
High Barbaree 214
High Cost of Loving, The 287
High Noon 249
High Road, The 67
High School Confidential 286
High Society 277, 378
'*High Society Calypso*' 277
High Wall 213
Highway to Freedom 172
Hill, Arthur 312
Hill, Elizabeth 144, 174
Hill, Ethel 202, 209
Hill, George 20, 28, 41, 42, 44, 69, 75, 81, 94, 127
Hill, George Roy 304, 368
Hill, James 156, 201, 306, 350
Hill, Mariana 357
Hill, Robert 293
Hill, The 326
Hiller, Arthur 313, 319, 331
Hiller, Wendy 138, 281
Hillier, Erwin 322
Hills of Home, The 219
Hilton, James 127, 149, 174, 176, 177
Hinds, Samuel S. 104, 105, 112, 126, 135, 139, 145, 149, 150, 158, 169, 181, 202, 219
Hines, Earl 'Fatha' 244
Hines, Johnny 85, 105, 145
Hingle, Pat 339, 364, 365, 368
Hird, Thora 228
Hired Gun, The 281
Hiroshima Mon Amour 300
Hirshbein, Peretz 186
His Brother's Wife 126
His Glorious Night 64, 66
His Hour 13, 16
His Secretary 27
Hit Man 362
Hit the Deck 270
Hitchcock, Alfred 54, 109, 156, 185, 210, 240, 291, 293, 296, 365
Hitler's Hangman 186
Hittleman, Carl 321
Hoban, Robert 368
Hobart, Rose 163, 168, 169, 171, 183, 186, 215
Hobbes, Halliwell 70, 80, 84, 89, 91, 94, 97, 100, 112, 133, 147, 149, 150, 154, 180, 183, 194, 215, 225
Hobson, Laura Z. 264
Hobson, Valerie 186
Hoch, Winton 218
Hodges, Eddie 296, 345
Hodges, Mike 356
Hodiak, John 186, 188, 191, 196, 204, 209, 215, 218, 219, 222, 225, 231, 237, 238, 243, 244, 247, 269
Hoerl, Arthur 313
Hoey, Dennis 179, 215, 224
Hoey, Michael 344, 345
Hoffe, Monckton 100, 105, 132, 165
Hoffenstein, Samuel 120, 136, 142, 146
Hoffman, Charles 178
Hoffman, Dustin 340, 346
Hoffman, Herman 273, 276, 281
Hoffman, Joseph 183
Hogan, Michael 134
Hohl, Arthur 135, 139, 154, 159
Holbrook, Hal 364
Hold On! 333
Hold That Kiss 140
Hold Your Man 91
Holden, Fay 134, 138, 140, 143, 149, 150, 156, 158, 165, 168, 169, 173, 174, 182, 197, 208, 232, 289
Holden, Gloria 145, 147, 183, 210, 213, 261
Holden, Jennifer 278
Holden, William 138, 210, 232, 259, 262, 266, 268, 278, 300, 304, 361
Holiday for Sinners 250
Holiday, Hope 319
Holiday in Mexico 208
Holland, Gretchen 64
Holland, Kristina 352
Holliday, Don 365
Holliday, Judy 230, 232, 296
Holliman, Earl 261, 276, 283, 338
Holloway, Jean 209, 218, 219
Holloway, Stanley 345
Holloway, Sterling 90, 97, 98, 102, 143, 154, 296, 345
Hollywood Party 102
Hollywood Revue, The 61, 63, 72, 154, 201, 377
Holm, Celeste 271, 277, 338
Holm, Ian 345
Holm, John Cecil 162, 188
Holmes, Brown 95
Holmes, Milton 302
Holmes, Phillips 74, 84, 90, 91, 94, 95, 97, 123, 176
Holmes, Stuart 12
Holmes, Taylor 233
Holt, David Jack 126
Holt, Jack 18, 51, 116, 125, 179, 202, 243
Holt, Nat 313
Holt, Patrick 252
Holt, Seth 289
Holtz, Tenen 43
Home from the Hill 299
Home of the Brave 223
Home Town Story 240
Home, William Douglas 286
Homecoming 218
Homecoming, The 214
Homeier, Skippy 206
Homes, Geoffrey 243
Homolka, Oscar 165, 174, 306, 314, 322
Hondo and the Apaches 339
Honeymoon 46
Honeymoon Hotel 319
Honeymoon Machine, The 303, 307
Hong, James 364
Honky Tonk 169
Honolulu 140
Hood, Darla 174
Hoodlum Saint, The 201
Hook, The 309
Hootenanny Hoot 313
Hoover, Herbert 82, 92
Hope, Bob 166, 185, 206, 223, 240, 302, 314
Hope, Edward 109
Hope, Frederic 100
Hopkins, Bo 367
Hopkins, Miriam 74, 95, 185
Hopkins, Robert 70, 72, 77, 78, 94, 125
Hopper, Dennis 298
Hopper, E. Mason 12, 57, 64
Hopper, Hedda 8, 15, 20, 24, 42, 56, 64, 69, 70, 71, 75, 77, 78, 80, 84, 86, 89, 91, 116, 134, 147
Hopwood, Keith 333, 345
Hordern, Michael 252, 280, 311, 317, 346
Horizontal Lieutenant, The 307
Horn, Leonard 352, 361
Hornblow, Arthur Jr. 188, 194, 202, 210, 214, 215, 228, 238, 245, 251, 259
Horne, James 110, 120
Horne, Lena 182, 183, 187, 188, 191, 192, 201, 209, 219, 222, 235, 271
Horner, Jackie 182
Horning, William 284, 290
Horovitz, Israel 352, 360
Horowitz, Lewis 337
Horton, Edward Everett 24, 84, 100, 102, 107, 168, 179, 209
Horton, Robert 253, 256, 258, 263, 333, 348
Horvarth, Charles 345
Hossein, Robert 321
Hot Millions 345
Hot Rods to Hell 339
Hot Summer Night 276
Hotel Paradiso 333
Hour of 13, The 252
House of Dark Shadows 355
House of Numbers 281
House of the Seven Hawks, The 295
House of Wax 254
Houseman, John 250, 252, 254, 264, 266, 268, 273, 274, 304, 307, 312
Houser, Lionel 149, 163, 174, 179, 183, 206, 209
Houston, Donald 346, 355
Hovey, Tamara 231
'*How About You?*' 171
'*How Am I to Know?*' 61
'*How Could You Believe Me . . .*' 237
How Green Was My Valley 166
How the West Was Won 304, 314
How to Marry a Millionaire 262
How to Steal the World 342
Howard, Ann 360
Howard, Cy 364
Howard, Esther 183, 202
Howard, John 160, 163
Howard, Kathleen 169, 214, 216
Howard, Leslie 66, 75, 77, 80, 87, 125, 152
Howard, Lewis 183, 203
Howard, Mary 138, 144, 145, 168
Howard, Norah 303
Howard, Ray 27
Howard, Ronald 280, 302
Howard, Ronny 287, 310
Howard, Sandy 338
Howard, Sidney 64, 97, 141, 152
Howard, Tom 312, 322
Howard, Trevor 309, 322, 331, 354, 365
Howard, William K. 91, 98, 105, 112
Howard, Willie 128
Howe, James Wong 102
Howland, Jobyna 72
Howlett, Noel 134, 293
Hoy, John 201
Hoyt, Arthur 20, 43
Hoyt, John 219, 243, 254, 266, 268, 269, 292
Hubbard, Lucien 36, 56, 69, 80, 90, 91, 92, 94, 95, 102, 103, 104, 105, 109, 111, 112, 115, 117, 122, 126, 133, 136, 138, 154
Huber, Harold 91, 104, 117, 122, 123, 125, 127, 132, 154, 163
Hucksters, The 210
Hud 310
Huddle 85
Hudis, Norman 338, 342
Hudson, Beverly 174
Hudson, Jeffery 364
Hudson, Rock 278, 281, 284, 291, 300, 317, 322, 344, 360, 366
Hudson, W.H. 293
Huff, Jack 20
Hughes, Carol 168
Hughes, Charles 228
Hughes, Howard 66, 75, 82, 184, 216, 225, 268
Hughes, Ken 316
Hughes, Lloyd 13, 35, 56, 57
Hughes, Mary Beth 147, 151, 174
Hughes, Rupert 10, 31
Hugueny, Sharon 321
Huie, Donald 162
Huie, William Bradford 319
Hulbert, Jack 82
Huldchinsky, Paul 194
Hulette, Gladys 20
Hull, Dianne 352
Hull, Henry 135, 138, 141, 142, 147, 150, 151, 152, 154, 214
Hullabaloo 162
Human Comedy, The 191
Humberstone, H. Bruce 117, 278, 287
Humbert, George 134, 143
Hume, Benita 94, 122, 125, 126, 127, 132
Hume, Cyril 16, 81, 86, 125, 132, 135, 151, 159, 166, 214, 273, 276, 281
Humphrey, William 299
Hunchback of Notre Dame, The 146
100% Pure 100
Hunnicutt, Arthur 232, 240
Hunnicutt, Gayle 347
Hunt, Marsha 147, 151, 158, 160, 165, 168, 169, 172, 174, 180, 181, 182, 183, 186, 187, 190, 191, 192, 202
Hunt, Martita 314, 319, 350
Hunter, Evan 268, 333, 364
Hunter, Glenn 214
Hunter, Ian 127, 147, 150, 151, 156, 162, 165, 168, 169, 174, 179, 188, 224
Hunter, Ian McLellan 187
Hunter, Jeffrey 298, 300, 319
Hunter, Tab 320, 325
Hunter, The 339
Huntley, G.P. Jr. 180
Hunyady, Sandor 90
Hurlbut, Gladys 127, 242, 256
Hurst, Brandon 40
Hurst, Fannie 80
Hurst, Paul 61, 105, 147, 152, 159
Hush, Richard 337
Hussey, Ruth 131, 136, 138, 140, 143, 147, 149, 150, 151, 154, 158, 160, 163, 168, 169, 174, 182
Hustler, The 300
Huston, John 238, 240, 245, 316, 360
Huston, Walter 54, 82, 84, 85, 90, 92, 139, 198, 218, 224
Hutchinson, A.S.M. 215
Hutchinson, Josephine 133, 215, 247, 264, 291, 296
Hutchison, Ken 364
Hutchison, Muriel 147
Huth, Harold 76
Hutsching, Edward 289
Hutton, Betty 234, 380
Hutton, Brian G. 339, 346, 354
Hutton, Jim 298, 302, 303, 304, 307, 320
Huxley, Aldous 160
Hyams, Leila 46, 56, 57, 61, 64, 66, 67, 69, 77, 78, 85, 87
Hyatt, Bobby 242, 261
Hyer, Martha 289
Hyland, Scott 360
Hyman, Arthur 85
Hyman, Bernard 49, 86, 91, 98, 100, 107, 112, 116, 117, 125, 127, 131, 136, 142
Hyman, Kenneth 326, 337
Hymer, Warren 91, 133, 136
Hysteria 327
Hytten, Olaf 174

I Accuse! 280
I am a Fugitive from a Chain Gang 90
'*I Concentrate on You*' 156
'*I Could Be Happy With You*' 358
'*I Cried for You*' 152
I Dood It 191
'*I Fall in Love Too Easily*' 201
'*I Got Rhythm*' 191
'*I Guess I'll Have to Change My Plan*' 254
I Live My Life 116
'*I Love Louisa*' 254
I Love Lucy 256
I Love Melvin 249
I Love You Again 162
'*I Love You, Samantha*' 277
I Married an Angel 179
'*I Remember It Well*' 284
'*I Should Care*' 201
I Take This Woman 146, 149, 150
I Thank a Fool 307
I Want to Live 291
'*I Wish I Were in Love Again*' 152, 219
'*I Won't Dance*' 209, 249
Ibanez, Vicente Blasco 20, 27, 33
Ice Follies of 1939, The 146
Ice Station Zebra 344
Idiot's Delight 145, 377
Idle Rich, The 61, 138
'*If I Were a Bell*' 271
'*If Love Were All*' 156
If Winter Comes 24, 214
If You Feel Like Singing 237
Ihnat, Steve 352
Il Etait une Fois 171
'*I'll Build a Stairway to Paradise*' 247
I'll Cry Tomorrow 67, 273, 302
'*I'll See You Again*' 156
I'll Wait for You 168
Illing, Peter 263, 277, 293, 295, 302, 306
I'm All Right Jack 296
'*I'm Falling in Love With Someone*' 110
'*I'm Glad I'm Not Young Any More*' 284
'*I'm Going Back to the Bonjour Tristesse Brassiere Company*' 296
'*I'm in Love with the Honorable Mr So-and-So*' 147
'*I'm In Love with Vienna*' 142
'*I'm Nobody's Baby*' 158
Imitation General 286
Imrie, Kathy 362
Imrie, Richard 322
Imperfect Lady, The 117
Importance of Being Ernest, The 249
Impossible Lover, The 85
Impossible Years, The 345
In Cold Blood 340
In Gay Madrid 67

In Old Arizona 54
In Old Chicago 138
In Old Heidelberg 36
In Old Kentucky 40
In the Cool of the Day 312
In the Good Old Summertime 225, 370
In the Heat of the Night 336
'In the Still of the Night' 128
'In Times Like These' 197
In Which We Serve 176
Ince, Thomas 7, 15
'Indian Love Call' 119
Inescort, Frieda 122, 151, 160, 165, 173
Informer, The 109
Inge, William 304
Ingraham, Lloyd 15
Ingram, Rex (director) 7, 8, 10, 12, 16, 20, 30, 36, 39, 250, 251
Ingram, Rex (actor) 146, 183, 294
Ingster, Boris 317, 331, 338
Innes, Hammond 293
Inside Straight 243
Inspiration 69
Inspiration Pictures 12
Intermezzo 146
Interrupted Melody 271, 273
Intolerance 30
Intruder in the Dust 228
Invasion Quartet 302
Invisible Boy, The 281
Invitation 242
Invitation to the Dance 275
Ireland, Jill 338
Ireland, John 216, 236, 286
Irish, Tom 233, 238
Irma la Douce 310
Iron Horse, The 10
Irving, Margaret 109, 122, 125, 141
Irwin, Margaret 257
Isham, Fredrick 117
Isham, Gyles 115
Isherwood, Christopher 174, 224, 273, 325
It Happened at the World's Fair 311
It Happened in Brooklyn 210
It Happened One Night 100, 146
It Started with a Kiss 292
'Italian Street Song' 110
It's a Big Country 242
It's a Date 231
It's a Dog's Life 273
It's a Gift 100
It's a Great Life 63
It's a Mad Mad Mad Mad World 322
'It's a Most Unusual Day' 377
It's a Wise Child 78
It's a Wonderful World 146
It's Always Fair Weather 270
It's in the Air 119
Iturbi, Amparo 192, 215, 231
Iturbi, Jose 187, 192, 201, 208, 215, 222, 231
Ivanhoe 252, 258, 271
'I've Got You Under My Skin' 123
Ivers, Julia 13
Ives, Burl 276, 287

Jack of Diamonds 338
Jackass Mail 183
Jackson, Anne 287, 352, 354
Jackson, Barry 350
Jackson, C.T. 35
Jackson, Charles 201
Jackson, Felix 143
Jackson, Freda 277
Jackson, Frederick 117
Jackson, Glenda 352, 358, 368
Jackson, Gordon 309
Jackson, Horace 102, 115, 127
Jackson, Kate 361
Jackson, Pat 228
Jackson, Ray 263, 287
Jackson, Sammy 339
Jackson, Selmer 172, 186
Jackson, Shirley 280, 312
Jackson, Thomas 71, 154, 202
Jacobi, Lou 331
Jacobs, Alexander 339, 361
Jacobs, Arthur 351
Jacobs, Seaman 311
Jacobs, W.W. 120
Jaeckel, Richard 225, 257, 298, 313, 337, 348, 366, 367
Jaffe, Carl 280, 287, 342
Jaffe, Sam (actor) 238, 291, 340
Jaffe, Sam (producer) 304
Jagger, Dean 122, 126, 133, 179, 266, 273, 303, 307, 341
Jai 304
Jailbirds 77
Jailhouse Rock 278
James, Gardner 31
James, Harry 188, 192, 195, 276
James, Polly 192
James, Ryan 173
James, Sidney 263, 302
James, Walter 22
Jameson, Pauline 319
Jandl, Ivan 218
Janice Meredith 12
Janis, Dorothy 56, 65
Janis, Elsie 67, 80
Janney, William 66, 97, 110
Janni, Joseph 367
Jannings, Emil 10, 44, 87
Janos, Vaszary 179
Janssen, David 303, 345
Janssen, Else 213
Jara, Maurice 257
Jardin, Pascal 317
Jarman, Claude Jr. 206, 214, 218, 222, 228, 236, 243
Jarre, Maurice 325
Jarrico, Paul 187, 188
Jarvis, Sidney 57
Jason, Rick 250
Jayne, Jennifer 327, 331
Jaynes, Betty 152, 187, 197
Jazz Singer, The 36, 46
Jeans, Isabel 284
Jeans, Ursula 302
Jefford, Barbara 345
Jeffreys, Anne 179, 306
Jeffries, Fran 327
Jeffries, Lionel 274, 277, 278, 287, 289, 306, 319, 327
Jenkins, Allen 178, 181, 331, 338
Jenkins, Jackie 'Butch' 191, 196, 203, 204, 206, 216, 218, 219
Jenkins, Megs 277, 302, 319
Jenkins, Paul 364
Jenks, Frank 134, 178, 187, 192, 237
Jennings, De Witt 35
Jennings, Talbot 119, 125, 127, 149, 159, 243, 258
Jenny Lind 72
Jensen, Eulalie 24
Jenson, Roy 338, 365, 367
Jeopardy 252
Jergens, Adele 228, 247, 273
Jergens, Diane 286
Jerome, Helen 160
Jerusalem File, The 360
'Jerry' 201
Jesse James 146
Jessup, Richard 329
Jesus Christ Superstar 336
Jevne, Jack 120, 123, 134, 142, 162, 174, 186
Jewell, Isabel 95, 97, 103, 105, 109, 111, 112, 119, 143, 149, 152
Jewison, Norman 329
Jezebel 138
Joe and Ethel Turp Call on the President 147
Joe Smith, American 172, 294
Joe, the Wounded Tennis Player 206
Johnny Eager 171
Johnny Get Your Hair Cut 31
'Johnny One Note' 152
Johns, Glynis 186, 203
Johns, Mervyn 224
Johns, Shirley 214, 218, 379
Johnson, Arch 281, 303
Johnson, Arte 298
Johnson, Ben 218, 361
Johnson, Bill 198
Johnson, Don 352
Johnson, Helen 72
Johnson, Kay 60, 61, 67, 70
Johnson, Laurence 67, 70, 78, 82, 85, 86, 97
Johnson, Melodie 357
Johnson, Noble 12
Johnson, Nunnally 117, 299, 337
Johnson, Owen 236
Johnson, Richard 259, 292, 304, 312, 322
Johnson, Rita 132, 133, 136, 138, 140, 143, 147, 149, 150, 154, 159, 163
Johnson, Robert Lee 85
Johnson, Van 178, 180, 183, 184, 187, 191, 192, 195, 196, 198, 201, 202, 206, 208, 209, 214, 216, 218, 222, 225, 232, 234, 235, 237, 242, 250, 251, 253, 256, 259, 263, 264, 266, 275, 281, 370, 380
Johnston, Agnes Christine 20, 24, 32, 35, 36, 44, 47, 143, 150, 173, 182, 197
Johnston, Johnnie 210
Johnston, William 84
Johnstone, Justine 20
'Joint is Really Jumpin', The' 187
Jolson, Al 36, 247
Jolson Story, The 206
Jones, Allan 111, 116, 119, 121, 125, 136
Jones, Arthur V. 123, 136
Jones, Barry 264, 266, 283
Jones, Buck 30
Jones, Carolyn 271, 276, 304, 315, 350
Jones, Christopher 354
Jones, Chuck 351
Jones, Dean 276, 278, 286, 287, 292
Jones, Freddie 361
Jones, Gordon 138, 143, 154, 169
Jones, Griffith 134
Jones, Grover 146
Jones, Henry 344
Jones, Jack 125
Jones, James 289
Jones, Jennifer 192, 222, 228, 249, 268, 275, 284
Jones, L.Q. 307, 344
Jones, Marcia Mae 191
Jones, Paul 216
Jones, Quincy 345
Jones, Shirley 310, 315, 327
Jones, Spike 197
Jordan, Bobby 159
Jordan, Dorothy 60, 67, 69, 72, 77, 80, 81, 84, 276
Jordan, Jack 188
Jory, Victor 152, 264
Joseph, Albrecht 186
Joslyn, Allyn 144, 151, 183, 187, 249, 277
Jourdan, Louis 216, 222, 228, 274, 276, 284, 311, 327, 379
Journey, The 287
Journey for Margaret 180, 190, 216
Journey's End 66
Joy House 317
Joy in the Morning 322
Joy, Leatrice 47
Joy, Nicholas 215, 218, 219, 244
Joyce, Alice 24, 66, 69
Joyce, Yootha 360
Juarez 146
Jubilee 156
Judels, Charles 133, 134, 135, 138, 143, 156, 169, 191
Judge Hardy and Son 150
Judge Hardy's Children 138
Judgment at Nuremberg 300
Julia Misbehaves 216
Julian, Arthur 277
Julie 276
Juliet of the Spirits 322
Julius Caesar 254
Jumbo 307
June, Ray 107, 121, 145
Jungle Book 340
Junkin, Harry 275
Jupiter's Darling 264
Jurado, Katy 269, 286, 344, 366
Jurgens, Curt 338
Just a Gigolo 78
'Just in Time' 296
Just This Once 242, 252
Juster, Norton 351
Justice for Sale 84
Justice, James Robertson 281, 302
Justin, Charles 337
Justin, John 263, 364
Justman, Robert 355

Kaestner, Eric 135
Kafka, John 168, 176
Kahn, Gordon 174, 179
Kahn, Gus 142
Kaley, Charles 61
Kallianiotes, Helena 362
Kallman, Dick 338
Kalmar, Bert 234, 372
Kameradschaft 82
Kamp, Irene and Louis 329
Kane, Helen 234
Kanin, Fay 179, 264, 276, 309
Kanin, Garson 230, 250
Kanin, Michael 172, 179, 187, 264, 276, 309, 317
Kansas City Bomber 362
Kantor, Hal 302
Kantor, Jay 360
Kantor, Mackinlay 120, 163, 194, 214
Kaper, Bronislau 242, 251
Kaplan, Jonathan 367
Kaplan, Marvin 234, 243
Karate Killers, The 338
Kardos, Leslie 244, 249
Karl and Anna 214
Karlen, John 361
Karloff, Boris 16, 22, 57, 71, 74, 85, 306, 331
Karlson, Phil 298
Karlweis, Oscar 271
Karns, Roscoe 76, 90, 154, 172
Karp, David 339
Karr, David 333, 339
Kashfi, Anna 286
Kastner, Elliott 339, 346, 355, 360
Kasznar, Kurt 242, 249, 250, 251, 256, 257, 258, 261, 264, 287, 295
Kata, Elizabeth 326
Katch, Kurt 198, 213
Katcha, Vahe 309
Katcher, Leo 286
Kathleen 173
'Katie Went to Haiti' 187
Katz, Peter 364
Katzin, Lee 339, 350
Katzka, Gabriel 347, 354
Katzman, Sam 313, 319, 320, 327, 333, 339, 344, 345
Kaufman, Charles 214, 300
Kaufman, George S. 60, 97, 111, 162, 214
Kaufman, Leonard 327
Kaufman, Millard 257, 266, 278, 292
Kaufman. S. Jay 24
Kaufman, Christine 307, 309
Kaus, Gina 225
Kaye, Claudelle 111
Kaye, Danny 210, 284
Kaye, Davy 339
Kaye, Stubby 271
Kazablan 368
Kazan, Elia 209
Keach, Stacy 352, 357
Keane, Doris 67
Kearney, Gene 365
Kearney, Patrick 56
Kearney, Philip 365
Keating, Fred 116
Keating, Larry 236, 242, 243, 251, 261, 306
Keaton, Buster 7, 8, 14, 15, 21, 28, 44, 56, 63, 69, 78, 85, 86, 98, 123, 162, 179, 191, 216, 225, 232, 296
Kedrova, Lila 331
Keel, Howard 222, 234, 242, 243, 247, 249, 252, 257, 258, 263, 264, 266, 267, 273, 377, 379, 380, 384
Keeler, Ruby 90
Keen, Geoffrey 289, 293, 302, 325
Keenan, Frank 13
Keene, Day 351
Keep Your Powder Dry 198
Keeper of the Flame 180
Keeping Company 156, 173
'Keeping Myself for You' 270
Keim, Betty Lou 276, 289
Keir, Ursula 280
Keith, Ian 23, 74, 77, 80, 98, 219
Keith, Robert 234, 249, 250, 270, 271, 273, 296
Kelland, Clarence B. 86
Kellaway, Cecil 165, 209, 234, 235, 257, 268, 271, 334
Kellerman, Annette 251
Kellerman, Sally 352, 366
Kelley, Albert 64
Kelley, Barry 216, 224, 236, 238, 259, 269, 276, 344
Kelley, DeForrest 286, 365
Kelley, John 352
Kellogg, Bruce 198
Kellogg, John 298
Kelly, Brian 333
Kelly, Claire 286, 289, 291
Kelly, Fred 267
Kelly, Gene 178, 180, 187, 195, 201, 208, 213, 219, 220, 224, 226, 227, 237, 242, 247, 249, 253, 263, 266, 267, 270, 271, 275, 277, 283, 287, 368, 372, 374, 378, 379, 380, 384
Kelly, George 104, 123, 209
Kelly, Grace 256, 262, 266, 268, 276, 277
Kelly, Jack 276
Kelly, Judith 196
Kelly, Mark 183
Kelly, Patsy 8, 100, 123, 136, 142, 298
Kelly, Paul 102, 122, 135, 149, 154, 158, 162, 168, 169, 181, 228, 242
Kelly, Paula 362, 367
Kelly, Sean 302
Kelly the Second 123, 136
Kelly, Tommy 165
Kelly's Heroes 354
Kelsey, Fred 39
Kelton, Pert 123,
Kemble-Cooper, Violet 112, 125, 152
Kemp, Jeremy 322
Kemp, Lindsay 364
Kemper, Charles 228
Kempson, Rachel 334
Kempy 57
Kendall, Cy 154, 168, 181
Kendall, Kay 271, 283, 286, 374
Kendrick, Bayard 181
Kennaway, James 352
Kennedy, Arthur 251, 269, 289, 302, 322, 341
Kennedy, Burt 315, 319, 326, 334, 339, 354
Kennedy, Edgar 109, 122, 128, 186, 201
Kennedy, George 337, 347, 352, 354
Kennedy, Jay Richard 273
Kennedy, Madge 274, 275
Kenner 345
Kent, Barbara 33, 77
Kent, Christopher: see Kjellin, Alf
Kent, Crauford 19, 21
Kent, Robert 150, 202, 339
Kent, Robert E. 320, 327, 339, 344
Kenward, Allan 186
Kenyon, Albert 22
Kenyon, Curtis 195
Kerkorian, Kirk 9
Kern, Hal 152
Kern, Jerome 116, 171, 191, 209, 247, 249
Kern, Robert J. 196
Kernan, Reginald 327
Kerouac, Jack 298
Kerr, Deborah 203, 210, 215, 222, 224, 232, 236, 245, 251, 254, 257, 261, 276, 287, 292, 316, 338, 340, 346
Kerr, Fred 67, 84
Kerr, Jean 298
Kerr, John 273, 276, 280
Kerr, Laura 234, 250
Kerrigan, J.M. 150, 159, 203, 240, 273, 277
Kerry, Norman 28, 36, 39
Kestrel Films 352
Key, Janet 355
Key, Kathleen 31, 32
Key to the City 230
Key Witness 298
Keyes, Evelyn 152
Keys of the Kingdom 192
Kibbee, Guy 76, 77, 78, 91, 135, 138, 139, 141, 143, 146, 151, 152, 154, 173, 174, 176, 179, 183, 191, 214
Kid, The 12
Kid from Texas, The 150
Kid Glove Killer 181
Kidd, Michael 263, 270, 271, 284
Kiki 28
Kilbride, Percy 180, 218
Kilburn, Terry 142, 143, 144, 149, 150, 175, 196
Kiley, Richard 268
Kilian, Victor 138, 146, 154, 159, 198, 243
Kill or Cure 306
Killer McCoy 210
Killer on a Horse 339
Kilpatrick, Lincoln 362
Kim 235, 240
Kimble, Lawrence 126, 182
Kind Lady 109, 244
Kinevox 255
King and I, The 274
King, Andrea 236
King, Bradley 43, 48
King, Charles 49, 63, 66
King, Dennis 92
King, Frank 312, 334, 350
King, Henry 12
King, Herman 312, 350
King, John 149, 150
King Kong 90
King Lear 364
King, Maurice 334, 350
King of Kings 300
King of Kings, The 44
King Sisters 208
King Solomon's Mines 128, 235, 236, 294
King, Walter Woolf 111, 143, 151, 162
Kings Row 176
King's Thief, The 273
Kingsford, Walter 110, 122, 126, 132, 134, 135, 139, 141, 142, 147, 150, 154, 158, 172, 173, 179, 182, 183, 187, 196, 284
Kingsley, Dorothy 191, 195, 209, 219, 220, 225, 232, 234, 243, 249, 253, 257, 259, 263, 264, 283, 293
Kingsley, Sidney 104, 218
Kingston, Winifred 80
Kinnear, Roy 326
Kinney National Service 330
Kinnoch, Ronald 299, 302, 304
Kinskey, Leonid 143, 187
Kinski, Klaus 325
Kipling, Rudyard 132, 235, 240
Kirby, Michael 202, 218
Kirgo, George 334, 338
Kirk, Lawrence 182
Kirk, Phyllis 234, 236, 237, 384
Kirkland, Alexander 85
Kirkwood, James 10, 15
Kirkwood, Pat 208
Kirsten, Dorothy 247
Kismet 194, 197, 273, 379
Kiss, The 58, 138
Kis Me Kate 257, 377
Kiss My Firm But Pliant Lips 345
Kissin' Cousins 320
Kissing Bandit, The 216
Kjellin, Alf 222, 228, 344
Klane, Robert 364
Klauber, Marcel 258
Klein, Allen 345
Kleinbach, Harry 100
Klemperer, Werner 287, 307
Klinger, Michael 256
Klorer, John 225
Klugman, Jack 289, 345
Klute 358
Knight, Don 367
Knight, Eric 191, 261
Knight, Felix 100, 110
Knight, Fuzzy 183
Knight, June 110, 141
Knight, Shirley 306
Knights of the Round Table 258
Knoblock, Edward 194, 273
Knopf, Christopher 273
Knopf, Edwin H. 117, 126, 165, 168, 171, 176, 186, 187, 202, 203, 208, 214, 215, 224, 225, 243, 244, 251, 253, 261, 264, 273, 276, 280, 281
Knox, Alexander 293, 312, 333
Knox, Mickey 210, 228
Kober, Arthur 94, 102, 109
Koch, Howard 289
Kohler, Fred 61
Kohner, Frederick 215, 231
Kohner, Susan 298
Kolb, Clarence 140, 142, 230
Kolker, Henry 27, 84, 125, 134, 135, 145, 151, 171
Kongo 85
Korda, Alexander 203
Korff, Arnold 71
Korjus, Miliza 142
Korman, Harvey 331
Koscina, Sylva 309, 331
Koshetz, Marina 208, 219, 333
Kosleck, Martin 172, 321
Koslenko, William 186, 208
Kossoff, David 287, 295
Koster, Henry 192, 209, 213, 276, 333
Kraly, Hans 36, 41, 56, 58, 60, 67, 72, 78, 80, 147
Kramer, Stanley 322
Krasna, Norman 123, 126, 133, 142, 143, 232, 315
Krasne, Philip 313
Krasner, Milton 115
Krauss, Werner 112
Kress, Harold 242, 253, 304
Krims, Milton 126
Kristofferson, Kris 366
Kroeger, Berry 219, 300
Kruger, Alma 141, 150, 151, 158, 162, 165, 173, 182, 183, 187, 198, 213
Kruger, Otto 92, 94, 95, 102, 104, 107, 112, 149, 314
Kruschen, Jack 276, 289, 292, 319
Kubrick, Stanley 306, 316, 342
Kuhn, Irene 85
Kulick, Barry 361
Kuller, Sid 169
Kuluva, Will 298, 322, 331
Kunen, James 352
Kurnitz, Harry 144, 151, 162, 171, 179, 186, 188, 192, 202, 277
Kwan, Nancy 309, 319
Kyne, Peter B. 20, 31, 43, 61, 125, 218
Kyo, Machiko 277
Kyser, Kay 187, 188

Laage, Barbara 215, 277
La Blanche, Ethel 143
La Boheme 24, 30, 35, 234
La Cava, Gregory 92, 105, 213
Lacey, Ronald 316
Lachman, Harry 76, 120
Ladd, Alan 46, 176, 262, 286, 360
Ladd, Alan Jr. 355
Ladd, David 361
Ladies in Retirement 166
'Ladies of the Town' 156
La Dolce Vita 300
Lady Be Good 171
Lady for a Day 102
Lady in the Lake 208
'Lady Is a Tramp, The' 152, 219
Lady Killer 90
Lady L. 326
'Lady Loves, A' 249
Lady of Chance 48
Lady of Scandal 67
Lady of the Night 15
Lady of the Tropics 146, 150
Lady to Love, A 64
Lady Without Passport, A 238
Lady's Morals, A 72
La Farge, Oliver 102
Laffan, Patricia 245
Laforet, Marie 338
La Frenais, Ian 360
Lagrange, Valerie 303
La Guerre est Finie 336
Lahr, Bert 77, 151, 180, 187, 197, 266
Laidlaw, William 218
Laine, Frankie 271
Laing, Hugh 266
Lake, Arthur 134
Lake, Florence 64, 67
Laks, Lucille 365
La Marr, Barbara 146
Lamarr, Hedy 146, 149, 150, 163, 165, 168, 174, 176, 181, 182, 188, 203, 238
Lamas, Fernando 243, 244, 249, 256, 259, 266
Lambrinos, Vassili 319
Lamont, Ducan 271, 291, 309, 313
Lamour, Dorothy 120
L'Amour, Louis 339, 361
Lampell, Millard 307
Lancaster, Burt 236, 249, 268, 274, 296, 304, 310, 346, 352
Lanchbery, John 360
Lanchester, Elsa 107, 110, 191, 224, 236, 264, 319
'Land Where the Good Songs Go, The' 209
Landau, Martin 291
Landers, Hal 346
Landi, Elissa 122, 123, 131

Landi, Marla 287
Landis, Jessie Royce 274, 291, 306
Landres, Paul 328
Lane, Burton 237, 256, 296
Lane, Charles 181, 257, 289
Lane, Lola 71
Lane, Richard 165, 174, 362
Lanfield, Sidney 249
Lang, Barbara 281, 286
Lang, David 174, 179, 281
Lang, Fritz 10, 123, 268
Lang, June 110
Lang, Matheson 39
Lang, Otto 294
Lang, Walter 94
Langdon, Harry 28, 143
Langdon, Sue Ane 319, 327, 333, 337
Langella, Frank 364
Langford, Frances 110, 123
Langley, Noel 134, 151, 163, 224, 251, 252, 258
Langton, Paul 194, 198, 202, 209, 257, 313
Lansbury, Angela 194, 196, 201, 204, 209, 214, 215, 218, 219, 222, 225, 244, 259, 286, 302, 304, 312, 333
Lansbury, Edgar 344
Lanza, Mario 222, 231, 234, 247, 251, 266, 281, 295, 378
La Plante, Laura 66, 206
Lardner, Ring Jr. 172, 187, 329
Larkin, John 234
La Rocque, Rod 18, 47, 57, 66, 70
Larsen, Keith 294
La Rue, Jack 102, 109, 132, 173, 331
Lasky, Jesse Jr. 179
Lass, Barbara 312
Lasser, Louise 366
'Lassie' 191, 202, 206, 218, 219, 222, 225, 242, 321, 384
Lassie Come Home 191, 202
Last Challenge, The 339
Last Chance, The 201
Last Command, The 44
Last Gangster, The 132
Last Hunt, The 273
Last Hurrah, The 284
Last of Mrs Cheyney, The 56, 84, 132, 244
Last of the Pagans 117
Last Run, The 360
Last Tango in Paris 366, 368
Last Time I Saw Paris, The 264
'Last Time I Saw Paris, The' 171, 209
Last Voyage, The 292
Laszlo, Miklos 219
Late Christopher Bean, The 97
Late George Apley, The 210
Latest from Paris, The 43
Latin Lovers 261
La Touche, John 183
Laugh, Clown, Laugh 52, 91
Laughing Boy 102
Laughing Sinners 76
Laughlin, Michael S. 361
Laughton, Charles 89, 90, 105, 107, 119, 141, 182, 188, 195, 219, 257, 275, 309
Laura 192
Laurel, Stan 8, 63, 64, 77, 82, 86, 92, 95, 100, 102, 110, 117, 120, 123, 136, 142, 143, 162, 186, 192, 317, 322
Laurel and Hardy's Laughing 20s 322
Lauren, S.K. 91, 169, 171
Laurence, Douglas 322, 333, 338, 344, 345
Laurent, Jacqueline 138
Laurents, Arthur 224
Laurie, Piper 278
Lauter, Ed 365
Laven, Arnold 275, 362
Lavender Hill Mob, The 249
La Verne, Lucille 21, 76, 119
Lavery, Emmet 232, 256
Lavi, Daliah 307, 361
Law, The 299
Law and Jake Wade, The 286
Law and the Lady, The 244
Law, Harold 136
Law of the Range, The 43
Lawbreakers, The 303
Lawford, Peter 142, 179, 194, 195, 198, 202, 206, 209, 210, 216, 219, 220, 222, 225, 232, 237, 242, 252, 292, 364, 368, 377
Lawlor, Mary 71
Lawrence, Barbara 258, 264
Lawrence, D.H. 296
Lawrence, Gertrude 80, 163
Lawrence, Marc 149, 159, 169, 172, 224, 238
Lawrence, Marjorie 271
Lawrence of Arabia 304
Lawrence, Reginald 91
Lawrence, Rosina 120, 123, 136
Lawrence, Vincent 43, 136, 145, 146, 201, 209
Laws, Sam 362
Lawson, John Howard 60, 61, 69, 71
Lawson, Priscilla 142, 145
Lawson, Ted 198
Lawson, Wilfrid 302
Lawton, Frank 76, 107, 122
Lay, Beirne 251, 313
Laye, Evelyn 107
Lazaga, Pedro 317
Lazarus, Paul III 366
Lazy River 102
Lazzlo, Nikolaus 154
Lea, Fanny Heaslip 136
Leachman, Cloris 275
Leader, Anton 312
Lean, David 278, 304, 325, 354
Lease, Rex 43, 51
Leasor, James 322
Le Baron, William 117
Lebedeff, Ivan 92, 97, 127, 135
Le Breton, Auguste 312
Leckenby, Derek 333, 345
Lederer, Charles 147, 149, 162, 165, 171, 188, 191, 253, 273, 276, 281, 292, 309, 314
Lederman, D. Ross 46
Lee, Anna 314, 329
Lee, Bernard 244, 263, 287, 289, 302
Lee, Bruce 347
Lee, Christopher 306
Lee, Gwen 27, 32, 36, 39, 42, 46, 47, 48, 60, 61, 69, 78, 133
Lee, James 296
Lee, John 302
Lee, Leonard 123, 132, 133, 169
Lee, Lila 71
Lee, Norma 57
Lee, Patricia 302
Lee, Robert 31
Lee, Rudy 276
Lee, Ruta 313
Lees, Hannah 228
Legend of Lylah Clare, The 344
Leggatt, Alison 237
LeGon, Jeni 220
Lehar, Franz 64, 100, 249
Lehman, Ernest 266, 277, 291, 314
Lehman, Gladys 177, 187, 192, 201, 203, 210, 219
Lehmann, Lotte 219
Leiber, Fritz 119, 236
Leibman, Ron 368
Leigh, Janet 214, 215, 216, 219, 222, 224, 225, 228, 242, 243, 250, 253, 296, 331, 364, 365, 384
Leigh, Nelson 240
Leigh, Vivien 134, 152, 164, 201, 240, 276, 322
Leighton, Margaret 244, 325, 329
Leisen, Mitchell 250, 271
Le Mesurier, John 299, 302, 306, 309, 312, 322, 331, 333, 338
Lemkow, Tutte 302
Lemmon, Jack 291, 310, 317, 322, 330, 346, 358, 366, 368
Lengyel, Melchior 148
Lennart, Isobel 183, 186, 190, 201, 208, 210, 216, 228, 237, 249, 261, 268, 271, 280, 284, 304
Lennon, John 352
Lennon, Thomas 143, 210
Lenya, Lotte 350
Lenzi, Umberto 326
Leonard, Barbara 71
Leonard, Elmore 357
Leonard, Herbert B. 361
Leonard, Hugh 354
Leonard, Jack 258
Leonard, Robert Z. 8, 12, 13, 15, 20, 24, 27, 30, 32, 35, 42, 46, 48, 64, 67, 70, 74, 78, 80, 84, 85, 92, 97, 107, 112, 116, 121, 126, 128, 134, 136, 142, 147, 156, 160, 163, 168, 171, 172, 182, 188, 196, 202, 203, 208, 213, 215, 219, 222, 225, 231, 234, 235, 242, 249, 251, 261, 264, 273
Leonard, Sheldon 169, 174, 181, 182, 213, 250, 271
Leone, Sergio 299
Lerner, Alan Jay 237, 247, 266, 284, 296
LeRoy, Mervyn 78, 95, 142, 143, 147, 151, 164, 169, 171, 172, 177, 191, 198, 216, 218, 222, 228, 244, 245, 249, 251, 261, 266
Les Girls 283, 374
Les Rois en Exil 24
Leslie, Joan 232
Lesser, Sol 278, 287
Lessey, George 158, 162, 169, 172
Lessing, Norman 322
Lessy, Ben 339
Lester, Bruce 160, 187
Lester, Mark 339
Let Freedom Ring 146
Let Us Be Gay 70
Letondal, Henri 244
'Let's Be Buddies' 182
Letter for Evie, A 202
Letter to Three Wives, A 223
Lettieri, Al 360
Letty Lynton 84
Levant, Oscar 224, 247, 254, 273
Levene, Sam 123, 141, 169, 171, 179, 181, 189, 191, 210, 236, 276, 278
Levien, Sonya 168, 202, 208, 215, 245, 247, 249, 266, 270, 271, 277
Levin, Henry 298, 303, 312, 314, 319
Levine, Nat 145
LeVino, Albert 24, 64
Levitow, Abe 351
Levitt, Alfred 261
Levitt, Gene 289
Levoy, Albert 151, 159, 163
Levy, Melvin 120, 186
Lewin, Albert 15, 32, 41, 43, 47, 49, 127, 194, 259, 281
Lewis, Albert 183, 209, 214
Lewis, Ben 273
Lewis, David 278, 283
Lewis, Diana 156, 158, 162, 163, 171, 173, 183, 186
Lewis, Edward 334, 344, 345, 346
Lewis, Fiona 360
Lewis, Jarma 271, 273, 278
Lewis, Jay 302
Lewis, Jerry 240, 262, 274, 278, 300
Lewis, Jerry Lee 286
Lewis, Joseph 238, 252, 258
Lewis, Mitchell 12, 18, 20, 57, 76, 80, 85, 97, 110, 132, 151, 154, 168, 179, 206, 244, 257
Lewis, Monica 243, 244, 247, 249
Lewis, Roger 362, 367
Lewis, Sinclair 215
Lewis, Ted (band) 117
Lewis, Ted (writer) 362
Lewis, Tom 235
Lewis, Tommy 235
Lewis, Vera 21
Lewton, Val 232
Libel 293
Libeled Lady 125, 209
Liberace 325, 327
Liberty Films 218
Licudi, Gabriella 331
Life Begins for Andy Hardy 173
Life of Emile Zola, The 128
Life of Her Own, A 237
Life with Father 210
'Life's Full of Consequences' 183
Light Fantastic, The 247
Light in the Piazza 302
Light Touch, The 242
Lightner, Winnie 98
Lighton, Louis D. 27, 126, 127, 132, 136, 145, 146
Lights and Shadows 64
Lights of New York 44
Lights of Old Broadway 19
Lili 251, 264
Lilies of the Field 310
Lillie, Beatrice 35
'Limehouse Blues' 201
Limelight 249
Lind, Della 143
Lindbergh, Charles A. 36
Linden, Eric 119, 120, 123, 135, 136, 152
Linden, Marta 177, 179, 182, 183, 186, 187, 191, 196, 197, 198
Linder, Stewart 334
Lindfors, Viveca 268, 280, 300
Lindon, Lionel 334
Lindop, Audrey Erskine 307
Lindsay, Howard 218, 259
Lindsay, Margaret 123, 133, 215, 298
Lindtberg, Leopold 201
Lion in Winter, The 340
Lipman, William 134, 165, 180, 186, 198, 203, 206, 213
Lippe, Jonathan 364
Lipscomb, W.P. 119, 287
Lipsky, Eleazar 244
Lipton, Lew 20, 32, 42, 44, 46, 48, 119, 147
Liquidator, The 331
Lisi, Virna 333, 337
Listen Darling 139
Lister, Moira 317
Litel, John 165, 181, 209, 215, 250, 281
Little Caesar 66, 78
'Little Curly Hair in a High Chair' 163
Little Foxes, The 166
Little Hut, The 280
Little Journey, A 30
Little Miss Marker 100
Little Mr Jim 206
Little Nellie Kelly 156
'Little One' 277
Little Robinson Crusoe 12
Little Sister, The 347
Little Women 216
Littlebird, Larry 367
Littlefield, Lucien 21, 86, 116, 169, 183
Litvak, Anatole 287
Live a Little, Love a Little 345
Live and Let Die 366
Live, Love and Learn 135
Livesay, Roger 316
Living Corpse, The 66
Living Idol, The 281
Living in a Big Way 213
Livingston, Margaret 47
Lizzie 280
Lloyd, Doris 23, 35, 86, 94, 109, 117, 180, 244, 257, 298
Lloyd, Euan 361
Lloyd, Frank 54, 119
Lloyd, Harold 18, 192, 232
Lloyd, Harold Jr. 294, 298
Lloyd, Norman 202, 208, 209, 216, 225, 242
Lloyd, Richard 327
Locke, Katherine 198
Lockhart, Calvin 341, 362
Lockhart, Gene 122, 127, 139, 143, 144, 146, 149, 154, 156, 164, 168, 214, 228, 232, 253
Lockhart, June 192, 198, 202, 206, 209
Lockhart, Kathleen 123, 127, 143, 144, 171, 190, 202, 208, 250, 253
Lockridge, Ross 278
Lockwood, Gary 311, 342, 360
Loder, John 57
Lodge, David 306
Loesser, Frank 225, 271
Loew, Arthur M. 7, 9, 143, 201, 216, 218, 235, 303
Loew, Arthur Jr. 252, 257, 258, 273, 275, 331
Loew, David L. 143, 216
Loew, Marcus 7, 8, 9, 12, 18, 143, 216
Loewe, Frederick 266, 284
Loew's Incorporated 7, 9, 54, 82, 128, 138, 146, 156, 166, 176, 206, 216, 222, 232, 240, 249, 262, 278, 290
Loew's Theatres 9, 290, 296
Lofts, Norah 329
Loggia, Robert 277, 313
Logue, Christopher 364
Lolita 306
Lollobrigida, Gina 292, 298, 299, 326, 333
Lolly Madonna War, The 365
Lolly Madonna XXX 365
Lom, Herbert 280, 281, 338
Lombard, Carole 90, 105, 128, 176, 178
Lombardo, Goffredo 299, 327
Lombardo, Guy 208
London After Midnight 39
London by Night 132
London Films 203
'London is London' 379
London, Julie 286, 338
London, Pauline 149
Lone Star 240
Lonelyhearts 284
Lonergan, Lenore 240
'Lonesome Polecat' 263
'Long Ago and Far Away' 209
'Long Before I Knew You' 296
Long, Long Trailer, The 256
Long, Lotus 117
Long, Richard 312
Long, Ronald 303
Long Voyage Home, The 156
Longdon, Terence 291
Longest Day, The 310
Longest Night, The 122
Lonsdale, Frederick 56, 67, 84, 86, 132, 244
'Look for the Silver Lining' 209
Looking for Love 320
Looking Forward 94
Loos, Anita 84, 87, 91, 92, 100, 102, 125, 131, 135, 147, 163, 168, 169, 171, 179
Loos, Mary 100
Lopez, Rafael 313
Lopez, Trini 327, 337
Loraine, Robert 107
Lord Byron of Broadway 61
Lord, Jack 281
Lord Jeff 142
Lord, Robert 213
Loren, Sophia 298, 300, 322, 326, 338, 339, 345
Loring, Ann 120, 122
Loring, Eugene 203
Loring, Hope 27
Loring, John 345
Lorraine, Louise 3 , 41, 43, 46, 48
Lorraine, Philip 338
Lorre, Peter 112, 165, 168, 187, 283
Lory, Milo 291
Losch, Tilly 127
Losey, Joseph 8, 316
Lost Angel 190, 204
Lost Horizon 128
Lost in a Harem 197
Lost Weekend, The 201
Lott, Milton 273
Louis, Willard 27, 32
Louise, Anita 141, 151
'Louisiana Hayride' 254
Love 40, 44, 115
'Love' 201
Love Affair 146
Love, Bessie 35, 49, 56, 61, 63, 69, 71, 289, 312, 361
Love Bug, The 352
Love Cage, The 317
Love Crazy 171
Love Finds Andy Hardy 138
Love in Las Vegas 320
Love in the Rough 72
Love is a Headache 134
Love is a Many-Splendored Thing 268
Love is Better Than Ever 247
'Love is Here to Stay' 247
'Love is Like a Firefly' 136
'Love is the Tender Trap' 271
'Love is Where You Find It' 216
Love Laughs at Andy Hardy 208
Love Me or Leave Me 270, 273, 377
Love, Montagu 52, 56, 133, 149, 182
Love on the Run 127
Love Parade, The 100
Love Song, The 35
Love Story 352, 361
Loved One, The 325
Lovejoy, Frank 263, 276
'Loveliest Night of the Year, The' 247
Lovelorn, The 43
Lovely to Look At 249, 377
'Lover Come Back to Me' 72
Lovers? 39
Lovers Courageous 84
Love's Blindness 31
Lovett, Josephine 36, 41, 49, 57
Lovey Mary 35
Lovsky, Celia 243, 264, 321, 367
Lowe, Edmund 21, 97, 122, 132, 162, 276
Lowell, Robert 198
Lowery, Robert 327
Lowndes, Marie Belloc 84
Lowry, Morton 194
Loxley, D.A. 203
Loy, Myrna 27, 31, 42, 54, 77, 84, 85, 86, 92, 94, 97, 98, 103, 104, 105, 107, 112, 121, 123, 125, 126, 128, 133, 136, 145, 146, 149, 154, 162, 163, 171, 187, 192, 209, 213, 291, 384
Lubin, A. Ronald 317
Lubin, Arthur 303, 333
Lubin, Lou 251
Lubitsch, Ernst 10, 36, 100, 148, 154
'Luck Be a Lady' 271
Luckham, Cyril 302, 333
Luckinbill, Laurence 361
'Lucky in Love' 71, 210
Lucky Night 146
Ludwig 365
Ludwig, Edward 116, 132, 174
Ludwig, Emil 186
Ludwig, William 138, 143, 150, 154, 171, 180, 197, 206, 208, 216, 218, 219, 225, 228, 247, 249, 266, 270, 271, 278, 281
Luez, Laurette 235
Lugosi, Bela 64, 74, 117, 148
Lukas, Paul 86, 111, 116, 132, 165, 235, 302, 339
Luke, Keye 112, 127, 169, 174, 183, 186, 187, 196, 197, 213
Lullaby, The 76
Lulli, Folco 300
Lumet, Sidney 326, 350
Luna, Barbara 313, 315
Lund, John 235, 261, 277
Lundigan, William 116, 173, 179, 182, 183, 186, 187
Lunt, Alfred 80, 145, 169
Lupino, Ida 206
Lupino, Richard 264, 273, 292
Lupo, Michele 362
Lupton, John 242, 252, 254, 257, 259, 261, 263, 273
Lust for Life 274
Lustig, Jan 176, 198, 224, 256, 258, 259, 268
Luther, Barbara 315
Lux Films 300, 303
Luxury Liner 219, 379
'Lydia the Tattooed Lady' 147
Lydon, James 202, 214, 232
Lyles, A.C. 313, 365
Lyn, Jacquie 82, 86
Lynch, Alfred 306, 326
Lynch, John 15
Lynde, Paul 333
Lyndon, Barre 237
Lynley, Carol 338, 347
Lynn, Diana 244
Lynn, Eleanor 138
Lynn, Emmett 252
Lynn, Jeffrey 240, 299
Lynn, Leni 152, 162
Lynn, Robert 302
Lynne, Sharon 120
Lyon, Ben 12, 66, 95
Lyon, Francis 313
Lyon, Richard 208, 307, 319
Lyon, Sue 306, 316, 329
Lyons, Chester 105
Lyons, Richard E. 315
Lytell, Bert 20

M 112, 164
M.A.S.H. 352
MGM British Studios 9, 76, 126, 134, 144, 149, 165, 186, 203, 224, 237, 244, 252, 256, 258, 263, 264, 266, 271, 274, 275, 280, 281, 283, 289, 293, 299, 302, 306, 307, 311, 312, 316, 319, 322, 333, 342, 345, 346, 350, 351, 352, 360
MGM Camera 65 278
MGM Grand Hotel 9, 368
MGM International 9, 204, 216
MGM Records 9
MGM Story, The 317
MGM Television 9, 303, 310, 313
MGM's Big Parade of Comedy 317, 322
MacArthur, Charles 66, 67, 69, 70, 76, 78, 86, 150, 307
MacBride, Donald 149, 171, 186, 188, 192, 203, 210, 293
MacCloy, June 162
MacDermott, Marc 10, 33, 36, 43, 47
MacDonald, J. Farrell 51, 75, 80, 92, 116, 132, 133, 134
MacDonald, Jeanette 54, 98, 100, 110, 119, 120, 125, 134, 136, 142, 144, 147, 156, 158, 169, 179, 187, 215, 218, 222, 266, 304, 379
MacDonald, Philip 100
MacDonald, Robert 290
MacDonough, Glen 100
MacDougall, Ranald 281, 295, 298
MacGill, Moyna 194, 214, 215, 244
MacGinnis, Niall 258, 264, 274, 345
MacGowran, Jack 182, 321, 338
MacGrath, Leueen 224
MacGraw, Ali 358
MacGregor, Edgar 71
Machaty, Gustav 149
MacInnes, Helen 184, 187, 331
Mack, Charles Emmett 20
Mack, Helen 97
Mack, Russell 102
Mack, Willard 12, 22, 27, 56, 57, 60, 61, 63, 64, 70, 71, 80, 95, 98
Mackaill, Dorothy 13, 28, 94
Mackay, Barry 143
Mackendrick, Alexander 338
MacKenzie, Aeneas 252
Mackenzie, Donald 289
MacLachlan, Janet 347
MacLaine, Shirley 289, 291, 303, 310, 317, 384
MacLane, Barton 143, 163, 174, 194, 319
MacLean, Alistair 344, 346
MacMahon, Aline 109, 116, 119, 176, 198, 206, 218, 296
MacMahon, Horace 132, 144, 149, 154, 158, 163, 164, 257, 268
MacMurray, Fred 120, 187, 242
Macnee, Patrick 283, 294
Macpherson, Jeanie 61, 67, 92
Macpherson, L. du Rocher 174
Macready, George 198, 238, 254
MacVeigh, Sue 181
Mad Dogs and Englishmen 360
Mad Holiday 122
Mad Love 112
Mad Masquerade 84
Mad Wednesday 232
Madam Satan 67
Madame Bovery 228
Madame Butterfly 147
Madame Curie 167, 191
Madame du Barry 141
Madame X 57, 76, 97, 131
Maddern, Victor 252, 277, 278, 283, 287
Maddow, Ben 228, 238, 242, 303
Made in Paris 327
Made on Broadway 92
Mademoiselle France 176
Mademoiselle Midnight 12
Madison, Noel 172
Maedchen in Uniform 82
Maesso, Jose 309
Magalona, Enrique 309
Magic Garden of Stanley Sweetheart, The 352
Magic Lamp, The 275
'Magic of Your Love, The' 151
Magician, The 30
Magnani, Anna 268
Magnificent Ambersons, The 176
Magnificent Obsession, The 120
Magnificent Yankee, The 232
Magrue, Roi Cooper 21, 42
Maguire, Kathleen 277, 311
Magwood, Paul 361
Maharis, George 322
Mahin, John Lee 82, 84, 89, 90, 92, 95, 97, 102, 107, 110, 126, 127, 132, 145, 165, 171, 174, 181, 186, 245, 247, 256
Mahoney, Jock 304, 312
Mahoney, Wilkie 182
Maibaum, Richard 123, 132, 135, 139, 159, 163, 273
Mail Order Bride 315
Main Attraction, The 309
Main, Laurie 365
Main, Marjorie 145, 146, 147, 149, 150, 162, 163, 165, 166, 168, 169,

171, 172, 174, 176, 182, 183, 186, 188, 192, 194, 203, 204, 208, 209, 222, 224, 236, 237, 242, 243, 244, 247, 256, 257, 266, 384
Main Street After Dark 197
Main Street to Broadway 257
Mainwaring, Daniel 300
Maisie 150
Maisie Gets Her Man 178
Maisie Goes to Reno 196
Maisie Was a Lady 162
Maitland, Colin 337
Maitland, Marne 277, 367
'*Make Believe*' 209, 247
'*Make 'em Laugh*' 374
Make Me a Star 214
Makeham, Eliot 165, 203
Mala 95, 117
Mala the Magnificent 95
Malamud, Bernard 345
Malaya 225
Malden, Karl 247, 257, 304, 312, 329, 345, 361
Malena, Lena 48
Malerba, Luigi 337
Mallalieu, Aubrey 165
Malle, Louis 307
Malleson, Miles 278, 299, 302, 319
Malloy, Doris 186
Malone, Dorothy 236, 281, 292
Maltese Bippy, The 347
Maltese Falcon, The 166
Malyon, Eily 154, 159, 198, 208
Mama Steps Out 135
Mamoulian, Rouben 98, 218, 283
Man and Maid 21
Man Called Dagger, A 337
Man for All Seasons, A 330
Man from Dakota, The 163
Man from Down Under, The 188
Man from U.N.C.L.E., The 322, 327, 328, 338, 342
Man in Possession, The 77, 131
Man in the Sky, The 277
Man Is Ten Feet Tall, A 277
Man of the People 133
Man on America's Conscience, The 182
Man on Fire 281
Man with a Cloak, The 244
Man with the Golden Arm, The 274
Man with Thirty Sons, The 232
Man Who Came to Dinner, The 166
Man Who Knew Too Much, The 109
Man Who Loved Cat Dancing, The 367
Man, Woman and Sin 43
Manchurian Candidate, The 310
Mancini, Al 337
Mandel, Frank 156
Mandel, Johnny 329
Mander, Miles 179, 181, 183, 184, 194, 202
Mangano, Sylvana 365
'*Manhattan*' 219
'*Manhattan Downbeat*' 224
Manhattan Melodrama 103, 179, 219
Mankiewicz, Don 269, 281
Mankiewicz, Herman J. 28, 97, 98, 104, 107, 112, 116, 132, 168, 182
Mankiewicz, Joseph L. 103, 107, 116, 123, 125, 127, 128, 133, 141, 143, 144, 146, 160, 165, 168, 169, 172, 176, 222, 232, 254, 271
Mankowitz, Wolf 322, 333
Manley, Walter 348
Mann, Anthony 222, 225, 228, 236, 243, 253, 296
Mann, Daniel 237, 277, 299, 302, 333
Mann, Delbert 268, 322
Mann, Hank 20
Mann, Louis 69
Manne, Shelley 303
Mannequin 133
Manners, J. Hartley 13
Mannheimer, Albert 150, 154, 159, 162, 172, 215
Manning, Bruce 231
Manning, Knox 174
Mannix, E.J. 117, 119, 122
Manoff, Arnold 216
Man-Proof 136
Man's Man, A 56
Man's World, A 24
Mansfield, Victor 117
Mantee, Paul 337
Mantell, Joe 333
Many Rivers to Cross 264
Marano, Ezio 365
Marauders, The 273
Marble, Alice 250
March, Alex 333
March, Fredric 54, 87, 105, 115, 128, 163, 174, 242, 249, 266, 275, 347
March, Joseph Moncure 143
March of Time, The 72, 95
Marchal, Georges 299
Marchant, William 355
Marcus, Lawrence 235, 361
Marcus Welby, M.D. 158
Mare Nostrum 20
Margetson, Arthur 177
Margheriti, Antonio 320, 337
Margo 120, 273
Margolin, Stuart 354
Margulies, Stan 364
Maria Candelaria 204
Marianne 64
Maricle, Leona 119
Marie Antoinette 103, 127, 141
Marie Walewska 136
Marihugh, Tammy 292, 303, 314
Marin, Edwin L. 102, 111, 112, 122, 126, 133, 136, 139, 140, 143, 147, 150, 151, 154, 159, 162, 163, 173
Marion, Frances 8, 20, 32, 35, 40, 41, 44, 47, 51, 52, 64, 69, 70, 71, 75, 76, 77, 84, 92, 95, 97, 116, 127
Marion, George F. 58, 64, 71
Marion-Crawford, Howard 289
Maris, Mona 85, 179
Marjorie Morningstar 284
Mark of the Vampire 117
Markey, Gene 69, 72, 77, 78, 89, 91, 92
Markham, Monte 364
Markle, Fletcher 243, 244
Marko, Zekial 326
Marks, Harry 360
Markson, David 354
Marlowe 347
Marlowe, Hugh 136, 192, 196, 342
Marlowe, Scott 276, 298
Marmont, Percy 24, 215
Marquand, John P. 174, 215
Marques, Maria Elena 243
Marquis, Don 135
Marriage Is a Private Affair 196
Marriage, Italian Style 345
Married Bachelor 169
Married Before Breakfast 136
Married Flirts 13
Marsh, Joan 69, 76, 77, 80, 84, 85, 145
Marsh, Mae 82, 218, 276
Marsh, Oliver T. 57, 100, 115, 117, 119, 121, 125
Marsh, Terry 325
Marshal, Alan 123, 128, 133, 136, 142, 145, 198, 276
Marshall, Bruce 225
Marshall, Dodie 334
Marshall, E.G. 281, 287
Marshall, George 86, 286, 289, 292, 304, 319
Marshall, Herbert 74, 95, 100, 103, 107, 111, 144, 171, 173, 187, 197, 213, 224
Marshall, Patricia 210
Marshall, Rosamond 298
Marshall, Tully 10, 13, 27, 46, 48, 57, 82, 85, 89, 119, 132, 134, 150, 162
Marshall, Virginia 24
Marshall, William 281, 322, 352, 361
Martin, Ana 334
Martin, Charles 208, 219
Martin, Chris-Pin 168
Martin, Dean 240, 262, 274, 278, 289, 291, 296, 302, 368
Martin, Dewey 261, 263, 278
Martin, Dick 333, 347
Martin, D'Urville 344
Martin, George Victor 204
Martin, Hugh 188, 192, 210
Martin, Marion 149, 162, 165, 169, 203, 230
Martin, Mary 257
Martin, Millicent 293, 302
Martin, Ross 289
Martin, Tony 168, 169, 209, 256, 267, 270, 384
Martin, Troy Kennedy 354, 360
Martinelli, Elsa 311
Martino, Giovanni 72
Marton, Andrew 194, 206, 236, 240, 253, 261, 263, 266, 289, 291, 327, 333
Marty 268
Marvin, Lee 266, 275, 278, 322, 337, 339, 346, 366
Marx, Arthur 314, 345
Marx Brothers 54, 78, 94, 111, 136, 147, 162, 168, 317
Marx Brothers at the Circus 147
Marx, Samuel 105, 122, 156, 172, 173, 174, 179, 183, 191, 198, 202, 206, 209, 234, 238, 249
Mary Names the Day 173
Mary Poppins 316, 330
Marzorati, Harold 295
Maschwitz, Eric 149, 151
Mascolo, Joseph 362
Mask of Comedy, The 32
Mask of Fu Manchu, The 85
Masked Bride, The 31
Maskerade 112
Masks of the Devil 47
Mason, Elliot 203
Mason, James 201, 224, 228, 251, 254, 256, 271, 289, 291, 306
Mason, LeRoy 52
Mason, Marlyn 351
Mason, Morgan 329
Mason, Portland 289
Mason, Reginald 102, 127
Mason, Sarah Y. 46, 56, 66, 72, 216
Massari, Lea 299
Massen, Osa 171
Massey, Ilona 128, 151, 208
Massey, Raymond 145, 196, 304
Massie, Paul 293
Master of Lassie 219
Masters, John 277
Mastroianni, Marcello 299, 307, 348
Mata Hari 76
Mate, Rudolph 295, 312
Mather, Aubrey 177, 183, 206, 210, 216, 224, 225
Matheson, Richard 294
Mathews, George 250, 261
Mathis, June 16, 18
Mating Game, The 289
Matter of W.H.O., A 302
Matthau, Walter 358
Matthews, Francis 277, 306, 319
Matthews, Jessie 109, 289
Matthews, Kerwin 342
Matthews, Lester 143, 174, 213, 252, 257, 344
Mattox, Martha 27, 32, 35
Mattox, Matt 263
Mature, Victor 251, 264, 300
Maugham, W. Somerset 24, 30, 67, 103, 174, 283, 316
Mauldin, Bill 240
Maurey, Nicole 293, 295
Maurice Guest 264
Maxwell, Edwin 69, 148, 154
Maxwell, James 313
Maxwell, Lois 312
Maxwell, Marilyn 182, 186, 187, 188, 196, 197, 209, 214, 218, 230
May, Anthony 357
Maya 333
Mayer, Edwin Justus 60, 66, 67, 77, 168
Mayer, Gerald 236, 243, 247, 250, 256, 273
Mayer, Louis B. 7, 8, 9, 10, 12, 16, 18, 19, 20, 21, 23, 27, 30, 35, 40, 41, 46, 47, 64, 69, 72, 78, 82, 86, 87, 91, 92, 94, 95, 97, 100, 102, 103, 104, 107, 116, 117, 125, 127, 128, 133, 134, 136, 138, 139, 141, 142, 146, 149, 150, 152, 163, 171, 172, 173, 179, 180, 182, 190, 191, 192, 206, 208, 209, 213, 216, 222, 224, 225, 237, 240, 245, 333
Mayerling 128, 164
Maynard, Ken 12
Mayne, Ferdy 302, 306, 338, 346, 355
Mayo, Archie 31
Mayo, Margaret 42, 82
Maytime 127, 134, 136, 267
Mazurki, Mike 195, 203, 225, 242, 273, 329
Mazursky, Paul 354
Mazza, Antonio 362
McAllister, Mary 32, 42
McAvoy, May 18, 31, 276
McBain, Diane 334, 338, 366
McCall, Mary Jr. 142, 150, 159, 162, 173, 187, 196, 198
McCallum, David 322, 328, 331, 333, 338, 339, 342
McCambridge, Mercedes 243, 296
McCarey, Ray 86
McCarthy, John P. 36, 43, 48
McCarthy, Senator Joseph 163, 188, 247, 345
McCarthy, Kevin 314, 361, 362
McCarthy, Neil 346
McCarthy, Nobu 303
McCartney, Paul 352
McClain, John 168, 171, 179
McCleary, Urie 169
McClory, Sean 268, 273
McCormack, Patty 296
McCormick, John 329, 345
McCowen, Alec 287, 312, 362
McCoy, Tim 30, 43, 51, 65
McCracken, Joan 210
McCrea, Jody 276
McCrea, Joel 61, 90, 109, 128, 185, 232, 236, 276, 307
McDaniel, Etta 178
McDaniel, Hattie 131, 141, 144, 152
McDermott, John 206
McDonald, Francis 15, 32
McDonald, Frank 143
McDonald, Marie 213
McDonald, Ray 169, 171, 173, 174, 187, 209, 210
McDowall, Roddy 191, 198, 202, 208, 298, 325, 360, 384
McDowell, Claire 18, 23
McEvoy, J.P. 85
McFarland, Spanky 117, 119, 123
McGee, Vonetta 362, 367
McGiver, John 292, 302, 304, 314, 327, 333
McGivern, William P. 264
McGoohan, Patrick 344, 357
McGowan, Jack 110, 123, 128, 152, 156, 171, 210
McGowan, John 44
McGraw, Charles 225, 228, 286, 296, 307, 361
McGregor, Malcolm 15, 24, 31
McGuinness, James K. 95, 110, 114, 131, 132, 142, 150, 163, 172
McGuire, Dorothy 201, 242, 269
McGuire, Kathryn 15
McGuire, Marcy 210
McGuire, William Anthony 43, 121, 128, 142, 168
McGunigle, Robert 172
McHugh, Frank 126, 162, 179, 201
McIntire, John 218, 225, 228, 231, 238, 240, 250, 273
McKee, Raymond 13, 15
McKellen, Ian 350
McKenna, Siobhan 300, 316, 325
McKenna, T.P. 321, 360
McKenna, Virginia 275, 293
McKenzie, Fay 100
McKern, Leo 345, 354
McKinney, Florine 94, 100
McKinney, Nina Mae 54, 116
McLaglen, Victor 23, 109, 146, 264
McLaren, Ian 219
McLeod, Catherine 206
McLeod, Mary 198
McLeod, Norman Z. 134, 142, 147, 165, 171, 182, 183, 187
McManus, Sharon 201, 202, 206, 210, 216
McNally, Horace (Stephen) 178, 180, 181, 183, 186, 188, 198, 202, 203, 204, 274
McNaughton, Charles 117
McNaughton, Jack 252
McNulty, Dorothy 71, 72, 123
McNutt, Patterson 141, 163
McPhail, Angus 165
McPhail, Douglas 152, 156, 174
McQueen, Butterfly 152, 183, 191
McQueen, Steve 284, 292, 303, 310, 329, 346
McRae, Carmen 298
McShane, Ian 360, 361
McSherry, Mary 261
McStay, Michael 342
McTeague 16
McWade, Margaret 10
McWade, Robert 95, 123, 135
Mead, Robert 360
Meadows, Jayne 208, 213
Meadows, Joyce 327
Medford, Don 322
Medford, Kay 187, 299
Medical Center 360
Medina, Patricia 208, 219, 292
Medioli, Enrico 365
Medwin, Michael 316
Meehan, Elizabeth 52
Meehan, John 67, 72, 75, 76, 77, 81, 84, 90, 92, 94, 95, 102, 103, 105, 126, 131, 138, 194, 202, 215
Meehan, John Jr. 172
Meek, Donald 100, 105, 109, 114, 117, 122, 123, 133, 154, 162, 163, 165, 168, 169, 171, 174, 178, 179, 180, 181, 183, 186, 187, 190, 192, 195, 196, 198
Meeker, George 77, 102, 141, 152, 171
Meeker, Ralph 235, 242, 250, 252, 253, 258, 302, 337
Meet John Doe 166
Meet Me in Las Vegas 271
Meet Me in St Louis 192, 216, 218, 370
Meet the Baron 94
Meet the People 197
Meighan, Thomas 18, 66
Meillon, John 304
Meins, Gus 100, 136
Melcher, Martin 276, 307, 333, 344
Melchior, Lauritz 201, 209, 210, 219
Melinda 362
Melly, Andree 289
Melnick, Daniel 368
Meloney, W.B. 208
Melson, Charles 143
Melton, James 201
Meltzer, Lewis 286, 294
Melvin, Murray 358
Men, The 232
Men Call it Love 78
Men in White 104, 105
Men Must Fight 91
Men of Boys Town 172
Men of the Fighting Lady 263
Men of the North 71
Mendelssohn, Eleanora 224
Mendes, Lothar 89
Menjou, Adolphe 10, 15, 72, 75, 77, 78, 210, 218, 237, 243
Menzies, William Cameron 152
Merande, Doro 292
Mercenaries, The 341
Mercer, Beryl 67, 69, 77, 84, 87, 117, 128
Mercer, Frances 147
Mercer, Johnny 204, 247, 259, 263
Merchant, Vivian 350
Mercier, Michele 303, 314
Mercouri, Melina 299
Meredith, Burgess 143, 145, 344
Meredith, Cheerio 314
Meredyth, Bess 18, 24, 51, 52, 57, 63, 67, 69, 71, 76, 77, 85, 94
Merivale, Bernard 122
Merivale, Philip 174, 176, 190, 192, 201
Merkel, Una 80, 85, 87, 90, 91, 94, 95, 97, 100, 102, 103, 105, 107, 110, 115, 116, 117, 119, 123, 126, 131, 135, 145, 154, 216, 243, 249, 289, 334
Merlin, Jan 317
Merlin, Milton 141, 154
Merman, Ethel 182, 187
Merrill, Dina 299, 310
Merrill, Gary 251, 333, 338, 339, 355, 360
Merrily We Go to Hell 82
Merrily We Live 142
Merritt, Abraham 122
Merry Andrew 284
Merry Widow, The 27, 36, 66, 100, 249, 261
Merry Wives of Gotham, The 19
Merton of the Movies 214
Mervyn, William 319
Mestral, Armand 303
Metro Pictures 7, 8, 46, 51, 195
Metrocolor 274, 287, 303, 344, 365
Metroscopix 256, 258
Mexican Village 250
Meyer, Emile 244, 367
Meyer, Greta 94, 110, 156
Michael, Gertrude 85
Michael, Ralph 312, 313, 319
Michaels, Beverly 228
Michaels, Nicola 276
Michaels, Sidney 298
Michell, Keith 312
Michener, James 278
Mickey Mouse 102
Middlemass, Robert 136, 150
Middleton, Charles 66, 86, 204
Middleton, Robert 269, 286, 313
Midnight Cowboy 346, 352
Midnight Mary 91
Midshipman, The 19, 51
Midsummer Night's Dream, A 109
Midwich Cuckoos, The 299
Mifune, Toshiro 334
Mighty Barnum, The 72
Mighty McGurk, The 206
Mike 30
Mildred Pierce 201
Miles, Bernard 256, 289
Miles, Sarah 336, 354, 367
Miles, Vera 303, 331
Milestone, Lewis 66, 216, 309
Miljan, John 20, 39, 56, 57, 60, 64, 66, 69, 71, 74, 75, 76, 78, 81, 82, 84, 85, 87, 92, 94, 98, 136, 151, 156
'*Milkman, Keep Those Bottles Quiet*' 191
Milland, Ray 70, 78, 82, 89, 201, 237, 243, 283
Millar, Ronald 237, 247, 250, 256, 264, 266
Millard, Helene 64, 74, 259
Millarde, Harry 33, 43
Millay, Edna St Vincent 186
Miller, Alice Duer 13, 15, 31, 32, 35, 43, 51, 57, 126, 154, 163, 198, 249
Miller, Ann 216, 220, 222, 227, 232, 243, 249, 257, 267, 270, 276, 377
Miller, Cheryl 327
Miller, Colleen 276
Miller, David 168, 179, 273, 276
Miller, Dean 249, 251, 261
Miller, Denny 293
Miller, Martin 186, 293, 311, 312
Miller Music 9
Miller, Sidney 172, 320
Millhauser, Bertram 90, 122, 154, 182
Milligan, Spike 302, 306
Million Dollar Mermaid 251, 380
Mills Brothers 103
Mills, Hugh 131
Mills, John 149, 287, 322, 354
Mills, Reginald 360
Milner, Martin 327
Milton, Franklin 290
Mimieux, Yvette 298, 302, 303, 314, 320, 322, 341, 364
Min and Bill 69, 75, 77
'*Mind If I Make Love to You?*' 277
Mineo, Sal 277, 333
Miniver Story, The 180, 237
Minnelli, Liza 220, 362, 368, 370
Minnelli, Vincente 183, 191, 192, 201, 203, 204, 208, 209, 220, 222, 228, 233, 238, 247, 252, 254, 256, 266, 273, 274, 276, 278, 284, 286, 289, 293, 296, 299, 302, 307, 310, 329
'*Minnie from Trinidad*' 168
Miracle Man, The 39
Miracles for Sale 147
Miracle Worker, The 304
Mirage, The 78
Miranda, Carmen 220, 231
Miranda, Isa 317
Mirren, Helen 364
Miss Susie Slagle's 201
Mission of Danger 294
Mistral, Jorge 328
Mitchell, Cameron 202, 206, 214, 215, 218, 247, 270
Mitchell, Grant 95, 97, 105, 122, 126, 127, 132, 149, 150, 156, 159, 164, 169, 174, 179, 186, 209
Mitchell, Gwen 361
Mitchell, James 225, 232, 234, 236, 254, 267, 268
Mitchell, Joseph 14, 15
Mitchell, Margaret 152
Mitchell, Millard 169, 181, 188, 243, 249, 253
Mitchell, Thomas 133, 152, 186, 201, 206, 214, 287
Mitchell, Warren 278, 302, 306, 309, 350
Mitchell, Yvonne 309, 365
Mitchum, Jim 294
Mitchum, Robert 198, 208, 214, 295, 299, 354, 361, 364
Mitford, Nancy 280, 292
Mittler, Leo 188
Mix, Tom 30
Mobley, Mary Ann 320, 322, 327
Mock, Laurie 339
Mockery 39
Modern Times 120
Modugno, Domenico 331
Moffa, Paulo 312
Moffatt, Geraldine 356
Moffatt, Ivan 277
Moffitt, Jeff 110
Moffo, Anna 362
Mogambo 256, 257
Mokey 178
Moll, Georgia 303
Molnar, Ferenc 64, 80, 128, 169, 197, 274
Monash, Paul 283, 303
Money Talks 31
Money Trap, The 326
Mong, William V. 66, 67
Monks, John Jr. 156, 236, 244
Monroe, Marilyn 236, 238, 240, 262, 268, 274, 281, 291
Monroe, Vaughn 197
Monsieur Beaucaire 10
Monsieur Verdoux 210
Monster, The 22
Montague, Lee 302
Montalban, Ricardo 211, 216, 219, 222, 225, 234, 236, 243, 250, 253, 261, 326, 333, 339
Montana Moon 70
Montand, Yves 299, 334
Monte Carlo 31
Montenegro, Conchita 77, 81
Montevecchi, Liliane 264, 268, 271, 281
Montgomery, Douglass 69, 80, 81, 164
Montgomery, George 294, 347
Montgomery, Robert 60, 64, 67, 69, 71, 72, 75, 77, 80, 81, 82, 84, 90, 92, 94, 98, 100, 102, 103, 107, 112, 115, 123, 126, 128, 131, 132, 135, 141, 142, 143, 151, 154, 165, 168, 171, 174, 186, 202, 208, 214, 218, 252, 316, 347
Moody, Ralph 264
Moody, Ron 319
Moon is Blue, The 315
Moon, Lorna 32, 39, 40
Mooney, Martin 109
Moonfleet 268
Moonlight Murder 126
Moonshine War, The 357
Moore, Archie 296, 367
Moore, Colleen 18
Moore, Dickie 91, 92, 128
Moore, Grace 72, 120
Moore, Juanita 273, 333
Moore, Kieron 295, 299, 307, 309, 328
Moore, Lisa 362
Moore, Matt 23, 24, 36, 43, 122, 178, 201, 225, 232, 242
Moore, Michael 339
Moore, Owen 23, 28, 31, 32, 33, 36, 42, 47, 89
Moore, Roger 264, 271, 273, 366
Moore, Terry 298, 337
Moore, Tom 13, 27, 36, 64, 126
Moore, Victor 201
Moorehead, Agnes 191, 198, 203, 204, 218, 224, 247, 256, 257, 261, 271, 274, 276, 278, 286, 302, 304, 333
Moorhead, Natalie 57, 66, 77, 78, 104, 147
Moran, Eddie 134, 142
Moran, Gussie 250
Moran, Lee 47
Moran, Lois 28, 78
Moran, Polly 39, 41, 42, 44, 46, 47, 51, 52, 56, 57, 60, 63, 66, 67, 69, 70, 76, 78, 82, 85, 228, 230
Morand, Paul 214
More, Kenneth 256, 341
More Than a Miracle 338
'*More Than You Know*' 72
More the Merrier, The 185

Moreau, Jeanne 317, 354
Morell, Andre 291, 341
Moreno, Antonio 20, 31, 32, 33, 110, 232
Moreno, Rita 234, 237, 249, 261, 300, 347
Morgan, Ainsworth 127, 132
Morgan, Byron 41, 48, 51, 56, 66, 85, 95, 110, 141
Morgan, Dennis: see Morner, Stanley
Morgan, Frank 90, 94, 95, 97, 98, 110, 112, 116, 117, 121, 126, 128, 131, 132, 133, 135, 142, 143, 144, 147, 151, 154, 156, 162, 163, 165, 168, 169, 171, 174, 181, 182, 186, 187, 198, 203, 206, 208, 209, 214, 218, 219, 222, 224, 228, 230, 234
Morgan, Helen 54
Morgan, Henry 179, 194, 228, 253, 258, 259, 292, 296, 304
Morgan, Michele 280
Morgan, Ralph 85, 86, 87, 109, 123, 126, 133, 134, 143, 151, 163, 186, 213
Morgan the Pirate 303
Morgan's Last Raid 65
Morhaim, Joseph 277
Morison, Patricia 186, 204, 213
Morley, Karen 69, 76, 77, 78, 81, 82, 84, 85, 87, 92, 97, 102, 160
Morley, Robert 141, 224, 266, 271, 287, 293, 296, 313, 316, 325, 333, 345
Morner, Stanley 121, 133, 135, 384
Morning Glory 90
Morocco 66
Moropticon 255
Morris, Chester 54, 67, 69, 87, 105, 112, 125, 126, 154
Morris, Dorothy 169, 173, 183, 186, 191, 197, 198, 204
Morris, Edmund 309
Morris, Howard 306
Morris, Kirk 327
Morris, Oswald 266
Morris, Peggy 183
Morris, Phyllis 186, 216, 224, 244
Morris, Rebecca 364
Morris, Richard 319
Morrison, E.G. 201, 218
Morrison, Joseph 13
Morriss, Ann 140, 143, 147, 156, 162, 163, 169, 276
Morrow, Doretta 251, 378
Morrow, Douglas 224
Morrow, Honore Willsie 139
Morrow, Jo 315
Morrow, Vic 268, 274, 296
Morse, Robert 319, 322, 325, 344
Mort du Cygne 214
Mortal Storm, The 162
Mortimer, Caroline 348
Mortimer, John 306
Morton, Charles 70
Morton, Clive 302, 333
Morton, Hugh 247
Morton, Tom 257
Mosley, Bryan 356
Moss, Arnold 225, 235
Moss, Jerry 360
'*Most Beautiful Girl in the World, The*' 307
Mostel, Zero 187
Moulder-Brown, John 365
Moulin Rouge 262
Mount, Peggy 333
Mourning Becomes Electra 210
Movietone 36
Movita 261, 309
Mowbray, Alan 76, 77, 84, 92, 100, 119, 134, 142, 172, 179, 182, 188, 214, 273
Mower, Patrick 355
Mozart, W.A. 210
Mr and Mrs North 169
Mr Buddwing 333
Mr Cinderella 123
Mr Deeds Goes to Town 120
Mr Griggs Returns 209
Mr Imperium 243
Mr Ricco 368
Mr Smith Goes to Washington 146
Mr Wu 39
Mrs Brown, You've Got a Lovely Daughter 345
Mrs McGinty's Dead 319
Mrs Miniver 172, 176, 198, 216
Mrs O'Malley and Mr Malone 236
Mrs Parkington 192
Mudie, Leonard 150
Mueller, Elisabeth 276, 295
Muir, Esther 136
Muir, Jean 163
Mulhall, Jack 140, 147
Mulhare, Edward 321, 338
Mullaney, Jack 280, 298, 303, 334
Mulligan, Gerry 296, 298
Mundin, Herbert 117, 119, 125, 142, 147
Muni, Paul 54, 90, 127, 128, 182
Munshin, Jules 220, 222, 226, 227, 231, 278, 283
Munson, Ona 152
Murat, Jean 243
Murder Ahoy 319
Murder at the Gallop 313
Murder for a Wanton 123
Murder in a Chinese Theatre 122
Murder in the Fleet 115
Murder in the Private Car 103
Murder in Thornton Square, The 194
Murder Man, The 116
Murder Men, The 303
Murder Most Foul 319
Murder on the Runaway Train 103
Murder She Said 302, 306
Murdock, Tim 198
Murfin, Jane 24, 143, 144, 147, 160, 165, 169, 198
Murger, Henry 24
Murphy, Audie 240, 284
Murphy, Dean 191
Murphy, Dennis 338
Murphy, Dudley 107
Murphy, Edna 32
Murphy, George 71, 128, 132, 156, 173, 177, 186, 191, 195, 203, 214, 215, 219, 222, 225, 242, 250
Murphy, Mary 257
Murphy, Michael 352
Murray, Charles 30, 35
Murray, Don 307
Murray, James 36, 39, 40, 43, 57
Murray, Jan 337
Murray, Ken 338
Murray, Mae 8, 12, 15, 27, 25, 44, 47, 214
Murray, Mary 345
Musante, Tony 326, 360
Muscle Beach 338
Muse, Clarence 119, 141, 159
Music for Millions 192
Musselman, M.M. 195
'*Must to Avoid, A*' 333
Mutiny on the Bounty 109, 119, 120, 214, 309, 310
My Brother Talks to Horses 206
My Dear Miss Aldrich 132
My Fair Lady 316
'*My Funny Valentine*' 152
'*My Heart is Bluer Than Your Eyes, Cherie*' 56
My Hero! 216
My Life is Yours 172
My Lover, My Son 355
My Man and I 253
My Sister Eileen 176
Myers, Carmel 18, 20, 28, 31, 32, 35, 51, 60
Myers, Harry 31, 35, 57
Myers, Peter 281, 286, 299
Myers, Zion 78
Myra Breckenridge 179
Myrtil, Odette 176, 184
Mysterious Island, The 56, 144, 350
Mysterious Lady, The 52, 76
Mystery of Mr X, The 100, 252
Mystery Street 236
Mystic, The 20

Nabokov, Vladimir 306
Nader, George 289
Nagel, Conrad 8, 10, 12, 13, 15, 19, 21, 24, 27, 31, 32, 35, 39, 41, 48, 52, 58, 60, 61, 63, 64, 66, 67, 76, 81, 84, 117
Naish, J. Carrol 82, 109, 120, 122, 126, 133, 179, 183, 186, 198, 203, 216, 222, 224, 231, 232, 234, 243, 270, 280
Naismith, Laurence 256, 274, 275, 280, 299, 344
Naked and the Dead, The 284
Naked Spur, The 253
Naldi, Nita 18, 280
Nancy Goes to Rio 231
Napier, Alan 177, 179, 184, 190, 191, 198, 211, 219, 225, 243, 247, 254, 268, 321
'Napoleon' 39, 46
Napoleon 44
Nash, Florence 147
Nash, Johnny 298
Nash, Mary 159, 160, 172, 183, 191, 203, 209
Nash, Ogden 122, 136, 144, 169
Nathan, Robert 204, 237
National Broadcasting Co. 146
National Velvet 196
Naturama 255
Natwick, Mildred 203, 216, 218, 347
Naughty Marietta 110
Navigator, The 15, 28
Navy Blue and Gold 135
Navy Blues 64
Nayfack, Nicholas 225, 236, 242, 247, 250, 259, 264, 273, 276, 281
Nazarro, Ray 281
Nazi Agent 172
Nazimova 164
Neagle, Anna 82
Neal, Lex 28
Neal, Patricia 251, 310, 329, 344, 360
Neal, Tom 141, 143, 145, 147, 149, 154, 165
Neame, Ronald 283
Nebel, Frederick 219
Nebenzahl, Seymour 164, 186
Nedell, Bernard 146, 149, 151, 165, 180, 196
Negri, Pola 10, 18, 35, 44, 64
Negulesco, Jean 143, 261, 292
Neil, James 61
Neilan, Marshall 8, 12, 20, 21, 30
Neilan, Marshall Jr. 232
Neill, Roy William 52
Neilson, James 334, 347
Nelson, Barry 171, 173, 174, 177, 181, 183, 184, 186, 191, 209, 213, 214
Nelson, Gene 313, 319, 320, 327
Nelson, Ozzie 345
Nelson, Ralph 326, 347, 364
Nelson, Ricky 256
Nelson, Ruth 209
Neptune's Daughter 225, 251, 380
Nero, Franco 337, 367
Nervig, Conrad 95
Nesbitt, Cathleen 360
Nesbitt, Derren 306, 346
Nesbitt, John 208
Netter, Douglas 368
Nettleton, Lois 304, 312, 315, 354
Neuman, E. Jack 331
Neumann, Kurt 132, 294
Never Let Me Go 256
Never Love a Stranger 284
Never on Sunday 300
Never so Few 292
Never the Twain Shall Meet 20, 77
New Adventures of Get-Rich-Quick Wallingford, The 78
New Moon 72, 156, 267
New Morals for Old 86
Newcom, James 152
Newcombe, Warren 214
Newhart, Bob 345
Newhouse, David & Rafe 339
Newhouse, Edward 242
Newland, Douglass 171, 179
Newland, John 328, 355
Newlands, Anthony 327
Newman, Joseph 179, 293, 303
Newman, Nanette 316, 350
Newman, Paul 275, 277, 278, 289, 300, 304, 306, 310, 314, 317, 326, 330, 346, 366
Newmar, Julie 347
Newmeyer, Fred 123
Newton, Robert 165, 240
Newton, Theodore 202, 277
Next Voice You Hear, The 237
Ney, Marie 228
Ney, Richard 176, 183
Niblo, Fred 8, 12, 18, 33, 36, 51, 52, 66, 69
Nicholas Brothers 220, 374, 384
Nicholas, Denise 368
Nicholls, Anthony 283, 287
Nicholls, Sarah 339
Nichols, Barbara 298, 320, 325, 338
Nichols, Dudley 102
Nichols, Mike 340
Nicholson, Jack 368
Nicholson, Kenyon 69
Nick Carter, Master Detective 154
Nicol, Alex 302, 309, 328
Nielsen, Leslie 273, 276, 286, 342
Nieto, Jose 281
Niggli, Josefina 250
Nigh, William 31, 39, 43, 51, 56, 61
Night and Day 206
Night at the Opera, A 111, 136
Night Court 84
Night Digger, The 360
Night Flight 98
Night Hostess 64
Night in Cairo, A 92
Night Into Morning 243
Night is Young, The 107
Night Must Fall 128, 154, 174, 316, 360
Night of Dark Shadows 361
Night of the Iguana, The 316
Night of the Lepus 365
Night of the Quarter Moon 286
Nightmare Alley 210
Nightmare Honeymoon 365
Nilsson, Anna Q. 214, 232
Nimmo, Derek 319, 331
Nimoy, Leonard 361
Ninotchka 148, 165, 283, 317, 372
Niven, David 119, 234, 240, 273, 280, 290, 291, 298, 316, 322, 326, 338, 340, 344, 345
No Blade of Grass 357
No Leave, No Love 208
No Minor Vices 216
No More Ladies 115
No, No, Nanette 72
No Questions Asked 242
Noble, William 187
Nobody's Baby 136
Noel, Chris 322
Nolan, Jeanette 219, 274, 313, 365
Nolan, Lloyd 159, 183, 186, 208, 209, 218, 273, 344
Nolan, Mary 47, 56
None But the Lonely Heart 192
Noone, Peter 333, 345
Norden, Denis 350
Nordhoff, Charles 119, 214
Norman, Leslie 287
Norman, Lucille 178, 208
Norris, Charles G. 15
Norris, Edward 133, 138
Norris, Frank 16
Norris, Kathleen 67
North by Northwest 291, 293
North, Jay 294, 327, 333
North, Sheree 346, 351, 355, 367
Northwest Passage 149, 294
Northwest Rangers 179
Norton, Edgar 70, 134
Norton, Grace 159
Norton, William 367
Norvo, Red 243
Not So Dumb 60
Not Too Narrow, Not Too Deep 165
Nothing But The Truth 166
Nothing But Trouble 192
Nothing Sacred 128
Noti, Karl 143
Novak, Kim 43, 274, 306, 316, 338, 344
Novarro, Nick 313
Novarro, Ramon 8, 10, 12, 18, 19, 32, 36, 39, 51, 56, 60, 67, 72, 76, 81, 84, 85, 86, 92, 98, 102, 107, 232, 236, 250
Novello, Ivor 86, 168
Novello, Jay 327
Novotna, Jarmila 218, 247
'*Now You Has Jazz*' 277
Nowhere to Go 289
Noy, Wilfred 77
Nugent, Eddie 47, 49, 51, 52, 56, 57, 60, 66, 69, 71, 77, 91, 94, 117, 119, 133
Nugent, Elliott 57, 60, 64, 67, 69, 71, 85, 232
Nugent, Frank 218
Nugent, J.C. 56, 57, 64, 66, 69, 71, 72
Nuisance, The 94, 140
Nunn, Larry 156, 162, 172, 174, 179
Nun's Story, The 291
Nusciak, Loredana 317
Nutmeg Tree, The 216
Nye, Carroll 51, 52, 57, 64, 152

Oakie, Jack 82
Oakman, Wheeler 52, 65
Oates, Warren 307, 315, 339, 345, 361
Ober, Philip 247, 251, 261, 287, 289, 291, 298, 303
Ober, Robert 64, 232
Oberon, Merle 203, 267, 384
'*Object of My Affection, The*' 109
Oboler, Arch 164, 202, 215, 255
O'Brian, Hugh 236, 312
O'Brien, Dave 257
O'Brien, Edmond 254, 275, 292, 364
O'Brien, Joan 287, 311
O'Brien, Margaret 180, 187, 190, 191, 192, 195, 201, 203, 204, 206, 214, 216, 219, 222, 224, 384
O'Brien, Pat 77, 97, 244
O'Brien, Robert 247, 346
O'Brien, Robert H. 9
O'Brien, Tom 15, 18, 31, 32, 41, 43
O'Brien, Virginia 162, 169, 171, 173, 180, 182, 187, 192, 197, 201, 204, 208, 209, 214, 384
O'Casey, Sean 321
Occhini, Illaria 304
O'Connell, Arthur 303, 317, 319, 320, 338, 364, 366
O'Connell, Helen 191
O'Connor, Carroll 339, 347, 354
O'Connor, Donald 249, 303, 368, 374, 384
O'Connor, Frank 15
O'Connor, Robert Emmet 51, 69, 97, 111, 186, 189, 194, 206
O'Connor, Una 105, 107, 117, 119, 127, 131, 177, 195
O'Day, Anita 352, 367
O'Day, Molly 43
Odd Man Out 210
O'Dea, Denis 256
Odets, Clifford 192
O'Donnell, Cathy 228, 237, 291
Odor of Violets 181
O'Driscoll, Martha 150, 163
Of Human Bondage 100, 283, 316
Of Human Hearts 139
Of Mice and Men 146
Offerman, George 150, 186
O'Flynn, Philip 321
Oh! What a Lovely War 346
O'Hanlon, James 196, 204, 206
O'Hara, George 52
O'Hara, John 215, 281, 299
O'Hara, Maureen 276
O'Herlihy, Daniel 240, 342, 364
O'Keefe, Dennis 126, 135, 140, 141, 150, 249
Oklahoma! 218, 263, 273
Oland, Warner 13, 15, 28, 51, 86, 103
O'Laughlin, Gerald 344
Old Acquaintance 185
Old Clothes 27
Old Hutch 123
Old Lady 31 162
Old Maid, The 146
Old Man and the Sea, The 284
'*Old Man Moon*' 134
'*Old Man River*' 209, 247
Old School Tie, The 123
Old Soak, The 135
Oliver! 340
Oliver, Edna May 94, 107, 115, 119, 125, 128, 132, 133, 135, 160
Oliver, Susan 317, 319, 320
Olivier, Laurence 74, 98, 160, 201, 223, 249, 345
Olmstead, Gertrude 22, 27, 31, 35, 36, 39, 41, 42, 51
Olsen, Moroni 172, 176, 202, 206, 209, 213, 218, 233, 238, 240, 242, 251, 256
Olympia 64
Omaha Trail, The 179
O'Malley, Pat 15, 20
O'Malley, Rex 127
Omooloo, Mutia 70
O'Moore, Patrick 169
On an Island with You 219
On Borrowed Time 154
'*On the Atchison, Topeka and Santa Fe*' 204
On the Beach 296
On the Buses 358
On the Town 227, 249, 270
On the Waterfront 262
'*On Your Toes*' 378
On Ze Boulevard 43
Once a Thief 326
Once Upon a Thursday 183
'*One Day When We Were Young*' 142
'*One Finger Concerto*' 192
One Hour with You 100
One is a Lonely Number 364
'*One Kiss*' 72
One New York Night 117
One Night in Rome 13
One of Our Spies is Missing 331
One Piece Bathing Suit, The 251
One Romantic Night 274
One Spy too Many 331
One Way Passage 82
O'Neal, Frederick 281
O'Neal, Patrick 344, 361
O'Neal, Ryan 361, 366
O'Neil, Barbara 141, 152
O'Neil, Nance 64, 67
O'Neil, Sally 20, 24, 27, 28, 36, 41, 43
O'Neill, Eileen 337
O'Neill, Eugene 58, 85, 119, 218
O'Neill, Frank 154
O'Neill, Henry 140, 141, 146, 156, 165, 168, 169, 171, 172, 173, 174, 181, 182, 184, 186, 187, 188, 189, 190, 191, 192, 198, 201, 203, 206, 209, 244
O'Neill, Jennifer 364
Only Eight Hours 105, 109
Only Thing, The 21
Only Yesterday 90
Opatoshu, David 286, 296, 331
Open City 210
Operation Crossbow 322
Operation Heartbeat 360
Operator 13 103
Ophuls, Max 224
Oppenheimer, Alan 366
Oppenheimer, George 112, 123, 125, 134, 135, 136, 143, 156, 162, 167, 169, 179, 183, 188, 191, 210
Opposite Sex, The 276
Orbach, Jerry 361
Orbison, Roy 339
Orczy, Baroness 132
Orfei, Liana 300, 304, 327
Oringer, Barry 304
Orlandi, Felice 367
Orr, William T. 150, 162, 172, 366
Orry-Kelly 247, 283
Orsatti, Vic 281
Orsini, Umberto 337, 365
Orth, Frank 173, 183, 233
Osato, Sono 216
Osborn, David 312
Osborn, Paul 97, 154, 186, 191, 206, 218, 242
Osborne, John 365
Osborne, Vivienne 115, 123
Oscar, Henry 280, 319
O'Shaughnessy's Boy 119
O'Shea, Oscar 133, 136, 139, 144, 149, 202
Ossessione 208
Ostrer, Bertram 350
Ostrow, Lou 126, 149, 150
O'Sullivan, Maureen 84, 85, 86, 89, 95, 103, 104, 105, 107, 109, 110, 111, 115, 117, 120, 122, 125, 132, 133, 134, 136, 140, 142, 143, 151, 159, 160, 162, 172, 180, 275, 278
O'Toole, Peter 299, 316, 351, 352
Ottiano, Rafaela 82, 84, 89, 134, 141
Our Blushing Brides 69
Our Dancing Daughters 49, 51, 57
Our Gang 8, 43, 77, 86, 119, 123
'*Our Love Affair*' 156
Our Modern Maidens 57
Our Mother's House 339
Our Relations 120
Our Vines Have Tender Grapes 204, 206
Oury, Gerard 314
Ouspenskaya, Maria 136, 150, 162, 164
Out West With the Hardys 143
Outcast Lady 107
Outfit, The 367
Outlaw, The 184
Outrage, The 317
Outriders, The 236
Outsider, The 76
Outward Bound 66
Over the Border 182
'*Over the Rainbow*' 151
Overland Telegraph, The 65
Overman, Lynne 136, 159
Owen, Catherine Dale 64, 67
Owen, Harold 39
Owen, Reginald 77, 84, 86, 98, 112, 115, 117, 119, 121, 123, 126, 127, 128, 131, 135, 136, 139, 141, 143, 146, 147, 151, 154, 162, 163, 168, 171, 172, 176, 177, 178, 179, 182, 183, 184, 186, 187, 191, 195, 196, 202, 203, 214, 215, 216, 219, 220, 222, 224, 225, 234, 235, 237, 261
Owen, Tudor 253
Owens, Patricia 286
Owsley, Monroe 85, 123
Ox-Bow Incident, The 185

Pabst, G.W. 82
Pace, Judy 362, 367
Pacific Rendezvous 179
Pack Up Your Troubles 86
Padden, Sarah 57, 138, 144, 146, 184
Padilla, Manuel 313
'*Pagan Love Song*' 56
Pagan Love Song 237, 377
Pagan, The 56, 60
Pagano, Ernest 56, 163
Page, Anita 44, 49, 51, 52, 57, 63, 64, 69, 70, 71, 75, 78, 82, 84, 85
Page, Bradley 169
Page, Genevieve 313, 334
Page, Geraldine 306
Page, Joy Ann 194
Page, Marco: see Kurnitz, Harry
Page, Patti 306
Page, Rita 156
Paget, Debra 273
Pagnol, Marcel 142
Paid 69, 149
Paige, Janis 283, 298, 302, 312, 339
Paige, Mabel 203
Painted Hills, The 242
Painted Veil, The 103, 283
'Pal' 202, 206
Pal, George 289, 298, 300, 314, 317, 338
Pal Joey 178
Palance, Jack 281, 326, 331
Pallette, Eugene 78, 90, 92, 117, 134, 159, 188
Pallos, Steven 322, 350
Palmer, Charles 247
Palmer, Lilli 216, 257, 322, 338
Palmer, Maria 243
Palmer, Stuart 236
Paluzzi, Luciana 322, 331, 348, 350
Pan, Hermes 234, 247
Panama Hattie 182, 187
Panama, Norman 216, 242, 243, 251, 347
Panavision 365
Pangborn, Franklin 35, 60, 126, 143, 147
Papas, Irene 274
Paper Moon 366
Paradine, Case, The 210
Paradis, Marjorie 91
Paradise for Three 135
Paramore, E.E. Jr. 125, 126, 141, 159
Paramount on Parade 63
Paramount Pictures 7, 8, 18, 28, 30, 35, 41, 44, 46, 57, 64, 67, 74, 82, 90, 98, 100, 103, 104, 109, 111, 128, 141, 146, 166, 168, 174, 176, 182, 192, 196, 206, 208, 209, 210, 214, 222, 224, 234, 240, 250, 284, 291, 296, 317, 330, 352, 362
Pardon Us 77
Paris 32
Paris Interlude 102
Paris, Jerry 263

Parisy, Andrea 327
Parker, Barnett 128, 132, 134, 135, 136, 139, 140, 141, 143, 147, 152, 162
Parker, Cecil 144, 293, 326
Parker, Cecilia 103, 110, 117, 119, 123, 136, 138, 141, 143, 150, 158, 165, 173, 181, 182, 183, 289
Parker, Dorothy 127, 144
Parker, Eleanor 210, 250, 251, 259, 264, 271, 280, 283, 299, 342
Parker, Frank 250
Parker, Jean 90, 92, 97, 102, 103, 105, 115
Parker, Lara 361
Parker, Willard 257
Parkhill, Forbes 143
Parks, Gordon 361, 362, 368
Parks, Larry 247
Parks, Michael 355
Parlor, Bedroom and Bath 78
Parnell 133
Parnell, Emory 230, 237, 253
Parrott, James 77, 120, 143
Parrott, Ursula 67, 78, 81
Parsonnet, Marion 133, 134, 147, 151, 162, 165, 174, 203
Parsons, Louella 47
Parsons, Nicholas 319
Partos, Frank 140
Party Girl 286
'Party's Over, The' 296
Pascal, Gabriel 201
Pascal, Jefferson 357
Pass, Mary Kay 362
'Pass That Peace Pipe' 210
Passenger, The 368
Passion Flower 67
Passionate Plumber, The 85
Passport to Oblivion 322
Password is Courage, The 306
Pasternak, Boris 325
Pasternak, Joe 183, 187, 188, 192, 201, 203, 208, 209, 210, 213, 215, 216, 219, 220, 225, 231, 234, 235, 237, 243, 244, 247, 249, 251, 256, 261, 263, 266, 270, 271, 276, 278, 280, 286, 291, 298, 307, 310, 315, 320, 322, 327, 331, 334, 370
Pat and Mike 250
Pat Garrett and Billy the Kid 366
Patch of Blue, A 326
Pate, Michael 254, 281, 293, 313, 319, 333, 334, 339
Paterson, Pat 145
Pathe Pictures 273
Patrick, Dorothy 206, 209, 213, 258, 259
Patrick, Gail 115, 165, 171, 172, 173, 202
Patrick, John (actor) 20
Patrick, John (writer) 277, 283, 289, 309
Patrick, Lee 178, 192, 198, 317
Patrick, Nigel 278, 365
Patsy, The 44, 46, 47, 60
Patten, Luana 206, 298, 299, 303
Patterson, Elizabeth 32, 86, 91, 97, 103, 123, 126, 151, 171, 179, 208, 216, 228, 251
Patton 352
Patton, Mary 218, 298
Paul, Elliot 171
Pavan, Marisa 273
Pavlow, Muriel 302
Paxton, John 273
Payment Deferred 89
Payne, Lawrence 291
Payton-Wright, Pamela 361
Pearce, Alice 227, 247, 276, 333
Pearl, Jack 94, 102
Pearson, Beatrice 216
Pearson, Richard 293
Pearson, Ted 138, 145
Peatman, James 337
Peck, Gregory 192, 201, 202, 206, 224, 240, 245, 278, 296, 304
Peck, Steven 289, 296
Peckinpah, Sam 307, 366
Peeples, Samuel 319
Peers, Joan 78
Peg o' My Heart 92
Pellissier, Anthony 203
Penalty, The 174
Pendleton, Nat 85, 94, 95, 97, 100, 102, 103, 104, 109, 115, 116, 117, 119, 121, 122, 126, 132, 133, 139, 140, 141, 143, 144, 146, 147, 149, 150, 154, 158, 159, 163, 165, 182, 183, 187, 188
Penelope 331
Penington, Jon 331
Penn, Leonard 133, 136, 138, 141, 142
Pennick, Jack 202, 218
Pennington, Ann 27
Pennock, Christopher 361
Penthouse 98, 147
People Against O'Hara, The 244
People vs. Dr Kildare, The 172
Peploe, Clare 348
Peploe, Mark 368
Peppard, George 298, 299, 304, 322
Percival, Lance 302, 311, 317, 345, 362
Percy 354
Percy, Eileen 35, 43, 44, 66, 234
Perelman, Laura 102, 159
Perelman, S.J. 102, 159
Perfect Gentleman, The 117
Perfect Strangers 203
Perier, Etienne 300, 309
Period of Adjustment 304
Perkins, Anthony 257, 293, 296, 312
Perl, Arnold 319
Perlberg, William 309, 313, 321
Perreau, Gigi 203, 213, 214, 228, 294
Perrin, Nat 162, 183, 188, 189, 203, 206, 208, 213
Perry, Eleanor 367
Perry, Joan 162
Perry, Margaret 86
Perry, Roger 312
Perschy, Maria 306
Perskey, Lester 358
Persoff, Nehemiah 286, 293, 314, 333, 338, 344
Personal Property 131
Perspecta Sound 255
Perugia, Luciano 367
Peter Pan 28
Peter Rabbit and Tales of Beatrix Potter 360
'Peter the Great' 15, 46
Peters, Brock 367
Peters, House 36
Peters, Susan 176, 177, 182, 183, 184, 187, 188, 195, 198
Peters, Werner 321
Peterson, Dorothy 82, 84, 89, 105, 107, 112, 122
Petit, Roland 264
Petrie, Daniel 309
Petrie, Howard 240
Petrovich, Ivan 30, 36, 287
Pettet, Joanna 350
Petticlerc, Denne Bart 355
Petticoat Fever 123
Pettingell, Frank 165, 306
Pevney, Joseph 287
Peyser, Arnold and Lois 351
Peyser, John 303
Peyton Place 284
Pflug, Jo Ann 361
Phantom of Paris, The 77
Phantom of the Opera, The 18, 366
Phantom Raiders 165
Phantom Tollbooth, The 351
Philadelphia Story, The 160, 169, 172, 204, 277
Philbrook, James 328
Phillips, Bill 186, 198, 201, 202, 204, 208, 209, 213, 224, 277
Phillips, Carmen 298
Phillips, Conrad 302
Phillips, Dorothy 32
Phillips, Eddie 15
Phillips, John 280, 299
Phillips, Leslie 275, 283, 295
Phillips, Mary 128, 133
Phillips, Sean 321, 351
Phipps, Thomas 179
Piccadilly Jim 126
Picerni, Paul 287
Pichel, Irving 123
Pick a Star 136
Pickens, Slim 286, 366
Pickford, Jack 30, 35
Pickford, Mary 10, 12, 32, 35, 47, 54, 143, 192, 274, 326
Picnic 274
Picture of Dorian Gray, The 194
Pidgeon, Walter 131, 132, 136, 139, 141, 142, 145, 147, 150, 154, 158, 165, 169, 174, 182, 191, 192, 201, 208, 215, 216, 218, 222, 224, 237, 240, 247, 251, 252, 261, 263, 264, 266, 267, 270, 275, 276, 364
Pied Pipers, The 219
Pierce, Maggie 339
Pierlot, Francis 156, 195, 202, 203, 204, 251
Pierre of the Plains 182, 240
Pierson, Arthur 240
Pillow Talk 291
Pilot No. 5 180
Pinero, Arthur Wing 47, 67
Pink Panther, The 316
Pinky 223
Pinocchio 156
Pinza, Ezio 243
Pirandello, Luigi 89
Pirate, The 220, 374
Pirosh, Robert 136, 225, 242, 251, 264, 286
Pistolero of Red River, The 339
Pitoeff, Sacha 314
Pitt, Ingrid 346
Pittman, Montgomery 278
Pittorru, Fabio 362
Pitts, ZaSu 16, 21, 27, 31, 67, 71, 80, 84, 94, 105, 122, 176, 280, 292
Place for Lovers, A 348
Place in the Sun, A 240
Plane Crazy 44
Planet of the Apes 342
Platinum High School 298
Platt, Edward 281, 287, 291, 300
Platt, Louise 149
Platt, Marc 263
Please Believe Me 232
Please Don't Eat the Daisies 298
'Please Don't Say No' 201
Pleasence, Donald 277, 278, 338, 360
Pleshette, Suzanne 333, 338
Plowman, Melinda 240
Plunkett, Patricia 287
Plunkett, Walter 247
Plymouth Adventure 250
Podesta, Rossana 320
Poe, James 289
Pogostini, S. Lee 365
Pohlmann, Eric 256, 271, 274, 278, 280, 295, 304, 306, 322
Point Blank 339, 345
Poire, Alain 312, 327
Poitier, Sidney 268, 277, 281, 291, 310, 326, 346, 358, 362, 366
Polanski, Roman 338
Politic Flapper, The 44
Politics 76
Polk, James Jr. 9, 346
Polk, Oscar 152, 183
Poll, Martin 350, 352, 367
Pollack, Barry 362
Pollard, Daphne 110, 120
Pollard, Harry 72, 77, 84, 85
Pollini, Francis 360
Pollock, Channing 36
Pollock, George 302, 306, 313, 319
Pollock, Nancy 298
Polly Fulton 215
Polly of the Circus 82
Polonsky, Abraham 216
Ponti, Carlo 322, 325, 326, 333, 336, 337, 338, 345, 348, 350, 368
Porcasi, Paul 72, 134, 147
Port of Seven Seas 142
Porter, Cole 123, 128, 156, 182, 187, 206, 220, 230, 257, 277, 283, 372, 374
Porter, Don 302, 345
Porter, Jean 191, 195, 197, 202, 203
Portrait of Maria 204
Poseidon Adventure, The 366
Posford, George 151
Posner, Phil 328
Possessed 78
Post, William Jr. 169, 179, 180
Posta, Adrienne 355
Postman Always Rings Twice, The 208
Postman's Knock 302
Potter, H.C. 141, 150, 154, 237
Poulsen, William Anthony 149
Povah, Phyllis 147, 250
Powell, Anthony 362
Powell, Dick 90, 109, 197, 234, 236, 243, 252, 291, 347
Powell, Eleanor 110, 123, 128, 140, 156, 171, 180, 187, 191, 208, 235, 372
Powell, Jane 208, 215, 219, 220, 222, 231, 234, 237, 243, 249, 263, 266, 267, 270, 377, 379
Powell, Norman 360
Powell, William 12, 21, 42, 64, 82, 103, 104, 105, 112, 116, 121, 123, 125, 128, 131, 132, 138, 149, 158, 162, 171, 176, 179, 188, 191, 192, 201, 209, 210, 213, 222, 242, 256
Power, Tyrone 120, 138, 141, 166, 176, 210
Power, The 338
Power and the Prize, The 276
Powers, Tom 225, 243, 244, 254
Poyner, John 337
Prairie Wife, The 16
Praskins, Leonard 77, 78, 119, 139, 146
Pratt, Purnell 69, 77, 82, 111, 119
Pravda, George 306, 322, 345
Preiss, Wolfgang 338
Preisser, June 150, 152, 154, 156, 165
Premier Productions 365
Prenez Garde a la Peinture 97
Prentiss, Paula 298, 203, 303, 307, 312, 320
Presenting Lily Mars 187
Presle, Micheline 314
Presley, Elvis 278, 300, 311, 317, 320, 322, 327, 330, 334, 336, 344, 345, 351, 352, 360, 366, 377
Presnell, Harve 319, 327, 377
Pressman, Lawrence 361
Preston, Robert 219, 304
'Pretty Girl is Like a Melody, A' 121, 378
Pretty Ladies 27
Pretty Maids All in a Row 360
Previn, Andre 210, 218, 234, 284, 298
Prevost, Marie 69, 71, 76, 78, 80, 81
Price, Ann 48, 56
Price, Dennis 306, 311, 319
Price, Eugene 361
Price, Kate 20, 24, 31, 43, 64
Price, Nanci 69
Price, Vincent 219, 351
Pride and Prejudice 160
Prime of Miss Jean Brodie, The 346
Pringle, Aileen 8, 13, 16, 20, 21, 39, 42, 46, 47, 51, 52, 122, 126, 132
Pringle, Brian 358
Prisoner of War 263
Prisoner of Zenda, The 7, 39, 128, 251
Private Life of Henry VIII, The 90, 105
Private Lives 80
Private Lives of Elizabeth and Essex, The 146
Private Parts 365
Private Pettigrew's Girl 141
Private Potter 313
Prize, The 314
'Prize Song' (Meistersingers) 209
Prizefighter and the Lady, The 92
Prodigal, The 77
Prodigal, The 268
Producers Associates 287, 306
Production Code Administration 290
Prosperi, Georgio 281
Prosperity 82, 125
Proud Flesh 20
Prouty, Jed 49, 63, 69, 81, 126
Provine, Dorothy 331
Prudence and the Pill 340
Prud'homme, Cameron 276
Psycho 296
Public Enemy, The 74
Public Hero Number One 109, 112, 168
Puglia, Frank 168, 180, 211, 224
Pully, B.S. 271
Pulver, Lilo 314
Purcell, Dick 156, 158
Purcell, Gertrude 98
Purcell, Irene 77, 78, 85
Purcell, Noel 274, 284, 309
Purdom, Edmund 254, 266, 268, 273, 293, 317
Pursall, David 302, 306, 313, 319, 333
Pursuit 112
Putnam, Nina Wilcox 15
'Puttin' on the Ritz' 337
Pygmalion 138

Qualen, John 112, 135, 140, 143, 154, 181, 187, 198, 201, 213, 266, 314, 317, 326
Quality Street 41
Quarrier, Iain 338
Quartaro, Nena 70, 71
Quayle, Anthony 322
Queen Christina 98, 103, 148
Quentin Durward 271
Quick, Before It Melts 322
Quiet American, The 284
Quiet Man, The 249
Quigley, Charles 171
Quigley, Juanita 144, 171, 179, 184, 196
Quigley, Rita 162, 163, 191
Quilici, Folco 327
Quillan, Eddie 95, 119, 133, 181, 266
Quimby, Fred 8
Quine, Richard 171, 176, 178, 182, 183, 218, 219, 357
Quinn, Anthony 258, 274, 333, 340, 345, 367
Quinn, Derry 322
Quo Vadis 235, 244, 290

RKO Radio Pictures 9, 64, 74, 97, 100, 107, 156, 168, 172, 177, 184, 191, 196, 224, 225, 240, 249, 268, 270, 278, 296
Rabin, Michael 264
Rachmaninov, Sergei 264
Rachmil, Lewis 367
Racimo, Victoria 352
Rack, The 275
Rackin, Martin 186, 251
Radd, Ronald 322
Raeburn, Frances 183
Rafferty, Chips 309, 336
Rafferty, Frances 183, 187, 191, 198, 202, 203
Raft, George 90, 264
Rag Man, The 12, 27
Rage In Heaven 174
Ragland, Rags 172, 173, 174, 178, 179, 182, 183, 187, 189, 191, 195, 196, 197, 201, 203
Rain 43
Rain, Douglas 342
Raine, Norman Reilly 95
Rainer, Luise 112, 121, 127, 132, 133, 141, 142
Raines, Ella 186
Rains, Claude 201, 313
Rains Came, The 146
Raintree County 278
Rall, Tommy 257, 263, 275, 284
Ralph, Jessie 105, 107, 112, 116, 117, 122, 123, 125, 127, 128, 132, 134, 140, 142, 145, 150, 168
Ralston, Esther 77, 102
Rambeau, Marjorie 69, 75, 76, 80, 81, 142, 144, 159, 228, 259, 275
Rambo, Dack 365
Rameau, Hans (Paul) 164, 172, 191
Ramirez, Carlos 192, 195, 201, 208, 209
Rampling, Charlotte 361
Randall, Tony 289, 296, 306, 317, 333
Randell, Ron 257, 300, 312, 319
Randolf, Anders 52, 58
Random Harvest 177, 191
Rank, J. Arthur 223
Rankin, William 204
Ransohoff, Martin 306, 313, 319, 325, 329, 338, 339, 344, 357
Ransom 273
Ransom, Lois 182
Ransome, Prunella 350
Rapf, Harry 7, 8, 49, 63, 94, 95, 97, 102, 107, 112, 116, 117, 122, 123, 126, 132, 135, 136, 139, 141, 143, 146, 154, 163, 206, 225
Rapf, Matthew 247, 252, 257, 258
Rapf, Maurice 123, 132, 135
Raphaelson, Samson 100, 132, 154, 204, 214, 243, 257
Rappeneau, Jean Paul 307
Rascel, Renato 281
Rashomon 317
Rasputin and the Empress 86, 91
Rasputin the Mad Monk 86
Rasulala, Thalmus 362, 368
Rasumny, Mikhail 208, 216
Rathbone, Basil 27, 56, 64, 67, 70, 107, 109, 115, 119, 125, 176, 179, 187, 195
Rationing 186
Ratoff, Gregory 84, 188
Rattigan, Terence 311, 317, 351
Rauh, Stanley 140
Ravel, Sandra 67
Ravetch, Irving 236, 299
Rawlings, Marjorie Kinnan 206, 218
Rawlinson, Herbert 16, 41, 132
Rawson, Clayton 147
Ray, Aldo 250, 284, 299, 338, 339
Ray, Charles 20, 24, 31, 32, 80
Ray, Nicholas 286, 300
Ray, Rene 215
Raye, Martha 307
Raymond, Cyril 283, 287
Raymond, Gene 89, 102, 169, 270
Raymond, Paula 222, 232, 234, 235, 236, 243, 247
Raymond, Robin 202, 286, 313
Readick, Bobby 186, 195
Reagan, Ray 201
Reagan, Ronald 168, 228, 250, 263
Realife 70
Rear Window 262
Reason Why, The 21
Rebecca 156, 160
Rebel Without a Cause 268
Reckless 116, 368
Red Badge of Courage, The 240, 242, 243
Red Danube, The 225
Red Dust 89, 150, 256
Red Lily, The 12
Red Mill, The 32
Redemption 66
Redford, Robert 336
Redgrave, Lynn 364
Redgrave, Michael 249, 277, 321, 326, 333, 351
Redgrave, Vanessa 336, 352
Red-Headed Woman 87, 100
Redmond, Moira 306
Reducing 70
Reed, Carol 309, 340
Reed, Donna 166, 168, 171, 173, 178, 181, 182, 183, 186, 187, 188, 191, 194, 202, 209, 214, 264, 273, 384
Reed, George 183, 196
Reed, Lydia 277
Reed, Mark 123
Reed, Oliver 361
Reed, Phillip 131, 142, 213, 327
Reed, Robert 347
Reed, Tom 133, 240
Reeves, Steve 266, 298, 303, 304, 317, 326, 327
Reeves, Theodore 105, 196, 228
Reformer and the Redhead, The 234
Regan, Phil 100, 234
Reggiani, Serge 333
Reicher, Frank 72, 132, 165, 172
Reid, Alastair 360
Reid, Beryl 306
Reid, Carl Benton 182, 247, 251, 259, 266, 287
Reid, Cliff 201
Reid, Elliott 187, 313
Reiner, Carl 292
Reiner, Ivan 337, 348
Reinhardt, Betty 159, 162, 178
Reinhardt, Gottfried 142, 146, 165, 167, 174, 224, 240, 242, 250, 256, 264
Reinhardt, Max 174
Reinhardt, Wolfgang 224
Reisch, Walter 112, 142, 148, 165, 178, 183, 188, 194
Reisner (Riesner), Charles 48, 56, 63, 70, 72, 76, 77, 78, 84, 94, 100, 102, 105, 119, 169, 173, 186, 197
Reisz, Karel 316
Relis, Harry 312
Relph, George 291
Relph, Michael 302
Reluctant Debutante, The 286
Remains to Be Seen 259
Remarque, Erich Maria 66, 141
Remember? 147
Remick, Lee 310, 313
Remote Control 66
Renal, Christine Gouze 307
Renaldo, Duncan 57, 70, 126
Renaldo, Tito 219, 225
Renard, Maurice 112
Rendelstein, Les 365
Rendezvous 112, 179
Rennie, Michael 338, 339
Renoir, Jean 228, 240
Republic Pictures 284
Rettig, Tommy 234, 244
Return of the Gunfighter 334
Reunion in France 176
Reunion in Vienna 90, 94
Revelation 13
Revere, Anne 172, 192, 196
Revill, Clive 345
Rey, Fernando 328
Reyher, Ferdinand 295
Reynolds, Adeline deWalt 163, 191
Reynolds, Burt 367
Reynolds, Charles 342
Reynolds, Clarke 328
Reynolds, Debbie 234, 243, 249, 256, 257, 266, 270, 271, 275, 289, 292, 304, 319, 333, 368, 374, 377, 380, 384
Reynolds, Gene 138, 139, 143, 151, 159, 162, 165, 174, 273
Reynolds, Marjorie 231, 240
Rhapsody 264
Rhapsody in Blue 201
Rhino! 321
Rhodes, Erik 133, 142
Rhodes, Hari 360
Rhodes, Marjorie 345
Rhue, Madlyn 345
'Rhythm of the Day' 97
Riano, Renie 203
Rice, Alice Hegan 35
Rice, Craig 214, 236
Rice, Florence 122, 126, 128, 133, 135, 136, 141, 143, 144, 145, 147, 150, 156, 165
Rice, Frank 65
Rich, Irene 77, 80, 81, 156, 162, 173
Rich, Full Life, The 214
Rich Man, Poor Girl 138
Rich, Young and Deadly 298
Rich, Young and Pretty 243
Richards, Addison 138, 141, 149, 150, 154, 158, 159, 162, 163, 165, 172, 179, 184, 196, 198, 202, 208
Richards, Ann 177, 183, 198
Richards, Jeff 243, 244, 250, 252, 257, 258, 263, 264, 273, 276, 283
Richards, Marc 346
Richards, Robert 219
Richardson, Henry Handel 264
Richardson, Ralph 144, 325
Richardson, Tony 310, 325
Richest Man in the World, The 69
Richman, Arthur 72
Richman, Mark 303, 342
Richmond, Kane 85
Richmond, Ted 302, 311, 319
Richmond, Warner 31, 46
Richter, Conrad 209
Richter, Daniel 342
Richter, W.D. 366
Ricketts, Tom 31
Rickles, Don 354
Rickman, Thomas 362
Rickson, Lucille 24
Ride the High Country 307
Ride, Vaquero 258
Riders of the Dark 51
Ridgely, John 213, 218, 219, 225
Ridges, Stanley 123, 141, 154, 181
Riesner, Charles: see Reisner
Riffraff 116
Rififi 312
Rififi in Tokyo 312
Rifkin, Ron 347
Rigaud, Jorge 299
Rigby, Edward 134
Rigby, Ray 322, 325
Rigby, Terence 356
Right Cross 236
Rilla, Walter 186, 304
Rilla, Wolf 299, 304, 314
Rimsky-Korsakov, Nicolai 197
Rinehard 92
Rinehart, Mary Roberts 176
Ring of Fire 303
Ring Up the Curtain 95
Ringside Maisie 173
'Rin-Tin-Tin' 36, 46, 191

'Rin-Tin-Tin Jr.' 122
Rio Bravo 291
Rio Rita 177
Riptide 100, 105
Risdon, Elisabeth 133, 146, 177, 180, 190, 195, 197, 213, 214, 216, 250
Rise of Helga, The 74
Riskin, Everett 184, 192, 194, 214, 216
Riskin, Robert 192
Ritt, Martin 277, 317
Ritter, Thelma 304
River, The 240
River, W.L. 67
Rivkin, Allen 94, 98, 172, 181, 225, 234, 244, 250, 263, 294
Rizzo, Carlo 253
Roach, Bert 10, 20, 31, 32, 40, 42, 44, 47, 51, 65, 92, 117
Roach, Hal 8, 71, 77, 86, 95, 100, 110, 117, 120, 123, 132, 134, 136, 142, 143, 147
Roache, Viola 237
Road to Mandalay, The 28
Road to Rome, The 264
Road to Romance, The 36
Robards, Jason Jr. 287, 366
Robbins, Clarence 23
Robbins, Gale 224, 234, 243, 247
Robbins, Jerome 227, 300
Robbins Music 9
Robbins, Peter 315
Robe, The 254
Rober, Richard 228, 232, 236, 243, 253
Roberta 249
Roberti, Lyda 136
Roberts, Ben 266
Roberts, Beverly 143
Roberts, Bob 216
Roberts, Bobby 346
Roberts, E.B. 107
Roberts, Edith 35
Roberts, Elizabeth Madox 76
Roberts, Kenneth 149
Roberts, Marguerite 164, 168, 169, 178, 198, 209, 214, 215, 219, 231, 240
Roberts, Meade 312
Roberts, Rachel 361
Roberts, Randolph 366
Roberts, Roy 216, 244, 367
Roberts, Stanley 213, 327
Roberts, Theodore 47
Roberts, William 252, 256, 257, 264, 289, 312, 314
Robertson, Cliff 315, 340
Robertson, Hugh 362
Robertson, John S. 36, 42, 57, 77
Robertson, Willard 95, 103, 119, 125
Robin, Dany 312, 350
Robin Hood of El Dorado, The 120
Robinson, Cardew 331
Robinson, Casey 214
Robinson, Dewey 64, 163
Robinson, Edward G. 66, 112, 132, 154, 166, 172, 182, 204, 257, 307, 314, 317, 329, 339, 360, 367
Robinson, Frances 169
Robinson, Frank 338
Robinson, John 287
Robinson, Thelma 203, 213
Robson, Flora 313, 321, 338
Robson, Mark 269, 280, 314
Robson, May 84, 85, 87, 90, 91, 92, 94, 95, 97, 102, 112, 115, 116, 126
Roche, Arthur Somers 112
Roche, Eugene 368
'*Rock Around the Clock*' 268
Rock of Friendship, The 51
Rock, Phillip 344
Roddenberry, Gene 360
Rodgers, Mark 347
Rodgers, Richard 97, 152, 179, 218, 219, 257, 307
Rodman, Howard 331
Roeg, Nicholas 365
Rogers, Bogart 188
Rogers, Charles 92, 100, 110, 120, 143, 186
Rogers, Charles 'Buddy' 54
Rogers, Ginger 90, 109, 120, 128, 138, 156, 160, 202, 222, 224, 270, 372, 384
Rogers, Howard Emmett 100, 107, 112, 122, 125, 132, 176, 178, 181, 184, 186, 244, 252
Rogers, Jean 173, 174, 179, 183, 186, 187, 189
Rogers, Jean Scott 306
Rogers, Paul 266, 344
Rogers, Roy 201, 206
Rogers, Will 82, 100, 109, 120
Rogue Cop 264, 268
Rogue Song, The 64, 72
Rogue's March 252
Rohmer, Sax 85
Rojo, Gustavo 281, 292
Roland, Gilbert 71, 85, 225, 232, 250, 252, 253
Roley, Sutton 342
Rolfe, Guy 252, 257, 300, 333
Rolfe, Sam 253, 322, 328
Romain, Yvonne 306, 336
Roman, Letitia 331
Roman, Ric 280
Roman, Ruth 242, 250
Roman Holiday 262
Romance 36
Romance 67
Romance for Three 135
Romance of Rosy Ridge, The 214
Romay, Lina 195, 201, 202, 208
Romberg, Sigmund 72, 107, 128, 134, 142, 146, 267, 377
Romeo and Juliet 125
Romeo in Pyjamas 78
Romero, Cesar 104, 112, 216, 345
Romola 12
Rookies 41, 48
Room at the Top 284
Rooney, Mickey 95, 102, 103, 116, 119, 127, 132, 134, 135, 136, 138, 139, 140, 142, 143, 146, 150, 152, 156, 158, 159, 165, 166, 171, 172, 173, 174, 179, 183, 185, 187, 191, 196, 197, 208, 210, 218, 219, 244, 261, 289, 294, 298, 327, 344, 368, 370, 379
Rooney, Mickey Jr. 339
Rooney, Teddy 289
Roosevelt, Eleanor 186
Roosevelt, Franklin D. 92, 209
Root, Lynn 159, 183
Root, Wells 76, 77, 102, 112, 126, 149, 154, 158, 168, 178, 182, 186, 188
Roots of Heaven, The 284
Roper, Brian 224
Ropes, Bradford 95, 142
Rorke, Hayden 244, 251, 252, 253, 319
Rory, Rossana 299
Rosalie 72, 128, 151
Rosamond, Marion 179
Rosay, Francoise 283
Rose, Billy 307
Rose, David E. 283, 295
Rose, George 278, 360
Rose, Helen 252, 273
Rose, Si 311
Rose, William 277
Rose Marie 36, 119, 240, 266, 379, 380
'*Rose Marie, I Love You*' 119
Rose Tattoo, The 268
Rosebush of a Thousand Years 13
Rosemond, Clinton 143, 169
Rosen, Phil 31, 39
Rosenberg, Aaron 286, 292, 298, 309
Rosenbloom, Maxie 123, 173, 188, 294, 331
Rosenfelt, Frank E. 9, 368
Rosher, Charles 44, 206
Rosi, Francesco 339
Rosmer, Milton 149
Ross, Herbert 351
Ross, Katharine 333, 364
Ross, Shirley 125
Ross, Terry Ann 289
Rossen, Carol 303
Rossi, Luisa 201
Rossiter, Leonard 333, 342
Rosson, Harold 80, 90, 107, 158, 198, 249
Rosson, Richard 110
Roth, Lillian 67, 273
Roth, Lois 333
Roth, Sandy 91
Rotha, Wanda 259
Rounders, The 319
Roundtree, Richard 361, 362, 367
Rouse, Russell 192, 277, 281
Roussin, Andre 280
Rouve, Pierre 306
Rouverol, Aurania 66, 136
Rouverol, Jean 344
Rowan, Dan 347
Rowe, Tom 348
Rowland, Roy 186, 190, 204, 206, 210, 214, 222, 225, 234, 236, 247, 264, 270, 271, 275, 276, 281, 328
Rowland, Steve 266, 281, 328
Rowlands, Gena 287
Royal Wedding 237, 368
Royle, Selena 197, 198, 204, 206, 208, 214, 215, 218, 220, 232
Rozsa, Miklos 290
Ruark, Robert 281
Ruben, J. Walter 112, 116, 123, 126, 135, 149, 150, 154, 158, 159, 162, 166, 168, 173, 178, 179, 182, 184
Rubens, Alma 47
Rubin, Benny 56, 63, 64, 70, 72, 242, 259
Rubin, J. Robert 7
Rubinstein, Artur 213
Ruby, Harry 196, 234, 249, 372
Ruby, Thelma 302
Rudley, Herbert 196, 198
Rueting, Barbara 322
Ruggles, Charles 28, 71, 103, 115, 151, 206
Ruggles, Wesley 71, 178, 186, 188
Ruick, Barbara 242, 249, 251, 252, 253, 257
Rule, Janice 250, 252, 298, 339
Ruman (Rumann), Sig 111, 134, 135, 136, 140, 142, 147, 156, 171, 176, 203, 209, 225, 264, 321
Runacre, Jennie 368
Runyon, Damon 122, 147
Ruric, Peter 181, 213
Ruskin, Harry 133, 134, 135, 139, 140, 147, 148, 150, 156, 158, 163, 165, 173, 174, 176, 182, 183, 186, 187, 196, 198, 202, 208, 213, 214, 216, 232, 236
Russell, Bryan 315
Russell, Charles 303
Russell, Gordon 354
Russell, Jane 184
Russell, John 12
Russell, Ken 358, 364
Russell, Kurt 317
Russell, Leon 360
Russell, Rosalind 105, 107, 110, 111, 112, 114, 116, 126, 128, 135, 136, 144, 147, 151, 168, 169, 174, 176, 210, 291, 310
Russell, Tony 337
Russell, William 24
Rutherford, Ann 135, 138, 139, 142, 143, 145, 150, 151, 152, 154, 156, 158, 160, 162, 163, 165, 172, 173, 174, 182, 183, 364, 384
Rutherford, Margaret 302, 311, 313, 319
Ruthven, Ormond 173
Ruttenberg, Joseph 142, 151, 176, 201, 277, 284
Ruymen, Ayn 365
Ruysdael, Basil 228, 276
Ryan, Edmon 228, 236, 319
Ryan, Elaine 139, 171
Ryan, Mitchell 361
Ryan, Peggy 133
Ryan, Robert 219, 224, 253, 264, 266, 284, 300, 337, 355, 365, 367
Ryan's Daughter 354, 361
Ryerson, Florence 31, 35, 42, 43, 91, 102, 103, 111, 122, 126, 136, 146, 150, 151, 154
Ryskind, Morrie 111

Saadia 259
Sabaroff, Robert 345
Sabata, Antonio 334
Sabatini, Rafael 30, 250
Sabre, Richard 266
Saddle The Wind 286
Sadie McKee 102
Safecracker, The 283
Sagal, Boris 303, 313, 317, 322, 327, 338, 360
Sagan, Leontine 82
Sahl, Mort 338
Saidy, Fred 191, 197
Sailor Takes a Wife, The 203
Saint, Eva Marie 278, 291, 304, 321, 329, 334
St Clair, Malcolm 46, 66, 70
St Jacques, Raymond 333, 362
St John, Betta 257, 261, 266, 306
St John, Christopher 361
St John, Jill 319, 331, 361
St Johns, Adela Rogers 15, 27, 57, 75
Sakall, S.Z. 163, 183, 214, 225, 242, 249, 266
Sale, Charles 'Chic' 84, 107
Sale, Richard 165, 287
Salerno, Enrico Maria 299
Salkow, Sidney 209
Salkowitz, Sy 339
Sallis, Peter 311, 360
Sally, Irene and Mary 27, 32, 69, 94, 168
Salmi, Albert 281, 317
Salt, Waldo 141, 168, 361
Salten, Felix 163
Salter, James 350
Salute to the Gods 141
Salute to the Marines 186
Salvatore, Renato 312
Samish, Adrian 294
Samson and Delilah 232, 238
Samuels, Lesser 154, 156, 172
San Francisco 120, 125
Sand, Paul 364
Sand Pebbles, The 336
Sanders, Clare 176
Sanders, Denis 352
Sanders, George 156, 173, 174, 179, 194, 242, 252, 264, 268, 273, 283, 292, 299, 304, 350
Sanders, Hugh 237
Sandokan the Great 326
Sandpiper, The 329
Sanford, John 169
Sangster, Jimmy 309, 327
Sanjust, Filipo 312
Sanmartin, Conrado 299
Santalucia, Ugo 365
Santell, Alfred 82
Santillo, Frank 344
Santley, Joseph 122, 123
Santschi, Tom 12, 32
Sapper (Hector McNeil) 244
Sarafian, Richard 365, 367
Saratoga 131
Sargent, Dick 345
Sargent, Joseph 331
Saroyan, William 191
Sarrazin, Michael 360
Saul, Oscar 367
Saunders, John Monk 110, 134
Savage Guns 309
Savage Messiah 364
Savalas, Telly 337, 338, 339, 354, 360
Save the Tiger 368
Saville, Philip 350
Saville, Victor 144, 149, 154, 156, 169, 171, 174, 180, 187, 208, 214, 215, 222, 228, 235, 244
Sawyer (Sauers), Joseph 102, 169
Saxon, John 286
'*Say a Prayer for Me Tonight*' 284
'*Say that We're Sweethearts Again*' 197
Sayers, Dorothy M. 165
Sayers, Jo Ann 139, 140, 146, 151
Scala, Gia 281, 283, 287, 295
Scandal at Scourie 261
Scapegoat, The 293
Scaramouche 7, 10, 39, 250, 251, 273
Scarborough, George 35, 86
Scarface 90
Scarlet Coat, The 273
Scarlet Letter, The 35
Scene of the Crime 225
Scent of Mystery 296
Schaefer, Jack 319
Schafer, Natalie 196, 198, 224, 244, 271
Schaffner, Franklin 352
Schary, Dore 9, 138, 156, 159, 169, 172, 183, 186, 190, 191, 216, 219, 222, 225, 232, 237, 240, 242, 243, 245, 250, 251, 252, 257, 261, 266, 273, 274, 278, 319
Schayer, Richard 28, 43, 44, 47, 48, 51, 54, 56, 57, 66, 69, 71, 72, 78, 80, 105, 127, 235
'*Scheherazade*' 197
Schell, Karl 307
Schell, Maria 281, 296
Schell, Maximilian 300
Schenck, Joe 56
Schenck, Joseph M. 7, 14, 21
Schenck, Nicholas M. 7, 9, 12, 78, 87, 127, 179, 191, 216, 237, 240, 255
Schermer, Jules 276
Schertzinger, Victor 8, 15, 21
Schiaffino, Rosanna 307
Schildkraut, Joseph 103, 141, 145, 147, 154, 165
Schlesinger, John 322
Schnee, Charles 225, 236, 237, 240, 243, 252, 253, 257, 258, 268, 269, 276, 277, 278, 281, 299, 307
Schneider, Maria 368
Schneider, Romy 355, 365
Schnitzler, Arthur 81
Schoenbaum, Charles 203
Schrank, Joseph 183, 195, 204
Schrock, Raymond 42, 44, 56, 77, 90
Schubert, Bernard 102, 109, 213
Schulman, Arnold 296
Schunzel, Reinhold 138, 146, 151, 251
Schwartz, Arthur 247, 254, 259
Schweizer, Richard 201, 218
Scofield, Paul 330
Scorpio Letters, The 344
Scott, Adrian 156
Scott, De Vallon 202, 203
Scott, Douglas 132
Scott, George C. 317, 352, 358, 360, 362
Scott, Gordon 278, 287
Scott, Hazel 191
Scott, Kathryn Leigh 355
Scott, Martha 291
Scott, Randolph 240, 307
Scott, Sir Walter 252, 271
Scott, Terry 319
Scott, Will 133
Scott, Zachary 215, 228
Scourby, Alexander 273
Screen Actors Guild 250, 274
Sea Bat, The 71
Sea of Grass, The 209
Sea Wolf, The 166
Seagulls Over Sorrento 263
Search, The 218
Searle, Jackie 102
Sears, Zelda 60, 67, 69, 74, 76, 77, 81, 82, 86, 91, 94, 95, 98, 102, 103
Seastrom (Sjostrom), Victor 8, 10, 18, 23, 24, 35, 42, 47, 52, 64
Seaton, George 136, 209, 309, 313, 321
Seawright, Roy 134
Sebastian, Dorothy 35, 42, 43, 47, 49, 51, 56, 57, 65, 69, 70
Secret Garden, The 224
Secret Heart, The 208
Secret Hour, The 64
Secret Land, The 218
Secret Life of Walter Mitty, The 210
Secret of Dr Kildare, The 150
Secret of Mme. Blanche, The 97
Secret of My Success, The 327
Secret Partner, The 302
Secret Six, The 75
Seddon, Jack 302, 306, 313, 319, 333
Seddon, Margaret 20, 41
Sedgwick, Edward 32, 42, 43, 43, 44, 48, 56, 69, 78, 85, 86, 98, 102, 115, 123, 136, 141, 186, 216
See Here, Private Hargrove 186
Seely, Tim 309
Seff, Manuel 125, 126, 127, 132, 169
Segal, Alex 273, 322
Segal, Vivienne 98
Seghers, Anna 198
Seiter, William 95
Seitz, George B. 94, 95, 102, 105, 109, 112, 122, 131, 132, 133, 135, 136, 138, 141, 143, 150, 154, 158, 165, 173, 174, 182, 197
Sekeley, Steve 345
Selby, David 361, 368
Sellars, Elizabeth 277, 299
Seller, Thomas 158, 176, 188
Sellers, Peter 289, 306, 316
Sell-Out, The 247
Selten, Morton 134
Seltzer, David 364
Seltzer, Walter 364, 367
Selwyn, Arch 69
Selwyn, Edgar 69, 71, 76, 78, 84, 91, 92, 94, 100, 107, 117, 146, 147, 150, 154, 156, 159, 162, 174, 182
Selwyn, Ruth 80, 82, 86, 91, 94, 117
Selzer, Milton 344
Selznick, David O. 94, 97, 98, 103, 107, 112, 115, 116, 119, 152, 178, 192, 194, 210, 225
Selznick International 152
Semple, Lorenzo 303, 368
Send Me No Flowers 322
Sennett, Mack 57
Separate Beds 313
Separate Tables 291
Sequoia 105
Serato, Massimo 337
Serenade 147
Sergeant Madden 149
Sergeant York 166
Serling, Rod 275, 286
Sernas, Jacques 304
Servant, The 316
Service 94
Service, Robert W. 48
Seven Arts Productions 306, 309, 314, 315, 316, 326, 330
Seven Brides for Seven Brothers 263, 379
Seven Chances 21
Seven Faces of Dr Lao 317
Seven Hills of Rome 281
Seven Seas to Calais 312
Seven Sweethearts 183
Seven Women 329, 344
Seven Year Itch, The 268
Seventh Cross, The 198, 218
Seventh Heaven 44
Seventh Sin, The 283
Seventh Veil, The 201
Severn, Christopher 176, 188
Severn, Raymond 179
Severn, William 180, 202
Sevilla, Carmen 300
Seward, Florence 319
Seyler, Athene 144, 307
Seymour, Anne 287, 298, 299, 344
Seymour, Dan 294
Shadow in the Sky 242
Shadow of a Doubt 185
Shadow of Doubt 112
Shadow of the Thin Man 171
'*Shadow of Your Smile, The*' 329
Shadow on the Wall 288
Shadows of Paris 32
Shadows of the Night 46
Shaft 361, 362
Shaft in Africa 367
Shaft's Big Score 362
Shaftel, Joseph 339
Shakespeare, William 109, 192, 254, 276
Shane 262
Shannon, Harry 234, 258, 273
Shannon, Peggy 94
Shannon, Robert 109
Sharaff, Irene 247
Sharif, Omar 317, 325, 339, 350
Sharp, Alan 360
Sharp, Margery 216
Sharpe, Albert 237, 266, 299
Shatner, William 281, 317
Shaughnessy, Mickey 278, 283, 286, 296, 304, 314
Shaw, Artie 154
Shaw, George Bernard 72, 287
Shaw, Irwin 307
Shaw, Oscar 32, 64
Shaw, Robert 293
Shaw, Victoria 322, 366
Shawn, Dick 276, 331
She Got Her Man 178
She Went to the Races 203
Shea, Michael 339
Shean, Al 147, 176, 186
Shear, Barry 338
Shearer, Douglas 46, 49, 69, 110, 125, 214
Shearer, Moira 256
Shearer, Norma 8, 10, 15, 20, 23, 24, 27, 32, 35, 36, 43, 46, 47, 48, 54, 63, 64, 67, 70, 75, 80, 81, 82, 85, 87, 100, 103, 105, 107, 125, 132, 141, 145, 147, 152, 164, 165, 172, 179, 187, 214, 244, 256, 275
Sheehan, Winfield 163
Sheekman, Arthur 250, 289, 302
Sheen, Martin 344, 355
Sheepman, The 286
Sheffield, Johnny 151, 152, 172, 180
Sheffield, Reginald 181
Sheldon, Edward 67
Sheldon, Sidney 220, 231, 234, 237, 242, 243, 259, 261, 307
Shelley, Barbara 299, 302
Shelton, John 156, 158, 162, 163, 164
Shelton, Marla 126, 131, 133
Shenson, Walter 302
Shepard, Sam 348
Sher, Jack 366
Sheridan, Ann 120, 276
Sherlock Jr. 14
Sherman, Lowell 42, 48
Sherman, Richard 178
Sherman, Vincent 240
Sherriff, R.C. 66, 149, 182
Sherry, John 339
Sherwood, Madeleine 289, 306, 366
Sherwood, Robert E. 90, 145, 164, 257, 264, 276
Sherwood, Roberta 310
Shiel, M.P. 295
Shields, Arthur 156, 179, 188, 196, 202, 225, 244, 261, 286
Shigeta, James 300, 361
'*Shine on Your Shoes, A*' 254
Shining Hour, The 144
Ship Ahoy 180, 201
Ship from Shanghai, The 60
Ship of Fools 322
Shipman, Samuel 13, 24
Shipmates 77
Shoemaker, Ann 149, 152, 156, 187, 198
Shoes of the Fisherman, The 345
'*Shoes with Wings On*' 372
Shoeshine 210
Shop Around the Corner, The 154, 225
Shopworn Angel, The 141
Shore, Dinah 209
Short, Gertrude 35
Short, Luke 231, 236
Shostakovich, Dmitri 187
Shotter, Winifred 123
'*Should I?*' 61
Should Ladies Behave? 98
Show, The 35
Show Boat 247, 249, 379
Show Girl 247
Show-Off, The 104, 209, 214
Show People 47
Shubert, Lee 7
Shuken, Phillip 338, 344
Shulman, Max 253, 257, 258, 271
Shy, Gus 71
Side Street 228
Sidewalks of New York, The 78
Sidney, George (actor) 43
Sidney, George (director) 168, 179, 180, 187, 195, 201, 204, 208, 215, 219, 222, 225, 230, 247, 250, 257, 264, 315, 320
Sidney, Louis K. 162, 168, 169
Sidney, Sylvia 74, 123, 128
Siegel, Sol C. 9, 277, 281, 283, 284, 289, 295
Sienkiewicz, Henryk 245
Signoret, Simone 313
Signpost to Murder 321
Silent Accuser, The 15, 46
Siletti, Mario 253
Silk Stockings 283, 372
Silliphant, Stirling 299, 347, 367
Sills, Milton 66
Silva, Henry 286, 293
Silva, Mario 213
Silver Casket, The 109
Silvera, Frank 298, 309
Silverheels, Jay 367
Silvers, Phil 168, 171, 174, 237
Silvers, Sid 110, 123, 128, 178
Silverstein, David 109
Silverstein, Elliot 365
Sim, Alastair 287
Simmons, Dick 180, 182, 187, 191, 208, 210, 213, 219, 235, 236, 242, 250, 251, 252, 263, 271
Simmons, Jean 254, 257, 271, 278, 280, 333
Simms, Ginny 191, 195
Simon, Michel 259
Simon, Robert 264, 275, 277, 302

Simon, S. Sylvan 143, 145, 150, 151, 154, 156, 159, 162, 166, 172, 174, 176, 177, 181, 183, 186, 189, 202, 203, 209
Simons, Richard 344
Simonton, Vera 182
Simpson, Ivan 156, 172, 177
Simpson, Russell 51, 74, 203, 240, 243
Sin of Madelon Claudet, The 76
Sinatra, Frank 180, 201, 209, 210, 216, 222, 226, 227, 243, 271, 274, 277, 278, 289, 292, 304, 310, 320, 340, 354, 368, 378, 379
Sinatra, Nancy 320, 344
Since You Went Away 192
Sinclair, Charles 348
Sinclair, Diane 84
Sinclair, Robert B. 142, 144, 147, 162, 163, 168, 169, 173
Sinclair, Ronald 135, 143, 154
Sinclair, Upton 84
Sinden, Donald 256, 360
'*Sing Before Breakfast*' 110
Singer, Ray 347
'*Singin' in the Rain*' 61, 63, 374
Singin' in the Rain 249, 270, 374
Singing Nun, The 333
Single Man, A 52
Single Standard, The 57
Singleton, Penny: see McNulty, Dorothy
Sinner Take All 123
Sinners in Silk 15
Sins of the Children 69
Siodmak, Robert 224, 307
Sioux Blood 65
Sirk, Douglas 186
Sirola, Joseph 368
Sisk, Robert 186, 187, 190, 194, 202, 204, 206, 208, 218, 219, 225, 228, 242, 243
Sitting Target 361
6,000 Enemies 154
Skelton, Red 158, 171, 172, 173, 178, 180, 182, 183, 187, 189, 191, 195, 201, 208, 209, 214, 216, 222, 225, 228, 232, 234, 243, 247, 249, 251, 258, 261
Skidding 136
Skinner, Otis 194
Skipper Surprised His Wife, The 232
Skipworth, Alison 67, 111, 127
Skirts Ahoy 249
Sky Full of Moon 252
Sky Murder 165
Skyjacked 132, 364
Skyscraper Souls 84
Slams, The 367
Slander 275
Slate, Lane 364
Slater, Humphrey 228
'*Slaughter on Tenth Avenue*' 219
Slave of Fashion, A 24
Sleeper, Martha 69, 71, 80, 85, 97
'*Sleepy Head*' 103
Slesar, Henry 331
Slesinger, Tess 127, 128
Slezak, Walter 220, 228, 253, 278, 314
Slide, Kelly, Slide 41, 51
Slight Case of Larceny, A 261
Slightly Dangerous 188
Slither 366
Sloane, Everett 247, 274, 277, 299
Sloane, Paul 102, 117
Slott, Henry 313
Sloyan, James 361
Small Town Girl 126, 249, 377
Smalley, Phillips 21, 42
Smart Set, The 51
Smight, Jack 357
Smilin' Through 87, 169
Smith, Alexis 222, 228, 384
Smith, Art 237, 242
Smith, Bernard 304, 329, 350
Smith, Betty 322
Smith, Bill 300
Smith, C. Aubrey 70, 76, 77, 78, 80, 81, 82, 84, 86, 92, 97, 98, 114, 125, 135, 149, 151, 162, 164, 168, 174, 191, 198, 216
Smith, Charles 28, 184, 234
Smith, Charles B. 169
Smith, Clifford 32
Smith, Dodie 94
Smith, Ethel 195, 202, 209
Smith, Frederick Y. 218
Smith, Gerald Oliver 176, 192, 203, 225
Smith, John 287, 339
Smith, Kent 122, 286
Smith, Leonard 206
Smith, Loring 250, 251
Smith, Maggie 289, 311, 321, 345, 346, 362
Smith, Paul Gerard 28
Smith, Pete 8, 208
Smith, Rebecca Dianna 365
Smith, Robert Paul 271, 294, 298
Smith, Stanley 71, 158
Smith, Thorne 134
Smith, Walton 85
'*Smoke Gets in Your Eyes*' 249
Snake Pit, The 223
Sneider, Verne 277
Snob, The 15
Snow White and the Seven Dwarfs 138
So Big 18
So Bright the Flame 251
'*So in Love*' 257
So This is College 60, 69
So This is Marriage 15
Sobbin' Women 263
Society Doctor 105
Society Lawyer 147, 154
Soeur Sourire 333
Sofaer, Abraham 245, 277, 312
'*Softly As in a Morning Sunrise*' 72
Sojin 20, 28, 43
Sokoloff, Vladimir 132, 133, 136, 165, 171, 176, 188, 209, 296
Sol Madrid 339
Soldati, Mario 291
Soldiers Three 240
Solitaire Man, The 95
Solow, Herbert 9
Solt, Andrew 216, 295
Sombert, Claire 275
Sombrero 250
Some Came Running 289
Some Like It Hot 291
Some of the Best 317
Somebody Up There Likes Me 275, 277
Something of Value 281
'*Something to Remember You By*' 254
'*Sometimes I'm Happy*' 270
Somewhere I'll Find You 178
Sommer, Elke 314, 326, 331, 355
Son-Daughter, The 86, 198
Son of a Gunfighter 328
Son of India 76
Son of Lassie 202
Son of Spartacus 304
Sondergaard, Gale 142, 228
Song of Bernadette, The 192
Song of Love 213
Song of Russia 188
Song of the City 133
'*Song of the Mounties*' 119
Song of the Thin Man 213
Song to Remember, A 201
'*Song's Gotta Have Heart, The*' 210
Sons and Lovers 296
Sons of the Desert 95
Sorel, Jean 367
Sorenson, Rickie 287
Sothern, Ann 126, 147, 150, 151, 159, 162, 171, 173, 178, 182, 183, 186, 187, 196, 203, 213, 219, 222, 228, 231
Soul Mates 21
Sound of Music, The 330, 340, 362
South Pacific 243, 296
Southern, Terry 325, 329
Southern Yankee, A 216
Soylent Green 367
Space, Arthur 188, 189, 204, 206, 209, 216, 253
Spain, Fay 294, 339
Sparks, Ned 20, 21, 24, 30, 31, 95, 103
Spartacus 304
Spats to Spurs 154
Speak Easily 86
Speed 126
Speedway 56
Speedway 344
Spellbound 201
Spence, Ralph 66, 85, 86, 100, 103, 105, 117
Spencer, Bud 346
Spencer, Elizabeth 303
Spencer, Franz 169, 174
Spencer, Kenneth 183, 186
Spencer, Marian 306
Spewack, Samuel and Bella 94, 95, 97, 98, 105, 112, 140, 143, 202, 257
Spies, Adrian 341, 344
Spigelgass, Leonard 191, 236, 243, 244, 251, 261, 266, 267, 283
Spinner, Anthony 338, 342
Spinout 334
Spinster 303
Spite Marriage 56, 191
Spivey, Victoria 54
Split, The 345
Spoilers of the West 43
Sporting Blood 80
Sporting Blood 159
Sporting Venus, The 20
Sprague, Chandler 184
'*Spring*' 263
'*Spring Came Back to Vienna*' 379
Spring Dance 143
Spring Fever 43, 51, 72
Spring Madness 143
Spy in the Green Hat, The 331
Spy 13 103
Spy with My Face, The 328
Square of Violence 306
Squaw Man, The 80
Squire, Ronald 292
Squire, Katherine 365
Squire, William 346
Stablemates 139
Stack, Robert 162, 220, 292
Stacy, James 347
Stafford, Hanley 257
Stage Door Canteen 185
Stage Mother 95
Stagecoach 146, 183
Stahl, John M. 8, 31, 39, 40, 133
Stainton, Philip 256
Stalag 17 262
Stallings, Laurence 18, 47, 67, 70, 98, 145, 149, 163, 218
Stamboul Quest 107
Stand By for Action 182
Stand Up and Fight 143
Stander, Lionel 116, 132, 143, 146, 325, 361
Standing Bear, Chief 65
Standing, Wyndham 70
Stanley and Livingstone 150
Stanley, Kim 361
Stanley, Phyllis 244
Stanton, Paul 172
Stanwyck, Barbara 54, 64, 126, 215, 228, 237, 244, 252, 266, 276
Stapleton, Jean 296
Stapley, Richard 216, 219
Star 340
'*Star Eyes*' 191
Star is Born, A 128
Star Said No, The 242
'*Star Spangled Banner, The*' 146
Stark, Ray 316
Stark, Richard 339, 345, 367
Stark, Wilbur 355
Starke, Pauline 20, 21, 30, 31, 42, 52
Starlight 42
Starr, Irving 179, 183, 186, 188, 209
Starr, Ronald 307
Starr, Sally 60, 64
Starrett, Charles 85, 117
Stars in My Crown 232
State Fair 95
State of the Union 218
Stay Away, Joe 344
Stehli, Edgar 300, 313
Steiger, Rod 235, 289, 325, 336, 337, 365
Steinbeck, John 181
Steinberg, William 213
Steiner, Max 152
Steinkamp, Fredric 334
Steinore, Michael 214
Stella Dallas 18, 128
Stepanek, Karel 228, 256
Stephani, Frederick 133, 134, 144, 151, 162, 163, 165, 169, 174, 181, 203
Stephen, Susan 275
Stephens, Harvey 105, 112, 116, 117, 119, 120, 122, 126, 172, 173, 322
Stephens, Martin 292, 299
Stephens, Robert 362
Stephenson, Henry 87, 100, 105, 107, 111, 112, 116, 117, 119, 132, 136, 141, 142, 151, 192, 208, 213, 216, 225
Stepping Out 78
Sterke, Jeanette 274, 283
Sterling, Ford 10, 24, 30, 69
Sterling, Jan 232, 236, 252, 286
Sterling, Robert 167, 168, 171, 173, 174, 178, 208, 247, 314
Stern, Stewart 235, 275
Stevens, Craig 384
Stevens, George 172
Stevens, Inger 281, 289, 295
Stevens, Mark 232
Stevens, Onslow 91, 92, 274, 298
Stevens, Paul 362
Stevens, Rise 169
Stevens, Robert 307, 312
Stevens, Stella 310, 319, 327, 339
Stevens, Warren 276
Stevenson, Philip 251
Stevenson, Robert Louis 126, 174
Stewart, Anita 20
Stewart, Donald Ogden 30, 87, 92, 95, 97, 98, 105, 115, 141, 160, 169, 171, 180, 204, 215, 224
Stewart, Elaine 252, 257, 258, 261, 266
Stewart, James 116, 119, 123, 126, 127, 132, 135, 139, 141, 146, 154, 160, 162, 163, 168, 222, 224, 225, 232, 251, 253, 262, 278, 304, 322, 368, 384
Stewart, Paul 171, 251, 252, 267, 273
Stickney, Dorothy 261, 275
Stiller, Mauritz 27, 33
Sting, The 368
Stock, Nigel 306
Stockwell, Dean 117, 201, 202, 206, 208, 213, 214, 215, 222, 224, 232, 235, 236
Stockwell, Harry 110, 117
Stone, Andrew 276, 289, 292, 303, 306, 327, 365
Stone, George E. 97, 103, 150, 271
Stone, Harold J. 275, 277, 281, 322
Stone, Irving 274
Stone, Lewis 10, 13, 24, 49, 51, 54, 57, 64, 67, 69, 75, 76, 77, 82, 84, 85, 86, 87, 91, 92, 94, 98 100, 102, 107, 109, 110, 112, 114, 122, 125, 126, 127, 131, 135, 138, 140, 141, 143, 146, 147, 150, 158, 159, 165, 166, 173, 182, 197, 201, 206, 208, 218, 222, 228, 230, 232, 234, 242, 243, 247, 250, 251, 257, 289
Stone, Marianne 306
Stone, N.B. Jr. 307
Stone, Virginia 289, 292, 303, 306, 327
Stone, W.S. 237
Stonehouse, Ruth 10
Stong, Phil 95
Stooges, Three 94, 97, 105
Stoppa, Paulo 299
Storey, Ruth 296, 298
Storm, James 361
Storm, Rafael 171
Storm at Daybreak 90
Story, Jack Trevor 302
Story of Gosta Berling, The 27
Story of Louis Pasteur, The 120, 128
Story of Three Loves, The 256
Stossel, Ludwig 169, 172, 203, 209, 210, 213
Stothart, Herbert 60, 119, 134, 151, 188
Stovin, Jerry 306
Strabel, Thelma 208
Stradling, Harry 194
Stradner, Rose 132
Straight is the Way 102
Strange, Glenn 243
Strange Cargo 165
Strange Interlude 85, 135, 174
Strange Interval 85
Stranger in Town 186
Strangers May Kiss 81
Strangers on a Train 240
Stranger's Return, The 95, 139
Strasberg, Susan 273
Stratton, Gil 191
Stratton, John 277
Stratton Story, The 224, 251
Straus, Oscar 169
Strauss, Johann II 142, 365
Strauss, Richard 342
Strawberry Statement, The 352, 360
Street Angel 44
Streetcar Named Desire, A 240
Streeter, Edward 233
Streisand, Barbra 340, 346, 358, 366
Stribling, Melissa 283, 302
Strickland, Robert 191, 210
Strictly Dishonorable 243
Strictly Unconventional 67
Strike Up the Band 156, 370
Strip, The 244
Stritch, Elaine 344
Strode, Woody 287, 292, 312, 329
Stromberg, Hunt 49, 84, 89, 92, 95, 97, 102, 103, 104, 107, 110, 119, 120, 123, 126, 128, 134, 136, 141, 144, 145, 147, 149, 160, 163, 168, 171, 179
Strong, Austin 206
Strong, Leonard 263
Strong, Michael 339
Stronger Than Desire 154
Stross, Raymond 295
Stroud, Don 347
Strudwick, Shepperd 144, 150, 158
Struss, Karl 44
Stuart, Giacomo Rossi 362
Stuart, Mel 364
Student Prince, The 36, 43, 267
Student Prince in Old Heidelberg, The 36
Student Tour 100
Sturges, John 222, 232, 236, 242, 244, 251, 252, 257, 259, 266, 273, 286, 292, 344
Sturges, Preston 142, 156, 243
Styne, Jules 210, 296
Subject Was Roses, The 344
Sublett, John 'Bubbles' 183
Subterraneans, The 298
Sudermann, Hermann 33, 57
Suicide Club, The 126
Sullavan, Margaret 90, 141, 144, 154, 162, 166, 186
Sullivan, Barry 222, 225, 228, 231, 234, 235, 236, 237, 242, 243, 247, 249, 252, 258, 264, 276, 303, 342
Sullivan, C. Gardner 41, 84, 85, 91, 117, 183
Sullivan, Ed 333
Sullivan, Francis L. 144, 225, 268
Sullivan, Sean 342
Sully, Frank 187, 192
Sully, Robert 188, 192
Sultan, Arne 306
Summer Holiday 218
Summer of '42, The 358
Summer Stock 237
Summertime 268
Summerville, Slim 154, 159, 201
Sun Comes Up, The 218
Sunday in New York 315
Sunday Punch 179
Sundberg, Clinton 206, 208, 210, 213, 216, 218, 219, 220, 222, 224, 225, 230, 234, 235, 236, 247, 257, 302, 314
'*Sunny*' 209
Sunrise 44
Sunset Boulevard 232
Sun-Up 21
Super Cops, The 368
SuperTotalScope 299
Surtees, Robert 198, 214, 236, 252, 290, 309
Susan and God 163
Susan Lenox, Her Fall and Rise 74
Suspicion 166
Susskind, David 277
Sutherland, Donald 337, 345, 354
Sutherland, Eddie 46
Sutton, Dudley 355
Sutton, Grady 86, 143, 183, 201
Sutton, John 219
Suzy 127
Swan, The 274
Swanson, Gloria 18, 47, 57, 232, 384
Swanson, Maureen 258
Swarthout, Glendon 298
Sweet, Blanche 8, 12, 20, 58, 64
Sweet Bird of Youth 306
Sweet Smell of Success, The 338
Sweethearts 144, 147
Swenson, Inga 360
Swerling, Jo 128, 271
Swimmer, Saul 345
Swinburne, Nora 144, 245, 264
Swing Fever 188
Swing Shift Maisie 187
Swingin' Set, The 320
Swiss Miss 143
Switzer, Carl 'Alfalfa' 162
Swofford, James 364
Swordsman of Siena 309
Sworn Enemy 126
Sydney, Basil 252
Sykes, Eric 302, 306, 331
Sylvester, William 342
'*Sympathy*' 136
Syms, Sylvia 322

Tabori, George 232, 287
Taeger, Ralph 339
Taggart, Errol 122, 133
Tahiti Landfall 237
Tailor-Made Man, A 80
Taka, Miiko 314
'*Take Back Your Mink*' 271
Take Me Out to the Ball Game 226, 379
Take the High Ground 257
'*Taking a Chance on Love*' 183
Talbot, Lyle 286
Talbot, Nita 322
Talbott, Gloria 294
Tale of Two Cities, A 119
Tales of Beatrix Potter 360
Talk About a Stranger 250
Tall Target, The 243
Tallchief, Maria 251
Talmadge, Constance 162
Talmadge, Norma 47, 66, 69, 87
Tamba, Tetsuro 346
Tamblyn, Russ 233, 238, 257, 263, 264, 270, 273, 277, 283, 286, 289, 296, 304, 312, 314, 328, 384
Taming of the Shrew, The 192, 253, 264
Tamiroff, Akim 98, 102, 105, 107, 110, 114, 181, 198, 211, 331, 333, 355
Tandy, Jessica 198, 202, 208
Tannen, William 169, 172, 179, 180, 182, 186
Target for Scandal 251
Tarita 309
Tarkington, Booth 187
Tarkington, Rockne 362
Tartars, The 300
Tartu 186
Tarzan and His Mate 107
Tarzan and the Lost Safari 278
Tarzan Escapes 125
Tarzan Finds a Son 151
Tarzan Goes to India 304
Tarzan the Ape Man 86, 293
Tarzan's Fight for Life 287
Tarzan's New York Adventure 180
Tarzan's Secret Treasure 172
Tarzan's Three Challenges 312
Tashlin, Frank 333
Tashman, Lilyan 20, 27, 31, 54, 100
Taste of Honey, A 304
Tate, Sharon 338
Taurog, Norman 138, 143, 146, 156, 159, 172, 174, 179, 187, 191, 201, 209, 216, 219, 222, 231, 232, 234, 236, 243, 311, 334, 336, 344, 345
Taxi Dancer, The 33
Taylor, Alfred 149
Taylor, Don 213, 222, 225, 231, 233, 238, 273, 309, 338, 346
Taylor, Dwight 85, 90, 192
Taylor, Elizabeth 191, 196, 198, 202, 206, 208, 214, 216, 220, 222, 228, 232, 233, 238, 240, 242, 245, 247, 252, 256, 264, 266, 278, 289, 296, 299, 300, 311, 317, 322, 329, 330, 336, 366, 384
Taylor, Estelle 47, 57
Taylor, Frank 236
Taylor, Joan 266
Taylor, Joyce 278, 300, 303
Taylor, Ken 350
Taylor, Kent 145, 150, 156, 174
Taylor, Laurette 13, 92
Taylor, Lawrence 238
Taylor, Robert 8, 102, 105, 109, 110, 115, 120, 126, 127, 128, 131, 134, 141, 143, 146, 147, 158, 164, 168, 171, 179, 182, 186, 188, 191, 194, 208, 210, 213, 218, 219, 222, 228, 231, 236, 240, 245, 249, 251, 252, 257, 258, 264, 271, 273, 276, 281, 286, 295, 313, 334, 339, 366
Taylor, Robert Lewis 317
Taylor, Rod 275, 278, 291, 298, 311, 312, 315, 321, 331, 333, 341, 348, 367
Taylor, Sam 35, 117, 192
Taylor, Valerie 312
Taylor, Wally 362
Taylor-Young, Leigh 361, 367
Tchaikovsky, P.I. 187, 188, 264
Tea and Sympathy 276, 289
Tea for Three 42
Teagarden, Jack 244
Teahouse of the August Moon, The 277
Tearle, Conway 13, 20, 35, 95, 98, 125
Tearle, Godfrey 209
Teasdale, Verree 84, 89, 150, 163
Technicolor 28, 31, 52, 56, 63, 64, 72, 144, 146, 147, 149, 151, 152, 156, 168, 169, 186, 187, 191, 192, 194, 195, 198, 201, 203, 204, 206, 208, 209, 210, 211, 214, 215, 216, 218, 219, 220, 225, 226, 235, 236, 243, 245, 249, 250, 256, 257, 159, 261, 263, 264, 166, 278, 281, 300, 304, 352
Technirama 281, 295, 320
Techniscope 326
Tell, Olive 54
Tell It to the Marines 28
Tell No Tales 149
Telling the World 44
Tempest, The 276
Temple, Shirley 100 109, 120, 126, 128, 151, 156, 173, 192
'*Temptation*' 95
Temptress, The 33
Ten Cents a Dance 64
Ten Commandments, The 10, 274
Ten North Frederick 284
Ten Thousand Bedrooms 278
Tender Trap, The 271
'*Tenement Symphony*' 169
Tennessee Champ 261
Tennessee Johnson 182
Tension 225
Tenth Avenue Angel 214
Terasaki, Gwen 300
Teresa 235, 242
Terrett, Courtney 92
Terriss, Tom 13
Terror on a Train 252
Terry, Alice 8, 10, 12, 13, 20, 24, 30, 36, 39
Terry, Ethelind 61
Terry, Hazel 306
Terry, Phillip 140, 145, 150, 151, 154, 186
Terry-Thomas 289, 302, 306, 314, 338, 344
Tess of the d'Urbervilles 12
Test Pilot 145, 165
Tetzel, Joan 322
Tetzlaff, Ted 252
Tewksbury, Peter 315, 338, 344, 351
Texas Carnival 243
Thacher, Russell 367
Thalberg, Irving 7, 8, 9, 10, 12, 18, 33, 35, 41, 43, 46, 47, 49, 51, 54, 64, 66, 69, 70, 72, 76, 78, 80, 82, 84, 85, 86, 87, 89, 92, 97, 100, 102, 103, 105, 107, 111, 114, 116, 119, 125, 127, 134, 141, 151, 160, 168, 176, 179, 198, 216, 225, 243, 247
Thalberg, Sylvia 12, 39, 42, 56, 60, 67, 70, 76, 82, 84, 97
'*Thank Heaven for Little Girls*' 284, 379
That Forsyte Woman 224
That Midnight Kiss 231, 234
That Mothers Might Live 181
'*That's Entertainment*' 254
That's Entertainment 283, 368, 370, 384
Thatcher, Heather 84, 131, 135, 172, 180, 194, 252
Thatcher, Torin 273, 309, 313
Thaxter, Phyllis 198, 202, 209, 213, 214, 364
Thayer, Tina 179
Theatre Guild, The 10
Thebom, Blanche 247
Theby, Rosemary 12
Their Own Desire 64

Then Came Bronson 355
'*There Are Two Sides to Every Girl*' 209
'*There But for You Go I*' 266
There You Are 35
'*There's Beauty Everywhere*' 201
'*There's Honey in the Honeycomb*' 183
'*There's No Business Like Show Business*' 234
There's No Business Like Shown Business 268
Thery, Jacques 203
These Glamour Girls 151
These Wilder Years 276
Thesiger, Ernest 271
Thew, Harvey 103
They All Come Out 149
'*They Can't Take That Away from Me*' 372
They Gave Him a Gun 132
They Knew What They Wanted 64
They Learned About Women 226
They Met in Bombay 168
They Only Kill Their Masters 364
They Shoot Horses, Don't They? 346
They Were Expendable 202
Thief of Bagdad, The 10
Thief of Baghdad, The 303
Thiele, William 133, 139, 146, 151, 163
Thin Man, The 97, 104, 122, 123, 144, 192
Thin Man Goes Home, The 192
Third Finger, Left Hand 163
Third Man, The 232
Thirteenth Chair, The 64, 131
Thirteenth Hour, The 39, 46
Thirty-Nine Steps, The 109
Thirty Seconds Over Tokyo 198
36 Hours 321
This Above All 176
This Could Be the Night 280
'*This Heart of Mine*' 201
This is Cinerama 249
This is the Army 184
This Mad World 70
This Man's Navy 198
This Modern Age 76
This Side of Heaven 91
This Time for Keeps 173, 210
This Time for Keeps
Thoeren, Robert 174, 192, 224
Thom, Robert 298
Thomas, A.E. 115, 135
Thomas, Danny 214, 219, 320
Thomas, Frank 149, 183
Thomas, Philip 368
Thomas, Ralph 355
Thompson, Carlos 263, 264
Thompson, J. Lee 338, 352
Thompson, Jimmy 266, 276
Thompson, Kenneth 49, 72, 85
Thompson, Marshall 197, 202, 203, 204, 206, 208, 209, 214, 215, 218, 219, 222, 225, 236, 243, 287, 327, 333
Thompson, Morton 206
Thompson, Natalie 171, 173
Thompson, Rex 257, 264
Thompson, Robert 333
Thompson, Thomas 286, 313
Thomsen, Robert 247
Thorburn, June 289
Thoroughbreds Don't Cry 135
Thoroughly Modern Millie 336
Thorpe, Jerry 331, 341
Thorpe, Richard 117, 120, 125, 126, 128, 134, 136, 141, 142, 143, 146, 151, 154, 159, 162, 168, 172, 174, 181, 182, 183, 186, 187, 192, 201, 202, 203, 210, 211, 218, 219, 220, 222, 224, 225, 234, 236, 242, 247, 251, 252, 256, 257, 258, 266, 268, 271, 278, 281, 295, 300, 303, 307, 312, 339, 344
Thorson, Russell 321
Those Magnificent Men in Their Flying Machines 322
Those Three French Girls 67
'*Thou Swell*' 219
Thousand Shall Fall, A 187
Thousands Cheer 187
Three Bites of the Apple 331
Three Coins in the Fountain 262
Three Comrades 141
Three Daring Daughters 215
3-Dimension films 254, 255, 256, 257, 258
Three Faces of Eve 278
Three Godfathers, The 125, 218
Three Guys Named Mike 237
Three Hearts for Julia 183
Three Little Words 234, 372, 380
Three Live Ghosts 117
Three Loves Has Nancy 143
Three Men in the Snow 135
Three Men in White 196
Three Musketeers, The 219
Three Weeks 13
Three Wise Fools 206
Three Wise Guys, The 122
Thrill of a Romance 201, 203, 210
Thring, Frank 291, 300
Thulin, Ingrid 302
Thunder 57
Thunder Afloat 154
Thunder of Drums, A 303
Thunderball 330
'*Thus Spake Zarathustra*' 342
Tibbett, Lawrence 64, 72, 77, 78
Tichenor, Edna 15
Tichy, Gerard 317, 325
Tick . . . Tick . . . Tick . . . 347
Ticklish Affair, A 315
'*Tico-Tico*' 195
Tide of Empire 61
Tidyman, Ernest 361, 362
Tiernan, Patricia 250, 253, 261
Tierney, Gene 176, 250, 256
Tiffany Productions 12
Tiffin, Pamela 312, 367
Tiko and the Shark 327
Tilbury, Zeffie 60, 135, 144, 146, 149
Till, Eric 345, 355
Till the Clouds Roll By 209, 220
Tillie the Toiler 43, 51
Tillie's Punctured Romance 41
'*Time After Time*' 210
Time Bomb 252
Time for Action 281
Time Machine, The 298, 300
Time, The Comedian 27
Time to Live and a Time to Die, A 284
Time to Sing, A 344
Times Square Lady 109
Tin Hats 32
Tingwell, Charles 302, 313, 319
Tinti, Gabriele 344
Tiomkin, Dimitri 142
Tip on a Dead Jockey 281
Tish 176
Titanus Productions 298, 299, 304, 320, 327
Tiu, Vicki 311
To Catch a Thief 268
To Have and Have Not 192
To Kill a Mockingbird 304
To Live in Peace 210
To Please a Lady 237
To Trap a Spy 322
Toast of New Orleans, The 234, 378
Tobacco Road 166
Tobey, Kenneth 289
Tobias, George 150, 151, 206, 333
Tobin, Dan 172, 208, 275
Tobin, Genevieve 142
Toby, Mark 310
Today We Live 90
Todd, Ann (American) 151, 154, 215
Todd, Ann (British) 202
Todd, Bob 302
Todd, Mike 274
Todd, Richard 322
Todd, Thelma 86, 92, 110
Todd-AO 255
'*Tokay*' 156
Toler, Sidney 57, 84, 86, 123, 125, 127, 128
Tolstoy, Leo 40, 44, 66, 115
Tom and Jerry 8, 259, 351, 380
Tom Jones 310
Tom Thumb 289
Tombes, Andrew 127, 168
Tomelty, Joseph 271, 299
Tomlin, Pinky 109
Tomlinson, David 244, 331
Tone, Franchot 90, 91, 92, 95, 97, 100, 102, 109, 115, 116, 117, 119, 122, 127, 128, 132, 133, 134, 135, 141, 143, 151, 180
Tonge, Philip 261, 294
Tonight at 8.30 172
'*Too Darn Hot*' 257
Too Hot to Handle 145
'*Too Late Now*' 237
Too Many Thieves 344
Too Young to Kiss 242
Toomey, Regis 112, 133, 149, 154, 182, 243, 244, 247, 271, 364
Toone, Geoffrey 273, 312
Topaze 92
Topper 134, 142, 209
Topsy and Eva 63
Torch Song 259
Torme, Mel 210, 219, 235, 294
Torn, Rip 300, 306, 329, 331, 339
Torpedo Run 287
Torrence, David 23, 24, 30, 36, 85, 105, 110
Torrence, Ernest 42, 43, 44, 51, 56, 57, 60, 67, 72, 77, 78, 80
Torrent, The 27, 33
Torres, Raquel 46, 57, 65, 71
Tors, Ivan 213, 224, 225, 232, 289, 311, 321, 327, 333
Tortilla Flat 181
'*Totem Tomtom*' 380
Toto 31
Tottenham, Merle 128
Totter, Audrey 197, 202, 203, 208, 209, 213, 222, 225, 228, 247, 384
Touch of Class, A 368
'*Touch of Your Hand, The*' 249
Tough Guy 122
Toumanova, Tamara 267, 275, 377
Tourjansky, Viachetslav 51
Tourneur, Jacques 149, 154, 165, 232, 294, 298
Tourneur, Maurice 20, 56
Tower of Lies, The 23
Townsend, Jill 361
Townsend, Leo 183, 224
Toy Wife, The 141
Trabert, Tony 367
Tracy, Lee 94, 98, 103, 104, 140, 145
Tracy, Spencer 66, 104, 105, 112, 116, 123, 125, 132, 133, 138, 145, 149, 150, 159, 165, 166 172, 174, 180, 181, 184, 186, 191, 198, 204, 206, 209, 215, 218, 222, 224, 225, 230, 233, 238, 240, 244, 250, 257, 266, 274, 284, 291, 304, 336
Tracy, William 154, 156, 165
Trader Horn 70, 86, 236, 367
Trail of '98, The 48, 163
Transamerica Corp. 336
Traubel, Helen 267
Traveling Executioner, The 357
Travels of Jaimie McPheeters, The 317
Travels with My Aunt 362
Travers, Bill 275, 277, 283, 302
Travers, Henry 90, 98, 112, 116, 154, 159, 162, 168, 176, 177, 182, 191, 198, 201, 206
Treacher, Arthur 107, 115, 116, 123, 146, 196, 231
Treasure Island 107
Tree, David 149
Tree, Dorothy 125, 165, 172, 238
Tree Grows in Brooklyn, A 201, 322
Treen, Mary 132
Trelawny of the Wells 46 l 67
Trevor, Austin 149, 333
Trevor, Claire 169, 176, 253, 307
Trevor, Elleston 287
Treynor, Albert 154
Trial 269
Trial and Error 306
Trial of Mary Dugan, The 54, 56, 75, 85, 131, 165
Tribute to a Bad Man 274
Triesault, Ivan 252, 257
'*Triplets*' 254
Trivas, Victor 188
'*Trolley Song, The*' 192
Trosper, Guy 168, 176, 181, 224, 236, 243, 264, 278
Trotti, Lamar 102
Trouble for Two 126
Trouble with Girls, The 351
Troup, Bobby 287
Trout, Tom 197, 214
Trowbridge, Charles 147, 201, 208, 209
Troy, Helen 135, 136
True Grit 346
'*True Love*' 277
Truex, Ernest 85, 146, 151, 183
Truman, Harry S. 209
Trumbo, Dalton 164, 184, 198, 204, 329, 345
Trunk Mystery, The 117
Truth Game, The 84, 168
Tryon, Glenn 81, 240
Tuchner, Michael 360
Tuchock, Wanda 47, 54, 60, 70, 74, 80, 84, 86
Tucker, Forrest 180, 206
Tucker, Larry 354
Tucker, Richard 110
Tucker, Sophie 54, 128, 135
Tucker's People 216
Tugboat Annie 95
Tugend, Harry 216, 226
Tully, Jim 67
Tully, Montgomery 342
Tully, Tom 201, 208, 210, 243, 247, 270
Tunberg, Karl 243, 244, 251, 261, 264, 266, 273, 283, 290, 292, 293, 307, 344
Tune, Tommy 358
Tunnel of Love, The 287
Tunnel 28 307
Tunney, Gene 36
Turn Back the Clock 94
Turnell, Dee 378
Turner, Bridget 355
Turner, John 350
Turner, Lana 57, 138, 142, 150, 151, 154, 156, 164, 168, 169, 171, 174, 178, 182, 187, 188, 191, 196, 198, 202, 214, 215, 218, 219, 222, 237, 243, 249, 252, 261, 263, 264, 268, 273, 302
Turner, Maidel 98, 218
Tushingham, Rita 325
Tutin, Dorothy 364
Tuttle, Lurene 218, 256, 257, 264, 275
Tuttle, W.C. 154
Tuttle, William 317
Twain, Mark 146, 296
Tweed, F.T. 92
Twelve Angry Men 278
Twelve Miles Out 43
Twelve O'Clock High 232
Twelvetrees, Helen 85, 109
Twentieth Century-Fox: see Fox Films
25th Hour, The 333
Twenty Mule Team 159
Twice Blessed 202
Twiggy 358
Twilight of Honor 313
Twiss, Clinton 256
Twitty, Conway 298
Two Are Guilty 312
Two-Faced Woman 167, 214
Two Girls and a Sailor 192
Two Girls on Broadway 156
Two-Gun Cupid 168
Two Loves 303
Two Sisters from Boston 209
Two Smart People 209
2001: A Space Odyssey 342, 360
Two Weeks in Another Town 307
Two Weeks with Love 234
Two Women 300
Tyler, Beverley 188, 206, 208, 209
Tyler, Judy 278
Tyler, Richard 276
Tynan, Kenneth 289
Tyrant of Syracuse, The 304
Tyzack, Margaret 342

Uggams, Leslie 364
Ukelele Ike: see Edwards, Cliff
Ullman, William 149
Ulric, Lenore 127, 209
Ultra-Panavision 344
Umberto D 268
Un Homme et une Femme 336
Unashamed 85
Uncle Tom's Cabin 69
Under Cover of Night 122
Under the Black Eagle 46, 47
Under the Clock 204
Undercover Girl 213
Undercover Maisie 213
Undercurrent 208, 228
Understanding Heart, The 31
Underwater Warrior 289
Underworld 44, 149
Unfinished Dance, The 214
Unger, Gladys 42, 61, 67
Unguarded Hour, The 122
Unholy Love 228
Unholy Night, The 57
Unholy Partners 172
Unholy Three, The 23, 71
United Artists 9, 28, 44, 100, 128, 142, 179, 216, 251, 274, 284, 290, 310, 336
'*United Nations on the March*' 187
Universal Pictures 7, 9, 54, 74, 85, 100, 128, 164, 176, 177, 183, 192, 197, 222, 231, 240, 243, 247, 254, 284, 368
Unknown, The 39
Unknown Man, The 247
Unsinkable Molly Brown, The 319
Untamed 60
Until They Sail 278
Up Goes Maisie 203
Up Pompeii 358
Up She Goes 203
Up the River 66
Upstage 32
Upton, Gabrielle 307
Ure, Mary 346
Uris, Leon 295
Urquhart, Robert 258, 287, 313
Ustinov, Peter 245, 266, 326, 336, 345

V.I.P.s, The 311, 317
Vacation from Love 141
Vacation from Marriage 203
Vaccaro, Brenda 361
Vadim, Roger 321, 360
Vadnay, Laslo 249, 256, 261, 313
Vagabond Lady 117
Vail, Lester 66, 78
Vailati, Bruno 298, 303
Vailland, Roger 299, 313, 321
Vajda, Ernst 76, 80, 87, 89, 90, 100, 105, 131, 141, 142
Valdengo, Giuseppe 247
Vale, Eugene 314
Valencia 35
Valentina, Anna 256
Valentino, Rudolph 10, 18, 28, 64, 327
Valerie, Joan 177
Valk, Frederick 256
Vallee, Rudy 54, 345
Valley of Decision, The 202
Valley of Hell, The 32
Valley of the Dolls 336
Valley of the Kings 264
Van, Bobby 249, 251, 257
Van, Gus 56
Vance, Ethel 164
Vance, Louis 321
Vance, Louis Joseph 13
Van Cleef, Lee 258, 261, 274
van der Meersch, Maxence 228
Van Devere, Trish 360, 364
Van Dine, S.S. 64, 111, 122
Van Doren, Mamie 286, 294
van Druten, John 86, 128, 133, 194
Van Dyke, Jerry 310
Van Dyke, Marcia 228
Van Dyke, W.S. 30, 43, 46, 47, 51, 56, 70, 76, 77, 78, 85, 86, 92, 95, 97, 102, 103, 104, 107, 110, 116, 117, 119, 123, 125, 126, 127, 131, 132, 141, 143, 144, 146, 149, 150, 156, 162, 169, 171, 173, 174, 179, 180, 194
Vane, Thaddeus 345
Vanel, Charles 312
Vanessa 112
Vanessa, Her Love Story 112
Van Every, Dale 44, 56, 64, 67, 132
van Eyss, Osso 224
Van Fleet, Jo 273, 361
Vanishing Virginian, The 171
Van Patten, Dick 366
Van Patten, Joyce 351
Van Riper, Kay 136, 138, 143, 150, 152, 171, 173, 204
Van Ronkel, Rip 287
Van Upp, Virginia 163
Varconi, Victor 133, 163, 165
Varden, Evelyn 266, 278
Varden, Norma 154, 177, 196, 198, 208, 224, 257, 264
Variascope 255
Variety 117
'*Varsity Drag, The*' 71, 210
Varsity Girl, The 41
Vasquez, Jose Luis Lopez 362
Vaughan, Peter 299, 350
Vaughn, Hilda 74
Vaughn, Robert 322, 328, 331, 338, 342
Vaverka, Anton 43
Vectograph 255
Veidt, Conrad 64, 112, 164, 171, 172, 187
Veiller, Anthony 179, 184, 201, 218, 316
Veiller, Bayard 54, 69, 76, 82, 84, 85, 131, 149, 165
Velez, Lupe 54, 57, 78, 80, 85, 102
Venable, Evelyn 117
Venetian Affair, The 331
Vengeance Valley 236
Ventantonio, John 365
Ventura, Lino 327
Ventura, Viviane 342
Venuta, Benay 234
Vera-Ellen 219, 222, 227, 234, 247, 257, 372
Verne, Jules 56, 350
Verne, Karen 165, 198
Verneuil, Henri 327, 333, 340
Vernon, Anne 252
Vernon, John 339
Vernon, Maurice 39
Vernon, Richard 299
Vernon, Wally 147
Very Private Affair, A 307
Very Warm for May 191
VeSota, Bruno 361
Vessel, Edy (Hedy) 303, 312
Vetluguin, Voldemar 228, 237
Vetter, Charles Jr. 287, 302, 342
Vibert, Marcel 36
Vice and Virtue 321
Victor, Charles 244
Victor, David 331
Victor, Henry 85, 154
Vidal, Gore 179, 275, 280, 291, 293
Vidor, Charles 242, 264, 270, 274
Vidor, King 8, 12, 13, 16, 20, 24, 30, 40, 44, 47, 54, 60, 70, 77, 95, 139, 144, 149, 165, 174, 183, 191, 198, 206, 274
Vie de Boheme 24
Viertel, Salka 98, 103, 115, 136, 167
Vignola, Robert 13, 24
Viking, The 52
Villechaize, Herve 361
Village of Daughters 306
Village of the Damned 299, 312
Villain 360
Villiers, James 313, 333
Vincent, Allen 213, 251
Vincent, Jan-Michael 361
Vinegar Tree, The 97
Vinson, Helen 116, 135, 192
Vintage, The 280
Violent Hour, The 236
Visaroff, Michael 32
Visconti, Luchino 208, 365
Vistarama 255
VistaVision 255, 291
Vitagraph Pictures 20
Vitaphone 36
Vitascope 255
Vitold, Michael 312
Viva Las Vegas 271
Viva Las Vegas 320, 344, 377
Viva Villa 103, 120, 135
Vogel, Joseph R. 9, 278, 300
Vogel, Paul 225
Voice of Bugle Ann, The 120
Voice of the City 56
Voice of the Turtle, The 210
Vollmer, Lulu 21
Volusia, Eros 177
von Berne, Eva 47
von Cube, Irmgard 213, 251
Von Eltz, Theodore 30, 74, 122, 127, 134
von Koszian, Johanna 295
von Seyffertitz, Gustav 13, 36, 52, 64, 87, 122
von Sternberg, Joseph 27, 31, 39, 82, 149, 150
von Stroheim, Erich 8, 16, 18, 27, 33, 89, 100, 122, 133, 232
Vorhaus, Bernard 31
Vortex, The 97
Vosselli, Judith 64, 69
Vroman, Mary 256
Vye, Murvyn 266, 280

Wadsworth, Henry 91, 104, 105, 110, 117
Waggner, George 294
Wagner, Robert 298, 339
'*Waiting at the End of the Road*' 54
Wakeman, Frederick 210
Walbrook, Anton 194, 280
Walburn, Raymond 105, 121, 122, 123, 128, 144, 146, 163, 218, 230, 247
Walcott, George 123
Waldman, Frank 195, 354
Waldman, Tom 354
Waldron, Bhetty 362
Waldron, Charles 163
Wales, Ethel 20
Wales, Ken 361
Walker, Clint 333, 337
Walker, June 71
Walker, Nancy 188, 191
Walker, Nella 162, 173, 181, 186, 209, 213, 231
Walker, Robert 186, 191, 195, 198, 202, 203, 204, 209, 213, 222, 232, 236
Walker, Robert Jr. 309
Walker, Walter 78, 84, 102
Walking Stick, The 355
Wall, Geraldine 202, 206, 208, 213, 214
Wallace, Ian 289
Wallace, Irving 314
Wallace, Jean 357
Wallace, Lew 18
Wallace, Parnum 339
Wallach, Eli 304, 352
Wallach, Ira 306, 313, 338, 345
Walley, Deborah 321, 334
Wallis, Hal B. 105, 209
'*Walls of Jericho*' 191
Walpole, Hugh 107, 109, 112, 244
Walsh, Arthur 198, 202, 208
Walsh, George 18
Walsh, Kay 257
Walsh, Percy 186
Walsh, Raoul 95, 117, 250
Walter, Eugene 75
Walter, Jessica 334
Walters, Charles 187, 188, 210, 220, 222, 224, 234, 237, 243, 247, 251, 256, 259, 264, 271, 277, 283, 291, 298, 303, 307, 319
Walters, Nancy 296, 302, 333
Walters, Thorley 302
Walthall, Henry B. 28, 35, 39, 57, 85, 103, 104, 119, 122
Walton, Douglas 94, 98, 119, 122, 127, 149, 194
Wanamaker, Sam 361
Wanger, Walter 92, 95, 98, 107
Waning Sex, The 32
War Against Mrs Hadley, The 183
War and Peace 203, 274
War Nurse 71
War Paint 30
Waram, Percy 232
Warburton, John 192, 198, 202, 203, 213
Ward, A.C. 360
Ward, Bradley 15
Ward, David 186
Ward, James 316
Warden, Jack 277, 303, 367
Ware, Clyde 328
Ware, Harlan 141
Ware, Wallace 303
Warfield, William 247
Warner Brothers 31, 36, 44, 46, 75, 78, 82, 84, 90, 94, 100, 103, 112, 132, 133, 135, 142, 143, 152, 162, 176, 182, 206, 210, 213, 254, 255, 274, 284, 316, 330, 331, 336, 352, 357
Warner, David 345
Warner, H.B. 33, 44, 54, 86, 97, 103, 119, 122, 126, 142, 146, 156, 163, 176, 213, 232
Warner, Richard 299
Warner, Sylvia Ashton 303
Warnerphonic Sound 255